Third Edition

THE CHILD

A CONTEMPORARY VIEW OF DEVELOPMENT

JUDITH RICH HARRIS

ROBERT M. LIEBERT
State University of New York at Stony Brook

PRENTICE HALL, Englewood Cliffs, New Jersey 07632

Library of Congress Cataloging-in-Publication Data

HARRIS, JUDITH RICH.
    The child: a contemporary view of development / Judith
Rich Harris, Robert M. Liebert.—3rd ed.
      p. cm.
    Includes bibliographical references p. ( ) and index.
    ISBN 0-13-131046-1
    1. Child development.   I. Liebert, Robert M., (Date).
II. Title.
RJ131.H288 1991
155.4—dc20   90-7318
                                       CIP

Editorial/production supervision: *Rob DeGeorge*
Interior design: *Lorraine Mullaney*
Prepress buyer: *Debbie Kesar*
Manufacturing buyer: *Mary Ann Gloriande*
Photo research: *Anita Dickhuth*
Photo editor: *Lori Morris-Nantz*
Cover photo: *Horst Fenchel/The Image Bank*
Cover design: *Lorraine Mullaney*

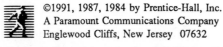

©1991, 1987, 1984 by Prentice-Hall, Inc.
A Paramount Communications Company
Englewood Cliffs, New Jersey 07632

Printed in the United States of America

10 9 8 7 6 5 4 3

ISBN 0-13-131046-1

PRENTICE-HALL INTERNATIONAL (UK) LIMITED, *London*
PRENTICE-HALL OF AUSTRALIA PTY. LIMITED, *Sydney*
PRENTICE-HALL CANADA INC., *Toronto*
PRENTICE-HALL HISPANOAMERICANA, S.A., *Mexico*
PRENTICE-HALL OF INDIA PRIVATE LIMITED, *New Delhi*
PRENTICE-HALL OF JAPAN, INC., *Tokyo*
SIMON & SCHUSTER ASIA PTE. LTD., *Singapore*
EDITORA PRENTICE-HALL DO BRASIL, LTDA., *Rio de Janeiro*

Contents Overview

Contents

Part Two: Infancy and Toddlerhood

5

The Baby   148

6

The First Social Relationships   181

7

The Beginnings of Intelligence and Language   217

Part Three: Early Childhood

8

The Preschool Child   258

9

Preschoolers Think and Communicate

10

Becoming a Member of Society

Part Four: Middle Childhood

Part Five: Adolescence

15

Preface

This is the third edition of *The Child,* and we have a new subtitle: instead of *Development from Birth through Adolescence,* it is now *A Contemporary View of Development.* We threw out the old subtitle because it didn't say very much and some of what it did say was misleading: development actually begins nine months *before* birth. We chose the new subtitle because it gives you a more accurate idea of how this book differs from other books on child development, including the previous edition of *The Child.*

What makes the third edition "a contemporary view of development"? One clue is the reference list at the back, the list of all the journal articles and other professional publications from which we derived the information contained in this book. There are 1140 references in that list, and only 419 of them are carry-overs from the previous edition of *The Child.* Of the 721 new references, 578 of them were published in the years 1987 through 1990. That means that over half of the references cited in this edition were published after the second edition of *The Child* appeared in print.

Not only does this edition contain the very latest findings of the people who do research in child development—it is equally up-to-date with regard to theory. There is less emphasis on older theories of development and more on modern approaches. A *transactional* view of development provides the underlying theme: children are seen as playing an active role in their own development, not as passive recipients of whatever the environment happens to deal out. Children differ from each other right from the start, and they respond differently to environmental events. They pick and choose different things from their environments. They evoke different reactions from their parents and other people. Parent-child relationships are seen as two-way transactions in which parents not only have effects on their children—children also have effects on their parents. This approach makes the study of development a good deal more complicated, but also a good deal more interesting, than it was in the days when researchers blithely assumed that anything children do is the result of how their parents act toward them.

What's new in the third edition? Too much to list here, so instead of answering that question directly we'll respond with another question—or, rather, with an assortment of questions:

If heredity is something you're "born with," why do its effects get stronger as you get older?

Why do identical twins reared apart often give similar descriptions of their childhood homes?

What is the one big advantage in performing surgery on an unborn fetus?

Why are toddlers virtually incapable of learning anything solely through the sense of touch?

How come fathers tend to "vanish" after the baby is born, even if they promised to share 50-50 in childrearing?

In what ways do American babies have more freedom than babies in other cultures, and in what ways do they have less?

Are young babies capable of feeling jealousy?

What specific type of mother-infant interaction does the most to advance the baby's language development?

Why is it unwise to insist that preschoolers clean their plates, or even to take "just one bite"?

How do children learn new words so rapidly?

Why do little girls start avoiding little boys by the time they're 3?

Are preschoolers capable of telling deliberate lies?

Is a carrot alive?

What time is it when an elephant sits on your fence?

Why do girls make better grades in math classes but lower scores on tests of math aptitude?

Why might it make sense to teach American children to count in Japanese?

Which proceeds faster, the development of self-knowledge or of knowledge about other people?

Can a child be both a bully and a victim?

What do adolescents and their parents argue about most?

Why can't homeless youth go home again?

Is it necessary to achieve emotional detachment from one's parents in order to feel like an independent adult?

In what ways are romantic relationships similar to infant-mother attachments?

How does "his" marriage differ from "her" marriage? Which is better?

Why is a man who has a single-minded attitude toward his work very attractive to a woman—until she marries him?

Answers to all these questions are in the sections that are new to this edition.

One thing we haven't changed is the overall organization of the book: from Chapter 4 on, *The Child* is chronologically organized, starting with prenatal development and continuing through late adolescence and early adulthood. But we have made an improvement in the organization: now Part 2 (Infancy and Toddlerhood), Part 3 (Early Childhood), and Part 4 (Middle Childhood) each begin with a chapter that presents an overview of that period of development, with the major focus being on the child who has just entered that period. This introductory chapter is followed by two more chapters on the entire period: one on social and personal development, and the other on cognitive development or (in the case of the school-age child) school achievement. Notice that we devote an entire chapter to the various factors that affect how well a child will do in school. Although the chapter itself is not new to the third edition, most of its contents are new. The topic of schooling and educational achievement is gaining increasing attention from researchers, and there are many new findings to report.

Another improvement is that there is now a list of key terms at the end of each chapter. Don't let this worry you: as in the previous editions of *The Child,* we avoid using technical jargon if we can say the same thing in plain English. Sometimes, however, there is a need for a specialized vocabulary. "Key terms" are words that you might not be familiar with, or words that look familiar but that are used here in a slightly different way. When a key term is introduced, it is printed in boldface, **like this,** and we tell you what it means. It appears again in the list at the end of that chapter. In general, key terms get listed only once, at the end of the chapter where they first appeared. But those that are introduced in Chapter 1 or Chapter 3 may be listed again, because those chapters are sometimes read out of order and they contain a great many new terms. Every key term appears again, along with its definition, in the Glossary at the back of the book. The Glossary also contains definitions of words that didn't quite make it into the category of "key terms."

While you're at the back of the book, be sure to notice our greatly improved and expanded subject index. And take another look at the reference section. In the previous editions of *The Child,* most of the articles we referred to came from a relatively small number of sources. But the reference list in the third edition contains articles from more than 175 different journals, ranging from *Infant Behavior and Development* to the *Journal of College Student Development,* from the *Pavlovian Journal of Biological Science* to *Educational Computing Research,* from *Mankind Quarterly* to *Psychology of Women Quarterly,* and from the *Australian and New Zealand Journal of Psychiatry* to the *International Journal of Humor Research.*

In reporting what we learned from these journals, we didn't want to present a dry parade of facts. Our goal was to provide a lively and vivid description of the developing child, so that someone who had never taken a college course in psychology or biology could read it with understanding and enjoyment. When writing about children in general would seem too vague or abstract, we have looked instead at one particular child. Many of the children who appear on these pages are real people. Others are composites, drawn from several typical or interesting cases.

Our focus, by and large, is on the normal development of the normal child. However, it is also necessary to acknowledge that things do not always go smoothly. In our "Problems in Development" boxes, set apart from the rest of the text, we examine difficulties that may occur during the course of development. Other boxes—the "Close-Ups"—provide an opportunity to go into more detail on some particular topic of interest. In the last type of box, labeled "The Child in Society," we look at issues of social importance or cross-cultural research. But cross-cultural topics are not confined to the boxes: the third edition of *The Child* contains a wealth of cross-cultural material, strewn all through the book. Cultures differ in their childrearing styles and in what they hope for and expect from children, and these differences are reflected in the children's thoughts, feelings, and behavior. It is informative to compare American parents and children with those who live in other parts of the world, and it is also informative to make such comparisons among the various subcultures *within* North America.

The study of child development is of value to anyone who likes children and/or finds them interesting, and to anyone who is or will be responsible for their welfare. One of the nice things about this field is that no one comes to it empty-handed: you bring to it all that you learned from having once been a child yourself.

Acknowledgments

Our goal for the third edition of *The Child* was to present a state-of-the-art view of data and theory in a user-friendly package. Many people have helped us in our efforts to achieve this goal. We gratefully acknowledge the contributions of the reviewers whose comments on the second edition, and on early drafts of this edition, provided us with helpful guidance and feedback. Thanks go to John C. Aston, Golden West College; Virginia Cronin, Mt. St. Vincent University; Sheridan DeWolf, Grossmont College; Thomas Fitzpatrick, Rockland Community College; Karan Hancock Gier, University of Alaska, Anchorage; Judy B. Lindamood, Bunker Hill Community College; Harriette B. Ritchie, American River College; Cosby S. Rogers, Virginia Polytechnic Institute and State University; Joe Siba, George Brown College of Applied Arts & Technology; Janet A. Simons, Des Moines Area Community College; and Roger J. Stouwie, Calvin College.

A number of people at Prentice Hall have contributed their talents and efforts to the third edition of *The Child*. We especially appreciate the help of Rob DeGeorge, who proved to be an ideal production editor—competent, conscientious, and kind-hearted. Lorinda Morris-Nantz, photo editor, and Anita Dickhuth, photo researcher, are to be thanked for the many fine photographs they provided for this edition. Leslie Carr was the development editor who got the third edition off to an excellent start, and Charlyce Jones Owen, editor-in-chief, had the difficult job of stepping in when this project was already in progress and seeing it through to completion. If you have any comments on the design or construction of the book, you can address them to the Psychology Editor at the Prentice Hall Building, College Division, Englewood Cliffs, NJ 07632. Any comments on the *contents* of the book should be directed to Judith Rich Harris, care of the Psychology Editor, at the same address. Your comments would be most welcome.

1

Some Basic Concepts

Look through your family photo album, next time you have a chance. Look at the photos of yourself as a baby, as a toddler, as a young child, as an older child. Can you remember what you were doing when those photos were taken, and what it was like to be a person of that age? Can you remember any of your thoughts or experiences from that time in your life? Do you feel that the person you see in those photos is the same *you* you are now, or have you changed so much in the intervening years that it's like looking at a picture of a different person?

All the differences between the adult you are now and the child you were then are summed up by the term *development*. Development is what this book is about. We hope that in reading it you will come to a better understanding of the child you used to be, of the adult you have become, and of how you got from there to here.

What Is Development?

Development* is defined as the physical, mental, and behavioral changes that take place in human beings over the course of time; these changes are generally permanent and irreversible. Included in this definition are all the changes that are programmed into the genes of a given individual and that reveal themselves gradually, over the course of time: growth in size and strength, the emergence of sexual maturity, the eventual signs of aging. It also includes all the changes that come about as a result of experience and learning: changes in knowledge and understanding, in the ability to use language, in the skill with which various physical activities are performed, in social behavior, in self-image and self-control, and so on.

Major Issues in Child Development

A book about child development must answer two separate but related questions. First, how does a "typical" or "normal" child grow and develop, progressing from a fertilized egg to a young adult? All young human beings must, to a great extent, travel the same path: along the way they grow considerably in size; they are born and must breathe and eat in order to survive; they learn to sit up, to crawl, and to walk; they form attachments to the caregivers upon whom they are dependent; they acquire a language; they continue to become larger, stronger, and more skilled in a multitude of ways; and eventually they become adults and in all probability have children of their own.

The second question, equally important, deals with uniqueness and variation: Why do children differ so much from one another? Although all children travel along the same broad path, each travels at his or her own rate, and each brings along a different bag packed with different things. They all start out pretty much the same—one fertilized human egg looks identical to another, though of course they are not. By the time babies are born they are already easily distinguishable from each other. The differences increase as babies turn into children and children into adults. The tasks of infancy are universal: to stand, to walk, to talk. The tasks of school-age children have already begun to vary, as some children lean toward development of their social skills, others toward development of their athletic skills, and still others toward academic achievement. By the late teens, it is clear that each person has his or her own agenda, though it might not yet be obvious—even to the individual in question—exactly what that agenda is.

**The Sources of
Differences**

The universals of human development are, presumably, built into our species. But what about the differences? Why are you different from all the other people whose pictures are in your family album—even people (your brother or sister) who have the same parents and grew up in the same home?

---

* The terms that are printed in bold type can be found, along with their definitions, in the Glossary at the back of the book.

The fact that children differ so widely from each other—in how they look, in how they act, and in how rapidly or slowly they develop—makes the job of describing their progress more difficult, but also more interesting. One of the major challenges is to discover the sources of these differences. Why is Shanna shy and quiet, while her brother Tyler is talkative and friendly? Why is Brian rough and aggressive with other children, while his classmate Daniel is kind and gentle? Why is Morgan running around and climbing on everything at an age when most babies are content to crawl? Why does Adaya love to read and Teresa prefer to ride her bike?

The answer, of course, is heredity and environment. Everyone knows that —everyone has known it for thousands of years. Sayings such as ''The apple doesn't fall far from the tree'' and ''Like father, like son'' acknowledge the obvious fact that people inherit many of their characteristics from their parents and grandparents. The importance of the environment—of what happens to children while they are growing up—has been recognized for an equally long time. The Bible says, ''Train up a child in the way he should go, and when he is old he will not depart from it.''

Although everyone already knows the importance of heredity and environment, it is not so easy to use that knowledge to account for the behavior of a particular child. For example, why is Shanna shy and quiet? Heredity? But both her parents are sociable, outgoing people, and so is her brother Tyler. Well, maybe it's environment, then. Maybe she felt she couldn't compete with so many sociable people, so she reacted by withdrawing. But then why is Courtney, who also has sociable parents and a sociable **sibling** (brother or sister), so outgoing?

It's easy enough to say *in theory* that children are a product of their heredity

Children differ from each other in how they look, how they think, how they act, and how rapidly or slowly they develop. What are the sources of these differences?

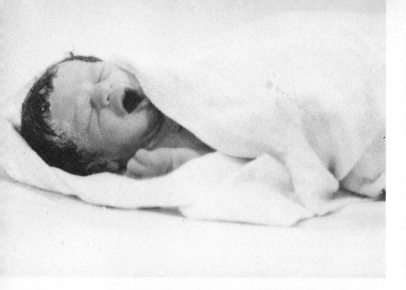
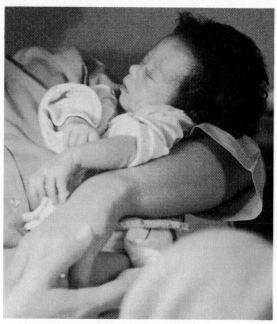
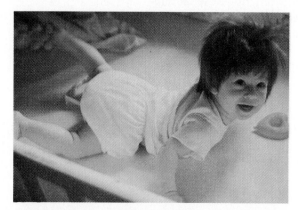

Development from birth to young adulthood.

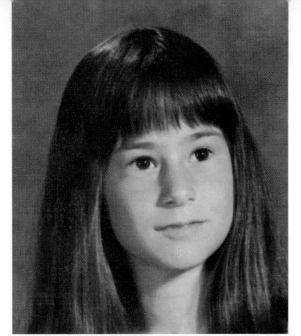

and their environment. But when we get down to individual children and specific characteristics, those generalities don't help much. It's seldom clear whether a given characteristic is inherited, or is due to environmental influences, or results from a combination of the two. The answer almost always turns out to be "results from a combination of the two," but that still leaves plenty of room for argument. A debate has gone on for decades over whether various qualities are *primarily* inherited or *primarily* a result of the environment. We'll listen to both sides of this debate in Chapter 2.

Continuity and Change in Development

Although you are still the same person as the child you used to be—the child in the photo album—you have changed a great deal. Development includes both continuity and change. Which aspects of an individual remain the same over the years of development? Which aspects change, perhaps in ways that are difficult to predict?

Newborn babies aren't all alike, but the variations are not as noticeable as the variations among children or adults. Can we look at the rather subtle differences between babies and get some idea of the much larger differences that will distinguish one from the other when they are older? Can we look at a baby and say "this one will be friendly," or "this one will be strong and active," or "this one will be very intelligent"?

These are not questions that have simple answers—they are ones that we will grapple with many times during the course of this book. But before we begin to do that, we want to give you an idea of the problems involved in answering this kind of question.

Take the subject of intelligence. Psychologists and pediatricians have been trying for decades to find some way of predicting how intelligent a given baby will turn out to be. There have been, over the years, many "intelligence tests" for infants: a baby is tested to find out how well she* can follow a moving object with her eyes, or reach for a rattle, or pass a toy from one hand to another, or put a peg in a hole, or build a tower of three blocks.

Although such tests might be able to distinguish between a child who is developing normally and a child who has some serious problem, they cannot distinguish between a potential theoretical physicist and a potential gas station attendant. For many years, the only clue we had about a baby's future intelligence was how intelligent her parents were.

Because tests of intelligence given in infancy had no value at all in predicting how intelligent a child would be five or ten years later, intelligence was believed to proceed in a *discontinuous* fashion. The idea was that infant development was more or less unrelated to what happens later on—different processes were involved. Whatever it was that made some babies seem brighter than others, it was not the same thing that made some school-age children seem brighter than others.

But just in the past few years, researchers have come up with new ways of testing infants that *can* tell us something about how intelligent these infants

---

* In this book we will sometimes refer to a child as "she" and sometimes as "he." We will generally speak of the child (meaning any child, no child in particular) as female when the context includes a male researcher or caregiver, and as male when the researcher or caregiver is a woman; this helps to avoid confusion. In other contexts, the masculine or feminine pronouns are chosen at random.

will be later on. The new techniques involve showing pictures to young babies. Babies, like everyone else, get tired of looking at the same picture after a while, so they stop looking at it. This onset of boredom is actually a kind of learning: the baby is saying, in effect, "I don't have to look at that picture anymore because I *know* it already." Researchers can find out how quickly a baby gets bored with a picture by watching his eyes and noticing when he stops looking at it. Then they give the baby another picture. If the new picture is exactly the same as the old one, naturally the baby will not find it interesting. But what if it's just a little bit different? If the baby notices the difference and is interested in it, he will look for a while at the new picture. If he doesn't notice the difference ("Just the same old picture again") or doesn't care ("Big deal—three pink dots instead of four"), he will remain bored.

How quickly the baby gets bored with an old picture, and how responsive and interested he is in a change, are measures of the baby's ability to pay attention and to learn. These measures can predict—not perfectly, but more accurately than any previous measures of infant intelligence—how well he will do on IQ tests later in life. (IQ tests are designed to measure those qualities that make some children seem brighter than others, such as the ability to learn things quickly. The IQ score is an approximate indication of a child's intelligence, although in some cases IQ tests can give misleading results. We'll have more to say on this topic in later chapters.)

We've seen that measuring a very simple kind of learning in a baby can tell us something about that child's ability to learn much more complex things later on. Thus, an aspect of development that was thought to be discontinuous, and to change in unpredictable ways over time, has been shown to have continuity after all (Bornstein and Sigman, 1986).*

We shouldn't assume, however, that when something seems to develop in a discontinuous fashion, it's only because we haven't yet found the underlying continuity. There may be traits or abilities that *do* develop in a discontinuous fashion.

SMOOTH DEVELOPMENT VERSUS STAGES. Discontinuity has another meaning in the study of development. Some theorists—B.F. Skinner, for example —think of the path of development as smooth, straight, and with a gradual upward slope: every day the child gets a little bit better at doing what she's supposed to do and a little bit less likely to do what she isn't supposed to. Other theorists—for example, Sigmund Freud and Jean Piaget—see the path as a series of **stages**, like the steps in a staircase. Each time the child steps up to a higher level, she gets a new outlook on things: she can solve a problem she couldn't solve yesterday, or she experiences a change in her relationships with others. The important feature of the different stages is that each one involves a *qualitative change*. The child is not just bigger or better. A small grasshopper simply grows into a larger grasshopper, but a caterpillar turns into something qualitatively different—a butterfly.

Another assumption is that the stages have to come in a certain order: you can't get to stage 3 unless you've first been in stage 1 and stage 2. However,

---

* The names in parentheses are the authors of the books or articles that are the sources of the information we have just given you; the dates indicate when these books or articles were published. Their titles can be found in the References at the back of the book. You can refer to these publications for additional information on a particular topic.

the rate at which these stages are achieved may vary considerably. Thus, stage theorists don't say that stage X always comes at age Y, but that that's the typical time. Some children may reach a given stage sooner, some later. And some may never reach it at all. A retarded child or one from a severely deprived environment may never progress to the highest stages of development. Stage theories allow for that possibility.

Finally, the transition from one stage to another is not assumed to be as clear-cut and sharp as our staircase and butterfly analogies would suggest. Transitional periods are allowed, and so are periods in which a child vacillates between two stages. We will look in more detail at this issue, and tell you more about Skinner, Freud, and Piaget, in Chapter 3.

The Sources of Development and Change

Whether children progress in a series of discontinuous jumps or in a smooth, uninterrupted climb, the fact is that they do progress. They change, mature, develop. Part of this development—the part usually referred to as **maturation**—results from the built-in instructions that are programmed into our genes.

But because we are humans and not caterpillars or frogs, nature hasn't programmed all our development in advance. Flexibility is a characteristic of our species. This flexibility permits babies and children to adapt to a wide range of possible environments and to profit from whatever advantages they happen to be offered. Thus, most aspects of child development depend not just on maturation, but also on adaptation and learning—processes that require a large dose of input from the environment, as well as from the child.

Theories of development differ in the roles they assign to the child and to the environment. Some theorists see children as more or less passive recipients of whatever the environment offers them. According to this view, children simply need to get a certain amount of experience (by being exposed to an adequate amount of environmental information) and they will develop. Learning a language, for example, would just be a matter of hearing enough words enough times in enough different sentences.

Other theorists give children a much more active role in their own development: it's not what the environment offers, it's what the child selects from it, seeks out in it, or even creates from it. Thus, language learning would depend—*does* depend, as we will see—not just on hearing enough words in enough sentences, but on a process of gaining insights and constructing theories of what words mean and how they can be combined. Language learning is one of the clearest cases of development resulting from what children make of their environment, rather than what the environment makes of the child. But even here, progress cannot occur without environmental support. If a child never hears a language, he will never learn to speak it.

If we assume that children play an active role in at least some aspects of their own development, and combine that assumption with the idea of children being different from one another right from the start, we get an inkling of how two children reared in the same home can develop in such different ways. If one child chooses to spend all his time watching TV while another prefers to play outdoors or to talk to his parents, they are, in that respect, growing up in two different environments. And if one child prefers to talk to his parents about stars or butterflies while another prefers to talk about what happened on the playground that day, in some sense they may even grow up with two different sets of parents. This is what we mean by a **transactional** view of development. A transaction (a business transaction, for example) is something in which two parties each have a role—what one does has an effect on what the other does, and vice versa. During development, it is the child and the environment that have these two-way transactions with each other. From the moment she is born, a baby begins to have an effect on her environment—on her parents, for example—just as the environment they provide has an effect on her. You will come to see how this works as we return to transactional effects many times in the next 14 chapters.

We've taken a brief look at some of the major issues in the field of child development. Now we will give you a quick overview of the trends and methods that have led to a greatly increased understanding of childhood in the past 100 years.

The Study of Child Development

People have been observing the stars and the planets for many centuries, carefully recording their observations and checking them against their theories. Yet the serious study of childhood is a relatively modern invention, dating only from the 1880s. This doesn't mean that no one had theories about children before that: there were theories, but they were based on philosophical or religious viewpoints, or on stories by writers of popular fiction. Even though these theories often conflicted with each other, for a long time there were no attempts to test them in a systematic way. Childhood was simply not considered to be a subject that one could study with the methods of science (Garwood, Phillips, Hartman, and Zigler, 1989).

The Discovery of Childhood

In olden times, children weren't even considered to be very important. When the only methods for limiting family size were the avoidance of sex or the abandonment of newborn babies, and when even those babies who were kept and cared for had less than a 50–50 chance of surviving to adulthood, it wasn't sensible to place much importance on the life of a child. There were times and places, in fact, when getting attached to one's offspring was downright discouraged. In 16th-century Paris, babies were not nursed by their mothers but were placed at birth in the homes of "wet nurses," who generally took care of several babies at a time. A large majority of these babies died; the others were accepted back into their families only after they had made it through the perilous ordeal of infancy. Banishment of this sort was comparatively benevolent: throughout ancient times and the Middle Ages, many babies were simply put out to die. This was especially likely in the case of babies who had the bad luck to be born female or with any other incurable defect, and babies that were conceived out of wedlock (Ariès, 1962).

Although this practice now seems unbelievably hardhearted, often the parents had no choice: there was not enough room in their houses or food in their cupboards to provide for the children they already had. Keeping the new baby would lower the chances of survival for the whole family. Moreover, it appears that many abandoned infants were rescued by the church or by people who could afford to rear them and who expected them to become useful. The lives of these rescued children were unlikely to have been pleasant, but their survival rates may actually have been higher than if they had remained in their original families (Boswell, 1988).

The modern view of the **nuclear family** (a husband, a wife, and their children) had its beginnings in 18th-century Europe, when the family began to be viewed as a unit held together by mutual affection, rather than by economic considerations. This led to a change in attitudes toward children, who became valued more for themselves and less for what they could contribute in the way of free labor. There was also a new understanding of childhood as a distinct phase of life; before that, children tended to be viewed as differing from adults only in size and competence (Ariès, 1962).

Other changes came about as a result of the industrialization of society in the 18th and 19th centuries. Men began to work at jobs that took them away from the home during much of the day. Women were increasingly seen as having the role of attending to the family's needs; this role—especially the job of caring for the children—began to be viewed as an important one. Around the same time, general health improved and more children were surviving to adulthood. Both of these trends led, around the beginning of the 19th century, to an increased interest in children and to the "discovery" of childhood as a special time of life (Hareven, 1985).

But long before this discovery was made, parents were already being given advice on how to raise their children. The advice-givers were invariably men, usually religious leaders, and their advice was often harsh. A Puritan minister who came to America with the Pilgrims wrote a sermon in 1625 that contained this warning for parents: "Surely there is in all children, though not alike, a stubbornness and stoutness of mind arising from natural pride, which must, in the first place, be broken and beaten down" (quoted in Moran and Vinovskis, 1985, p. 26).

Religion also provided a motive for teaching children to read at the earliest possible age: they should learn to read the Bible so their souls (tarnished with "original sin") could be saved. Early reading books for children were religious in nature. In New England, in the early decades of the 19th century, there was a movement to put 2- and 3-year-old children into "infant schools" where they could be taught to read. By 1840, as many as 50 percent of 3-year-olds in Massachusetts may have been enrolled in such schools. But there were already other voices warning of the dangers of this practice: in 1833, a physician warned parents that early education could lead to insanity. By 1860, the infant school movement was over and educators were recommending that schooling should begin at age 5 with kindergarten, where reading was not taught (Moran and Vinovskis, 1985).

Asking Questions

Although many were willing to construct theories or give advice about children, it was not until the early 1880s that people began to look at actual children for information about childhood. The study of child development was launched by the work of the American psychologist G. Stanley Hall. What Hall did to assure his place in history was quite simple: he asked children questions. Actually, his job was even simpler, since he didn't ask the questions himself: he decided what questions to ask and distributed them in the form of questionnaires to the schoolteachers of Boston. The teachers did the asking and reported the results to Hall. In this way, Hall learned that 80 percent of 6-year-olds in Boston knew that milk comes from cows, even though some of them had never seen a cow. Almost all the 6-year-olds (94 percent) knew where their stomachs were, but only 55 percent could locate their hips and only 10 percent could locate their ribs (Boring, 1950).

Asking children to answer questions has always been a useful method in the study of child development. Hall's work was soon followed by that of Alfred Binet, in France, whose efforts led to the construction of the first IQ tests in the 1890s. Fifty years later, the Swiss developmental psychologist Jean Piaget based his theories, in part, on children's answers to his questions.

But asking questions of children—especially if they're quite young— clearly has its perils. A modern developmental psychologist named Jeremy Anglin has used this method in studying how children learn what words mean, and whether a young child's idea of a word is different from that of an older person's. Here, for example, is what happened when a child named Peter, age 2 years, 8 months, was questioned about his ideas on the meaning of the word "car":

INTERVIEWER: Can you tell me what a car is, Peter?
PETER: Okay. A car is a truck and a truck is a car (laughs).
INTERVIEWER: What does a car look like?
PETER: A truck.
INTERVIEWER: A truck? What does a car do?
(Peter crawls on hands and knees away from table, demonstrating what a car does.)
INTERVIEWER: Peter, Peter, come on back. . . . Can you tell us what a car does?
PETER: Voom, voom. (He demonstrates by acting like a car again.)
INTERVIEWER: It vooms. What else does it do?
PETER: Yeah.
INTERVIEWER: What else does it do?
PETER: It goes and they run.
INTERVIEWER: Oh, that's very good, Peter. What does it look like?
PETER: Voom, voom, voom (demonstrating again).
INTERVIEWER: Peter, what does a car look like!
PETER: Voom, voom, voom. (He acts like a car.)
INTERVIEWER: Peter, OK, why don't you drive back here.
PETER: No.   (Anglin, 1977, p. 193)

Observation

Another time-honored way of studying children is by the simple procedure of observing them and writing down the observations. In fact, this method preceded Hall's questionnaire studies: the practice of keeping a detailed diary to record the progress of one's own children goes back at least to the 1870s and probably much earlier. The observation method is still in use. For example, a sociologist named William Corsaro, who is interested in the social behavior of 3- and 4-year-olds, spent several months in a nursery school, observing and recording. What did he observe?

A researcher studying the social interactions of children in a nursery school found that these "peer episodes" tend to be brief and that children who are playing together are likely to exclude newcomers.

First, he reported that few of the children enjoyed playing alone— a child who found herself alone generally tried to find one or more other children to play with. Corsaro calls a period in which two or more children were playing together a "peer episode," **peer** meaning another child of the same age (**agemate** means the same thing). These peer episodes tended to be brief: only half lasted more than five minutes. Here, in the language of a sociologist, is how a peer episode commonly ended:

> The children had to be prepared for the breakdown of interaction at any time, because playmates often simply left a play area and terminated the activity without a formal, verbal marker.   (Corsaro, 1981, p. 215)

In other words, when one child got tired of playing with another child, she just walked off without even saying goodbye.

Children who found themselves suddenly left without a playmate almost immediately tried to gain entry into another group. Here is what often happened:

> [Linda approaches Barbara and Nancy, who are playing together with some toy animals.]

BARBARA TO LINDA:	You can't play!
LINDA:	Yes I can. I can have some animals too.
BARBARA TO LINDA:	No, you can't. We don't like you today.
NANCY TO LINDA:	You're not our friend.
LINDA:	I can play here, too.
BARBARA TO NANCY:	No, her can't—her can't play, right Nancy?
NANCY:	Right. (p. 214)

Corsaro carefully noted how many times a group of two or more children refused to allow a new child to join them. He found that the newcomer was rejected 54 percent of the time.

CASE STUDIES. A study that involves only a single subject—in other words, one child—is called a **case study**. The study may involve only observation and recording, like the diaries people kept about their children. Or it may, in addition, involve some kind of testing or treatment. Sigmund Freud, for example, wrote a case study about a child he called Little Hans, who had an extreme fear of horses (see Chapter 3). Little Hans was treated under Freud's direction and recovered from his phobia; the description of the treatment and of its effects on the child were part of the case study, which was first published in 1909.

One of the most intriguing case studies ever reported began over a century earlier. In 1799, a boy of 11 or 12 was captured in a forest in France. The child, who became known as "The Wild Boy of Aveyron," had evidently been living on his own in the forest for some time; he could not speak and in many ways he acted more like a wild animal than a human being. A young French doctor, Jean Itard, took charge of the boy, whom he named Victor. Itard kept a journal of his efforts to civilize Victor—to teach him to wear clothing, eat with a spoon, keep himself clean, and so on. But, to his great disappointment, Itard never succeeded in teaching Victor to say more than a few simple words.

No one knows why Victor never learned to speak in sentences. One theory is that he was too old: it may be difficult or impossible to acquire a first language after the age of 12. Another theory is that Victor was retarded; perhaps he was abandoned in the forest for that reason. The problem with studies that deal with only a single child (often one who is unusual or especially interesting in some way) is that it is very difficult to tell whether the results can be generalized to other children. On the other hand, by going deeper into the lives of their subjects, case studies can make up in depth what they lack in generality, and provide us with fascinating information that we couldn't otherwise obtain.

Measurements and Samples

G. Stanley Hall reported the percentages of children who answered a given question correctly, and William Corsaro reported the percentages of children who wouldn't let other children enter their games. Now we come to studies that collect numerical data of another sort, obtained by testing or measuring large numbers of children. The measurements serve as a standard of comparison, enabling us to compare an individual child with others of the same age. For example, physicians and anthropologists have been recording data about children's height for over a century. Such information can be used to reassure worried parents that their child is growing normally or to alert a pediatrician that a child's growth is slower than it should be.

When we measure the heights of many children of a given age, the measurements (like other data of this sort) fall into what is known as a **normal** or **bell-shaped curve**. Figure 1–1 shows an example: this is what the data would look like if we took a very large number of measurements—measuring the height of every 8-year-old girl in America, for instance. Data that fall into such a curve are said to be **normally distributed.**

The average 8-year-old American girl is 50 inches tall, or 127 centimeters (cm). Thus, the center of the curve, and its highest point, is at 50 inches (127 cm); 50 inches is the **mean** (average) measurement. A large number of 8-year-old girls are about 50 inches tall, or slightly shorter or slightly taller than

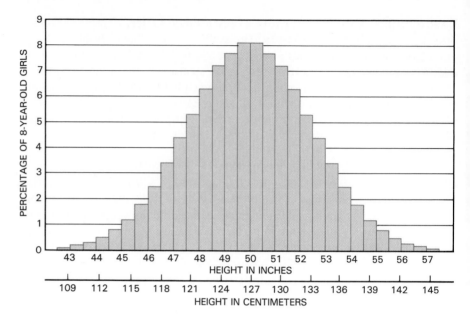

FIGURE 1-1
A normal or bell-shaped curve. If we measured the height of a very large number of 8-year-old girls, the results would look approximately like this.

that. The number of girls who are much shorter or much taller than 50 inches decreases rapidly, the farther away from 50 inches we get. Fewer than 5 percent are shorter than 45 inches or taller than 55 inches.

Although an 8-year-old girl who is 43 or 58 inches tall may be unusual, that doesn't mean she is "abnormal." The "normal" in "normal curve" refers only to the mathematical description of its shape. The curve tells us nothing about what is normal or what is abnormal—only about what is common and what is rare. Any further distinctions are arbitrary—a question of where to draw the line.

For example, IQ data are also normally distributed, with a mean IQ of 100; children with IQ scores below 70 or above 130 are rare. Children with IQ scores below 70 are often labeled "mentally retarded," and those with IQ scores above 130 are sometimes called "gifted." These labels mean only that their IQs fall below or above an arbitrary cutoff point on the curve. Thus, a child with a measured IQ of 69 might be considered retarded, while a child with a measured IQ of 71 (not noticeably different at all) will be classified as "low normal." This is not to imply that there's no use trying to make distinctions. We distinguish between night and day, and there, too, it's hard to say where one ends and the other begins.

One more point should be made about normal curves. When we said that "The average 8-year-old American girl is 50 inches tall, or 127 centimeters," we were talking about a girl who is average in *height*. Any given 8-year-old girl who is average in height might be far from average in weight, or strength, or intelligence, or musical ability, or in countless other ways. In fact, it would be impossible to find a child who is average in everything. Thus, when we speak of an "average child," we are referring to a theoretical child who measures at the mean in one particular characteristic—the characteristic we are interested in at the moment.

FIGURE 1-2
Motor milestones in the first 15 months of life, according to Shirley (1933).
Modern data don't agree with Shirley's: nowadays, the average baby
walks at about 12 months.

VARIABILITY. The first big surge of research in child development came in the 1920s and '30s. A good example of the work done in those days is the research reported in 1933 by a psychologist named Mary Shirley. Shirley studied 25 infants as they grew to toddlerhood, recording their **motor development**—the development of the ability to move and coordinate the parts of the body, as in crawling, walking, and grasping things with the hands. A summary of Shirley's findings is shown in Figure 1–2. Clearly, there is a need for this sort of information. People who deal with children—parents, for instance—want to know what to expect from a child and roughly when to expect it. But there are problems with Shirley's data. The age she gives for walking, for example, is 15 months; modern studies put the age of walking at about 12 months. Why is Shirley's estimate so far off?

One reason may be that the babies Shirley studied were almost certainly not what we call a **representative sample** of American babies. A representative sample contains individuals from different racial and ethnic groups, different social and economic backgrounds, different geographic locations, and so on, in roughly the same proportions that they occur in the population as a whole. But Shirley carried out her study in Minnesota, and her subjects were Minnesotan babies. Most of them were probably of Northern European ancestry; almost certainly, all these babies were white. Such a sample gives us some idea of what to expect from a baby born in Minnesota to white parents of Northern European ancestry; but what if the baby we're interested in is born in New York City to parents of Italian ancestry, or in South Carolina to African-American parents, or in Arizona to Mexican-American parents? Can we simply apply Shirley's data to all these babies and hope it will work? No, we can't: we have to test babies of all different backgrounds and ancestries if we want to draw conclusions about babies in general. The fact that Shirley didn't do this is one reason that the **norms** (or averages) she gave for the ages of the motor milestones do not agree with more recent figures. A black baby, on the average, begins to walk a little earlier than a white baby. If Shirley had included black babies in her sample, she would have gotten a slightly lower number for average age of walking.

But even for white babies, Shirley's figure of 15 months is too high. Perhaps, for unknown reasons, modern babies learn to walk a little earlier than babies did in the '30s. But it is more likely that Shirley's group of 25 babies simply happened, by chance, to contain a few extra babies of the type who are in no hurry to get up and walk. With such a small sample—only 25 babies—it's easy to have the results thrown off by chance factors, also known as bad luck: the kind of luck that can cause a driver to miss the green light a dozen times in a row, or that can cause a card player to get one bad hand after another.

Shirley's sample of 25 babies is also too small to provide an idea of the **variability** of motor development—of how widely spread out, or narrowly lumped together, the measurements are on the normal curve. Are all babies quite similar in when they learn to walk, or are there great differences from one to another? This becomes an important question in the case of a child who is unusually slow to walk. What if the child is still not walking at 18 months, or at 20 months, or at 24 months? At some point we must begin to realize that there is a problem. But when?

There can be no hard-and-fast answer to this kind of question. If Shirley had studied 250 babies instead of 25, she might have found that 95 percent of them walked between, say, 9 months and 18 months. Then we would know that a nonwalking 20-month-old is quite unusual and should certainly be given a careful examination by a pediatrician.

Doing Experiments

Some people may think there is something hardhearted about the idea of doing experiments with children; they think of an "experiment" as something cold and possibly ruthless. In a very few cases, this concern is well-founded; see Box 1–1. Fortunately, most researchers who use babies or children as subjects carry out their work with great care and sensitivity.

In 1961, at a time when a great surge of interest in the newborn baby was just beginning, an experimental psychologist named Michael Wertheimer did a test on his own child, a baby girl just a few minutes old. He wanted to find out whether newborn babies can localize sounds—whether they can tell which direction a sound is coming from. So he clicked a toy "cricket" on one side of the baby and then on the other, and observed that the baby's head turned in the direction of the sound.

These results were recorded, written up, and published in the journal *Science*, but no one was really convinced. It was a case study— only a single child was involved—and everyone knows that the children of psychologists are a bit peculiar! So the question of sound localization in newborn infants was still an open issue in 1979, when a pair of Canadian researchers decided to investigate it more thoroughly.

We have seen that asking questions of lively 2½-year-olds has its hazards, but they are nothing compared with the difficulties of doing experiments with newborn babies. Very young babies spend most of their time sleeping; when they are awake they are generally being fed or diapered, or are crying. They are capable of being asked experimental "questions" only during those few precious moments when they are doing none of the above. Carrying out research on very young babies requires, as much as anything else, a tremendous amount of patience.

The researchers in question, Darwin Muir and Jeffrey Field, started out with 12 babies from the newborn nursery in a Canadian hospital. The experiment was performed in a quiet room next to the nursery. (It was necessary, of course, to have the permission of the hospital and of the babies' parents to carry out this research.) The babies—six boys, six girls—were all healthy and normal in size and weight, and all were less than a week old. The experiment could be performed only when a baby was in an alert, receptive state, neither sleeping nor crying. The researchers had to give up on three of the 12 babies, because these babies never seemed to be in an appropriately receptive mood. The remaining nine were tested one at a time.

Each baby was held in a researcher's hands, face upward, in an almost horizontal position. The other researcher was holding two medicine bottles, one in each hand, and the baby's head was placed between them. Both bottles were then shaken. One bottle was empty and made no noise, but the other contained hard pellets and made a rattling sound (the bottles were opaque, so the pellets couldn't be seen). The rattling went on for 20 seconds or until the baby turned her head to one side or the other and held it there for at least 5 seconds. If the baby tended to turn her head to the side with the rattling sound, it couldn't have been that she was attracted by the sight of the moving bottle because there was a moving bottle on both sides of her head.

The test was given from five to eight times to each baby, depending on how long the baby remained cooperative. The rattling bottle was sometimes on the right, sometimes on the left, in a random order. Two people—one researcher and one other person—wrote down which way the baby had moved her head on each trial. (If a baby turned in both directions during the course of a trial, they decided which direction her head had turned the farthest.) The two observers almost always agreed in their judgments.

The results seemed to indicate that the babies could tell which direction the sound was coming from: they turned their heads in the direction of the rattling sound on a total of 52 of the 60 trials. Their movements, according to

The Child in Society

Box 1-1
The Ethics of Child Development Research

In 1939, Myrtle McGraw, a professor at Briarcliff College, reported on her research on "Swimming Behavior in the Human Infant." Her paper described the results of experiments performed on a total of 42 babies, ranging in age from 11 days to 2½ years.

McGraw was interested in the question of whether human babies have any inborn ability to swim. Her method of testing them was straightforward: she put them in a large tub of water.

> At each examination the baby was placed in three different positions: (1) With the hands of the experimenter placed under his chin and on the crown of his head, he was supported in such a way that his body and extremities could move freely while his nose and mouth were protected above the water level; (2) he was submerged in a prone (face-down) position without any support whatsoever; and (3) he was submerged without support in a supine (face-up) position. (McGraw, 1939/1967, p. 128)

McGraw reports that very young babies do have some swimming ability:

> The movements of the infant only a few weeks old are striking when he is placed in water in a prone position. . . . These movements (of the legs, arms, and body) are ordinarily sufficiently forceful to propel the baby a short distance through the water. . . . Another outstanding feature of the infant's behavior during the newborn phase is breath control. Apparently a reflex inhibits his breathing while he is submerged, since he does not cough or show disturbances common among the older babies after they have been submerged. (pp. 128–129)

Unfortunately for them, babies lose these remarkable abilities when they are about 4 months old. Infants of 4½ or 5 months (still too young to sit without support) failed to swim when McGraw immersed them in water. Their movements, she reported, "are of the struggling order"; the babies "clutch at the experimenter's hand" or "try to wipe the water from the face." They are obviously upset and their distress is understandable—they no longer have the benefit of a reflex to keep them from breathing water into their lungs:

> It was apparent during this phase that the baby had more noticeable difficulty with respiration, or controlling respiration, when he was submerged. Often the ingestion of fluid was considerable, and the infant would cough or otherwise show respiratory disturbance when he was taken out of the water. (pp. 129–131)

McGraw doesn't tell us whether any of these babies suffered ill effects as a result of their unwilling participation in her experiment. Nor does she tell us where and how she obtained these babies. We can safely assume, however, that she did not seek or obtain the permission of the babies' parents: What parent would allow an 11-day-old infant to be "submerged in a prone position without any support whatsoever"?

Nowadays, research of this nature could not be carried out in the United States. It is very unlikely that it would even be proposed. In 1973, a special committee of the American Psychological Association drew up guidelines for research with human subjects. Among their recommendations was a question that must be asked of every research project in child development: "Whether there is a negative effect upon the dignity and welfare of the participants that the importance of the research does not warrant" (APA, 1973, p. 11). McGraw's experiment would fail this test by cur-

the researchers, suggested that the babies were making a deliberate attempt to look for the source of the sound: "They hunched their shoulders, actively pulled their heads up, turned to the side of the stimulus, and then seemed to inspect the sound source visually" (Muir and Field, 1979, p. 432).

But the researchers were not satisfied. The experiment we've just described has a flaw: both the person holding the baby and the people recording her responses knew which way the sound was coming from. It's possible that the researcher who was holding the baby would involuntarily look in the direction of the rattling sound himself, and that the baby was responding to his eye movements. Or perhaps the way he was holding the baby was influenced by

Ethical considerations are particularly important when research involves children.

rent standards. It *did* involve "a negative effect upon the dignity and welfare of the participants," and the research would not be considered important enough to justify inflicting that effect on them.

The American Psychological Association's guidelines also listed a number of specific points that a researcher must consider. For instance, when children are used as subjects, the researcher is expected to obtain their parents' *informed* consent. This means that the parents must be told about any aspects of the experiment that might influence their decision to let their children participate. Researchers are also expected to avoid the use of deception, except where deception is necessary to the purpose of the experiment; in this case they are supposed to undeceive the participants ("debrief" them) when the experiment is over.

It is not always easy to put these guidelines into practice; occasionally it may be impossible. In some experiments, it's necessary to keep the participants from knowing that they are subjects in an experiment. An example might be an experiment in which a "lost" wallet is left in a school corridor and the researcher watches to see what the finder does. The use of deception is also necessary in some cases. In a study of the development of moral behavior, a researcher might give children the impression that they are being left alone in a room and then watch them through a pane of one-way glass to see how well they can resist temptation. Afterward the researcher would be expected to tell the children of this deception and also to relieve them of any feelings of guilt that might follow from a failure to resist temptation. But if the children were going to be tested again at a later time, the researcher wouldn't want to tell them about the one-way glass—it would affect their behavior the next time they were tested.

Another case in which deception might be required is in research involving the children of convicted criminals or mentally ill patients. If such a study required that these children be observed in a school setting, it would be necessary to conceal from the children's classmates and teachers the reason for studying those particular children. It might even be necessary to conceal which particular children were being studied. And in this case —in order to keep these children's backgrounds from becoming public knowledge—the deception would have to be permanent.

These examples show that ethical considerations are not always easy to apply—often it's a matter of weighing the importance of one principle against the importance of another. Most universities now have committees that review proposed research in advance and decide whether it is ethical.

In order to learn about human beings, we must study human beings. Given the present-day standards of ethics in research, the risks to the subjects are usually negligible. Whatever small risks remain are outweighed by the potential benefits.

his expectation that she would be turning her head in a certain direction. (If the baby *were* actually responding to these subtle hints from the researcher, that would be at least as interesting as an ability to localize sounds, but it's not what the researchers were trying to prove.) Another possibility is that the people recording the responses may also have been biased by their expectations. If the baby moved her head once in one direction and once in the other within a given trial, they were supposed to record the direction of the larger head movement. But what if the two head movements were equal or almost equal—wouldn't they be more likely to write down the response they were expecting (or hoping) to get?

To answer these objections, Muir and Field did a second experiment, using 12 new babies. This time the rattling sound was recorded in advance and played through one of two stationary loudspeakers, one located on each side of the baby's head. This time the researcher holding the baby couldn't tell which side the sound was coming from: he was wearing earphones that piped a continuous rattling sound into both his ears, and the sound that the baby heard was controlled by someone else. And this time the people who recorded the babies' responses also didn't know which side the sound was coming from: instead of watching the experiment itself, they viewed a silent video-tape that showed the babies' movements during each trial. The observers viewed the videotapes, decided which way the babies turned their heads, and wrote down their judgments; afterward these judgments were compared with records indicating which side the sound had come from on each trial.

The results of this second experiment are shown in Table 1–1. This table shows how many times each baby turned his or her head in the direction of the sound.

Now it's pretty clear-cut. Of the 12 babies, 11 turned in the direction of the sound more often than in the opposite direction. (The twelfth turned in the two directions equally often.) Altogether, 82 percent of the head-turns were in the direction of the sound. These results can't just be due to the babies' having a preference for turning their heads in one particular direction, because the sound came equally often from the left and from the right.

If the babies had just been turning their heads at random, we would expect roughly 50 percent of the babies to turn their heads more often in the direction of the sound. But 11 out of 12 babies turned their heads in the right direction—considerably more than 50 percent. Such a sizable effect is unlikely to be a mere coincidence.

We didn't say, however, that it *couldn't* be a coincidence. Improbable things sometimes do happen just by chance: you can flip an ordinary coin high into the air 12 times in a row and it's possible for it to land heads up on 11 of the 12 tries. It's possible, but highly unlikely. We can say exactly how unlikely: by

TABLE 1–1
Results of the Sound-Localization Experiment

BABY	HEAD-TURNS TOWARD SOUND	HEAD-TURNS AWAY FROM SOUND
1	7	1
2	7	1
3	8	0
4	7	1
5	7	1
6	5	2
7	7	1
8	3	3
9	6	2
10	5	1
11	3	2
12	7	1

(Based on data from Muir and Field, 1979, p. 433. © The Society for Research in Child Development, Inc.)

the laws of mathematical probability, the chances are 12 in 4096, or roughly .003, of having an unweighted, fairly tossed coin turn up heads 11 times out of 12. When a result is this unlikely to have occurred purely by chance, statisticians say that the result is *significant*. Statisticians will generally use the label **significant** for any result that has less than a .05 probability (less than one chance in 20) of being a coincidence. Thus, there is a small but real possibility that a result that is called "significant" *did* occur just by chance. Note also that a result can be significant in the statistical sense without being the least bit interesting or important.

Correlational Studies

It isn't always possible to perform an experiment in which you do something and then watch to see how your subjects react. In some cases, what you want to study might not be under your control—for instance, you might want to study the effects of parents' childrearing methods or of how many siblings a child has. Or perhaps what you want to study might have harmful effects on children—obviously you can't try it out in order to find out exactly how harmful it is. Let's say you are interested in the long-term effects of watching violent TV shows: you want to find out if watching televised violence makes children more likely to push or hit their classmates, and you suspect that the answer is yes. You probably wouldn't want to test this theory by sitting a bunch of children in front of a TV screen and showing them scenes of violence, week after week. One thing you *could* do, however, is to find out how many violent TV shows children watch on their own, and then see whether the ones who watch a lot of these shows are more aggressive on the playground than children who watch few or none of these shows. This is called a **correlational study.**

In a correlational study, the idea is to look at a number of children, measure each of them in two different ways, and then see if those measurements are **correlated.** In the case of TV watching and aggressiveness, the first measurement would be the number of violent TV shows each child watched per week, and the second would be some measure of the child's aggressiveness. Do the children who watch many violent shows tend to be high in aggressiveness? Do the children who watch relatively few of these shows tend to be low in aggressiveness? If so, there is a **positive correlation** between watching violent shows and acting aggressively. If the correlation goes the other way —if the children who watch many violent shows are *less* aggressive—the correlation would be **negative.**

Just about any two sets of measurements, taken on the same group of children, can be tested (using the methods of mathematical statistics) to see if they are correlated. You could measure the height of a group of children and also measure their weight, and you would find that there was a positive correlation between height and weight: the taller children weigh more, on the average, than the shorter ones. Or you could measure *pairs* of children, such as twins, to see how similar they are to each other.

Correlations can range from +1.00 (the strongest possible positive correlation) through zero (no correlation at all, meaning that the two things being measured are unrelated to each other), to −1.00 (the strongest possible negative correlation). For example, the heights of identical twins raised together are very similar: if one twin is tall, it is extremely likely that the other twin is also tall. The correlation between the heights of identical twins is +.94 (Tanner, 1978). Let's say we measured 25 pairs of 8-year-old identical twin girls and put one point on a graph for each pair of twins. Figure 1–3 gives the expected results of this procedure: this graph shows what a correlation of +.94 looks like.

If each pair of twins were exactly equal in size, the correlation would be +1.00 and all the points would be right on the diagonal line. If, instead of measuring twins, we measured pairs of unrelated girls chosen at random, the correlation would be close to zero (the measurements would be uncorrelated) and the points would be scattered around instead of clustering near the line.

What about the effects of TV watching on children's aggressiveness? A correlational study on this topic was carried out some years ago by Leonard Eron, of the University of Illinois, and three of his colleagues. The subjects were a group of 875 9-year-old girls and boys. To find out about the children's TV-watching habits, the researchers asked the mothers of the children to name their child's favorite programs. To find out which children were most aggressive, they asked all the children in the school questions such as "Who pushes and shoves other children?" and "Who starts a fight over nothing?" The researchers ended up with two scores for each child: a score for liking to watch violent shows, and a score for aggressiveness based on ratings by his or her classmates. The boys, by the way, were significantly more aggressive than the girls.

There was no relationship between aggressiveness and viewing habits in girls, but the researchers found a positive correlation of .21 between violent TV watching and aggressive behavior in the third-grade boys. That is not, however, a very high correlation; if all we knew about a boy was his viewing

FIGURE 1-3
A positive correlation of .94. This is approximately what the data would look like if we measured the heights of 25 pairs of 8-year-old twin sisters. Each point on the graph represents one pair of twins. For example, the lowermost point represents a pair in which the first twin we measured was 45 inches tall and her twin sister was 44½ inches. If two sisters are exactly the same height, their point will fall on the diagonal line.

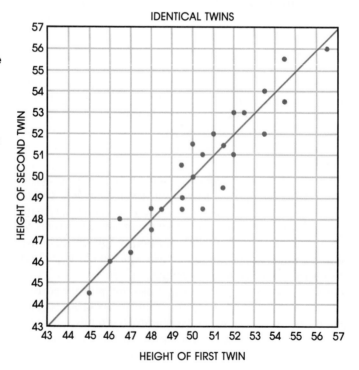

habits, we wouldn't be able to make a very accurate guess about how he is likely to behave on the playground.

More important, we don't know *why* the two measures are correlated. Even if the correlation had been very high—let's say, .70 or .80—it would not prove that the TV watching was responsible for the aggressive behavior. It could work the other way around: boys who are aggressive may prefer to watch violent TV shows. A correlation cannot prove that one thing *caused* another—that TV viewing, for example, *caused* aggressiveness. All a correlation shows is that two things are mathematically related.

However, the researchers did not stop there. Ten years later they rounded up as many as they could find of the original group of 875 children. Some could not be located and others refused to participate again, so the researchers were left with a group of 427 19-year-olds. The 19-year-olds were retested. This time there was no correlation at all between current viewing of violent TV shows and aggressive behavior (the correlation for both sexes was —.05, which is essentially zero). But there was a significant positive correlation (+.31) between boys' TV viewing habits at the age of 9 and their aggressiveness at age 19.

Thus, for boys (though not for girls), watching violent TV shows at age 9 appeared to lead to an increase in aggressiveness at age 19. Clearly, the relationship couldn't have worked the other way round: a tendency to be aggressive at age 19 couldn't possibly have had an effect on the boys' TV viewing habits ten years earlier (Eron, Lefkowitz, Huesmann, and Walder, 1972).

LONGITUDINAL VERSUS CROSS-SECTIONAL STUDIES. When the same children are measured or tested more than once over a period of time, as the children in the TV-watching study were, it is referred to as a **longitudinal study.** The important thing about longitudinal studies is that the *same children* are examined again at a later point in their lives. Patience is indeed a valuable attribute in people who study child development: those researchers had to wait ten years to complete their study!

For researchers who want quicker results, another method is available. Let's say we were studying how memory develops as children get older, and we decide to use a simple test: we read out loud a short list of numbers, for example "five, eight, two, three," and ask the child just to repeat it back to us. This is a test of the child's **memory span.** Memory span increases as children get older: a 4-year-old can repeat back a list of three or four numbers, a 6-year-old can handle four or five, and an 8-year-old five or six. How do we know this? Not by testing a child at 4, waiting two years and testing her again at 6, and waiting two more years and testing her once again. Instead, we test a group of 4-year-olds, a group of 6-year-olds, and a group of 8-year-olds. This is called a **cross-sectional study.**

The advantages of cross-sectional studies, as opposed to longitudinal ones, are obvious. First, we don't have to wait years to get the data. Second, we don't lose so many subjects. In a longitudinal study, in order to end up with a large enough group of subjects, the researchers have to start out with a great many more. Families move away; children who are willing to participate at one age may refuse when they are older. In the TV-violence study, the researchers started out with 875 9-year-olds and ended up with 427 19-year-olds.

The *disadvantages* of cross-sectional studies are less obvious. One problem is that we are dealing with groups of children who differ in age, but who may also differ in other ways, because they were born in different years. Researchers call this the **cohort** effect, a *cohort* being a group of people who were all born at about the same time. A cohort of children born in 1986 will probably not differ much from a cohort born in 1984, but they will differ considerably from a cohort born in 1966—a time when there were no home computers, no *Sesame Street*, and relatively few mothers of toddlers who worked outside the home.

Some questions can *only* be answered with a longitudinal study. For example, earlier in this chapter we discussed the question of whether tests given in infancy can predict how well a given child will do on an IQ test when he is several years older. There is no way of answering this question other than by testing a child in infancy and testing the same child again later on.

Easy to Say, Hard to Prove

There are many methods of doing research in child development; each method has the potential for producing misleading results. For example, a cross-sectional study can yield misleading results due to the cohort effect. It used to be thought that intelligence declines steadily in adulthood, as people grow older. This belief was based on cross-sectional studies which showed that 40-year-olds score lower on IQ tests than 20-year-olds, and 60-year-olds score lower than 40-year-olds. The trouble is that the 60-year-olds grew up at a time when educational and cultural opportunities were quite different from what they were when the 20-year-olds were growing up. Longitudinal studies give more optimistic results: they show that if particular individuals are examined over a span of many years, around half of them reach their 70s without showing any noticeable decline in intellectual abilities, and a smaller proportion retain their abilities well into their 80s (Schaie and Willis, 1986).

But longitudinal studies, too, have the potential to mislead. The problem is that the researchers always end up with fewer subjects than they started out with, and the subjects they end up with may not be a fair sample of the original group. In the study of TV and aggression, the group of 427 subjects who were retested at the end of ten years differed in an important way from the original group of 875. This is because only 27 percent of the most aggressive children in the original group came back to be tested, whereas 57 percent of the *least* aggressive children remained in the study. Thus, because they lost so many of the highly aggressive children, the researchers ended up with a less aggressive group of subjects (Eron and others, 1972).

What effect did this have on their results? We don't know. But, especially since the research was *about* aggressiveness, we can't rule out the possibility that the change in the nature of the group may have influenced the results.

THE DIRECTION OF EFFECTS. The boys who watched many aggressive shows at age 9 were more aggressive at age 19. Does this mean that their TV-watching during childhood *caused* their aggressiveness ten years later? Perhaps it did; this is how the researchers interpreted the results. But there are other possibilities. Sometimes when two things are correlated, neither one has caused the other: instead, both may be the result of a third factor. Take the example of the correlation between the heights of identical twins. It would

Does watching TV cause children to be aggressive? Researchers think so, but it's not easy to prove.

make no sense to say that one twin's height "caused" that of the other twin. Rather, the heights of both twins are the result of a certain combination of genes plus an environment that provided them with the essentials for growth.

In the same way, other (unmeasured) factors may account for the correlation between watching violent TV shows at age 9 and aggressiveness at age 19. Perhaps the aggressive 19-year-olds had received inadequate supervision from their parents all through childhood and adolescence. Perhaps they were reared by aggressive parents who themselves enjoyed violent TV shows and encouraged their sons to watch too. Although it's very possible that watching those shows was the reason, or one of the reasons, why the boys became aggressive, that still hasn't been proved.

This leads us to a much more common problem with correlational studies. Very often, such studies involve finding a correlation between the way a parent treats a child and the way the child behaves. For instance, it has been noted many times that children whose parents behave in an aggressive fashion toward them—children who are punished frequently and severely—tend to be more aggressive and disobedient than children who are punished mildly and seldom. In the past it was assumed that the punishments produced the misbehavior—that too many spankings produce an aggressive, uncooperative child. That may very well be true. But it's also possible that the child's behavior influences the parents—that parents who punish their children harshly may be reacting to their children's behavior, rather than (or in addition to) producing it.

Twenty or thirty years ago the direction of causality was always assumed to be from the parent to the child—the child's characteristics were invariably seen as a result, never as a cause. Now there is much greater awareness of the transactional nature of parent-child relationships: the fact that children have effects on their parents, just as parents have effects on their children. Nonetheless, it is still common to make the mistake of assuming that the parents' behavior is always the cause and the children's behavior always the result.

In the real world, there seldom are clear-cut "causes" and clear-cut "effects." Often the effects work in both directions at once, as in the case of punishment and misbehavior. Sometimes these two-way effects lead to "vicious circles": the child misbehaves, the parents punish, the punishment produces more misbehavior, and so on. It is rare to find a single, simple cause for a given kind of behavior. Children's behavior generally results from many factors—inherited tendencies, the parents' behavior toward them, the reactions of their peers, chance events—all working at once.

What Should Our Role Be?

Researchers from a variety of fields—psychology, education, medicine, home economics, sociology, anthropology—study children for a variety of reasons. One thing we all have in common is that every one of us was once a child; maybe that's why we find children so interesting. We also find children appealing. They are attractive and lively people—sometimes troublesome but never boring.

Beyond that, the motivations differ. Some researchers are driven mainly by the same kind of curiosity that makes other scientists study sea worms or black holes. Some are urged on by a desire to help children, to make their lives better, to make childhood a happier time and adult life more successful.

Both types of people are needed. The people who want to help children require precise, scientific knowledge if they are to be effective. And the people who produce the precise, scientific knowledge would be working in a vacuum if they didn't have the feeling that their work would one day be put to practical use.

It is not always easy to decide, however, what kind of practical use child development research *should* be put to. Let's say, for example, that researchers come across a certain way of changing the environment that causes development to be speeded up, so that children learn to talk or read or do higher mathematics at an earlier age. Is it clear that we want to give this kind of environment to every child (or to *any* child)? Is it clear that faster is better? Some authorities—Piaget, for example—don't think so.

An even more difficult question involves prediction. What if we learn how to predict development so accurately that we could tell in advance how a child will turn out? What if we could predict which children will grow up to be murderers, which ones will cheat on their taxes? What would we do with this knowledge? Such questions do not have right or wrong answers, but they are the kinds of questions that need to be thought about.

In this chapter we have tried to give you some feeling for what the study of child development is like. You have had a glimpse of the kinds of questions researchers ask and the kinds of problems they are up against in their attempts to answer them. You have also seen some of the dangers of being too quick to accept a result at its face value.

A tremendous amount of research in child development has been carried out and published in the past 25 years. We will try to distill for you, out of all this work, an accurate and complete picture of the developing infant, child, and adolescent.

Summary

1. Development is defined as the physical, mental, and behavioral changes that take place in human beings due to the passage of time or to what has occurred during that time. These changes include both those that are programmed in the genes and those that come about as a result of experience.

2. Two major issues in child development: How does a "typical" child develop, and what are the sources of differences between individuals?

3. We know that heredity and environment are the sources of children's individual characteristics, but it is difficult to use that knowledge to account for the behavior of a particular child.

4. Development involves both continuity and change. Which aspects of an individual change during development, and which remain the same? Intelligence, for example, was previously thought to develop in a discontinuous fashion, but now an underlying continuity has been found.

5. Some theorists believe that development proceeds in **stages,** and that what occurs in one stage is qualitatively different from what occurred in an earlier stage. Other theorists believe that development is a smooth, even progression.

6. What causes development to occur? One factor is **maturation,** which results from the built-in instructions programmed into our genes. But humans are flexible, which means that development can vary: children can adapt to a wide range of possible environments.

7. Some theorists see children as passive recipients of environmental information, whereas others see them as actively selecting or creating their own environments.

8. One reason why children in the same family may develop in different ways is that their different interests and preferences may cause them to choose different environments for themselves and to have different relationships with their parents. The recognition of the two-way transactions between the child and the environment is what we mean by a **transactional** view of development.

9. The scientific study of childhood dates only from the 1880s. Although people had theories about childhood long before that, no attempt was made to test them in a systematic way. A change in attitude toward family life, and an increased likelihood that a child would survive to adulthood, led to a greater interest in children.

10. The first researcher to study childhood in a systematic way was the American psychologist G. Stanley Hall. His method was to ask questions of children to find out how much they knew. Another early method for studying children was observation. Modern researchers still use these methods.

11. A **case study** typically involves only a single subject, such as "Little Hans," or "The Wild Boy of Aveyron." The trouble with a study based on a single child is that it's never clear whether the findings can be generalized to other children.

12. Measurements such as height and IQ are **normally distributed**—that is, they fall into a **normal** or **bell-shaped curve.** The highest point of the curve is at the **mean** (average). Measurements close to the mean are common; measurements farther from the mean are rare but are not necessarily "abnormal." Labels such as "mentally retarded" or "gifted" are based on arbitrary cutoff points on the curve of IQ scores.

13. Early studies such as Shirley's study of **motor development** may have given misleading results because the researcher failed to obtain a **representative sample.** Shirley also did not test enough babies to provide an idea of the **variability** of the measurements.

14. Research with children must take ethical considerations into account. Researchers are expected to avoid producing negative effects on their subjects' dignity or welfare that are not justified by the importance of the research.

15. Newborn babies who were tested in an experiment frequently turned their heads in the direction of a sound; this result was statistically **significant,** indicating that they almost certainly could tell from what direction the sound was coming. It's possible, but unlikely, for a significant result to happen purely by chance.

16. Correlational studies are designed to investigate the relationship between two (or more) sets of measurements made on the same subjects. A **correlation** is a numerical description of such a relationship. **Positive correlations** range from just above zero to +1.00; **negative** ones from just below zero to −1.00. A zero correlation means that the two sets of measurements are unrelated.

17. In a **longitudinal** study, the same children are tested more than once over a period of time. A longitudinal study of TV watching and aggression found a positive correlation between watching violent TV shows at age 9 and aggressiveness at age 19.

18. The disadvantages of longitudinal studies are that it may take years to collect the data and subjects tend to drop out of the study. The group that remains may not be a fair sample of the original group.

19. In a **cross-sectional** study, different age groups are tested in order to measure a developmental change. The results may be misleading because of the **cohort** effect: one cohort of children may differ from another because they were born and reared at different times.

20. The fact that two measurements are correlated does not indicate that one thing caused the other. Sometimes when two things are correlated, both may be the result of a third factor.

21. When a relationship is found between a certain type of parental behavior and a certain type of child behavior, it used to be assumed that the parents' behavior *caused* the child to act that way. Now it is recognized that children have effects on their parents, just as parents have effects on their children. Often, the effects work in both directions at once. Sometimes these two-way effects lead to ''vicious circles.''

22. People from many fields study child development; some are motivated chiefly by scientific curiosity and others by the hope of helping children.

Key Terms

development
sibling
maturation
stage
transactional view
nuclear family
peers
agemates
case study

normal curve
bell-shaped curve
normally distributed
mean
motor development
representative sample
norm
variability
significant

correlational study
correlated
positive correlation
negative correlation
longitudinal study
memory span
cross-sectional study
cohort

2

Heredity and Environment

When Wolfgang Amadeus Mozart was 4 years old, his father found him one day with pen and paper. "What are you doing?" he asked his son. "Writing a concerto for the piano," the child said. "Let me see," said the father, and took the paper, stained with ink blots, from his son. "But this is so difficult that nobody could play it!" the father exclaimed. "One must practice it," said the child. "Look, this is how it goes," and he played the music on his father's piano.

By the time Mozart was 7, he was touring Europe, amazing his audiences with his ability to perform on the piano, organ, and violin. He became one of the world's most prolific composers, writing sonatas, concertos, symphonies, operas, and choral music. Melodies poured out of him like water from a faucet—it was just a question of getting them down on paper (Turner, 1954).

Both **heredity** and **environment** were involved in Mozart's extraordinary talents. His father was a violinist who gave lessons in violin and piano; he was also a composer. The son was given access to musical instruments at an early age and was trained by his father, who derived satisfaction and profit from his son's precocious talents. But many other children have been reared in homes just as musical, by parents just as anxious to cultivate (or exploit) their children's talents, and they have not turned into musical geniuses. Environment alone cannot account for Mozart. On the other hand, heredity is also not sufficient. The uniquely musical brain he happened to be born with wouldn't have done him much good if he had been born into a peasant farm family and spent his entire life on the farm, without ever setting eyes on a musical instrument. Mozart would probably not have made a very good farmer.

Heredity and environment are responsible not just for outstanding characteristics like Mozart's musical talent—they are responsible for *all* of our characteristics: things we share with every other member of the human race, such as the ability to walk erect or to communicate with language; things we share with every other mammal, such as the ability to see, hear, and maintain a stable body temperature; even things we share with lower forms of life, such as the ability to digest food and to reproduce. But questions of heredity and environment are more likely to come up when we talk about *differences* among people. Children differ from each other because they have inherited different genes from their parents and because their environments also differ.

Sometimes, instead of heredity and environment, the terms **nature** and **nurture** are used. *Nature*, in this context, is a synonym for heredity—the characteristics people are born with, which they've inherited from their ancestors. *Nurture* refers to the way a child is reared. The term *environment* actually covers a lot more than that, because it refers to everything that happens to a person, from the time of conception to the time of death. Everything you have ever seen, heard, felt, smelled, tasted, eaten, breathed, or experienced is part of your environment.

We will begin this chapter with a quick overview of the major environmental influences on children. (In later chapters we will deal with some of these influences in greater detail.) Then we will briefly review the mechanisms of heredity. In the last section of this chapter we will discuss the ways in which genetic and environmental influences interact with each other, and the ways in which researchers have tried to tease apart their effects.

Basic Environmental Influences

If we look at the world as a whole, and back over history, we see that children's environments vary across a tremendous range. Ancient Egyptians and 18th-century Austrians, Sri Lankans and Swedes, the Masai of Africa and the Navajos of Arizona—all have different views on how children should be reared. In some countries, at some times, children are coddled and given a lot of attention and affection. In other times or places, they are ignored or treated harshly. Children may be expected to start acting like adults when they're 7 or

8, or they may be permitted to remain dependent on their parents until their 20s. These widely different attitudes toward children reflect basic differences among cultures.

A group of people who share common traditions, activities, beliefs, behaviors, and values, and who speak the same language, share a common **culture.** The ways that adults act toward children differ widely from culture to culture. Consider the following conversation between a 4-year-old girl and her aunt. Here's what the aunt says to the child:

> What a beautiful new shirt you have. Why don't you die so I can have it? Don't you want to die? Don't you want to die? Do die, then I can have the shirt.   (Kagan, 1979, p. 888)

Most Americans would never dream of talking like this to a child. But this conversation took place between two members of the Inuit (Eskimo) society of Baffin Island, in northern Canada. This kind of teasing is perfectly acceptable in Inuit society. The child was not in the least upset by her aunt's teasing—she was smiling happily the whole time her aunt was speaking.

The conversation between the Inuit aunt and her niece illustrates an important point: one cannot look at an isolated bit of a child's environment out of context. What effect a given sample of adult behavior will have on a child—how she interprets the adult's words or actions—depends partly on her previous experiences. And the child's previous experiences depend to a large extent on her culture (Kagan, 1979).

A **society** is a group of people with a common culture. One of the tasks of a society is to rear its children in such a way that they become acceptable members of that society. The children must acquire the appropriate patterns of behavior, knowledge and skills, and beliefs and attitudes. A method of childrearing that produces an acceptable American might produce a very unacceptable Inuit, and vice versa.

There are many possible ways of carrying out the job of rearing children. It is easier to see this if we look first at the way it is done in a culture other than our own.

THE HUTTERITES. The childrearing methods of a society serve to prepare the child for adult life in that society. A good illustration is the childrearing practices of a group of people called the Hutterites. The 230 Hutterite colonies in Canada and the northern United States contain a total of about 24,000 people. These people live communally, sharing their farmlands, buildings, and equipment, and eating together in community dining halls. They belong to a religion that calls for adult baptism and total pacifism. The rules of the community are very strict. For example, the women must wear long-sleeved, full-length dresses that button to the neck, even when working outdoors in hot weather. Their heads are always kept covered, first with a cap that buttons under the chin, and on top of that a black polka-dotted scarf. Girls must dress in this way from the time they reach school age.

An anthropologist named Gertrude Enders Huntington, who lived with a Hutterite colony in Canada for many months, has provided us with a detailed description of their method of childrearing. According to Huntington, a Hutterite baby is regarded as a gift from God. When a baby is born, the mother (who has worked hard throughout her pregnancy) is relieved of all responsibility other than the care of the newborn. The grandmother or another woman of the community takes over all her other chores. But the baby's mother resumes her regular duties three months after the birth, and from that time on the baby will be fed, played with, or left alone according to the community's schedule. When it's time for the adults to go to church or dining hall, the baby is put in a crib and left there.

When out of the crib, however, the Hutterite baby is the center of attention. Everyone in a Hutterite colony wants to hold a baby, and the infant is passed from hand to hand—spoken to, played with, tickled.

By toddlerhood the children are already under pressure to belong to the community rather than to their parents. And by the age of 3 the period of indulgence is definitely over. A Hutterite 3-year-old might be whipped for refusing to go to a person other than his parents, for quarreling with other children, for refusing to share, or for being noisy. After the punishment the child is immediately comforted.

Hutterite 3- to 6-year-olds spend their days in a group called the "kindergarten"; they are kept in a small building under the care of a "kindergarten mother." They are taught obedience, and they memorize prayers that they cannot yet understand. The idea of kindergarten is to break the "stubborn will" of the child and to make him or her into a conforming member of the group. Quiet, cooperative behavior is praised. Bad behavior is prevented with threats ("If you go outside a bear will get you!") or punished by means of a willow switch. But the children are not made to feel guilty for their misbehavior, since "it is only natural for a child to sin" (Huntington, 1981, p. 42).

At age 6, Hutterite children enter the community school, where they learn to read and write in English and German, and they study religion and Hutterite history. They're praised for working hard, but a fast learner is not given any special attention.

Hutterite kindergarten girls at nap time.

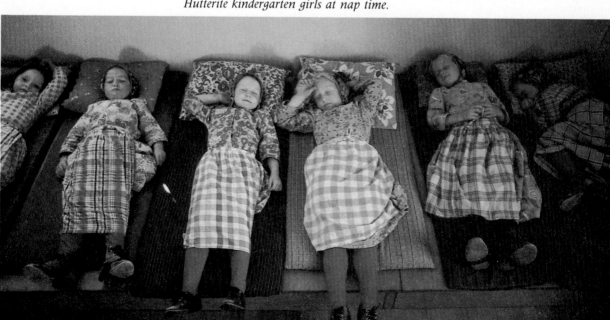

At 15 the Hutterite joins the adult work force and is allowed to eat in the adult dining hall. Physical punishment is no longer given. Young people must do their work and speak respectfully to their elders, but the community tolerates a certain amount of disregard for its rules. They are allowed to yield to some of the temptations of the outside world as long as they do it in private. Boys of this age sometimes smoke secretly; girls might use nail polish on their toenails—which they then hide under their thick black shoes. Teenagers of both sexes often own transistor radios on which they secretly listen to popular music. The community permits these little indulgences, because it knows that in another couple of years the young Hutterite will turn away from them and back to the community. He or she will humbly request baptism and will voluntarily become a full-fledged member of the Hutterite colony. The years of training and discipline will have accomplished their purpose.

DIFFERENT CULTURES, DIFFERENT GOALS. The Hutterites want their children to be obedient, cooperative, and faithful to their religion; their childrearing methods are successful in achieving those goals. But different societies have different goals for their children. Table 2–1 shows the results of a recent survey that asked mothers in five countries—the United States, the Philippines, Korea, Taiwan, and Turkey—what qualities they most desire their children to have. As you can see, there is little agreement from one country to another (Hoffman, 1988).

Within a given culture, childrearing goals may change dramatically over time. Mothers in the United States, and Chinese mothers in Taiwan, have not always wanted their children to be independent and self-reliant. In 1924, mothers in Muncie, Indiana, gave "strict obedience" and "loyalty to the church" as the two most important qualities they wanted their children to have. In 1978, mothers in the same town chose "independence" and "tolerance" as the qualities they most desired in their children (Alwin, 1988).

The traditional Chinese childrearing pattern also had obedience as its primary goal. Their culture prescribed a sharp distinction between the sexes, with the mother taking full responsibility for the children until they were about 6 years old. Typically, she was a devoted and indulgent parent. The father took over the education of his sons when they became capable of "understanding"; girls were not considered important, so they remained under the supervision of their mother. The traditional Chinese father was a harsh disciplinarian whose sons were expected to respect and obey him: he

TABLE 2–1
The Qualities Mothers in Five Countries Want Most in Their Children

UNITED STATES	PHILIPPINES	KOREA	TAIWAN	TURKEY
To be a good person	To mind their parents	To be independent and self-reliant	To be a good person	To mind their parents
To be independent and self-reliant	To be a good person	To do well in school	To mind their parents	To be a good person
To mind their parents	To do well in school	To be a good person	To be independent and self-reliant	To do well in school

Source: Hoffman, 1988.

The traditional Chinese family consisted of a stern father, a devoted mother, and children who gave their parents unquestioning obedience and respect.

was feared, rather than loved. But the sons continued to respect and obey their fathers all their lives, even after they had children of their own—thus, it was the grandfather, not the father, who had the real power in the family. This pattern has changed considerably. In Taiwan today, girls and boys have similar upbringings, fathers are less strict and more involved in the care of their young children, and children no longer think of their grandfather as someone who makes important family decisions and who must be obeyed (Ho, 1989).

Different societies have different ideas of what children are like, and this also affects their childrearing patterns. Americans view children as requiring a considerable amount of nurturing from their parents; the parents are held to be responsible if the child doesn't live up to expectations. In contrast, Hindu culture in India views the child's characteristics as passed down from previous existences. Thus, the parents are assumed to play a minor role in how the child turns out (Miller, 1986).

A society's ideas about what children are like and what to expect from them are likely to be reflected in the children's behavior. An anthropologist studied two farming villages in southern Mexico, both inhabited by native speakers of a language called Zapotec. The two towns are not far from each other; their people plant the same crops and lead the same kind of life. But in one town, La Paz, the people view children as basically good and respectful, whereas in the other, San Andres, children are seen as mischievous and unruly. La Paz parents disapprove of fighting in their children; they tell their children to stop even if the fighting is only in play. Their childrearing methods are gentle; they seldom use physical punishment. In San Andres, on the other hand, children are often beaten with sticks, and fights between children are taken as a matter of course: "One San Andres mother, upon seeing two sons throwing rocks at each other, did nothing to stop this rather dangerous activity and simply remarked that her boys always fought." In San Andres, the children are always fighting. They continue to do so after they become adults. The homicide rate in San Andres is more than five times that of La Paz (Fry, 1988, p. 1016).

AMERICAN CHILDREARING METHODS. In Hutterite society and in other communal societies such as those of mainland China and the Israeli kibbutz, children are encouraged to cooperate, to share, and to work for the good·of the group. American society places more emphasis on individual achievement than on group goals. The American child tends to be independent and assertive, rather than obedient and cooperative. Most American toddlers are encouraged to explore their environment and to use initiative. In other societies, parents worry more about toddlers getting chilled, dirtying their clothes, or falling into an open fire; the toddlers in those societies are much more restricted in their movements (Richman and others, 1988).

But it is an oversimplification to talk of "American childrearing methods," just as it would be to lump together the residents of La Paz and San Andres under the heading "Zapotec childrearing methods." American culture (like Zapotec culture) is divided into a number of **subcultures.** Children in Muncie, Indiana, are not reared in exactly the same way as children growing up in the hills of West Virginia or the valleys of southern California. African Americans, Asian Americans, Hispanic Americans, Americans whose ancestors came over on the Mayflower, and Americans whose ancestors were here long before the Mayflower set sail—each group brings its own attitudes and experiences to bear on the job of nurturing the next generation. And childrearing patterns also vary according to socioeconomic status.

THE EFFECTS OF SOCIOECONOMIC LEVEL. A family's **socioeconomic status** (or level) depends on the income, occupation, education, and social status of its members. A family that includes a doctor, a judge, or the president of a big company is at a high socioeconomic level. A family whose chief wage earner has a low-paid, unskilled job or is frequently unemployed is at a low socioeconomic level.

Cultural differences across the world are diminishing, as more and more societies are affected by technological advances and by increased contact with other societies. But socioeconomic differences are not diminishing. The result is that children's environments may be affected more by the socioeconomic status of their families than by their cultural background. Two children from different cultural groups but whose families are similar in socioeconomic status may lead fairly similar lives. Two children from the same cultural group, one reared in a rich family and the other in a poor one, will lead very different lives (Richman and others, 1988; Kagitcibasi and Berry, 1989).

In the United States, one child in three is now living in a family whose income is below the poverty line. About 2½ million American children live in a persistent state of poverty and an additional 3½ million experience briefer periods of economic deprivation (Duncan and Rodgers, 1988). Babies born into poverty are more than twice as likely to die before they reach their first birthday as babies born into middle-class homes (Stockwell, Swanson, and Wicks, 1987). A child who grows up in poverty is more likely than a middle-class child to be abused or neglected, to be left back in school, to have lower scores on intelligence tests, to drop out of high school, to become a teenage mother or father, to become a drug user, and to get into trouble with the law. Americans like to think that a child from a poor background can grow up to be president. But 33 of our 40 presidents have come from upper- or upper-middle-class backgrounds (Shenkman, 1988). Children reared in poverty are far more likely than those from upper- or middle-class homes to end up in low-paying jobs or unemployed.

Although socioeconomic class sometimes gets mixed up with racial issues (because the different racial groups in a society tend to differ, on the average, in socioeconomic status), the effects of poverty can also be seen in societies where people are all of the same race. In Poland, for example, Polish children

The Child in Society

Box 2-1
Physical and Sexual Abuse of Children

How bad can an environment be? Rosa Swain found out the hard way. When she died she had welts on her body and burn marks on her feet, ankles, and buttocks. Her teeth were broken and there were scars on her face and body. Rosa was 2½ (Kruse, 1985).

Child abuse, the presumed cause of Rosa's death, is nothing new: it has occurred throughout human history. But stories like Rosa's are more likely to get into the newspapers nowadays, and cases of child abuse—especially when they result in the child's death—are less likely to be covered up. It is estimated that three children die every day in the United States from the results of physical abuse or neglect (Sedlack, 1989).

Who is doing the abusing? More than half of physically abused children are abused by their own parents. Despite the fact that mothers spend much more time with their children than fathers do, mothers and fathers are equally likely to be implicated in child abuse. When children are physically abused by people other than their own parents, at least 80 percent of the time the abuser is a man, often a stepfather or the mother's boyfriend. In the case of sexual abuse, close to 95 percent of the abusers are male, and most of them are *not* the child's father. Stepfathers are five times more likely to sexually abuse a stepdaughter than fathers are to abuse a daughter (Sedlack, 1989; Wolfe, Wolfe, and Best, 1988).

What kind of person could beat a toddler to death or rape a little girl? Insanity is not usually the explanation: serious mental illness is uncommon in child abusers (Wolfe, 1985). What *is* common is poverty. Although child abuse occurs at all socioeconomic levels, it is almost seven times more common in homes where the annual income is under $15,000 than in homes where the income is higher (Sedlack, 1989).

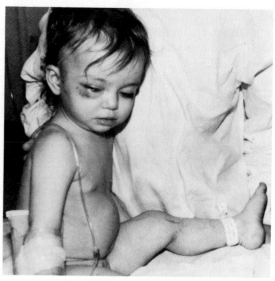

Fifteen-month-old Jody recovers in a hospital, after a court order removed her from the home in which she had been physically abused.

Whatever the income level, things are not likely to be going well in a home where a child is abused. Perhaps the man of the house is absent, or unemployed, or an alcoholic, or a drug user. The parent or parents may be socially isolated, without close friends or relatives they can call on for help. The adults and children in the home tend to get along poorly with each other. The number of unpleasant interactions between family members far exceeds the number of pleasant ones. But that may seem normal to them, because the home the parents grew up in was probably much the same. Many child abusers were themselves abused as children, and many continue to be abused in adulthood by their husbands or boyfriends (Wolfe, 1985; Ney, 1988).

Who are the children receiving the abuse? Boys

from families of low socioeconomic status tend to score lower on IQ tests than Polish children from wealthier families (Galkowski, Jacunska, and Scott, 1987).

There are many reasons for the differences among children of differing socioeconomic classes. Children reared in poverty start out with a disadvantage even before they are born: their mothers are more likely to be teenagers and less likely to receive good prenatal medical care and nutrition. This lack of good medical care and nutrition tends to continue after the child is born. In

are slightly more likely than girls to be the victims of physical abuse, and younger children sustain more serious injuries than older ones: about half of the serious injuries involve children under the age of 3. For sexual abuse, most victims (nearly 85 percent) are girls, and two-thirds are under the age of 13 (Rosenthal, 1988). Children who are unusually difficult to deal with, or who cry or whine a lot, appear to be at greater risk of physical abuse. Although some of these characteristics could be a result of abuse rather than the cause of it, certain children do seem to try the patience of their caregivers. When such children are removed from the abusing home and placed in a foster home, they sometimes become the target of further abuse (Vasta, 1982). Rosa Swain, the child who found out how bad an environment could be, was living with adoptive parents at the time she received her fatal injuries. She had been taken away from her biological mother when she was an infant: her mother had broken both of Rosa's legs (Kruse, 1985).

Ignorance of what children are like or what can be expected of them doesn't seem to be the major cause of child abuse. What matters more is how the parent reacts when the child behaves in an unpleasant way. They may take the child's behavior too personally: the mother of a 1-month-old, who had herself been brutally battered as a child, said about her baby, "I don't think she even likes me" (Pawl, 1987, p. 17).

Aggressive behavior is a common response—in animals as well as humans—to any kind of prolonged or severe discomfort, physical or psychological. The chief goal of aggressive behavior is to inflict pain or harm. For a person whose life is going badly, it may take very little to arouse this response, which will then be turned against anyone who happens to be handy or who is too weak to fight back. Thus, when stress (due to poverty, marital conflicts, or other problems) builds up, it may take only a little additional stress (spilled milk,

a crying baby) to put people into a state in which their chief purpose is not to make the child "behave," but to inflict pain (Emery, 1989).

How can we stop abuse? No one knows whether teaching children to beware of potential sex offenders is protecting them or just increasing their anxieties, especially since most sexual abuse is committed by someone the child knows. With regard to physical abuse, programs designed to teach parents better ways of dealing with family problems have had some success, but regardless of the method used, at least a quarter of abusing parents continue to dish out abuse (Ferleger, Glenwick, Gaines, and Green, 1988). Criminal prosecution of abusers and, if necessary, removing the child from the home are sometimes the only ways of assuring the child's safety.

What happens to the children who are abused? Only a very small fraction of them die; most live to be abused again. Many of these children blame themselves, not their parents, for the abuse. Five-year-old Melanie said she deserved her punishment because she had "evil thoughts" and did not honor her mother: "I was rebellious when she burnt me with cigarettes," she confessed (Clarkson, 1988, p. 92). As adults, the victims of abuse are more likely than other people to suffer from depression, low self-esteem, and difficulty in trusting others; they are more likely to become alcoholics or drug abusers, and they are more likely to abuse their own children (Schaefer, Sobieraj, and Hollyfield, 1988).

But—and this is where we finally get to the good news—they probably won't. The majority of people who suffered abuse as children do *not* abuse their own children. Many of these people simply decided, often while they were still children themselves, that they would not treat their own children the way their parents treated them (Rocklin and Lavett, 1987). And they succeeded in living up to this resolution.

addition, the child is less likely to live in a family consisting of both a father and a mother, and is more likely to be one of several siblings close together in age. Housing is usually crowded, at best; homelessness is an increasing problem for America's poor.

Babies born into poverty, if they are in good health, achieve the milestones of early development as quickly as middle-class babies. The differences start to show up after the first year, and widen as the disadvantaged children fall further and further behind their more fortunate agemates. One reason for this widening gap is that parents who live under conditions of economic deprivation tend to be under a great deal of stress, and thus do not have much time and energy to devote to childrearing. Such parents are less able to provide the kind of stimulation and attention that advances their children's social and intellectual development. This is true not just in our own society: all over the world, differences in childrearing styles are found between parents who differ in family income. Two researchers studied a society called the Gikuyu, in a small agricultural village in central Kenya. They found that Gikuyu mothers from lower-income families played with their babies less and paid less attention to them than mothers from wealthier families (Leiderman and Leiderman, 1977).

But, as we will see later in this chapter, some children thrive even under the most unfavorable environmental conditions. A child reared in poverty is not inevitably doomed to a life of deprivation and failure.

The Family and Cultural Change

Cultures, subcultures, and socioeconomic levels do not act directly on the very young child: they act upon the child's family. It is the family, not the cultural or socioeconomic group, that provides the context for the child's earliest experiences.

What sort of context does the family provide? Not quite the same as in the past. The traditional American family consisting of a married couple and their children, with the father going to work every day and the mother staying home and taking care of the children, has become increasingly rare. A number of factors have contributed to the decline of the traditional family:

- High divorce rate: about half of all marriages now end in divorce.
- High remarriage rate: 73 percent of divorced women with one or two children eventually marry again, as do 57 percent of those with three or more children. There were 9 million children living in stepfamilies in 1987.
- Large number of births outside of marriage: in 1986, 16 percent of births to white women and 61 percent of births to black women were to unmarried mothers. Overall, 23 percent of babies were born to unmarried women.
- Large number of single-parent homes: in 1986, 24 percent of all children were living with only one parent. Thirty percent of black homes and 9 percent of white homes are headed by a single parent.
- Large number of mothers in the workforce: in 1987, 71 percent of married mothers with school-age children and 53 percent of married mothers with babies under 1 year were working outside the home (Glick, 1988, 1989; Hoffman, 1989).

Let's look more closely at the effects of these trends on today's children.

MOTHERS WITH MULTIPLE ROLES. Most mothers of babies and young children now have jobs outside the home. Does this mean that mothers and fathers are sharing the childrearing responsibilities equally? No, as a matter of fact (as we will see in Chapter 6), it doesn't. Mothers in our society, as in every other society, have the primary responsibility for taking care of babies and children. Fathers, especially if they are well-educated and liberal in their thinking, may be nice enough to "help out," but it is not clear that they help out more when the mother is employed full time than when she is not employed. If there is such a tendency, it is a small one.

As a result, employed mothers put in many more hours at jobs, housework, and childcare chores than employed fathers do: an average of 80 hours a week, as opposed to 50 hours a week for fathers. In families with children under 3, working mothers put in a total of 90 hours a week!

Sounds pretty stressful. Oddly enough, however, there is no evidence that this heavy workload is taking a toll on the mental or physical health of these women. Employed mothers are as healthy as unemployed mothers and are less likely to suffer from depression. And although the majority work out of financial necessity, most say that they would continue to work even if they didn't need the money.

So the mothers are doing all right. What about the children, though? Rest easy: the children are doing all right, too. There have been many, many studies of the children of employed mothers versus the children of full-time homemakers, and few consistent differences have been found. The effects are minor, and most of them are beneficial. Children of employed mothers—especially in middle-class families—tend to be more independent and to have less stereotyped views of males and females (they are less likely to see women as helpless and incompetent). The daughters of working mothers are, on the whole, more self-confident and do better in school.

What negative effects there are tend to be found in the males of the family. There is some evidence that the mother's employment may have mildly negative effects on her relationship with a male toddler or preschooler. One possible reason for this is that boys, on the average, are somewhat more active and less cooperative than girls, and perhaps these characteristics are harder to deal with for a mother who works 90 hours a week. There is also some evidence that men who work in blue-collar jobs (who tend to have fairly traditional views) feel threatened by their wives' employment, and that this may put some strain on the father–son relationship. If the father expects his son to look up to him because he is the family breadwinner, you can see how this

Although fathers are helping out with childcare chores more than they used to, the primary responsibility for taking care of the baby still belongs to the mother.

could happen. At any rate, the worst news is that divorce is more common in families in which both parents work. However, it is not clear whether this is due to a decrease in marital happiness or is a result of the wife's greater financial independence (Hoffman, 1989; Scarr, Phillips, and McCartney, 1989).

WHO'S TAKING CARE OF THE CHILDREN? Of course, the effects of the mother's employment on her children will depend very much on where the children are and on who is taking care of them while their mother is at work. Parents have three basic choices for childcare. The first is home care: either a relative or a paid employee takes care of the children in their own home. The second alternative is family day-care, in which someone—almost always a woman—takes care of several children (often including her own) in her home. The third alternative is the day-care center. For children under the age of 3 whose parents both work full time, 19 percent are cared for at home, 54 percent in family day-care, and 27 percent in day-care centers. The proportion in day-care centers rises to 57 percent for children between 3 and 5 (Scarr and Weinberg, 1986).

Home- and family-based forms of childcare vary tremendously: their effects on the child's development will depend on the stability of the arrangement and on the competence and involvement of the caregiver. Thus, no general statements can be made about these kinds of childcare arrangements.

In contrast, much is known about the effects of center-based childcare. Although we will discuss this topic at greater length in Chapter 6, we can summarize the findings here. Children who are cared for in good-quality day-care centers (where the physical facilities are adequate and where there are no more than four infants or eight preschoolers per adult caregiver) do very well. If they are children from disadvantaged homes, they may do better in day-care than they would without it, because the day-care center might provide them with some of the advantages their homes lack.

For children from middle-class homes, there are pros and cons. On most measures there are no differences between day-care children and home-reared children. When differences are noted, they usually consist of a tendency for the day-care children to be a little less strongly attached to their parents in toddlerhood, a little less likely to comply with their parents' requests, and a little more aggressive with other children. According to one authority, these results indicate that the day-care children are somewhat

Children who attend a good day-care center while their parents work are no worse off, on the whole, than children who stay home all day. For children from disadvantaged homes, the day-care center may provide some benefits their homes lack.

more independent, "that they think for themselves and that they want their own way" (Clarke-Stewart, 1989, p. 269).

School-age children whose parents work full time may go to day-care centers after school hours, but some of them—particularly the older ones— may be left to fend for themselves. These are the "latchkey children" who let themselves into empty houses and wait till their parents come home. "It's not as bad as it used to be," says Karen, age 13. "I used to be kind of scared. Now I'm just kind of lonely." She is alone in the house until her father comes home from work at 6:30 P.M. (Martin, 1989, p. B7). Ninety percent of latchkey children are age 9 or older. Most of them are not from poverty-level homes —they are more likely to be from middle- or upper-middle-class families (Chollar, 1987).

A study of 8- to 12-year-old latchkey children showed that these children were as well adjusted as other children of their age; however, those who spent some of their unsupervised time in the company of their peers were more likely to do things their parents disapproved of (Lovko and Ullman, 1989). This goes along with the findings of another study, which looked at older latchkey children—young adolescents. These young people were twice as likely to use alcohol, marijuana, or cigarettes as others of the same age who hadn't been left unsupervised (Richardson and others, 1989).

THE EFFECTS OF DIVORCE. The rate of divorce rose precipitously between 1965 and 1980. Although it has now leveled off, it remains high. From 40 to 50 percent of the children born in the last decade will experience the divorce of their parents. What effect will this have on their lives?

Mavis Hetherington and her colleagues at the University of Virginia have been studying the effects of divorce on children for many years. According to Hetherington, most children feel a considerable amount of grief, anger, and anxiety when their parents divorce. They may become depressed or blame themselves for the marital breakup; they may be confused and disturbed by the rapid changes going on in their lives; they may become aggressive and refuse to obey their parents. Behavioral and emotional upheavals are common in the period immediately following the divorce.

What happens next depends, in large part, on whether the parents can manage their divorce any better than they managed their marriage. If things calm down and the parents stop fighting with each other, the children are likely to do fairly well. Children who live in a well-functioning single-parent or stepparent family have fewer problems than those whose parents have not divorced but are in a constant state of conflict (Hetherington, Stanley-Hagan, and Anderson, 1989).

They do not, however, do as well as children from well-functioning intact homes. The children of divorce—particularly the boys—continue to be less well adjusted than children whose parents remain married. They have higher rates of school failure, aggressiveness, and delinquency, and poorer relationships with peers and siblings. But these problems may not all be due to the divorce itself. Studies show that couples who eventually divorce usually go through a long preliminary period of tension and conflict. During this period, neither parent is likely to be doing a good job of meeting the needs of their children (Block, Block, and Gjerde, 1988; MacKinnon, 1989).

Divorce does not put an end to the child's misery if there is continued conflict between the divorced parents. Jennifer, age 8, whose parents have been divorced for two years, wonders "Why do they have to keep arguing all the time? I thought the divorce was going to stop all the fighting." Years after the divorce, some couples are still at each other's throats. What they're fighting about now, mainly, is the children. These parents trade insults, constantly remind the child that the other parent is a jerk, and bicker over the smallest issues of childcare—who's going to drive the child to soccer practice on Friday, and whether they should come at 2:30 or 2:45. The children of such parents are likely to have more behavior problems and to be more aggressive than children whose divorced parents are reasonably cooperative with each other. Since children have a tendency to follow in their parents' footsteps (due to heredity as well as environment), it is not surprising that parents who fight a lot and don't cooperate with each other have aggressive, uncooperative children (Camara and Resnick, 1987, p. 166).

Although some children "continue to feel that divorce has cast a long and unhappy shadow over their childhood," other children eventually make it out into the sunshine again. For these children, according to Hetherington, the experience of having coped successfully with the crisis of their parents' divorce may actually bring them some long-term benefits in toughness and resiliency (Wallerstein, 1985, p. 117; Hetherington and others, 1989).

THE SINGLE-PARENT HOME. Due to the large numbers of American couples who get divorced, and the large number of unmarried women (and teenage girls) who have babies, more than half of American children will spend at least part of their childhood in a single-parent home. In 1988 there were 7.3 million of such homes in the United States; 85 percent of them were headed by women (Glick, 1989).

For homes without fathers, the most serious problem is likely to be poverty: 60 percent of families headed by women have incomes under the poverty line (Martin, 1989). Divorced women are not much better off than never-married women in this respect: only a small proportion of them receive regular child-support payments from their ex-husbands. It has been estimated that the standard of living of a divorced woman and her children declines by 73 percent in the first year after a divorce, whereas that of the divorced man *increases* by 42 percent (Devillier and Forsyth, 1988).

Due to the drastic drop in the divorced woman's income, the necessity of finding a job (if she didn't have one already), and all the other unfavorable changes in her life, the first year after a divorce is difficult for the mother and for the children in her custody. Emotionally, she is probably in no shape to provide the understanding and attention that her children need now more than ever. Thus, life in the mother-headed home may be chaotic for a while. The children react by becoming more demanding and argumentative, and less cooperative and sympathetic. With girls, this reaction is usually temporary; two years later, a daughter is likely to have settled down and to have developed a close relationship with her mother. With boys, the trouble tends to continue: two years after a divorce, a son is probably still giving his mother a hard time.

It seems to be the absence of the father that causes problems in the male children of divorce: a boy who lives with his father rather than his mother, or who remains in close contact with his father, or whose mother remarries before he reaches adolescence, is likely to show fewer behavioral problems than a boy whose mother is his only parent (Hetherington and others, 1989). However, most boys, especially if they are very young, do live with their mothers after a divorce, and their fathers tend to grow increasingly remote. Even when the father tries very hard to keep in touch, there may be a big difference between how well *he* feels he is doing at this and how the *child* perceives it: in one study (Johnson, Klee, and Schmidt, 1988), 76 percent of the divorced fathers said they saw their children at least once a week, but only 42 percent of their children said they saw their fathers at least once a week!

Because mothers and fathers do not play equal and symmetrical roles in two-parent families, neither parent can completely fill the shoes of the missing parent. A major problem for single mothers is getting their sons to listen to them. From toddlerhood on, a boy is less likely than a girl to do what his mother tells him to, and less likely to obey his mother than his father. In some single-parent homes, the mother seems to have given up hope of ever controlling her son's behavior, and the son adopts a leadership role in their relationship. This lack of parental control is probably a chief source of the behavior problems shown by the sons of divorced parents (Phelps, Huntley, Valdes, and Tompson, 1987).

One of the ways that fathers and mothers differ in two-parent families is that fathers tend to make much more of a distinction between sons and daughters, whereas mothers generally treat girls and boys pretty much the same. Fathers are gentle with daughters; they are rougher, more stimulating, and stricter with sons. Although researchers have speculated that the absence of the father should therefore result in less masculine sons and less feminine daughters, there is no evidence that this happens. In fact, the aggressiveness of fatherless boys can be interpreted as a sign of *greater* masculinity (Siegel, 1987; Stevenson and Black, 1988).

Recently there has been an increase in the number of divorced fathers who are awarded custody of their children, and this arrangement may have some advantages for the children. First, they are less likely to suffer the deprivations of poverty: fathers have considerably higher incomes, on the average, than mothers. Second, the children are less likely to end up losing contact with the noncustodial parent: mothers who do not win custody of their children generally keep in closer touch with them than noncustodial fathers. Third, boys who live with just their fathers tend to be better behaved and to have higher self-esteem than boys who live with just their mothers; however, they are also likely to be less communicative and less affectionate.

Interestingly enough, girls who live with their divorced fathers show some of the same behavior problems as boys who live with their mothers. The small amount of information we have on father-headed single-parent homes suggests that these girls tend to be more aggressive, less cooperative, and less friendly than girls who live with their mothers (Hetherington and others, 1989).

For both girls and boys, the long-term effects of losing a mother may be more serious than the effects of losing a father. Severe depression is more common in adults whose mothers died when they were children than in those whose fathers died (Finkelstein, 1988).

STEPPARENTS. Since most divorced parents with children get married again, most children of divorce will eventually have stepparents. Although their parents' remarriage may ultimately be beneficial for them, the initial effect is to disrupt the stability that has finally returned to their lives after the turmoil of the divorce. It may actually take longer for children to adjust to their parents' remarriage than to the divorce itself—partly, perhaps, because the remarriage puts a damper on their hopes that their parents will someday get back together again. Moreover, the parents' second marriage may turn out to be no better than the first: in fact, second marriages end in divorce more frequently, and more quickly, than first marriages. Children may actually contribute to the quicker breakup of the second marriage, because they have much less motivation, the second time around, to try to keep the family together (Hetherington and others, 1989; Guisinger, Cowan, and Schuldberg, 1989).

Assuming the second marriage does work out, what are the effects on children of living in a family with a stepfather or stepmother, and perhaps stepsiblings and half-siblings as well? First of all, the presence of unrelated stepsiblings in the home—children from the stepfather's or stepmother's previous marriage—makes the child's adjustment to the new family arrangement more difficult. If the parent and stepparent go on to produce children of their own, the child is likely to experience still more difficulty. Families in which the children are "his," "hers," and "ours" may look good on TV, but in real life they are complicated situations, full of tension.

A number of other factors will affect how well the stepchild–stepparent relationship works. Younger children adapt more easily than older ones—an older child, especially one just entering adolescence, is more likely to see the parent's new partner as an intruder, to resent displays of affection between them, and to refuse to accept the stepparent's role in making family decisions.

The sex of the child will also make a difference. Although boys have more problems in adjusting to their parents' divorce, it appears that girls have more problems adjusting to their parents' remarriage. For a boy whose mother remarries, the entrance into the family of a substitute father—especially if he is warm, involved, and not too bossy—may solve some of the difficulties the boy has had in living in a female-headed house. But for a girl, the close relationship that has developed between her and her mother is threatened by the new stepfather. Regardless of how he acts to her, she may refuse to accept him (Hetherington and others, 1989).

The most difficult stepparenting role is that of stepmother. The woman who moves into a home occupied by a father and his children has a tough job cut out for her. For one thing, the children are likely to have remained in close contact, physically and emotionally, with their "real" mother, and the stepmother's presence is seen as a threat to that relationship. For another thing, a stepmother is usually less willing than a stepfather to remain in the background—she may expect to have more closeness and influence with her stepchildren than she can actually achieve. She may go all out in an effort to win their affections, and feel hurt and resentful when her efforts are rejected (Whiteside, 1988).

With more fathers being awarded custody of their children and with rates of remarriage remaining high, more women are taking on the role of live-in stepmother. Perhaps in the future it will become an easier role to fill, when children are more likely to have friends who also have live-in stepmothers, and when they no longer have to base their idea of a stepmother on the stories of Cinderella and Snow White.

Adults are not the only people who matter in a child's environment: siblings also play an important role in children's lives, and they may remain important through the entire lifespan. Relationships between siblings run the gamut from close and affectionate to downright murderous, like those two brothers in San Andres (p. 34) who amused themselves by throwing rocks at each other.

When a firstborn child becomes a sibling, upon the birth of her baby brother or sister, some drastic changes occur in her life. There is likely to be a sharp decline in the amount of attention she receives from her mother. Fortunately, the attention she receives from her father does not decline—it may even increase, because the child may turn to him for attention and affection when she finds that her mother is busy with the new baby.

For a while after the second child is born, the older sibling might behave in "babyish" ways—crying or whining more, having more toileting accidents, wanting a pacifier or a bottle. These behaviors seem to be an effort to regain her mother's attention: "My mother appears to be awfully interested in someone who cries, wets his pants, and drinks from a bottle, so I'll cry, wet my pants, and drink from a bottle." When she finds that this strategy doesn't win back her mother's undivided attention, the child soon gives it up. After the first few months, the presence of a younger sibling is likely to lead to an *increase* in maturity and independence for the older one. By the time the younger sibling is a year old, most firstborns have decided that having a baby in the house is not so bad. In one study, 80 percent of firstborns expressed favorable feelings toward their 12-month-old younger siblings, and most said that they wouldn't mind having *another* baby brother or sister (Stewart, Mobley, Van Tuyl, and Salvador, 1987).

Although a mother usually gives more attention to her younger child than to the older one, this is seldom due to a tendency to favor one child over the other: more often it is simply a response to the younger child's greater needs. In fact, a mother's behavior toward a baby or toddler is remarkably consistent, whether the child is her firstborn or her second. In other words, the way the mother behaves toward her second-born when he is 12 months old is very similar to the way she behaved toward her firstborn, when *she* was 12 months old. In contrast, the way the mother behaves toward a 24-month-old is very different from the way she behaves toward a 12-month-old (Dunn, Plomin, and Daniels, 1986).

Even though these differences in the mother's behavior are based on the child's age, they can cause trouble between the siblings. The greater the difference in the way she treats the two siblings—the more attention and affection she gives to the younger one at the expense of the older one—the worse the sibling relationship is likely to be. In families where the mother behaves very differently toward the two children, the siblings are likely to play together less and to fight more. The personalities of the two children will also

Brothers and Sisters

The birth of a baby brother or sister has a dramatic impact on the life of a firstborn child.

affect their relationship. If either sibling is very active or emotional, there is less of a chance that their relationship will be friendly and peaceful (Brody, Stoneman, and Burke, 1987; Stocker, Dunn, and Plomin, 1989).

Two other factors often thought to affect sibling relationships are the age difference between the children and their sexes. As far as age difference is concerned, researchers have found no consistent effects: in some studies, children who are further apart in age get along better; in other studies it's the opposite. With regard to sex, there seems to be a tendency for two sisters to get along better than two brothers, and for same-sex pairs to get along better than opposite-sex pairs, but in young children this trend is slight and not very consistent. However, it appears to get stronger as the siblings get older: female college students report much closer relationships with their sisters than males do with their brothers, and same-sex relationships are closer than opposite-sex ones (Pulakos, 1987).

In a relationship between two young siblings, the older child is almost invariably the dominant one—the one who issues more commands and invitations to play, who gives more affection and expresses more hostility. But there is no evidence that this unequal relationship is bad for either sibling. The younger one does not turn into a wimp; younger children are as capable as their older siblings of taking a dominant role in their relationships with their peers. The older one does not turn into a bully; in fact, older children who *don't* act bossy with their younger siblings—who are unusually kind and affectionate toward them—are the ones who are most likely to have trouble getting along with their peers. Or perhaps it's the other way around: children who have trouble making or keeping friends may look to their younger siblings for the companionship and closeness they fail to get from their peers (Abramovitch, Corter, Pepler, and Stanhope, 1986; Marvinney and Fury, 1989).

Although many parents complain that their children "fight like cats and dogs," they may be failing to notice the quiet periods when their children are *not* fighting. In the majority of families, friendly interchanges between siblings far outnumber the moments of hostility (Abramovitch and others, 1986).

BIRTH ORDER AND FAMILY SIZE. It is usually assumed that a child's position in the family—oldest, youngest, or in the middle—will have an important effect on what kind of person he or she will become. But, although there are some personality differences between firstborn, last-born, and middle children, they are minor. This doesn't mean that brothers and sisters in the same family are likely to have similar personalities: in fact, as we will see later in this chapter, siblings usually have very different personalities. But we can't guess in advance what they'll be like just on the basis of their birth order (Plomin and Daniels, 1987).

With regard to intelligence and achievement in school and careers, birth order does have a small but detectable effect: firstborns tend to be more verbal and to have slightly higher IQs; they are more likely to do well in school and to be high achievers (Zajonc and Markus, 1975).

Much more important than being the oldest or the youngest is how many children there are in the family. Here the findings are quite clear: children in smaller families do better in school and go further in their education; children

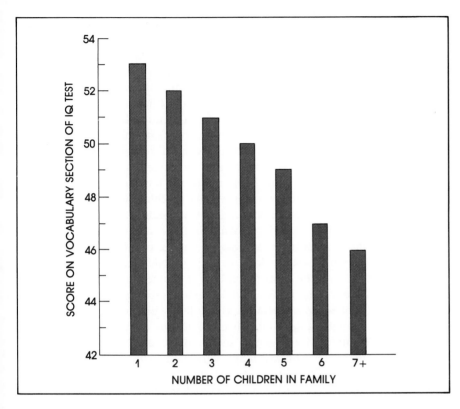

FIGURE 2-1
The relationship between family size and verbal IQ (from Blake, 1989). The school-age children who took the test were matched for socioeconomic status, parents' education, region of residence, and whether the family was intact. Average score on the test was 50.

with many siblings are far more likely to drop out of high school. On the average, the more children there are in the family, the fewer years of education each one gets. This is not due to the fact that parents with many children can't afford to send them to college, because most of the difference results from the higher rates of high school dropout in larger families. And it's not due just to socioeconomic factors: even in middle-class families, children with many siblings don't do as well, on the average, as children with few. What seems to happen is that in larger families the children have fewer opportunities for one-on-one interactions with their parents—each child gets less attention and less verbal stimulation. As a result, they score lower on tests of verbal intelligence. Figure 2–1 shows the relationship between family size and scores on a verbal IQ test obtained by 4500 school-age children (Blake, 1989).

The same effect of competition for the parents' attention can be seen in children who are close together in age. For a given family size, children who are born close together have slightly lower IQs, on the average, than those born three or four years apart. The children born closest together in time are twins and triplets. Twins have IQs that average 4 or 5 points lower than children born singly, and this difference is apparently due to the fact that they almost always must share their parents' attention (Zajonc, 1976).

THE ONLY CHILD. If having to fight for one's share of parental attention leads to a lowering of intelligence and achievement, then the only child should be the smartest and the highest achiever of all. But, although the only child does score highest in tests of verbal intelligence, in most respects the child who has one or two younger siblings comes out a little ahead of the only child. There are a number of possible reasons for this. One is that the oldest child in a two- or three-child family has an opportunity to serve as a teacher for the younger siblings (Zajonc and Hall, 1986). Another is that children who have siblings may be more competitive than those who don't. A final possibility is that only children have, in the past, tended to come from families that had some kind of trouble—marital breakup, for example. Statistics from the early '80s showed that only children were more likely to grow up in single-parent homes than children who had siblings (Veenhoven and Verkuyten, 1989).

Now that people are marrying later and having fewer children, only children are becoming more common—especially in China, where the one-child family is the official standard. Although only children may score high on intelligence tests and do well in school and in their careers, don't people who grow up without siblings have more psychological problems?

According to many studies done in the United States and Europe, the answer is no: only children do just fine. They do not feel lonelier or less happy than other children, they do not have lower self-esteem, and their peers do not consider them to be unsociable. Overall, in childhood and adulthood, only children are indistinguishable from firstborns in two-child families in terms of achievement, intelligence, sociability, character, and adjustment (Falbo and Polit, 1986; Veenhoven and Verkuyten, 1989).

But things may be different in China. In a study done in Beijing, only children were found to be more self-centered, less cooperative, and less popular with their peers than children with siblings (Jiao, Ji, and Jing, 1986). If these results hold up—if it is true that only children are worse off in China than they are in other countries—researchers will have to try to find out the reasons for this puzzling contradiction.

The Workings of Heredity

In our sampling of environmental influences, we've tried to touch on the many ways that one child's environment might differ from another child's, and on the many ways these differences might affect children. Now we confront the fact that children themselves differ right from the start—they differ genetically.

Inherited characteristics, also called genetic characteristics or genetic traits, are transmitted by the **genes.** As you probably remember from your high school biology course, genes are located in the nucleus of every cell that makes up a human, an animal, or a plant. They are composed of long, twisted molecules of **DNA** (deoxyribonucleic acid) and are coiled together in tiny strands called **chromosomes.** Humans have 46 chromosomes. However, the egg cells in a woman's ovaries have only 23 chromosomes, and so do the sperm cells formed in a man's testicles. During conception an egg cell unites with a sperm cell, and the result is a fertilized egg containing 46 chromosomes—23 from the mother and 23 from the father.

Among the 23 pairs of chromosomes in the fertilized egg, there is one pair called the **sex chromosomes.** Sex chromosomes are of two kinds, called X and Y because that's what they look like. Each of a woman's egg cells contains a single X chromosome; each of a man's sperm cells contains either an X or a Y. If a sperm with an X chromosome fertilizes the egg, the fertilized egg will have two X's and will develop into a baby girl. If a sperm with a Y does the job, the result will be an X and a Y: a baby boy.

Genes and Heredity

The fertilized human egg with its allotment of 46 chromosomes divides and divides again, and eventually turns into a baby. It is the genes that are responsible for this remarkable transformation: the genes trigger the formation of specific proteins in particular places and at particular times during development. In this way they determine whether the new creature will be tall or short, male or female, dark or fair—or, for that matter, human or frog.

Although people have been interested in heredity since ancient times, the principles of genetics were unknown until 1866, when a monk named Gregor Mendel published his theories. The reason it took so long to work out these principles was the seemingly unpredictable way in which heredity works. A family may contain one child who looks just like the mother, another who looks just like the father, and another who doesn't look much like either parent. Yet we know that all three of these children have inherited half of their genes from their mother and half from their father. What's particularly puzzling is when a child has some trait that neither parent has. One way this can happen is through the action of *dominant* and *recessive* genes.

DOMINANT AND RECESSIVE TRAITS. Janet and Frank are healthy, normal people, but their daughter Valerie was born with a disorder called **PKU** (phenylketonuria). Valerie has lighter hair and eyes than her parents and siblings; her urine and perspiration have a characteristic "mousy" odor. Fifty years ago, Valerie would have had no chance of leading a normal life—she would have ended up in an institution for the mentally retarded. PKU is a metabolic defect that makes it impossible for the body to excrete a substance called phenylalanine. As a result, excess phenylalanine can build up, causing severe and irreversible brain damage. But babies in the United States are now tested for PKU when they are a few days old, and Valerie's disorder was detected. She will be put on a special diet, very low in phenylalanine, and this will enable her brain to develop normally—she will not become retarded.

Valerie inherited PKU from a mother and father who don't have the disorder. PKU is a **recessive trait,** which means that a baby who has it must have inherited two genes for the trait, one from each parent. Babies who inherit only one copy of the PKU gene will not have the trait, because the normal gene—the gene that carries the instructions for excreting phenylalanine—is **dominant.** But they will be **carriers** of it—the gene will remain hidden in their chromosomes and can be passed on to their descendants. Both parents of a child with PKU are carriers of the trait. The gene is present in half of the mother's eggs and in half of the father's sperm, so each time they have a baby there is a 25 percent chance that the baby will inherit both PKU genes and be born with an inability to excrete phenylalanine. There is a 50 percent chance that the baby will inherit just one PKU gene and will be another carrier.

A computer model of DNA, showing the spiral structure of the molecule. Genes are made of DNA; chromosomes are made of thousands of genes strung together.

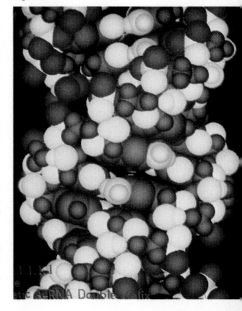

Only traits that are controlled by a single pair of genes behave in this simple dominant–recessive manner. Almost all normal human characteristics, including hair and eye color, are controlled by more than one pair of genes, so the rules of inheritance are more complicated. Single-gene traits in humans most often consist of genetic disorders and defects, and most of them are recessive, which means they are usually inherited from parents who don't themselves have the disorder.

In contrast, dominant traits show up in everyone who inherits even a single gene for the trait—thus, dominant genes can't be hidden. An example of a single-gene dominant trait is brachydactyly, or abnormally short fingers. A person who has inherited brachydactyly must have a parent who also has that trait. On the average, half of his children will inherit the gene for brachydactyly and will also have short fingers. The other half will not inherit the gene—they will not have the trait and they will not be carriers.

Because everyone who has the gene has the trait, very serious disorders are unlikely to be transmitted by dominant genes. The exception is when the disorder doesn't show up until late in life—after the person has had children, perhaps, and passed the gene on to half of them. An example is Huntington's disease, a brain disorder that makes its first appearance in middle age. The victims' movements become jerky and their mental processes begin to deteriorate; the deterioration leads to paralysis and eventually to death. In the past, the children of people stricken with Huntington's disease had to watch their parents die, knowing that they had a 50–50 chance of ending up the same way. Now the gene that causes Huntington's has been located on chromosome 4 and there is a way of testing people to see if they are carrying it. Thus, young adults can find out before they have children whether there is a risk of passing the disorder on to them. Older adults at risk of inheriting Huntington's—those for whom childbearing is no longer an issue—are faced with the decision of whether or not to take the test: would they rather live in hope, or would they rather know for sure? One of the scientists who was responsible for finding the Huntington's gene was Nancy Wexler, whose own mother died of the disorder and who thus has a 50–50 chance of having inherited it. Wexler is often asked whether she has taken the test, but she is understandably reluctant to make her decision public (Jaroff, 1989).

MUTATIONS. Occasionally, a child is born with a dominant-gene disorder that neither parent has. When this happens, it's due to a **mutation:** a gene has changed into some other kind of gene, perhaps because of exposure to radiation or to some chemical, or perhaps for no particular reason at all. Certain genes seem to be more prone to mutate than others. A spontaneous mutation of this sort is responsible for a growth disorder called achondroplasia. People with this disorder have normal-sized heads and bodies but very short arms and legs. Achondroplasia is a dominant trait, so the child of a person with this disorder has a 50–50 chance of inheriting it. If two achondroplastic people marry, their children have only one chance in four of growing to normal size.

SEX-LINKED TRAITS. A number of genetic disorders are far more common in males than in females. Most of these disorders are **sex-linked traits.** Color-blindness is an example. The gene for color-blindness is located on one of the sex chromosomes, the X chromosome. Girls have two X chromosomes, and if one of them contains a gene for color-blindness but the other does not, they will have normal color vision. A girl will not be color-blind unless she inherits the gene from both her parents, which is unlikely. But a boy has only one X chromosome, so if that chromosome contains the gene for color-blindness he will be color-blind.

Since both of the boy's parents have normal color vision, how has he inherited this trait? He inherited it from his mother, who carries the gene for color-blindness on one of her X chromosomes. The son can't have inherited the trait from his father, because his father only has one X chromosome and the son didn't inherit it: fertilized eggs that contain the father's X chromosome turn into girls, not boys. For the same reason, this boy can't pass his color-blindness to his own sons: only his daughters will receive his X chromosome with the color-blindness gene. Thus, all his daughters will be carriers; they will pass the affected gene to half of their own children. Half of their daughters (the granddaughters of the color-blind man) will be carriers, and half of their sons will be color-blind.

Thus, sex-linked traits are passed from fathers to daughters to grandsons. Other sex-linked traits are hemophilia and Duchenne muscular dystrophy. The genes for both of these disorders have now been identified.

Problems Involving Chromosomes

Not all genetic disorders are caused by defective genes; in fact, not all of them are inherited, in the usual sense of the word. A man and a woman with entirely normal chromosomes can have a child with a disorder caused by an abnormality of the chromosomes. What has happened is that something went wrong during the formation of an egg or a sperm, so that instead of having the normal complement of 23 chromosomes it has too many or too few. Then the fertilized egg ends up with 45 or 47 chromosomes, instead of the normal 46.

Most often, when this happens, the fertilized egg is unable to develop properly and it dies, either right away or after a few weeks. A good proportion of early miscarriages are believed to result from chromosomal abnormalities. But sometimes, depending on which chromosomes are missing or extra, the fertilized egg continues to develop. A fertilized egg with an extra copy of chromosome 21, one of the smallest human chromosomes, is especially likely to survive; the result is a baby born with **Down syndrome.**

Down syndrome children are generally short, with small heads, flat noses, and a characteristic slant to their eyes; they suffer from a variety of mental and physical problems. All are mentally retarded, though the degree of retardation varies. Many have heart defects, visual problems, and frequent infections. There is a greatly increased risk of developing leukemia. In the past, few Down syndrome people survived to the age of 20, but now most do. The increased lifespan has revealed another problem that these people face: abnormally rapid aging. The physical changes that occur in their brains by the age of 35 resemble those found in much older people who don't have Down syndrome but who have Alzheimer's disease, the memory loss and intellectual impairment that used to be called senility (Patterson, 1987).

The chances of conceiving a child with Down syndrome increase as the mother gets older: it is 1 in 1500 for mothers under 30 and gradually rises to 1 in 60 for mothers over 45. However, it is possible to test for the presence of

These children were born with Down syndrome.

Down syndrome early in pregnancy, and most doctors recommend that this be done if the pregnant woman is over 35. The test is usually performed with a procedure called **amniocentesis,** around the fourth month of pregnancy. A needle is carefully inserted into the woman's uterus and some fluid is withdrawn. This fluid contains some of the cells of the developing fetus. The cells are grown in a culture medium and then the chromosomes are photographed and sorted out, as shown in Figure 2–2. If there are three copies of the twenty-first chromosome—a condition called **trisomy 21**—the fetus has Down syndrome.

Institutions for the retarded used to be full of people with this disorder; now fewer Down syndrome babies are born and they are much less likely to be institutionalized. In a supportive environment and with the help of their parents and siblings, they can make considerable progress and eventually lead nearly independent lives.

THE EFFECTS OF EXTRA OR MISSING SEX CHROMOSOMES. A developing fetus with an extra or missing copy of chromosomes 1 through 20 has little chance of surviving for more than a few months. One with an extra copy of 21 survives, but has a multitude of problems. In contrast, the effects of extra or missing sex chromosomes are comparatively mild—so mild that most people born with this problem are never diagnosed. According to one estimate, as many as one baby in 400 may be born with a sex-chromosome abnormality.

Boy babies who are born with an extra X chromosome (XXY instead of XY) have Klinefelter syndrome. As adults they tend to be tall and poorly coordinated; their testicles do not develop normally during puberty and they are infertile. An extra Y chromosome (XYY) also results in a tall adult male; most of these men are physically normal. Girl babies born with only one X chromosome (X0) have Turner syndrome. They tend to be short, with broad chests and wide necks. Their breasts do not develop at puberty and they are infertile. Girls with an extra X chromosome (XXX) are the least likely to have any obvious abnormalities, though they tend to develop more slowly in infancy and childhood.

All these people are likely to have somewhat lowered IQs and to have prob-

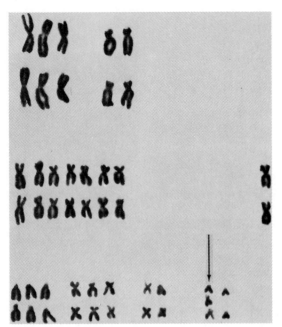

FIGURE 2-2
Human chromosomes sorted out by the process known as karyotyping. The arrow is pointing to the chromosomal abnormality that produces Down syndrome: three of the twenty-first chromosome (trisomy 21). The two large chromosomes on the right are X chromosomes, indicating that this fetus is female.

lems with schoolwork and social relationships. Turner syndrome girls have normal verbal abilities but very poor spatial skills (for example, they have no sense of direction), poor handwriting, and trouble with math. Girls and boys with an extra X have problems with language; the boys are often reading-disabled. Reading disabilities are also common in boys with an extra Y. Girls with an extra X may have problems with remembering things (such as the digits in a telephone number) in the right order. Although the XXX girls have fewer specific disabilities than the children with other sex-chromosome abnormalities, on the average they have the lowest IQs (Berch and Bender, 1987).

THE FRAGILE X SYNDROME

By the time her third child was walking and talking, the young mother was haunted by guilt. Her second child, a boy, had been diagnosed variously as autistic, hyperactive, or brain-damaged. Now her third child, also a boy, had similar behavioral and mental problems. Meanwhile, her first child, a 10-year-old girl, was showing signs of a learning disability; she seemed unable to grasp arithmetic. "I kept asking myself, 'What am I doing wrong?'" the mother says. (Bishop, 1986)

All three of these children turned out to have **fragile X syndrome:** they had inherited from their mother an X chromosome that has a tendency to break. About 90 percent of boys born with a fragile X are retarded, and the rest are borderline or low-normal. The symptoms of girls with a fragile X are much milder, because females have an extra X chromosome.

Boys with fragile X often have large, protruding ears and "double-jointed" fingers; as adults they have long faces and enlarged testicles. About 30 percent are severely retarded (most are institutionalized); those who are mildly retarded generally do all right in group homes. All fragile X males—even

Box 2-2 Genetic Counseling

Bob and Marlene Lippman had been married ten years when their first child, Evelyn, was born. She was a lovely baby, with doll-like features and big, long-lashed eyes. Even Evelyn's pediatrician was impressed. At her 1-month checkup he told Marlene, "I can't fault your baby. She's perfect."

At 6 months Evelyn was smiling and alert, just starting to reach for toys. She wasn't sitting up yet, but Bob and Marlene figured that she "just wasn't in any hurry."

Five months later Evelyn still wasn't sitting, and Marlene and Bob were starting to worry. They brought Evelyn to their pediatrician and he examined her carefully. He saw that her movements were "floppy" and that her eyes were no longer following moving objects. He recommended that the Lippmans take Evelyn to a pediatric neurologist—a children's doctor who specializes in problems of the brain and spinal cord.

The neurologist spent only ten minutes examining Evelyn. He pulled no punches when he gave them the diagnosis: "Your daughter has Tay–Sachs disease. She will die, probably within two years. Before that she will become blind, deaf, and paralyzed. She'll lose the ability to swallow. You'll have to put her in an institution." He explained that Tay–Sachs disease is an inherited metabolic disorder carried by recessive genes. Babies who inherit two Tay–Sachs genes lack an enzyme that is necessary for metabolizing a certain kind of fat molecule. Without that enzyme the molecule gradually builds up in the brain, eventually destroying it.

Stunned and grief-stricken, Bob and Marlene took their baby home. The neurologist's prediction came true, except that Evelyn didn't die until she was 5 years and 10 months old. She remained at home for most of her short life and her parents

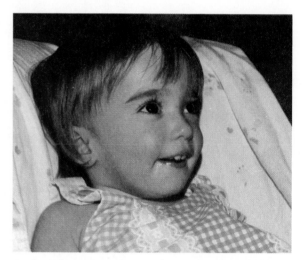

Evelyn Lippman at 17 months. Evelyn died of Tay–Sachs disease about four years after her parents took this picture.

gave her excellent, loving care. But Evelyn smiled her last smile at the age of 17 months. For the last three years of her life she was unable to see or hear. When she lost the ability to swallow, her parents had to feed her through a tube that went from her nose to her stomach. She was unable to respond to them in any way.

During the years they were caring for Evelyn, the Lippmans came to an important decision. They decided that they still wanted children—normal, healthy children. But they'd never have another child if there was any chance of having another Tay–Sachs baby.

Most large medical centers contain a genetics clinic. The Lippmans made an appointment to see a genetic counselor at a medical center near their home. Genetic counselors are trained in the medi-

those whose IQs place them in the low-normal range—have problems with language. Many also show behavioral abnormalities such as hyperactivity, hand-flapping, and hand-biting. As children they are often diagnosed as autistic. (We will discuss autism in Chapter 10.)

Although girls with fragile X syndrome are unlikely to be severely affected, about 30 percent are mildly retarded. However, even those with normal IQs often have learning problems, especially in math. Many also have emotional or personality problems such as depression or difficulty in making friends.

An estimated one baby per 1000 is born with the fragile X chromosome—it is the second most common cause of mental retardation, after Down syn-

cal aspects of genetics and can give advice to people like the Lippmans—people who want children but who have reason to fear that their children might not be normal. The genetic counselor explained to the Lippmans that if they conceived another child there was a 1-in-4 chance that their second child would also have Tay–Sachs. But, she told them, it is possible to test a fetus for the disorder during pregnancy, by the process of amniocentesis (see p. 52). If the test showed that the fetus had Tay–Sachs, what would the Lippmans do? There was no question in their minds: Marlene would have an abortion. Neither she nor Bob could see any point in letting a pregnancy continue if it would result in a baby doomed to die, slowly and horribly.

Marlene became pregnant a few months later. Amniocentesis showed the fetus to be normal. Julia, the Lippmans' second daughter, is a lively, talkative little girl, with hazel eyes and dark-blond hair.

Many couples who seek genetic counseling, like the Lippmans, have already had a child with a serious defect or have a close relative with such a child. Or they may be members of a group with an elevated risk of having an abnormal child—women over 35, or members of a racial or ethnic group that is known to be at risk for a genetic disorder. About 1 in 350 Americans is a carrier of the Tay–Sachs gene, but the proportion of carriers is ten times higher among Jews whose ancestors came from Eastern Europe.

A number of other recessive genetic disorders also occur with greater frequency in particular population groups. The gene for sickle-cell anemia, a painful and sometimes crippling blood disorder, is most common among African Americans. The gene for cystic fibrosis is most common among European Americans—this disorder affects one white baby in 2,000. Children with cystic fibrosis have abnormally thick mucus in their lungs and suffer from respiratory and digestive difficulties; they are frequently hospitalized and seldom live beyond their 20s (Kolata, 1990). Tests are now available for these disorders and many others: parents can be tested to see if they are carriers, and the fetus can be tested for the disorder itself. A new procedure called **chorionic villus sampling** is much quicker than amniocentesis and can be done as early as the ninth week of pregnancy.

Genetic counseling is not limited to recessive disorders. Potential parents can be tested for Huntington's disease, a dominant-gene disorder. Fetuses can be tested for Duchenne's muscular dystrophy and hemophilia, which are sex-linked disorders, and for chromosomal abnormalities such as Down syndrome and fragile X syndrome. And fetuses can be tested for disorders that are only partially inherited or inherited in more complex ways, such as spina bifida. Babies with spina bifida are born with a serious abnormality of the spinal cord that can lead to permanent paralysis. A blood test given during pregnancy is used to detect fetuses that are at risk of having spina bifida; if the test is positive, an ultrasound scan is performed to get a closer look at the fetus. This procedure uses sound waves to produce a sonogram, a moving picture of the fetus, which can then be checked for spina bifida and for a number of other abnormalities.

A severely retarded or permanently ill child is an enormous burden for a family, emotionally and financially. The goal of genetic counseling is to enable people to have children without fear of this kind of burden. More often than not, the tests give reassuring news, but their value rests on the possibility of abortion if the news is not good. If abortion is not a possibility, people like the Lippmans are likely to feel that the risk is too great—they may give up the idea of having children, or try to adopt a child.

drome. Prenatal testing is available to determine if a fetus has fragile X (Hagerman and Sobesky, 1989).

Polygenic Inheritance

So far, our discussion of the basic mechanisms of heredity has concentrated on all the things that can go wrong. The reason for this pessimistic approach is simple: just as you're likely to learn more about how your car works when it breaks down than when it's running fine, it's easier to find out how genes and chromosomes work when a mistake occurs.

Fortunately, things usually *don't* go wrong. But the inheritance of normal traits tends to be a lot more complicated than the inheritance of defects and disorders, because almost all normal traits are **polygenic.** This means that they're controlled by many genes, not just a single pair. Inheritance of polygenic traits is more complicated than single-gene traits because so many combinations of genes—and so many variations of the trait—are possible. A baby either has or doesn't have Tay–Sachs disease or PKU. But when it comes to polygenic traits such as size, coloring, strength, or musical ability, there is a tremendous range of possibilities. A person's adult height can be anywhere from over 8 feet to under 2. Musical ability can range from Mozart to tone-deaf. It's typical of polygenic traits that the two extremes are very rare. Most people fall somewhere in the middle.

It's also typical of polygenic traits that they're more flexible—more capable of being influenced by environmental factors—than single-gene traits. Accomplishment in music, for example, depends on the existence of inborn talent but also on music training. Even physical characteristics such as skin color (which is affected by exposure to the sun) and height (which is affected by diet and health care during childhood) are influenced by environmental factors. Between 1870 and 1970, children in many countries grew taller with each generation, so that Americans born in 1970 are two or three inches taller than those of a century earlier. Improved nutrition and health care are believed to be responsible for this trend (Roche, 1979).

With a polygenic trait such as height, something is inherited, but it isn't a specific number of inches or centimeters. A child inherits a *range* of possible heights. Within this range, the final height is determined by environmental factors. If everything goes well and nutritional needs are met in abundance, the child will end up at the tall end of his or her potential range. If nutrition is just barely enough to keep the child alive, and health is poor throughout the growth period, final height will be at the short end of the range. Generally, neither of these extremes occurs and people end up somewhere in the middle of their potential range of heights.

Since the inherited range sets a limit to potential height, once the upper limit is reached, further improvements in the environment will have no effect. Americans are no longer increasing in height: future generations will probably be no taller than their parents.

Virtually all the interesting characteristics of children, if they have any hereditary basis at all, are inherited polygenically. Thus, these traits depend not just on the genes but on the interaction between the genes and the environment. In the next section we will discuss what is known about these interactions.

Interactions between Heredity and Environment

In Chapter 1 we raised the question of human differences: Why are children so different from each other? What makes them turn out the way they do? The answer is obvious, we said: their heredity and their environment. Now that we have looked at some basic environmental influences and reviewed some facts about heredity, we can return to the question: What makes children turn out the way they do?

Researchers have carried out countless studies in an effort to find out the effects of various environmental factors on children. A typical study was published in 1975 by Bettye Caldwell, Robert Bradley, and Richard Elardo. Caldwell and her colleagues wanted to determine which factors in the home environment would have a favorable effect on the intelligence of a young child. The researchers found that the most intelligent children tended to come from homes in which mothers were warm and responsive, bought the children suitable toys, and played with them a lot. In other words, there was a positive correlation between maternal behavior of this sort and the IQ of the child. But does that mean that the behavior of the mother *caused* her child to be more intelligent?

Heredity and Environment: Deeply Intertwined

It could mean that. But, as the researchers themselves pointed out, other explanations are also possible. In an important theoretical paper, developmental psychologists Sandra Scarr and Kathleen McCartney (1983) have spelled out three different ways in which effects that appear to be environmental may be at least partly due to genetic factors.

PASSIVE EFFECTS. Scarr and McCartney call the first of these genetic factors **passive effects.** The children and their responsive, toy-buying mothers are close relatives—genetically quite similar. The same mother who provides the child with much of his environment has also provided him with half of his genes. Scarr and McCartney point out that there's no way to separate the genetic influences from the environmental ones. For example, parents who do a lot of reading tend to have children who are good readers. Is this because the parents provide an environment in which reading is encouraged, or is it because their children have inherited the ability to become good readers? In all probability, both environmental and genetic factors are involved.

To take another example, we said in the box on child abuse that many abusing parents were themselves abused as children. Does this prove that the experience of having been abused caused these people to become abusers? An alternative explanation is that the tendency to abuse others—a tendency toward aggressiveness—was inherited from their abusing parents. Note that the two explanations are by no means mutually exclusive. Both effects can work simultaneously, and it's very likely that they do.

REACTIVE EFFECTS. The second factor involves what Scarr and McCartney called "evocative effects" but that later researchers have renamed **reactive effects** (Plomin and others, 1988). The idea is that children evoke responses from the people around them—people *react* to the child's characteristics. Different children evoke different reactions. People react one way to a lively child, another way to a quiet one. Their behavior with a girl is not the same as their behavior with a boy. A child who learns quickly is treated differently from a child who learns slowly.

Consider the finding that intelligent children tend to have responsive mothers who play with them a lot. Suppose that some children are innately brighter than other children, due to their genetic characteristics. Now suppose that grownups find bright children more interesting, more fun to be with, than other children. Suppose that the mothers of bright children enjoy them more and therefore play with them more than do the mothers of other children. Perhaps they buy these children better toys because the intelligent children are more capable of expressing their desire for certain toys or more sensible in their choice of which toys to ask for.

If these suppositions are true, then they could account for the correlation between the children's IQ and their mothers' tendency to play with them a lot and to buy them suitable toys. But, as we will see in Chapter 7, the correlation works both ways—children who are bright to begin with tend to get more attention from their mothers, and more attention from the mother tends to make the child brighter. If intelligent children bring out certain behaviors in parents, and these very behaviors increase the children's intelligence, we have a sort of "vicious circle," which in this case is anything but vicious.

The circle may indeed be vicious, however, in the case of abused children. Suppose that there is some genetic component involved in the behavior of child abusers—that their tendency to lash out at others is partially inherited. Suppose that a person's experiences also have an effect: someone who was abused as a child will grow up with the idea that beatings are an appropriate method for dealing with children. If both of these factors are involved in child abuse, then they will tend to operate together: those children who may have inherited a tendency to behave aggressively are precisely the ones whose parents are more likely to abuse them. Thus, the cycle of child abuse may be handed down in two different ways, from one generation to the next.

Reactive effects often have this "vicious circle" quality, so that children who are different in some way from other children will tend to become more so. But these effects can also work in the opposite direction, to *reduce* differences among children. A child who is very active, for instance, will be told over and over again to sit down and keep still, while an inactive child might be admonished to go out and play, or be enticed into games of catch or tag (Bell and Chapman, 1986).

There is evidence to show that adults do attempt to "normalize" children's behavior in this fashion. Researchers have studied how adults behave with children and found that an adult's behavior depends on how the child acts. In one study, adult females were asked to play a game of checkers with a 10-year-old boy they had never met before. The boy, who was collaborating with the researchers, had been trained to act in two very different ways with the women who were the subjects in this experiment. With some of the women he acted shy and withdrawn, saying little. With others he behaved in a belligerent fashion, acting defiant and uncooperative. The adults behaved very differently toward this boy, depending on which way he was acting:

> When the child was shy and incompetent, the adults responded with higher rates of verbal helping and rewards in order to stimulate activity. On the other hand, when the child exhibited aggressive and defiant behavior, the adults responded with higher rates of ignoring, commands, and discipline in an attempt to reduce child activity to acceptable levels. (Brunk and Henggeler, 1984, p. 1080)

So reactive effects can work in either direction: sometimes they serve to decrease differences among children and sometimes to increase them.

ACTIVE EFFECTS. The final way that genetic factors can lurk behind what appear to be environmental influences is through **active effects.** This refers to the tendency, most noticeable in older children, to seek out their own environments—to find the environment that suits them best, or to modify their environment according to their preferences. Bright children will not grow up under the same conditions as those who are less bright, because they will choose different activities, toys, and friends. They may ask their parents to buy them books, rather than talking teddy bears, or a computer rather than a car. They will seek out other intelligent children to be their friends. They will choose more challenging courses in high school and will go to a more prestigious university. All these choices will lead to a further increase in their intelligence.

Children are not simply passive recipients of whatever the environment happens to deal out. They have effects on their environment and on the people with whom they associate. And—more and more as they grow older—they can voluntarily determine many aspects of their own environment.

Clearly, the interactions between environmental and genetic influences are extremely complex. How can they be disentangled?

Genetic and Environmental Influences on Intelligence

When we ask, "What makes children turn out the way they do?" what we really want to know is what determines the differences among them. Why, for example, is one child more intelligent than another?

As it happens, intelligence (as estimated by IQ tests, which we'll discuss in later chapters) has probably been the subject of more research than any other characteristic of children. One reason for this is that intelligence matters. A child's future will be affected in important ways by his or her intelligence. The other reason is that researchers have a convenient way of measuring it. Although no one thinks that a score on an IQ test is a perfect measure of a person's real intelligence, it is a reasonably good indication. Other characteristics that also matter—persistence, optimism, good looks, kindness—are much harder to measure.

Let us, therefore, begin our discussion of interactions between heredity and environment with a look at intelligence.

EXPERIMENTS WITH ANIMALS. Even rats differ in something that could reasonably be called intelligence. Some rats learn their way through mazes more quickly than others. These differences show up even if all the rats have exactly the same environment—the same cages, the same food, and so forth. When the effects of environment are **controlled** in this fashion (by being held constant), any differences among the rats are probably genetic. That they *are* genetic is proved by the fact that they can be passed on: the offspring of bright rats are brighter than the offspring of the dull ones (Thompson, 1954).

It is also possible to control rats' heredity and to vary their environment. The rats that are ordinarily used for laboratory experiments have been purposely **inbred** for many generations. Inbreeding means mating close relatives to each other—fathers to daughters, brothers to sisters, and so on. Generation after generation of inbreeding produces strains of animals that show hardly any variation from one individual to another. They all have practically the same genes.

Now we can take some of these carbon-copy animals and divide them randomly into two groups. One group can be raised in an "enriched" environment—a big pen with interesting toys to play with and mazes to explore. The other group can be raised in an "impoverished" environment—small cages with bare walls and no frills.

Experiments of this sort have been done many times. What is found is that the rats reared in the enriched environment turn out brighter (Rosenzweig, 1966). They do better than the impoverished rats on various tests, and they even have bigger brains!

STUDIES OF HUMAN FAMILIES. With rats, we can control both heredity and environment. But we can't tamper with the heredity of humans. We can't even do much to change their environments, except in small ways or for short periods of time. The problem in studying humans is that their heredity and environment tend to vary together, and we can't hold one factor constant in order to see what effect the other has.

Early researchers overlooked this important fact. In 1912, Henry Goddard published a study of the descendants of a man named Kallikak, who fathered the child of a mentally retarded barmaid. The descendants of the barmaid's child, according to Goddard, were clearly an inferior bunch. They included criminals, alcoholics, prostitutes, and mentally retarded people. Goddard claimed that the members of this family had inherited their deficiencies from the barmaid. But what kind of environment had these people grown up in— "enriched" or "impoverished"? Perhaps these people had inherited their deficiencies; perhaps they were the result of an unfavorable environment. Most likely, both were involved. But there is no way of telling, because the two factors went together, as they so often do.

Since Goddard's time, it has often been observed that members of different socioeconomic classes tend to differ in IQ. The average doctor, lawyer, or engineer has a higher IQ than the average unskilled worker. Moreover, the children of the doctor, lawyer, and engineer have higher IQs than the children of the unskilled worker. Is this because they have inherited their intelligence from their parents, or is it because they grew up in an environment that met all their needs with abundance? Studies of twins and adopted children can help to answer that question.

TWIN STUDIES. Although it is never possible to give two people exactly the same environment, nature occasionally blesses us with two people who have exactly the same heredity: **identical** (or **monozygotic**) **twins.** Identical twins are formed when a fertilized egg splits in two at some early stage of development. The two halves—each containing an identical set of 46 chromosomes—grow into two babies. These babies are always the same sex and generally look so much alike that it is difficult to tell them apart. Their bodies are composed of exactly the same proteins; their blood type is always the same.

Only about a third of twins are identical. The rest are **fraternal** (or **dizygotic**) **twins,** born of two different egg cells that have been fertilized by two different sperm. Fraternal twins happen to be born at the same time, but they are no more alike genetically than any other pair of siblings. They are not necessarily the same sex. Like siblings born at different times, fraternal

Identical twins. These boys developed from a single fertilized egg, so they have exactly the same genes.

twins have, on the average, 50 percent of their genes in common. In contrast, identical twins have 100 percent of their genes in common—that is, they have exactly the same genes.

Not only do identical twins have the same genetic makeup: if they are raised in the same home (and they almost always are), they also grow up in very similar environments. Thus, they should be very much alike. Fraternal twins, if they are raised in the same home, also have very similar environments. However, only about half of their genes are the same, so they will be less alike than identical twins. Twin studies make use of this difference. The assumption is that if identical twins are very much alike in regard to some trait, and fraternal twins are often different in regard to that trait, then that trait must be mostly genetic. For example, identical twins are usually very similar in height—the correlation in height for identical twins reared together is .94 (see our discussion of correlation in Chapter 1). The correlation for fraternal twins of the same sex is considerably lower: .60 (Tanner, 1978). Differences in height are largely due to genetic factors.

Identical twins are also a good deal more alike in intelligence than fraternal twins. In a survey that combined the results of a large number of IQ studies on twins—111 studies in all, from all over the world—the average IQ correlation for identical twins reared together was found to be .86. For fraternal twins the correlation was about .60. Mathematical analysis of the results led to the conclusion that about half of the variation in IQ in this group of people was due to heredity. In other words, these studies suggested that the **heritability** of IQ was around 50 percent (Bouchard and McGue, 1981).

But more recent studies indicate that this estimate of heritability may have been too low and that heredity may actually be more important than environment in determining intelligence. Most of the older studies looked at IQ measurements made in childhood. It turns out that if you measure people's IQs after they reach adulthood, twin studies yield a higher estimate of the heritability of IQ. This means that, as people get older, heredity appears to play a greater role in determining IQ and environment plays less of a role (Loehlin, Willerman, and Horn, 1988; Tambs, Sundet, Magnus, and Berg, 1989).

That statement seems contrary to common sense: Why should your environment have less and less of an impact, the longer you remain in it? And if heredity is something you're "born with," why do its effects get *stronger* as you get older? Two reasons: active genetic effects and reactive genetic effects. As children get older, their genetic characteristics are likely to become more pronounced, due to their increasing freedom to choose their own environ-

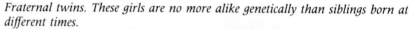

Fraternal twins. These girls are no more alike genetically than siblings born at different times.

ments and to the "vicious circle" action of reactive effects. The influence of the family is probably greatest in the early years, when the family is the child's entire environment and she has little choice about how or with whom she will spend her time.

ADOPTION STUDIES. Additional information comes from studies of adopted children. When children grow up with their **biological parents** (the father and mother from whom they inherited their genes), it is difficult to separate the effects of heredity and environment. But when children are adopted at an early age by parents who are unrelated to them, we have what amounts to a controlled experiment: one set of parents has contributed the heredity and a different set of parents contributes the environment. If adopted children are more like their biological parents in some respect, then heredity was evidently more important in determining that characteristic. If they are more like their adoptive parents, then the environment counted for more.

With regard to IQ, although the environment definitely has an impact, adopted children are slightly more like their biological parents than they are like their adoptive parents. This is shown most clearly by a study recently carried out in France. The researchers searched through the French adoption records until they found a group of children whose biological parents had been of low socioeconomic status but who were reared by adoptive parents of high socioeconomic status. Such children were not hard to find—in fact, this is the typical situation for an adopted child. But the researchers also wanted to find children with high-status biological parents and low-status adoptive parents—in other words, children who had been born to people from wealthy, well-educated families but reared by people whose incomes and education were at the low end of the scale. They found only eight such cases. So the study involved only 38 adopted children in all: the eight who were born rich and reared poor, plus ten who were born poor and reared rich, and twenty who remained in the socioeconomic classes they had been born in.

Table 2–2 shows the results. Regardless of how they were reared, the children born to biological parents of high socioeconomic status had higher IQs (average: 114) than those born to biological parents of low status (average: 98). But regardless of who their biological parents were, the children reared in upper-middle-class homes had higher IQs (average: 112) than those reared in less advantaged homes (average: 100). As you can see, heredity makes a big difference: 16 IQ points. Environment makes slightly less of a

---

TABLE 2–2
IQs of Adopted Children as a Function of Heredity and Environment

| | | SOCIOECONOMIC STATUS OF ADOPTIVE PARENTS | | |
		Low	High	Low + High
SOCIOECONOMIC STATUS OF BIOLOGICAL PARENTS	Low	92	104	98
	High	108	120	114
	Low + High	100	112	

Source: Capron and Duyme, 1989.

Close-Up

Box 2-3
Identical Twins and Triplets Raised Apart

In September 1980, 19-year-old Bobby Shafran enrolled in a community college in upstate New York. Always a sociable young man, Bobby wasn't surprised when his fellow students seemed very glad to see him, but he was a little puzzled about why everyone kept calling him "Eddy." He found out why when someone showed him a photo of Eddy Galland. "It was like looking in a mirror," Bobby said.

Eddy Galland had attended the same community college the year before, but had transferred to a college on Long Island, closer to his home. He was at home one evening at 9 o'clock when the phone rang. It was Bobby, who said, "Eddy, I think you're my twin brother."

The two young men wasted no time getting together and comparing notes. They had been born in the same Long Island hospital on the same day: July 12, 1961. Both had been adopted in infancy.

They hit it off right away. "It was incredible," said Eddy, "we became instantaneous best friends. He'd start sentences, and I'd finish them. It was like we never met, but we knew each other all our lives" (Lyman, 1989).

The story of the reunited identical "twins" made the local newspapers. A day or two later, the phone rang again at the Galland home. Eddy wasn't home this time and Mrs. Galland answered the phone. The caller said, "You're not going to believe this, Mrs. Galland, but my name is David Kellman and I think I'm the third."

It was true: there were three of them, so much alike that it's hard to tell them apart. They had

Bobby Shafran (left), David Kellman (center), and Eddy Galland.

been adopted from the same adoption agency; none of the adoptive families had been informed of the multiple birth (Battelle, 1981).

Identical triplets, all from the same fertilized egg, are produced when the developing cells split twice: first one cell (or group of cells) splits into two parts, and then one of these parts splits into two more parts. If the splitting occurs once or twice more, identical quadruplets or even quintuplets might be produced. It's also possible for multiple births to be a mixture of identical and fraternal—triplets may consist of an identical pair plus a fraternal sibling.

---

difference: 12 points. But 12 extra IQ points are not to be sneezed at—they could mean the difference between being in the bluebird reading group or the chickadees, taking algebra or remedial math, attending Harvard or the state university (Capron and Duyme, 1989).

Incidentally, the children in this study were tested at an average age of 14. There is a good possibility that if the researchers were to test them again in four or five years, heredity would prove to be even more important (McGue, 1989).

DON'T JUMP TO CONCLUSIONS. What does it mean to say that heredity is a little more important than environment in determining a person's intelligence? Not as much as you probably think.

The reunited triplets found that they had much in common besides their looks. Bobby, Eddy, and David all have high IQs but have trouble with math. They are all outgoing, lively young men who excel in wrestling and have similar tastes in food, music, and women. As it happened, they also grew up in rather similar environments. All three were raised in upper-middle-class homes in the New York City area, with parents who were business or professional people. All three had older adoptive sisters. With identical genes and similar environments, it's not surprising they had a lot in common.

But even when they're reared in very different environments, identical twins or triplets may be so much alike that it's almost eerie. There is the case of Oskar Stöhr and Jack Yufe. Separated in infancy, they saw each other only once after that, when they were in their 20s. But when the two men arrived in Minnesota to participate in a study of identical twins reared apart, both had wire-rimmed glasses and mustaches, and both wore blue double-breasted shirts with epaulets. Oskar had been reared in Germany as a Catholic, Jack by his Jewish father in Trinidad. But they had similar personalities: both had a quick temper and a peculiar sense of humor—they both liked to startle people by sneezing in elevators (Holden, 1987).

Identical twins—even those reared apart—also tend to be very similar in intelligence. There is the case of the British sisters, separated in infancy. One was adopted into the family of a wealthy lawyer and attended expensive private schools. The other was adopted into a lower-middle-class family in a poor section of London; she quit school at the age of 16 in order to get a job. Tested in adulthood, the sisters' IQ scores were only one point apart (Drexler, 1989). Although most twins reared in such different environments don't end up quite

as closely matched as that, there is seldom a big difference in IQ. In studies of identical twins reared apart, the correlation between the IQs of separated twins averages .72; the correlation for identical twins reared together is about .86. Identical twins reared apart are more similar in IQ than fraternal twins reared together (Bouchard and McGue, 1981).

How different is the environment of twins reared in separate homes? Attempts to answer this question have led to some unexpected findings. Adult twins in Sweden who had spent all or most of their childhoods in separate families nonetheless gave fairly similar descriptions of their childhood homes, when asked about such things as the warmth of their adoptive parents or how much emphasis was put on achievement. In fact, the descriptions given by the separated twins were only a little less similar than descriptions given by twins reared in the *same* homes. The researchers proposed two reasons for why identical twins reared in different families might give similar descriptions of those families: one is that identical twins might perceive things in similar ways (for example, both twins might have a tendency to see their childhoods through "rose-colored glasses"), and the other is that identical twins might evoke similar reactions from the other members of their families—even though they were reared in different homes, they might have been treated in similar ways (Plomin and others, 1988).

Thus, whether they're reared together or in two separate homes, identical twins might grow up in fairly similar environments (or in environments they *perceive* as similar, which may amount to the same thing). But the point is that these similar environments are, at least in part, a *result* of their being genetically identical.

First, the studies we've discussed have all involved a limited range of environments. The children whose IQs are tested in twin and adoption studies are not likely to have been abused, neglected, or to have undergone periods of starvation. They were reared in the United States, Canada, or Western European countries, where childrearing patterns vary over a much narrower range than they do in the world as a whole. The presence of a TV set in virtually every one of these homes means that virtually every one of these children had been exposed to the lowest common denominator of Western culture.

How much environment matters will depend on how widely children's environments differ: if every child grew up in exactly the same environment, then the environment wouldn't play any role in producing differences among them, and whatever variations there were among the children would be due to genetic factors. If you give all the corn you plant the same amount of fertilizer and the same amount of sunshine, then any variations in the height of the corn will be due to genetic differences in the seeds. If you give half of the corn much more fertilizer and sunshine than the other half, then the variations in height will be due largely to environmental factors. So the results of twin and adoption studies will depend on how wide a range of environments is tested and will hold true only for that range.

Second, saying that something is inherited is not at all the same as saying that it's fixed, unchanging—that whatever number you get in the genetic lottery, you're stuck with it. Height is mostly genetic; yet height can certainly be affected by environmental factors. Between 1946 and 1982, the average height of young adult males in Japan increased by more than 3 inches (8 cm). Changes in a single generation obviously can't be due to genetic factors, so environmental factors such as diet and health care must be responsible (Angoff, 1988).

Curiously enough, IQ scores have also gone up over the same period of time, all over the world; the increases have ranged from 5 to 25 points. Between 1952 and 1982, the average IQ score of young adult males in the Netherlands increased by more than 20 points. No one knows for sure what environmental factors are responsible for this increase, but some possible candidates are a higher overall standard of living, a tendency for children to get more years of schooling, their greater exposure to sources of information such as TV, and their greater experience in taking tests (Flynn, 1987).

But the most dramatic increases in IQ involve children like Valerie—children born with PKU (see p. 49). A couple of generations ago, children born with this inherited metabolic disorder were doomed to a lifetime of severe mental retardation. Now, due to improvements in medical care—*environmental* improvements—children with PKU will not be retarded: their IQs will be in the normal range. The gain in IQ points might be 30 points or more.

Intelligence, insofar as it is inherited, is a polygenic trait. For polygenic traits, as we said before, what is inherited is not a certain number of inches or a certain number of IQ points, but a *range* of possibilities. Different children inherit different ranges of possibilities, so when they're reared in similar environments they do not turn out the same. But the environment will determine whether they end up at the lower end of their range or at the upper end. The difference, for a child who does not have PKU, can be as much as 20 or 25 IQ points (Weinberg, 1989).

Genetic and Environmental Influences on Personality

Long before parents have any clues about how intelligent their baby is going to be, they are gathering information about his or her personality. Some babies are full of smiles; others spend most of their time screaming. Some are in constant motion; others lie peacefully in their cribs. Such differences reflect differences in **temperament.**

TEMPERAMENT. It is clear that infants differ in certain basic aspects of personality and that some of these characteristics continue to be noticeable all through childhood—perhaps all through life. We use the term *temperament* for these fundamental, long-lasting aspects of personality. Temperament includes the tendency to be active or inactive, emotional or cool, cheerful or cranky, outgoing or shy, sensitive or tough, adaptable or rigid, distractible or persistent (Goldsmith and others, 1987).

The very fact that such qualities tend to be noticeable at an early age and to be maintained as a child grows older suggests that they are built in. Researchers have observed babies in the first couple of months of life and then observed them again a year or two later, and found many consistencies in behavior: young babies who are very active, or who smile or cry a lot, are likely to turn into toddlers who are very active, or who smile or cry a lot (Riese, 1987; Worobey and Blajda, 1989).

This doesn't mean, however, that temperament can't change. Measurements of temperament made in the first month of life are least likely to be consistent with later measurements. Also, consistency is more likely to be found over short periods of time than over longer ones. If you observe a child's temperament at one age and then again 6 months later, there is not likely to be much difference; but if you wait five or six years to make the second observation, there may be a great deal of difference. Even basic, presumably innate aspects of personality can change in response to environmental pressures. Shy, fearful children, for example, can become less shy and fearful.

SHY CHILDREN. For several years, Jerome Kagan and his colleagues at Harvard University have been studying a group of unusually timid children. Kagan calls these children "inhibited," because when they are confronted with anything new or anything they're not sure about—unfamiliar people or places, or things that look scary or make loud noises—they tend to freeze up. They stop doing whatever they were doing and back off; if their mother is handy, they may cling to her or hide behind her.

A group of inhibited toddlers were identified when they were 21 months old, and observed several times as they grew older. They were compared with a second group of children who had been unusually uninhibited and fearless at 21 months. The differences between the two groups continued to be clearly visible, year after year. At 7½ years, when they were last observed, the children who had been inhibited as toddlers were still noticeably less outgoing and more cautious than the uninhibited children. Kagan and his co-workers believe that the inhibited children were born with an unusually sensitive nervous system that has a hair-trigger reaction to any kind of stress. These children were found to have higher levels of stress-related hormones and higher heart rates than their uninhibited agemates (Kagan and others, 1988).

But not all the inhibited children remained shy and fearful, and not all the uninhibited children remained outgoing and bold. About 25 percent of each group changed as they got older: some of the inhibited group became more friendly and talkative, and some of the uninhibited group became shy and quiet. The researchers attribute these changes to the children's environments. The shy, fearful children were under pressure from their parents to become less so—the mothers of most of these children had admitted that they were worried about their child's shyness and timidity and were encouraging their child to be bolder and more sociable. The researchers found it harder to explain why some formerly outgoing children had become shy and quiet, but they thought that in some cases it was due to problems in the home and in others to the parents' preference for quiet, reserved behavior (Reznick and others, 1986; Kagan and others, 1988).

Reactive effects, as we said on page 58, can work to reduce differences among children—to "normalize" children's behavior. Parents react to the characteristics they see in their child, and if these characteristics are too extreme, the parents try to bring the child's behavior closer to what they consider ideal. But there is a limit to how much they can accomplish. The inhibited children who were most likely to become more outgoing and bold —more "normal" by American standards—were those whose inhibition had been relatively mild. The children who had been the most inhibited at 21 months were the least likely to change.

"DIFFICULT" CHILDREN. Reactive effects can also work in the opposite direction, to exaggerate children's differences and make extreme characteristics more extreme. This sometimes happens when children have characteristics that make them unusually difficult to take care of. Alexander Thomas and Stella Chess, psychiatrists at New York University Medical Center, have described how children's inborn temperaments affect their relationships with their parents. The babies they describe as "difficult" tend to be cranky rather than cheerful, they adapt slowly to change, and their eating and sleeping patterns are irregular. They react negatively to most things and their reactions are often intense. Although many babies outgrow these characteristics, some do not. The parents of a "difficult" child may blame themselves for their child's behavior and may lose confidence in their ability to be good parents. Worse still, they may blame the child. In either case, they may tend to do things that make the situation worse, not better (Thomas and Chess, 1977).

The results of this "vicious circle" might be a poor parent-child relationship and, over the long run, perhaps a child with serious behavior problems. Children with difficult temperaments tend to evoke negative reactions from their parents and other people—they are likely to get more criticism than praise, more anger than affection. A child whose parents are usually angry at him is not likely to have a happy childhood and is less likely to develop into a well-adjusted adult. Some researchers in Sweden studied a group of children

Some babies react negatively to most things; their temperaments make them difficult to take care of.

who were rated as "difficult" at age 2 and found that only about half of them had gotten easier to handle by age 6—the other half were still "difficult." And a Canadian researcher found that children whose temperaments were extremely difficult at age 7 had a greatly increased risk of being referred to a child psychiatrist by the time they were 12 (Persson-Blennow and McNeil, 1988; Maziade, 1988).

RESILIENT CHILDREN. Some children do poorly even in what appears to be an ideal environment. At the other end of the spectrum are children who thrive under the most adverse conditions. Emmy Werner of the University of California has been studying a group of such children—she calls them "resilient" children—over a period of 30 years. The children were born and reared on Kauai, one of the Hawaiian islands; they were from a mixture of racial backgrounds, predominantly Polynesian, Filipino, and Japanese. All had encountered at least four of the following risk factors:

- Their mothers had suffered complications of pregnancy or delivery when they were born.
- They were born into poverty.
- They were reared by mothers with very little education.
- They lived in a family environment marred by parental discord, desertion, or divorce.
- One or both of their parents were mentally ill or alcoholic.

Most of the children born and reared under these conditions did not do well: two-thirds of them developed serious learning or behavior problems in childhood, or had mental health problems, delinquency records, or teenage pregnancies in adolescence. But the other third—the resilient children—managed to develop into "competent, confident and caring people." Here's Werner's description of what these children were like as babies:

> Even as infants, the temperamental characteristics of the resilient children elicited positive attention from family members as well as from strangers. By the age of one, both boys and girls were more frequently described by their caregivers as "very active"; the girls as "affectionate" and "cuddly," the boys as "good-natured" and "easy to deal with." The resilient infants had fewer eating and sleeping habits that distressed their parents than did the high-risk infants who later developed serious learning or behavior problems. (Werner, 1989, p. 73)

So they were "easy," lovable babies. They became good-natured, alert, and sociable toddlers; as school-age children they got along well with their teachers and their peers. In adolescence they were self-confident, responsible, and achievement-oriented. Three-quarters of them managed to get some college education. Now, at 30, the great majority describe themselves as happy or satisfied with their lives.

Not all their success was due to qualities they had been born with, however—the resilient children did have somewhat better environments than the ones who developed learning or behavior problems. They tended to come from slightly smaller families (four or fewer children), with the children not too close together in age. All the resilient children had been well cared for in their first year of life by a parent or a grandparent, and they had formed a close relationship with that caregiver. But later, if their parents or grandparents were no longer around or could no longer take care of them, they had the ability to find someone else—a teacher, a minister, a relative, a friend of the family, or even an agemate—who could give them the emotional support they needed. These were children who, if life handed them lemons, could make lemonade.

THE HERITABILITY OF PERSONALITY. Temperament is only part of what we mean by personality. Personality also includes attitudes, values, motivations, self-image, habitual ways of dealing with frustration or disappointment, and so on—characteristics that aren't detectable in a newborn baby and that emerge during development. Does that mean that these aspects of personality are determined by the environment, and not by heredity?

No, heredity continues to play a role. Research on identical and fraternal twins, reared together or apart, indicates that most personality characteristics are, like intelligence, affected by both heredity and environment. A study in England of adult twins who had been reared together found roughly 50 percent heritability for a number of personality traits—altruism, empathy, nurturance, aggressiveness, and assertiveness. This means that half the variation in these traits was due to genetic factors (Rushton and others, 1986). The importance of heredity was confirmed in another study, in which personality traits such as "traditionalism," "social potency," and "harm avoidance" were measured in identical twins who had been reared apart. The personality traits of these twins were almost as similar (correlation: .49) as those of identical twins reared together (correlation: .52). The heritability estimate here, too, was about 50 percent (Tellegen and others, 1988).

Adoption studies lead to similar conclusions. The correlation between the personality characteristics of adopted children and those of their adoptive parents is close to zero. The correlation for adopted siblings reared together is also close to zero. Thus, adopted children have virtually no resemblance in personality to the people they grew up with (Plomin and Daniels, 1987).

But biological brothers and sisters are not much alike, either. The personality traits of genetically related siblings, reared in the same home, show a correlation of only .20—quite low. And, what's particularly puzzling, even this paltry similarity is due almost entirely to the siblings' shared genes, the 50 percent of their genes they have in common. The fact that they grew up in the same family contributes virtually nothing to the small correlation between their personalities. Robert Plomin, a behavioral geneticist at Pennsylvania State University, points out that this does not mean that family environmental influences are unimportant:

> Rather, the data imply that environmental influences important to behavioral development operate in such a way as to make children in the same family different from one another. That is, environmental influences do not operate on a family-by-family basis but rather on an individual-by-individual basis. They are specific to each child rather than general for an entire family.   (Plomin, 1989, p. 109)

WHY ARE CHILDREN REARED IN THE SAME HOME SO DIFFERENT FROM EACH OTHER? What does it mean to say that environmental influences within the family operate on an "individual-by-individual basis" rather than a "family-by-family basis"? It means that whatever it was in Jeffrey Smith's environment that influenced the development of his personality, it wasn't the fact that he grew up in the Smiths' house rather than the Joneses'. Jeffrey Smith and Jordan Smith, who grew up in the same home, were reared by the same parents, ate the same foods and went to the same schools, will be similar in personality only to the degree that they have genes in common. If they have all their genes in common (if they are identical twins) they will have fairly similar personalities; if they have no genes in common (if they are adopted) they will resemble each other about as much as two children who are chosen at random from two different homes.

The aspects of his environment that have mattered most in forming Jeffrey's personality are not the aspects we can easily measure. They are far more subtle than that. They have to do with Jeffrey's role in his family and his relationships with his parents and siblings. They have to do with the "niche" he occupies in the family, and how the other members of the family think of him and react to him. Every child, even one who is a member of a large family, plays a unique role in the network of relationships within the family.

Every child is seen by his parents and his siblings as a unique individual, even if he is an identical twin. When identical twins are born, their families are quick to notice any small differences between them. For example, one twin might appear to be a little more alert than the other one or might happen to cry a little less. This twin might be typecast by family members as "the bright one" or "the cheerful one." Then the differences in the family's behavior to the two children may increase the differences between them. This is called the **contrast effect,** and it works on fraternal twins and on nontwin siblings, too.

Researchers have found some direct evidence for the contrast effect. In one study, mothers were asked to say whether each of their children was "difficult" or "easy." The researchers found that a mother who rated her first child as "easy" was likely to rate her second child as "difficult"; those who said that the first one was "difficult" generally thought the second one was "easy." The mothers saw their children as opposites—they didn't say "They were both easy children, but the first one was a little easier," or "The first one was difficult, the second is average" (Schachter and Stone, 1985). Because parents are so prone to see their children as opposites, the children tend to be driven further apart in personality. Small differences are magnified and become large differences.

Parents don't treat their children all alike—they *can't* treat them alike if the children are different and behave in different ways. (This is the reactive effect we talked about earlier.) Despite their best intentions, parents may love one child more or find one more annoying. In a study of twins, fraternal twins often differed on how "accepting" or "rejecting" they said their parents were toward them. Evidently, one twin felt more "accepted" by her parents than the other (Rowe, 1981). When there is a difference of this sort, both children are likely to be keenly aware of it.

We have seen (in the box on identical twins and triplets reared apart) that

Problems in Development

Box 2-4
Psychiatric Disorders in Children

Wayne believes that his dog talks to him and tells him what to do; once he said that his dog told him to bite his mother. Alison is unable to enter her house through the front door without going back and forth seven times and touching both doorposts. Jenna doesn't want to go to school, says her stomach hurts, and follows her mother around the house. Tom is constantly getting sent to the principal's office for refusing to obey his teacher and for hurting his classmates; his mother reports that he lies, steals, and breaks family rules. Bill sits in his room, stares out of his window, and says "I wish I was never born." These are some of the symptoms shown by children who are brought to psychiatrists and mental health clinics.

The psychiatric disorders of children fall into three major groups. The first consists of the behavioral disorders, which include **hyperactivity** (the children who "never sit still") and **conduct disorder** (children like Tom, who constantly break rules and get into trouble). The second category consists of the emotional disorders, which include **depression** (Bill), **anxiety disorder** (Jenna), and **obsessive–compulsive disorder** (Alison). The third category is called pervasive developmental disorders, which means that everything is affected— behavior, emotions, thought processes, and social relationships. **Autism** falls into this category, and so does **childhood schizophrenia**—Wayne is schizophrenic.

Autism will be discussed in Chapter 10; it's a serious disorder that appears very early in development and is probably due to something wrong with the brain. Childhood schizophrenia appears much later in development, usually after the age of 7. Schizophrenia is not rare in adults—it's found in about 1 percent of the population—but it almost always makes its first appearance in adolescence. It is extremely rare in children. When it does appear in childhood, the symptoms are similar to those seen in adult schizophrenics: delusions and hallucinations like Wayne's, peculiar behavior and distorted thinking, and emotional responses that are either inappropriate or absent. Although drug therapy can control the symptoms of schizophrenia, there is currently no cure—Wayne is likely to be schizophrenic all his life (Russell, Bott, and Sammons, 1989).

Jenna, on the other hand, will probably be all right. Anxiety disorders are quite common in children, and most of them go away without any special treatment. Children who are nervous or fearful, or who wet their beds, bite their nails, or wake up in the night screaming in terror, have an excellent chance of turning into adults who are as normal as the rest of us (Lerner and others, 1988).

The outlook for Tom is uncertain. Although his behavior is likely to improve once he is past mid-adolescence, his chances of getting into serious trouble will remain much higher than average. He runs an increased risk of becoming a delinquent, a drug user, or an alcoholic; as an adult he may commit crimes, have difficulties in getting or staying married, or abuse his wife and children. As many as 9 percent of boys, but only 2 percent of

identical twins raised in different homes tend to perceive their environments as similar, either because they perceive things in similar ways or because they tend to evoke similar reactions from people (or both). For the same reasons, children who are not identical twins, but who are reared in the same home, might perceive their environments as different. Perhaps they only perceive things differently, or perhaps their environments really are different, because they evoke different reactions from the members of their family. One is given more affection; the other is yelled at more. One is under more pressure to achieve; the other is expected to cause more trouble.

Such environmental differences *within* the family apparently have far more effect on a child's personality than environmental differences *between* families. This means that the passive effects we described on page 57 can't play much of a role in determining personality, because passive effects—the tendency for genetic and environmental factors to work together in families that are biologically related—should have the same influence on all the

girls, show symptoms of conduct disorder (Clarke and Clarke, 1988; Tuma, 1989).

Obsessive–compulsive disorder is uncommon in children; not much is known about it. Children like Alison, who feel compelled to go through rituals such as hand-washing or counting, usually appear to be normal in other respects, although some may be depressed or have "tics" (nervous twitches). These children don't enjoy performing their rituals—they wish they could stop. A drug that has been used in treating depression is now being tried for obsessive–compulsive disorder, with promising results (Swedo and others, 1989).

That brings us to Bill, the depressed child. It used to be thought that depression was rare in children, but now some authorities believe that as many as 2 percent of young children, and 5 percent of older ones, may suffer at least one period of depression. During this period they may act lethargic, sleep or eat too much or too little, cry a lot, talk about feeling worthless and hopeless, and perhaps mention death or suicide. Although Bill will probably recover from this period of depression, there is a good chance that he will have additional spells in adolescence or adulthood. These periods of depression may alternate either with periods of normalcy or with periods in which he is "manic" (active, excitable, and either happy or irritable). In either case, the disorder can be treated fairly successfully with drugs and psychotherapy. Depression in children is found equally often in both sexes, but in adolescents and adults it is considerably more common in females (Kovacs, 1989).

With the exception of autism, which appears to be something that babies are born with, all the disorders we have discussed are caused by a combination of genetic and environmental factors. All of them "run in families." For example, the chances of a child becoming schizophrenic are about 1 percent if she has no relatives with the disorder, 10 percent if one of her parents or siblings has it, and 45 percent if her identical twin is schizophrenic (Plomin and Daniels, 1987).

Notice that it's quite possible for one twin to be schizophrenic and the other not. This shows that children don't inherit the disorder itself—only an increased likelihood of developing it, an increased vulnerability. Whether or not they actually develop the disorder will depend on environmental factors. Children are at greater risk of developing a psychiatric disorder if they are reared in poverty, or in a large family, or by parents who treat them badly (Goldstein, 1988). More surprisingly, they are at greater risk of developing a psychiatric disorder if they had a serious physical illness in childhood (Cohen, Velez, Brook, and Smith, 1989). Psychiatric disorders are apparently caused by a combination of inherited vulnerability plus environmental stress, but stress can be physical as well as psychological, and environment can include the environment inside the womb. Some researchers in Finland found that children were more likely to become schizophrenic if their mothers had the flu while they were pregnant (Kopp and Kaler, 1989).

All children are vulnerable to some extent. The outcome of their interactions with the environment will depend on their own particular vulnerabilities and their own particular environment.

children in the family. Passive effects would make children reared in the same home more alike, not more different.

But reactive effects and active effects can readily account for the differences among children reared in the same home. Children start out different and they become more different from each other as they get older, because people react to them in different ways (ways that tend to increase the differences between them), and because as they get older they become more free to choose different environments for themselves. To some extent, siblings may be different because they *choose* to be different.

It is important to remember that the parents' behavior toward a child is only one factor in the child's development, and it might not be the most important one. Many influences—both genetic and environmental—will have an effect on what kind of person the child turns out to be. Parents need not take all the credit, nor all the blame, for their children's characteristics (see Box 2–4).

The Child and the Environment

The child's environment is the context for the child's development: what he or she becomes is partly determined by the environment. But in another sense, the child is the context for the environment, because the effect of a given environmental influence depends on the child. Unlike genetic messages, messages from the environment must be interpreted. How a child interprets an environmental message depends on many factors. It depends on the child's past experiences: an Inuit child and an American child will have very different reactions to an aunt who says, "Why don't you die?" It depends on temporary states such as fatigue or hunger. And it depends on the characteristics of the individual child. One child grows up in poverty and deprivation and becomes a successful, well-adjusted adult, while another grows up in the same environment and is defeated by it.

Children do not only receive messages—they also send them. A child's behavior has an important effect on the behavior of parents and other adults. This two-way interaction often makes it difficult to interpret the correlations that researchers find between adults' behavior and children's behavior. The correlations may result from adult-to-child influences, from child-to-adult influences, or from two-way influences. It's usually impossible to distinguish among these alternatives.

The view that there is a two-way interaction between the child and the environment is what we call a **transactional** approach to the study of child development. A business transaction, for example, requires two parties, both of whom play an ongoing role in determining the outcome. Similarly, children's dealings with the environment—for example, with their parents—involve complex and constantly changing mutual influences, influences that go in both directions. A transactional view of child development is the basic theme that underlies this book.

Summary

1. **Heredity** and **environment** are responsible not just for characteristics such as musical talent, but for *all* our characteristics—those we share with others as well as those that make us different from each other.

2. Children's environments vary across a tremendous range, partly due to differences in the **cultures** in which they are reared. How a child interprets an adult's words or actions will depend in part on the child's culture.

3. A **society** is a group of people with a common culture. One of the tasks of a society is to rear its children in such a way that they become acceptable members of that society.

4. Mothers in some societies want their children to be obedient; others want them to be independent. Changes occur over time: although mothers in the U.S. currently value independence in their children, in 1924 they valued obedience.

5. Different societies have different ideas of what children are like and what to expect from them, and this affects their childrearing patterns and the children's behavior. One Zapotec society in Mexico views children as good and discourages fighting; another views children as naturally unruly and takes fighting as a matter of course. In the second society, children (and adults) fight a great deal.

6. American childrearing methods emphasize independence and assertiveness rather than obedience and cooperation. American toddlers are given more freedom to explore their environment than toddlers in many other societies.

7. Childrearing practices differ according to **socioeconomic status**. Children reared in poverty have many disadvantages: they are more likely to be born to teenage mothers and to have many siblings; they are less likely to be reared by two parents and to have good medical care and nutrition. Their parents do not have as much time and energy to devote to them. After infancy, the disadvantaged children fall further and further behind their agemates from middle-class homes.

8. About three children die every day in the U.S. as a result of physical abuse or neglect. Most physical abuse comes from parents. About 95 percent of sexual abusers are male, generally not the child's biological father.

9. Boys receive more physical abuse, girls more sexual abuse. Children may blame themselves, rather than their abusers, for the abuse; as adults they may suffer from depression and low self-esteem. Some (but not most) go on to abuse their own children.

10. Changes have occurred in the American family due to the high divorce and remarriage rate, large numbers of unmarried mothers and single-parent homes, and large numbers of mothers of young children working outside the home.

11. Women with jobs still have primary responsibility for childcare, even if fathers "help out." Although working women with children put in much longer hours than their husbands, there is no sign that this heavy workload is harming them.

12. The children of working mothers are not very different from the children of nonworking mothers. A mother's employment appears to have mildly beneficial effects on a daughter but may have mildly negative effects on her relationship with a son (and on the son's relationship with his father).

13. In good day-care centers, children do as well as, or better than, they would at home. Day-care children are a little less dependent on their parents, a little less likely to obey them, and a little more aggressive.

14. Nearly 50 percent of today's children will experience parental divorce. At first there are behavioral and emotional upheavals. Later things calm down, but children of divorce, especially boys, remain less well adjusted than children from intact families. Problems are worsened if the parents continue to fight.

15. For children in single-parent homes headed by women, the most serious problem is poverty. Girls in such homes usually develop a close relationship with their mothers, but boys continue to give their mothers a hard time. Boys who live with their fathers or remain in close touch with them, or whose mothers remarry before they enter adolescence, show fewer behavioral problems.

16. It may take longer for children to adjust to their parents' remarriage than to the divorce itself, especially if there are stepsiblings or half-siblings. Young children and boys accept a stepparent more easily than do older children and girls; a stepfather is accepted more readily than a stepmother.

17. After the birth of a sibling, an older child may act babyish for a while in an attempt to recapture her mother's full attention, but in the long run a sibling's birth is likely to lead to increased maturity and independence for the older child.

18. Mothers generally give more attention to younger children than to older ones, and this may cause trouble between siblings. The siblings' personalities will also affect their relationship.

19. Birth order does not have a consistent effect on personality, but firstborns tend to be more verbal and to be higher achievers. Children from large families, especially when they are born close together, are less verbal and more likely to drop out of school. Lack of one-on-one interaction with a parent apparently leads to lower verbal skills.

20. In general, only children are similar in character, adjustment, and achievement to children with one or two younger siblings.

21. Genetic characteristics are transmitted by the **genes.** Humans have 46 **chromosomes,** 23 from each parent. One pair is the **sex chromosomes:** girls have two X chromosomes, boys have an X and a Y.

22. A baby who has a **recessive trait** has inherited two genes for that trait, one from each parent. Babies who inherit only one gene for the trait will be **carriers.** Twenty-five percent of the children of two carriers will have the trait.

23. A **dominant trait** shows up in everyone who inherits a single gene for it. If a person has a dominant trait, each of his or her children has a 50–50 chance of inheriting the trait.

24. When a child is born with a dominant-gene disorder that neither parent has, it is usually due to a **mutation.**

25. The gene for a **sex-linked trait** is located on the X chromosome. Sex-linked traits are far more common in boys than in girls. A boy with such a trait has inherited the gene from his mother.

26. Chromosomal abnormalities occur when a fertilized egg has too many or too few chromosomes. An extra copy of chromosome 21 leads to a baby born with **Down syndrome.**

27. Missing or extra sex chromosomes have relatively mild consequences, though there is an increased risk of mental retardation and minor physical abnormalities.

28. Boys with **fragile X syndrome** are usually retarded; many show behavioral abnormalities. Girls with this syndrome are less severely affected.

29. Most normal human traits are **polygenic**—controlled by more than one pair of genes. With polygenic traits, the child inherits a range of possibilities: the environment determines whether he will end up at the low end, the high end, or the middle of this range.

30. Correlations are often found between various aspects of the environment (such as parental behavior) and various characteristics of children. Although these appear to be environmental effects, they may be due (at least in part) to three kinds of genetic effects: **passive, reactive,** and **active.** Passive effects occur because the parents who provide the child's environment have also provided the child's heredity.

31. Reactive effects occur because different children evoke different responses from people. Adults' reactions may serve to increase (or exaggerate) a child's characteristics, in "vicious circle" fashion, or to decrease (or "normalize") them.

32. Active effects occur when children are able to seek out their own environments in accordance with their own interests and inclinations (which may be at least partly genetic).

33. **Identical twins** can help us distinguish the effects of heredity and environment, because they have exactly the same genes. **Fraternal twins,** like separately born siblings, have only 50 percent of their genes in common. If a trait is mostly genetic, identical twins will be very much alike and fraternal twins will be much less alike with respect to that trait.

34. The **heritability** of adult IQ is probably over 50 percent, which means that heredity is somewhat more important than environment in determining intelligence. The IQs of identical twins reared in different homes are more similar than those of fraternal twins reared together.

35. As people get older, heredity plays a greater role in determining their characteristics and environment plays a smaller role. This is because of reactive and active genetic effects.

36. The finding that heredity is slightly more important than environment in determining intelligence applies only to the range of environments that were tested.

37. Babies are born with different **temperaments.** The fact that such differences are present in infancy and tend to persist as a child grows older suggests that they are built in. But temperaments can change in response to environmental pressures.

38. Adopted children show virtually no similarities in personality to their adoptive parents or siblings. Biological siblings are not much alike in personality, either; their similarities are mostly due to shared genes rather than a shared environment. Environmental influences are specific to the individual child rather than general to the family.

39. The **contrast effect** acts to widen any personality or intellectual differences between children in the same family. Mothers who felt that their first child was "easy" are likely to see their second child as "difficult," and vice versa.

40. Parents don't treat all their children alike, because children have different characteristics. Reactive and active effects explain why children who are reared in the same home are so different from each other.

41. Psychiatric disorders of children fall into three categories: (1) behavioral disorders such as **conduct disorder;** (2) emotional disorders such as **depression, anxiety disorder,** and **obsessive–compulsive disorder;** and (3) pervasive developmental disorders, which include **autism** and **childhood schizophrenia.**

42. Most of these disorders result from a combination of inherited vulnerability plus environmental stress. The stress may be physical as well as psychological.

43. Children receive "messages" from the environment; how they react to these messages will depend on their past experiences and on the characteristics of the individual child. Children also send messages to the environment. The recognition of the complex two-way interactions between the child and the environment is what we call a **transactional** approach to child development.

Key Terms

heredity	subculture	PKU
environment	socioeconomic status	recessive trait
nature	genes	dominant trait
nurture	DNA	carrier
culture	chromosomes	mutation
society	sex chromosomes	sex-linked trait

Down syndrome
amniocentesis
trisomy 21
chorionic villus sampling
fragile X syndrome
polygenic trait
passive effects
reactive effects
active effects
controlled

inbred
identical twins
monozygotic twins
fraternal twins
dizygotic twins
heritability
biological parents
temperament
contrast effect

hyperactivity
conduct disorder
depression
anxiety disorder
obsessive–compulsive disorder
autism
childhood
   schizophrenia
transactional view

3

Theories of Development

What is the point of having theories of child development? Why can't we just look at what children do and report what we see?

Without a theory we would have no way of deciding what to look at, what to report. One child may do hundreds of things within a day, hundreds of thousands of things within a year. And there are millions of children. Theories tell us what matters and what doesn't. A new theory may direct our attention to something that was previously considered unimportant. Toilet training was never considered to have any significance, until Sigmund Freud brought it into the spotlight. The grammatical errors children make when they're learning to speak were thought to be cute but of no consequence, before linguists used them to analyze the ways that children learn a language.

Theories also give us a way of organizing our observations, of summarizing what we see. A good theory makes sense out of what would otherwise be a random collection of data. Even a bad theory is sometimes useful: it can stimulate researchers to prove that it is wrong and to come up with alternative proposals.

But even good theories don't deal with *everything* that happens as children develop, because so many different things are going on, all at once. Thus, most of the theories we will describe in this chapter look only at certain aspects of development. Some theorists concentrate primarily on personality and social development—on the changes that occur in a child's social behavior, personal relationships, and emotional makeup. Others focus primarily on cognitive development—on the changes that occur in a child's ability to think, reason, and acquire information. The reason we need *theories* of child development, and not just a single theory, is that no one theory is currently capable of doing the whole job.

A Greek sculpture, 2100 years old. The two smaller figures were meant to be little boys.

Early Theories

In ancient times, childhood was not viewed as a special period of life or as different from adulthood in any important way. Children were seen simply as undersized adults, differing from grownups only in height, weight, and the number of facts they had in their heads. Ancient people didn't even realize that children have different bodily proportions from adults. Until late in the Middle Ages, pictures and statues of children didn't look like children at all, because most artists depicted them simply as miniature adults.

Just as a baby was considered a miniature adult, a developing fetus was considered a miniature baby. In the ancient world, prenatal development was accounted for by the theory of **preformation.** According to this notion, an infinitesimally small grownup was contained in the egg or the sperm (take your pick), and this tiny but perfect creature just grew and grew—first into a baby, then into a child, and finally into the adult it was destined to become. This belief remained popular right up to the 1800s. Even the invention of the microscope didn't put an end to preformationism. When no one could detect the tiny person through the microscope, preformationists claimed that it was too tiny and too transparent to see, even under the finest lens (Crain, 1980).

An idea that went along with preformationism was the **doctrine of innate ideas.** Most people who lived before the modern era believed that certain ideas are inborn—that the mind comes already furnished with the knowledge of such things as Truth, Beauty, and God. This doctrine was called into question by a paper published in 1690, entitled *An Essay Concerning Human Understanding.* Its author was a British philosopher named John Locke.

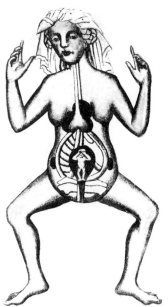

Preformationists believed that the womb of a pregnant woman contains a miniature adult.

Locke's Tabula Rasa

Locke maintained that the mind of a newborn baby is a **tabula rasa**—an "empty slate" with nothing written on it. What gets written on this slate is what the baby experiences—what he or she sees, hears, tastes, smells, and feels. All that we know, says Locke, comes to us through these five senses. No knowledge or ideas are built in. Locke's view of the mind—an empty room until it is furnished by experiences provided by the environment—makes him the first important environmentalist, the first to take the side of nurture rather than nature.

Back to Nature with Jean-Jacques Rousseau

Jean-Jacques Rousseau.

The pendulum soon swung back to nature again, but nature in a different sense—nature meaning "natural," the opposite of "civilized" or "artificial." In 1749 an uneducated Swiss named Jean-Jacques Rousseau won an essay contest sponsored by the Academy of Dijon, France. In his winning essay Rousseau argued that the progress being made in the arts and sciences was bad, not good, for the human race. Civilized society corrupts people, claimed Rousseau. He believed that "savages," such as the natives of North America, needed no laws and were happy, healthy, and self-sufficient.

Rousseau was a strange fellow who lived a strange, troubled life. His troubles began on the day he was born: his mother died in childbirth. He was raised by his father, a watchmaker, who was kind to Jean-Jacques except when he was reminding the boy of his responsibility for his mother's death. But when Jean-Jacques was 8, his father injured a man in a fight and had to leave Geneva in order to avoid imprisonment. For the next eight years, the child was tossed around from relative to relative and was unsuccessfully apprenticed out to various tradesmen, who treated him badly—or so Rousseau later claimed. But Rousseau usually ended up thinking that *everyone* treated him badly.

Rousseau ran away at the age of 16 and began a life of wandering—of fleeing, really, from one place after another. He lived in Switzerland, France, Italy, and England. Everywhere he went he made influential friends and then quarreled with them. He got along best with women, especially older women. For a while he lived in the home of a wealthy widow whom he addressed as "Mama" and who became his mistress. The chief love of his life, however, was a woman named Thérèse who worked as a servant at an inn; she could neither read nor write. Rousseau lived with Thérèse for many years, on and off. According to his own account, she bore him five children. But Rousseau refused to play the role of father, and each child was delivered, soon after birth, to an orphanage!

Thus, Rousseau never reared a child of his own. Yet he had very definite ideas about how *other* people's children should be reared. He believed that children are born good and should be left alone to develop naturally. In one of his books, Rousseau described how he would educate a fictional boy named Émile. Émile would pretty much educate himself, by exploring his environment with no more than some subtle encouragement from his teacher. There would be no rules, no commands—the child would simply progress as his nature intended him to.

The "back-to-nature" theme keeps recurring from time to time; it was very popular in the 1970s. The idea that anything natural is good and anything artificial is bad forms part of the theme. Another part of it—more relevant to our interests—is a certain view of childhood. Children are seen as wise and capable individuals, better than any adult at determining the course of their own development, their own education. Rousseau influenced educational philosophy by introducing the theme of the self-directed child. The "open classroom" of the 1970s, in which children were given considerable freedom to decide how to spend their time in school, was one product of this philosophy.

Darwin on Instinct

A major event in the history of science was the publication in 1859 of Charles Darwin's *The Origin of Species.* Darwin was a member of a distinguished British family that gave rise to many prominent scientists, physicians, philosophers, and poets. When he was a child, his parents thought that he was destined for failure; he attended Cambridge University but he was not a particularly good student. His leanings toward science finally emerged at the age of 22, when he was selected to accompany the expedition of the Beagle as the ship's biologist. During this voyage, which took him to exotic places like the Galapagos Islands, Tahiti, and New Zealand, Darwin collected the data that led to his famous theory of evolution by means of natural selection.

Darwin is important to child development theorists for two reasons. Before 1859 the human species was considered to be unique, exempt from the laws of nature that were acknowledged to control the actions of animals. By convincing the scientific world that humans are a kind of animal, Darwin made human behavior a proper subject for a natural science. In a way, he made it possible to do research on child development.

The second reason for Darwin's importance is what he had to say about **instincts** (such as nest-building). Earlier thinkers spoke of inborn ideas, but instincts are inborn *patterns of behavior.* Darwin believed that such patterns are inherited in the same way as physical features and that they evolve in the same way. Different members of a species would inherit slightly different patterns of instinctive behavior (just as they would inherit slightly different shapes of noses or colors of hair). The individuals with the most successful variations would survive and pass on these behavior patterns (or noses or colors) to their descendants.

The existence of built-in patterns of action—now called **species-specific behavior**—was recognized in animals long before Darwin's time. Darwin went further when he said that people, too, are born with instincts—many instincts. This became the prevailing view for the next half-century.

Psychoanalytic Theories

Now we come to Sigmund Freud, the most famous of all those who have constructed theories of human thought and behavior. From Darwin, Freud got his idea of the human baby as a little animal, full of instincts and primitive desires. Like Rousseau, Freud saw this baby in an unavoidable conflict with society. But there the similarities end. Freud's theory was entirely original—not because every one of his ideas was original, but because of the innovative way he brought these ideas together. The school of thought he founded became known as **psychoanalytic theory,** because it was based on **psychoanalysis,** the method Freud developed for investigating the nature and contents of the human mind.

Sigmund Freud

Born in 1856, Freud lived almost all of his life in Vienna. He was his mother's first and favorite child; she was only 20 when he was born. His father, who had children from a previous marriage, was 40.

A brilliant student throughout his school years, Freud was attracted to all the sciences. He settled on medicine, specializing in neurology. He soon became interested in patients who had what were then called **hysterical symptoms.** A patient who had hysterical blindness had nothing wrong with

Sigmund Freud.

her eyes. A patient who had hysterical numbness of the hand—no sensation from the wrist down—had nothing wrong with the nerves in her hand. Freud believed that these symptoms, which in those inhibited Victorian times were much more common than they are today, were psychological in origin.

To get at the source of hysterical symptoms, Freud first tried hypnotizing his patients. Under hypnosis, patients were sometimes able to connect the appearance of their symptoms to some **traumatic** (highly upsetting) event in their lives. Reliving this event and talking about it was often all that was needed to make the symptom go away.

Later, Freud discovered that even hypnosis was not necessary: talking was sufficient. He devised a method for getting at what was bothering his patients by encouraging them to say whatever came into their heads, and by analyzing their dreams, slips of the tongue, and so on. This is the technique he named *psychoanalysis.*

Through psychoanalysis of his patients and through careful self-analysis, Freud arrived at a new view of the human mind. He believed that most of the psychological problems of adults had their origins in childhood experiences —making childhood a much more important time of life than was previously believed. Furthermore, he felt that most of these problems were sexual in origin. By "sexual," Freud meant not only the sensations connected with the genital organs, but other kinds of pleasurable sensations as well: sucking, eating, being stroked, urinating, defecating, and so on. However, the greatest emphasis was placed on the sorts of things that the word *sexual* usually does refer to.

It must have taken courage to talk about such matters at a time when "nice" people didn't even use the word *leg* in public. For several years, Freud was shunned or ignored. But the times were changing, and by the early years of this century he had a few followers, including Carl Jung and Alfred Adler. In 1909 Freud visited the United States, where he acquired new adherents to his theories. Gradually his fame spread. In the long run his American followers proved more faithful than the European ones. Some members of his original circle—including Jung and Adler—later developed their own variations of psychoanalytic theory. In his old age, Freud spoke with great bitterness about those who he felt had turned against him (Freud, 1938).

THE FREUDIAN VIEW OF DEVELOPMENT. According to Freud, the adult human mind consists of three different "agencies" or aspects: the *id,* the *ego,* and the *superego.* They develop in that order. The **id,** present from birth, is the home of powerful instinctive desires or **drives,** such as hunger, thirst, and (especially) the sexual urge. The aggressive urge also forms part of the id. The mind of a baby at first contains nothing other than those inborn drives—no concept of self, no idea that anyone else exists. The id is interested only in the instant gratification of its desires.

The baby's conflict with society, represented by the parents, is immediate and inevitable. The baby wants to be fed the minute she feels hungry, but her parents may not be able (or willing) to drop everything and run. When the child is older, she may want to grab food from others, bite or kick, urinate and defecate when and where she wishes. All these urges must eventually be brought under control. Freud does not see the baby as innocent and virtuous, the way Rousseau did. His view is closer to the opposite: the baby is a greedy, self-centered creature whose fierce desires must be curbed if she is to become a decent, responsible person.

The experiences the young baby has with reality—that she *can't* have everything she wants the moment she wants it—produce the **ego.** The ego is the "thinking" mind, the part that "stands for reason and good sense" (Freud, 1933/1965, p. 76). It directs the child's actions in a rational way, trying to fulfill the id's desires and at the same time keep the child from getting into trouble. Freud used the analogy of a powerful horse controlled by its rider: the id is the horse, the ego the rider.

Later, between the ages of 3 and 5½, the **superego** develops. It is similar to a conscience. The superego is in favor of what society regards as "good" behavior; it is opposed to "bad" behavior. A child's ego might keep her from doing something because it knows she won't be successful, but her superego stops her for a different reason: Don't do it because it's *wrong.* If the child goes ahead and does it anyway, the superego is what makes her feel guilty. When she's a little older, her superego will make her feel guilty even for having forbidden thoughts. Such thoughts may eventually become **repressed,** or driven down into the unconscious mind. There they remain, likely to cause trouble later, until rooted out by psychoanalysis.

Freud made a clear distinction between the conscious mind (mostly ego) and the unconscious (mostly id). The unconscious is depicted as a seething pool of desires and impulses, repressed thoughts and "forgotten" memories. Some of these things leak out in the form of dreams or slips of the tongue ("Freudian slips"). Some are **displaced.** For example, an unacceptable aggressive urge against a parent or teacher might be repressed, but it will emerge in another form. This **displaced aggression** might be directed toward a younger sibling, a classmate, or even an animal. In other cases a repressed impulse might be transformed into its exact opposite—instead of hitting her little brother, the child kisses him. This is called **reaction formation.**

THE FREUDIAN STAGES. Freud was the first important theorist who saw development as a series of stages, rather than as a smooth, continuous process (see Chapter 1). The path from birth to adulthood can be viewed either as an inclined plane, like a wheelchair ramp, or as a set of stairs. Freud—and many later theorists—chose the staircase model. Each step in the staircase represents a stage in development. The stages have to come in a certain order, but the transitions between stages are not necessarily clear and sharp, and the rate at which these stages are achieved can vary considerably. Thus, stage theorists don't say that a given stage *always* comes at a certain age, but that that's the *typical* time. Some children may reach a given stage sooner, some later, and some may never reach it at all.

According to Freudian theory, the first stage lasts from birth to around 1½ years. This is called the **oral stage,** because it focuses on the mouth. The important sources of pleasure are sucking, biting, and chewing.

When the child is weaned, he progresses to the **anal stage.** Here the pleasurable sensations involve the bowel—withholding bowel movements or letting go. During the anal phase there is a struggle between the child (who wants to choose when and where he will defecate) and his parents (who want him toilet trained).

A lot depends on the outcome of these stages. According to the Freudian view, if things don't go well a person may be **fixated** at a certain stage of development. A child fixated at the oral stage may suck his thumb; as an adult he may become a habitual smoker or pencil-chewer. Fixation at the anal stage produces one of two possible results. A child who fights toilet training by defecating when and where he pleases may become an impulsive, messy adult. One who reacts to harsh training by holding back bowel movements may become an overly controlled adult—compulsively neat and clean, inhibited and stingy.

The anal stage normally ends at about age 3. It is followed by the **phallic stage** (phallus means penis). During this stage, attention is focused on the pleasurable sensations produced by the genitals. Masturbation is discovered as a way of achieving these sensations. The child is also greatly interested in other people's genitals and notices the difference between males and females. A boy becomes sexually interested in his mother, a girl in her father.

The phallic stage is really what all the fuss was about. Freud was saying that little children have sexual feelings, and most people found that notion unacceptable. Even more unacceptable was that these feelings are directed, incestuously, toward the parents. But Freud's depiction of what happens during this period (especially what happens with boys) forms a central part of his theory.

The boy in the phallic stage wants to be near his mother, wants to touch her, wants her all to himself. But he must share her with his father. This causes him to have aggressive feelings toward his father, and these feelings, in turn, cause him anxiety. He imagines that his father is aware of his feelings and fears that punishment may result. The punishment he fears, according to Freud, is **castration**—he fears that his penis will be cut off! He sees that women and girls don't have one and assumes that they have already suffered that punishment. Bear in mind that in those days a little boy who was caught masturbating was threatened with dire consequences: that his penis would "drop off," or even that someone would cut it off. Indeed, it was probably due to Freud's influence that parents stopped making such threats.

Freud named the struggle he claimed was taking place in the boy's mind the **Oedipal conflict** (after Oedipus, a character in a Greek myth, who killed his father and married his mother). He said that a girl goes through a parallel ordeal, the **Electra conflict.** The girl, however, thinks her penis has *already* been cut off. The result is **penis envy,** which Freud thought was eventually transformed into a desire for a baby—in particular, a baby boy. Again, this belief must be seen in the context of its time. In those days, boys were considered superior beings who were expected to grow up and become famous. Girls were seen as inferior creatures who were expected to grow up and become mothers. A girl might well have envied a boy, though not necessarily for his penis!

The Oedipal and Electra conflicts are resolved when the child faces the fact that he cannot have his mother, that she cannot have her father. Instead, the child begins to **identify** with the parent of the same sex—the boy wants to be like his father, the girl like her mother. He takes on his father's moral rules and standards; she takes on her mother's. Thus, identification with the same-sex parent gives rise to the superego. By the time the phallic stage ends, at age 5 or 6, the child's personality is assumed to be almost completely formed. This assumption—that nothing really important happens after age 6—is one of the more controversial aspects of Freudian theory.

After the phallic stage comes the **latency period.** Strictly speaking, this is not a stage—rather, it is a period *between* stages, during which nothing much happens (nothing that Freud was interested in, at any rate). Sexual feelings are repressed; girls play only with girls and boys play only with boys. The child concentrates on other matters, such as acquiring skills and knowledge.

The final stage is the **genital stage,** which begins at adolescence. Due to biological maturation, the submerged sexual feelings become too powerful to suppress and they reappear. This time, if all goes well, they find a proper outlet: a love relationship with a suitable person of the opposite sex.

CURRENT EVALUATIONS OF FREUD. Freud was the first theorist to put major emphasis on childhood—to point out that what occurs during the first few years of life can have very long-lasting effects. Both heredity and environment are given their due: the child is seen as being born with certain characteristics, which interact with and are modified by the environment.

Although Freudian theory had a tremendous impact on modern thought, not all of it has stood the test of time. Freud based the developmental aspects of his theories not on his personal observations of children, but mostly on the memories of adults (including himself)—adults reared in the sexually inhibited atmosphere of Victorian times. Perhaps this was why he placed so much emphasis on sex. Although that emphasis doesn't shock people anymore, many modern readers are put off by Freud's blatant male chauvinism. Females really didn't count for much in his scheme of things, except in their role of mother. Some critics have complained that *facts* also didn't count for much in his scheme of things—"Some of Freud's cases just don't stand up in light of historical fact," one said recently (Goleman, 1990a, p. C1).

Researchers have found it difficult to devise ways of testing Freud's theory experimentally. When experimental tests *have* been carried out, the results, as often as not, have gone against predictions derived from the theory. Although Freud's methods are still frequently used in clinical settings to treat patients with problems, his views are no longer popular among people who use the methods of science to study child development (Miller, 1989).

Erik Erikson was born in Germany of Danish parents. He was never much of a scholar and he didn't go to college; for a while he considered becoming an artist. Later he moved to Vienna, where he worked as a schoolteacher and, by chance, met Anna Freud, Sigmund's daughter. She encouraged Erikson to become a psychoanalyst and saw to it that he received the proper training. In 1933, when Erikson was 31, the rise of Hitler made him decide to leave Europe. He settled in the United States and became Boston's first psychoanalyst. Despite his lack of a formal degree, he eventually became a professor at Harvard.

Erikson's theories are extensions and modifications of those of Freud. His view of development is similar to Freud's in that it involves stages; moreover, most of Erikson's stages parallel the Freudian stages. But Erikson differs from Freud in what he believes goes on *within* these stages. Erikson places more emphasis on social interactions—interactions between child and family, between child and society. There is less importance placed on sexual matters.

Erikson's Psychosocial Theory

Erik Erikson.

Thus, Erikson speaks of **psychosocial** stages of development, whereas Freud's are called **psychosexual.**

Another difference is that the Freudian stages end at adolescence. Erikson believes that development continues throughout life, and he defines three further stages that encompass adulthood. Erikson places less emphasis on events that happen in infancy and early childhood. He doesn't believe, for example, that traumatic experiences occurring in childhood necessarily lead to trouble. "There is little," he says, "that cannot be remedied later" (1963, p. 104). In other words, good experiences at a later stage can make up for bad ones at an early stage. It's a more cheerful outlook than Freud's.

ERIKSON'S STAGES OF DEVELOPMENT. According to Erikson's view, each stage revolves around a different theme or conflict. In stage 1, which corresponds to Freud's oral stage (see Table 3–1), the theme is *trust versus mistrust.* The focus is on the way the new baby interacts with his parents. If the parents are reliable and consistent in their handling of the child, he comes to feel that he can rely on them and that his needs will be met. That is, he develops **basic trust.**

In the second stage, toddlerhood, the major issue is *autonomy versus shame and doubt.* **Autonomy** is the ability to do as one pleases, not to be pushed around by others. This is the famous "No!" stage, in which the child begins to show that he is an individual in his own right. At the same time, he has doubts about whether he is capable of doing what he wants to do. He also feels shame for the first time—he wants people to think he is "good" and fears that they won't.

The third stage, which takes place during the preschool period, involves *initiative versus guilt.* Initiative refers to the child's ability to work toward a goal, to make plans and carry them out. One of his ambitions, as in Freud's phallic stage, is to win his mother away from his father—a goal he can never attain. He comes to feel that he was wrong to wish to possess his mother. He develops a superego and experiences guilt.

The next stage covers the years of middle childhood, the elementary school years. Freud thought that nothing much happens during this time—according to psychoanalytic theory, everything important has already happened. But Erikson sees middle childhood in a different light: this is a period of **ego growth,** in which the personality continues to develop and, if things go well,

TABLE 3-1
The Psychoanalytic Stages of Development

APPROXIMATE AGE	FREUD'S FIVE STAGES (AND THE CONFLICTS INVOLVED)		ERIKSON'S EIGHT STAGES
Birth to age 1½	Oral	(Weaning)	Basic trust versus mistrust
Age 1½ to 3	Anal	(Toilet training)	Autonomy versus shame and doubt
Age 3 to 5½	Phallic	(Oedipal and Electra)	Initiative versus guilt
Age 5½ to 12	Latency	—	Industry versus inferiority
Adolescence	Genital	—	Identity versus role confusion
Young adulthood	—	—	Intimacy versus isolation
Middle adulthood	—	—	Generativity versus stagnation
Late adulthood	—	—	Ego integrity versus despair

children become more sure of their abilities. They work industriously at learning the skills that society requires of them. But it is also a period in which feelings of inferiority are common, because the price of failing (socially or academically) is so high. Erikson names *industry versus inferiority* as the major issue of middle childhood.

Puberty comes next, with what Erikson calls the **identity crisis**—the "Who am I?" stage. Adolescents must develop an identity of their own, apart from their family identity. At the same time they are faced with a rapidly changing physical appearance and with the necessity to start making decisions that will determine the course of their lives.

By early adulthood, the psychologically healthy person has established his or her identity. When that happens—and not before—the person becomes capable of mature, unselfish relationships with other people (such as a husband or wife). This stage leads naturally to the next one, in which the emphasis is on creating something: children, works of art, scientific discoveries, or the like. Finally, in old age, people look back and ask, "Has it been worthwhile?" If they can answer yes, they have achieved **ego integrity.**

CURRENT EVALUATIONS OF ERIKSON. Erikson, like Freud, began as a clinician. Thus, both started off thinking of people as patients, not as subjects. Later, both men became interested in discovering things about humans in general. But the methods they used to study people were clinical methods, not experimental methods. The evidence they used to support their theories was gained from individual patients in one-to-one sessions. In that kind of situation, patients probably have a tendency to say what they feel they are expected to say, and psychologists probably have a tendency to hear what they expect to hear. The clinical situation does not produce objective data, the kind of data we might get from a controlled experiment.

Although Erikson can be criticized on many of the same points as Freud, somehow his theory seems more compatible with modern thought, more persuasive. The things he says about children often ring true. His theory may be closer to art than to science, but this doesn't prevent it from containing some important insights about human development.

Learning Theories

At around the same time that Freud, in Vienna, was turning out volume after volume of writing on psychoanalytic theory, a very different movement was under way in America. It was called **behaviorism,** and its methods were as far removed from those of the psychoanalysts as they could possibly be.

Behaviorism

Psychoanalysts are interested in what their patients say about their feelings, thoughts, and dreams. Behaviorists are not interested in feelings, thoughts, or dreams; for that matter, they're not interested in what their subjects have to *say.* They're interested chiefly in what their subjects *do*—or, as a behaviorist would put it, in their **responses.** Responses are assumed to depend on external events, such as **visual** and **auditory stimuli** (sights and sounds); on how long it's been since the subjects ate, drank, or slept; and on the past history of the subjects—what they did in the past and what happened to them when they did it. Internal events, such as thoughts and feelings, are not taken into consideration, because there is no way of directly observing them. Hereditary factors also are given no role. Behaviorism takes no official notice of individual differences among members of a species. Even genetic differences *between* species are pretty much ignored. Subjects are called **organisms,** a word that can be applied equally well to people and to animals.

In Chapter 2 we discussed the nature-nurture debate and we described the long-standing conflict between the theorists who favor heredity and those who think that environment is what really counts. For many years, the environmental view was the prevailing one among child development researchers. That view grew directly out of behaviorism. Behaviorism had a very strong influence on researchers in all fields and varieties of psychology, including child development.

John B. Watson.

GIVE ME THE BABY. The most famous quote in all of behaviorism is this one, from the pen of John B. Watson:

> Give me a dozen healthy infants, well-formed, and my own specified world to bring them up in and I'll guarantee to take any one at random and train him to become any type of specialist I might select—doctor, lawyer, artist, merchant-chief, and, yes, even beggarman and thief, regardless of his talents, penchants, tendencies, abilities, vocations, and race of his ancestors. (Watson, 1924, p. 104)

Watson was not the founder of behaviorism (that honor belongs to a psychologist named Edward Thorndike, who did experiments with cats). Rather, he was its first popularizer. That statement we just quoted shows his style, his boldness. Watson was willing to go out on a limb.

He showed some of the same traits in his personal life. In 1929 Watson was accused of becoming romantically involved with a young woman who was his research associate. (He was 51 at the time.) His wife divorced him, and the resulting scandal lost him his position at Johns Hopkins University. He ended up working for an advertising agency.

Although he was an experimental psychologist, Watson is remembered for only one important experiment—and that experiment was not very good and not at all ethical, by present standards. It involved a single subject: an 11-month-old child known as ''little Albert.'' Watson had read about the work of the Russian researcher, Ivan Pavlov. Pavlov had **conditioned** a dog to salivate at the sound of a bell by **pairing** food with the sound of the bell—in other words, by feeding the dog whenever the bell rang. Watson decided to produce **conditioned fear** in little Albert by pairing a loud noise with the sight of a harmless white rat. Albert was afraid of the loud noise; he wasn't afraid of the rat. But after the experimenter had several times made a loud noise behind Albert's back while he was looking at the rat, Albert became afraid of the rat. Moreover, he became afraid of *other* white furry things, such as a toy rabbit and a man with a Santa Claus beard (Watson and Rayner, 1920).

Watson had planned to ''decondition'' little Albert and get him to like white rats again. But before he was able to do so, the child was removed from the hospital where the experiment had taken place. Albert was still afraid of white furry things when he went out into the world and disappeared from the recorded history of child development research (see Box 3–1).

B. F. SKINNER. In 1929, the year that Watson's career in psychology came to an abrupt end, the career of another behaviorist was just beginning. B. F. Skinner was a first-year graduate student in Harvard's psychology department, having spent the previous year in an unsuccessful attempt to become a writer. (He ended up writing anyway, with countless articles and more than a dozen books to his credit.) The young Skinner was a man of many talents. He was a fine musician (who once played saxophone in a jazz band) and adept at languages (he could read German, French, and Italian). He also possessed unusual mechanical ability—he was a tinkerer. In one of the old Cambridge houses where he lived as a graduate student, he rigged up a device that automatically opened the damper of the furnace every morning (Skinner, 1979). Later, when his second daughter was born, he used his mechanical talent to build her a special enclosed area called an ''air crib.'' The air crib was provided with warm, filtered air, so that the baby could play or sleep without the restrictions of clothing. Skinner had always been fond of children and was a devoted father.

B. F. Skinner.

It was Skinner's love of tinkering that led him to invent, in 1930, the device for which he became famous: the **Skinner box,** as it's now called. This is simply an animal cage, built originally for a rat (but later used for other animals, such as pigeons). In the cage is a movable metal bar called a lever. When the rat pushes the lever it activates a switch, which causes a pellet of food to drop into a feeding tray. With this simple device Skinner worked out his theories of behavior. Skinner's basic claim is that the behavior of humans and animals is lawful—it is controlled by rigid laws of cause and effect, just like the ricocheting billiard balls on a pool table. If we knew all the laws and if we could completely control the environment, then human behavior would be perfectly predictable.

OPERANT CONDITIONING AND REINFORCEMENT. Skinner made a clear distinction between **classical conditioning,** as in Pavlov's experiments, and what he called **operant conditioning.** Classical conditioning involves the conditioning of a simple, automatic, inborn response called a **reflex**—salivating or becoming afraid are two examples. To condition the response, a stimulus that normally produces it is repeatedly paired with a neutral stimulus: food (which produces salivation) is paired with the sound of a bell, or a loud noise (which produces fear) is paired with the sight of something white and furry. Eventually the neutral stimulus alone is able to produce the response.

Operant conditioning, on the other hand, is capable of producing a brand-new response. A nonbehaviorist would just call it *learning.* For example, a rat learns to press a lever, a pigeon learns to peck at a lighted plastic disk. Both animals are rewarded with food for their responses. But Skinner doesn't call the food a reward, he calls it a **reinforcer,** because it reinforces (or strengthens) the tendency to make the response. Anything an animal or a

Problems in Development

Box 3-1
Phobias: Two Old Theories and a New View

Most children have fears. When a fear gets out of hand and starts to interfere with the child's day-to-day activities, it is called a **phobia.** A child who has a phobia of dogs, for example, may be so afraid of meeting one that he may refuse to go outside.

One of Sigmund Freud's most famous case histories concerns a 5-year-old boy referred to as "little Hans." Little Hans had a phobia of horses. Since he lived in the days before motor cars, when the streets of Vienna were teeming with horse-drawn vehicles, this was a real problem. His parents sought Freud's aid. The boy was psychoanalyzed. Eventually, Freud decided that little Hans's phobia was due to an Oedipal conflict and that horses symbolized Hans's big, powerful father. Hans unconsciously feared that his father would discover that they were both in love with the same woman (Hans's mother); he feared that his father would retaliate by castrating him. Since these fears were unacceptable to Hans's conscious mind, they were converted into a fear of horses (Freud, 1909/1950).

Hans had long since gotten over his phobia of horses when a child called little Albert developed a phobia of a similar sort. Albert was the child in Watson's experiment who was conditioned to fear white rats. Afterwards, Albert would shrink in terror from the sight of any white, furry animal. Although Hans and Albert reacted in much the same way when they encountered a creature they feared,

Freud and Watson had very different explanations for their behavior. An Oedipal conflict or conditioned fear—which explanation was correct?

Little Hans himself probably would have sided with Watson. His own explanation of how he became afraid of horses was nothing like Freud's: he linked his phobia (which he called "the nonsense") to a frightening incident involving a horse that was pulling a bus. Hans described how the horse had fallen down and kicked its feet, violently and noisily. "When the horse in the bus fell down, it gave me such a fright, really! That was when I got the nonsense" (Freud, 1909/1950, p. 192).

So, if Hans was right, a single scary incident involving a horse— not very different from Albert's experience in Watson's laboratory—was enough to give him a fear of horses. Does this mean that phobias are just conditioned fear? If so, why don't we develop a fear of whatever we happen to be looking at (let's say, the TV set) whenever something scary (a loud noise, an earthquake) happens while we're looking at it?

As a matter of fact, phobias hardly ever involve objects such as TV sets. They don't even involve potentially dangerous things such as electric outlets or razor blades. What they usually involve are things like dogs, cats, snakes, spiders, heights, or lightning and thunder. In the years after Watson's experiment, other researchers tried repeating his procedure, using different children and different stimuli. They were unable to condition their subjects to be afraid of inanimate objects such as curtains and wooden blocks (English, 1929; Bregman, 1934).

Why was it so easy to teach little Albert to fear a white rat, and so difficult to teach another child to

---

person is willing to work for is a reinforcer—food or water to a hungry or thirsty organism, a kind word or a pat on the head to a child or a dog.

In Skinner's terms, a hungry rat is **reinforced** with food when it presses the lever. The first lever-press was accidental, but the **reinforcement** increases the likelihood that the rat will press again and yet again. If we *stop* giving the rat food when it presses the lever (and feed it in some other way instead), it will eventually stop making the response. This is called the process of **extinction.** The response has been **extinguished** by the absence of reinforcement.

One of Skinner's important findings was that reinforcement does not have to be given consistently in order to work: **partial reinforcement** works too. For example, we can feed the rat after every 10 lever presses, or after every 25. Or the number of required presses can vary—the rat may be reinforced after 9 responses on one trial, after 5 on the next, and after 16 on the next. In

fear a wooden block? We believe that the explanation has two parts. The first was provided by Martin Seligman, of the University of Pennsylvania. Seligman (1972) has proposed a concept he calls **preparedness**. According to this concept, people are genetically **prepared** to become afraid of certain things. These are things that, far back in the history of our species, were associated with real danger. Seligman doesn't believe that we're born with these fears: what we're born with is a tendency to acquire them very readily. It might take only one or two unpleasant experiences to make a child fear heights or spiders, whereas it would be extremely difficult to condition him to fear something he was not genetically prepared to become afraid of.

The second part of our explanation was provided by Jerome Kagan, of Harvard University, whose work with shy, inhibited children was described in Chapter 2. Kagan believes that some children are born with exceptionally sensitive nervous systems, so that they tend to overreact to anything stressfull or scary (Kagan, Reznick, and Snidman, 1988). We suspect that Hans and Albert were both children of this sort—children whose fearfulness is easily aroused. Thus, in order to produce a severe case of conditioned fear in a child, two ingredients may be required: a stimulus that a child is genetically prepared to become afraid of, and a child who is very prepared to become afraid. Once you have those two ingredients, the techniques of classical conditioning are likely to be quite successful in producing a phobia.

So Watson was right about the nature of the environmental event that is capable of producing a phobia in a child. But he was wrong about the nature of the child. "Give me the baby," he said —*any* baby. We doubt that he could have produced a phobia in just any baby. A given environmental event does not have the same effect on every child. Freud was well aware of that.

Are phobias curable? Yes, though it is not easy to cure them. One reason for this is that a phobic person is usually so successful in avoiding the object of his fear that he never has a chance to get over it. Perhaps the reason why little Hans eventually stopped being terrified of horses was that it was impossible to avoid them completely in turn-of-the-century Vienna. An often successful method for treating phobias is to introduce the phobic person to whatever it is he fears, doing it so gradually that his fear always remains manageable. Watson called this method *deconditioning* —breaking the association between the stimulus and the fear.

Two other methods used for treating phobias in children are pairing the feared stimulus with something the child likes, such as ice cream, and letting him watch other children playing happily with whatever it is he is afraid of. All of these methods have been in use for a long time. In 1924, a researcher named Mary Cover Jones used them to cure a phobia in a 2½-year-old boy named Peter. Like Albert, Peter was afraid of small, furry animals. Jones gave Peter good things to eat while a white rabbit was gradually brought closer and closer to him. She also had Peter watch other children playing with the rabbit. Peter's fear gradually went away, and eventually he got brave enough to pet the rabbit himself.

such situations the rat eventually ends up pressing the lever very rapidly, over and over. The interesting thing about partial reinforcement is what happens in extinction, when pushing the lever no longer produces any food at all. If reinforcement has been continuous, the rat soon stops pressing the lever when the food stops coming. But if it has been partial, the rat may go on pressing, over and over again, making thousands of responses before it stops. That's because, in its past, unreinforced responses were eventually followed by reinforced ones. If a child out shopping with his mother keeps whining for candy, and every now and then she gives in and buys him some, she's given him partial reinforcement for whining. Now if his mother decides to *stop* buying him candy, he will go on whining for a very long time—longer than if she had bought him candy every time he asked for it!

With reinforcement, organisms can eventually learn to perform complicated actions that are quite different from those they would normally perform. The process of teaching them such actions is called **shaping.** A pigeon can be taught to turn around in circles, for example, by this method. First you reinforce any sideways movement. Once this response is learned, you gradually increase your requirements—reinforce the bird only for a quarter of a turn, then only for half a turn, and so on. Soon the pigeon is pirouetting like a ballerina. Skinner even taught a pair of pigeons to play Ping-Pong with each other by the method of shaping.

One important thing to remember about reinforcement is that it primarily affects the last response made—the one that occurred just before the reinforcement was given. If a pigeon turns around, then lifts its wing, then stretches its neck, and then is reinforced, it's the neck-stretching that has been reinforced. The same principle holds for punishment.

PUNISHMENT. **Punishment** consists of administering an unpleasant stimulus, such as one that causes pain (or in removing a pleasant stimulus, such as food). Punishment *decreases* the strength of a response, just as reinforcement increases it. The response that is primarily affected is the last response before the punishment. So if your dog does something wrong and you call him over to you and smack him, you've actually punished him for coming to you when you call!

Although many behaviorists believe that punishment is an effective way to eliminate an undesirable response, Skinner does not. He believes that the best way to get rid of an unwanted kind of behavior is to extinguish it—to avoid reinforcing it until it goes away. He practiced what he preached. When his older daughter, Julie, was 5 years old he announced to her that she would never be punished again. "For a month or two she tempted us, beginning to act in punishable ways and watching us closely, but it did not last. For one thing, having abandoned punishment, Yvonne [his wife] and I looked for and found better ways of treating her" (Skinner, 1979, p. 279). The "better ways" consisted of using reinforcement to increase desired behavior, rather than punishment to decrease unwanted behavior. Evidently, Skinner was satisfied with the effects of this method on Julie's behavior.

CURRENT EVALUATIONS OF SKINNER. Skinner and his followers have shown that many kinds of behavior are affected by reinforcement. But it's a long step to go from saying that reinforcement works to saying that *all* learning depends on reinforcement. As we will see in the next section, children learn many things they have never been reinforced for doing. By ruling out thought, the behaviorists have painted themselves into a corner. Human understanding modifies the effects of many supposed reinforcers and punishments. For example, although calling your dog to you and then punishing him might decrease your dog's tendency to come when you call, the same rule doesn't necessarily apply to children. If you call Jason over to you and scold him for throwing sand at Jacqueline, he will probably associate the scolding with throwing sand and not with coming when you call him.

Classical behaviorism fails to take account of the fact that children are different from rats and pigeons. Almost as serious is its failure to take account of the fact that children are different from *each other*. Although Jason and Jacqueline might behave in similar ways in the restricted environment of a

Skinner box, in the sand box they behave quite differently—for reasons that Skinner's theory is incapable of explaining.

NEOBEHAVIORISM. Behaviorism, like Freudian psychology, has not died, though it has declined in popularity and has changed to some extent. Modern behaviorism—called *neobehaviorism* or *behavior analysis*—is not as narrow and rigid as the classical variety, but it still emphasizes the study of observable events and it still puts its faith in reinforcement. The reinforcers, however, can consist of less tangible things such as approval, and the effects of the reinforcers can vary according to the context in which they're given (Baer, 1989).

Sometimes a behavior-analytic approach can be quite useful. A team of researchers studied the home environments of boys with conduct disorders —these boys are highly aggressive and disobedient. The researchers found that the parents of these boys, instead of reinforcing their sons for good behavior and punishing them for being bad, were ignoring good behavior and actually reinforcing bad behavior. When a child had a temper tantrum, for instance, his mother would often reward his behavior by giving in to him. If the mother tried to ignore the tantrum, the child was likely to escalate the aggressiveness of his behavior—perhaps even physically attacking his mother—until she did provide whatever reinforcement he wanted. Thus, the parent was selectively reinforcing increasingly aggressive behavior. To escape from this vicious circle, the parents have to be trained how to modify their behavior, so that they consistently provide reinforcement for good behavior and punishment for bad. Physical punishment is not recommended—a brief period of isolation or the withdrawal of a privilege are acceptable forms of punishment (Patterson, DeBaryshe, and Ramsey, 1989).

Social Learning Theory

Social learning theorists agree that reinforcement and punishment affect behavior, but they don't think that's *all* that is going on. The fact is that children do many things they have never been reinforced for. Reinforcement does not seem to be necessary in order for learning to occur: much of human behavior is learned by observing another person's behavior and, in some cases, imitating it. The other person is called a **model,** and what the model does is called **modeling** the behavior.

Social learning theory had its origins in the 1940s, when two Yale theorists published a book called *Social Learning and Imitation* (Miller and Dollard, 1941). But the name that has been most closely associated with this view-point is that of Albert Bandura, a professor at Stanford University. Bandura has made important contributions both to the development of the theory and to the experimental evidence that supports it.

The best known of Bandura's experiments dealt with the modeling of aggressive behavior. The subjects were preschool children; they watched an adult model perform in a short movie film. The adult was shown attacking a large, inflated plastic toy called a "Bobo doll," which bounces back up each time it's knocked down. The model sat on the doll, punched it, and hit it with a mallet, yelling things like "Pow, right in the nose," and "Sockeroo . . . stay down." Bandura filmed two different endings for the movie. One group of

After seeing a movie that shows an adult attacking a Bobo doll (top row), these children (middle and bottom rows) imitated the model's behavior.

children were shown a version that ended with the model being praised by another adult and given rewards of candy and soda. The second group saw a film with a different ending—the model was hit with a rolled-up newspaper by the second adult, who exclaimed, "You big bully!"

After seeing the videotape, the children were brought one at a time into a room containing the Bobo doll. Each child was left alone in the room and observed through a one-way screen. Many of the children who had seen the movie with the reward ending imitated the model's behavior—they sat on the Bobo doll, hit it with the mallet, and so on. The children who had seen the model punished were much less likely to do these things (Bandura, 1965).

Imitative behavior, then, is affected by reinforcement and punishment. But in this case it's the consequences experienced by the model that counts. Bandura calls this **vicarious reinforcement** and **vicarious punishment**—rewards and punishments that we see someone else get. We learn by watching other people and by seeing what happens when they do something. This is considerably more efficient than if we had to try everything out for ourselves. A child who sees another child burned when he touches a hot stove, or scolded by the teacher for speaking out of turn, doesn't have to try it herself. She already knows the consequences.

Thus, learning occurs whether the model is rewarded or punished. In one case the child learns what to do; in the other, what not to do. Both groups of children in the Bobo doll experiment could later tell the researcher exactly what the model had done. For this reason, Bandura distinguishes between acquiring information about new responses and actually performing them. Children pick up information from watching a model, but whether they will

One of the ways that children learn is by observing the behavior of models. Their first models are their parents.

perform what they learned depends on other factors—on whether they saw the model rewarded or punished, and on what happened when they performed similar acts in the past. So rewards and punishments matter, but they needn't be experienced "in person."

Of course, children don't just imitate undesirable behavior such as aggressiveness—they imitate more approved kinds of behavior, too, such as sharing, helping, and self-control. As we will see in later chapters, modeling is often an effective way of teaching children to act the way we want them to.

SOCIAL COGNITIVE THEORY. Recently, Bandura (1986) has presented an updated version of social learning theory, which he has named *social cognitive theory.* The name change reflects a decreased emphasis on traditional learning theory and an increased emphasis on **cognition,** which means thinking, reasoning, and understanding. This hybrid school of thought acknowledges the contributions of Piaget (whom we'll discuss in the next section) and thus falls right on the borderline between learning theories and cognitive theories.

Social cognitive theory still talks about rewards and punishments, but now these consequences are assumed to have their effect only by way of a special kind of observational learning, in which the behavior that is observed is one's own behavior. Children learn from observing the results of their *own* behavior in exactly the same way they learn from observing the results of others'. On the basis of such observations, they develop ideas about what behaviors are appropriate and, if necessary, modify these ideas on the basis of additional experience.

The new theory also recognizes children's ability to use forethought (as in anticipating the consequences of doing something) and symbols (such as words), to set standards for themselves and form opinions about their own ability to meet these standards. If a child thinks she is less capable than she really is, she is less likely to attempt a challenging task and more likely to fail if she does attempt it (Perry, 1989).

Another addition that social cognitive theory has made to social learning theory is the recognition of the transactional relationship between the child and the environment: in a sense, the child creates her own environment. The child who acts in a bullying way to other children lives in a world where other children dislike and avoid her—a very different world from the one inhabited by a kind and friendly child. The child who chooses to watch TV all day exposes herself to different learning experiences than a child who plays soccer or practices ballet (Miller, 1989).

Social cognitive theory differs from plain cognitive theories in two important ways. First, the main focus is still on what the child actually *does* and on whether the child finds the consequences of those actions pleasant or unpleasant. Second, social cognitive theory, like other learning theories, holds that development is a gradual process. In contrast to the psychoanalytic theories we discussed in the previous section and most of the cognitive theories we will discuss in the next, it is not a stage theory.

Cognitive Theories

The stage theories of Freud and Erikson dealt with the emotional life of the child and with the changing relationships between children and other people (primarily parents). Behaviorism went in the other direction, ignoring the child's emotions and social relationships and concentrating entirely on the child's actions. Now we come to the third distinct way of looking at development: once again we are allowed to peer into the child's mind, but now the emphasis is on thoughts, ideas, and knowledge, rather than on feelings. The study of **cognitive development**—the development of the capacity to reason and understand—owes as much to Jean Piaget as psychoanalysis owes to Freud.

Jean Piaget   Piaget, like Rousseau, was born in Switzerland and spent part of his early life in France. But there the resemblance ends. Piaget was a highly educated man and a dedicated scientist right from the start. At the age of 10 he published his first scholarly article; by 21 he had earned a doctorate in science. Piaget and his wife had three children. Unlike many European fathers of the 1920s (and *very* unlike Rousseau), he found his children fascinating. He spent long hours observing them and recording their behavior. Jacqueline, Lucienne, and Laurent Piaget were Jean Piaget's first and best subjects.

What interested Piaget was the way children learn about the world by systematically exploring it. In his view, children do not simply receive information from the environment: they actively seek it. They achieve knowledge and wisdom through their own efforts. Their drive to do this is built in; it's one of the characteristics of the human species. Piaget sees cognitive develop-

Jean Piaget with one of his colleagues, studying cognitive development in children.

ment from the point of view of a biologist—as a kind of biological **adaptation.** All living species have ways of adapting to their environment: plants send down longer roots in dry climates; animals learn to avoid places where predators lurk and to seek out areas where food is plentiful. Humans are the most adaptable of all. They adapt by using their intelligence, by the active process of gaining understanding of their environment.

Piaget divides childhood into four major periods (see Table 3–2). However, development is seen as a continuous process, and transitions from one period to another are gradual rather than abrupt. Is this a stage theory, then? Yes, because there are assumed to be *qualitative* differences between one period and another—major reorganizations in the way children think, the way they understand the world.

THE SENSORIMOTOR PERIOD. The first period of development begins at birth and lasts for about two years. Even at birth, babies are not entirely helpless. For example, they can suck—they are born with a sucking reflex. They can look at things and can track a slowly moving object with their eyes. Later they learn to grasp objects—first with the entire hand, eventually with the thumb and forefinger. Piaget calls such patterns of action **schemes.** Schemes can be inborn, like sucking, or acquired later, like grasping. They can also be modified—a baby learns to grasp a stuffed animal in one way, a small piece of food

Piaget's Stages of Cognitive Development

TABLE 3-2
Piaget's Stages of Cognitive Development

APPROXIMATE AGE	STAGE	CHARACTERISTICS
Birth to age 2	Sensorimotor period	Infant develops concept of permanent objects and the ability to use mental representations.
Age 2 to 7	Preoperational period	Egocentric thought; child centers on one aspect of the situation.
Age 7 to 11	Period of concrete operations	Child can decenter but cannot reason abstractly.
Age 11 on	Period of formal operations	Abstract reasoning and systematic experimentation are now possible.

in another way. And schemes can be extended or combined, forming ever more complicated schemes.

During the sensorimotor period, the baby develops the concept of **object permanence.** According to Piaget, babies start out with no conception of the permanence of objects or people—they are aware of the existence of things only when they can actually see them or feel them. When the object disappears, the baby instantly forgets it: out of sight, out of mind. Here is Piaget's description of his daughter Jacqueline at 9½ months:

> Jacqueline is seated and I place on her lap a rubber eraser which she has just held in her hand. Just as she is about to grasp it again I put my hand between her eyes and the eraser; she immediately gives up, as though the object no longer existed.   (Piaget, 1954, pp. 21–22)

Lucienne at about the same age watches her father hide a doll under a piece of cloth. She does nothing until her father pulls back the cloth to reveal the doll's feet, whereupon she grabs them and pulls out the doll. After several more trials, Lucienne learns to find the doll even when it is completely hidden by the cloth. But then Piaget hides the toy in a different place, under a blanket. Instead of searching there, Lucienne again looks for the doll under the cloth—even though she *saw* her father put the doll under the blanket!

By the end of the sensorimotor period, toddlers can think of a toy as being in a place other than where they last saw it or last found it—object permanence is complete. At age 1½,

> Jacqueline throws a ball under a sofa. But instead of bending down at once and searching for it on the floor she looks at the place, realizes that the ball must have crossed under the sofa, and sets out to go behind it.   (p. 205)

Jacqueline has to make a detour around a table in order to get behind the sofa. Her ability to do this shows that she has an overall idea of the locations of various objects (such as furniture) in the room. Her ability to go to a certain place by an indirect route also shows that she is capable of making a plan, of thinking ahead. All these new abilities require the use of what Piaget called **representations**—mental images (or, later on, arbitrary symbols such as words) used to represent real actions or things.

By the end of the sensorimotor period, children are also capable of

deferred imitation—they can imitate an action they saw previously. Jacqueline at 16 months saw a little boy having a tantrum and watched him with interest. The next afternoon she screamed and stamped her feet on the floor of her playpen, just as the little boy had done the day before (Piaget, 1962).

THE PREOPERATIONAL PERIOD. From around age 2 to age 7, the child is in the second of Piaget's developmental stages. This period is marked by the increasing use of representational thought—words and other symbols are used as substitutes for actual objects or actions, in solving problems and in recalling past events. Their growing skill with language also enables children to communicate their thoughts to others.

What are the characteristics of preoperational thought? For one thing, according to Piaget, it's **egocentric.** By this term Piaget doesn't mean selfishness or conceit—he means the inability to see a situation from the point of view of another person. For instance, a preschool child is shown a model of three mountains constructed out of cardboard. A doll is also in the room, "looking" at the mountains. The child is asked, "What does the doll see?"

> The child describes what he himself sees from his own position, without taking into account the obstacles which prevent the doll from seeing the same view. When he is shown several pictures from among which he is to choose the one which corresponds to the doll's perspective, he chooses the one which represents his own. (Piaget, 1954, p. 365)

Another limitation of preoperational thought, according to Piaget, is the inability to understand the concept of **conservation,** the principle that the amount of something doesn't change merely because you've changed its shape. In his famous experiment on the conservation of liquid, Piaget showed his subjects two identical glasses, each filled to the same level with a liquid such as juice. The child is asked, "Which glass has more juice?" "They both have the same amount," is the reply. Now, as the child watches, the juice from one glass is poured into a tall, narrow beaker. The same question is asked again—which has more? Most children see that the level of juice in the beaker is way above that in the glass and reply that the beaker has more. A few children notice that the glass is wider than the beaker and reply that the glass has more. In neither case will the child agree that the two containers still hold the same amount of fluid! Similar results are found in other situations: the young child believes that a ball of clay contains more clay when it is flattened out into a pancake or when it is divided up into several smaller pieces.

Why are these children unable to see that the quantity of liquid or clay remains the same? Because, according to Piaget, they **center** on only one aspect of the situation at a time—the height of the liquid or the diameter. They can't **decenter**—they cannot yet consider both aspects at the same time. But they will be able to do this later, typically by the end of the preoperational period (Piaget and Inhelder, 1941).

THE PERIOD OF CONCRETE OPERATIONS. By age 7 or 8, children have acquired the concept of conservation—they understand that the amount of liquid stays the same, whether it's poured into a tall, narrow container or a

Which container holds more? Most children under the age of 7 don't realize that the amount of liquid stays the same, whether it's poured into a tall, narrow container or a short, wide one.

wide, flat one. They can consider several aspects of a situation at once. But their understanding is tied to real events, real (concrete) objects. They cannot, according to Piaget, abstract a general principle from particular examples. Nor can they disregard reality and temporarily put aside what they believe to be true, for the sake of argument. Piaget asked some 8- to 10-year-olds whether a rapidly swinging object would still make a breeze if the room were empty of air. "Yes," was the reply, "because there is always air in the room." "But in a room where all the air had been taken away would it make any?" "Yes . . . because there would be some air left" (Piaget, 1928, p. 68).

THE PERIOD OF FORMAL OPERATIONS. At around age 11 or 12, children begin to reason logically and abstractly. They can now draw conclusions even from impossible suppositions—they are no longer troubled by a question such as "If dogs had six heads, how many heads would 15 dogs have?" (Piaget, 1928). Given a scientific problem to solve, such as what determines the amount of time it takes for a pendulum to complete its swing, they can carry out systematic operations to find out the answer. In a study done in Piaget's laboratory, children of different ages were asked to try to solve the pendulum problem. They could vary the length of the string, the weight of the object swung by the string, or the height at which the object was released. Concrete-operational children couldn't solve the problem because they didn't know how to test the possibilities systematically. Formal-operational children, however, realized that they must vary only one factor at a time, holding the others constant, in order to test its effects. One 15-year-old girl first tried two different lengths of string with a 100-gram weight and then the same two strings with a 200-gram weight. "It's the length of the string that makes it go faster or slower," she correctly concluded. "The weight doesn't play any role" (Inhelder and Piaget, 1958, p. 75).

CURRENT EVALUATIONS OF PIAGET. There is no doubt that Piaget made a tremendous contribution to our understanding of cognitive development. Still, as with Freud and other pioneering theorists, many of Piaget's ideas have been called into question by later research. For example, Piaget's statement that 2- to 6-year-olds are capable only of egocentric thought has been knocked down again and again. Young children are capable of taking another's point of view in some situations. If you ask a 3-year-old to show you a picture, she will hold it up with the picture facing *you*, not facing her. A 4-year-old who has gone on a trip with his nursery-school class and who later talks to his mother about it will take into account the fact that his mother was not there. He will *tell* his mother about the trip, whereas with his nursery school teacher he will *refer* to it (Siegler, 1986). With regard to preschoolers' alleged inability to decenter, it has been shown that 4-year-olds and even some 3-year-olds can be taught to understand that the amount of liquid in a glass doesn't change merely because it has been poured from one container to another (Field, 1981).

Piaget tended to underestimate the abilities of infants and preschoolers. On the other hand, he seemed to *over*estimate the abilities of teenagers. Many teenagers—many adults, for that matter—would be unable to solve his pendulum problem.

Despite criticisms of this sort, Piaget's basic ideas have held up well. But Piaget's greatest contribution is not contained in the details of his theories, or even in his basic ideas. Piaget is a central figure in child development because he was the first to call attention to the importance of cognition. Thus, he opened up a whole new topic for investigation. Until the time that Piaget's works were translated into English and began to be widely read, research in child development was dominated by a behavioristic approach that frowned on asking questions about the child's mind and that ignored the contribution that children make to their own development. It was Piaget, more than anyone else, who was responsible for the decline in popularity of behaviorism.

The Information-Processing Approach

Right now you are processing information. Your eyes are looking at the letters printed on the pages of this book, and your mind is translating the letters into words and the words into meaningful (we hope) ideas, and storing these ideas in your memory, from where (you hope) you will be able to retrieve them when you need them. While you are processing this information, other information in your environment is *not* being processed: you may be failing to notice the music coming from the room next door, the slight smell of your roommate's deodorant in the air, or the fact that it has become a little chilly. If the music, the smell, or the temperature does happen to capture your attention, you will find that you have stopped processing the information contained on this page, even though your eyes might continue to move

The Child in Society

Box 3-2
The Development of Moral Reasoning

One aspect of cognitive development that researchers have studied is the development of moral reasoning —concepts of good and bad, right and wrong, moral and immoral. Piaget (1932) asked children of various ages to make moral judgments about characters in stories he told them. He found that the children's judgments were related to their level of cognitive development: a child in the preoperational period might say that a boy who broke a trayful of teacups by accident was "naughtier" than one who broke a single cup while trying to steal some jam.

An American researcher named Lawrence Kohlberg extended Piaget's work, using the same method: tell children stories, then ask them questions. Kohlberg's stories presented a moral dilemma: in one, for example, a man had to decide whether to break the law in order to steal an expensive drug that might save the life of his dying wife. The important question was not "What should the man do?" but "Why?" Kohlberg (1981, 1984) found that moral reasoning became increasingly sophisticated as children got older, and proposed a stage theory of moral development (see Table 3–3).

According to Kohlberg, there are three major levels of moral reasoning: **preconventional, conventional,** and **postconventional.** Preconventional moral reasoning is based on self-interest: achieving one's own goals and avoiding "getting caught." A child at this level might say "No, the man shouldn't steal the drug because he'll probably get caught and sent to jail." Conventional moral reasoning focuses on upholding society's rules: "No, the man shouldn't steal the drug because it's wrong to steal." Postconventional moral reasoning admits the possibility that some principles might be more important than society's

TABLE 3-3
Kohlberg's Stages of Moral Development

Level 1: Preconventional Moral Reasoning
Stage 1: Obedience and Punishment. Children are concerned about obedience to rules. Obedience is valued both for its own sake and as a way of avoiding punishment.
Stage 2: Self-Interest and Fair Exchange. Children follow rules because it's to their own advantage to do so. You do things for other people so that they will do something for you.

Level 2: Conventional Moral Reasoning
Stage 3: Approval and Conformity. Children try to live up to the expectations of others; they want to be considered "good."
Stage 4: Law and Order. Breaking rules is bad because "What if everybody did it?"

Level 3: Postconventional Moral Reasoning
Stage 5: Social Contract and Individual Rights. Laws are designed to protect society and thus should generally be upheld, but some values are more important than upholding the law.
Stage 6: Universal Ethical Principles. Self-chosen ethical principles, based on concepts such as justice and equality, are thought out and followed consistently.

Source: Kohlberg, 1981; Snarey, 1985.

rules: "Stealing is wrong, but it would be worse to just let a person die."

Kohlberg believes that all children start at level 1 and most go on to level 2. But admission to level 3 is restricted to a select few. In fact, one of the weaknesses of Kohlberg's theory is that studies of people in other societies have found *no* level-3 individuals in some societies. It's possible that Kohlberg's theory is not applicable to cultures in which the customs and values are very different from our own (Snarey, 1985).

mechanically over the letters. The environment is rich in information, but at any given moment we can process only a small fraction of it.

Research on **information processing**—on how information is selectively taken in, acted on by the brain, stored in memory, and then perhaps retrieved from memory and acted on again—began by studying adults. Only in the past ten years has it been extended to children. This came about partly because of the growing interest in cognitive development and partly because it was

Even within our own society, Kohlberg's theory has a serious limitation. The children he questioned in his early studies, and on whose responses he based his descriptions of the various stages, were all boys. Evidently, girls' replies to his questions didn't fall as neatly into his categories or were more difficult to interpret (Gilligan and Attanucci, 1988). So the test Kohlberg constructed to measure children's level of moral development was based only on boys' responses. And—not surprisingly—boys tend to do better on Kohlberg's test than girls do, despite the fact that in tests of moral *behavior,* girls are more likely to come out ahead.

Carol Gilligan, of Harvard University, feels that Kohlberg's test is biased in favor of males because it ignores the fact that moral development follows a different path in females. Gilligan (1982) proposed that boys' ideas about right and wrong generally develop according to a concept of *justice,* whereas for girls morality involves *caring and concern for others.* In her research, which is mostly based on interviews with adolescents and young adults, she asks her subjects to talk about moral decisions they have actually been faced with, such as whether to use drugs or whether to have an abortion. The responses are categorized according to whether the focus is mainly on caring and interpersonal relationships, or mainly on abstract principles such as justice. A caring orientation is exemplified by a student who didn't turn in someone who had broken the school's rule against drinking, because what was important was "to be concerned about someone without antagonizing them or making their life more difficult." A focus on justice is demonstrated by a student who decided not to take drugs, even though pressured to do so by friends, because "I know for me what is right is right and what's wrong is wrong—it's like a set of standards I have." In the study from which these quotes were taken, 35 percent of the female subjects, and only 2 percent of the males, were found to have a caring orientation; 65 percent of the

male subjects were focused mainly on justice (Gilligan and Attanucci, 1988, p. 226).

Recently, Gilligan's ideas on male-female differences in moral development have been tested in younger children. Children between the ages of 6 and 11 were told a story about a porcupine who needed a home for the winter so he moved in with a family of moles. The moles, who had agreed to share their burrow with the porcupine, later regretted this decision because they kept getting pricked by the porcupine's sharp quills. The children were asked how they would solve this dilemma. There were no differences between the sexes in the 6- to 9-year-olds. But the responses that involved aggression—"Pluck the porcupine" or "The moles should shoot him"—were given only by 10- and 11-year-old boys (Garrod, Beal, and Shin, 1989).

It remained for Nancy Eisenberg, of Arizona State University, to tie the loose ends together. In longitudinal studies, she traced the development of moral decision making in children between the ages of 4 and 16. What she found was that girls and boys start out pretty much the same in the responses they give when they're presented with moral dilemmas. The differences start to appear around the age of 11 or 12. From that age on, girls show an increasing tendency to sympathize with the feelings of the person (or porcupine) in need—to put themselves in someone else's shoes (or quills): "I know how *I'd* feel if. . . ." Boys demonstrate less of this kind of reasoning and it takes them longer to achieve it (Eisenberg, 1989a; Eisenberg and others, 1987).

Two final points to make. First, remember that the male-female differences we referred to are *statistical* differences. There are many 12-year-old boys who are very concerned about the feelings of others, and many 16-year-old girls who hold abstract notions of justice and equality. Second, society needs both kinds of people. Neither kind of moral judgment is "better" than the other.

natural to ask: if adults are limited in how much information they can process, aren't children likely to be even more limited?

Information-processing theorists have been particularly interested in the aspect of cognitive activity they call **encoding.** Robert Siegler, of Carnegie-Mellon University, defines encoding as "identifying the most informative features of objects and events, and using the features to form internal representations" (1986, p. 13). Siegler is using the term *representations* in the same

Young children do not process information as quickly or efficiently as adults.

way Piaget did, to mean mental images, ideas, or thoughts. When a child views a scene, some features of that scene are encoded, which means that they become representations in the child's mind. Other aspects of the scene are not encoded—they just don't register. As children get older, they get better at encoding the important aspects of a scene or an event. Since they can encode only a limited amount of information at a time, knowing which kinds of information to encode and which kinds to ignore is crucial. Thus, the 5-year-old thinks that the tall, narrow beaker contains more juice than the shorter, wider glass because she has encoded only the height of the beaker and ignored its diameter.

Another thing that changes as children get older is what Siegler calls **automatization.** As children gain experience in using their mental processes, they become more and more efficient at the job. Their processing becomes faster and requires less effort and attention. For instance, when a child first begins to walk to school she needs to pay close attention in order to go in the right direction, turn at the right corner, and cross the street at the right time. Later, these actions become automatized, so the child no longer has to concentrate on them and can instead pay attention to the scenery or to a conversation with a friend. Automatization of reading skills is what allows older children to read with greater ease and speed than younger ones. Automatization of memory processes is one reason older children can remember more than younger ones. As Siegler points out, you can pack more into the trunk of a car once you have learned how to pack it efficiently.

Some information-processing theorists have found it useful to compare the child's mind to a computer. Like a computer, the mind can be described as consisting of "hardware" and "software." The hardware of the system consists of structural features such as built-in memory capacity. The software consists of programs—rules or strategies—for using the mind's capacity. Development involves changes in both hardware and software: progress is due both to the physical maturation of the brain and to the creation of more complex programs that make use of these physical capacities. On the basis of information provided by the child's experiences, she is able to "debug" her programs so that they run more efficiently and produce more accurate results (Klahr and Wallace, 1976).

CASE'S THEORY OF COGNITIVE AND EMOTIONAL DEVELOPMENT. Robbie Case, of the Ontario (Canada) Institute for Studies in Education, has recently proposed an interesting theory that ties together Piagetian thought with an information-processing viewpoint. The latest version of his theory not only describes cognitive development—it deals with emotional development as well (Case, 1985; Case, Hayward, Lewis, and Hurst, 1988).

Like Piaget, but unlike most other information-processing theorists, Case believes that cognitive development proceeds in stages; the four stages he proposes are roughly equivalent to the four Piagetian periods, though the ages are a bit different. Also like Piaget, Case uses the word *scheme* to describe the contents of the child's mind. For Case, a scheme can be any cognitive event—a representation or a pattern of action. Each scheme also has an emotional value, either positive (a scheme that is experienced as enjoyable or interesting), negative (a scheme that gives rise to unpleasant feelings), or neutral. The child, even in infancy, is assumed to have some control over the schemes she experiences. The motivation that produces cognitive development is her desire to move from negative schemes to positive ones. She does this by means of various actions, which Case calls *operative schemes.* Simple operative schemes, such as turning one's head or eyes to look at something, are innate; more complex ones are acquired as the baby gets older. The young baby utilizes her inborn ability to move her eyes in order to keep an object in view, because she finds looking at this object more interesting (positive scheme) than looking at a blank wall. Later she learns how to reach out and grab objects, and then crawl toward them, and later climb on top of a table in order to reach them. As motor and cognitive abilities are acquired and practiced, they gradually become smoothly running "programs," requiring less and less energy to maintain.

At the same time, the emotions the child experiences grow more complex. The newborn infant, says Case, can experience only two strong emotions, distress versus contentment, plus two weak ones, interest versus boredom. As the baby gets older, emotions such as anger, delight, and fear emerge, followed later by jealousy, shame, and pride. The appearance of these emotions rests on the advances made in cognitive development. Anger emerges when the baby has learned to perform some action to accomplish a goal and that action is interfered with: for instance, the baby tries to reach for an object but someone restrains her arm movement. Delight appears when a goal is reached, as when the baby succeeds in causing a mobile to turn or making her mother smile. Fear appears when the baby becomes capable of anticipating some negative experience, as when the pediatrician picks up his syringe. Jealousy appears when the baby becomes capable of understanding the connection between (A) "My mother isn't paying enough attention to me" and (B) "She's paying too much attention to that other person." According to Case, the ability to understand the connection between A and B doesn't appear until the transition between the first stage and the second, which in Case's theory comes at about 18 months.

Within each of Case's four stages of development, the child becomes able to combine more and more simple schemes into increasingly complex schemes. Movement from one major stage to another comes when the child is able to use schemes that are on a different level of abstraction. During the first stage the child is capable of being afraid of physical things, such as people or things she associates with pain. During the second stage the child is capable of being afraid of imaginary monsters. In the third stage the child might fear that people will judge her to be inadequate in abstract things such as "goodness" or "intelligence." In the last stage, the child might fear even more abstract things, such as "conspiracies" and "social injustice." In the same way, the goals the child sets for herself, and the kinds of things that bring her pleasure, increase in complexity and abstractness: in the first stage the child enjoys getting her mobile to turn; in the second she likes games such as tag and follow-the-leader; in the third it's games based on rules, and in the fourth she may derive satisfaction from getting a computer program to run.

Both genetic and environmental factors play a role in Case's theory. In the early years, the child becomes able to combine schemes into more complex schemes mainly because of the physical maturation of her brain, which enables her to think about two or three things at a time instead of only one. As she gets older, physical maturation plays less and less of a role. Cultural and educational factors, plus the child's own individual characteristics, become ever more important, because they determine what experiences the child will have and, therefore, what she will learn.

Case's theory of cognitive and emotional development is still so new that it's too early to tell whether research will support its assumptions. But the way it ties together several different lines of thought makes it look very promising.

Biological Theories

The last two theories we will discuss, ethology and sociobiology, are descendants of Darwin. Both focus primarily on innate behavior and on behavior that is presumed to have evolutionary significance, because it increases the chances that the members of a species will survive. Both fields are at least as much concerned with the behavior of subhuman animals as with human behavior. Nonetheless, ethologists and sociobiologists do have things to say that are relevant to child development.

Ethology

Ethology is the study of species-specific behavior (also known as instinctive behavior), especially when it is performed by animals living in their natural environment. Species-specific behavior is behavior that is present in all the members of a species—or, to be more precise, all the normal members of a species of a given sex and condition, such as all normal females that have just given birth. (Whether or not the behavior is also present in the members of *other* species doesn't matter.) Although the behavior is resistant to change once it is established, environmental factors and learning may play a role in the early stages. Some species of birds have to learn to sing the characteristic song of their species by hearing it sung by other members of their species. However, these birds are predisposed to learn only their own song and not the songs of other species they may happen to hear. The notion that humans are genetically prepared to become afraid of certain things (see Box 3–1) fits in very well here.

Not everybody agrees with the preparedness explanation of phobias, but it is clear that *some* species-specific behaviors exist in humans. The reflexes babies are born with fall into this class. As we will see in Chapter 5, babies are born with many reflexes, some of which are essential to life. Walking erect and smiling at people also qualify as built-in traits that are characteristic of the members of our species.

The existence of other types of species-specific behavior in humans is more controversial. One likely candidate is babies' attachment to their parents, which we will discuss in Chapter 6. Attachment emerges quite reliably in all normal babies when they are about 8 months old. The parents' response to the baby also appears to have some built-in components. Most human adults have an "aw, shucks" reaction to the sight of cute babies, and this reaction is not confined to the young of our own species: kittens, puppies, and baby porcupines are just as capable of evoking it. As we will see in Chapter 5, young mammals have certain physical characteristics that tend to bring out a protective or nurturing response in older humans. The evolutionary significance of this response is obvious: if humans didn't generally feel protective and nurturing toward their young, the species would be unlikely to survive. Similarly, the baby's attachment to his mother (which conveniently appears just at the age when the baby starts to become mobile) makes him stick close to her and decreases the chances that he will wander off and get lost or be eaten by predators.

Ethologists like to study animals in their natural environments, not in laboratory settings with artificial constraints on their behavior. Videotaping has become a useful tool for this kind of research. By studying videotapes of young humans, ethologists have found that teenage girls in nine different cultures flirt in exactly the same way—they use the same facial expressions and the same movements of the head and eyes (Eibl-Eibesfeldt, 1975; Miller, 1989).

Sociobiology

"A chicken is just the egg's way of making another egg." That saying sums up fairly well the philosophy of the sociobiologists. According to this view, all living things are driven by their genes to produce more copies of their genes, and then to take care of these copies (their offspring) so that they will survive and produce still more copies. The adult members of a given species are simply fancy packaging for their DNA, designed to preserve it, protect it, and (most important) pass it on. Furthermore, by extension, these adults are also predisposed to protect other close relatives, since they share some of the same genes.

Nor is this behavior confined even to close relatives. In species that live in groups, such as many birds and hoofed mammals, a member that spies a predator will give an alarm cry or signal as a warning to all the members of its group. Although by doing this the individual increases the risk to itself, it decreases the risk to the group as a whole. In this way the group's shared genes are preserved and the group's chances of survival increased. And the group's survival is essential to the survival of the individual and its descendants.

Thus, apparent acts of unselfish heroism—such as rescuing a stranger from a burning building—can be interpreted as a selfish attempt on the part of the rescuer's genes to protect other possessors of the same genes. Sociobiologists would predict that if the rescuer has a choice he will concentrate his efforts on rescuing those people with whom he shares the most genes: first his own children, then his nephews or nieces, and only then the neighbor's child. A further prediction is that mothers will make a greater effort to rescue their children than fathers will, because a mother knows for certain that her child is really her biological offspring (and the carrier of half her genes), whereas a father can never be 100 percent certain.

As this example suggests, sociobiologists have more to say about adults' behavior toward children than about children per se; it also shows why many people find this viewpoint offensive. But the theory generates large numbers of predictions that have an annoying way of being confirmed: for example, that a child is more likely to be abused by a stepfather than by a man who believes the child is his, that parents tend to favor a child who closely resembles them over one who doesn't, and that grandparents generally show more interest in their daughter's children than in their son's (Crawford, Smith, and Krebs, 1987; Smith, 1990).

Sociobiology and ethology are not, at present, central to the study of child development. However, the recent surge of interest in genetic influences on development may bring them into greater prominence in the future.

Will the Right Theory Please Step Forward?

We've come to the end of the chapter. We've told you about a number of different approaches to child development. Now you're probably waiting for us to answer the big question: Which theory is right? Let's evade that question for a minute and instead answer an easier one: Which theories are *wrong?*

Preformationism was wrong. There really *isn't* a tiny humanoid inside of the egg and/or sperm, ready to inflate (gradually) to adult size. Locke's basic idea was wrong too. The baby isn't born with an empty slate. As we'll see in Chapter 5, the newborn baby's slate already has quite a lot written on it. He or she comes with a lot more standard equipment than Locke realized, to say nothing of the custom features.

None of the other theories can be labeled *wrong.* Each contributes something useful to the study of child development. Freud, Skinner, and Piaget represent extreme positions and for that reason it's easy to find flaws in what they say, but each has had some valuable things to tell us about childhood.

Since they focus on different aspects of development, the different theories are not necessarily incompatible. Thus, current theorists pick and choose from the older theories that we have described here, skimming off the best of each of them and blending these parts into new theories that may be more complicated and less easy to explain, but closer to the truth. Development *is* a complicated process! It's no accident that most of the newer approaches we have described, such as Bandura's social cognitive theory and Case's theory of cognitive and emotional development, are combination models that put together the theoretical advances from two or more different schools of thought.

Current theoreticians also take more notice of the transactional nature of development: they recognize that children's characteristics affect their relationships with others, and that children to some extent determine their own environments. Inborn differences among children are no longer ignored. In fact, genetic interpretations are in danger of becoming *too* popular. One researcher in the field of behavioral genetics observed recently,

> During the 1970s, I found I had to speak gingerly about genetic influence, gently suggesting heredity might be important in behavior. Now, however,

I more often have to say, "Yes, genetic influences are significant and substantial, but environmental influences are just as important." (Plomin, 1989, p. 110)

No extreme position, whether it says "everything is inherited," "everything is learned through reinforcement," or "it all boils down to sex," is likely to be correct; yet, each may have something to tell us. The study of child development is like a woven tapestry, with each of the theories we've described here contributing some of the threads. You will see the threads reappear, woven together in various ways, throughout the rest of this book.

Summary

1. Two beliefs popular in former times were **preformationism,** the notion that the egg or the sperm contains a miniature version of the adult it is destined to become, and the **doctrine of innate ideas,** the notion that babies are born with their minds already furnished with certain ideas.

2. Locke denied the doctrine of innate ideas. He believed that the baby's mind is empty—a **tabula rasa**—until it is furnished with experiences provided by the environment.

3. Rousseau believed that children are capable individuals and should be left alone to develop naturally.

4. Darwin's work persuaded the scientific world that humans are a kind of animal, and hence that humans are subject to the same laws of nature that control the behavior of animals. Darwin believed that people, as well as animals, are born with **instincts.**

5. Freud was the founder of **psychoanalysis.** He believed that most of the psychological problems of adults have their roots in childhood experiences, and that most of these problems are sexual in origin.

6. According to Freud, the human mind consists of the **id,** the **ego,** and the **superego.** The id is present from birth and is the home of powerful instinctive **drives.** The ego results from the baby's conflicts with society; it directs the child's actions in a rational way. The superego is similar to a conscience; it develops during the preschool period.

7. Freud offered the first important stage theory of development; the five stages are called **oral, anal, phallic, latency,** and **genital.** During the phallic stage (age 3 to 5½), the **Oedipal conflict** occurs: little boys become sexually interested in their mothers and fear that their fathers will punish them with **castration.** Girls are presumed to go through a parallel experience, called the **Electra con-** flict. The resolution of these conflicts causes children to **identify** with the same-sex parent. This identification gives rise to the superego.

8. Erikson's stage theory is **psychosocial**—compared to Freud's, there is more emphasis on social interactions, less on sexual matters. Development does not stop at adolescence but continues throughout life.

9. In the first of Erikson's eight stages, infancy, the important issue is trust versus mistrust—if the infant's parents are reliable and consistent, the infant will develop **basic trust.** In toddlerhood, the issue is **autonomy** versus shame and doubt—toddlers want the freedom to determine their own actions but doubt their capabilities. In the preschool period, the issue is initiative versus guilt—the Oedipal conflict plays a role here. In middle childhood, a period of **ego growth,** the issue is industry versus inferiority. In adolescence, teenagers go through the **identity crisis.** Erikson's last three stages occur during adulthood.

10. Behaviorism is concerned with people's and animals' **responses,** and not with their thoughts, feelings, or dreams. Responses are assumed to depend on external **stimuli** and on the past history of the subjects.

11. Watson, the first popularizer of behaviorism, performed only one important experiment: he produced **conditioned fear** of white rats in an 11-month-old boy called little Albert.

12. After Watson's experiment, little Albert had a **phobia** —he was terrified of white rats. Little Hans, a 5-year-old boy described by Freud, had a similar phobia of horses. Freud attributed Hans's phobia to the Oedipal conflict, but it is more likely that it resulted from the same kind of conditioning process that produced Albert's phobia.

13. Children are genetically **prepared** to become afraid of certain things, such as animals and insects. Also, some children are genetically more fearful than others. Both of these ingredients may be necessary in order to produce a phobia in a child.

14. Skinner distinguished between **classical conditioning** and **operant conditioning.** In classical conditioning, a neutral stimulus is **paired** with a stimulus that produces a **reflex;** eventually the neutral stimulus alone can produce the reflex. In operant conditioning, a response is **reinforced** with a reward such as food or praise; this **reinforcement** makes the response more likely to occur again. If reinforcement is no longer given, **extinction** occurs: the response eventually stops being made. Extinction occurs more rapidly if reinforcement was continuous than if it was **partial**.

15. Punishment, the administration of an unpleasant stimulus, decreases the tendency to make a response. The response that is affected is the last one that occurred before the punishment.

16. Social learning theorists such as Bandura believe that children can learn without reinforcement by observing the behavior of other people, called **models.** A child's tendency to imitate a model's behavior will be influenced by the rewards or punishments received by the model. Such **vicarious reinforcement** or **vicarious punishment** affects only the *performance* of new responses—learning occurs whether the model is rewarded or punished.

17. Piaget awakened interest in **cognitive development**—the development of the ability to think, to reason, and to understand. In his view, children do not simply receive information from the environment—they actively seek it. Piaget sees cognitive development as a kind of biological **adaptation.**

27. Piaget's first stage is the sensorimotor period (birth to age 2). During this period, the simple **schemes** (patterns of actions) that babies are born with develop into more complex schemes, and babies acquire the concept of **object permanence**—the understanding that objects continue to exist even when they cannot be seen or felt. Babies also develop the ability to use mental **representations,** and **deferred imitation** becomes possible.

18. In the preoperational period (age 2 to 7), preschoolers tend to **center** on a single aspect of a problem. According to Piaget, their thought is **egocentric**—they can't see a situation from the point of view of another person.

19. In Piaget's period of concrete operations (age 7 to 11), children can consider several aspects of a situation at once, but their understanding is tied to real (concrete) objects. They cannot temporarily put aside what they believe to be true for the sake of argument.

20. Piaget's fourth stage is the period of formal operations (which begins around age 11). Children now become able to reason logically and abstractly, and to solve problems by systematically testing the alternatives.

21. According to Kohlberg, there are three levels in the development of moral reasoning, each consisting of two stages. In the **preconventional level,** moral reasoning is based on achieving one's own goals and avoiding "getting caught." In the **conventional level,** moral reasoning is based on upholding society's rules. Reasoning in the **postconventional level** recognizes that some principles might be more important than upholding society's rules. The third level is rare in our society and nonexistent in some other societies.

22. Gilligan believes that moral development is different in girls and boys: boys focus on *justice,* girls on *caring.*

23. The **information-processing** approach looks at how information is selectively taken in, acted on by the brain, stored in memory, and later retrieved. We can process only a small fraction of the information in the environment.

24. Information is taken in through the process of **encoding,** by which the informative features of objects and events are turned into mental representations. Learning which kinds of information to encode is an important part of cognitive development. **Automatization** enables children to use their mental processes faster and more efficiently.

25. According to Case's theory of cognitive and emotional development, *schemes* are cognitive events with an emotional value. The desire to move from negative schemes to positive ones provides the motivation for cognitive development. The infant can only experience distress, contentment, interest, and boredom, but later—as cognitive development advances—other emotions make their appearance.

26. Ethology is the study of **species-specific behavior** —behavior that is found in all the normal members of a species. Although this kind of behavior is resistant to change once it is established, learning may play a role in its early stages. Possible species-specific behaviors in humans are walking, smiling, flirting, and babies' attachment to their parents.

27. According to the sociobiologists, all living things are driven by their genes to produce more copies of their genes, and then to take care of these copies (their offspring) so that they will survive and produce still more copies.

28. Current theorists put together ideas from two or more different schools of thought to produce new theories that are more complicated but perhaps closer to the truth.

Key Terms

preformation
doctrine of innate ideas
tabula rasa
instinct
species-specific behavior
psychoanalytic theory
psychoanalysis
hysterical symptom
traumatic
id
drive
ego
superego
repressed
displaced
displaced aggression
reaction formation
oral stage
anal stage
fixated
phallic stage
castration
Oedipal conflict
Electra conflict
penis envy
identify
latency period
genital stage

psychosocial
psychosexual
basic trust
autonomy
ego growth
identity crisis
ego integrity
behaviorism
response
visual stimulus
auditory stimulus
organism
condition
pairing
conditioned fear
phobia
preparedness
prepared
Skinner box
classical conditioning
operant conditioning
reflex
reinforcer
reinforce
reinforcement
extinction
extinguish
partial reinforcement

shaping
punishment
model
modeling
vicarious reinforcement
vicarious punishment
cognitive development
cognition
adaptation
scheme
object permanence
representations
deferred imitation
egocentric
conservation
center
decenter
preconventional moral
   reasoning
conventional moral reasoning
postconventional moral
   reasoning
information processing
encoding
automatization
ethology

4

From Conception to Birth

The scene is a delivery room in a suburban hospital, around 3:30 in the morning. The characters: Dr. Gordon, an obstetrician; Karen Schisano, age 27, about to give birth to her first child; Don, her husband, age 29; and two nurses.

DR. GORDON: Push, Push!
KAREN: Aah . . . Uh!
DON: I can see the baby's head!
DR. GORDON: Push again!

The baby's head emerges, nose down, into the obstetrician's hands. The doctor clears out the baby's nose and mouth with a suction device and then turns the head a little to the side and eases out first one shoulder, then the other. The rest of the body slips out easily, along with a gush of watery fluid.

"It's a boy!" exclaims the doctor, and the parents' first big question is answered. Slightly more than half of births—about 51.5 percent—are males. The second big question quickly follows: "Is he all right?" asks Karen. "He's terrific," replies Dr. Gordon. "Here, see for yourself." The doctor places the baby, now crying vigorously, on his mother's still bulging stomach.

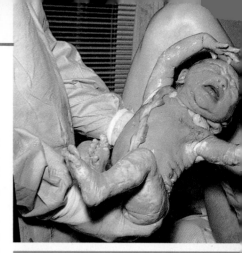

KAREN (looking thrilled):   Oh, wow! Look at him!
DON (looking a little dazed):   He's turning pink!
             KAREN: Isn't he lovely? He has your nose!

The baby is still attached to his mother by way of the **umbilical cord,** but he is already breathing on his own. The doctor delivers the **placenta** (afterbirth) and clamps and cuts the umbilical cord. Now the baby is wiped off and weighed. His weight, 7½ pounds (3400 g), is about average for a baby boy. Girls weigh a few ounces less, on the average.

The baby is wrapped in a blanket and returned to his mother, who is glowing with pride and happiness. She looks and smiles at her child; she examines his toes and fingers, his face and ears. The baby has stopped crying and now lies quietly next to his mother.

KAREN: Oh, look, he's opening his eyes! Hello, there!
  DON: What color are his eyes? They look sort of grayish. Hello, baby!
KAREN: Say hello to your Daddy. Oh, he's holding your finger!
  DON: He has quite a grip!

If Karen and Don are delighted with their new baby, it's clearly a case of beauty being in the eyes of the beholder. Baby Michael (as his parents have decided to call him) is not, at this point, anything that an objective observer would call ''lovely.'' His hair is still plastered down to his head, which is oddly elongated due to being squeezed temporarily out of shape during the birth process. His eyes are puffy; he seems barely able to open them. His facial expressions change rapidly and apparently at random. He has hardly any chin and no neck at all. Nonetheless, he is that most remarkable of creatures: a newborn human child.

But newborn isn't the same as new. Although Michael has so far had no environment other than the interior of the **uterus** (womb), he has already had nine months of development. In this chapter we'll look at what went on during those nine months. We'll return for a closer look at the **neonate**—the newborn baby—in Chapter 5.

Development in the Prenatal Period

Development in the uterus takes place during a period of time called the **prenatal period** (or, alternatively, the **period of gestation**). In humans, this period averages 266 days, or 38 weeks—one week short of nine months. The prenatal period begins at the moment of **conception.** It ends when the baby is born. To put it another way, the prenatal period begins when two cells—one from a man and one from a woman—unite to form a single cell.

Conception

When a sperm from a man's **testis** (testicle) unites with an egg from a woman's **ovary,** conception has occurred. The ovaries generally put forth a single egg (or **ovum**) each month, about midway through the menstrual cycle. In contrast, there may be as many as 400 million sperm cells released in a woman's vagina during sexual intercourse. Some small proportion of these sperm make their way through the uterus and up the **Fallopian tubes,** which lead from the uterus to the ovaries. Only a single one of those 400 million sperm will fertilize the egg. It is in the Fallopian tubes where this event ordinarily takes place, most often within 24 hours after intercourse.

INFERTILITY. It has been estimated that one out of every six American couples would like to have a child but are having trouble conceiving (Frank and Vogel, 1988). There are dozens of possible causes of infertility—they range from minor problems that are easily corrected to major abnormalities of the male or female reproductive system. Medical science has made considerable progress in recent years in diagnosing and treating many of these problems.

Despite this progress, however, the proportion of infertile couples has increased in the past 20 years. There are at least two reasons for this increase in infertility: a tendency to marry and have children later, and a tendency to have sex earlier and with a wider variety of partners. The first factor, later marriage and childbearing, means that couples are now trying to have children at an age when their fertility has already begun to decline. A woman has more trouble getting pregnant once she is past her late 20s; a man's fertility declines too, though far less rapidly. The second factor, earlier sexual activity and a greater number of partners, has produced a sharp increase in the spread of sexually transmitted diseases. Some of these diseases, especially gonorrhea and chlamydia, can permanently damage a woman's reproductive organs and make it difficult or impossible for her to become pregnant.

A third possible cause of decreased fertility may, ironically, be the current emphasis on fitness. The thin, muscular bodies that are today's ideal of beauty turn out not to be ideally suited for childbearing. Female athletes and ballet dancers often have irregular menstrual cycles or do not menstruate at all; they may fail to **ovulate** (their ovaries may fail to produce an egg) even in months when they do have a period. This is because a certain amount of body fat is necessary in order for ovulation to occur. On the average, 28 percent of the weight of an 18-year-old woman consists of fat. If this percentage drops below 22 percent, she will have difficulty becoming pregnant (Frisch, 1988). Fortunately, infertility of this sort is easy enough to remedy: gaining weight or easing up on training is usually all that's required.

Other causes of infertility are more difficult to diagnose and to treat. But there is now a wide choice of possible alternatives for a couple who have so far been unable to produce a baby.

ALTERNATIVE PATHS TO PARENTHOOD. The first choice for many childless couples is adoption. Although the increased use of abortion and the growing acceptability of single motherhood have greatly reduced the number of babies available for adoption, the situation is not hopeless. Couples who are willing to consider a child who is not perfect, or not white, or not an infant can usually succeed in their quest.

In at least 40 percent of cases, an infertility problem can be traced to the male (Andrews, 1984). When the woman is fertile but the man is not, an alternative that has been in use for almost a century is **artificial insemination.** With this procedure, sperm from a donor is injected with a syringe into the woman's **cervix** (the opening into the uterus). Sometimes the husband's

Louise Brown and her parents. Louise, born in England, was the world's first "test-tube baby."

sperm is used for artificial insemination, if he produces fertile sperm but is incapable of normal intercourse. If the husband's sperm are inadequate or if he is known to be a carrier of a serious genetic defect, sperm from a donor will be used.

What if the man is fertile but the woman is not? A common cause of infertility in women is blockage or abnormalities of the Fallopian tubes. For women whose tubes cannot be repaired surgically, an increasingly possible alternative is **in vitro** (or "test-tube") **fertilization.** With this procedure, eggs are surgically removed from the woman's body and are combined with sperm in a glass laboratory dish. Conception takes place there, in the dish. One or more fertilized eggs are then injected into the woman's uterus. The first "test-tube baby," Louise Brown, was born in England in 1978. America's first test-tube baby, Elizabeth Carr, arrived three years later. In vitro fertilization is now being performed in clinics all over the world; thousands of babies have been conceived this way (Holmes, 1988).

Once the idea of conception outside the human body became a reality, many other alternatives became possible. Fertilized eggs can now be kept frozen for several months and then thawed and implanted into a woman's body. The woman need not be the same one who donated the egg—she may be a **surrogate mother,** who becomes pregnant with someone else's biological child and gives birth to that child. (The term *surrogate mother* is also used to refer to a woman who becomes pregnant through artificial insemination and thus is the biological mother of the baby she has agreed to bear for someone else.)

Theoretically, it is now possible for a baby conceived through in vitro fertilization to have five different parents. The egg and the sperm used in the fertilization process may be obtained from donors; these donors are the baby's biological mother and father. The woman in whose uterus the fertilized egg develops is the baby's surrogate mother or **birth mother.** And the people who rear the child are her legal mother and father. Such a child will get her coloring, her facial features, and all her other inherited characteristics from the genes she received from her biological parents—the genes contained in the egg and sperm. The instructions contained in these genes will be put into effect during the nine months spent in the uterus of the birth mother.

Stages of Prenatal Development

In the nine months it takes for a fertilized egg to become a baby, one cell becomes millions of cells, organized in a complex and minutely detailed fashion. How does this amazing transformation come about? Prenatal development is divided into three stages: the **germinal** stage (the first two weeks, starting at conception), the stage of the **embryo** (from two weeks to two months), and the stage of the **fetus** (from two months to birth).

THE GERMINAL STAGE. The fertilized human egg (or zygote) is a single cell containing 46 chromosomes. Like other cells, it multiplies by dividing in two. When a cell splits in half, the chromosomes also split into two identical halves, so each of the two new cells has the same number of chromosomes, containing the same genes, as the first cell. Soon the two cells divide again, becoming four cells—all containing the same chromosomes. Then four become eight. Only 20 such divisions are needed to put the number of cells over a million.

Occasionally the developing cells split into two or more separate parts and form two or more babies—identical twins, triplets, or quadruplets. But most multiple births are fraternal twins, triplets, or quadruplets. With this type of multiple conception, two or more eggs are released from a woman's ovaries during a single menstrual cycle, and each egg is fertilized by a different sperm.

Rapid cell division continues during the two weeks of the germinal stage. In the first three or four days after a natural conception in the Fallopian tubes, the small clump of dividing cells—now called the **blastula**—travels down the tube and into the uterus (see Figure 4–1). The blastula is a hollow ball of cells filled with fluid. At first it floats freely in the uterus. Soon, however, its outermost layer of cells produces threadlike structures that work themselves into the soft lining of the wall of the uterus. This implantation process is not always accomplished successfully. When it's unsuccessful, the blastula is expelled during the woman's next menstrual period.

If all goes well, the blastula is firmly implanted in the uterine wall by the tenth or twelfth day after conception. Some of the cells from its outermost layer will develop into the umbilical cord, the placenta, and the **amnion** (the

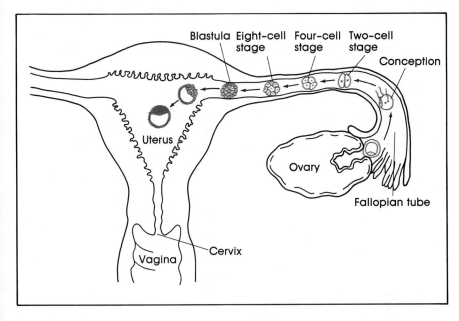

FIGURE 4-1
Conception normally takes place in a woman's Fallopian tube. The ovum leaves the ovary and is fertilized by a sperm. Then the fertilized egg (which has already started to divide) travels down the tube into the uterus, where it implants itself into the uterus wall.

protective sac, filled with fluid, that encloses the growing baby throughout prenatal development).

The inner mass of cells of the blastula is the part that's destined to become the baby. This mass of cells now undergoes **differentiation,** a process that begins when it separates into three distinct layers. The cells in these layers are then assigned to do specific jobs: cells from the outer layer form the baby's skin and nervous system, those from the inner layer form most of the internal organs of the body, and those from the middle layer form the remaining organs, the muscles, and the bones.

THE STAGE OF THE EMBRYO. Once this differentiation of cells has taken place, the developing organism is called an embryo. The stage of the embryo begins two weeks after conception. The embryo grows rapidly, with growth in the top half of its body going faster than in the lower half—a **cephalo-caudal** pattern of growth—and growth in the central part going faster than in the outer parts—a **proximodistal** pattern. In other words, the head and upper torso take shape before the lower torso; the arms develop before the legs. Likewise, the internal organs and torso develop before the arms and legs; the arms and legs develop before the fingers and toes.

The stage of the embryo ends two months after conception (see Table 4–1). At this point the embryo is only a little over one inch (2.5 cm) in length, but it already bears a rough resemblance to a human being. Its head is disproportionately large and is bent over. Its heart, also large in proportion to its body, has begun to beat. The embryo—from now until birth to be called the *fetus*—floats in a watery fluid (the **amniotic fluid**) within the baglike amnion.

THE STAGE OF THE FETUS. The rate of growth reaches a peak in the early part of the stage of the fetus. By the time the mother is through the first **trimester** (three-month period) of her pregnancy, all the essential parts of the fetus's body are present, though many are still quite primitive in form. Each part was

TABLE 4-1
The First Nine Months

	STAGES OF PRENATAL DEVELOPMENT	WHAT IS OCCURRING	STAGES OF PREGNANCY	
Conception →	Germinal Stage	Implantation in uterine wall Differentiation of cells	First Trimester	← Conception
Two Weeks →	Stage of the Embryo	Formation of heart and basic body structures		
Two Months →				← Three Months
	Stage of the Fetus	Most body parts and organs have now been formed	Second Trimester	
		Movement of fetus detectable by mother, heartbeat audible through stethoscope		
		Growth and further development of body parts and organs		← Six Months
		If delivered prematurely, survival is possible	Third Trimester	
		If delivered prematurely, survival is likely		
		Fetus is fully developed		
Birth →				← Birth

formed at a very specific stage of prenatal development: the fingers and toes, for example, were formed between the sixth and eighth week of pregnancy. That two-week interval is called the **critical period** for the formation of fingers and toes. If anything (such as a harmful drug) interferes with prenatal development during this critical period, the fingers and toes may not develop properly. The damage cannot be repaired later, because finger and toe formation occurs only during its appointed time (Smolak, 1986).

Most organs and body parts form during the first trimester. Thus, the critical periods for those parts occur during the first three months of pregnancy. That is the time that an unfavorable prenatal environment can have the most serious effects on the developing embryo and fetus. (We'll have more to say on this topic shortly.)

At the end of the first trimester of pregnancy, the fetus can move freely in its watery environment. It can clench its fists and move its arms and legs. Swallowing and urination are possible now; the fetus swallows amniotic fluid and urinates it out again. It is still very small, however: only 2½ to 3 inches (7 cm) in length and about half an ounce (15 g) in weight.

During the second trimester of pregnancy, the organs and body parts that

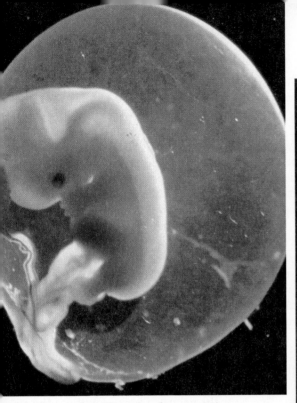

A human embryo 7 weeks after conception.

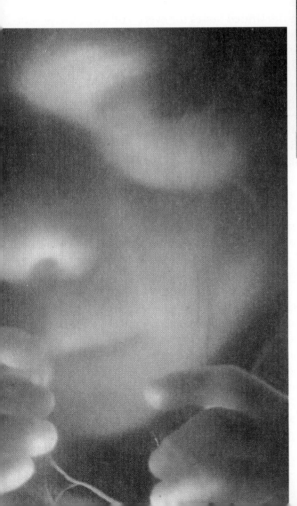

The fetus at 5¹/₂ months.

The fetus at 14 weeks.

were formed earlier become larger and more complete. The bones harden; the fetus's heartbeat becomes strong enough to be heard through a stethoscope. Fingernails, toenails, hair, eyelashes, and eyebrows appear. Most pregnant women become aware of the fetus's movements about four months after conception. At this time the first hint of individual differences also appears —some fetuses move around a great deal while others are relatively quiet. Later in the second trimester comes clear evidence that the fetus's sense of hearing has begun to function. A fetus can hear loud noises in its mother's environment and may react to them with startled movements.

At the end of the second trimester, the 6-month (26-week) fetus is about 13 inches long (33 cm) and weighs about 2 pounds (750 g). Thirty years ago, babies born at this stage of development had only a 10 percent chance of surviving; today, half of them survive. But the prospects for a baby born less than 23 or 24 weeks after conception have not improved, and most physicians feel that they will not do so in the foreseeable future. The lungs and the kidneys are simply not mature enough before 23 or 24 weeks to sustain life outside the uterus (Kolata, 1989).

Normally, the fetus waits until it is around 38 weeks old to make its first public appearance. During the last trimester in the uterus, the fetus gets larger and acquires a protective layer of fat; its brain grows rapidly and its lungs, kidneys, and other organs mature. Now the baby can survive without the aid of modern medical technology.

Boy or Girl?

About 106 boys are born in the United States for every 100 girls; the proportion of males is even higher at conception. Evidently, the sperm carrying the boy-producing Y chromosome have a slight edge over those carrying the girl-producing X (see Chapter 2). It almost looks as though nature permits more males than females to be conceived as a way of compensating for the greater fragility of the male, because all through life the human male is more fragile —physically less durable—than the female. From prenatal development through old age, the death rate for males is higher than that for females. This applies not only to deaths due to natural causes, but also to accidents, homicides, and suicides. As Table 4–2 shows, the numbers of males and females become equal around the age of 18. The ratio of men to women continues to dwindle over the years: by the age of 87, only half as many men as women are still alive (Strickland, 1988).

Embryos destined to be male and embryos destined to be female start out the same, inside and out. The sex differences aren't evident until two months after conception, when the embryo becomes a fetus. By that time the primitive internal glands that were present in the early embryo have begun to develop either into ovaries, the female sex glands, or into testes, the male glands. Ovaries will be formed if the embryo has two X chromosomes; testes will be formed if the embryo has an X and a Y. These glands soon start to produce **hormones**—biochemical substances that are present in the blood in very small amounts. It is the hormones that determine which kind of external sex organs will develop. Testes secrete the male hormones called **androgens;** these hormones cause a penis to form. Ovaries secrete the female hormones called **estrogens.** However, the fetus need not produce any hormones at all in order to develop female sex organs. In the absence of androgens a female

TABLE 4-2
Sex Ratios from Conception through Age 100

AGE	NUMBER OF MALES	NUMBER OF FEMALES
Conception	125	100
Birth	106	100
18 Years	100	100
55 Years	90	100
87 Years	50	100
100 Years	20	100

Sources: Strickland, 1988; "Ratio of Sexes," 1987.

body will be formed, probably due to the influence of estrogens secreted by the mother.

Hormones produced by the fetus or present in the mother's body are also believed to have subtle effects on the development of the brain. These effects are evidently responsible for some of the differences in behavior between girls and boys. On rare occasion, something goes wrong with this process: the fetus's body may be unable to utilize its own hormones in the normal way, the mother's immune system may destroy them, or the mother may have received an injection of an artificial hormone in the course of a medical treatment. The result can be masculinization of a female fetus or feminization of a male, both physically (the genitals may be ambiguous in appearance), and, later, in the way the child behaves (Bjorklund and Bjorklund, 1988).

Development of the Nervous System

The job of controlling and coordinating all the various parts of the body belongs to the **nervous system.** The nervous system includes the brain, which specializes in processing and storing information, and the nerves and the spinal cord, which specialize in transmitting information. The brain and the spinal cord together make up the **central nervous system.**

Nerves are of two types, **sensory** and **motor.** Sensory nerves carry messages *to* the central nervous system from the sense organs, the skin, the muscles and joints, and the internal organs. Motor nerves carry messages *from* the central nervous system to the muscles, directing them to move this way or that. Everything you have ever seen, heard, tasted, smelled, or felt has arrived at your brain by way of sensory nerves. Every movement or action you have ever performed has been controlled by messages sent out through the motor nerves.

Like the other parts of the body, the nervous system is composed of cells. The basic unit of the nervous system is a long, skinny cell called a **neuron.** Nerves are made up of bundles of parallel neurons. A nerve's message is carried by a tiny electrical pulse that moves rapidly down the length of a neuron until it reaches the end. At that point the message might be relayed to one or more other neurons through a junction called a **synapse.** A message from the eye or the toe is carried by a number of neurons and passes through a number of synapses before it reaches its destination in the brain.

GROWTH OF THE BRAIN. The nervous system develops from cells on the outer layer of the early embryo. Within a month after conception these cells have formed a hollow tube. The tube becomes the spinal cord; its front end enlarges to become the brain. The brain develops extremely rapidly. Nine months after conception it contains an estimated 100 billion neurons—as many as there are stars in our galaxy! The rate of brain cell formation during prenatal development averages out to a fantastic 250,000 cells a minute (Cowan, 1979). But that average is misleading, because developing cells don't increase in number at an even rate. They increase by dividing in two, doubling in number each time. The increase in the number of cells is slow at the beginning (when 1 becomes 2, 2 becomes 4) and very fast at the end (when 1 billion becomes 2 billion). To get from 1 cell to 100 billion, it takes only 35 doublings, or one doubling every seven or eight days throughout the pregnancy.

Figure 4–2 shows how the brain changes in size and appearance during prenatal development. The brain of a five-month fetus is smooth, like that of a cat or a rat. Not until seven months after conception does the human brain begin to develop its characteristic wrinkles. These wrinkles are formed because the outer layer of the brain, the **cortex,** grows faster than the inner portions. The cortex is the seat of all those special abilities that are unique to the human species—the ability to communicate in spoken and written language, to think up plans and theories, to contemplate the future and the past, and even to make jokes and laugh at them. This important part of the brain grows most rapidly during the last three months of prenatal development.

MAKING CONNECTIONS. The nervous system is not just a tangle of neurons. If it is to function properly, the cells must be hooked up correctly—they have to form synapses with certain other cells. For example, visual information from the eye has to cross several synapses before it gets to the part of the brain where "seeing" actually occurs. These synapses have to make connections between exactly the right cells, so that a signal from a particular neuron in the eye ends up in exactly the right spot in the brain.

For another example, consider the **reflex.** A reflex is a simple, automatic response to a stimulus. Your leg swings forward when the doctor taps it under the knee (the knee-jerk reflex); the pupil of your eye contracts when a light shines into it (the pupillary reflex). Not many synapses are involved in a reflex—in some cases only a single neuron intervenes between the sensory neuron that carries the signal to the brain or spinal cord and the motor neuron that carries the command back to the muscle. But the synapses and the neurons have to be the right ones. If the connections were wrong, the reflex wouldn't work the way it was supposed to—when you're tapped under your knee, your arm would swing up, or when a light shines into your eye, you would sneeze!

As we will explain in the next chapter, babies are born with reflexes and visual systems that generally work exactly the way they're supposed to. The neurons in question have somehow managed to find the right cells to form connections with, out of all the billions of cells in the nervous system. Neurologists are only beginning to discover how this impressive feat is accomplished.

There is reason to believe, however, that many of the initial connections made during prenatal development are either incorrect or turn out to be useless. An important aspect of nervous system development in the first few months after birth is the pruning out of unneeded cells or unwanted syn-

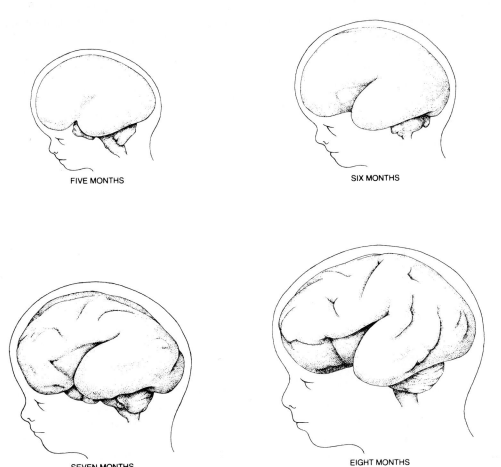

FIVE MONTHS

SIX MONTHS

SEVEN MONTHS

EIGHT MONTHS

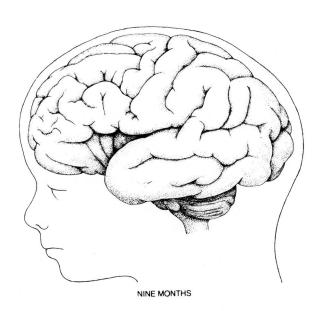

NINE MONTHS

FIGURE 4-2
The development of the human brain, from 5 months to 9 months after conception. (Adapted from "The Development of the Brain," by Maxwell Cowen. Copyright © September 1979 by Scientific American, Inc. All rights reserved.)

apses. The ones that don't work properly or that serve no useful purpose are dismantled; the useful ones are strengthened. It is the baby's experiences and actions in the early months of infancy that will determine which cells or synapses are kept and which are discarded. In this way, the baby's environment can have a lasting effect on the actual structure of her nervous system (Greenough, Black, and Wallace, 1987).

Factors That Influence Prenatal Development

The developing human life floats in its watery surroundings, cushioned within the walls of the uterus. Nature has provided it with excellent protection against many possible sources of harm. Even if its mother suffers a serious accident—a fall down the stairs, for instance—the pregnancy is likely to continue in the usual way. Yet, in another sense, the embryo and fetus are extremely vulnerable, because their health and normal growth depend entirely on their mother.

Crossing the Placenta

During prenatal development, oxygen and nutrients from the mother's bloodstream are transmitted to the fetus. At the same time, carbon dioxide and other waste products from the fetus are deposited into the mother's bloodstream for disposal by her body. This exchange takes place in the placenta, to which the fetus is attached by way of the umbilical cord. Though it is destined to be discarded as soon as the pregnancy ends, the placenta is a complex organ: it contains the blood vessels of the mother and those of her unborn child, woven intricately together. The connection is not direct, however—the two blood supplies never actually mingle. But the mother's blood vessels lie close enough to the fetus's to permit molecules to pass from one to the other. Substances transmitted in this way are said to **cross the placenta.** Virtually any substance that is dissolved in the mother's blood can cross the placenta.

THE RH FACTOR. Among the substances found in the mother's bloodstream are proteins called **antibodies.** Antibodies are formed by the body's immune system as a way of fighting infection; thus, they are usually beneficial. The antibodies in the mother's blood can cross over to the fetus's, and this means that babies are born with at least partial immunity to many diseases.

In one case, however, a mother's antibodies can be harmful to her unborn child. If the mother's blood type is Rh negative and she has developed a sensitivity to Rh positive blood—blood that contains a substance called the **Rh factor**—her immune system will form antibodies to Rh positive blood cells. These antibodies can cross the placenta and attack the blood cells of an Rh positive fetus. In severe cases the baby may be brain-damaged or may die soon after birth.

Only about one out of seven women is Rh negative, so the Rh factor is not a danger in the majority of pregnancies. Furthermore, first pregnancies are seldom affected, because the mother will not form antibodies to Rh positive blood unless she has previously been exposed to it. Such exposure normally happens only during a delivery, miscarriage, abortion, or amniocentesis involving an Rh positive child. Thus, the first pregnancy of an Rh negative woman is unlikely to present any problems. It is the later pregnancies of these women that are at risk.

Fortunately, there is now a way of protecting the subsequent pregnancies of an Rh negative woman. A special serum can be given to her by injection during and immediately after each pregnancy involving an Rh positive baby. This injection will prevent her body from forming antibodies to Rh positive blood and thus provides protection for her next baby.

Once a woman's body has started to produce antibodies to Rh positive blood, there is as yet no way to stop this process. Her later pregnancies will have to be monitored very closely, and her babies will probably be given a blood transfusion immediately after birth or perhaps even before birth.

INFECTIOUS DISEASES. An infection in a pregnant woman poses a serious threat to her unborn child, because many kinds of disease-producing micro-organisms can cross the placenta and infect the fetus. It has been known for many years that the sexually transmitted disease syphilis can be passed from a woman to her unborn child; the most common result is death of the child, either before birth or soon afterward. If the child survives, the syphilis micro-organism can attack any organ in his body, especially the nervous system. Antibiotics that are effective against syphilis have been available since the 1940s; for a time, it looked as though the disease might be wiped out entirely. But recently the number of cases has begun to increase again (Wendel, 1988). A blood test for syphilis is an essential part of prenatal care; if the mother is found to be infected, antibiotic treatment will protect both her and her fetus.

Another infectious organism that is particularly harmful to the developing embryo is the **rubella** virus. Rubella, commonly known as German measles, is an illness that produces no more than a short-lived rash and a fever in a child or an adult. A woman who has a mild case of the disease may not even realize she is sick. But if she is in the early stages of pregnancy, the virus will attack the embryo, almost always causing serious birth defects such as blindness, deafness, heart abnormalities, and mental retardation. There is a vaccine to prevent rubella, but many women have not been inoculated and the inoculation is occasionally ineffective: an estimated 15 to 20 percent of women of childbearing age remain susceptible to the disease (Freij, South, and Sever, 1988). A blood test can determine whether a woman is protected against rubella. If she is not, she should be inoculated before she becomes pregnant.

Toxoplasmosis is a condition caused by a parasite sometimes present in raw meat and, more frequently, in cat droppings. A woman who has previously been exposed to this parasite has probably become immune to it; her previous infection poses no danger to a fetus. But an estimated 50 to 60 percent of women of childbearing age have *not* acquired an immunity to the toxoplasmosis parasite. A susceptible woman who is infected during pregnancy will experience, at most, only minor symptoms, but the parasite can cross the placenta and cause serious damage to the eyes or brain of her fetus (Lee, 1988). Although there is, as yet, no inoculation against toxoplasmosis, there is a test that can determine whether a woman is susceptible. If she has not already developed an immunity to the parasite, a pregnant woman should guard against infection by avoiding close contact with cats and cat litter, and by making sure the meat she eats is thoroughly cooked.

The **herpes** viruses are so widespread in the world's population that almost everyone becomes infected with one or more of them, sooner or later. This family of viruses includes *herpes simplex,* one variety of which causes genital herpes, and the *cytomegalovirus,* an even more prevalent virus that produces few or no symptoms in children and adults. Cytomegalovirus can harm a fetus if a woman is infected for the first time during pregnancy; however, this is an unlikely possibility. Genital herpes is more likely to be a problem, since a woman can pass on the virus not only at the time she is first infected with the disease but also each time she experiences a new outbreak. The risk, in this case, is that the baby could be exposed to the virus while being born, during the passage through the vagina. There is currently no cure for herpes infections. If a woman has an active case of genital herpes when she goes into labor, her obstetrician will probably perform a cesarean section to avoid the danger of a herpes infection in the baby (Freij and Sever, 1988).

The disease that worries people most today, and for good reason, is **AIDS** (acquired immune deficiency syndrome). A woman can become infected with the AIDS virus through intravenous drug use, or by having sex with someone who has the disease, or from a contaminated blood transfusion (this last possibility has become unlikely, due to careful screening of donated blood). Once the virus has invaded her body, symptoms of the disease usually appear within five years. It's still not certain whether everyone who gets the disease will eventually die of it, but the odds are not in their favor.

The odds are a little bit better for the unborn child of a pregnant woman who is infected with the virus. Although it is still too early to be sure, it appears that only about half of the babies of AIDS-infected mothers will be born with the virus (Feinkind and Minkoff, 1988). But these babies are probably doomed to a slow and painful death. Any woman who is at risk for AIDS should be tested for the virus early in her pregnancy or, preferably, before she becomes pregnant.

OTHER HEALTH PROBLEMS IN PREGNANCY. Not all diseases that threaten the fetus are caused by microorganisms. **Pre-eclampsia,** formerly known as *toxemia of pregnancy,* is a relatively common disorder that affects only pregnant women, most often in the last trimester of a first pregnancy. Its cause is unknown. The symptoms of pre-eclampsia include high blood pressure, swelling and weight gain due to an excess of water in the tissues, and protein in the urine (a sign that the kidneys aren't working properly). The pregnancy of a woman with pre-eclampsia must be carefully monitored by a physician. If untreated, the condition can progress to full-fledged eclampsia, which causes convulsions and can lead to the death of the mother, as well as of the fetus. The risk is greater if the mother's blood pressure was already high before she became pregnant.

Careful medical supervision is also essential for pregnant women with diabetes, asthma, heart or kidney disease, sickle-cell anemia, lupus, cystic fibrosis, or inflammatory bowel disease. All these conditions increase the risks associated with pregnancy, but with proper diagnosis and treatment, a successful outcome is likely (Carlson, 1988).

Anything in the body or the environment of a pregnant woman that is capable of causing abnormalities in the embryo or fetus is called a **teratogen.** The microorganisms we discussed in the preceding section are teratogens because the infections they cause can cross the placenta. Radiation (for example, from exposure to radioactive substances) is a teratogen that may reach the fetus directly through the wall of the uterus, without passing through the placenta. No woman voluntarily exposes herself to disease germs or radioactive fallout, but there are many other teratogens that she should also make an effort to avoid (see Box 4–1).

PRESCRIPTION AND OVER-THE-COUNTER DRUGS. Thalidomide is not the only drug that can have devastating effects on a fetus. There are many others that are capable of crossing the placenta, sometimes with damaging effects. Table 4–3 lists the kinds of prescription drugs that are known to have teratogenic effects on a fetus. No over-the-counter drugs have been *proved* to be ter-

Teratogens

TABLE 4-3
Prescription Drugs Known to Cause Birth Defects

THE DRUGS AND HOW THEY ARE USED	BIRTH DEFECTS CAUSED BY THESE DRUGS
Accutane or other vitamin A derivatives, used to treat severe acne	Abnormalities of the brain, skull, eyes, ears, or heart; cleft palate; mental retardation
Anticancer drugs (e.g., 6-mercaptopurine, chlorambucil)	Death of the fetus; multiple and serious defects
Drugs used in the treatment of epilepsy (e.g., Dilantin, Valproic acid)	Mental retardation; cleft lip; spina bifida; various other defects
Drugs used to prevent blood clots (e.g., dicoumaral, warfarin)	Underdeveloped bone and cartilage, especially in the nose; bleeding; mental retardation; blindness
Drugs used to treat malaria and to regulate heart rhythm (e.g., quinine, chloroquine)	Death of the fetus; blood disorders; deafness or blindness
Drugs used to treat overactive thyroid gland (e.g., radioactive iodine)	Destruction or enlargement of the fetus's thyroid gland
Hormones used to prevent miscarriage or for birth control	Abnormalities of the fetus's genital organs
Iodides used in some cough medicines and asthma drugs	Enlargement of the fetus's thyroid gland
Local anesthetics used by dentists and surgeons	Slowing of the fetus's heart; in extreme cases, death of the fetus
Tetracycline and related antibiotics, used to treat infections	Staining of the teeth; abnormal development of tooth enamel
Thalidomide, a drug used to prevent nausea and vomiting	Absent or deformed limbs; other serious deformities

Source: Copyright © 1987 by Aubrey Milunsky, M.D. Adapted by permission of Simon and Schuster, Inc.

Problems in Development

Box 4-1
Birth Defects

If the first question parents ask about their new baby is "Boy or girl?" don't be misled: that's not ordinarily their biggest concern. Perhaps they ask that question first just so they'll know what pronoun to use for the crucial second question: "Is she all right?" or "Is he all right?" No matter how deeply parents may desire a baby of a particular sex, their first wish is to have a normal, healthy child. In the great majority of cases, this wish comes true.

But sometimes, unfortunately, it doesn't. Birth defects range in severity from merely annoying to quickly fatal. The minor ones include the dark-red birthmarks that mar the faces of some newborns but gradually fade away as they grow older. The most serious ones include anencephaly, the absence of most of the brain. Many birth defects are correctable by surgery: for instance, pyloric stenosis, an overdeveloped muscle at the top of the intestine that prevents the passage of food; and cleft lip or cleft palate, where the two sides of the upper lip or the roof of the mouth have failed to join together during early prenatal development.

Some birth defects, such as deafness and muscular dystrophy, may not be detected until months or years later. With others, such as Down syndrome (see Chapter 2) and spina bifida (a serious malformation of the spine), the parents know almost at once that their child will probably never be able to lead a normal life. Some of these babies die in the first days or weeks after birth. The spina bifida survivors are often left partially paralyzed, unable to use their legs or to gain control of bowel and bladder.

In Chapter 2 we described abnormalities that are due to defective genes or chromosomal accidents, and we mentioned two methods of testing during pregnancy, amniocentesis and chorionic villus sampling. With the use of these tests, over

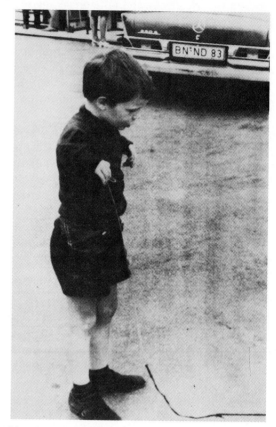

This German child was born with deformed arms because his mother took thalidomide in early pregnancy. At the time she took the drug (prescribed to her by her doctor), no one realized that thalidomide caused terrible birth defects.

100 genetic disorders can now be identified prenatally, including Down syndrome, Tay-Sachs disease, cystic fibrosis, sickle-cell anemia, and some

atogenic, but some, including antihistamines, aspirin, and acetominophen, are suspected of causing birth defects if used in excess. A pregnant woman should therefore avoid taking any drug unless absolutely necessary, and then only under the supervision of a physician who is aware of her pregnancy.

Sometimes drugs have teratogenic effects that don't show up until months or years later. The synthetic hormone called DES (for diethylstilbestrol) was used in the 1950s and '60s to prevent miscarriages in pregnant women. Its use was discontinued when researchers found abnormalities of the reproductive systems in the teenage or adult daughters of women who had been given

types of muscular dystrophy. Another test that is routinely used by most obstetricians today is called the **alpha-fetoprotein (AFP)** test. This requires only a sample of the mother's blood, taken around the 16th week of pregnancy. A high AFP level means there is a possibility that the fetus has anencephaly or spina bifida; further tests (such as ultrasound scans) are then used to check on this possibility.

If the tests do show that the fetus has a serious defect such as Tay–Sachs disease or anencephaly, most parents elect to terminate the pregnancy by abortion and to begin a new pregnancy as soon as possible. In the case of milder types of birth defects there are other alternatives. It is now possible to give blood transfusions and to perform certain kinds of surgery on the unborn fetus. Hydrocephalus (an accumulation of fluid in the brain) has been successfully treated by inserting a tube in the fetus's skull while it is still in the uterus. The tube drained off some of the excess fluid, thereby preventing brain damage (Birnholz and Farrell, 1984). Another fetus has been treated for an irregular heartbeat by means of injections of a heart medication into the umbilical cord (Kolata, 1988a). It is even possible to perform complex surgical procedures on a fetus, such as correcting a blocked urinary tract. The interesting thing about surgery performed on fetuses is that they heal without scars. Thus, it might soon be possible to correct a cleft lip or palate before birth in such a way that the surgery is undetectable later on (Kolata, 1988b).

Birth defects can be divided into three classes: (1) those due solely to genetic or chromosomal factors (Tay-Sachs and Down syndrome are in this category), (2) those due to a combination of inherited and environmental factors, and (3) those due primarily to environmental factors. Defects in the second category include cleft lip and spina bifida. With this type of defect, the embryo does not inherit the abnormality itself, but only an increased risk of developing it: its appearance

depends both on inheriting unfavorable genes and also on the presence of unknown environmental factors in the uterus. Since the abnormality doesn't depend solely on heredity, even identical twins may be affected differently. When one identical twin is born with a cleft lip, the other twin is normal 60 percent of the time (Nyhan, 1976).

In the third category of birth defects are those due primarily to environmental factors. Sometimes what seems to be a random stroke of fate can be traced to a specific causal factor. That was what happened in the case of the thalidomide disaster in the early 1960s. Occasionally, for no obvious reason, a baby is born missing an arm, or both arms, or both legs. Usually this defect is extremely rare, so when a German geneticist saw a sudden increase in the number of babies born with missing limbs, he began to investigate. A prescription drug named thalidomide was eventually found to be the culprit. Fortunately, thalidomide was never approved for release in the United States, but in Canada, Europe, and England an estimated 8000 babies were born with missing or deformed arms or legs. Their mothers had taken thalidomide during the first trimester of pregnancy to quell nausea and vomiting.

Because most body parts are formed during the first trimester of pregnancy, environmental influences are likely to have their greatest impact at this time. Harmful environmental influences during early pregnancy are responsible for nearly all nongenetic birth defects, including structural deformities such as missing limbs and sensory defects such as some forms of deafness and blindness.

The thalidomide case illustrates an important point: prenatal development does not take place in a totally isolated, protected environment. What the pregnant woman eats or doesn't eat; what she smokes, drinks, or injects into her body; the viruses and bacteria to which she is exposed—all are potentially capable of harming the tiny embryo inside her, an embryo that she may not yet even know she is carrying.

this drug during their pregnancies. These young women, who had been exposed to DES before they were born, run a much greater than normal risk of developing cancers of the reproductive organs. The DES daughters are also more likely than other women to experience complications during their own pregnancies (Linn and others, 1988).

Drinks containing caffeine, a mild stimulant, are popular all over the world. There is no evidence that the moderate use of caffeine—a daily intake of two to four cups of coffee or tea—does any harm to the human fetus (Leviton, 1988). However, caffeine does cross the placenta and it has been found to cause birth defects in laboratory animals, so it is sensible to avoid drinking large amounts of coffee or tea during pregnancy.

ALCOHOL. The babies of alcoholic mothers are at risk of being born with **fetal alcohol syndrome.** Such babies generally have a wide variety of problems, including characteristic abnormalities of the face and hands, heart defects, mental retardation, and growth deficiencies. The more the mother drinks during pregnancy, the more likely these defects are to occur and the more severe they are likely to be. Even moderate drinking (two to four glasses a day of wine, beer, or distilled spirits) increases the risk, especially during the first trimester of pregnancy.

The effects of prenatal exposure to alcohol do not appear to be outgrown: they are still detectable in the 4-year-old children of mothers who had more than two or three drinks a day during pregnancy. Many of the children have abnormally formed facial features, ears, hands, or fingernails; they tend to have small heads and to be undersized both in height and in weight. There are behavioral and intellectual problems, too. These children have difficulty in keeping their attention focused on a task, and they have significantly lower IQs than the children of nondrinkers (Graham and others, 1988; Streissguth and others, 1989).

Alcohol harms prenatal development in three ways. First, it crosses the placenta and has a direct effect on the fetus itself, damaging cells or inhibiting their growth. Second, it also damages the cells of the placenta, thus interfering with the fetus's supply of oxygen and nutrients. And third, it leads to poorer nutrition in the mother, partly because alcohol furnishes her with ''empty calories'' that diminish her hunger without supplying her with neces-

This baby was born with fetal alcohol syndrome. The thin upper lip and the wide, flat bridge of the nose are typical of the facial abnormalities found in the babies of alcoholic mothers.

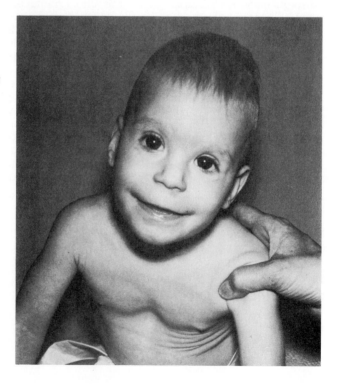

sary vitamins, minerals, and protein; and partly because it actually lowers the body's supply of certain minerals by causing them to be excreted in the urine. As one researcher sums it up, "The bottom line is that chronic [alcohol] intake may cause poor maternal nutrition, thereby robbing the developing fetus of a balanced and adequate supply of essential nutrients" (Fisher, 1988, p. 101).

CIGARETTE SMOKING. "WARNING," it says right there on the pack. "Smoking By Pregnant Women May Result in Fetal Injury, Premature Birth, and Low Birth Weight." Cigarette smoke contains nicotine, a potent drug; carbon monoxide, a poisonous gas; plus smaller amounts of over 2000 other chemicals, including cyanide (Maurer and Maurer, 1988). The dangers of cigarette smoking during pregnancy have been summarized by a physician who is experienced in this field:

> About one-third (32 percent) of pregnant women in this country are cigarette smokers at the start of pregnancy. We know that pregnant women who smoke are more likely than nonsmokers to deliver babies who are born prematurely, are small or underweight, have respiratory and cardiovascular problems or die within the first year of life. Perinatal mortality—death in the eight weeks before or seven days after birth—among babies of heavy smokers is about 35 percent greater than among the babies of nonsmokers. It is estimated that maternal smoking causes 5,000 extra perinatal deaths each year in the United States. . . .
> Smoking during pregnancy may also adversely affect the child's physi-

Just say no. Smoking can harm the developing fetus.

cal growth, intellectual development, and behavior characteristics. Some studies have shown that babies of smokers score lower on math and verbal tests than babies of nonsmokers.   (Edelman, 1988, p. A30)

A woman who smokes gives birth to a baby who weighs almost half a pound (200 g) less, on the average, than the baby of a nonsmoker (Finnegan and Fehr, 1980). The smoker's baby is small not because it is born too early (although premature delivery is also common), but because it hasn't grown as much as it should have in the uterus. Smoking during pregnancy has also been linked to a higher risk of various abnormalities such as cleft lip, cleft palate, and reduced head size.

Smoking rates are declining in this country, especially among people with a college education. Unfortunately, the one population group in which smoking has not decreased is young women. More than 20 percent of female high school seniors smoke, as opposed to 16 percent of males. Among college students, 18 percent of females smoke, versus 10 percent of males (Sullivan, 1987). If these young women continue to smoke during pregnancy, the toll of their addiction will be reckoned against their children's health, as well as their own.

MARIJUANA. After smoking one joint of pot, the marijuana user has five times as much carbon monoxide in her bloodstream as a tobacco user has after smoking one cigarette (Oliwenstein, 1988). The drug crosses the placenta; the babies of regular marijuana users tend to show some of the same symptoms (though in milder form) that are found in the babies of narcotics users—for example, a tendency to startle easily, shakiness, and abnormalities in the way they respond to visual stimuli (Fried, Watkinson, Dillon, and Dulberg, 1987). Long-term effects of marijuana are as yet unknown. Like any other unnecessary drug, pot should be avoided during pregnancy.

NARCOTICS. Narcotic drugs such as heroin, methadone, morphine, and codeine (a prescription painkiller that can be addictive) cause serious harm to the unborn children of users. There is a greatly increased risk of fetal death, prematurity, and retarded growth. The babies of addicted mothers are likely to be born with a physical addiction themselves and will show withdrawal symptoms after they are born. There is also evidence for long-term effects such as hyperactivity (Householder, Hatcher, Burns, and Chasnoff, 1982). A recent study of the babies of users of methadone (a drug prescribed as a legal substitute for heroin) found these babies to have a higher death rate than babies born to nonusers of similar socioeconomic status. At the age of 12 months the methadone babies had smaller heads than their agemates (which suggests that their brains might not be developing at a normal rate) and a significantly higher rate of physical and behavioral problems (Rosen and Johnson, 1988).

COCAINE. The use of cocaine, especially in the form known as "crack," has increased rapidly over the last decade. The effects of maternal cocaine use on prenatal development are just starting to be known. It appears that cocaine is more dangerous to the fetus than alcohol, cigarettes, marijuana, and perhaps even heroin. A single cocaine "hit" will be cleared from a woman's body within 48 hours, but it will continue to affect her fetus for four or five days, contaminating the amniotic fluid so that every time the fetus swallows some fluid it gets another dose of the drug. One use of cocaine by the mother might be enough to cause a stroke in the fetus, leading to brain damage or death. Smoking crack causes the uterus to contract, which may result in the premature delivery of a baby born too early to survive (Brody, 1988; Revkin, 1989).

The babies of cocaine users share many of the risks of the babies of the other drugs we have discussed, such as higher death rates before and soon after birth, growth retardation, and abnormally small heads and brains. However, the frequency and severity of these effects appear to be higher with cocaine than with the other drugs. In addition, there is a significantly increased risk of serious birth defects, including malformations of the heart and the head (one cocaine baby was born with his brain outside his skull) and deformities of the genital and urinary organs.

A recent survey done at 36 hospitals around the country found that 11 percent of the mothers of newborn babies had used illegal drugs during pregnancy. Cocaine was the most widely used of all (Bingol and others, 1987; Brody, 1988).

ENVIRONMENTAL POLLUTANTS. Not all dangers to the fetus are as easy to avoid as cigarettes, alcohol, and cocaine. Some hazards, such as exposure to toxic wastes, may be an invisible part of our environment. Toxic wastes often include chemicals called PCBs (polychlorinated biphenyls). Exposure to trace amounts of PCBs has been linked to a number of relatively mild problems in babies, notably a tendency to be sluggish and unresponsive and to have weak reflexes (Jacobson and others, 1984). Eating fish can be a source of exposure to PCBs, because lakes, rivers, and coastal waters are often contaminated by industrial wastes. Eskimo women in northern Canada, whose diet includes large quantities of fish, were recently found to have dangerously high levels of PCB exposure ("High PCB Levels," 1989).

Lead poisoning is usually thought of as a problem in children, not fetuses; we associate it with children who live in tenements where old, lead-based paint is peeling off the walls. But the toxic effects of exposure to lead are not limited to any age group or socioeconomic class. Lead contamination can come from the air (air pollution in cities or near busy highways) or from the water (water pipes may contain lead solder) or from food or beverages stored in certain kinds of pottery containers. Exposure to lead either before birth or afterward lowers IQ and increases the risk of learning disabilities.

Other Influences on Prenatal Development

A number of other factors have been shown to affect the outcome of a pregnancy. One of these factors is maternal age: women between 18 and 35 years of age have the fewest problems of pregnancy and childbirth and bear the healthiest babies. Pregnancy and childbirth are particularly risky for the babies of teenage girls and for these girls themselves; this is especially true when they fail to receive adequate prenatal care, as is so often the case.

On the other hand, pregnancy later in life, even after the age of 40, appears to involve fewer risks than is generally believed. It is true that the risk of conceiving a child with Down syndrome is higher, but that can be ruled out with amniocentesis. An older woman is likely to have more difficulty becoming pregnant, and there is also a greater chance that she will have developed some sort of chronic health problem, such as high blood pressure, diabetes, obesity, or an addiction to alcohol or tobacco. But if she is able to conceive and if none of these health problems is present, the pregnancy of a woman over 40 is no more likely to lead to complications than that of a younger woman (Kopp and Kaler, 1989).

NUTRITION. One reason why pregnancy and childbirth are hazardous for the teenage girl is that she may have not have completed her own growth. Physically, she is in no position to provide for the growth demands of an unborn child. Even if she is fully mature physically, she may not have enough stored reserves to meet the demands of pregnancy. Because the embryo and fetus grow so rapidly—building a body "from scratch"—the mother's body has to be able to meet the fetus's nutritional needs as well as her own.

It used to be thought that the fetus would take what it needed from the mother's body, if what she ate did not provide enough for the fetus's requirements. For example, it was believed that the mother's teeth and bones might be robbed of their calcium in order to build the fetus's bones. This theory is misleading, however, because it implies that only the mother will suffer from the deficiency, and not the child. The truth is that if the mother's diet is deficient in something the fetus requires, both the mother *and* the fetus are likely to be affected—in other words, the teeth and bones of a woman with a calcium-deficient diet *will* lose some of their calcium, but there will probably still not be enough for the baby's bones. This principle applies not only to specific nutrients, but to overall caloric intake as well. A woman who gets too little to eat during pregnancy—whose caloric intake is insufficient to meet the needs of her expanding body—will not only lose fat from her own body: she will also have a smaller, thinner baby than a well-fed woman.

A weight gain of 25 to 30 pounds (11.3 to 13.6 kg) during pregnancy is ideal. About 7½ pounds (3.4 kg) of this weight is the baby. The placenta, amniotic fluid, and growth in size of the uterus will contribute a little over 5 pounds (2.3 kg) of the extra weight. Most of the remainder of the weight gain comes from enlargement of the breasts, an increased blood supply, and an increased amount of water in the tissues. Only about 7 pounds (3.2 kg) is extra fat, laid down by nature to assure that the mother has something in reserve for nourishing her baby (Eisenberg, Murkoff, and Hathaway, 1988).

The diet of the pregnant woman should be high in nutritious foods such as dairy products, fish and poultry, fruits and vegetables, complex carbohydrates (potatoes, pasta, and beans), and whole grains. It should be low in simple carbohydrates such as sugar and refined starches (white bread, white rice). Simple carbohydrates supply calories and thus satisfy the appetite, but they are deficient in the vitamins, minerals, and protein that are necessary for the health of the woman and her unborn child.

EMOTIONAL STRESS. When we experience a strong emotion, our bodies react in a number of ways—increased heartbeat and breathing, a dry mouth and wet underarms. These kinds of reactions are accompanied by the secretion of hormones such as adrenalin. Because hormones can cross the placenta, it is reasonable to assume that the emotional state of a pregnant woman may influence the development of her child. Research with subhuman animals supports this view. Severe stress in pregnant sheep or rodents lowers the chances of a normal birth and healthy offspring. There may also be an effect on the later behavior of the young animals, such as increased fearfulness (Thompson and Grusec, 1970).

The situation is far less clear when it comes to humans. In fact, there is reason to believe that the human fetus may be better protected against maternal stress than are the fetuses of lower animals. Over the past 35 years there has been much research on the question of whether a pregnant woman's anxiety, or stressful events in her life, leads to an increase in problems of pregnancy and childbirth. A recent review of this research led to an unexpected conclusion: there is no solid evidence that stress alone increases the risks to the mother or the baby (Istvan, 1986). Earlier results that appeared to show an effect of stress on the outcome of pregnancy may actually have been due to the effects of stress on the mother's *behavior*. For example, if she reacts to stressful situations by smoking more cigarettes or drinking more alcohol, or by not eating well or not getting regular checkups, she and her baby are likely to experience more problems of pregnancy and childbirth.

THE ROLE OF THE FATHER. One of the most helpful things a woman can have during her pregnancy is the emotional support of the baby's father. The man's concern for her health and for that of their child is an important factor in how well the expectant mother takes care of herself and in the kind of medical supervision she receives. He can make life easier and safer for her during pregnancy, go to childbirth classes with her and participate in the delivery, and share in the caregiving after the baby is born. Some men become so emotionally involved in the pregnancy that they even experience some of the same symptoms, such as nausea or backache.

Less commonly, a man may withdraw from his partner or even become hostile to her. If the relationship was not going well to begin with, a pregnancy is not likely to improve it. A man who has a history of battering his partner will not necessarily stop when she gets pregnant; in fact, battering sometimes begins or gets worse during pregnancy (Helton and Snodgrass, 1987). In a study of women given emergency-room treatment in a city hospital, 21 percent were there because they had been battered by men. If they were pregnant at the time of the abuse, they were twice as likely to have a miscarriage as pregnant women who hadn't been assaulted (Stark and others, 1981). For a woman who is unhappily married or not married at all, complications of pregnancy and childbirth are less likely to occur if she has a network of family and friends who will be there when she needs them (Hopkins, Marcus, and Campbell, 1984).

Birth

At the beginning of this chapter we described the birth of an infant named Michael. Now that the presence of the father in the delivery room is considered to be the norm, the events we described are those that occur most typically or frequently. Most babies in this country are delivered in a hospital by a physician (Havemann and Lehtinen, 1986). The great majority are born head first and are full-term, healthy infants.

The birth process most often begins between 38 and 42 weeks from the date of the last menstrual period. Sometimes it begins when the amniotic sac ruptures, and a flow of amniotic fluid precedes the onset of labor. More often, it begins with contractions of the uterus that gradually increase in intensity, frequency, and painfulness.

The term "labor pains" has gone out of favor. According to the view of childbirth popularized by the British obstetrician Grantly Dick-Read, labor is painful only because women have been taught to fear it. In his book, *Childbirth without Fear* (1944), he proposed his theory of "natural childbirth." Dick-Read believed that if you educate women so that they know what to expect and how to cope with it, they won't be afraid and therefore they won't feel pain.

Dick-Read based his theory on two experiences he had, early in his practice of medicine. The first occurred when he was an intern in a London hospital, assisting a woman in labor. He offered her an anesthetic and she refused it, explaining afterward that the birth hadn't hurt: "It wasn't meant to, was it?" The second experience came when he was an army surgeon during World War I and he came across a Flemish woman giving birth in a field. She refused his offer of aid and calmly delivered her baby herself (Edwards and Waldorf, 1984, p. 15).

But these women may not be typical. There is a certain amount of variability in the human nervous system: no two people—not even identical twins —are wired up in exactly the same way. A modern British physician believes that childbirth is totally painless for around 3 or 4 percent of women. All the rest experience at least some pain. He doesn't believe the pain is an effect of cultural expectations:

> Observation of people still living in primitive societies around the world appears to show that there is no culture in which childbirth is painless, and in many cultures women have a much worse time than in our own. (Macfarlane, 1977)

The reason labor is painful is that evolution has enlarged the human brain to the point where the baby's head just barely makes it through the opening in the woman's pelvis (the girdle of bones inside the hips). According to an anthropologist who has studied the evolution of the pelvis and the skull, "The human birth process is one of the most difficult in the animal kingdom" (Lovejoy, 1988, p. 123). For the human baby to pass through the birth canal, his head has to go through the first part sideways and through the last part nose down (see Figure 4–3).

Women nowadays tend to feel that they've somehow failed if they experience pain during childbirth. It's neither helpful nor accurate for them to feel this way about the job.

Stages of Labor   In a first pregnancy, the delivery process may begin as much as a month before the due date, as the fetus begins its head-first descent into the birth canal. This process is called **lightening,** because it relieves some of the pressure on the stomach and diaphragm, so the pregnant woman can breathe

A Baby Is Born

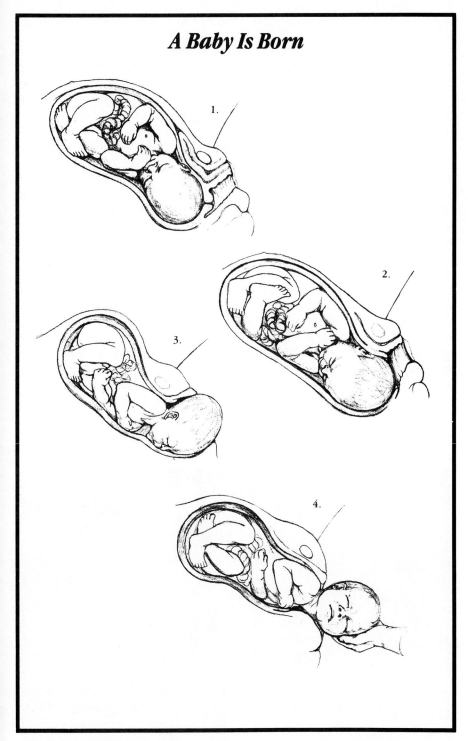

FIGURE 4-3
Birth. (1) At the start of labor, the cervix has not yet begun to dilate. (2) The cervix is now fully dilated; the baby's head passes through the pelvic bones sideways. (3) The baby's head has now turned to a face-down position; it is somewhat molded to fit the shape of the birth canal. The top of the head has "crowned." (4) Once the head is through, the rest is easy. (From Eisenberg, Murkoff, and Hathaway, 1988, p. 268)

more easily. With later pregnancies, lightening may not occur until she is actually in labor.

In the last month or so before delivery, many women experience contractions of the uterus that are known as **Braxton–Hicks contractions.** Generally these practice contractions are painless, but sometimes they are hard to distinguish from those of genuine labor. Unlike real labor, however, they tend to occur at irregular intervals and not to become more severe or more frequent.

The delivery itself involves three stages of labor. The first stage, **dilation,** begins with the onset of real labor. Sometimes this is preceded by the rupture of the amniotic sac and the dribbling out of amniotic fluid; sometimes the first sign is the discharge of the plug of mucus (often stained with a little blood) that sealed the entrance to the uterus. But it's also possible for the mucus plug to pass, unnoticed, several days before delivery, and for the amniotic sac to remain intact during most of the first stage of labor.

The involuntary contractions of the uterus that occur during labor serve to widen the opening of the **cervix**—the door of the uterus through which the baby will pass. This stage of childbirth takes about 12 hours, on the average, for a woman delivering her first child. Later births are faster and easier. Occasionally, especially in later pregnancies, the first stage of labor is almost over before the woman realizes she is about to give birth. Although it may seem to her that she was in labor only for a few minutes, in all probability she was having mild, painless labor contractions for several hours or even days, and didn't notice them (Eisenberg, Murkoff, and Hathaway, 1988).

As the dilation stage progresses, the contractions become more intense,

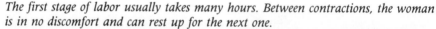

The first stage of labor usually takes many hours. Between contractions, the woman is in no discomfort and can rest up for the next one.

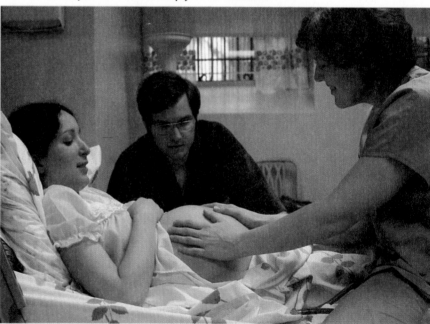

longer, and more frequent, until they are finally coming as rapidly as one every minute. By now the amnion has probably ruptured, letting out some of the watery fluid that surrounded the fetus during pregnancy. At the end of the dilation stage, the woman experiences some very long, intense contractions as the cervix is stretched around the baby's head. This is called **transition;** it is often the most uncomfortable and exhausting part of the delivery process.

Birth occurs during the second stage of labor, which generally takes from 30 minutes to two hours. The contractions are still intense, but now the woman may feel a surge of energy and a lifting of her spirits—she may even feel exhilarated. If she has not been anesthetized, she will feel the urge to push, and her efforts help move the baby through the birth canal and into the world.

The baby emerges with the umbilical cord attached to his belly at the point where his naval will be. The other end of the umbilical cord is attached to the placenta, which is still inside the mother. Shortly after the birth, the physician or midwife will clamp or tie the cord and then cut it. By now the placenta has been loosened from the wall of the uterus. The last stage of labor consists of expelling the placenta, which usually occurs several minutes after the birth of the baby.

Complications of Childbirth

Although the usual outcome of childbirth is a healthy baby, occasionally there are problems. The day of birth is the most hazardous time in a child's life. In the absence of good medical care, it can be a hazardous time in the mother's life as well.

ANOXIA. Complications during the birth process can cause the baby to suffer **anoxia**—an insufficient supply of oxygen. Anoxia can occur during delivery if the placenta detaches too soon or if the umbilical cord is squeezed shut or knotted. It can occur immediately after birth if the baby fails to begin breathing right away. Anoxia can also occur during prenatal development if the mother is anemic or if she smokes.

Severe anoxia can be fatal; less severe anoxia can destroy some of the baby's brain cells. The brain damage may later show up as cerebral palsy or mental retardation. However, even for babies who do not breathe on their own and have to be resuscitated, the risk of serious brain damage is still low. The neonate's brain can apparently withstand a much longer period of oxygen deprivation than the brain of an older person.

Nevertheless, even mild or brief anoxia may have effects that can be detected later, though they are not as severe or as lasting as mental retardation or cerebral palsy. Several studies have found that babies who suffered mild oxygen deprivation at birth tend to cry more than other infants and later show higher rates of learning disabilities and behavior difficulties, although the problems appear to lessen with age (Stechler and Halton, 1982).

UNUSUAL BIRTH POSITIONS AND CESAREAN DELIVERIES. A common complication of childbirth occurs when the fetus is not in the typical head-first position at the beginning of labor. This condition is more frequently found in premature deliveries than in those that are full term. Some babies emerge feet

Problems in Development

Box 4-2
Low-Birthweight Babies

Average weight of an infant at birth is a little over 7 pounds (3200 g), with boys weighing slightly more than that, girls slightly less. Traditionally, any baby that weighs in at less than 5½ pounds (2500 g) has been labeled "premature." About 7 or 8 percent of American babies fall into this category. But this group actually includes two kinds of low-birthweight babies: those who were truly born too soon, and those who are small despite being full-term or nearly full-term.

Babies in this second group are called **small for gestational age (SGA),** also known as *small for date.* Pre-eclampsia or other health problems in a pregnant woman increase the risk of having an SGA baby. A small baby is also more likely if the mother smokes, if she is a teenager, or if she doesn't get adequate nutrition during pregnancy. Even in the absence of any of these factors, small babies are more commonly born to black women than to white women (Kleinman and others, 1988). The reason for this difference is not clearly understood, but genetic factors may be involved.

The majority of low-birthweight babies have simply been born too soon. The exact cause of a premature birth, defined as delivery three weeks or more before the due date, is often impossible to determine. However, in the case of multiple births, prematurity is the rule rather than the exception. Twins are born three weeks early, on the average. Triplets and quadruplets are usually earlier still. These sharers of a crowded uterus are also apt to be SGA. But weight may vary considerably: even identical twins may differ in birthweight by a pound or two, evidently because one had a more favorable location in the uterus than the other. The lighter twin is likely to remain somewhat smaller

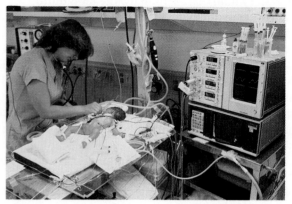

A premature baby in the intensive-care unit of a hospital nursery.

than the heavier one all through life. Babies who are born small because they are born early will generally catch up in the long run, but SGA babies tend to remain slightly smaller than average (Teberg, Walther, and Pena, 1988). These babies do all right in other ways, though. One researcher tested a group of twins that had differed considerably in birthweight, with the larger twin outweighing the smaller one by an average of almost 2 pounds (815 g). At age 6 there was no difference in IQ between the heavier twin and the lighter one (Wilson, 1985).

In the past, any baby weighing under 2000 grams at birth (about 4½ lb) had a relatively poor chance of surviving. But advances in medical technology have led to a dramatic improvement in the survival rates of very small newborns. Now babies weighing as little as 1000 grams (2.2 lb) and born as much as three months early are routinely

---

or buttocks first; this is known as a **breech birth.** A breech birth is hard on the child, and if things are not going well, most obstetricians will perform a **cesarean** (also known as a *C-section*). In this surgical procedure, an incision is made through the woman's abdomen and uterus so that the baby can be removed through the incision, rather than having to pass through the vagina. Cesareans are a matter of necessity when the fetus is positioned sideways in the uterus or when the mother's pelvis is too narrow for the baby's head to pass through. Many obstetricians now use electronic monitoring of the baby's heartbeat, and some will perform a cesarean if there is any sign that the baby might be in trouble.

cared for in the neonatal intensive-care units of hospital nurseries. They are kept in isolettes—special cribs designed to protect them against infection and to maintain controlled levels of temperature and humidity. Their heartbeat and breathing are carefully monitored. Very young premature babies can't suck or swallow properly, so they're given nutrients through a feeding tube that runs from the nose to the stomach. With all the tubes, with their sticklike limbs and their skin so thin that the blood vessels are clearly visible, they hardly look human. But the majority of these babies are going to graduate from their isolettes and go home with their parents.

What does the future hold for these miniature infants, born so early and so small? One recent study tracked a group of very low birthweight babies born in a hospital in Cleveland. All the babies weighed less than 1500 grams (3.3 lb) at birth; the average was 1189 grams (2.6 lb). Of these babies, 73 percent survived infancy. Only 8 percent of the survivors had serious handicaps such as cerebral palsy, blindness, and mental retardation (Breslau, Klein, and Allen, 1988).

The rest of the children in the group were reexamined at the age of 9. Although all these children were considered normal, they measured 7 points lower on IQ tests, on the average, than a group of full-term control children from similar backgrounds. The boys in the low-birthweight group were rated significantly less attentive in school, more aggressive, and less socially competent than the boys in the control group. These differences in behavior and IQ may be due to minor injuries to the brain that result from being born so early. Often, the problems are compounded by an environment that is less than ideal, because of the fact that low-birthweight babies are more commonly born to teenage or economically disadvantaged mothers. In a highly supportive environment, with attentive and responsive parents, low-birthweight babies are likely to become indistinguishable from their agemates over the course of time (Beckwith and Parmelee, 1986).

But being an attentive and responsive parent to a low-birthweight baby is not an easy job: it is difficult for the relationship to get off to a good start in the high-tech atmosphere of the neonatal intensive-care unit. Even when they finally get their babies home, the parents may feel nervous and overprotective or emotionally drained. Simply knowing (or believing) that a baby was born prematurely has an effect on an adult's behavior. Some researchers did an experiment in which women were asked to play with a baby—a normal, full-term baby. Half the women were told that the baby had been born prematurely; the others were not. The ones who thought that the baby was premature touched him less, gave him less challenging toys, and rated him less cute and less likable than the ones who thought he was full-term (Stern and Hildebrandt, 1986).

Recently, efforts have been made to overcome the negative effects of low birthweight on the parent–child relationship. A group of parents was coached in how to respond to their low-birthweight babies in a sensitive and stimulating fashion, and given reassuring information about their babies' development. By the age of 4, the children in this group were performing significantly better on developmental tests than a low-birthweight control group whose parents hadn't had the training sessions. In fact, these 4-year-olds were doing as well as children who had spent a full nine months in the uterus and had weighed a normal amount at birth (Rauh and others, 1988).

FORCEPS DELIVERIES. A medical procedure that is sometimes used when there are birth complications is a **forceps delivery.** Forceps are metal tongs shaped to fit around the baby's head. The physician may use forceps during the second stage of labor to hasten and ease delivery in the case of a breech birth or when there are signs that the baby is in difficulty. However, the procedure can lead to complications of its own. If forceps are applied too early in labor or too roughly, the baby's face or head can be bruised or, on rare occasion, seriously injured. For this reason, forceps deliveries have become less common and newer devices, which use suction to hasten birth, are being used instead.

MEDICATION DURING CHILDBIRTH. Pain-killing drugs and sedatives are used quite commonly during childbirth. Medication may be used to reduce the pain of labor or to relieve the mother's anxiety. Although such drugs may benefit the mother and in some cases make delivery easier, they can cross the placenta and may have unfavorable effects on the fetus. This is one reason why general anesthetics (which produce unconsciousness) are now seldom used in childbirth, and why other kinds of anesthetics are used as little and as late in labor as possible.

Newborns who have been exposed to pain-killers or sedatives before birth may be somewhat sluggish after they are born. They may be less active and less alert, and they may cry more (Smolak, 1986). Depending on the drug that is used, its dosage, and its timing, these effects might last anywhere from a few hours to a few weeks.

POSTPARTUM DEPRESSION. Postpartum depression, also known as the "new-baby blues," is a period of weepiness and emotional ups-and-downs that affects as many as 40 percent of women in the first few days or weeks after childbirth, usually reaching a peak around the third or fourth day (Condon and Watson, 1987). It is believed to be related to the hormonal changes that occur in a woman's body during and after delivery: these hormonal changes seem to make the new mother feel *all* emotions—joy as well as sorrow—more intensely than usual. In fact, as one team of researchers reported, "Some women experience themselves to be both happy and miserable at this time" (Hapgood, Elkind, and Wright, 1988, p. 304).

Postpartum depression is usually short-lived and mild, but sometimes it is severe and long-lasting and may interfere with the mother's ability to care for her child. Not surprisingly, a woman who has a history of depression or other psychiatric illness, or who felt depressed or pessimistic during pregnancy, is more likely to suffer from postpartum depression (Carver and Gaines, 1987).

Research on other factors that might make a woman more or less likely to become depressed after delivery has yielded contradictory results. Some studies have shown that a strong network of social support—from the baby's father and/or friends and relatives—decreases the chances of a severe depression (Hopkins, Marcus, and Campbell, 1984), although other studies have failed to find such a connection (Hopkins, Campbell, and Marcus, 1987). Similarly with stress: some studies have found that a stressful life during pregnancy increases the chances of postpartum depression; others find it makes no difference. A more important factor seems to be stress *after* delivery, and the leading cause of stress after delivery is the baby. It is stressful to care for a baby with major health problems or a difficult temperament (see Chapter 2). A woman experiencing that kind of stress appears to be at greater risk of a serious postpartum depression (Hopkins and others, 1987).

Alternatives in Childbirth

Many couples now look for ways of having their babies that seem to them to be more "natural." They want more control over what goes on during labor and delivery. They want a warmer, more homelike atmosphere, with the husband present and perhaps other friends or relatives as well. They want fewer medical interventions such as drugs and forceps. Sometimes a midwife is used instead of an obstetrician. Although these practices can occasionally present some dangers to the mother or child if there are unexpected complications, the major result of the trend has been to increase the chances that childbirth will be an emotionally satisfying experience for everyone concerned.

"NATURAL CHILDBIRTH." As we mentioned earlier in this section, Grantly Dick-Read was the first to popularize the idea that a woman who is properly prepared for childbirth will have an easier time of it. Currently, the most widely used technique of natural childbirth is the **Lamaze method.** Fernand Lamaze was a French obstetrician who visited the Soviet Union in 1951 and was very impressed by the childbirth methods used there. Lamaze's book, *Painless Childbirth,* was published in France in 1956 and translated into English in 1958.

A Lamaze class in childbirth preparation. The father plays an important role: he is taught to time the mother's contractions and to provide guidance and encouragement while she is in labor.

Lamaze's method, sometimes called the **psychoprophylactic method,** includes education about the physical aspects of childbirth. In addition, the pregnant woman is trained in breathing and relaxation techniques, and her husband is taught to coach her during labor and to provide emotional support. He may also help by stroking or massaging her or by giving her candies or ice chips to suck on. People who believe in the Lamaze method don't claim that it makes childbirth painless—just that it reduces pain and makes the woman feel more in control and more positive about the experience. She is not prevented from using drugs if she feels she needs them.

Studies of the childbirth experiences of Lamaze-prepared women have found that these women use significantly less pain-killing drugs during labor than other women. There is no reduction in the length of labor, but there is some decrease in the incidence of various complications. When questioned later, women in the Lamaze group generally have more favorable things to say about their childbirth experiences and seem to be getting along better with their husbands and their babies (Markman and Kadushin, 1986; Wideman and Singer, 1984).

THE LEBOYER METHOD. Another variation on the theme of childbirth is the **Leboyer method.** Frederick Leboyer, another French obstetrician, pioneered the concept of "gentle birth." He felt that the way newborns were usually introduced into this world was needlessly cruel and frightening—they emerged from a world of warmth and darkness into a cold, noisy room with bright lights shining at them. They were held upside down; sometimes they were even slapped. The umbilical cord was cut almost at once, so babies had to learn to breathe on their own immediately.

According to Leboyer (1975), the newborn should be welcomed into the world with gentleness and compassion. The room should be dimly lit and quiet. The baby and the mother should not be separated immediately after delivery: the baby should be placed on the mother's abdomen, and the cord should not be cut until the blood vessels in it cease to throb. Then the newborn should be placed in a warm bath.

Although only a minority of births in this country follow all the rules that Leboyer laid down, his philosophy has definitely had an impact on hospital procedures. Research has supported Leboyer's idea that babies are born fully able to see, hear, and feel—that they are more sensitive and aware than previous generations believed. Due to this evidence and to Leboyer's influence, there has been a noticeable improvement in the way the baby is treated in the delivery room. Although physicians usually object to turning out the lights (after all, the baby is perfectly capable of closing her eyes if the light bothers her), some of Leboyer's other suggestions are now routine delivery room procedures.

OTHER VARIATIONS. There are several other variations in childbirth practices. Home deliveries have gained some popularity in recent years, and this option generally works well enough in the case of a healthy woman experiencing an uncomplicated birth. However, it can be hazardous if unforeseen complications arise.

Birthing centers offer a compromise between home and hospital. A birthing center might be associated with a hospital or it might be a separate facility. It features a homelike, relaxed atmosphere in which family and friends are welcome.

One of the things that women have objected to in the traditional hospital delivery was being strapped down to the delivery table on their backs, with their feet in the air. An alternative to this procedure has recently been gaining in popularity: it is the **birthing chair,** which allows the woman to sit nearly upright. She has a place to rest her legs to aid her in pushing, and she has gravity working in her favor. There is less pressure on her back—this is said to reduce the backaches that often follow a conventional delivery (Goldman and Goldman, 1986).

CHILDBIRTH IN OTHER TIMES AND PLACES. Like the clothes we wear, the food we eat, and the music we hear, childbirth procedures are subject to trends and fads. Fifty years ago husbands were never allowed in the delivery room. Women were given general anesthesia during childbirth; they remained in the hospital for two weeks and, during this time, saw their babies only when it was convenient for the hospital staff.

We can assure you, because some of our best friends were born under such conditions, that those babies nonetheless turned out perfectly all right. Babies do thrive under a remarkable variety of conditions. Consider Margaret Mead's description of birth in a primitive society:

> The baby is born on an unsheltered hillside, where the mother and attending women crouch shivering over a tiny fire until finally the baby falls with a soft little thud on a cold, dew-coated leaf—to be left there, perhaps five minutes, while the mother herself cuts and ties the cord, packs up the placenta, and wipes out the baby's eyes and nose. Only then can the squirming, exposed little creature be gathered up and laid against the mother's breast. (Mead, 1955, pp. 54–55)

Perhaps birth is bound to be a shock to a baby, no matter how "gentle" Leboyer would like it to be. The great differences in childbirth customs from one time or country to another may be insignificant compared to the much greater difference between life in the uterus and life outside of it:

> At birth itself, whether the mother kneels squatting holding on to two poles or to a piece of rattan hung from the ceiling—whether she is segregated among females or held around the waist by her husband, sits in the

middle of a group of gaming visitors or is strapped on a modern delivery table—the child receives a sharp initial contact with the world as it is pulled, hauled, dropped, pitched, from its perfectly modulated even environment into the outer world, a world where temperature, pressure, and nourishment are all different, and where it must breathe to live. (Mead, 1955, p. 54)

Summary

1. The **prenatal period** begins at the moment of **conception** and ends at the moment of birth. In humans, this period averages 266 days (38 weeks) in length. Conception, when a man's sperm unites with a woman's egg, ordinarily takes place in one of the woman's **Fallopian tubes.**

2. About one out of six American couples has trouble conceiving. Childless couples may decide to adopt a baby, or they may try **artificial insemination** or **in vitro fertilization** in order to have a baby of their own.

3. Prenatal development can be divided into three stages: the **germinal stage** (the first two weeks), the stage of the **embryo** (two weeks to two months), and the stage of the **fetus** (two months to birth).

4. In the germinal stage, the fertilized egg (a single cell containing 46 chromosomes) begins to divide, producing more and more cells. The cells form a hollow ball called a **blastula,** which implants itself in the walls of the **uterus.** Some of the outer cells of the blastula develop into the **umbilical cord,** the **placenta,** and the **amnion** (a protective sac filled with fluid).

5. The rest of the blastula undergoes **differentiation:** the cells from the outer layer form the skin and the nervous system, those from the inner layer form some of the internal organs, and those from the middle layer form muscles, bones, and the remaining internal organs.

6. The growth of the embryo is **cephalocaudal**—the head develops before the feet—and **proximodistal**—the arms and legs develop before the fingers and toes. Two months after conception the embryo roughly resembles a human being, though it's still very small.

7. Growth rate reaches a peak in the early part of the stage of the fetus. By the end of the first **trimester** (three-month period) of pregnancy, all the essential parts of the body are present. Each has been formed during its own **critical period** of development.

8. During the second trimester of pregnancy, the mother can detect the fetus's movements for the first time. Later in the second trimester, a fetus will react to loud sounds in the mother's environment. A 6-month fetus now has a 50 percent chance of surviving if it is born early.

9. Visible sex differences don't appear until the end of the stage of the embryo. The primitive sex glands of the early embryo become the **ovaries** of a female or the **testes** of a male. Testes secrete hormones called **androgens,** which cause male sex organs to form. Ovaries secrete hormones called **estrogens.** In the absence of androgens, female sex organs are formed.

10. The **nervous system** consists of the brain, the spinal cord, **sensory nerves,** and **motor nerves.** The basic unit of the nervous system is a cell called a **neuron.** Brain growth is fastest in the last three months of prenatal development.

11. Neurons transmit messages to other neurons at locations called **synapses.** Babies are born with many **reflexes** and they're generally all in working order, which indicates that most of their neurons have managed to form the proper connections with other neurons. Connections that are useless or don't work right are dismantled in the first few months after birth.

12. In the **placenta,** the mother's blood vessels are interwoven with those of the developing child in such a way that molecules can pass between them. In this way, nourishment from the mother is provided to the embryo or fetus; its waste products are transferred to the mother.

13. Most substances dissolved in the mother's blood are able to **cross the placenta.** Sometimes this is beneficial, as when the mother's immunities are transmitted to the unborn child. Sometimes it is harmful, as when the immune system of an Rh negative mother produces antibodies that destroy the red blood cells of a fetus whose blood contains the **Rh factor.**

14. A **teratogen** is anything that can produce abnormalities in the developing embryo or fetus. Disease-producing microorganisms may have this effect, especially the **rubella** virus. Genital **herpes** can be transmitted to a baby during birth, producing a potentially fatal infection. When a mother is infected with the **AIDS** virus, about 50 percent of the time the disease will be passed to her fetus.

15. Birth defects range from minor annoyances to fatal malformations. Many defects, especially those caused by defective genes or chromosomal accidents, are now detectable before birth.

16. Women who took the drug thalidomide during the first trimester of pregnancy had babies with missing or deformed limbs. Because most body parts are formed during the first trimester of development, teratogens pose the greatest danger during this time. Some prescription drugs are known to cause birth defects; some over-the-counter drugs are suspected of causing defects if used in excess.

17. Alcoholic mothers run the risk of giving birth to a baby with **fetal alcohol syndrome,** which includes mental retardation and various physical abnormalities.

18. Cigarettes have a harmful effect on prenatal development. The child of a smoker is smaller at birth than that of a nonsmoker, at greater risk for various abnormalities, and is significantly more likely to die, either before birth or soon after.

19. Drugs such as heroin and cocaine increase the risk of fetal death, birth defects, brain damage, and long-term behavioral problems. The baby of a user is likely to be born with a physical addiction to the substance.

20. Women between the ages of 18 and 35 have the healthiest babies. Pregnancy is particularly risky for teenage girls and their babies. Pregnancy in older women is less hazardous than was previously believed, unless the woman has a chronic health problem.

21. Although severe stress has been found to produce complications of pregnancy and delivery in animals, there is no good evidence that a woman's anxiety, or stressful events in her life, have bad effects on her fetus. The stress may, however, have a negative effect on the way she takes care of herself during pregnancy.

22. The baby's father can help during pregnancy by giving emotional support to the mother and by showing concern for her health.

23. Birth usually occurs between 38 and 42 weeks after the last menstrual period. The human birth process is difficult because the baby's head is so large.

24. In the first stage of labor, **dilation,** contractions of the uterus widen the opening of the cervix. This stage takes an average of 12 hours for a first pregnancy but may be much shorter for women who have given birth before. Birth occurs during the second stage of labor. The last stage consists of expelling the placenta.

25. Anoxia, a failure to get enough oxygen, is a danger to the baby during and immediately after birth. Anoxia can destroy some of the baby's brain cells, sometimes producing mental retardation or cerebral palsy. However, the brain of a newborn baby can withstand much more oxygen deprivation than that of an older person.

26. A **breech birth,** in which the feet or buttocks are delivered first, is harder on the baby than the usual head-first delivery.

27. Postpartum depression affects many women in the first few days after delivery; it may be related to hormonal changes. Usually it is short-lived and mild, but in some women—particularly those who have a history of psychiatric illness or who were depressed during pregnancy—it may be severe and long-lasting. Caring for a sick baby or one with a difficult temperament also increases the risk of postpartum depression.

28. The average baby weighs a little over 7 pounds (3200 g) at birth; girls weigh slightly less than boys. Low-birth-weight babies weigh less than 5½ pounds (2500 g). Most of these babies were simply born too early, but some are **small for gestational age (SGA).** Nowadays babies weighing as little as 1000 grams (2.2 lb) can often be saved.

29. With the **Lamaze method** of "natural childbirth," the mother is trained in breathing and relaxation techniques; the father is trained to provide coaching and emotional support during labor. The **Leboyer method** of "gentle birth" is designed to make birth less frightening and unpleasant for the baby.

30. Childbirth procedures differ greatly from one time and place to another. Such differences probably have less impact on the newborn baby than the much greater difference between life within the uterus and life outside it.

Key Terms

umbilical cord	prenatal period	ovum
placenta	period of gestation	Fallopian tubes
uterus	conception	ovulate
neonate	ovary	artificial insemination

cervix
in vitro fertilization
surrogate mother
birth mother
germinal stage
embryo
fetus
blastula
amnion
differentiation
cephalocaudal
proximodistal
amniotic fluid
trimester
critical period
testes
hormones
androgens
estrogens

nervous system
central nervous system
sensory nerve
motor nerve
neuron
synapse
cortex
reflex
cross the placenta
antibodies
Rh factor
rubella
toxoplasmosis
herpes
AIDS
pre-eclampsia
teratogen
alpha-fetoprotein test (AFP)

fetal alcohol syndrome
lightening
Braxton-Hicks contractions
dilation
transition
anoxia
breech birth
cesarean
forceps delivery
postpartum depression
small for gestational age (SGA)
Lamaze method
psychoprophylactic method
Leboyer method
birthing center
birthing chair

5

The Baby

The baby whose birth we witnessed at the beginning of the last chapter now lies quietly in his mother's arms. Although he's not even half an hour old, he already has a name: Michael. Michael appears to be unimpressed with his new environment; the vast difference between his life within the uterus and his present surroundings does not seem to have fazed him. One has the impression that he's neither frightened nor confused. He looks rather peaceful, in fact.

To his parents, and also perhaps to us, the newborn baby is one of the world's most interesting people. And yet, he can't tell us a thing! There are so many questions we wish we could ask him: What was it like being born? What was it like in the uterus? Are you glad to be here? When you dream, what do you dream about? Alas, we can get no answers to any of these questions. But there are many questions to ask about the newborn that can be answered. In fact, we now know a great deal more about the neonate—the newborn baby—than we did ten or fifteen years ago. Research on the neonate has been a very active and productive field.

Characteristics of the Newborn Baby

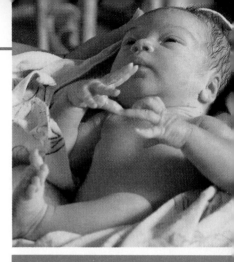

At this point, Michael bears little resemblance to the smooth, dimpled babies shown in diaper commercials. His hair is still plastered down with **vernix,** a fatty substance that protected his skin in the uterus and helped to grease his passage down the birth canal. His skin is blotchy and bruised. His eyelids are puffy. He's decidedly hairy, especially on the upper back. (This fine hair, called **lanugo,** will fall out in a few weeks.) But his color is a healthy pink now; he was somewhat blue for the first minute or two after birth, due to a temporary drop of oxygen in his blood. That blueness is usual in newborns —it takes a little while for the lungs to clear and start working properly.

Because a quick glance doesn't always discriminate a healthy newborn from one who is in serious trouble, most hospitals rate the condition of babies one minute and five minutes after birth by a scoring system known as the **Apgar test** (after Virginia Apgar, its originator). Five different aspects of the baby's physical condition are quickly judged (see Table 5–1) and each is given a score of 0, 1, or 2. Thus, the total score can range from a low of 0 to a high of 10. The lowest scores are generally found in babies who were born too early or who have a serious physical defect, and those for whom the delivery did not go smoothly. A baby with a low Apgar score has a greater risk of dying and a slightly greater risk, if he or she survives, of being brain-damaged.

States of Sleep and Wakefulness

Having successfully navigated the crucial transition from fetus to neonate, Michael falls asleep. As everyone knows, newborn babies generally spend much of their time sleeping.

Sleep used to be considered a do-nothing time, a time of rest and recuperation from the day's activities. That made it hard to understand why young infants need to sleep so much. Now sleep is known to consist of active periods as well as quiet ones. In **active sleep,** also known as **REM** (for rapid eye movement) **sleep,** the eyes can be seen moving beneath the closed lids. Mus-

TABLE 5–1
The Apgar Test

WHAT IS OBSERVED	APGAR SCORE		
	0	1	2
Baby's heart rate	heart not beating	heart beating weakly	heart beating strongly
Breathing, crying	no breathing, no crying	some breathing, weak cry	steady breathing, strong cry
Muscle tone	limp	moderate muscle tone	good muscle tone
Response to a pinch	none	weak response	withdrawal of limb, crying
Skin color	blue, pale	body pink, hands and feet blue	all pink

cles twitch and breathing is faster and less regular than in quiet sleep. Adults who are awakened during active sleep usually say they have been dreaming. Only about a quarter of adults' sleeping time is spent in active sleep. The newborn is in this state about half of his total sleep time—that's about eight hours of active sleep a day, on the average (Roffwarg, Muzio, and Dement, 1966).

But active sleep and quiet sleep in the newborn are not exactly the same as active and quiet sleep in the adult. In newborns the two kinds of sleep are less distinct—even in quiet sleep their bodies occasionally twitch or jerk and their lips make sucking motions. Moreover, sleep in a young baby (either kind of sleep, active or quiet) is not as different from being awake as it is for an adult. Adults who are deeply asleep are not conscious of their surroundings and their brains are able to block out stimuli—lights, sounds, and touches—unless these stimuli are strong enough to wake them up. Newborn babies don't seem to be capable of that kind of deep sleep—they are never totally unresponsive to stimuli (Maurer and Maurer, 1988).

HOW DO BABIES SPEND THEIR SPARE TIME? When they are not being fed, bathed, or diapered, what do young infants do? To say that they're either asleep or awake is an oversimplification: just as there is more than one kind of sleep, there is more than one kind of wakefulness. Researchers use the word **state** to describe these various types of sleep and wakefulness. Although it is not always possible to make clear distinctions between one state and another, six different states have been defined—two for sleep (we've already described these), three for wakefulness, and one for a state between sleep and wakefulness, called drowsiness, in which the baby lies fairly quietly while her eyes open and close sleepily. The baby goes from state to state in an irregular fashion during the course of a day.

The three waking states are crying, fussing, and **quiet alertness.** Crying includes vigorous movements of the face and body, as well as the conspicuous

FIGURE 5-1
How newborn babies spend their time. (Sources: Berg, Adkinson, and Strock, 1973; Roffwarg, Muzio, and Dement, 1966.)

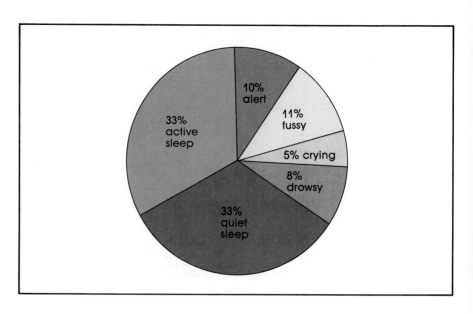

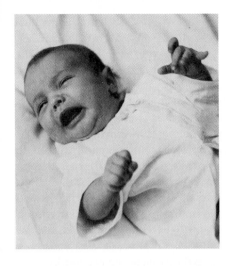
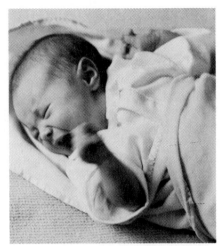
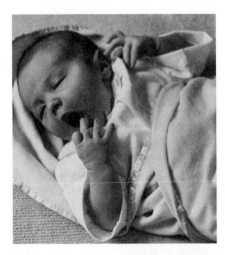
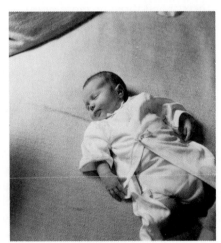
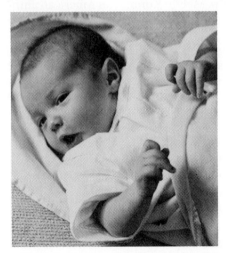

Five states of the young baby: fussiness (upper left), crying (upper right), drowsiness (middle left), sleeping (middle right), and quiet alertness (bottom).

sound effects. Fussing, also known as *active alertness,* is less dramatic: the baby whimpers occasionally and moves her arms and legs, but not so vigorously as when she's crying. Quiet alertness is the state that parents and developmental psychologists like best of all. The baby lies quietly but fully awake, with her eyes wide open—she appears to be very attentive to the sights and sounds around her. When researchers investigate the abilities or preferences of babies, they generally must wait until babies are in this state.

Researchers have studied the behavior of neonates as they lie in their cribs between feedings. Figure 5–1 shows how a typical infant spends his or her time. But individual babies might differ considerably from the percentages shown in this figure. An infant named Charles, whose behavior was observed during his first week of life, spent more than a third of his time in the state of quiet alertness. Another baby, Ted, was seldom in this state—he spent most of his time sleeping. Dorothy also slept a lot, but when she was awake she was almost always crying (Brown, 1964).

Babies do differ enormously in how much they cry. Some cry hardly at all; others spend three or more hours a day at it—most commonly in the early evening. Although this type of crying is called "colic" (meaning a pain in the gut), there is no evidence that anything is wrong with the babies' digestive systems. The crying tends to increase in the first few weeks after birth, reaches a peak when the baby is about 2 months old, and then declines fairly rapidly. Since this kind of crying is more common in our culture, where babies spend most of their time lying in their cribs, than in cultures where babies are carried around during the day, some researchers wondered what would happen if American mothers carried their babies around more. The researchers found that babies who were carried around for an extra two hours a day cried only about half as much as babies who didn't get the extra carrying (Hunziker and Barr, 1986; St James-Roberts, 1989).

Different cultures have different beliefs and practices regarding the care of young babies. Whereas American and European mothers believe that babies should spend most of their time lying down, a mother of the !Kung San people of southwest Africa holds her infant sitting or standing in her lap or in a cloth sling on her hip. Melvin Konner, an American anthropologist who studied childrearing practices among the !Kung San, reports:

> Infants are rarely permitted to lie down while awake. [!Kung San] mothers consider that this is bad for infants and that it retards motor development. This is the opposite of the folk belief in the Northwestern United States where vertical posture is considered bad, at least for very young infants. (Konner, 1977b, p. 291)

Konner found that !Kung San babies score very high on tests of motor development. He speculates that their "vertical posture" may have something to do with their rapid progress.

What Can the Newborn Do?

Immediately after birth, the new baby is capable of responding to a wide variety of stimuli. Most of these responses are of the kind we call reflexes. A reflex is a simple, automatic response to a stimulus—an involuntary movement that results, not from thought or intention, but from built-in neural connections in the nervous system.

REFLEXES OF THE NEONATE. A number of reflexes are essential for life outside the uterus. Human babies share these mechanisms with all baby mammals. The most important are those associated with breathing. Breathing rhythms are not firmly established in the newborn; normal, healthy babies occasionally neglect to breathe for brief periods of time. But this causes carbon dioxide to build up in the blood and the excess carbon dioxide triggers a reflex: breathing deepens and quickens, and the baby takes extra breaths in order to "catch up." Other reflexes connected with breathing are sneezing and coughing, both ways of ridding the breathing passage of obstructions.

Second in importance are the reflexes associated with feeding. A full-term newborn is capable of sucking and swallowing immediately after birth. However, a baby born two or three months early usually can't suck or swallow adequately. Such a baby has to be fed through a tube that carries liquid directly to the stomach.

When Michael is put to his mother's breast, he shows a reflex called **rooting.** A touch of the nipple near his mouth or on his cheek causes him to turn his head and move his lips toward the touch, enabling him eventually to get the nipple into his mouth. He'll do the same thing if you touch his cheek with your finger.

Among the responses that are important for the baby's survival, we should include crying. It's the baby's signal to his parents that he's hungry or in pain, too hot or too cold. The piercing sounds of a baby's cries are *supposed* to be unpleasant: their function is to motivate the parent to turn them off, by meeting the baby's needs.

Although the baby is entirely dependent on his caregivers for relief from hunger, there are other reflexes for dealing with pain and temperature regulation. A painful stimulus to a limb causes the baby to withdraw the limb. When a doctor must take a few drops of blood from the heel of a newborn baby, the baby will try to pull the leg away. When that proves impossible, the other foot comes up and tries to push away the doctor's hand.

Babies react to heat and cold in the same ways as older people. Heat causes the blood vessels in the skin to expand, so that more heat can be lost through the skin. Cold produces the opposite reflex: the blood vessels in the skin contract, so that heat is conserved inside the body. It's easy to tell when babies are cold—they turn pale, then blue. (These color changes are usually detectable even in babies who are destined to be dark-skinned, since the skin is not fully pigmented at birth.) Babies do need to be protected against chilling, because their response to cold is much less efficient than an adult's. They lack the layer of fat that helps to insulate the body of an older person. Furthermore, their small size means that even when most of their blood supply is withdrawn from the skin, it's still much closer to the surface than it is in an adult.

One more reflex that should be mentioned here, because it is present in the newborn, is yawning. For a long time, yawning was assumed to be a breathing reflex: it often follows a period of shallow breathing, so it was thought to have something to do with taking in oxygen or getting rid of carbon dioxide. But recent experiments in which college students were given air containing different amounts of oxygen and carbon dioxide found no relationship between what they breathed and how much they yawned. (In fact, the best inducer of yawning in college students was not oxygen deprivation but a lecture on calculus!) At present, scientists have to admit that they just don't know what purpose yawning serves, although the fact that it occurs in every animal from amphibians to zebras shows that it must serve *some* purpose (Huyghe, 1989).

"USELESS" REFLEXES. There are a number of reflexes present in the normal newborn that serve no useful purpose at all. Most of these gradually disappear during the first three or four months of life. The **Babinski** and **Moro reflexes** are in this class. The Babinski reflex is a response to being stroked on the sole of the foot: when Michael's foot is tickled, his big toe sticks up and the other toes fan outward. The Moro reflex is a startle response to a loud noise or a sudden loss of support. The baby's arms are first flung wildly outward, then are quickly brought toward the chest again.

Other "useless" reflexes appear to be relics—leftovers from an earlier evolutionary stage. The **swimming reflex** is one of these: when placed on his stomach, Michael may rhythmically extend his arms and legs. The **grasp**

Three reflexes of the newborn baby: the Babinski reflex (upper left), the walking reflex (upper right), and the grasp reflex (bottom).

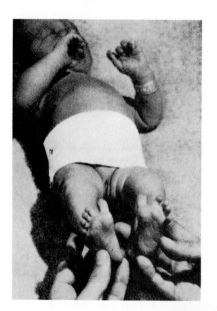
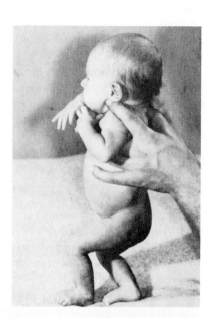
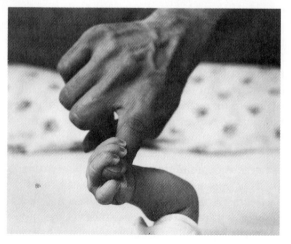

reflex causes him to close his hand tightly if something is pressed in his palm. He grasps so tightly that he can support almost his entire weight by the grip of his two little fists. Premature babies grasp even more tightly—they will grip an adult's index fingers firmly enough to be lifted entirely into the air! The grasp reflex is present in baby monkeys, too. It enables them to cling to their mothers as they are carried through the trees.

Some "useless" reflexes look forward, rather than backward, in time. The most interesting of these is the **walking** (or stepping) **reflex.** If Michael is held firmly in an upright position with his feet touching a solid surface, his legs will make stepping movements, very similar to real walking—except that, of course, his little legs can't possibly hold the weight of his body. This reflex usually disappears within a few weeks, and real walking doesn't appear until many months after that. But the walking reflex of the newborn appears to be related in some way to the walking of the toddler. A group of infants were "walked" for a few minutes at a time, several times a day, during the first two months of life. Later, these children began to walk independently some five to seven weeks earlier than children who hadn't had this practice (Zelazo, 1983). Notice that during the walking practice the infants were being held upright, like the !Kung San babies—and apparently with similar results. What isn't yet known is whether there are any long-term advantages in walking early. Rapid progress in one area of development is not necessarily related to progress in other areas of development or to development at a later stage.

A REMARKABLE ABILITY OF THE NEWBORN. No one expects a newborn baby to do anything very remarkable. However, a surprisingly complex response has been reported in newborn babies: imitation of adults' facial movements (Meltzoff and Moore, 1983; Field and others, 1983). The photographs on p. 156 show a baby girl only 6 days old sticking out her tongue in imitation of her mother's action. Babies can imitate other facial expressions, too, such as opening the mouth or pursing the lips. They can also imitate gestures such as opening and closing the hand.

When the first reports of imitation in newborn babies were made public, many experts in child development were skeptical. They couldn't believe that a week-old baby was capable of such a sophisticated kind of behavior. How could an infant who had never seen herself in a mirror make the connection between her mother's tongue and her own tongue? How could she copy a movement that she can only see, and produce a similar movement of her own that she cannot see but can only feel?

By now so many researchers have reported imitation in young babies that it is no longer possible to doubt its existence. Getting the babies to perform this trick isn't easy—the room has to be quiet and free of distractions, and the adult must make the gesture clearly and then not move for several seconds—but under the proper conditions it can be shown in babies only a few hours old. However, many authorities still don't accept the idea that a newborn baby is capable of understanding the relationship between her own mouth and someone else's, or her own actions and the actions she sees someone else perform. Their view is that this kind of imitation is simply a reflex—a very simple, wired-in behavior that requires no thought or understanding at all on the baby's part (Bjorklund, 1987a; Wyrwicka, 1988).

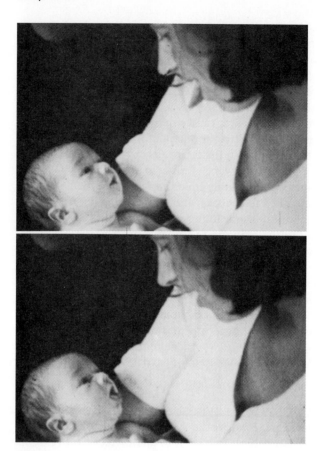

A mother sticks out her tongue and her 6-day-old baby imitates her.

There is good evidence to support this view. Like a number of other reflexes found in the newborn, the ability to imitate disappears as the baby gets older: it is rarely seen in babies over 6 weeks of age (Abravanel and Sigafoos, 1984). Imitation doesn't reemerge until the baby is several months older. There seems to be no relationship between the very simple and limited kind of imitation found in newborns and the far more complex and flexible kind found in older babies. The early imitation does not lead to the later kind —it just goes away. Perhaps it serves some function in the first weeks of life (for instance, to improve babies' social relationships with their caregivers), or perhaps it is just another one of those "useless" reflexes put there to entertain people who do research on neonates.

The Perceptual World of the Infant

A hundred years ago, the noted American psychologist William James concluded that newborn babies must perceive the world as a "blooming, buzzing confusion." For many decades after James, the prevailing belief was that babies start out seeing only a meaningless blur of lines and colors swimming around in their visual field, and gradually learn to interpret these stimuli as stationary or moving objects of various shapes and sizes. But we have already given you some evidence against that point of view: the photograph of the 6-day-old baby imitating her mother. Even if this behavior is merely a reflex, it wouldn't be possible if the baby saw her mother's face only as a formless blob. Notice, too, how intently the baby is staring up at her mother. One gets the impression that she's extremely interested in what she sees.

What *are* newborn babies able to see, hear, smell, taste, and feel? How do their sensory capacities develop during infancy? Modern methods for studying the abilities of babies have revealed that they are a lot less confused than William James thought, and a lot more capable of perceiving things (see Box 5–1).

Vision

Puppies, kittens, and rats are born with sealed eyes that don't open until a week or two after birth. But newborn monkeys, apes, and humans are born with eyes that are ready to function immediately. Even a baby born two months prematurely can see at birth: the essential working parts of the eye are complete at seven months after conception. The body of a newborn human is only a twentieth of its adult weight; the brain is a fourth. But the human eye only doubles in volume during the course of development (Maurer, 1975). A baby's eyes look big because they *are* big, compared with the size of the baby!

A normal neonate like Michael can track a slowly moving object with his eyes, right from the start, and will even turn his head to follow it. But the movements of his eyes, either in tracking a moving object or in shifting his gaze from one stationary object to another one, are jerky and imprecise, unlike the smooth and accurate eye movements of older people (Banks and Salapatek, 1983).

Other factors combine to make everything the newborn sees appear somewhat blurry and washed-out. First, some parts of his **retina**—the light-sensitive membrane at the back of the eye, corresponding to the film in a camera—are not yet fully formed. Second, the newborn cannot at first adjust the focus of his eyes to near or far stimuli, the way an older infant can. He can focus best on things that are about 8 to 12 inches (20 to 30 cm) away from him—about the distance of his mother's face when she holds him in her arms. The ability to focus develops rapidly and so does the retina. The newborn's vision sharpens to near-adult levels by the time he is 6 or 8 months old, though it takes another four years for children's eyes to reach their full adult level of acuity (Maurer and Maurer, 1988). The important point, however, is that even newborns can make out most of the important features of their environment, and their vision improves with breathtaking speed over the first few months of life.

WHAT DO BABIES LIKE TO LOOK AT? Because things look blurry and washed-out to a young baby, the patterns they can see most clearly—and the ones they prefer to look at—are composed of sharply contrasting areas of stark black and white. The size of the black and white areas matters too, especially for newborns: a pattern with large squares, for example, is preferred to a pattern with small squares. The larger squares are less apt to blur together in the babies' vision. Babies of all ages also prefer patterns that are moderately complex, containing a fair number of lines or contours, rather

Close-Up

Box 5-1
Some Methods for Finding Out about Babies' Perceptions

Systematic testing of infant visual perception was first performed by Robert Fantz in the late 1950s. Fantz's technique was simple: he put a baby in a little booth and placed two pictures on the ceiling of the booth, not far above the baby's face. Then he watched to see which one she looked at. (He could see the baby's eyes through a peephole in the top of the booth. The lighting was arranged in such a way that whatever the baby looked at was reflected on the shiny surface of her eyes.)

What Fantz found was that babies would usually look at one of the pictures significantly more than at the other, regardless of whether that picture was on the right or the left. Certain kinds of pictures seemed to be preferred over other kinds, and the preferences sometimes changed as the babies got older. These preferences tell us more than just the likes and dislikes of babies: it shows that they could tell the pictures apart. They couldn't consistently choose one picture over another (regardless of position) unless they could see that the pictures were different (Fantz, 1958).

So if a baby prefers to look at one picture (or one object) instead of at another, we can be pretty sure that she can see them and that she can tell them apart. But the reverse is not true: if the baby looks equally often at two pictures, that doesn't mean she can't see any difference—perhaps she just likes them equally well. Thus, Fantz's **preferential-looking technique** doesn't enable us to tell if the baby can discriminate between two

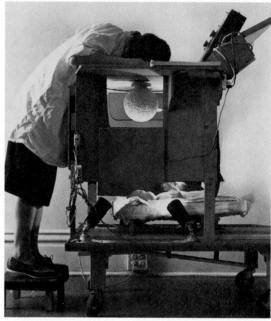

Fantz's apparatus for studying the visual preferences of babies.

very similar pictures, since similar pictures are likely to be similarly attractive.

However, there is a way of testing the baby's ability to tell the pictures apart: it's called the **habituation technique.** First, a baby is shown one picture and given a chance to look at it. After a while, this picture no longer arouses her attention or interest—she **habituates** to it, she learns to ignore it. Then she's shown two pictures, the old

than simple patterns or extremely complicated ones. They prefer patterns with curved lines to ones with straight lines (Fantz, Fagan, and Miranda, 1975).

By the time they are 2 or 3 months old, babies are able to recognize the essential features of a human face, even in a fairly crude drawing. They would rather look at a drawing that resembles a face than at a similar drawing (similar in terms of contrast, number of lines, and so on) that doesn't look like a face (Dannemiller and Stephens, 1988).

COLOR VISION. Because black and white produce the greatest contrast and sharpness, a 1- or 2-month-old baby will look at a black-and-white pattern in preference to a colored one. This preference for sharp contrasts and a relative lack of interest in color has made it difficult to study color vision in babies. If

one and a new one. Almost invariably, babies (like anyone else) will prefer to look at a new picture, rather than one they've seen before—that is, if they can tell the two pictures apart. So if the two pictures are looked at equally, researchers assume that the baby can't tell them apart. This technique allows us to test whether babies can detect fairly subtle differences between stimuli. It also enables us to test the baby's memory: if the two-picture test isn't made until a month after one of the pictures is shown, and the baby still prefers the newer one, then she must have some memory of the one she saw previously.

More complex abilities can also be tested with the habituation technique. One study used this method to demonstrate that young infants can "count": they can tell the difference between two and three, though not between four and six. Week-old babies were repeatedly shown pictures of three black dots in various arrangements; eventually they became bored with looking at dots in threes. They looked with renewed interest when they were then shown new pictures with two dots. Similarly, after repeated exposure to two dots they looked longer at pictures with three. But babies first shown pictures with four dots showed no great interest in groups of six, or vice versa (Antell and Keating, 1983).

The habituation technique is not restricted to studies of vision—it can be used to study other senses as well. For example, an experiment was performed to find out whether babies could discriminate between sounds of different pitch. The babies were sucking on a pacifier; when a musical tone was played, they showed their interest by slowing or briefly stopping their sucking. After several repetitions of the sound they ceased to pay attention to it. But when a higher or a lower sound was played they once again stopped sucking on the pacifier, showing that they could hear the difference (Bronshtein and Petrova, 1967).

There are other methods for studying vision and hearing, some of them quite high-tech indeed, compared with Fantz's simple setup of one baby and two pictures. Neurologists paste electronic sensors onto a baby's scalp and study the electrical changes that go on inside her head when a stimulus comes in through her eyes or her ears. Ophthalmologists (physicians who specialize in the eye) study a baby's visual acuity (the sharpness or clearness of her vision) by peering into her eyes with the various tools of their trade. But visual acuity can also be studied with the preferential-looking technique. A baby will always look at a striped black-and-white pattern in preference to a solid sheet of gray, so we just have to find out how narrow the stripes have to be before the baby stops preferring them. At some point the stripes will blur together in the baby's vision and she will no longer be able to tell the difference between the stripes and the solid gray. It turns out that the stripes can be no narrower than one-tenth of an inch wide (2.5 mm) for newborn babies to see them at a distance of 1 foot (30 cm). A 2-month-old can see stripes that are half as wide, a 4-month-old can see them a quarter as wide, and an 8-month-old can see them an eighth as wide (Maurer and Maurer, 1988).

William James should be pardoned for his views of infants: very little was known in 1890 about what a baby could see or hear. We know much more now, thanks to a combination of ingenious methods and extraordinarily patient investigators. The baby who couldn't tell us a thing one hundred years ago now has a rich lode of information to give us.

we habituate a baby to a pale gray square, for example, and then show him a red one and he looks interested, how do we know he is not just responding to the difference in darkness between the red square and the gray one? It is necessary to use a wide variety of grays, pale ones and darker ones, in order to be sure that color alone is what the baby is responding to. Daphne Maurer and her colleagues at McMaster University in Canada have used this technique to study the development of color vision in babies. Here's what they found:

We bored babies with an assortment of grays, then showed them a color to see whether they perked up: if they did, they could tell the color was not gray. We found that newborns distinguish yellow, orange, red, green, and turquoise from gray. However, they do *not* distinguish blue, purple, or chartreuse. . . .

After birth, a baby's color vision improves rapidly. By one month he can distinguish blue, purple, and chartreuse from gray, as well as the yellow, orange, red, green, and turquoise he could distinguish at birth; by two months he can distinguish yellow from green; and by three months he can distinguish yellow from red as well. By the time the baby is three to four months old, his color vision is substantially adult.   (Maurer and Maurer, 1988, pp. 124–125)

Babies not only can see colors: they also categorize them in the same way that adults do—as shades of red, blue, yellow, or green. Three- and 4-month-olds evidently see one shade of blue as being similar to another shade of blue and noticeably different from any shade of green: if they get tired of looking at blue things they will look again at something green, and vice versa. They seem not to like in-between colors: 4-month-old babies, like adults, prefer clear, bright, primary colors, especially red and blue (Teller and Bornstein, 1987).

WHERE DO BABIES LOOK? When babies look at a picture, an object, or a face, where do they look? The answer depends on the age of the baby. Newborns tend to look at the edges of things, at the contours where contrast is greatest. For example, when 1-month-old babies are shown a pattern such as a square with some spots inside it, they will look at the edge of the square instead of at the spots. Similarly, when looking at a face, they tend to point their eyes at the line between the forehead and the hair, or at the edge of the chin or jaw. Figure 5–2 shows where one baby looked when examining an adult's face, first at 1 month (left) and then at 2 months of age (right). At 1 month the baby looked at the edge of the adult's chin; his gaze remained in one place for a while, then moved a little and got stuck again at another part of the chin. By 2 months he was able to scan the face and to focus on some of its important features (Maurer and Maurer, 1988).

The ability to look at the features inside a contour emerges at about the fifth or sixth week. At that point, a parent might notice that the baby has finally begun to "look me in the eye," or to make eye contact.

DEPTH PERCEPTION. The ability to see things in three dimensions—some things closer, some farther away—is an important part of human vision. Even with one eye closed you have some **depth perception** (three-dimensional vision): you can tell the approximate distances of the objects in an unfamiliar room, for example. You judge by the sizes of the objects, by the fact that the things that are closer to you block your view of things that are farther away, and by the way in which nearby things shift relative to the background when you move around. But the world seen with one eye has a flat, unconvincing appearance, like a photo instead of the real thing. The world assumes its most vivid three-dimensional appearance only when seen with two eyes. Psychologists call this **stereoscopic vision.** It depends on the fact that the left eye's view is slightly different from the right eye's view. There are specialized neurons in the brain, called **binocular cells,** that receive inputs from both the left eye and the right eye. These cells are responsible for stereoscopic vision.

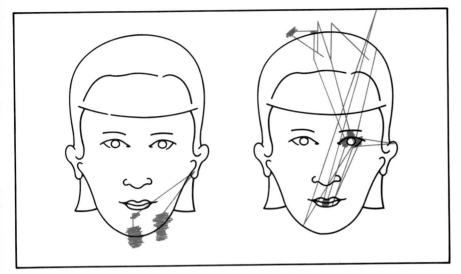

FIGURE 5-2
How young babies look at faces. The marks on these drawings show where a baby looked when he was 1 month old (left) and 2 months old (right). At 1 month, the baby's eyes got stuck on the edge of the chin, but at 2 months he was able to scan the features of the face. (From Maurer and Maurer, 1988.)

For a baby to see stereoscopically, she must be able to coordinate her two eyes so that both point in the same direction—both eyes are looking at the same thing. This ability is present from birth to some extent, but it is not nearly as precise as it needs to be. Because the newborn's eyes are so poorly coordinated at first, and because the necessary brain mechanisms are not yet fully developed, it takes about four months for stereoscopic vision to emerge (Aslin and Smith, 1988).

The emergence of stereoscopic vision, plus an increased ability to control the movements of their hands, enables 4-month-old babies to swipe with fair accuracy at a toy dangled above them; to do this, they must have a pretty good idea of how far away the toy is. It generally takes them another three or four weeks to become successful at grasping the toy, but that is a matter we'll deal with later, in the section on motor development.

An experiment with 5-month-olds provides evidence for the sophisticated visual abilities present at this age. The babies were given a choice of two objects to grab for: a brightly patterned object close enough for them to reach, and a similar but larger object that was farther away. The sizes and distances were arranged in such a way that the images of the two objects on the babies' retinas were the same size. Thus, if they reached for the nearer object rather than the farther one, it showed that they were able to tell how far away the objects were. Some babies were tested with a patch over one eye; the others used normal two-eyed vision. The babies who could see with one eye had only a slight tendency to reach for the nearer of the two objects. But those who could see with both eyes reached for the nearer object 89 percent of the time. This experiment shows that 5-month-olds do use stereoscopic vision to tell them how far away things are (Granrud, Yonas, and Pettersen, 1984).

Although we now have good evidence that most babies have stereoscopic vision by the time they are 4 or 5 months old, this was not known in the early '60s. Thus, an experiment that showed depth perception in crawling babies, 6 to 14 months old, was big news back then. The experiment was carried out at Cornell University by Eleanor Gibson and Richard Walk (1960). It made use

A baby being tested on the visual cliff.

of a setup called a **visual cliff.** This is basically a big table with a top made out of heavy-duty glass and a solid platform across the middle. A patterned surface is visible directly under the glass on one side of the platform. On the other side, the patterned surface is several feet below the glass—this is the "cliff" side. In the experiment, babies of crawling age were put on the platform and their mothers called them, either from the cliff side or the shallow side of the table. Gibson and Walk found that babies were willing to crawl across the shallow side to get to their mothers, but they generally refused to go onto the cliff side. Some babies just sat and cried; some actually crawled in the other direction.

A baby who is afraid of heights must have depth perception; however, a baby who has depth perception may nonetheless lack this fear. This was shown by a later series of experiments performed at the University of Denver by Joseph Campos and his colleagues. Babies have depth perception *before* they learn to crawl. They usually don't start worrying about heights until a couple of weeks *after* they start crawling. It isn't just a question of being a little older: noncrawlers who were placed on the cliff side of the table showed no signs of being afraid (there was no increase in the rate of their heartbeat), but crawling babies of the *same age* showed clear signs of fear when they were placed on the cliff—their hearts began beating faster (Kermoian and Campos, 1988).

What causes babies to start worrying about heights? The obvious answer is: they have had a fall or two, and now they are worried about falling again. But this obvious explanation is not correct. It turns out that a baby who cannot yet crawl, and who has never fallen, will learn to be wary of heights if she is allowed to push herself around in a walker. (A walker is a baby seat with wheels, which holds the baby upright and lets her feet touch the floor.) Evidently, in order to develop a healthy respect for heights, the baby has to have some experience with moving around voluntarily in her environment. Being carried or pushed by someone else is not enough to make her vividly aware of her own position in three-dimensional space. But it isn't necessary for her to move *entirely* on her own—moving around in a walker seems to be sufficient (Bertenthal and Campos, 1987).

We should mention that some authorities object to the use of walkers. These wheeled seats can occasionally be dangerous (especially around stairs), and they don't give babies much opportunity to exercise their arms.

THE EFFECTS OF EARLY VISUAL EXPERIENCE. Although babies need to have experience in moving around in the world in order to become afraid of heights, experience is not necessary for the development of most aspects of vision—for example, depth perception and color vision. Babies do not have to *learn* to see the world in three dimensions and in full color. The sense of color is weak at birth and depth perception is absent, but this is because the various parts of the visual system are not yet completely developed. These parts have to undergo some additional physical maturation before they are in complete working order (Banks and Salapatek, 1983).

Although babies do not have to learn to see, their visual experiences in the first months of life are nonetheless important. If a baby *fails* to have normal visual experiences during this period, the physical structure of his visual system can be permanently affected. In our discussion of the development of the nervous system (Chapter 4), we said that useless or erroneous neural cells and connections are eliminated in the first months of life. Neurons and synapses are kept or discarded on the basis of experience—on what proves to be useful, what turns out to be unnecessary. Thus, the structure of the nervous system is not entirely determined in advance—there is a certain amount of flexibility, or what neurologists call **plasticity.** This plasticity enables the brain to tailor itself to the environment: the neural circuits that work best in one environment may be worthless in another.

But plasticity has its disadvantages, too. The clearest example of a disadvantage involves stereoscopic vision. The binocular cells in the brain simply disappear—or become some other kind of cell—if they do not receive inputs from both eyes in the first few months of life.

Much of the data we have on this topic was gathered by two Nobel-prize-winning neurologists from Harvard Medical School, David Hubel and Thorsten Wiesel. Their subjects were not humans, but cats and monkeys. The monkey's visual system is very similar to that of humans; even a cat's is not that different.

What Hubel and Wiesel found was that an animal's visual system could be permanently impaired if one of its eyes was kept covered for a few weeks early in its life. If, during this period, the binocular cells in the brain receive inputs from one eye only, they cease to be binocular cells. Even when the animal is later allowed to see through its covered-up eye, these cells no longer respond to inputs from that eye. The animal is **stereoblind**—it lacks stereoscopic vision (Hubel and Wiesel, 1970; Wiesel, 1975).

According to one estimate, 2 percent of human children and adults are stereoblind (Julesz, 1971). Stereoblindness will result if a baby is born with crossed eyes and they are not corrected by surgery in the early months of life. It may also result from anything that impairs the sight of one eye, even if the impairment is temporary. Crossed eyes or the impairment of vision in one eye may also lead to **amblyopia,** sometimes called "lazy eye." Amblyopia is the failure to use one eye for vision, even though the eye itself may be perfectly normal. The "lazy" eye is, in effect, partially blind. But the blindness is not in the eye itself: it's in the brain, where the part of the cortex that is normally assigned to that eye has been taken away (because it wasn't being used) and given some other job.

By the time a baby is 4 or 5 months old, his eyes should be well coordinated and seldom look crossed. If they are still turning in or out, the baby may have a muscular imbalance or a visual problem such as nearsightedness or farsightedness in one eye. If the condition is not corrected before the baby is about a year old, he may become permanently stereoblind and will probably have amblyopia as well. There is still time to improve the child's appearance —crossed eyes can be corrected by surgery at any age—but it will be too late to save the binocular cells in the brain (von Noorden, 1985).

This makes it sound as though the plasticity of the brain has mainly harmful effects. However, plasticity is very beneficial in some situations. For example, if a child receives an injury to some part of her brain, other areas can take over the functions of the damaged portions. The earlier in life the damage occurs, the more completely the brain can compensate for it. But even in late adulthood, a person who has lost the ability to speak because the language portion of her brain was destroyed by a stroke is often able to recover that ability (Rubin, 1989).

OBJECT PERCEPTION. Experts no longer think that the infant sees the world as a "blooming, buzzing confusion," but does that mean that small babies perceive the world pretty much the same way we do? For example, if a baby reaches toward a brightly colored toy, can we assume that she actually sees it as an object, and not simply as an interesting patch of contrasting color or brightness? Until recently, most researchers doubted that babies perceived objects as unified, distinct things, separate from their surroundings.

The work of Elizabeth Spelke, of the University of Pennsylvania, has shed new light on this question. Spelke and her colleagues have done some interesting experiments with 3- and 4-month-old babies—too young to have had much experience in reaching for objects. Using a habituation procedure, Spelke (1982) showed that when two objects are placed next to each other with their surfaces touching, babies see them as one object. When the two objects aren't touching, even if one is in front of the other so that it's partly blocking it from view, they're seen as two separate things. In another study, babies were shown a rod moving back and forth behind another object in such a way that the top and bottom of the rod were visible but its middle was not. Babies saw this as a single, unified rod with its middle blocked out—just the way an adult sees it. The babies didn't perceive the top and bottom pieces of the rod as two separate things, even though the connecting part was not visible (Kellman and Spelke, 1983).

So a baby sees objects as unified—as one object—if the various parts of them move together or if they have no empty space between them. These same principles also work for things that are touched and felt, rather than seen. Four-month-old babies were given two rings to hold, one in each hand. A sheet blocked their view of their hands and the rings—the babies could only *feel* the rings, not see them. Sometimes the two rings were connected by a wooden bar, so that the rings and the bar formed one inflexible object; sometimes the rings were connected by an elastic cord so that they could be moved independently. The researchers found that the babies could tell the two types of motion apart and that only the rings with the wooden bar between them were perceived as a single object (Streri and Spelke, 1988).

Thus, whether they are using vision or their sense of touch, babies tend to perceive unitary, solid objects as unitary, solid objects—very much the way the rest of us do.

Hearing

A baby is born with his eyes in working order but he has had no previous opportunity to use them: there was not much to see inside the uterus except for slight differences in darkness or brightness. But Michael's ears had already been functioning for three months or more before he was born, and there were definitely things to hear during that time. In the last third of her pregnancy, Michael's mother noticed that her child would "jump" if a loud noise, such as a car horn, sounded nearby. The assorted thumps, swishes, and gurgles of her heart and digestive system must have been clearly audible to him.

There is good evidence that babies can also hear the sound of their mother's voice before they are born. Experiments have shown that babies only three days old can distinguish their mother's voice from the voices of other mothers, and that they prefer listening to their own mother's voice (DeCasper and Fifer, 1980). Their preference was probably based on what they were able to hear *before* they were born, rather than on their three days of experience since birth. This conclusion was supported by another experiment, in which pregnant women were asked to read a story out loud twice a day during the last few weeks of their pregnancy. After the babies were born, they were allowed to choose to listen either to that story or to another one (the rate at which they sucked on a pacifier determined which story they would hear). Almost all the babies chose to listen to the story that had been read to them before they were born (DeCasper and Spence, 1986).

Even very young babies seem to be particularly attuned to the sounds of human speech. Newborns who have heard a recording of a repeated speech sound such as "ti-ti-ti-ti" will stop paying attention to it, but will listen with renewed attention if a new sound, such as "pah-pah-pah-pah," is played (Weiss, Zelazo, and Swain, 1988). Month-old infants can detect subtle differences between two speech sounds: after they have habituated to a recording that goes "pah-pah-pah," they will respond to a new recording that goes "bah-bah-bah," and vice versa (Eimas, 1975).

The odd thing is that babies can hear the difference between some speech sounds that adults cannot tell apart. There are many speech sounds that have separate meanings in some languages but are lumped together in others. People who learn to speak a language that doesn't distinguish between a certain pair of speech sounds eventually lose the ability to hear the difference between those two sounds. Babies can distinguish these speech sounds from birth, so they can discriminate between two sounds that appear identical to their parents. A study of babies in Kenya, Africa, showed that the Kenyan babies could hear a difference between two speech sounds that were treated as a single sound in Kikuyu, the language their parents spoke (Streeter, 1976).

A researcher in Toronto wanted to find out whether young Canadian babies could distinguish two sounds used in the Czechoslovakian language. She ordered a tape recording of the two sounds. When it came she thought the language lab must have made a mistake—no matter how many times she listened to the tape, she heard only a single sound, repeated again and again. But when she phoned the lab to complain, they told her there was no mistake: the sounds were different. And sure enough, although she couldn't hear the difference between the two sounds, the Canadian babies in her experiment could (Maurer and Maurer, 1988).

SOUND LOCALIZATION. Some years ago, a psychologist named Michael Wertheimer, whose specialty is perception, performed a simple test on his brand new baby daughter. He clicked a metal "cricket" noisemaker to the baby's right, and the baby turned her eyes to the right. When he clicked it on the left, the baby looked to the left. This baby was only a few minutes old! Similar results have since been found with many other newborns, though perhaps not quite as new as the Wertheimer baby. But this ability to localize sounds—to respond to the direction the sound is coming from—appears to be only a reflex: like other surprising abilities found in newborns, it disappears after a month or two. In this case, however, the disappearance is a brief one:

babies regain their ability to tell what direction a sound is coming from by the time they're about 4 months old (Wertheimer, 1961; Muir, 1985).

A newborn is better at localizing high-pitched sounds than low-pitched ones, so he is more likely to look at his mother when she talks than at his father when he does. The baby seems to make the connection between his mother's voice and his mother's face at a very early age, and he expects them to appear in the same place. One researcher devised a setup in which a stranger's voice seemed to come from the baby's mother, or the mother's voice came from the stranger's face. Babies as young as 2 weeks of age reacted by turning actively away from the confusing stimuli in apparent dismay (Carpenter, 1975). In another experiment the baby saw his mother in one location and heard her voice (through a loudspeaker) coming from another location. This, too, was a distressing experience for young infants (Aronson and Rosenbloom, 1971). It appears that babies are able, quite early in life, to associate what they hear with what they see.

The Link between Vision and Hearing

Piaget believed that infants are at first totally unable to coordinate the perceptions from two different senses such as vision and hearing. Along with most other theorists of the time, Piaget felt that a child must learn through long experience that certain sounds and certain sights bear some relationship to each other—that they "go together." The ability to make this sort of connection is called **intermodal perception.**

Recent evidence shows that babies are much better at intermodal perception than Piaget had supposed. They are so good at it, in fact, that it seems unlikely they could have learned about the complicated relationship between the various senses through experience alone. Babies must have some kind of built-in tendency to associate what they see with what they hear or feel. A number of experiments have shown that they do make these connections. In one, babies saw two films of women talking, shown side by side. A loudspeaker located between the two screens played the soundtrack from one of the films—the sound of one of the women talking. These 4-month-old babies were able to coordinate the sound with the appropriate film: they watched the film that matched the sound and not the film that didn't (Spelke and Cortelyou, 1981). In another experiment, babies saw a film of an angry-looking woman on one side and a film of a happy-looking one on the other. When an angry voice was played they generally looked at the angry woman; when a happy one was played they looked at the happy woman (Walker, 1982).

How much of this ability is due to built-in connections between the senses? How much of it is due to rapid learning of what to expect, based on the babies' experiences since birth? The relationship between innate factors and learning was examined in a recent experiment. Three-month-old babies watched a film that showed a clear plastic cylinder being shaken up and down; either one large marble or many small ones were visible inside the cylinder. At the same time, a soundtrack played a rattling sound. Some babies heard the soundtrack that was appropriate to the film—the recording was made with the right number of marbles in the cylinder and it was synchronized with the picture. Other babies heard a soundtrack with an inappropriate kind of rattling or heard it out of synchrony. Only the babies who heard the appropriate, synchronized soundtrack were able to learn the connection between the picture and the sound (as shown by their later performance in a preference test). They made this connection extremely quickly: it took only 2 minutes of watching the film paired with the appropriate soundtrack. The researcher concluded that babies do learn to associate sights with sounds and that they can do this on the basis of a very small amount of experience. However, they can accomplish this only if the sight and the sound are well matched, so they must have a built-in tendency to link up a given sight with the appropriate sound (Bahrick, 1988).

"Newborns," says Lewis Lipsitt of Brown University, "come into the world with all of their sensory systems functioning at a level that enables them to assimilate and 'appreciate' their environment" (1980, p. 96). Lipsitt and his colleagues have conducted a number of studies on babies' responses to tastes and smells.

Taste

A newborn infant sucking on a nipple doesn't suck steadily—she sucks in bursts and pauses. If each time she sucks she receives a drop of a sweet liquid such as sugar water, her rhythm of sucking will depend on the sweetness of the liquid. The sweeter it is, the more times she will suck per burst, with shorter and fewer pauses between bursts. But—and here's what seems odd at first—the sweeter the liquid, the slower she will suck within a burst. Lipsitt explains it this way:

> The slower sucking . . . suggests that the baby is savoring fluid that goes into his/her mouth. The phenomenon is not unlike that found in adults who tend to slow down their sucking and licking behavior when savoring an especially delectable substance.   (1980, p. 81)

If the baby is switched from a sweet liquid to one that is less sweet, she will react with apparent "distaste" by sucking less—less than if she hadn't first tasted the sweeter substance. For this reason, Lipsitt warns that it is unwise to try to "prime a baby with something very sweet before putting the baby to the breast" (p. 93). The baby is more likely to reject the milk after a taste of sugar water.

Babies don't have to learn to like sweet-tasting substances—the preference is innate. So is their dislike of sour and bitter tastes: if a researcher puts a drop of something sour or bitter on a newborn's tongue she will screw up her face in an expression of dismay and disgust, though she does not cry or gag. The reaction to a salty taste is less consistent; in fact, it is not at all clear that babies can tell the difference between a salty fluid and plain water. This can occasionally have tragic results: three newborns in a hospital were given formulas that had mistakenly been made with salt instead of sugar. The babies drank the mixture without complaint, and all died. But even with sour and bitter mixtures, which babies clearly don't like, they will usually go on drinking. Their reflex to suck and swallow is so strong that they seem to be unable to stop (Rosenstein and Oster, 1988; Maurer and Maurer, 1988).

Smell

The sense of smell is fully developed at birth. Newborn infants demonstrate the same clear-cut likes and dislikes as adults. The smell of rotten eggs causes them to grimace in apparent disgust and to turn their heads away. The smell of vanilla or honey is evidently pleasant to them—sometimes they will even smile when they get a whiff of these scents (Steiner, 1979).

Perhaps babies are even more sensitive to smells than older people are. Research has shown that a baby as young as 2 weeks of age can distinguish his own mother from other women purely by the sense of smell. In this experiment, cotton pads that the mothers had worn under their clothing were hung near the babies' heads. The babies tended to turn their heads toward the pads worn by their own mothers, in preference to those worn by other women (Cernoch and Porter, 1985).

The Skin Senses

Traditionally, there are supposed to be five senses, of which the fifth is commonly called "touch." But touch itself actually consists of several different senses: sensitivity to pressure, to pain, to heat, and to cold (the four **skin senses**); and **proprioception,** the sense that tells you the positions of the parts of your body even when your eyes are closed. When the parts of your body are moving, the sense that tells you the direction and speed of their movement is called **kinesthesis.** We'll discuss proprioception and kinesthesis in the next section, under visual–motor coordination.

Sensitivity to pressure begins very early in prenatal life: several months before it's due to be born, a fetus will twitch if its skin is touched (for instance, during amniocentesis). A newborn infant responds to touches on various parts of her body with the reflexes described earlier—a touch on the cheek, for example, produces the rooting reflex. Babies also show that they can tell approximately *where* they are touched. An irritating stimulus on her nose or on her leg will cause the neonate to swipe in the appropriate direction with her hand or her other leg. Mild stimulation of a baby's skin—for instance, patting her on the stomach—will sometimes temporarily soothe a fussy baby. The stronger stimulation produced by swaddling (wrapping a young baby tightly in cloth) is more effective and is used for that purpose in many societies.

How sensitive to pain is a newborn baby? This is currently a controversial topic and one that is very difficult to answer. Babies let out loud, shrill cries in response to procedures such as circumcision (the surgical removal of the sheath of skin that covers the tip of the penis in male babies). On the other hand, they calm down quickly as soon as the procedure is over (Porter, Miller, and Marshall, 1986).

Daphne Maurer, the Canadian authority on newborns whom we mentioned earlier in this chapter, thinks that young babies are not very sensitive to pain because they haven't had enough experience to know which sensations are normal and which aren't, and only abnormal sensations are perceived as pain. According to Maurer and her co-author (her husband),

> Fewer stimuli seem abnormal to them. Therefore, they are less likely than adults to feel pain. An indication of how much less comes from the pediatric ophthalmological clinic where we have one of our laboratories. We routinely study babies just one month old when they are first being fitted with a hard contact lens to replace the eye's natural lens after surgical removal of a congenital cataract. When a skilled technician inserts the lens (which takes less than a second), the babies seem to take no notice at all, nor do they later seem in the least bothered by it. Yet to an adult, a mote in the eye

feels painful, and it takes days of inurance before a hard contact lens stops feeling like an implanted chisel.   (Maurer and Maurer, 1988, p. 35)

But the fact that babies don't mind contact lenses doesn't mean that they don't mind getting jabbed with a safety pin. It is better to assume that babies feel pain just as much as the rest of us do, until we have firm evidence to the contrary.

Motor Development

Among the most striking characteristics of the newborn human is his lack of motor abilities. Michael can't do very much with his body—his arms and legs wave around pretty much at random. From the neck up, however, he is considerably more sophisticated: he can already turn his head from side to side; open, close, and move his eyes; suck and swallow; open and close his mouth; and move his tongue around. Within a few weeks he will be able to hold his head up steadily and look around when he is on his stomach or is held upright.

In general, motor development proceeds in a cephalocaudal pattern—it starts at the top and works its way down. Michael will gain control of his head before he can use his hands for accurate reaching. He will use his hands for reaching before he can use his legs for walking. Table 5–2 shows the average ages at which American children achieve the major motor milestones. The table also lists the age ranges within which 90 percent of children achieve these milestones.

Motor development also follows a proximodistal pattern, which means that it proceeds from the center of the body outwards toward the extremities. Mastery of the legs and arms comes before mastery of the feet and hands; progress is made from large muscles to small ones. For example, reaching and grasping actions start with clumsy swipes at an object, using mostly arm muscles rather than hand muscles. Grasping at first is with four fingers

TABLE 5–2
Motor Milestones and When They Are Achieved

MOTOR BEHAVIOR	AVERAGE AGE IN MONTHS	USUAL RANGE IN MONTHS
Sits with support	2.3	1 to 5
Sits alone steadily	6.6	5 to 9
Stands up holding on to furniture	8.6	6 to 12
Crawls	10.0	7 to 14
Stands alone	11.0	9 to 16
Walks alone	11.7	9 to 17
Walks downstairs alone (both feet on each step)	25.8	19 to over 30

Based on the Bayley Scales of Infant Development (Bayley, 1969) and the Denver Developmental Screening Test (Frankenburg and Dodds, 1967).

A 5-month-old baby grasps things with his whole hand, but a 1-year-old (like this toddler) can use his thumb and forefinger to pick up small objects.

against the palm, then with the thumb and palm, then with thumb and fingers. Finally, at the end of the first year, a baby can pick up very small objects with his thumb and index finger.

Maturation versus Experience

Esther Thelen, a behavioral biologist at the University of Indiana, has described how babies gear themselves up for motor milestones by repeating certain movements over and over again, in a rhythmic fashion. Such repetitive movements, which include kicking, rocking, waving, and bouncing, take up an average of 5 percent of an infant's day. Thelen has observed that babies tend to perform certain types of motions shortly before the appearance of a motor milestone that uses the same group of muscles:

> For example, kicking movements had their greatest frequency just before the onset of locomotion [crawling and walking]. . . . Rocking on hands and knees appeared just before crawling, and rhythmical hand and arm movements appeared before complex manual skills.   (Thelen, 1981, p. 239)

A reasonable interpretation of these observations is that babies learn to crawl and walk through practice—they repeat the movements until they get good at them. But it is also possible that motor milestones in human babies are achieved mainly through *maturation.* Maturation is development that is due to the carrying out of plans pre-programmed in the genes, and not to the child's actions or experiences. It occurs when the child reaches a certain age or size, and is more or less independent of environmental influences and practice.

An early experiment on the question of maturation versus practice involved tadpoles, the fishlike creatures that grow up to become frogs. Frogs' eggs are transparent, so the tadpoles are visible even before the eggs hatch. Thus, it is possible to see that tadpoles begin to make swimming movements with their tails before they are hatched, and that these movements gradually become smoother and more vigorous. The tadpoles are able to swim as soon as they are hatched. For the experiment, which was performed in the 1920s, a researcher kept unhatched tadpoles under light anesthesia for several days. Their growth was unaffected but they couldn't move. As soon as the anesthetic wore off, however, the tadpoles were able to swim just as well as unanesthetized tadpoles that had been practicing swimming movements for several days. The experimenter concluded that the swimming of tadpoles results from maturation and not from practice (Carmichael, 1927). Thus, the ability of tadpoles to move around in their environment appears to be determined by the animals' genes; experience plays no role.

The results of another experiment performed at about the same time suggested that in human babies, too, the ability to move around is largely a function of maturation. A pair of identical twin girls were the subjects. One twin was given lessons in stair-climbing; the other wasn't. At a year of age the trained baby could crawl up a flight of stairs far more rapidly than her untrained twin. But only two weeks later the untrained twin caught up and could climb the stairs as quickly as her sister (Gesell and Thompson, 1929).

A third study, a decade later, involved Hopi Indian babies who spent most of their first year of life tightly swaddled and strapped to a cradleboard, in the traditional Hopi manner. These babies learned to walk at the same age—about 15 months—as other Hopi children who hadn't been tied down (Dennis and Dennis, 1940).

A Hopi Indian baby strapped to a cradleboard.

All these findings seem to imply that the motor milestones of human babies occur at a certain stage of physical maturation and that experience doesn't much matter. However, these studies leave some questions unanswered. Traditionally reared Hopi babies were removed from their cradleboards before they were a year old. Thus, those babies had at least three months to ready themselves for walking. In the stair-climbing experiment, the "trained" twin was simply moved passively up the stairs in the practice sessions. Probably a better way to prepare for stair-climbing is to practice crawling around on the floor. Both twins were evidently allowed to do that.

It is true that normal children reared in a normal environment will invariably learn to sit, to stand, and to walk. But under certain extreme conditions the normal schedule of events can be interfered with. Children who were reared under very deprived conditions in an orphanage in Lebanon were very delayed in their motor development. These children were kept in bare cribs, with nothing to look at and nothing to do. They received a minimum of adult attention. Some of these children couldn't sit alone at 1 year or walk at 2 (Dennis, 1973).

Motor development can also be speeded up somewhat. Earlier in this chapter we described an experiment in which babies under 2 months of age were given practice in using the walking reflex. Later these babies learned to walk unusually early. Although the walking reflex usually disappears by the time a baby is 2 or 3 months old, it didn't disappear in the practiced babies (Zelazo, 1983).

But speeding up motor development in this way may not be such a good idea. Babies may tend to fall more easily if they walk at an unusually early age, because their bodies are quite top-heavy during the first year of life. They may tend to "get into trouble" more quickly, since walking is faster than crawling and they lack the cognitive skills that would serve to keep them out of danger. Even Philip Zelazo, the researcher who discovered that early practice leads to early walking, has his doubts: "I don't think there's any benefit to being a few weeks earlier in walking. It's more of an issue for scientists who are trying to understand more about early motor development" (quoted in Schuman, 1985, p. 75).

Visual–Motor Coordination

Sitting, crawling, and walking are motor skills—to do them, all the baby needs is her own sturdy little body and the surface beneath it. But reaching for an interesting-looking object, or stacking one block on another block, or getting a spoon under a piece of food, or drawing a circle are **visual–motor skills:** the baby must learn to guide her movements by what she sees. Another name for this ability is **eye–hand coordination.**

Reaching for a visible object is the earliest form of eye–hand coordination. Under certain conditions, babies may swat at objects even in the first month of life. In general, however, reaching for things doesn't begin in earnest until babies are about 4 months old. At this age, for the first time, the majority of the babies' reaches hit their target. But they are still very poor at grasping an object they reach for: they may contact it with the wrong part of their hand, or close their hand too soon or too late. By 5 to 6 months, most babies are able to grasp the objects they reach for, using arm movements to bring the hand to the object and hand movements to grasp it (von Hofsten and Fazel-Zandy, 1984).

By moving her hand and watching it move, the baby gets visual feedback that helps her to gain control over her hand and arm movements.

What is going on during the first four or five months of life, before babies are able to do much in the way of successful grasping? What the babies are doing during this period is watching their own hands. They are, in fact, quite fascinated by the sight of their moving hands. It may be precisely this fascination that keeps 1- or 2-month-old babies from reaching for things. When a baby of this age sees something she might start to reach for it, but then she catches sight of her hand—and her attention immediately switches to her hand. At 1 or 2 months, a baby can't pay attention both to an object and to her hand. The hand wins (Bower, 1977).

But all this gazing at the hand will soon make accurate reaching possible. By moving her hand and watching it move, the baby is getting **visual feedback** from her actions—she's seeing the visible results of what happens when she directs a particular set of muscles to contract. She's also developing accurate proprioception and kinesthesis in her hands and arms—a sense of exactly where the parts of her body are and which way they are moving. These senses can't be built in, the way accurate vision is, because the limbs (unlike the eyes) change so drastically in size during development. So the greater accuracy of the visual system is used to "calibrate" proprioception and kinesthesis: the baby comes to feel her arms and legs in the positions she sees them in, and to feel them moving the way she sees them move (Harris, 1980).

The brain devotes much more space to vision than to any other type of sensation; from infancy on, vision is dominant over the other senses. If you

Problems in Development

Box 5-2
Sudden Infant Death

Stephen Richard Raring was born on November 18, 1970, in Washington, D.C. He was what we called in Chapter 2 an "easy baby"—good-natured, adaptable, and regular in his habits. In his routine medical checkups, his pediatrician gave him a clean bill of health.

Here's how Stephen's father describes the last day of his son's life:

> On February 8, 1971, just short of 12 weeks of age, he awoke at his usual time of 7 a.m., and had his early liquid breakfast, as usual, followed by a period of conversation with his mother, a short nap, a bath, more conversation and play, and a second breakfast, became sleepy—again on schedule—and did not object to retiring for his regular 11 a.m. nap. During the next hour his mother looked in to see that all was well—again a usual procedure. The third time she found him face down in the center of his crib—in a non-normal position and very still. (Raring, 1975, p. 42)

Stephen was dead—a victim of what used to be called "crib death" and is now called **sudden infant death syndrome,** or **SIDS.**

The next 24 hours were a nightmare for Stephen's parents. The doctor on duty at the emergency room of Georgetown University Hospital pronounced Stephen dead, "cause unknown." An autopsy was ordered. A homicide detective arrived at the Rarings' home to question them— child abuse is often suspected in cases of SIDS. The

next morning, Stephen's father had to go to the morgue to identify his son's corpse. The tiny body, with the marks of the autopsy clearly visible, lay on a gray slab. Raring describes these painful events in the third person: "When the father was able to speak," he says, "he identified the body of his dead son."

The hospital sent the Rarings a bill for their services, but provided them with no information about the cause of the baby's death. It was the Rarings' own pediatrician who told them that Stephen had died of SIDS. But the emergency-room doctor was correct, in a way: the precise cause of SIDS was unknown in 1971. And, though there have been many promising theories in the intervening years, the cause of SIDS is still unknown.

There have always been theories of SIDS, because SIDS has always been with us. An early theory is recorded in the Old Testament, in one of the stories about King Solomon: "And this woman's child died in the night, because she overlaid it." When babies slept in the same beds with their mothers, it was reasonable to suppose that the mothers caused these deaths by rolling onto their babies. When it became customary to keep the baby in a separate bed, the death was blamed on suffocation by a blanket (although even a newborn can push a blanket out of the way) or by a cat (the cat was supposed to have "sucked the life" out of the baby!).

What makes SIDS so puzzling is that ordinarily there are no signs of a struggle; parents who have been nearby have heard no sounds of distress. The baby goes to sleep in the usual way and, while he's asleep, he simply stops breathing. In the United

---

see something happen in one place and the sound comes from somewhere else, as with a ventriloquist and his dummy, your vision will dominate and you will perceive the sounds as coming from the dummy's mouth. Similarly, if an experimenter puts you in a situation (using mirrors, perhaps) in which vision and touch disagree—you see one thing and feel another—your vision will triumph and your sense of touch will be disbelieved. Visual dominance begins quite early in life: by 5 or 6 months of age. This is when the movements of the hand come under the close control of vision. Infants older than 5 months are likely to get upset, or to refuse to play the game, if you ask them to handle an object but prevent them from seeing their hands. The ability to learn things through the sense of touch alone is virtually absent in babies between 5 and 20 months, and is poor in older babies. The hands serve mainly to do the eyes' bidding: to bring an object closer to the face and to turn it this way and that, so the eyes can see it from all angles (Hatwell, 1987).

States an estimated 7000 infants die each year in this way—it's the leading killer of babies between 1 month and 1 year of age. SIDS claims about one infant out of every 500, most often when they are 2 or 3 months old. Deaths due to SIDS are rare in the first month of life (Naeye, 1980).

Because many babies who die of SIDS have symptoms resembling those caused by suffocation, medical research has for a long time focused on the respiratory system. According to one theory of SIDS, these babies were born with inadequate breathing reflexes. All babies stop breathing for brief periods from time to time, but some babies seem to have a weaker-than-normal impulse to begin again and to "catch up." Pediatricians have attempted to identify such babies and to protect them by hooking them up to monitors that sound an alarm if the baby stops breathing. But these efforts have not proved successful: the number of crib deaths has not decreased since the use of monitors became common (Blakeslee, 1989).

Most SIDS deaths occur while the baby is sleeping, so some researchers have proposed that SIDS may be due to a disturbance of the sleep-wake cycle. Perhaps these babies sleep too deeply and are unable to wake up in time if something interferes with their breathing (Navelet and others, 1984). But if this were the case, why is it that parents are sometimes unable to revive a baby who has stopped breathing, even if they are trained in resuscitation techniques and begin their efforts as soon as the monitor sounds the alarm?

The latest theories focus on the nervous system. One blames SIDS on abnormalities in the nerves that regulate the heartbeat: if the nerves to the two sides of the heart develop unevenly, this would cause the heart to beat irregularly and, eventually, to stop beating (Rosen and Johnson, 1988). Another theory places the abnormalities in the brain, in the areas that control breathing, heartbeat, or even the muscles of the tongue (Blakeslee, 1989).

Eventually we may find that the deaths lumped under the SIDS label do not have a single cause—several factors may be operating at once, or there may be different causes in different babies. About half the babies who succumb to SIDS had mild colds at the time of their deaths, which suggests that infection may play a role in some cases. This would explain why breast-fed babies are less likely to die of SIDS than bottle-fed babies: breast milk conveys partial immunity to many viruses and bacteria, so breast-fed babies are more resistant to infections.

A number of other factors are associated with an increased risk of SIDS. Babies whose mothers used narcotics or cocaine during pregnancy have the highest rates of SIDS (Rosen and Johnson, 1988). Cigarette smoking by the mother also significantly increases the risk to the child. SIDS babies are more likely to have had low Apgar scores and to have weighed less than 5½ pounds (2500 g) at birth. Boys are at greater risk than girls, later-borns are at greater risk than firstborns. But these are just statistics. They're of little consolation to the non-smoking, non-drug-using parents of a firstborn girl who weighed 7½ pounds at birth, who was breast-fed, and who appeared to be in perfect health at the time of her death.

From Infancy to Toddlerhood: Physical Growth

Another noteworthy characteristic of the human newborn is his small size. Michael's weight is only about one-eighteenth of his mother's weight; his length is less than a third of his mother's height. Within a year he will add 10 inches (25 cm) to his height, 15 pounds (7 kg) to his weight. Then his rate of growth will slow considerably. Dramatic changes in size and shape won't occur again until adolescence.

Many people wonder whether it is possible to predict from a baby's size how tall he or she will be as an adult. For a newborn baby, the answer is *no:* size at birth correlates hardly at all with size at maturity. In fact, we can do a better job of predicting ultimate height by ignoring the baby's size at birth and measuring the parents instead.

The future height of the individual child begins to be detectable early in the first year: babies destined to be tall adults will grow faster than those destined to be short. By age 2 there is already a good indication of how tall the child will eventually become—height at age 2 correlates .80 with height at maturity. We can make a rough estimate of eventual adult height by doubling the height at 2 years for a boy or multiplying it by 1.9 for a girl. But that estimate is only an approximation—it may be off by as much as 2 or 3 inches, one way or the other (Tanner, 1978).

Gender Differences in Growth

The formulas we just gave for predicting height mean that a boy has achieved about half of his adult height by age 2. A girl has achieved more than half of her adult height, despite the fact that since birth she's been slightly shorter and slightly lighter in weight than her male agemates. To put it another way, a 2-year-old girl is physically closer to being an adult than a 2-year-old boy is. As early as four months before birth, female fetuses are physically more mature than male fetuses. At birth there is a difference of four to six weeks in physical maturity (Tanner, 1978).

The Brain after Birth

Almost all the cells in our bodies continue to divide after birth—continue, in fact, all our lives, so that dead or damaged cells can be replaced with new ones. Neurons are an exception. For some reason, neurons lose their ability to divide at about nine months after conception. The 100 billion neurons in the brain of that newborn baby are just about all he's ever going to have. And yet his brain is only a quarter of the size of an adult brain. In six months it will have almost doubled in weight; in two years it will have tripled.

What causes this rapid increase in brain size, if there is no increase in the number of neurons? Three factors are involved. The first is **myelination.** During the first years of life, many neurons develop a coating of a fatty substance called **myelin.** This insulating jacket greatly speeds the transmission of neural signals. One consequence of this is that the brain works faster and more efficiently.

The second factor is an increase in another type of cell in the brain, called the **glial cell,** whose chief function is to support and nourish the neurons. Glial cells continue to multiply in number all through childhood; by adulthood they outnumber the neurons by about 10 to 1. If a neuron dies it is not replaced—instead, the gap is filled by a glial cell. (But don't worry too much about your neurons dying. It has been estimated that only 3 percent of the brain's neurons die during a normal lifetime.)

The third cause of brain growth after birth is an increase in the size of the neurons themselves: they send out more branches, form more synapses (junctions) with other neurons. The rate of formation of new synapses is extremely rapid during the first year of life. On the other hand, the rate of pruning out of unneeded synapses is also high. These two factors, reflecting both the physical maturation of the brain and the effects of the infant's experiences during the first months of life, underlie many of the important developmental changes that occur during this period (Fischer, 1987).

The newborn isn't just smaller than an adult: he's shaped differently. His body proportions are different. Compared with an older child or an adult, his limbs are very short, his head is very large. In fact, the head makes up only an eighth of an adult's total height, but it's a full quarter of the baby's length. Before birth the head is even larger, compared to the rest of the body. We might say that the head is "physically more mature" than the rest of the body, because all during prenatal life, infancy, and childhood, it is closer to its adult size than any other part of the body (except the eyes). The head grows rapidly during infancy and early childhood; by age 10 its growth is virtually complete, although the body as a whole has reached only about half of its adult weight.

A big head is characteristic not only of human babies—it's characteristic of animal babies as well. In general, the young of all warm-blooded species have small limbs and bodies and relatively large heads. The head itself is proportioned differently from an adult's: the eyes are comparatively large and are located lower down on the head; the other features are small and close together. As you can see in Figure 5–3, these characteristics make a face look babyish and cute. Human babies have other characteristics that add to their appeal, such as soft skin, long eyelashes, pink lips, and round cheeks (Berry and McArthur, 1986).

Changes in Body Proportions

FIGURE 5-3
The location and relative size of the facial features are what determine whether a face looks babyish and cute.

CUTENESS COUNTS. Newborn babies are totally dependent on other, older members of their species. This is true of all baby mammals—a newborn kitten, calf, rabbit, or monkey will usually die if its mother abandons it. But mammal mothers don't ordinarily abandon their young. A female rat will repeatedly cross an electrified grid in order to reach her squealing pups, even though she gets a shock that is painful enough to keep her away from food when she is hungry, from water when she is thirsty (Warden, 1931). Even female animals that have never given birth, even (in some cases) male animals, will nurture young members of their species. And even the boundaries between species do not necessarily interfere with this willingness to nurture: mother cats have suckled puppies, gorillas have cuddled kittens, humans of both sexes have tenderly bottle-fed the orphaned young of virtually every mammal on the face of the earth.

Konrad Lorenz, a well-known ethologist, has proposed the theory that this nurturing impulse is "released," or triggered, by the babyish features of young animals. According to Lorenz (1971), this response is innate and instinctive—in humans as well as in animals. In other words, the big heads and eyes and the small, low-set features of baby mammals evoke in most of us an automatic, involuntary response of affection and protectiveness. The existence of such an instinctive response would clearly have adaptive value for any species, since it would increase the chances that the young of that species would survive.

Whether this "maternal" reaction is due to nature or nurture, there is no question that it does exist in many humans. Moreover, it exists in males as well as females. In several studies, a majority of people of both sexes judged pictures of young humans or animals to be more appealing and likable than pictures of older humans and animals. Some of these studies found this preference to be stronger in women than in men; others found no overall difference between the sexes. However, the preference does seem to appear at an earlier age in girls than in boys. Children of both sexes under the age of 11 prefer pictures of *adult* humans and animals. Girls switch to a preference for baby humans and animals by about age 13, boys by about 17. Interestingly enough, it appears that this preference for babies is related to sexual maturity: in a study of 12- and 13-year-old girls, it was the girls who had begun to menstruate who most preferred to look at pictures of babies (Jackson and Jackson, 1978; Goldberg, Blumberg, and Kriger, 1982).

Human babies are not able to move around and find food on their own a few hours after birth, the way the young of some species can. But they can do something that's perhaps even more remarkable: they can make the older members of their species *want* to feed them and take care of them.

Summary

1. The **Apgar test** is a quick way of assessing the physical condition of a neonate (a newborn baby).

2. Babies sleep an average of 16 hours a day; roughly half of this time is spent in quiet sleep, the other half in **active (or REM) sleep.**

3. Babies' behavior can be described in terms of **states.**

Six states that have been described are active sleep, quiet sleep, drowsiness, crying, fussiness, and **quiet alertness.** The baby is most attentive to visual and auditory stimuli in the state of quiet alertness.

4. Babies are born with a number of reflexes. The most important of these are associated with breathing: breathing deepens and quickens if there is too much carbon dioxide in the blood; obstructions of the breathing passages produce coughs or sneezes. Temporary lulls in breathing are normal in newborns.

5. Reflexes associated with feeding include sucking, swallowing, and **rooting,** in which a touch on the cheek causes the baby's head to turn in that direction.

6. The **walking reflex** can be seen in newborns when they're held upright with their feet touching a solid surface. A group of babies were "walked" in this way during their first two months; later these babies began to walk independently at an earlier age than babies who hadn't had this practice.

7. Very young babies have a remarkable ability to imitate adults' facial and hand movements. This ability, which disappears by the time the baby is about 6 weeks old, appears to be a type of reflex behavior and is not related to the more complex kind of imitation found in older babies.

8. The **preferential-looking technique** is a way of finding out about a baby's visual perception. If a baby looks at one picture significantly more than at another, she must be able to see that the two pictures are different. However, even if there's no preference, the baby may still be able to see the difference. One way of finding this out is to **habituate** the baby to one picture, and then notice if she looks more at a new picture.

9. Human babies can see at birth and can track moving objects with their eyes, but things look somewhat blurry to them at first. Their vision improves rapidly and reaches near-adult levels in six or eight months.

10. Although they show little interest in color, newborns can distinguish red, orange, yellow, and green from gray; 1-month-olds can also distinguish blue and purple. Color vision is fully developed in three or four months.

11. Newborn and 1-month-old babies tend to look at the edges of patterns (or faces), rather than at what's inside them. By the fifth or sixth week, they start to look at the features inside the contours—their parents' eyes, for example.

12. Even with one eye closed you have some **depth perception**—that is, you see the world in three dimensions. But the most vivid kind of three-dimensional vision, **stereoscopic vision,** requires two eyes: it depends on the fact that the left eye's view is slightly different from the right eye's. **Binocular cells** in the brain, which receive inputs from the two eyes, are responsible for stereoscopic vision.

13. Babies do not have stereoscopic vision at birth, partly because their eyes are not perfectly coordinated at first. It takes about four months for stereoscopic vision to develop.

14. The **visual cliff** experiment showed that babies of crawling age not only can perceive depth—they are afraid of heights. Later experiments showed that babies acquire this fear not through falling, but by moving around on their own in the environment.

15. The structure of the nervous system has a certain amount of **plasticity** at first, which means that it can be affected by experiences in the early months of life. If the binocular cells do not receive inputs from both eyes during this time, **stereoblindness** will result.

16. Three- and 4-month-old babies evidently see objects the way we do—as separate, unified things. Things that are seen or felt to move independently are perceived as two objects, rather than one.

17. Fetuses are able to hear sounds in the uterus three months before they are born. Newborns can recognize sounds they heard in the uterus. They are attuned to the sounds of human speech and can hear the difference between two similar speech sounds—even some sounds that their parents cannot tell apart.

18. Newborns respond to the direction a sound is coming from by turning their heads in that direction. This ability briefly disappears but is reestablished by the time they are 4 months old.

19. Babies have a built-in tendency to associate what they see with what they hear; this ability is called **intermodal perception.**

20. Newborn infants like sweet-tasting liquids. They screw up their faces to sour and bitter tastes, but they don't show a consistent reaction to salty liquids.

21. The sense called "touch" consists of the four **skin senses** (pressure, pain, heat, and cold); plus **proprioception,** which tells us the positions of the parts of our bodies even when our eyes are closed; and **kinesthesis,** which tells us the direction and speed of movement of the parts of our bodies.

22. Motor development tends to follow a cephalocaudal pattern: it starts at the head and works its way down. It also follows a proximodistal pattern, which means that it proceeds from large muscles to small ones—babies can control their arm movements before they can control their finger movements.

23. Tadpoles' ability to swim when they are hatched is due to maturation, not to practice. There are some indications that the same may be true of motor development in humans. However, children reared under extremely deprived conditions may be delayed in their motor development. Motor development may also be speeded up somewhat—for example, in babies who are given practice in using the walking reflex.

24. Stacking blocks and reaching for objects are **visual–motor skills**—these actions require **eye–hand coordination.** Four-month-old babies usually succeed in touching objects they reach for; by 5 or 6 months they can also grasp the objects. Younger babies spend a lot of time looking at their hands. This **visual feedback** helps them to gain accurate senses of proprioception and kinesthesis.

25. Sudden infant death syndrome (SIDS) claims an estimated 1 out of 500 babies, most often when they are 2 or 3 months old, generally when they are asleep, and often when they have a cold. Its cause is still unknown.

26. Size at birth correlates hardly at all with size at maturity, but height at age 2 can be used to predict adult height. At age 2 a boy is roughly half his adult height; a girl is more than half of her adult height. Girls are physically more mature than boys all through infancy and childhood.

27. The newborn's brain is a quarter of its adult size. The brain doubles in size in the first six months and triples in size in the first two years. It will have achieved nearly all its growth by age 10.

28. The neurons in the brain do not continue to divide after birth. Increase in brain size after birth is due partly to **myelination,** which speeds neural transmission. Other factors involved in the increase in brain size are an increase in the number of **glial cells** and an increase in the size of the neurons themselves. Neurons form many new synapses in the first year of life, but there is also a high rate of pruning of unneeded synapses as a function of the baby's experiences.

29. The proportions of the baby's body are different from those of an adult: a baby's head is relatively large and the limbs are short. The big heads, high foreheads, and large, low-set eyes of baby humans and animals make them look cute and appealing.

Key Terms

—

vernix	**stepping reflex**	**intermodal perception**
lanugo	**preferential-looking technique**	**skin senses**
Apgar test	**habituation technique**	**proprioception**
active sleep	**habituate**	**kinesthesis**
REM sleep	**retina**	**visual–motor skill**
state	**depth perception**	**eye–hand coordination**
quiet alertness	**stereoscopic vision**	**visual feedback**
rooting	**binocular cells**	**sudden infant death syndrome**
Babinski reflex	**visual cliff**	**(SIDS)**
Moro reflex	**plasticity**	**myelination**
swimming reflex	**stereoblind**	**myelin**
grasp reflex	**amblyopia**	**glial cell**
walking reflex		

6

The First Social Relationships

An adult who doesn't happen to like people can get along without them. He or she can live alone and become a recluse. But living alone is hardly an option for a child, much less for an infant. Young humans don't have any choice: they *have* to associate with other people in order to survive. And the course of their lives will be very much affected by how successful these relationships are. The first relationship is the one between the baby and his or her parents. This will be of central importance during infancy and toddlerhood, and it is likely to remain important well into adulthood.

Much is known about the relationships between babies and their mothers. Much less is known about the relationships between babies and their fathers. There are three basic reasons for this difference. First, researchers in the past were less interested in father–child relationships than in mother–child relationships, so they accumulated no stockpile of data to serve as a foundation for later studies. Second, although fathers are certainly no busier than mothers, they tend to be busy in ways that make them less available to researchers.

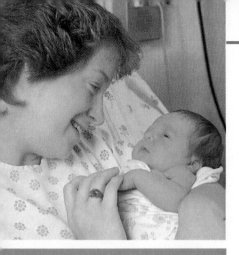

Finally, it is still the case that the mother is the primary caregiver, the one who takes chief responsibility for the baby, in the overwhelming majority of homes. This has been true in every known human culture, throughout human history (Konner, 1977a), and it is still true today (see Box 6–1). Although modern fathers may change diapers or spoon baby food into little mouths, they are not the ones who keep track of when the child has to go to the pediatrician. And, as for changing diapers and spooning baby food, they spend only about a third as much time at such chores as mothers do, even in families where the mothers are employed (Lamb, 1987; LaRossa, 1988).

In this chapter we will summarize the vast amount of data on interactions between mothers and babies. We will also tell you what is known about interactions between fathers and babies.

Parent–Infant Interactions

The newborn baby is not a particularly sociable person. Very young infants are in a receptive state—a state of quiet alertness—only for brief periods. More often they are sleeping or crying or being fed. Pediatrician T. Berry Brazelton and his colleagues have described what happens if you prop up a 1-week-old baby in an infant seat and ask the mother to "communicate" with her child.

> Our mothers were faced with the problem of communicating with infants who, if they were not crying or thrashing, were often hanging limply in the infant seat with closed or semiclosed eyes or, just as frequently, were "frozen" motionless in some strange and uninterpretable position—staring at nothing. While infants in the first few weeks did seem to look directly into the faces of their mothers, the communicative aspects of eye-to-eye contact sometimes were dampened when the mothers moved their heads and found the infants still staring off in the original direction. (Brazelton, Koslowski, and Main, 1974, p. 67)

The baby's talents as a social partner improve rapidly. During the first three weeks, a mother may occasionally notice a little smile appearing while the infant is drowsy or asleep. By the end of the third week, this smile sometimes occurs in response to the sound of her voice. Around the fifth week the baby starts to focus on her face and true eye-to-eye contact begins. By 6 or 7 weeks the baby is looking right at her and smiling, and perhaps making cooing noises as well. Social interactions have begun.

A baby's smile is a delightful event. Most parents find it irresistible—it's nearly impossible not to smile back. But eye contact may be even more important than the smile in establishing a bond between parent and child. Once eye contact is made, the parents feel that their baby is "becoming a person." Some mothers report their first feelings of love at this time (Robson, 1968). This is when parents begin playing with their babies instead of simply taking care of them.

Child psychiatrist Daniel Stern has videotaped many hundreds of hours of mothers and babies at play. He has studied three aspects of the mothers' behavior with their infants: their speech, their facial expressions, and the direction of their gaze. In all three kinds of behaviors, Stern finds, mothers act quite differently with babies than they would with an adult. Their speech contains exaggerated variations in pitch and loudness and is very slowed down, especially in the duration of the vowels:

> Hi- swee-e-e-et-ee, Hi-i-i, Hi-i-iya, watcha lookin' at?, Hu-u-uh? O-o-o-o-o-o. Yeah, it's mommy, ye-e-a-ah.   (Stern, 1974, p. 192)

Stern believes that this slowed-down "baby talk" is a better match to the baby's perceptual abilities than the pace of normal adult speech would be.
Mothers' facial expressions, too, are highly exaggerated:

> The often seen "mock surprise" expression of mothers is a good example. The eyebrows go way up, the eyes open very wide, the mouth opens and purses and usually emits a long "Ooooooooo," and the head comes up and forward, sometimes to within inches of the baby's face. This expression may take many seconds to slowly come to a full bloom and then may be held for an unusually long time. Such an expression directed toward an adult would be experienced as quite bizarre.   (p. 192)

Finally, mothers and babies gaze at each other for exceptionally long periods of time—sometimes for 30 seconds or more. Such long gazes seldom occur among adults, except between people who are in love or people who are challenging each other to a fight.
The three kinds of behavior—looking, talking, and facial expressions—generally go together. However, there is one time the gaze occurs alone: mothers often look steadily at their babies during a breast- or bottle-feeding. These gazes tend to be one-way: the infant seldom looks back. Such is the potency of social stimuli for the infant that if eye contact is made and the mother smiles or speaks, the baby may stop sucking in order to return her smile.

THE BABY'S BEHAVIOR DURING SOCIAL INTERACTIONS. During play—while the mother is speaking, gazing, and changing her facial expressions—what is the infant doing? By 2 months of age, a baby's response to a human face is already different from the response to an inanimate object. When confronted with an interesting object—say, a stuffed animal—babies look at it intently and look away only occasionally and briefly. They wave their arms around in an apparent attempt to reach for the object. In contrast, their response to a person tends to be more on-and-off in nature—a short period of gradually increasing interaction followed by a short period of withdrawal. It seems that social interactions are so intensely stimulating for young infants that they must take frequent breaks, either to avoid becoming overstimulated or to rest up for the next interaction (Tronick, 1989).
A typical interaction begins with the mother looking at the infant. The baby looks back at her and she smiles. His face brightens and he turns his body and face in her direction; he pays close attention to her. She smiles more

Playful Interactions

The Child in Society

Unburdening his soul, a man named Nicholas Morgan recently wrote in his college alumni magazine on his feelings about fatherhood. His confession begins, "It is not working out the way I figured."

"Growing up," Nicholas continues, "I knew that we were part of a generation that was going to initiate change. I saw my Dad going off to work every day . . . Mom stayed home with us kids." The time he spent with his father was limited to "a couple of hours every night and a little more on weekends." Nicholas figured that he and his wife could do better than that. "We were going to be different. . . . We were going to be fifty–fifty."

It started out in a most promising way: he put his wife through college, then she put him through college. They shared the household chores "on a strict rotation" basis. But pretty soon, "things began to slip a little." And then they had children.

> Things really slid when the kids came. Only one of the sexes can nurse a baby. Thus, the other sex must go out and drag home the woolly mammoths. . . . If I could earn the bread while Marjie nursed the children, wasn't that the most efficient division of labor? Raising children is such exhausting work that you begin to specialize. (Morgan, 1988, p. 13)

So Nicholas specialized in his professional work and in taking care of the family car and lawn, while Marjie specialized in the children and the house. It was a comment from his younger child that made Nicholas realize how far he had come from the image of the "fifty–fifty" dad he had started out with, and how much he had become like his own father. He was saying goodnight to his 5-year-old son when the boy patted him on the shoulder and told him, "Don't worry Dad, you're a great dad, even though I only see you for a few hours every night." In shock, Nicholas protested,

> "But Eric, I'm here as much as I can be. I have to bring home the woolly mammoths. Besides, I see you all weekend." "Yeah, but you're so busy, always mowing the lawn or something." I heard myself saying weakly that the work had to get done. Eric just patted me on the shoulder. (p. 14)

Nicholas thinks of his son's remark as he drives to the office every day, and he muses about the roles he plays in his children's lives: "The Breadwinner, the Slayer of Mammoths. The Guy Who Drops In and Evaluates Your Day. The Weekend Project Coordinator." That wasn't the kind of father he had intended to be.

Nicholas's experience is not unique. Many college-educated fathers start out with the idealistic goal of sharing the childrearing chores with their wives. Only it seldom seems to work out that way. Research has shown that during the first year after the baby is born, most couples become more traditional, with fathers doing less of the child care at the ninth month than they did at the third month. One father, interviewed when his daughter was 3 months old, said that he "was not going to be an absentee father . . . I love babies." But only three months later, the researcher reports,

> He had indeed become very much the absentee father. In fact, almost every evening since the first interview he had left the house after dinner to play basketball, or participate in an amateur theater group, or sing in the local choir. Since what he was doing contradicted what he said he would do, he was asked by his wife to "account" for his behavior. . . . He offered no fewer than 20 different explanations (including) "I help out more than most husbands do" and "I'm not good at taking care of the baby." At one dramatic point during the second interview, the husband and the wife got into a verbal argument over how much of the husband's contribution to child care was "fact" and how much was "fancy." (La-Rossa, 1988, p. 455)

Unfortunately, this scenario is also typical. A

broadly and begins to talk to him and touch him. He responds by widening his smile and waving his arms and legs. If she says something to him and then is quiet for a moment, he may **vocalize** (make some sounds); he is less likely to vocalize if she talks without stopping. As the intensity of the interaction builds up, the baby's movements become more vigorous. Then, gradually, he begins to relax. His smile fades and his eyes lose their bright look. At this point he appears to withdraw his attention from his mother; he looks away.

number of studies have shown that marital satisfaction declines after the first child is born. A recent investigation confirmed the finding that women are less happy with their husbands after their babies are born than they were before, and linked this to the fact that "women reported doing much more of the housework and child care than they had expected" (Ruble, Fleming, Hackel, and Stangor, 1988, p. 78).

Although men are doing more parenting than they used to, what has changed most in the past 20 years is not how the father acts after the baby is born, but how the mother and the father *feel about* how he acts. Both the mother and the father have high expectations about the father's role in childrearing. When the father fails to live up to those expectations, the mother reacts by feeling put-upon and resentful, and the father reacts by feeling guilty and resentful.

Why are the majority of men not living up to modern expectations about the father's role in childrearing? Here are two clues:

First, a study showed that men rated themselves *lower* in parenting ability after their first child was born, compared with how they rated themselves before the birth. Similarly, women's judgments of their husbands' ability to take care of children went *down* after the birth of their child (Entwisle and Doering, 1988).

Second, in one extensive investigation of parenting practices, every couple that was interviewed spoke at least once of the father "helping" the mother with child care. No parent ever said anything about the mother "helping" the father take care of the children (LaRossa and LaRossa, 1981).

So both the father and the mother see the mother as being in charge, and both see the father as playing the role of a somewhat incompetent "helper" ("I'm not good at taking care of the baby"). If someone feels incompetent at a job, he's not likely to enjoy doing it.

There is ample evidence that women come to parenthood with more knowledge of babies and

A father's eagerness to help take care of the baby is diminished if he feels that he is incompetent at the job.

children than men do. Because mothers know more about the job to begin with, they tend to take over. The father, in turn, discovers that all he has to do is to act a little more incompetent than he actually is, and he will be partially relieved of his duties. Soon the mother's slight edge in parenting skills becomes a wide gap: the mother, because she has taken over the chief responsibility, gets more practice in performing the chores of childcare and in interpreting the baby's signals. And the better she gets at it, the more impatient she becomes with her husband's performance as a "helper."

The current myth of the involved father is at odds with the reality of the father as reluctant occasional helper (Mackey, 1989). Perhaps society will eventually progress to the point where fathers really do share fifty-fifty in childrearing. Or perhaps we will discard the new myth and return to the old one: the belief that childrearing is a job that men can do, but women can do better.

But he is still aware of her, because if she now looks away, he's likely to return his gaze to her face. A brief period without eye contact seems to be what he wants. If he gets it—if the mother doesn't insist on trying to maintain his attention—he will soon be ready for another interaction, perhaps in a matter of seconds (Brazelton and others, 1974; Cohn and Tronick, 1987).

Whether the mother and baby enjoy these interactions, whether all goes smoothly, depends to a large extent on the mother's sensitivity to her baby's

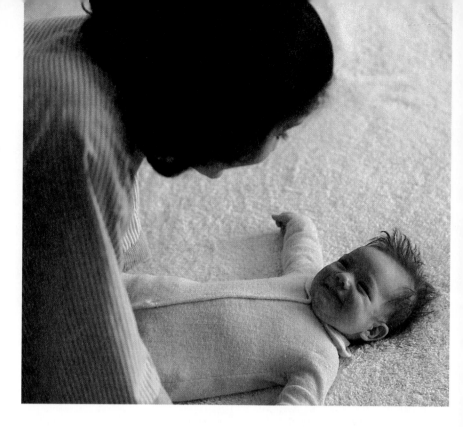

signals. If she gives him time to respond, if she allows him his "time-outs" without overwhelming him with stimulation, if she adjusts her behavior to his rhythms, then their interactions are likely to be successful. But if she ignores his signals and continues to try to get the infant's attention when he's had enough, her efforts may backfire. He may respond to her less and less. Stern describes an extreme example of an unsuccessful interaction of this kind: the case of Jenny, a 3-month-old baby girl, and her mother. Whenever Jenny looked at her mother, her mother would overwhelm her with exaggerated facial expressions, continuous speech, tickling, and so on.

> Jenny invariably broke gaze rapidly. Her mother never interpreted this temporary face and gaze aversion as a cue to lower her level of behavior, nor would she let Jenny self-control the level by gaining distance. Instead, she would swing her head around following Jenny's to reestablish the full-face position. Once the mother achieved this, she would reinitiate the same level of stimulation with a new arrangement of facial and vocal combinations. Jenny again turned away, pushing her face further into the pillow to try to break all visual contact. Again, instead of holding back, the mother continued to chase Jenny. . . . With Jenny's head now pinned in the corner, the baby's next recourse was to perform a "pass-through." She rapidly swung her face from one side to the other right past her mother's face. When her face crossed the mother's face, in the face-to-face zone, Jenny closed her eyes to avoid any mutual visual contact.   (Stern, 1977, pp. 110–111)

Having an Effect on the World

One reason why things went badly for Jenny and her mother was that Jenny's behavior didn't seem to have any effect on her mother's actions—her mother wasn't paying attention to Jenny's signals. Babies—like everyone else—get frustrated and unhappy if what they do doesn't seem to make any difference. They like to feel that people are responding to them. (Think how frustrating it is to try to communicate with someone who ignores your questions and never gives any signs of having noticed what you said.) Perhaps the feeling of having an effect on what's happening is particularly important for babies, because there are so few things they can actually *do*.

When babies find out that something they *can* do makes something else happen, they are delighted. For example, in one study mothers simply imitated the actions of their 3½-month-old babies—they did whatever their babies did. When these babies realized that they were "controlling" their mothers' behavior, they smiled and laughed. In fact, they smiled and laughed more when their mothers imitated them than when their mothers played with them in the ordinary way (Field, 1977).

Robert McCall (1979) has described how one baby reacted when her father made his own responses **contingent** (dependent) on her vocalizations. This father sat his 8-week-old baby girl on his knee, and every time she cooed or gurgled or sighed he would immediately give her a big smile, bounce her gently on his knee, and say "bumpety-bump." Since he was reinforcing her vocalizing (see the discussion of operant conditioning in Chapter 3), it's not surprising that the baby's vocalizing increased. By the third day she had turned into a real chatterbox. But the point here is that the baby delighted in this game, once she found out how to make her father go "bumpety-bump." In fact, within a week the baby was bursting into smiles and coos whenever she saw her father.

CRYING AND HELPLESSNESS. Not all babies can make their fathers go "bumpety-bump." But all babies can cry. Crying is usually the most effective way a baby has of producing a response from the people around her. A tiny baby has been known to move a full-grown adult up an entire flight of stairs, just by the force of her cries!

When parents respond reasonably quickly and reasonably consistently to their babies' cries, the babies seem to acquire what Erikson calls **basic trust.** They come to see the world as a friendly place, a place where their needs will be met, a place where what they do matters. Not surprisingly, these babies turn into reasonably contented toddlers who cry relatively little (Bell and Ainsworth, 1972).

Babies who are usually ignored are in danger of developing what has been called **learned helplessness.** They come to feel that nothing they do makes any difference, so why bother? The extreme case of this was seen in babies in old-fashioned institutions where there were too few caregivers and too many babies. The babies were fed on schedule; their cries had little or no effect on their caregivers' behavior. By the end of the first year they were crying very little, just like babies with highly responsive parents. But the institutionalized babies hadn't only stopped crying—they had stopped laughing as well. Their faces were expressionless, they showed little interest in their surroundings, and their motor and language development were retarded (Provence and Lipton, 1962).

Babies whose cries are answered promptly, and babies whose cries are not answered at all, end up crying the least. The babies who cry the most are those with parents in the middle category: parents who respond slowly or inconsistently. But maybe the causal connection works the other way around:

Babies whose cries often go unanswered may come to feel that the world is an unfriendly place and that what they do doesn't make any difference.

Wouldn't parents be likely to stop responding quickly when they have a baby who cries a lot? Some babies do cry more than others, right from the start. Naturally, parents who have a baby who cries constantly would have a tendency to pay less and less attention to her cries—especially if they find that they're seldom able to stop her from crying by feeding her or picking her up.

There is, in fact, evidence that this sort of reaction occurs—that babies who "cry wolf" too often are in greater danger of being ignored. Research has shown that if a baby does a lot of crying during one three-month period, her mother is less likely to pay attention to her cries during the next three-month period. But the reverse is true, too: a mother who ignores the baby's cries during one period will have a baby who cries more during the next one (Bell and Ainsworth, 1972). So it appears to be another one of those "vicious circles" we've mentioned before: the baby cries, the mother ignores the crying, the baby cries more, the mother pays even less attention, and so on. It is precisely this kind of two-way influence that we have in mind when we speak of the parent-child relationship as being *transactional* in nature.

Babies Are Not All Alike

From the point of view of the baby, the best kind of parents are ones who respond quickly and appropriately to her cries and to her other efforts at communication. Parents who act in this way tend to have successful interactions with their babies (Tronick, 1989).

But it takes two to make a successful interaction. Babies are not all alike.

Some babies are born experts at letting their parents know what they want and at rewarding their parents when they do the right thing. (All the baby has to do is stop crying—that's a sufficient reward for the parents. A smile is even more rewarding.) Most babies are amazingly good at "training" an inexperienced parent. Some, however, are not (see Box 6–2).

GROUP DIFFERENCES. There are group differences as well as individual differences among babies. For example, it has been reported that Japanese babies tend to be more inhibited and to react less intensely than Caucasian babies; they also have a tendency to be less cheerful and less adaptable (Miyake, Chen, and Campos, 1985). Babies in the Zinacanteco Indian tribe of southeast Mexico are less active than North American babies. They cry less often and less hard, their sleep is not as deep, and they move more gradually from one state to another (Brazelton, 1977). Babies in the Gusii tribe of Kenya, on the other hand, move from state to state rapidly and irregularly; they tend to be more irritable than American babies but they are also better at soothing themselves by putting their fingers in their mouths (Bornstein, Gaughran, and Homel, 1986). Although some of these differences probably result from cultural differences in infant care, it is also likely that there are innate differences in temperament between groups.

CUDDLERS AND NONCUDDLERS. Babies may differ in many ways, but all babies need their minimum daily requirement of hugs and cuddling, right? Wrong! Some infants not only don't seem to need cuddling—they show a definite dislike for it. They struggle and protest when their mother (or anyone else) tries to hold them close. Here, for example, is a letter from a perplexed mother to a newspaper columnist:

> Our son, who is 5 . . . has always been a big snuggler. If I wasn't still nursing my daughter, however, I don't think I'd get to snuggle her at all. She is super active and wiggly, never calm and relaxed. . . . When anyone picks her up, she wants to get down and crawl. [She plays on the floor for a while], then she wants to be picked up. Before she's fully in my arms, however, she's straining to get down. (Kelly, 1988, p. C19)

It is difficult to hug or cuddle a baby who doesn't want to be hugged or cuddled; eventually, the mothers of such babies stop trying. Fortunately, there is no evidence that these babies suffer any psychological harm from their lack of cuddling. Nor is there reason to think that they are any less capable than other babies of forming close ties with their parents.

These findings first emerged in a longitudinal study of 37 infants, carried out in Scotland. About half of the babies and toddlers in this study loved being cuddled. All through infancy they enjoyed being held, hugged, and carried. "She would be up on my lap all day if I let her," reported one mother. Other mothers said that their baby "snuggles into you" or "cuddles you back."

But a sizable proportion of the children—about a quarter of them—*never* liked cuddling, even when they were tired or ill. The comments of the noncuddlers' mothers were sometimes rather wistful: "He's just like his father—not one for a bit of love."

The remaining babies fell in between the two extremes—they liked cud-

Problems in Development

**Box 6-2
The "Difficult"
Baby**

When interactions between babies and parents don't go well, many parents (especially inexperienced ones) think that it's their fault—that they must be doing something wrong. But some babies are more difficult to deal with than others. Consider, for example, Jillian, the third daughter of a child psychiatrist:

> Jillian arrived on a cold winter morning in early 1974. Within a day the head nurse in the newborn nursery remarked: "That one is going to be trouble." A restless, irritable baby, totally unpredictable in her feeding and sleeping, she always seemed to be screaming. Neither Lucille, an experienced mother, nor a baby-nurse could soothe her. Sleepless nights were the rule in our home. . . . The pediatrician assured us that the baby was normal, but at times her erratic behavior made this hard to believe. . . .
>
> By the time she was 2, Jillian, with Lucille's continuing efforts, had settled into somewhat more predictable routines. Still, when Jillian was upset, a very loud, very long tantrum usually followed. Often it was so hard to understand why she had such extreme reactions. Dressing her, bedtime, going for a walk—virtually any new experience—could cause problems. (Turecki and Tonner, 1985, pp. 1–2)

Jillian showed all four characteristics of the typical "difficult" baby: her feeding and sleeping patterns were irregular and unpredictable, her mood was usually unhappy rather than cheerful, her negative reactions were strong in intensity, and she was not adaptable—she disliked anything new. Having a baby like Jillian changed her father's whole outlook toward his profession:

> Professionally, my whole focus was shifting. No longer did I view problem behavior in young children as only a reaction to their parents or as a developmental "phase." . . . I clearly started to see that many parent-child problems were not caused by the parents alone. (p. 3)

This father realized that neither he nor his wife was to blame for Jillian's characteristics—"Some children are born difficult," he discovered. His training in child psychiatry may have helped him to see that, but what helped even more was the fact that he and his wife had already had experience with two previous babies. It's harder on parents when their first child is difficult. Another father, looking back on his children's early years, was asked what he would have done differently if he had it to do over again. He replied,

> I wouldn't have taken my first child's difficult disposition so personally. My second child had the same parents, same house, same everything, and she's Miss Sunshine. (Williams, 1986, p. 87)

It's clear that babies differ from birth in the way they respond to people and to situations. These differences reflect differences in temperament, which we discussed in Chapter 2. In an important longitudinal study of temperament, psychiatrists

---

dling some of the time. Being a cuddler or a noncuddler didn't depend on the babies' sex or on birth order: girls and boys, firstborns and later-borns, didn't differ significantly in this respect.

The noncuddlers didn't shun their parents altogether—like other babies they went to their mothers when they were frightened. They allowed themselves to be held during feedings (at least until they were old enough to sit in a high chair). In play they didn't mind being kissed, stroked, or tickled, as long as they weren't being held. They enjoyed being bounced or swung around just as much as the cuddlers did, even though these activities did involve being held. What they seemed to mind was the restraint of movement that resulted from being cuddled or hugged. These babies were generally more active and restless than the cuddly babies. They disliked being wrapped up or having their clothes put on. Interestingly enough, these wriggly babies were significantly ahead of the cuddly ones in motor development.

The researchers concluded that babies are cuddlers or noncuddlers right from the start—they found no evidence that these characteristics resulted

Alexander Thomas and Stella Chess (1977) followed a group of 133 babies from birth to adulthood. Of the babies in this group, 40 percent were classified as "easy." These babies were cheerful, adaptable, and regular in their habits. Another 15 percent of the babies were classified as "slow to warm up." These babies reacted negatively to anything new; however, their reactions were mild, not intense. Only 10 percent of the babies were labeled "difficult." These babies were like Jillian—irregular in their eating and sleeping habits, intense in their negative reactions, unadaptable, and often unhappy. (The remaining 35 percent of Thomas and Chess's sample fell into none of these three categories—some babies show no clear-cut patterns of behavior.)

According to Thomas and Chess, the quality of the relationship between parents and baby depends partly on the "goodness of fit" between the baby's characteristics and the parents' expectations and attitudes. A difficult baby seldom provides a good fit to the parents' expectations. Whether the parents blame themselves for their baby's characteristics or blame the baby, the results can be a rapidly escalating vicious circle. The relationship between the baby and the parents might go from bad to worse:

> The vicious circle can start early. In infancy, one of the central temperament issues is irregularity. The mother cannot "cue in" to the child, meaning that the child isn't giving out definite cues on a regular basis as to what he wants. The cues are erratic and are not picked up by the mother. And this is not because she's a bad mother; no one could pick up these cues. . . . You can't tell when he's hungry and when he's not; you can't establish any patterns with this baby. The baby screams a great deal and doesn't sleep for any regular period. The mother tries to soothe the child and is unsuccessful. The pediatrician says it's colic, but after several months the colic doesn't go away. . . . The mother gets more tired and angry. The father, if he shares any responsibilities for taking care of the child, is under pressure as well, and out of this anger and tiredness come patterns of blame. (Turecki and Tonner, 1985, pp. 31–32)

Stanley Turecki, Jillian's father, has established a "difficult child" clinic at Beth Israel Hospital in New York City, where he counsels the parents of such children. Turecki agrees with Thomas and Chess in believing that the parents of a difficult baby can be helped to understand, to accept, and to deal successfully with their baby's temperament. If the parents and the baby can be shown the way out of their vicious circle, the difficult baby is less likely to turn into a problem child.

At last report, Jillian Turecki was 11 years old. According to her proud father,

> Jillian is charming, exuberant, outgoing, and happy. She is popular in school and at summer sleep-away camp. Her schoolwork is good; she works hard and persistently and writes creative stories. . . . She has . . . an intuitive and empathetic soul that makes her sensitive to the feelings of others. (p. 205)

from differences in the way their mothers acted toward them. Nor was there any evidence that the noncuddlers had a need for cuddling that was not being met: they showed no signs of insecurity or of looking for other ways to satisfy a frustrated need for physical contact. In fact, the noncuddlers were less likely than the cuddlers to become thumbsuckers or to become attached to a favorite blanket or stuffed animal (Schaffer and Emerson, 1964).

By the way, there is also no evidence that an attachment to a favorite blanket or stuffed animal is a sign of insecurity or emotional problems—nor, for that matter, any evidence that such attachments *prevent* emotional problems. About a third of American children become deeply attached to a blanket or soft toy by the time they are 18 months old. Researchers have found no important differences between these children and the ones who become only mildly attached to a **security object,** or who have no attachments to objects at all. It is interesting to note, however, that such attachments are far more common in countries where babies sleep alone than in countries where babies sleep with their mothers (Passman, 1987).

GENDER DIFFERENCES IN BABIES. Among the factors that affect a baby's relationship with parents and other people, surely one of the most important is the baby's gender. "What a cute baby," strangers say. "Is it a girl or a boy?" Unless the baby is dressed in pink ruffles or a blue baseball suit, it's not easy to tell, is it? Girls and boys seem pretty much alike at this age.

There are measurable differences between male and female infants, even in the first week or two of life. But these differences are small—statistical differences between the "average boy" and the "average girl." The differences between one baby boy and another, or between one baby girl and another, are likely to be far greater than the differences between the averages for the two sexes.

What, though, are these gender differences? The most reliable ones are the differences in size and strength. Boys are somewhat longer and heavier at birth and remain slightly larger, on the average, during most of childhood. A boy baby tends to have a bigger head and a bigger face than a girl, and to have less fat and more muscle (Tanner, 1974). He is able to hold up his head at an earlier age.

The other differences between male and female infants are slight enough so that they show up in some studies and not in others. Some of these differences may be due to the fact that at birth girls are a little more advanced in physical development than boys. Infant girls have been found to be more sensitive to various kinds of stimuli, especially touch, cold, pain, and taste. Some studies find that boys tend to cry more than girls and are a little harder to soothe; they also tend to startle more easily (Korner, 1974).

As babies get older, the differences between girls and boys become more numerous and noticeable. This increase in gender differences is due partly to biological factors and partly to the fact that parents and other people act differently toward male and female babies. For example, some researchers in England taped conversations between mothers and babies, and between babies and their older siblings. They found that when mothers and older children were talking to baby girls they made about twice as many references to "feeling states" (such as hunger, pain, tiredness, surprise, fear, affection, and pleasure) as when they were talking to baby boys. And by the time they were 24 months old, the toddler girls were themselves talking about "feeling states" more than twice as often as the toddler boys (Dunn, Bretherton, and Munn, 1987).

By the preschool period, it is usually possible to guess a child's gender even if clothing and hairstyle provide no clues. We'll return in later chapters to the important matter of gender differences.

Parents Are Not All Alike Either

Because parents are human beings, each brings to the role of parenthood their own characteristics, including educational and cultural background, personality, their previous experiences with young children, the happiness or unhappiness of their marital relationship, and any medical or psychological problems. All these factors (and others) are likely to have an effect on parent–child relationships.

GENDER DIFFERENCES IN PARENTS. There are only minimal differences in behavior between male and female infants, but the behavioral differences between male and female *parents* are considerable. The most important dif-

Fun with Daddy. Fathers and mothers interact with babies in different ways: fathers' interactions are less likely to involve caregiving and more likely to involve active, physical play.

ference is one we have already discussed (see Box 6–1): mothers spend much more time with their babies and perform a much larger proportion of the childcare chores than fathers do. This is true even when both parents are employed. When fathers *are* around, they tend to be less available to their young children than mothers are: they are more likely to be watching TV or engaging in some other activity (LaRossa, 1988).

When fathers do interact on a one-to-one basis with their offspring, they are more likely than mothers to be playing with the baby and less likely to be feeding, diapering, or giving other kinds of care. Although mothers actually play with babies more than fathers do, a much greater proportion of a father's interactions with his child consists of playing (Lamb, 1987).

Fathers and mothers also play with babies in different ways. A father's play is more physical and less verbal; it is less likely to involve a toy or a game such as peek-a-boo; it is less carefully "tuned" to the baby's abilities (Ninio and Rinott, 1988). A father's speech to his infant is also not as well adjusted to the baby's level of development as a mother's speech (Kruper and Uzgiris, 1987). Fathers know less about infant development than mothers do and they are aware of it. If a father has a problem in dealing with an infant, he usually turns to his wife for help, whereas a mother is more likely to seek assistance from a friend, relative, or pediatrician (Stevens, 1988).

Finally, fathers make more of a distinction between girl babies and boy babies than mothers do—mothers treat girls and boys pretty much the same. Fathers roughhouse with boys but play in gentler ways with girls (Kruper and Uzgiris, 1987). A father is likely to show less involvement with a daughter than with a son (Grossman, Pollack, and Golding, 1988).

EMPATHY AND SENSITIVITY. We've said that infants are better off if they have parents who respond to their needs quickly, consistently, and with sensitivity. Regardless of the characteristics of the baby, some parents are more likely than others to give care in a sensitive, responsive way. It appears that this difference hinges in part on a difference in **empathy,** which is the ability to share in the feelings of others—to feel sad when another person is sad or happy when another person is happy. Some researchers gave a group of young women (college students) a test designed to measure their empathy. Then the women were shown videotapes of infants crying. The women who had scored high on the empathy test showed more of a sympathetic reaction to the crying babies than did the low-empathy women—they expressed a greater desire to pick up the babies and comfort them (Wiesenfeld, Whitman, and Malatesta, 1984).

People who lack sensitivity to the feelings of others are less likely to respond appropriately to their babies' signals. They are also more likely to become abusive parents. A recent study compared mothers who had abused their children with nonabusing mothers. The two groups of mothers were shown photos of babies' faces and asked to identify the emotions on the babies' faces ("What is this baby feeling?"). The abusive mothers did poorly on this test: for example, when they were shown a photo of a frightened baby they often said "anger" or "sadness"; occasionally they even mistook positive emotions such as joy for negative ones such as distress. The nonabusing mothers never made this mistake (Kropp and Haynes, 1987). Obviously, a mother cannot respond appropriately to her baby's signals if she can't even tell what he is signaling.

PARENTS WITH PROBLEMS. Sometimes a mother is unable to respond to her baby's needs, or to interact with him in a mutually satisfying way, because she has serious problems of her own—for example, mental illness or alcoholism. In addition, the infant himself might have characteristics that make him more difficult than usual to care for: the babies of alcoholic mothers are often born with birth defects (see Chapter 4), and the babies of mentally ill mothers may have inherited some tendencies toward mental illness (see Chapter 2). There may also be a reverse effect of the baby on the mother: mothers of babies with difficult temperaments have been found to be at increased risk of postpartum depression (see p. 142). The causal connections are cloudy but the hazards are clear: a serious problem in a mother is likely to be a serious problem for her child.

Depression is not uncommon in new mothers; sometimes it is only a temporary reaction to the physical stresses of childbearing and infant care, but sometimes it is a symptom of a prolonged mental illness. Depression might also alternate with emotional highs. Whether the mother acts sad and withdrawn most of the time, or cycles unpredictably between periods of sadness and periods of being "hyper," normal interactions with the baby are disrupted.

A study of depressed mothers and their babies found that by the age of 6 months the babies were very withdrawn and seldom smiled. Some of these mothers were themselves withdrawn and generally ignored their babies, whereas others were very intrusive and would pull or poke at their babies in order to get their attention, paying no attention to the babies' reactions. Both groups of mothers were completely out of touch with their babies' feelings. In a normal mother–baby interaction, the two participants mirror each other's emotions: when one smiles, the other is likely to smile also; when one looks unhappy, the other looks concerned. If a normal (nondepressed) mother pretends to be sad, her baby is likely to smile hopefully and then turn his face away. He'll glance back at her from time to time with a wary expression and then, if she continues to act sad, he is likely to begin to cry. But the babies of depressed mothers no longer react to their mother's sadness; they have given up on her (Cohn and others, 1986). What's more disturbing is that they seem to have given up on social relationships in general: they show "depressed" behavior not only with their own mothers, but also with other adults (Field and others, 1988).

As they get older, the children of depressed mothers are likely to show other effects of their disrupted relationships. As toddlers they are more distractible and less able to focus their attention, and as preschoolers they don't talk as much as other children (Breznitz and Friedman, 1988; Breznitz and Sherman, 1987).

CULTURAL DIFFERENCES IN BABY CARE. It isn't surprising that having an "abnormal" relationship with a parent can be harmful to a baby: what's surprising is how wide and varied the range of "normal" parent–child relationships is and how well babies generally adapt to them. This is most obvious when it comes to cultural differences in childrearing styles. We will take a quick look at the patterns of infant care in four contrasting societies that have recently been studied: the Gusii people of Kenya, Africa; Yucatec Mayans of the Yucatán peninsula in Mexico; Italians in a small town in central Italy; and middle-class Americans in suburban Boston.

Gusii and Yucatec Mayan babies are seldom put down or left alone: they are held almost all the time, either by their mothers or by other female relatives (often, their older sisters). The babies sleep with their mothers at night and are breast-fed every time they cry, even at the slightest whimper. By the time they are 3 or 4 months old, these babies are very calm and quiet—they cry very little. They also do less cooing and babbling than American babies. The mothers show great concern for the physical well-being of their babies, but other aspects of development are not given much attention. The type of mother–infant interactions that are common in our own society—with mutual eye contact and smiling, "baby talk" from the mother and cooing sounds from the baby—tend to be rare in preindustrialized societies. Moreover, when the Gusii and Yucatec Mayan babies are 9 or 10 months old and are capable of sitting up by themselves and crawling, their mothers continue to hold them or to otherwise restrict their movements. They are given no toys and are not permitted to explore their environments the way American babies do at this age. In these homes, cooking is done over an open fire, and a baby who crawls around on the floor is at risk of being burned (Howrigan, 1988; Richman and others, 1988).

Italian babies are also discouraged from crawling around on the floor, but for different reasons. Italian mothers worry about drafts on cold, tiled floors and are very concerned about keeping their babies clean; toddlers are prevented from doing anything that might get their clothes dirty or that would expose them to sun or cold. The Italians believe that a plump baby is a healthy baby, so there is much emphasis on feeding: mothers spoon-feed toddlers who are capable of feeding themselves and will resort to force-feeding if they think the baby isn't eating enough. The babies in this society are seldom left alone

—they are talked to and given a lot of attention by parents and by visiting friends and relatives. Babies sleep in their parents' bedroom and have their naps on someone's lap or in a carriage in the kitchen. They are awakened—perhaps with a pinch on the cheek—whenever someone wants to play with them. Interactions often consist of the adult teasing the baby, perhaps by holding a toy just out of reach or by offering nonexistent candy. Then, when the baby starts to cry, everyone laughs and the baby is consoled with hugs and kisses (New, 1988).

Unlike the babies in these other cultures, babies in the Boston suburbs are expected to be independent and self-reliant at an early age. Instead of restricting the child's movements, American mothers make an effort to "childproof" the environment so that an older baby can move around in it safely. Younger babies spend much of their time in "containers" other than their mothers' arms: cribs, playpens, high chairs, and infant seats. Babies are often left alone in cribs or playpens and are expected to entertain themselves, with the aid of plentiful toys. They are never force-fed and are allowed, at least to some extent, to determine their own eating schedules. On the other hand, they are expected to conform to the sleeping schedule set down by their parents. These mothers are very concerned that their infants get "enough sleep" (14 hours a day, on the average) and persist in their efforts to get them to nap or to go to sleep at night (alone), even if the child protests loudly. Although American babies engage in intense periods of play and social interaction with their parents, they are also expected to learn that they can't have these social interactions whenever they want them (Richman, Miller, and Solomon, 1988).

In periods of rapid cultural change, patterns of childrearing change, too. Often there is conflict between a mother's views on infant care and the views of *her* mother. On the Yucatán peninsula, Yucatec Mayan mothers have switched in one generation from breast-feeding their infants to using a commercial formula for daytime feedings. The modern Yucatec mother sees breast-feeding as "old-fashioned," though the baby's grandmother continues to believe that breast milk is more nutritious than powdered formula. The grandmother, in this case, is right. Because breast milk provides protection

American babies are permitted more freedom to explore their environment than babies in most other cultures. The parents of this adventurous toddler are obviously not overly concerned about cold drafts!

against infections and commercial formula does not, Yucatec babies who are predominately bottle-fed are far more likely than breast-fed babies to suffer from bouts of severe diarrhea. As a consequence, the bottle-fed babies tend to be smaller and thinner—a difference that is still detectable at 4 years of age (Howrigan, 1988).

Attachment

When Sarah was 3 or 4 months old, any kind person could care for her—rock her or diaper her or give her a bottle. In those days Sarah smiled at everyone: little old ladies in the supermarket, visiting aunts and uncles, even her pediatrician. But now Sarah is 12 months old, and the situation has changed. Just anybody won't do. There are times—times when Sarah is tired, frightened, or in pain—when she wants her mother and only her mother. If her mother is available, Sarah will cling to her and be comforted. If her mother is not around, Sarah may cry and cry, refusing to be consoled, until her mother returns. If her mother is gone for a period of time that seems endless to a 1-year-old—a week, say—Sarah may fall into a deep depression.

A special relationship now exists between Sarah and her mother, a relationship that didn't exist six months ago. Developmental psychologists call this relationship **attachment;** others might simply call it love. Attachment is an emotional tie that Sarah feels toward her mother—a tie that developed over a period of time. It causes Sarah to want to be near her mother, especially when she is in need of security or comfort.

Attachment is a remarkably universal aspect of development. Virtually every normal child becomes attached to someone (provided, of course, that there is someone there to become attached to). Moreover, the age at which attachment first begins to affect the baby's behavior—between 6 and 8 months—is virtually the same in societies all over the world. Babies generally

cry, or at least look unhappy, when a person to whom they are attached leaves them alone in an unfamiliar place. This is called **separation distress** (or **separation anxiety**), and it shows up at pretty much the same age in babies raised in a wide variety of settings,

> [in] American cities, Latin American barrios, Israeli kibbutzim, or !Kung San bands in the Kalahari. Such crying usually emerges when babies are about eight months old, rises to a peak in the middle of the second year, and then declines in all those cultures.   (Kagan, 1978, p. 72)

Social Referencing

Although the effects aren't evident until the baby is about 8 months old, the roots of attachment begin to form much earlier, in the first few months of life. One aspect of the attachment process that can be seen even in young babies is their response to the emotions displayed by their parents. As was clear in the case of the babies who were upset when their mothers acted sad (p. 195), babies are capable of responding to the emotions of their caregivers at a surprisingly early age. In an interesting experiment, mothers of 2½-month-old babies were given training in displaying three different emotions: happiness, sadness, and anger. The mothers then portrayed these emotions to their babies, at the same time saying, "You make me very happy" in a happy voice, or "You make me very sad" (or mad) in a sad (or angry) voice. Although these babies were not yet 3 months old, their responses showed that they could discriminate these emotions. They looked happy when their mother portrayed happiness. When she looked sad they stopped smiling, turned their gaze downward, and sucked on their lips or tongue in an apparent effort to console themselves. And when the mother looked angry, the babies turned their gaze to one side and stopped moving. Some of them began to cry. At this age they cannot yet discriminate emotions by vision alone (it was their mother's face *plus* the tone of her voice), but by the age of 5 or 6 months, looking at their mother's face is sufficient (Haviland and Lelwica, 1987).

By the time they are 12 months old, babies are looking at their parents' faces for information about how to react to something; this is called **social referencing.** When a baby is uncertain about what something means or what to do about it, he looks at his mother to see how *she* is reacting. His mother's facial expression and gestures help him decide what to do. For example, in one experiment using the "visual cliff" (see p. 162), the cliff in question was just deep enough to make babies uncertain about whether they wanted to cross it. They resolved their uncertainty by looking at their mother's face. If the mother looked happy or interested, most babies crossed. If the mother looked angry, very few ventured onto the cliff. And if she looked fearful, *none* did (Sorce, Emde, Campos, and Klinnert, 1985).

Babies get valuable information about the world through social referencing. The person they look at to get this kind of information need not be their mother—a father is just as good (Dickson and Parke, 1988), and any friendly adult will do in a pinch. In an experiment to test social referencing, 12-month-old babies were confronted with an unfamiliar toy—a slightly scary-looking robot. Two adults were also present: their mother and a friendly female researcher who had played with them for a while. The mother was told to show no expression at all when the toy rolled into the room. It was the researcher whose face showed a reaction: with half of the babies, she looked happy when the toy appeared, with the other half she portrayed fear. Almost all the babies looked at the researcher's face as well as at their mother's face for information about how to react to the toy. They approached the toy far more readily when the researcher looked happy about it; when the researcher looked fearful they were more likely to retreat from the toy and go to their mother (Klinnert, Emde, Butterfield, and Campos, 1986).

Fear of Strangers

During the first year of life, while a baby's attachment to her caregivers is increasing, there is a corresponding change in her reaction to strangers. Although she might look at the face of someone she doesn't know very well for information about the world, she no longer smiles at them as readily as she did when she was younger. By 12 months, many babies will burst into tears if a person they don't know tries to pick them up.

Unlike attachment, however, fear of strangers is not universal. Babies have positive feelings, as well as negative ones, toward friendly strangers. Which feeling wins out depends in part on who the stranger is and on what he or she does. Babies are seldom afraid of other babies or of children; they are less afraid of women than of men (Brooks and Lewis, 1976). Adult strangers are more likely to get a favorable response from a baby if they approach her slowly, if she is in a familiar setting, and if her mother is nearby.

A baby is more likely to smile at someone she doesn't know if she has previously seen her mother talking in a friendly manner with the stranger (Feiring, Lewis, and Starr, 1984). Here we have another example of the use of social referencing: the baby glances back and forth from the stranger's face to her mothers' face, so she can see how her mother reacts to the stranger before she has to make up her own mind about what to do (Dickson and Parke, 1988). Watching her mother converse with the stranger also gives the baby an opportunity to study the stranger without making eye contact. Meeting the eyes of an unfamiliar adult seems to be an emotionally arousing experience for many 1-year-olds (Perry and Bussey, 1984).

A final factor, but one of the most important ones, in determining how a baby acts toward a friendly stranger is the baby's temperament: some babies are more sociable than others, some are more fearful. Some tend to be cheerful most of the time, others frown or cry more readily. Recently some of these temperamental differences have been linked to built-in differences in patterns of brain-wave activity. Researchers found that differences in brain-wave patterns could predict how a baby would react when her mother left the room and a stranger entered. The babies who had the kind of brain-wave pattern that is associated with negative emotions were far more likely to cry than the babies with a "happy" pattern of brain-waves (Fox and Davidson, 1987).

To Whom Are Babies Attached?

Most babies are attached not just to their mothers but to their fathers as well. Babies often become attached to both parents at around the same age, usually between 7 and 9 months. At 12 or 13 months, the majority of babies appear to be equally attached to both parents—under normal conditions they show no consistent preference for one parent or the other. However, in stressful situations, when they are upset, 12-month-old babies generally go to their mothers for comfort (Lamb, 1978). This is probably because the mother is the primary caregiver in most families. The amount of caregiving does make a difference. In one study, babies' attachment to their fathers was found to be related to the number of times per week the father changed the baby's diaper (Ross, Kagan, Zelazo, and Kotelchuck, 1975).

ATTACHMENT WITHOUT CAREGIVING. But caregiving isn't the only factor involved in forming attachments. In order to become attached to someone, a baby must have many opportunities to interact with that person. There are other ways, besides having diapers changed, for these interactions to occur. Babies often become attached to people who never take care of them at all— not only to fathers but also to siblings, grandparents, and even the family dog (Kidd and Kidd, 1987). Moreover, babies sometimes *fail* to become attached to people who *do* take care of them—people such as housekeepers and day-care-center workers. Babies who spend their days at a day-care center are generally more attached to their mothers than to the people who take care of them at the center (Clarke-Stewart, 1989).

What seems to count most in the attachment process is not who changes the diapers or how much time (within reasonable limits) the baby and the parent spend together. What is important is the *quality* of their interactions: the sensitivity of the older person's response to the baby, the emotional intensity of their interactions, the sheer delight each takes in the other's company.

The Unattached Child

Toddlers who have formed attachments to their parents are often desperately unhappy if they must be separated from them. As one researcher has put it, "Young children may well respond to an involuntary separation with an intensity appropriate to matters of life and death" (Ainsworth, 1977, p. 56). If the separation is prolonged, the child's frantic unhappiness gives way in time to sadness and depression. Eventually, though, the wounds are healed and new attachments are formed (Rutter, 1974).

Far more serious are the consequences of a failure to form attachments in the first place. There is only one situation in which this is likely to happen: when a child is reared in an institution where there are many caregivers, all of the "here today, gone tomorrow" variety. If a child never has the chance to interact with one particular person over a period of time, he or she will form no attachments. Even in a "good" institution, where the care is adequate and the children are given many things to look at and play with, the long-range forecast is not promising. These children will probably turn out to be of near-average intellectual ability, but their social and emotional development will probably not be normal. As toddlers they tend to follow and cling to any available adult. As preschoolers they are likely to be overly friendly toward strangers and very demanding of attention. By middle childhood they are often restless and disobedient, and they tend to get along poorly both with adults and with other children. Few appear to form lasting relationships with anyone (Rutter, 1979).

These effects are found in children who remain institutionalized too long —longer than three or four years. Children who are adopted by age 3 generally become normal adults, able to form lasting, loving relationships. Those adopted after age 4 may form very close ties with their new family, but the damage has been done. In school they show the same social and emotional

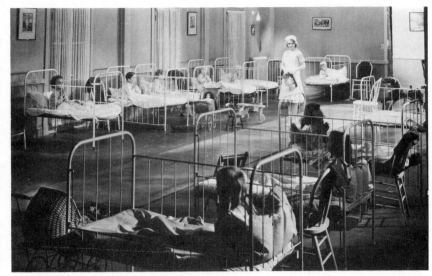

For babies who grew up in old-fashioned orphanages like this one, there were no opportunities to form lasting attachments.

problems as the children who remain in the institution. So infancy and toddlerhood appear to be a crucial time for the formation of human attachments. An attachment to someone in the first two or three years of life is necessary for normal social and emotional development (MacDonald, 1985).

Even if there is no mother, no permanent caregiver, given half a chance, babies will form attachments. This was poignantly illustrated many years ago by some young Jewish children who had spent their infancy in a Nazi concentration camp. Their parents were dead. They were kept together in the concentration camp and cared for by an ever-changing series of adults, all of whom were killed before the war was over. At the end of the war these six children were sent to England, where they came to the attention of Anna Freud, Sigmund's daughter. She was amazed to discover that these 3½-year-olds cared not a bit for any adult. They were attached solely and completely to one another!

> The children's positive feelings were centered exclusively in their group. It was evident that they cared greatly for each other and not at all for anybody or anything else. They had no other wish than to be together, and became upset when they were separated from each other, even for short moments. . . .
>
> On walks they were concerned for each other's safety in traffic, looked after children who lagged behind, helped each other over ditches, turned aside branches for each other to clear the passage in the woods, and carried each other's coats. In the nursery they picked up each other's toys. After they had learned to play, they assisted each other silently in building and admired each other's productions. At mealtimes handing food to the neighbor was of greater importance than eating oneself. (A. Freud and Dann, 1967, pp. 497, 500)

Attachments to Other Children

Can such attachments to other children take the place of attachments to caregivers and lead to normal social development? It would be of great interest to know how the concentration camp children turned out—whether, despite their early experiences, they developed into reasonably normal adults—but we have no information about these children's later lives. However, if attachments to peers could serve as an adequate substitute for attachments to caregivers, why aren't children reared in institutions able to develop normally?

Perhaps they would be, if they were permitted to remain together for a long enough period of time. But babies living in institutions probably have few opportunities to interact with each other until they are able to walk around, so they are unable to form attachments to each other in infancy (Dontas and others, 1985). Then, as they get older, children little by little leave the institution, as adoptive homes are found or their biological parents become able to take care of them. So a child remaining in an institution until age 3 or 4 may have already formed several attachments to other children and then lost them when the other children were taken away. Forming attachments and then losing them several times during infancy and toddlerhood "may finally make the child unwilling to engage in this task yet again," as one researcher has put it. Thus, the institutionalized child ends up with "the inability to form a loving relationship with anyone" (Bretherton, 1980, p. 206). The same thing could happen with young children in foster care, if they were tossed around from one foster home to another.

Why Do Babies Form Attachments?

Fortunately, most babies do have mothers and do become attached to them. But what causes them to form these attachments? Early theorists—Freud, for example—linked attachment to the fact that the mother nurses the baby. Freud thought that the baby first becomes attached to his mother's breast and then to the rest of her. Theorists with other viewpoints have also connected the baby's attachment to his mother with the fact that she feeds him. Behaviorists, for example, have theorized that a baby tries to remain near his mother because he has come to associate her with good things such as food and warmth (Bijou and Baer, 1965; Gewirtz, 1972).

Although this theory sounds reasonable, it can't account for all that we know about attachment. Babies don't become attached just to their mothers, and they don't become attached just to the people who feed them or take care of them. Pleasurable sensations such as those connected with nursing or being held and stroked also do not seem to be necessary. In fact, *visual* contact between the baby and the other person seems to be more important than *physical* contact (Roedell and Slaby, 1977). But visual contact is not essential either: babies who are blind from birth do form attachments (Fraiberg, 1977). And finally, even babies whose mothers have beaten them or neglected them become attached to their mothers (Egeland and Sroufe, 1981).

THE ETHOLOGICAL APPROACH. Because babies have such a strong predisposition to form attachments, even under the most unfavorable conditions, many researchers in child development now believe that this is a built-in characteristic of the human species. The study of animals' and humans' built-in patterns of behavior is the concern of a field known as **ethology.**

John Bowlby, a British theoretician, was the first to propose an ethological interpretation of attachment.

Bowlby (1969) pointed out that attachment of the infant to its mother is not unique to the human species—it is found in most bird and mammal species as well. Baby ducklings, for example, follow their mother wherever she goes. Their tendency to follow is innate and instinctive, but ducklings must *learn* to recognize their mother. The way they learn this is through a process called **imprinting:** ducklings will follow the first moving object they see after they hatch. Normally this is their mother, but occasionally it turns out to be something else—a large, featherless ethologist, perhaps. Some ducklings became imprinted on the ethologist Konrad Lorenz and followed him wherever he went; they were totally uninterested in full-grown female ducks. Once ducklings are imprinted on someone or something, it's virtually impossible to *un*imprint them.

Another feature of imprinting is that it must take place soon after the duckling is hatched or it won't take place at all. The period of time during which the duckling can be imprinted—the *critical period*—lasts only about a day. If the duckling is not allowed to see its first moving object until after it is 24 hours old, little or no imprinting will occur (Hess, 1970).

Imprinting is a quick and simple form of attachment. The attachment process is more gradual and flexible in the higher animals such as monkeys and apes. The end result is similar, though: the attached baby animal stays close to its mother. A newborn monkey at first clings to its mother only by reflex—it doesn't recognize her yet. But a month or so later, when it has begun to explore its environment, its attachment to its mother is clear. At the first sign of danger the baby monkey leaps toward its mother and clings to her tightly (Bowlby, 1969).

Ethologist Konrad Lorenz and his devoted followers.

Unlike ducklings, monkeys have no critical period during which attachments must be formed and after which they cannot be changed. Instead, there is a **sensitive period**—a period during which attachments are formed most readily. An orphaned young monkey can become reattached to a substitute mother; one reared by a human caretaker will eventually accept a new caretaker. As the monkey gets older, its capacity to form new attachments gradually declines.

The tendency for a young animal to become attached to its mother and to remain close to her is adaptive—it increases its chances of survival. A baby mammal that remains with its mother is less likely to be taken by predators or to lose its only source of food. Thus, the tendency to become attached is passed on from generation to generation, preserved by the process of natural selection. According to the ethological view, the same is true of the human baby's tendency to form attachments: the predisposition has been inherited by human babies because, in the primitive environment of the early humans, it had survival value.

In line with this idea, we might point out that attachment occurs just at the time it's needed most—just when the young organism develops mobility and is most likely to stray into danger. Ducklings can walk almost as soon as they hatch, and ducklings become imprinted almost immediately. Young rhesus monkeys start to move around on their own at about 2 weeks of age; it takes them only a week or two for them to become attached to their mothers (Harlow and Harlow, 1965). Human babies begin to develop attachments at 8 or 9 months, just when they're starting to crawl. Their attachment behavior—their clinginess—tends to reach a peak at around 13 months, precisely the age when they begin to walk.

SECURITY AND COMFORT. In human babies, as in young monkeys, attachment behavior is a compromise. Two different desires motivate the young human or monkey: the desire to stay close to its mother, and the desire to explore its environment and to play. In both human and monkey babies we can see the pull of these two opposing interests. The typical human baby of 12 to 18 months will explore and play happily within sight of his mother, now and then returning to her (or glancing at her) for reassurance. The child is using the mother as a "secure base from which to explore" (Ainsworth, 1977, p. 59).

Attachment reveals itself most clearly when a child is in pain, afraid, tired, or ill. Anything that worries or frightens a young child is likely to increase his or her clinginess, and that includes being punished or threatened for clinging too much! The same is true in baby ducklings. A researcher who studied imprinting in ducks noticed that if he accidentally stepped on the toes of a duckling that was beginning to follow him around, the duckling followed him more closely than ever (Hess, 1970). In a similar manner, human babies become attached even to caregivers who physically abuse them: the child in pain may go for comfort to the very person who caused his pain. One little boy who was badly beaten by his mother was removed from his home and placed in a children's residential center. When the nurse in the center held him in her arms, he looked up at her and said dolefully, "Nobody holds me when I hurt like my mama does" (Blount, 1981, p. 5).

In the past two decades, the most influential theorist in the field of attachment has been Mary Ainsworth, a professor at the University of Virginia. Ainsworth began to formulate her ideas on attachment in the course of a study of babies and mothers in Uganda, Africa, in the 1950s. Since then, however, she has devoted herself to American babies and their mothers. As we shall see, some of her ideas do not transfer readily to babies reared in other cultures.

Ainsworth's main interest has been in the *quality* of the attachment relationship. She believes that a baby is either attached to someone or not attached, and that it makes no sense to talk about the *strength* of the attachment. How attached a baby appears to be at a particular moment depends on the situation and on whether the baby is frightened or not, happy or not, and so on. But attachment relationships do vary along another dimension, a qualitative dimension. Ainsworth (1977) calls this dimension the **security** of the child's attachment. Virtually all children are attached by 12 or 14 months, but some are **securely attached** and some are **insecurely attached**.

To assess the security of babies' attachments, Ainsworth and her colleagues developed a procedure called the **Strange Situation** (Ainsworth, Blehar, Waters, and Wall, 1978). This procedure has now become the standard way of testing infant attachments—it has been used in hundreds of studies.

The Strange Situation begins with the baby and his mother being brought into a room where they've never been before, a room with toys for the baby to play with. They remain in the room for a little while and the baby is allowed to play. Then, during the course of the next 20 minutes, the mother leaves the room twice. The first time there is another person in the room—a woman whom the baby doesn't know. The second time the baby is left alone.

Many babies cry when their mothers leave, whether or not the stranger is present. Crying isn't the important thing, though. Securely attached babies may or may not cry; the same is true of insecurely attached babies. What the investigators look at is the whole pattern of the baby's behavior during the course of the session. A securely attached baby will generally be attracted to the toys and will play happily as long as his mother is there. (He's using his mother as a "secure base from which to explore.") When his mother leaves he may not cry, but he'll stop playing or play with less enthusiasm. Then, when his mother returns, he'll greet her joyously. If he wasn't greatly upset by her leaving, he may just smile or babble at her. If he was upset, he'll rush to her and cling to her, and he'll calm down quickly.

That's the typical pattern for the securely attached child. Children with insecure attachments are more variable in their behavior. Some do little playing and exploring, even when their mothers are present—they may cry or cling even before their mothers leave. But it's their reaction to their mothers' return (after the mother does leave) that is most revealing. An insecurely attached child will not greet his mother with unmixed joy. He may alternate between clinging to her and pushing her away, and he may continue to cry in an angry way and refuse to be comforted. This is called the **resistant** pattern of reunion. Or he might ignore his mother completely when she returns. This is called the **avoidant** pattern. Most studies show that at age 12 months about 70 percent of babies from middle-class American

The Quality
of Attachment

homes are securely attached to their mothers. About 20 percent of babies are classified as avoidant and 10 percent as resistant.

Bear in mind that attachment is a *relationship*. The security or insecurity of a child's attachment to someone is presumed to reside in the child's relationship with that person, and not necessarily in the child. Thus, a child may be insecurely attached to one parent and securely attached to the other parent (Belsky and Rovine, 1987). Furthermore, relationships may change over time, perhaps as a function of changes in family circumstances. A child may be securely attached to his mother at one point in time and insecurely attached to her a few months later, or vice versa (Egeland and Farber, 1984).

THE CONSEQUENCES OF BEING SECURELY OR INSECURELY ATTACHED. Securely attached and insecurely attached children have been found to differ in a number of ways. These differences have been found at the age when the security of their attachments is measured and also at later ages.

Securely attached children are generally friendlier to unfamiliar adults, both as toddlers and as preschoolers. They are also friendlier to other children (Thompson and Lamb, 1983; Lütkenhaus, Grossmann, and Grossmann, 1985; Pastor, 1981).

In general, securely attached children appear to be more competent. This competence shows up in their greater ability to deal with novelty and to cope with failure, their greater persistence and enthusiasm for problem solving, and their greater self-esteem (Sroufe, 1985). Even their motor skills seem to be better—children rated securely attached were found to fall down, bump into things, and drop things less often than insecurely attached children (Cassidy, 1986).

Children who are judged insecurely attached at 12 months are at greater risk for a variety of problems later on. As preschoolers, avoidant children tend to be more aggressive and impulsive and less cooperative. Resistant children are more timid and withdrawn (Erickson, Sroufe, and Egeland, 1985). Both types of insecurely attached children are less skillful at getting along with their peers. They are dependent, clingy, and whiney with their nursery school teachers (Sroufe, Fox, and Pancake, 1983). At age 6, they are at greater risk of being judged emotionally disturbed (Lewis, Feiring, McGuffog, and Jaskir, 1984). In general, these unfavorable effects are more likely to be found in boys than in girls and are more common when there is no father present in the home.

WHAT DETERMINES THE QUALITY OF AN ATTACHMENT? We said earlier that what seems to be important in the attachment process is the quality of the interactions between the baby and the other person. Consequently, it is not surprising to find that children who have been physically or emotionally abused by their mothers are less likely to be securely attached to them. In one study, only 30 percent of a group of abused and neglected children were found to be securely attached to their mothers. At 12 months, most of the insecurely attached children showed the resistant pattern of reunion, but at 18 and 24 months they showed an increasing tendency to avoid their mothers (Schneider-Rosen, Braunwald, Carlson, and Cicchetti, 1985).

In general, it has been found that the security of a baby's attachment to his mother (assessed in the Strange Situation at age 12 months) is correlated with

the quality of the care she has given him and with the quality of their interactions. Babies who are judged to be securely attached to their mothers at 12
months tend to have mothers who have responded to their cries and signals in
a consistent and sensitive way. Their interactions with each other have been
successful and mutually enjoyable. It is safe to assume that both mother and
baby contributed to these mutually enjoyable interactions.

Insecurely attached babies are less likely to have had successful interactions with their mothers. Babies who show the resistant pattern (the ones
who refuse to be comforted and alternate between clinging to their mother
and pushing her away) tend to have mothers who ignored their cries and who
were emotionally uninvolved and distant. And the insecure–avoidant pattern
(displayed by babies who pay no attention to their mother when she returns)
is correlated with an interfering and obtrusive style of mothering, sometimes
combined with thinly veiled hostility toward the baby (Belsky, Rovine, and
Taylor, 1984; Lyons-Ruth, Connell, Zoll, and Stahl, 1987).

It has been shown that women who behave in an uncaring way to their
children are often the product of very poor mothering themselves—many of
them were rejected, mistreated, or abandoned by their own mothers (Ricks,
1985). Such women are particularly unlikely to have securely attached babies
if they are single parents who must handle the childcare chores without
assistance. The presence of a man in the household increases the chances of a
secure attachment to the mother (Egeland and Farber, 1984). Women suffering from serious depression also tend to have insecurely attached children. If
they have a husband living with them—even if the husband is depressed too
—there is a better chance that the child will become securely attached to the
mother (Radke-Yarrow, Cummings, Kuczynski, and Chapman, 1985). Having
no assistance and no time-outs can make motherhood seem like an overwhelming burden, especially for a woman who already has problems of her
own.

Some researchers have claimed that what happens in the first few hours
after birth has a long-term effect on the mother–child relationship. A group
of mothers were permitted some time alone with their babies immediately
after delivery. Later, these mothers appeared to have more affectionate relationships with their infants than other mothers whose babies had been
whisked off to a hospital nursery. The investigators concluded that a period of
togetherness in the first few hours after birth is necessary for successful
bonding—the mother's attachment to her baby (Klaus and Kennell, 1978).

Although this report received quite a lot of publicity, later research failed to
support the original finding (Myers, 1984). On the whole, what happens
immediately after birth doesn't seem to have any consistent effect on a baby's
later relationships. A baby who is separated from his mother soon after birth
due to medical complications (prematurity, a cesarean delivery, or the like)
does not run a greater risk of developing an insecure attachment (Entwisle
and Alexander, 1987; Goldberg, Perrotta, Minde, and Corter, 1986).

EFFECTS OF THE MOTHER'S EMPLOYMENT. Now that over 50 percent of
mothers go back to work before their babies are a year old, the question of the
effects of day-care on infants has become a pressing one. Can babies form
normal attachments if they are away from their parents for eight or ten hours
of the day? Will they suffer some kind of emotional deprivation due to a lack

She'll drop off the children at the day-care center on her way to work. Today more than 50 percent of mothers are employed outside the home before their babies are a year old.

of parenting? This is an issue that has not yet been settled and one that evokes strong feelings.

There have been 14 studies assessing the quality of mother–infant attachment in the babies of employed and unemployed mothers. Some of these have found significant differences in security of attachment; others have not. One researcher, Alison Clarke-Stewart of the University of California at Irvine, has put all the data from these 14 studies together—data from 1247 infants and mothers. She found that, overall, 64 percent of the babies of full-time employed mothers were judged to be securely attached, versus 71 percent for babies whose mothers worked part-time or not at all. The increase in insecure attachments was found mostly in the avoidant category (Clarke-Stewart, 1989).

Though a 7 percent difference in security of attachment is not a big one, it is enough to worry some people. One team of researchers concluded that full-time maternal employment is a "risk factor for the development of avoidant infant–mother attachment relationships." They warned that babies who have to undergo "repeated, daily separations" from their mothers interpret these separations as a sign of rejection (Barglow, Vaughn, and Molitor, 1987, p. 952). The researchers do point out, however, that the majority of babies of full-time employed mothers nonetheless manage to form secure attachments.

What's curious is that the babies of employed mothers who *were* judged insecurely attached did not seem to have the other problems that usually go along with insecure attachments. These babies were not lacking in friendliness, competence, or self-assurance; in fact, according to Clarke-Stewart, "The infants of working mothers who were coded as insecure in the Strange Situation have been found to perform better than the infants of nonworking mothers on a variety of other tasks" (1989, p. 268).

Clarke-Stewart believes that the explanation for these seemingly contradictory findings lies in the Strange Situation itself. This test was designed to bring out attachment behavior in babies by putting them through a fairly stressful procedure—the idea is to arouse their anxiety in order to see how they act toward their mother when they're upset. But the babies of full-time employed mothers are *used* to being left in places other than their homes, with people other than their parents. Thus, if the baby of an employed mother ignores her when she comes back, instead of going to her for comfort, it may just be that he wasn't worried by her absence and isn't in need of comforting.

IS THE STRANGE SITUATION A FAIR TEST? The children in dual-career families are not the only ones who might flunk the Strange Situation test for the wrong reasons. When the test is given to babies in other countries—for example, Japan, West Germany, and Israel—the proportion of babies who appear to be insecurely attached is higher than in the United States (Bretherton and Waters, 1985). The implication is not that children in other countries are less secure than American children, but that the Strange Situation test might not be appropriate for children reared under different cultural conditions. Babies in other cultures do not necessarily have the same kinds of experiences that American babies have.

In one study of Japanese babies, for instance, over 40 percent of the babies were classified as insecure–resistant, because they became so upset during the separation that their mothers had great difficulty in calming them down. But babies in Japan are seldom apart from their mothers during their first year of life and are virtually never left with babysitters. So these babies were simply not prepared for the type of separation they experienced in the Strange Situation (Miyake, Chen, and Campos, 1985).

What about babies who are *not* Japanese but who nevertheless get so upset in the Strange Situation that their mothers can't calm them? Isn't it possible that some of these babies have had fewer experiences with strange people and strange places? And, more important, isn't it possible that inborn differences in temperament—in fearfulness, in emotionality—will affect a child's behavior in the test?

Differences in temperament definitely do affect behavior in the Strange Situation. A recent review looked at 38 experimental studies of attachment and concluded that the baby's temperament is one of the factors that determines the outcome of the test. Babies who tend to have strong negative reactions to anything new are more likely to be rated insecure–resistant. The reviewers also confirmed the connection between security of attachment and a sensitive, responsive mother. The correlation with maternal responsiveness is not a strong one, but the mother's behavior matters a bit more than the baby's temperament (Goldsmith and Alansky, 1987).

Remember, though, that a mother's responsiveness to her baby may be determined, in part, by her baby's characteristics. And the mother–baby relationship can change over time—it may improve or it may get worse. A mother who finds it burdensome to take care of a 3-month-old infant might have highly successful interactions with a 3-year-old. For all these reasons, there is no need to worry excessively about a child, nor to place all the blame on his mother, just because they don't receive a gold star in the Strange Situation.

The Beginnings of Friendships

Children begin to be interested in other children very early in life. Attachments to older siblings are often among babies' first attachments, even though the older siblings may be scarcely out of toddlerhood themselves.

To study how relationships with agemates develop, some researchers put babies or toddlers of various ages into a room with another child of the same age and watched to see what would happen. (There were toys in the room, too, and the babies' mothers were present.) The study showed that as early as 10 months of age, babies' responses to another baby were mostly friendly and positive—they looked at the other baby and smiled and vocalized. This was different from their response to a new toy—a toy was touched and manipulated. So babies aren't attracted to other babies because they look like interesting *things*. Even to a 10-month-old, another baby is a *person* (Eckerman, Whatley, and Kutz, 1975).

The older babies in this study (16 to 24 months) didn't just look and smile at each other: sometimes two toddlers actually played together. For example, one child might hand the other a toy, or both children might play side by side with the same kind of toy. Sometimes they even imitated each other's actions. (Imitation is a firmly established ability by the end of the first year.) Of

The first interactions with agemates can't really be described as "playing together."
These babies are only a year old.

course, not all the things the toddlers did were friendly. They were about as likely to take a toy *away* from the other child as to give her one, and sometimes that led to a struggle.

The older the two babies in the room were, the more attention they paid to each other and the less attention they paid to their mothers. By the end of the second year, the bonds of attachment are starting to loosen, and peer relationships—interactions with agemates—are starting to gain in importance. Toddlers who have had regular experience with other children in playgroups or day-care centers tend to be particularly sociable with their peers (Clarke-Stewart, 1989).

Not surprisingly, the toddlers who get along well with other children tend to be the same ones who had successful interactions with their mothers in infancy, and who were securely attached at age 12 months. Perhaps because these toddlers are very good at evoking favorable responses from others, their mothers generally behave in a responsive manner toward them. And they, in turn, are likely to behave in a responsive manner toward others—for example, by smiling back when another child smiles at them (Pastor, 1981; Vandell and Wilson, 1987).

The Toddler's Struggle for Autonomy

As Sarah approaches her second birthday, she shows less and less of a need to remain in close contact with her mother. Her interest in play and exploration remains high. She can walk well now. Her new mobility, coupled with her increased willingness to leave her mother's side, enables her to explore more of her environment. During toddlerhood, children are moving toward independence. (To *toddle* means to take short, uncertain steps. Roughly speaking, **toddlerhood** is a period that begins in the second year of life, when the child begins to walk. It ends around age 2½, when the child becomes a preschooler.)

Erikson has pointed to the struggle for **autonomy** as the big issue in the toddler's life. Autonomy means self-determination. It means "Me do it!" It means "No!" The 2-year-old, in her drive to achieve independence, often becomes stubborn and contrary—in fact, this period has become notorious as the "terrible twos." A child who was pleasant and cooperative only a couple of months earlier will, at 24 months, kick her feet and scream while her parents are trying to put on her shoes, and then kick and scream some more when she tries to put them on herself and is unable to. Some researchers attribute the orneriness of the 2-year-old to the gap between what she wants to do and what she is able to do. The baby didn't *mind* if she couldn't put on her own shoes; the toddler finds it extremely frustrating (Bullock and Lütkenhaus, 1988).

Because toddlers of this age are so intent on doing things *their* way, a 24-month-old who hasn't yet learned to use the potty (see Box 6-3) is unlikely to agree to give it a try. Thus, for children who have reached the age of 2 without being toilet trained, it might be better to wait until the "terrible twos" subside and they become more cooperative.

But there are other kinds of training that can't be put off. Toddlerhood is the time when **socialization** begins in earnest—when a child must begin to learn the behaviors, attitudes, knowledge, and skills that are necessary to get along in his society. Thus, the child's desire to do what he wants conflicts with the pressures on him to conform to the rules of the society.

Socialization of a toddler is primarily the parents' job. When a parent asks a toddler to do something (or not to do something), what are the chances that he will obey? A study of children between the ages of 15 months and 3½ years looked at how well toddlers comply with their mothers' requests and commands. On the average, the children in this study (who were tested in a homelike setting) complied with a little over half of their mothers' instructions: boys obeyed 53 percent of the time, girls 65 percent. The usual pattern, when a child failed to comply with a request or command, was simply to ignore it: boys did this 32 percent of the time, girls 18 percent. There were no gender differences in the other responses to commands: girls and boys were equally likely to refuse ("I don't want to"), defy (refusal plus a show of temper), or negotiate ("I'll do it later"). There was an age difference, however: older children in this study were less likely just to ignore a command and more likely to use negotiation (Kuczynski and others, 1987). Other studies have found that as toddlers turn into preschoolers they become more compliant: they are more likely to cooperate with their parents suggestions and instructions, and they have more self-control—they are less likely to break rules when their parents aren't watching (Howes and Olenick, 1986).

Aside from gender and age, a number of other factors have been found to affect toddlers' compliance. Toddlers who had been judged securely attached at 12 months were found to be more obedient at 21 months than those who had been judged insecurely attached (Londerville and Main, 1981). Toddlers whose parents fight with each other are less obedient, and this is especially true of boys (Jouriles, Pfiffner, and O'Leary, 1988). Toddlers who had been enrolled in day-care before the age of 12 months were found to be less compliant with their parents than children cared for at home (Clarke-Stewart,

The Child in Society

Box 6-3
Toilet Training

Every human society places some restraints on its members with regard to elimination—nowhere are people allowed to urinate or defecate wherever and whenever they please. Eventually, all young children are expected to conform to the toileting customs of their culture. But societies differ greatly in when and how this demand is made. Children may be trained harshly or with gentleness. They may be trained in early infancy or in late toddlerhood.

Gentle, late training is often found in preindustrial societies where the climate is warm and toddlers go naked (at least from the waist down). The practices of the Siriono, a South American Indian people, are a good example. The Siriono make no effort to train babies until they can walk. After they can walk, children learn by imitation, and with some encouragement from their parents, not to soil near the family's sleeping quarters. Gradually the children learn to indicate their needs, and gradually their parents lead them further away in order to urinate and defecate. By the age of 3, they have learned "not to pollute the house" (Whiting and Child, 1953, p. 75).

We tend to think of this style of toilet training as gentle and of early toilet training as harsh. But there is no necessary connection between gentleness and timing. The Digo of East Africa train their babies early, but the training is by no means harsh. Babies in this society are generally trained by 6 months! Here's how it's done:

> Bowel and bladder training are initiated simultaneously and extremely early, at about 2 to 3 weeks of age. The mother takes a teaching role and assumes all responsibility in the initial phase of the training process. She places the infant in a special training position outside the house, at first at times when she senses that the infant needs to eliminate (after feeding, when waking from naps, etc.), with the idea that he will soon learn to let her know more independently.
>
> At about 2 to 3 weeks of age, the mother begins by putting the infant in a position assumed to facilitate elimination. For voiding (urination), the mother sits on the ground outside, with her legs straight out in front of her. The infant is placed between the mother's legs, facing away from her, in a sitting position, supported by the mother's body. The mother then makes a "shuus" noise that the infant learns to associate with voiding. This is done many times during the day and at night. When the infant voids as the "shuus" sound is made, he is rewarded for his behavior by feeding, close contact, or other pleasurable activity. Gradually, the infant is expected to become more articulate in communicating his needs or by

This Digo baby has learned to urinate in response to his mother's signals.

1989). However, another study showed that toddlers who had attended high-quality day-care centers, adequately staffed and with well-trained caregivers, were just as compliant and had *more* self-control than children cared for at home (Howes and Olenick, 1986).

What can parents do to increase the likelihood that their toddler will obey them? Research has shown that harsh methods of discipline, such as shouting and physical punishment, or low levels of parental involvement in which dis-

climbing to the appropriate position. He is expected to urinate in position and on command at least by 4 to 5 months.   (deVries and deVries, 1977, p. 173)

The procedure is similar for bowel training; only the baby's position is different.

The Digo do not regard bladder and bowel training as private or unclean—rather, it is accepted in a relaxed way as a normal part of infant care. During the first year, occasional slips are taken casually, perhaps only with an exclamation of surprise. After the baby is walking he is scolded if he eliminates in the house, but apparently that happens very rarely.

In our own culture, toilet-training practices have changed drastically over the years. In the 1920s, mothers were told to begin training when the baby was a month old and to adhere to a strict schedule: the baby should be held over a potty at certain times of day, and these times mustn't vary by as much as five minutes (Wolfenstein, 1967). Nowadays children are seldom put under any pressure to use the potty until after their second birthday, and even then the pressure tends to be far milder than it was in the past.

From the child's point of view, the timing of training probably matters less than the *manner* of training—whether the trainer is impatient and critical or gentle and understanding. But what about timing? In one way, late training may actually be *more* difficult for the child. Urination and defecation start out as simple reflexes, triggered by the pressure of a full bladder or bowel. Like other reflexes, they can be linked with neutral stimuli, if the neutral stimuli are often present when the reflex occurs (see the discussion of classical conditioning, p. 89). The Digo's training technique makes use of this principle. The sounds the mother makes and the position in which she puts the baby become associated with urination or defecation, and eventually these stimuli can themselves trigger the reflexes.

We don't use those techniques in our culture, but that doesn't mean that the reflexes don't become linked to other stimuli. Babies in our society have spent two or three years urinating and defecating into their disposable diapers. Then we take their diapers off and expect them to perform under totally different conditions, sitting down on the potty with a bare bottom. Even if they're perfectly willing, it might not be that easy. Our astronauts discovered how difficult it is to get the reflexes to function under unfamiliar conditions. Here's astronaut Russell Schweickart describing what it's like to urinate in space:

> You just . . . urinate into it (a bag) through the one-way valve. There are lots of little cute problems and uncertainties. Unless you're an extremely unusual person, since the time you were about a year and a half old or so, you probably have not taken a leak laying flat on your back. And if you think that's easy, let me tell you, you've got some built-in psychological or survival programs, or something which you've got to overcome.   (Schweickart and Warshall, 1980, p. 14)

Most modern parents (and pediatricians) deny that it is possible to toilet train a baby before the age of 2; they say younger babies are too immature to control their reflexes or to understand what is being asked of them. If you politely refrain from mentioning the Digo and merely point out that most American babies in the 1930s and '40s were trained by the age of 12 or 14 months, they reply, "It was the *mother* who was trained, not the baby." This is true in a sense: the mother had to be willing to remain within hailing distance of a potty (because 14-month-olds can't hold in their urine very long), had to respond quickly when the child signaled a need to urinate, and had to cope with occasional accidents. But if they were willing to go to the trouble, they could—without ever being mean or harsh or shaming the child—usually produce a 14-month-old who was dry during the day.

Today, most American parents find it a good deal more convenient just to keep their toddlers in disposable diapers. But those who worry about the environmental impact of 2000 discarded diapers per child per year may be happy to hear that there is an alternative.

obedience is often ignored, go along with disobedient behavior by the child. But here we have a which-came-first-the-chicken-or-the-egg problem: is the parent's behavior the *cause* of the child's disobedience, a *reaction* to it, or both? In all probability, the answer is both, which means that a "vicious circle" is in operation.

One way of getting a child to do what you ask is to do what *he* asks occasionally. In an interesting study, mothers and their young children were randomly placed in one of two experimental conditions. In one, the child and the mother were allowed to play freely with the toys in a playroom; then the mother instructed the child to put away the toys. The child was unlikely to obey. In the other experimental condition, the mother was told to follow her child's lead in playing with the toys during the play period—she was supposed to allow the child to control the situation and to go along with his suggestions. In that condition, the child was significantly more likely to cooperate when his mother then asked him to pick up the toys (Parpal and Maccoby, 1985). No one likes to have to follow orders *all* the time.

Even children who are usually cooperative are likely to say "I don't want to" when it's time to pick up their toys. But a child who refuses to put his toys away may be quite willing to listen to his mother's advice about how to solve a tricky problem (Matas, Arend, and Sroufe, 1979). A toddler may like to feel that he is independent and autonomous, but of course he really isn't. He still has a lot to learn, and he still needs his parents' help. The path is smoother for a child who knows when he needs assistance and who can accept it when it's offered to him.

Summary

1. Although there has been some increase in the amount of caregiving provided by fathers, the mother is still the primary caregiver, the one who takes chief responsibility for the baby. Mothers know more about babies to begin with, and most fathers end up in the role of reluctant, somewhat incompetent helpers.

2. Newborn babies are not, at first, very sociable, but by the time they are 6 or 7 weeks old they have begun making eye contact and smiling at people.

3. Mothers act differently with babies than they do with adults—their speech and facial expressions are slowed down and exaggerated.

4. When babies play with their parents, they want brief periods of interaction followed by brief periods without eye contact. If a mother tries to get her infant's attention during these "time-outs," their interactions may be unsuccessful.

5. Babies enjoy having an effect on someone—they like to feel that people are responding to them. When the other person makes his behavior **contingent** on what the baby does, the baby is delighted.

6. Babies whose parents respond quickly and consistently to their cries end up crying less, perhaps because they have developed what Erikson calls **basic trust**. Babies who are completely ignored also end up crying little— they cease to feel that what they do makes a difference, which is called **learned helplessness**.

7. Babies whose parents respond slowly or inconsistently to their cries end up crying the most. This relationship works in a transactional, "vicious circle" fashion: parents tend to stop responding if the baby cries a lot, and babies whose cries are often ignored tend to cry more.

8. Parents who respond quickly and appropriately to their babies' cries and other efforts at communication have the most successful interactions with their babies.

9. A "difficult" baby is one whose feeding and sleeping patterns are irregular, who reacts negatively to anything new, whose negative reactions tend to be intense, and who is often unhappy. These characteristics reflect the baby's built-in temperament.

10. Only a small proportion of babies can be described as "difficult." Many more are "easy" or "slow to warm up." The quality of the relationship between parents and baby depends partly on how well the baby's characteristics fit the parents' expectations.

11. There are group differences as well as individual differences among babies. For example, Japanese babies, babies in the Zinacanteco Indian tribe in Mexico, and babies in the Gusii tribe in Kenya all show differences in temperament compared to North American babies.

12. Some babies don't like to be cuddled. The tendency to be a cuddler or a noncuddler appears to be present from birth.

13. Gender differences are negligible in infancy; nonetheless, parents treat male and female infants differently. Gender differences increase as children get older, due partly to biological factors and partly to the differences in the ways parents act with boys and girls.

14. A father is more likely to pick up a baby for play; a mother is more likely to pick up a baby for caregiving. Fathers' play is more physical, less verbal, and less carefully attuned to the baby's level of development than mothers' play. Fathers make more of a distinction between girls and boys than mothers do.

15. People differ in how much **empathy** they have for the feelings of others. Parents who are low in empathy are less likely to respond appropriately to their babies' signals and more likely to become child abusers.

16. If a mother is alcoholic or severely depressed, she may be unable to have satisfactory interactions with her baby. The babies of depressed mothers tend to become withdrawn and to act depressed themselves. If a normal mother pretends to be sad, her baby may become upset.

17. Gusii babies in Africa and Yucatec Mayan babies in Mexico are held most of the time and are fed every time they cry. However, these babies have fewer face-to-face interactions with their mothers than American babies do, and fewer opportunities to explore their environment.

18. American mothers keep young infants in "containers" such as cribs and allow older ones much freedom to explore their environment. Though they engage in intense periods of parent–infant interaction, the babies are expected to learn to play by themselves and to go to sleep alone, at a schedule set by their parents.

19. Every normal child develops an **attachment** to someone, if there is someone to become attached to. Babies show **separation distress** when a person to whom they are attached leaves them alone in an unfamiliar place; this behavior emerges at about 8 months of age in babies all over the world.

20. Twelve-month-old babies will look at the faces of their caregivers (or other adults) to gain information about how to react to something; this is called **social referencing.**

21. By 12 months, many babies will cry if someone they don't know tries to pick them up. But fear of strangers varies: it depends on who the stranger is, on what he or she does, and on the baby's temperament.

22. When children are separated from the people to whom they are attached, they are desperately unhappy at first and then become depressed. Eventually they form new attachments. Failing to form attachments at all has far more serious consequences. Children who have no opportunity to form attachments before the age of 4 may later be unable to form deep and lasting relationships with anyone.

23. In the absence of parents or permanent caregivers, children sometimes form deep attachments to other children. A child who keeps forming attachments and then losing them may eventually become unable to form new attachments.

24. A duckling becomes attached to its mother by a quick form of learning called **imprinting,** which can occur only within a critical period lasting about a day after it is hatched. Attachment is a slower process in monkeys; there is no critical period, but rather, a **sensitive period** during which attachments are formed most readily.

25. According to the ethological view, the tendency of human babies to become attached to their mothers is a built-in characteristic of our species, inherited because it had survival value for early humans.

26. A baby of 12 to 18 months has two opposing desires: to remain near his mother, and to explore and play. If his mother is nearby, he will use her as "a secure base from which to explore."

27. Ainsworth distinguishes between **secure attachments** and **insecure attachments**; the difference shows up in babies' reactions to the **Strange Situation.** A securely attached baby tends to play happily while his mother is there; he will greet her joyously when she returns after a brief absence. Insecure attachments are of two kinds: **avoidant** and **resistant.**

28. Abused children are likely to be insecurely attached to their mothers. Mothers who responded to their infants' cries and signals in a sensitive and responsive way are most likely to have securely attached children. The presence of a man in the household increases the chances that the baby will be securely attached to the mother.

29. Although the chances of being judged securely attached to their mothers are slightly less for babies whose mothers work full time, in general the children of employed mothers are *more* competent than children of mothers who don't work. The Strange Situation does not appear to be a fair test for these babies. It also may not be a fair test for babies who were raised in other cultures or for babies whose temperaments are unusually fearful or emotional. Temperament affects behavior in the Strange Situation almost as much as having a sensitive, responsive mother.

30. As early as 10 months of age, babies show friendly responses to other babies. As they get older, they pay more attention to one another and less attention to their mothers. Toddlers who have had good interactions with their mothers are likely to get along well with their peers.

31. Toddlerhood starts when the child begins to walk and ends around age 2½, when the preschool period begins. According to Erikson, the struggle for **autonomy** is the major issue in the toddler's life. The 2-year-old, in her drive for independence, is likely to become stubborn and contrary (the "terrible twos").

32. Toilet-training practices differ from culture to culture. Gentle training is not necessarily late training: the Digo people of East Africa train their babies very early (by 6 months!) but the training is gentle.

33. On the average, toddlers obey a little over half of their mother's commands; girls obey more than boys. Parents who use harsh methods of discipline or who ignore disobedience tend to have disobedient children, but the parents' behavior could be a reaction to their children's behavior as well as a cause.

Key Terms

vocalize
contingent
basic trust
learned helplessness
security object
empathy
attachment
separation distress

separation anxiety
social referencing
ethology
imprinting
sensitive period
security of attachment
securely attached
insecurely attached

Strange Situation
resistant
avoidant
bonding
toddlerhood
autonomy
socialization

The Beginnings of Intelligence and Language

Stephanie was born four days ago. She's just come home from the hospital and lies in her crib, awake. As neonates go, she's a rather attractive one, with a full crop of dark hair and big, alert-looking eyes.

Someday Stephanie may become a mathematician, or a concert pianist, or a writer of best-selling novels. Right now, though, she doesn't appear to be awfully bright. She can't add 1 and 1, she can't hum a few bars of "Rockabye Baby," she can't even speak English! Stephanie has a long way to go.

But before Stephanie learns to count or sing or even to speak, she has some much more basic things to find out. She must learn about herself— which parts of what she experiences are "me" and which parts are "the world out there." She must learn about the shape and size of her own body, and how to make its various parts move where she wants them to. She must learn that people and objects exist "out there," and that her actions can have an effect on those people and objects. She must learn some simple laws of physics: if you let go of a rattle it will fall down; you can stick your hand into water but not into the floor. She must learn about relationships like *under* and *on top of, behind* and *inside*.

Stephanie may seem dumb, but in fact she is one of the most efficient learning machines on the face of the earth. A baby chimpanzee is way ahead of her at this point, but in less than two years she will be doing things that no chimpanzee has ever learned to do. She will be doing things that no computer has ever been programmed to do. How will it come about—this remarkable transformation from the ignorant creature she is now to the clever person she is destined to become? We are talking now about **cognitive development** —the growth of intelligence, reasoning, knowledge, and understanding.

Cognitive Development in Infancy

The pioneering investigator in the field of cognitive development was Jean Piaget, whose theories we summarized in Chapter 3. Because Piaget has had such an overwhelming influence on this field, we will start out with a look at his description of cognitive development in infancy.

The Piagetian Approach As we said in Chapter 3, Piaget believes that cognitive development proceeds in stages. Each child must go through the same stages in the same order. However, the rate of progress may vary considerably from child to child, and transitions from one stage to another are usually gradual rather than clear and distinct.

What causes the child to progress from stage to stage? According to Piaget, cognitive development depends both on maturation—the gradual unfolding of a genetic plan—and on the child's interactions with the environment. Maturation provides the child with the necessary biological equipment. Children put that equipment to good use in their active exploration of the environment.

Above all, human beings are *adaptable.* Adaptability means that a child can adjust to the demands of the environment and then *re*adjust if the environment changes. Thus, **adaptation** depends both on the challenges provided by the environment and on what the child is capable of doing and understanding. In the chameleon, adaptation may result only in a change of skin color. In the young human, adaptation leads to cognitive development.

Adaptation, according to Piaget, occurs in two different ways. The first he calls **assimilation.** Assimilation means applying something you already know (or already can do) to something new. You've learned to draw with crayons; now you can also draw with felt-tip pens. You've counted ten pebbles; now you can count ten raisins.

The other kind of adaptation is called **accommodation.** In accommodation you don't do (or think) the same thing—you modify your **scheme** (Piaget's term; see p. 97) to suit some new situation. You do this because the old scheme wouldn't work.

Here's an example of the two kinds of adaptation. Young Alex, age 14 months, sits on the floor putting small objects into his pail. (He's using his putting-things-into-the-pail scheme.) We hand him several objects he's never seen before: a sea shell, a walnut, a pocket watch, a small box. He *assimilates* them all into his putting-things-into-the-pail scheme: in other words, he puts them all into the pail. Now we hand him a cardboard tube from a roll of paper towels. He tries to put it in the pail, but he's holding it crosswise and it's too long to fit in that way. So he *accommodates:* he turns the tube sideways so it can go into the pail vertically.

When he's older, Alex's *ideas,* as well as his actions, will undergo assimilation and accommodation. Alex may believe, for example, that all dogs are friendly and playful. Then he meets a dog that backs off and runs away when Alex approaches. Alex can assimilate this experience to his previous belief ("The dog did that because he was trying to get me to play with him") or he can accommodate and modify his idea ("Not all dogs are friendly").

Using assimilation and accommodation, children constantly widen their ability to cope with a variety of situations—increasingly complex situations. We will see how this happens during the first major period of development, which Piaget calls the **sensorimotor period.** The sensorimotor period itself is divided into six separate stages (see Table 7–1), the six stages of cognitive development in infancy. Bear in mind that the ages given for these stages are all very approximate.

THE SIX STAGES OF SENSORIMOTOR DEVELOPMENT. During the first stage of the sensorimotor period (the first month of life), the baby makes use of inborn schemes such as sucking and rooting. Adaptation occurs even with schemes this basic: for example, Stephanie quickly becomes more skillful at finding the nipple and taking it into her mouth. Looking at things is another built-in scheme that shows adaptation during this period: the baby gets better at focusing her eyes and tracking moving objects.

The second stage (1 to 4 months) marks the entrance of what Piaget (1952) calls "the first acquired adaptations." Thumb-sucking is a good example. The baby's hands flail around at random at first, but occasionally one hand lands on her face and, through the rooting reflex, she is able to get her thumb into her mouth. In this way she discovers that sucking her thumb feels good. She isn't able to take full advantage of this discovery right away, because it takes her a while to gain control over her hand movements, but she practices and pretty soon she is moving her hand to her mouth reliably and on purpose. She has learned to repeat an action that first occurred only by accident, because she found the results enjoyable. This is an example of what Piaget calls a **circular reaction:** "The child does something at random, and when he gets an interesting result, he repeats the action indefinitely. In this way, he learns to suck his thumb, to seize objects, to make noises by knocking hard things together, and so on" (1927/1977, p. 202).

A new kind of circular reaction appears in the third stage (4 to 8 months): now the adaptation involves not just the baby's own body, but also the interesting effects the baby can produce on his environment. Piaget (1952) hung a rattle over his son Laurent's crib; then he tied a string to the rattle and attached the other end to Laurent's right hand. When Laurent moved his arm, the rattle made a noise. At first it startled him, but soon he began to wave his arm around in order to produce this interesting result. He clearly enjoyed this game—he smiled and laughed when he succeeded in shaking the rattle.

Piaget credits the stage-3 baby with understanding that his actions—in this case, his arm movements—were what produced the interesting result, the rattling noise. Stage-3 babies are able to understand that something they did made something else happen, but they don't understand why or how it

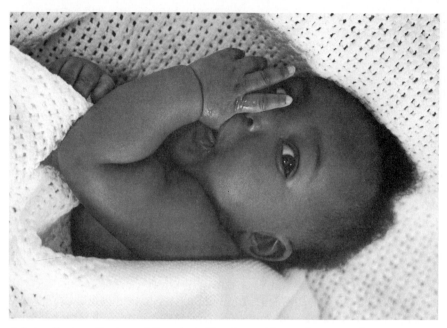

A baby discovers the joys of thumb-sucking by accident, when a random arm movement happens to bring his thumb near his mouth.

happened—the connection between their action and its result is still a "magical" one.

In stage 4 (8 to 12 months), we see the beginnings of "intelligent" behavior and a new appreciation of cause-and-effect relationships. When Piaget's daughter Jacqueline was 9 months old, Piaget took her toy duck and tangled it in the strings leading to two other toys suspended above her crib. Jacqueline wanted the duck but it was too high for her to reach. So she tried different ways of pulling on the strings—pulling them harder, pulling from higher up—until the duck finally fell out. Jacqueline's actions were not novel: she had already learned various ways of pulling on strings. But now she was able to apply these methods in an appropriate way to a new situation.

The dawning intelligence of stage-4 babies is also shown in the way they act when you give them something they've never seen before. When Piaget gave Jacqueline a new object, she examined it carefully. Then she tried out all her old schemes on it: she shook it, tapped it, rubbed it against the side of her crib, put it in her mouth, and so on. She seemed to be trying to understand this new thing by systematically exploring all of its possibilities.

When they reach stage 5 (12 to 18 months), toddlers can work out *new* schemes to suit new situations. Piaget (1952) calls their method for doing this "discoveries of new means through active experimentation." A stage-5 child may perform a series of experiments just to see what will happen. Piaget gives many examples of the kinds of "experiments" his own children performed. Laurent, for instance, spent a lot of time discovering that objects of all shapes and sizes would fall down when he let them go. He varied the position of his hand or arm and they still fell down. Jacqueline, with similar concentration, spent many hours investigating the properties of water. She filled containers of all sorts with water, studied it as she poured it out, let the water run along

TABLE 7–1
The Six Stages of Piaget's Sensorimotor Period

STAGE	APPROXIMATE AGE	DESCRIPTION
1	Birth to 1 month	The use and adaptation of built-in reflexes.
2	1 to 4 months	The first acquired adaptations. Simple circular reactions.
3	4 to 8 months	More complicated circular reactions. Procedures to make interesting events happen again.
4	8 to 12 months	Applying known procedures to new situations.
5	12 to 18 months	The discovery of new procedures through active experimentation.
6	18 to 24 months	The invention of new procedures through mental representations. Insight and planning.

her arm, squeezed it from a sponge, and so on. Jacqueline studied the behavior of water in much the same manner, and with the same seriousness of purpose, that Piaget studied the behavior of Jacqueline!

The stage-5 child approaches problems in a flexible, sometimes even inventive way. Jacqueline tried over and over again to put the chain from her father's watch into a small matchbox. She put one end of the chain into the box, but when she released it in order to grab the other end, the first part slid out. She did this 14 times in a row! Then she tried a different method: she held the chain by the middle and got both ends into the box before she let go. That worked better, but sometimes the middle part fell outside the box and then the chain slipped out again. Finally, she had a new idea: she rolled the chain into a ball and put it all into the box at once (Piaget, 1952).

The last stage in the sensorimotor period, stage 6 (18 to 24 months), is when children become able to solve problems not just by trial and error, but by a flash of insight. When Piaget's younger daughter Lucienne was just entering stage 6, Piaget handed her a matchbox with his watch chain already inside it. Lucienne wanted to get the chain out, but the matchbox was partly closed and the opening was too narrow to permit the chain to slip out. Here's what Lucienne did (this is a very famous passage):

> She looks at the slit with great attention; then, several times in succession, she opens and shuts her mouth, at first slightly, then wider and wider! . . . Lucienne, by opening her mouth thus expresses . . . her desire to enlarge the opening of the box.

Then,

> Lucienne unhesitatingly puts her finger in the slit and, instead of trying as before to reach the chain, she pulls so as to enlarge the opening. She succeeds and grasps the chain.   (Piaget, 1952, p. 338)

Piaget explains that Lucienne, at this point, still couldn't think out the situation in words or in clear visual images. So she used mouth-opening as a symbol, as a means of representing to herself what she wanted to do. What's particularly interesting about Lucienne's behavior is that it marks a transition between stage-5 and stage-6 abilities. In stage 5, children actually have to try out solutions to problems. Later in stage 6, they can *think* out the possibilities —do them mentally. This is a real breakthrough. It enables children to plan ahead, to envision the consequences of their actions without actually having to experience them. Here's Jacqueline in stage 6, age 20 months:

> Jacqueline . . . arrives at a closed door—with a blade of grass in each hand. She stretches out her right hand toward the knob but sees that she cannot turn it without letting go of the grass. She puts the grass on the floor, opens the door, picks up the grass again and enters. But when she wants to leave the room things become complicated. She puts the grass on the floor and grasps the doorknob. But then she perceives that in pulling the door toward her she will simultaneously chase away the grass. . . . She therefore picks it up in order to put it outside the door's zone of movement.   (1952, p. 339)

Thus, we have reached the point where the child can work things out in her head, using mental **representations,** as Piaget calls them. Representations are something like ideas and something like memories—they can be mental images of things seen, of things heard, or even of actions performed. They can also be words or sentences, but they don't have to be. The child has mental representations before she has words. Jacqueline, at age 16 months, imitated a little boy she had seen having a tantrum the day before. At that age she couldn't possibly have described the scene in words. Her **deferred imitation** (see p. 99) was based on her mental representation of the event.

THE CONCEPT OF OBJECT PERMANENCE. The stage-6 child understands that she lives in a world which also contains other people and objects. She understands that these people and objects have a permanent existence, even when she can't see them or feel them. According to Piaget, this understanding is not present in young babies—it develops slowly, over the course of the first two years of life. Here is Piaget's theory of how the concept of **object permanence** develops.

By the end of stage 1, according to Piaget, the month-old baby is able to recognize certain sights and sounds: the sight of the nipple from which she gets her milk, the sight of her mother's face, the sound of her mother's voice. But, says Piaget, this kind of simple recognition does not mean "that in the first weeks of life the universe is really cut up into objects, that is, into things conceived as permanent, substantial, external to the self, and firm in existence" (1954, p. 5). There are simply "pictures" that come and go, and some of the pictures start to look familiar after a while. The disappearance of one of these pictures causes no particular concern. If the baby sees her mother's face she may gaze at it for a time, but if it goes away she simply stops looking and does something else (Ginsburg and Opper, 1969).

In stage 2 (1 to 4 months), the baby begins to show some expectation that things looked at or touched can be looked at or touched again. For instance,

Lucienne looked at her father, looked away, and then looked back again—clearly expecting to see him in the same place. However, this kind of behavior is very limited. It consists only of continuing to do something that was done a few seconds before. If her father isn't there when the baby looks for him again, he's quickly forgotten (Piaget, 1954).

The first hints of object permanence appear in stage 3 (4 to 8 months): now when Laurent sees his father drop a toy, he'll look for the toy on the floor and not just in his father's hand. He will do this, however, only if he has actually seen the toy fall. What happens when you cover up an object that he's been looking at? According to Piaget, this is a problem a stage-3 baby can't solve. Piaget showed Laurent a small bell and then, when Laurent started to reach for it, hid it behind his other hand.

> [Laurent] immediately withdraws his arm, as though the little bell no longer existed. I then shake my hand, always revealing the back of it and gripping the little bell in my palm. Laurent watches attentively, greatly surprised to rediscover the sound of the little bell, but he does not try to grasp it. I turn my hand over and he sees the little bell; he then stretches out his hand toward it. I hide the little bell again by changing the position of my hand; Laurent withdraws his hand.   (pp. 39–40)

For the stage-3 baby, when an object is "out of sight" it is immediately "out of mind."

Piaget says that as long as any little piece of the bell was visible, Laurent would try to grab it. But when it was totally covered he acted as though it was totally gone.

In stage 4 (8 to 12 months), babies begin to unravel the mystery of disappearing objects. Their developing concept of object permanence—the knowledge that things don't cease to exist just because you can't see them anymore—is also extended to people. As we mentioned in the previous chapter, babies first show signs of attachment to their parents at around 8 months of age, the beginning of Piaget's stage 4. One of the signs of attachment is separation distress, the protest that a baby puts up when he is parted from his mother. A younger baby doesn't show separation distress and this fits in very well with Piagetian theory: how can the baby be upset by his mother's absence if she doesn't exist when he can't see her? The emergence of separation distress, at around 8 months of age, implies that the baby now realizes that his mother is a "permanent object"—that even if she isn't here, she must be *somewhere* (Phillips, 1975).

As it turns out, babies evidently come to believe in the permanence of people a little before they draw the same conclusion about inanimate objects. Piaget (1954) described how Jacqueline, at 8½ months, uncovered her father when he was hiding behind a blanket. She was still stumped, though, when he hid one of her toys in the same way.

Other researchers have supported Piaget's finding that "person permanence" comes a little before object permanence. In one study, a number of babies were tested several times between the ages of 8½ and 13½ months. Each baby was given two kinds of tasks: to find a hidden toy, and to find Mommy (who hid behind a screen or a couch). The results showed that the babies' concept of person permanence was ahead of their concept of object permanence. Moreover, the babies who did best on both kinds of tests were the ones who had formed secure attachments to their mothers (see Chapter 6). As we said in that chapter, securely attached children tend to have mothers who respond quickly and appropriately to their cries for help. So these findings fit together nicely: a baby who learns that his mother can be counted on to appear when he really needs her will naturally begin to believe that she exists all the time, not just when he can see her. Once he has had this realization about a person, he can apply it to inanimate objects as well (Bell, 1970).

By the middle of stage 4, most babies have enough understanding of the permanence of objects that they will search for a vanished toy. But Piaget discovered a strange limitation to their understanding. Here's Laurent at 9½ months:

> Laurent is placed on a sofa between a coverlet A on the right and a wool garment B on the left. I place my watch under A; he gently raises the coverlet, perceives part of the object, uncovers it, and grasps it. The same thing happens a second and a third time. . . . I then place the watch under B; Laurent watches this maneuver attentively, but at the moment the watch has disappeared under garment B, he turns back toward coverlet A and searches for the object under that screen. I again place the watch under B; he again searches for it under A.   (Piaget, 1954, p. 53)

TABLE 7–2
Piaget's View of the Development of Object Permanence

STAGE	APPROXIMATE AGE	DESCRIPTION
1	Birth to 1 month	No signs of object permanence.
2	1 to 4 months	No particular reaction if objects vanish, but there seems to be some expectation that an object looked at or touched can be looked at or touched again.
3	4 to 8 months	Still "out of sight, out of mind" for hidden objects, but if an object is seen to fall it may be searched for on the floor.
4	8 to 12 months	The child now searches for a hidden object, but if it is hidden in a new place the child may continue to search for it in the place where it was previously found.
5	12 to 18 months	The child searches for hidden objects in new as well as old locations, but only if the movements of the object are visible.
6	18 to 24 months	Invisible movements of objects can now be followed in the imagination, by means of mental representations. Object permanence is complete.

Laurent searched in a place where he had previously found the watch, even though he saw his father put it in a different place. It's hard to believe that a clever baby like Laurent would make such a stupid mistake! But Jacqueline and Lucienne behaved in a similar way at that age, and so have many other babies—babies whose last names were Thompson or Romero or Chen, and not Piaget.

Piaget's explanation for this behavior is that the baby's concept of the object is still not complete at stage 4. The baby does not yet have an understanding of the object as a permanent thing that is independent of his actions and independent of its surroundings. Take the case of Piaget's nephew Gérard. Gérard was playing with a ball. It rolled under an armchair and he got it out. Then the ball rolled under the sofa. Gérard tried to get it out from under the sofa but was unable to. So he crossed the room and again searched for the ball under the armchair! At this age, Piaget explains, Gérard doesn't have a concept of the ball as an object in itself but only as part of a larger context. It's perfectly possible for the child to have two contexts that include the ball: "ball-under-the-armchair" and "ball-under-the-sofa." When Gérard failed to find the "ball-under-the-sofa," he went in search of the "ball-under-the-armchair" (Piaget, 1954).

By stage 5 (12 to 18 months), the toddler knows that things can be moved from place to place (see Table 7–2). He searches for an object in the place where he saw it hidden, and not necessarily where he previously found it. The only limitation to his concept of object permanence is that he still cannot take account of the movements of objects unless he actually sees them happen. Piaget took a potato that Jacqueline had been playing with, put it in a box, put the box under a rug, dumped the potato out of the box, and brought out the empty box.

> I say to Jacqueline, who has not stopped looking at the rug and who has realized that I was doing something under it: "Give papa the potato." She searches for the object in the box, looks at me, again looks at the box minutely, looks at the rug, etc., but it does not occur to her to raise the rug in order to find the potato underneath. (1954, p. 68)

This problem can at last be solved when the child reaches stage 6 (18 to 24 months), according to Piaget, because at this age children become capable of forming mental representations. The stage-6 child is able to follow all the movements of the potato, even when she can't see them happen, because now she can imagine them.

PLAY AND IMITATION. Piaget was very interested in children's play, for two reasons. First, when children play, they are engaging in exactly those activities—exploration, experimentation, and practice—that are necessary to advance their cognitive development. Second, the skills children make use of when they play are an indication of the cognitive stage they have reached.

The earliest kind of play is called **sensorimotor play** or **mastery play.** According to Piaget (1962), the baby repeats actions that she has already performed, such as grasping or throwing, just for the pleasure of mastering the activity and proving to herself that she can do it. Piaget's children got so accustomed to having their father put barriers in front of toys that the act of pushing aside the barrier became a game in itself, and the children would laugh when they did it.

The second kind of play, **pretend play** or **symbolic play,** emerges some

The earliest kind of play is sensorimotor play: the baby may repeat an action over and over again, just for the sheer pleasure of mastering it.

time after the first birthday. It begins as an extension of the earlier form of play: the child repeats an action she has done in the past, but in a "make-believe" way. Jacqueline, at 15 months, saw a fringed cloth that reminded her of the fringes on her pillow. She took the fringe in her fist, put her thumb in her mouth, and lay down on her side as though she were going to sleep, laughing as she did so. She was *pretending* to perform her going-to-sleep ritual, and she was using the fringed cloth to represent her pillow. Piaget (1962) says that this behavior is an intermediate stage, not yet fully symbolic. True symbolic play doesn't appear until mental representations are possible, in stage 6 (18 to 24 months). At this point, props are no longer necessary: the stage 5 baby might pretend to drink from an empty cup or even from a block, but the stage 6 baby can drink from a purely imaginary cup.

Other researchers have added more details to Piaget's description of the development of pretend play. The 14-month-old can apply imagination only to herself, as when she pretends to drink from a cup. Later, between 15 and 20 months, she also begins to apply it to others, as when she pretends to give her doll a drink from a cup. At the same time, her use of imagination becomes more abstract, less tied to real objects. The 14-month-old may pretend to talk into a toy telephone, but the 18-month-old will talk into a banana. The 22-month-old can imagine her doll drinking from the cup by itself (Brownell, 1986; Acredolo, 1988).

Imitation, according to Piaget, may start as early as stage 2 (1 to 4 months): if an adult mimics what a baby has just done, the baby might do it again. Thus, in "imitating" the adult, the baby is simply repeating her own action. In stage 3 (4 to 8 months) she can imitate an adult's action even if she hasn't just performed that action, but it has to be something she already knows how to do and something she can see or hear herself do—for example, she can imitate a sound that she already knows how to make. According to Piaget, a stage-3 baby cannot yet imitate something that she can't see or hear herself do, such as a facial expression. In stage 4 (8 to 12 months), babies become able to imitate facial expressions, though perhaps not very accurately; they can also imitate novel actions if they are simple enough. In stage 5 (12 to 18 months) they are able to imitate more complex actions. Imitation reaches its full development in stage 6 (18 to 24 months), when the child becomes able to imitate actions she has seen several hours or even days before, based on her mental representations of the actions.

Current Views on the Cognitive Capacities of Babies

Given that many of the things Piaget was talking about had never been studied before, and given that his own three children were virtually his only subjects for his work on infancy, his description of cognitive development in the first two years has held up remarkably well. But quite a bit has been learned since Jacqueline, Laurent, and Lucienne climbed out of the Piagetian crib. Today, many researchers feel that Piaget underestimated babies. Lacking the sophisticated experimental techniques that are now available, Piaget was unable to detect some of the less obvious capabilities of his young subjects.

For example, Piaget believed that the ability to imitate something you can't see yourself do, such as a facial expression, doesn't appear until stage 4 (8 to 12 months). But babies only a week old appear to have the built-in ability to imitate simple facial gestures (see Chapter 5). In 1973, a Greek graduate

Close-Up

Box 7-1
The Origins of Self-Awareness

Jean Piaget and Sigmund Freud had very different views of infant development, but they agreed on one point: that the newborn baby has no concept of self, no idea of the distinction between "me" and "not me." The baby at first doesn't realize that the sounds he hears are his own cries, that the moving thing passing in front of his eyes is his own hand. As Piaget put it,

> When a baby discovers his own body—his fingers, feet, arms—he looks at them no differently than he regards other objects, without any idea that he himself is the one responsible for moving the particular objects that he is admiring. . . . To begin with, a baby has no sense of self at all. (1927/1977, p. 200)

The concept of self develops gradually during infancy. Many aspects of the baby's experience are responsible for this development. He discovers that he can control the movements of his hands and feet, but that he can't make the wall move, nor the table, nor the dog. He discovers that his hands and feet and mouth and chest are always there, while other things—such as Mommy and Daddy—come and go. He learns that certain sensations derive from the "me" parts of the world and not from the other parts: biting down hard on his toe feels dramatically different from biting down hard on a teething ring!

By the second year of life, most babies in our society have access to another way of finding out about themselves: mirrors. Babies' reactions to their own mirror images change as they get older (Brooks-Gunn and Lewis, 1984). A 5- or 6-month-old baby seems to regard his mirror image as an entertaining playmate—another baby who is playing an amusing game called "I do everything

This 11-month-old baby is still too young to realize that the entertaining playmate in the mirror is "me."

that you do." He smiles enthusiastically at this appealing companion.

In the second half of the first year, babies begin to make deliberate, repetitive movements in front of a mirror, apparently in an effort to systematically explore the mirror's possibilities (the same way Jacqueline, in stage 4, explored a new object). They might also look *behind* the mirror, or kiss or hit their mirror image—still without any recognition, apparently, that the baby in the mirror is "me."

Around the middle of the second year, the baby begins to show signs of self-consciousness, silliness, or coyness when he sees his mirror image.

student named Olga Maratos visited Piaget in his home in Switzerland and told him that she was sticking out her tongue at young babies. "And do you know what they are doing?" she asked him. "They are sticking out their tongues right back at me! What do you think of that?" The dignified old professor reflected for a moment. "I think that's very rude," he replied (Friedrich, 1983, p. 55).

Piaget said that deferred imitation—imitation of an action at a later time, not immediately after it is seen—cannot occur until stage 6, which begins at 18 months. This is because deferred imitation depends on mental representations, which (according to Piaget) babies don't have until stage 6. But one

He may also point at himself in the mirror, as if to say "Look at me!"

Can we tell when the baby first recognizes that the image in the mirror is himself? There is a clever technique that researchers have used to answer this question: a red mark is put on the baby's nose without his knowing it—his mother puts it on while pretending to wipe his face. Then the baby is shown his face in a mirror. What will he do when he notices the red mark? He might just stare at himself or touch the mirror, but if he realizes that the red-nosed baby in the mirror is himself, he will probably touch his own nose.

This experiment was tried on 96 babies. The results are given in Table 7–3. You can see that self-recognition increases as the baby grows older: no 9- or 12-month-old babies touched their reddened noses, but 75 percent of the 21- and 24-month-olds did so (Lewis and Brooks, 1975).

TABLE 7–3
Self-Recognition of Mirror Image in Babies of Different Ages

	NUMBER TESTED	PERCENT OF BABIES WHO TOUCHED THEIR NOSES
9 and 12 months	32	0
15 and 18 months	32	25%
21 and 24 months	32	75%

Source: Lewis and Brooks, 1975, p. 124.

A similar procedure has been used to test various species of animals. Only apes (chimpanzees and orangutans) seem to be capable of recogniz-ing that what they see in the mirror is themselves. Chimps can even use a mirror as a grooming aid! On the other hand, monkeys (which are lower on the evolutionary scale than apes) show no signs of self-recognition (Brooks-Gunn and Lewis, 1984). We might say that in this respect the 12-month-old baby is at the level of the monkey, whereas the 21-month-old has reached the more advanced level of the chimpanzee.

By 21 months, many toddlers can also recognize photographs of themselves, and can even discriminate such photos from photos of other babies of the same sex and age. In a test of these abilities, a 21-month-old named Erika was shown a photo of herself and was asked, "Who is that?" "Erika," she replied. When she was shown a photo of a different 21-month-old girl, her response was "No, not Erika." Erika also recognized a photo of her mother ("Mommy," she said) and labeled a photo of another woman "lady." Not all the children in this study did as well as Erika. Only 7 out of 25 toddlers correctly identified photos of themselves—six gave their own names and one said "Me." But the toddlers did just about as well in identifying themselves as they did in identifying their mothers (Lewis and Brooks, 1975). That's rather remarkable, since a baby presumably spends much more time looking at her mother's face than at her own face.

This finding, however, fits in well with Piaget's view of the stage-6 child (18 to 24 months). Piaget believes that the development of the child's self-image progresses hand in hand with the development of the concepts of object and person permanence. Once representation is possible, Piaget says, the child can visualize her own body as "an object among other objects," localized in space and existing through time (1954, p. 86).

researcher recently reported deferred imitation in babies only 9 months old. The babies in this study were shown several objects that could be acted upon in ways that they were unlikely to have seen before: there was a wooden block that was attached to a base with a hinge in such a way that it could be tipped over, another block containing a button that could be pushed (with interesting results) by reaching a finger into a recess on the block, and a plastic egg that made an unexpected noise when shaken. The experimenter demonstrated all these actions to the babies without letting the babies try them out for themselves. A day later the babies were given the three objects and allowed to handle them. Half of these 9-month-olds imitated at least two of the three actions that they had seen demonstrated the day before; nearly 20 percent of the babies performed all three actions. The deferred imitation shown by these 9-month-olds suggests that children still in stage 4 can form some sort of mental representation of a simple motor response and store it in their heads for 24 hours (Meltzoff, 1988).

DIFFERING OPINIONS ON OBJECT PERMANENCE. Show a stage-3 baby (4 to 8 months) an appealing toy and then quickly throw a blanket over it, and she'll immediately lose interest in the toy. According to Piaget, this is because stage-3 babies have no concept of object permanence. But an ingenious experiment by Renée Baillargeon, of the University of Illinois, has cast doubt on his theory.

The experiment involved showing 3½- to 4½-month-old babies an "impossible" event (see Figure 7–1). The babies were seated in front of a table with a sheet of cardboard mounted on it in such a way that the cardboard could be tilted forward (until its front surface was touching the table) or backward (until its back surface was touching the table), like a drawbridge being raised and lowered. A wooden block, painted to look like a clown, stood behind the drawbridge. The baby could see the wooden block when the drawbridge was lowered onto its front surface. When the drawbridge was raised, it cut off the baby's view of the block. As the drawbridge continued to rotate away from the baby, it would normally hit the block and come to a stop—except that sometimes the block was secretly removed by the experimenter, through a hole in the bottom of the apparatus, and the drawbridge continued its rotation until it was flat on its back surface. This gave rise to the "impossible" perception of the drawbridge moving through the space that was occupied by the wooden block. (When the drawbridge began to rotate forward again, the experimenter replaced the block so that the baby could see it again when the drawbridge reached its forward position.)

How did the babies react to this demonstration? The 4½-month-olds showed definite signs of being surprised or puzzled: they stared at the moving drawbridge significantly longer when this "impossible" scenario was enacted than when the drawbridge behaved in a normal fashion and came to a stop against the wooden block. Even some of the 3½-month-olds seemed to notice the difference between the normal sequence of events and the sequence in which two objects appeared to occupy the same place at the same time.

Baillargeon (1987) concluded that by 4 months of age babies already have formed some expectations in regard to objects: they expect objects to continue to exist even though they're briefly out of sight, and they don't expect one solid object to pass through the space occupied by another. We said in Chapter 5 that babies perceive objects as objects by the time they are 3 or 4 months old. Now we see that, by 4 months of age, they also have some ideas about the nature and behavior of these objects.

Why, then, don't 4- and 5-month-olds search for a toy that has been hidden beneath a blanket? Some researchers have attributed the baby's loss of interest in the hidden toy to a deficiency of memory: babies simply forget things too quickly, because some parts of their brains are not yet fully formed (Kagan, 1984). But then why don't babies forget about the wooden block as soon as it's out of sight behind the drawbridge? Baillargeon feels that babies don't search for a covered-up toy because the task requires the coordination

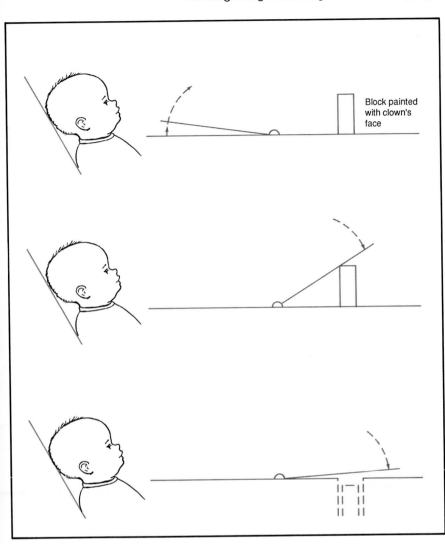

Block painted
with clown's
face

FIGURE 7-1
Baillargeon's experiment.
When the drawbridge was in
its forward position (top), the
baby could see the block.
Normally, as the drawbridge
continued to rotate, it would
hit the block and stop
(middle). But sometimes the
block was removed while it
was hidden behind the
drawbridge, and the
drawbridge continued until it
was flat on the table.

of two separate actions performed on two different things: first, lifting up the
blanket, and second, grasping the toy. Organizing a double-barreled attack of
this sort is too complex for a 4-month-old.

THE STAGE-4 ERROR. In stage 4 (8 to 12 months), babies do search for hidden
objects; however, there is something odd about the way they search. On page
225 we described how Laurent, at 9½ months, found his father's pocket
watch three times under a blanket, and then looked for it again under the
blanket even though he saw it being hidden somewhere else. The tendency to
search in an old familiar hiding place in preference to a new one has been
observed often enough in babies of this age that it has become known as the
stage-4 error. However, stage-4 babies do not invariably commit this error:
sometimes they do search in the new hiding place, or choose one place or the
other at random. A factor that has proved to be important in determining
whether they will search in the old place or switch to the new one is *timing:* if
there is any delay between when babies see the object hidden and when they

are allowed to search for it, they are more likely to search in the place where they found the toy on previous occasions. If they are allowed to search immediately, they are more likely to search in the place where they just saw it hidden. Since a delay makes it necessary for the baby to remember where he saw the object hidden, memory must play some role in this behavior (Kagan, 1984).

Recently, researchers have come up with an unexpected finding about the stage-4 error: babies who know how to crawl are less likely to make this error (and more likely to search in the right place) than babies of the same age who haven't yet started crawling. Perhaps you're thinking that the early crawlers must be smarter than the later crawlers, but there's no correlation between age of crawling and intelligence. Furthermore, superior search ability has also been found in infants who have not yet begun to crawl but who have had experience in propelling themselves around in a wheeled contraption called a walker. It seems that infants who are able to move around on their own, either on their hands and knees or suspended in the seat of a walker, are better at searching for things than their less mobile agemates. And infants who have been mobile for several weeks are better searchers than those whose experience with self-propelled mobility has been briefer (Kermoian and Campos, 1988).

Why should moving around on his own increase a baby's search skills? Three factors are thought to be involved. First is spatial understanding: through moving around in his environment, the baby develops the ability to locate objects in three-dimensional space. Second is goal-directedness: the child who can move around on his own has more opportunity to go after what he wants and to succeed in getting it. Last is the ability to focus his attention—to "keep his eye on the ball," as it were. Babies who watch a researcher hide a toy and then keep their attention focused on the hiding place are unlikely to search in the wrong place; babies who are easily distracted are much more likely to make errors. And babies who can crawl have been found to be more visually attentive than babies who haven't started crawling. Once a baby starts moving around in his environment, he has more need to keep track of the location of objects—he discovers the importance of keeping his eyes on his goal (Acredolo, 1988; Horobin and Acredolo, 1986).

An Overview of Cognitive Development in Infancy

How can we sum up the cognitive changes that take place during the first two years of life? A useful way of looking at these changes is to say that the child becomes able to keep track of more and more actions, objects, or ideas at the same time, and to combine them in increasingly complex ways. The baby at first can focus on only one thing, then she becomes able to see the relationship between two things, and still later she becomes able to compare or combine two relationships (Case, Hayward, Lewis, and Hurst, 1988).

The very young baby cannot pay attention to two things at once: if she reaches for something, the sight of her hand at first distracts her from what she is reaching for. If the object she reaches for is covered up, her attention instantly switches to the cover or to the person who did the covering. By 9 months, when the baby begins to search for hidden objects, she is able to keep in mind several things at once: the hidden object, whatever is covering it, the action she will have to take to remove the cover, and the action she will have to take to get the object. At 12 months she can keep track of all these things for *two* different hiding places. At 18 months a toddler can solve a search problem of the following sort: a small toy is held in the researcher's hand, the hand is put under one cover and then taken out, the hand is opened to show that the toy is still there (or is gone), then the hand is put under a second cover and is taken out and opened up again. Solving this problem, by searching under the correct cover, requires that the toddler keep track of two possible hiding places and two different events—the researcher's hand goes under a cover and comes out again twice (Haake and Somerville, 1985).

In only 18 months, babies can solve a problem this complex! But from birth on, they have been working at increasing their skills in combining things. Between 9 and 13 months, babies spend a good deal of time experimenting with putting things into, under, behind, or on top of other things: "They seem to be entertained ceaselessly by putting kitchen pans in and out of each other, taking lids off and putting them back on, filling up and emptying containers, and playing "peek-a-boo" (Acredolo, 1988, p. 370). This practice in using concepts such as *inside of* and *under* makes it easier for toddlers to use these concepts in more complex combinations.

The same ability to combine ideas or actions in increasingly complex ways shows up in many other aspects of the child's life. A 9-month-old can imitate an adult's action only if it is a very simple one consisting of a single motion, but a 20-month-old can imitate a sequence of three actions and a 27-month-old can imitate a sequence of six (Brownell, 1988).

These cognitive advances spill over into the child's social and emotional life. Relationships with peers develop as the child becomes able to imitate another child's actions or to combine various behaviors into overtures of friendship—to smile, say hi, and hand another child a toy. Her deepening understanding of the relationship between "self" and "other" (or between "me" and "you") is shown by her ability to apply her imagination to others, as when she pretends to drink from a block and then offers her companion a sip of block-juice. The older toddler can begin to form partnerships with other children and to cooperate with them in play (Brownell, 1986).

COGNITIVE DEVELOPMENT AND EMOTIONAL DEVELOPMENT. The development of complex emotions parallels the development of complex thought, starting from a simple distinction between distress and pleasure in the newborn baby and becoming increasingly differentiated into anger, fear, jealousy, pride, joy, and so on. The newborn baby reacts with distress to loud noises and the feeling of being dropped; this reaction is not "fear" because fear has to do with anticipating the future and a newborn baby knows nothing of the future. An older baby becomes afraid when he sees or hears something that he associates with pain—for example, the pediatrician. He is afraid because he anticipates pain, a future event. By the time he is 3 or 4 years old, a child can be afraid of an idea, such as an imaginary monster (Case and others, 1988).

Consider the emotion *jealousy*. Jealousy is a complex emotion because it requires an awareness of two different relationships: your relationship with someone else, and that person's relationship with a third person. You are jealous when you recognize that your relationship with someone you love is being threatened by your loved one's relationship with a third party. (Since you are at an advanced stage of cognitive development, your loved one's relationship with the third party need not be a real one—it can be as imaginary as the 4-year-old's monster.) To understand this connection between two relationships is beyond the capabilities of a young infant, and indeed, young infants show no signs of jealousy.

A recent study examined the development of jealousy in babies and toddlers; the children were tested in the following way. First, a child and his mother were brought into a room with toys in it, and the child was allowed to play for a short time. Then the mother was instructed to get up, go over to a second child who was also in the room, put the other child on her lap and read him a story, and ignore her own child.

Babies under 12 months showed no signs of being jealous of the other child; a few of them did seem a little unhappy, but they appeared to be reacting to their mother's unavailability, rather than to her behavior toward the other child. At about 14 months of age, many toddlers began to whine or cry when their mothers turned their attention to the other child. Jealousy reached a peak at about 24 months, an age when a toddler becomes capable of understanding that his mother isn't paying attention to him *because* she is paying attention to someone else (Case and others, 1988).

Variations in Intelligence: Infancy and Later

One thing is very clear about babies' development: some babies progress more rapidly than others. This was true even in Piaget's own family—at any given age, Lucienne and Laurent were ahead of Jacqueline.

A question that is often asked about these differences in rate of development is: Will an advanced baby turn into an intelligent child, a slow baby into a dull one? The answer is: not necessarily. The babies who are quicker at learning to reach for toys, or to crawl or walk, do not turn out to be any brighter, on the average, than their less ambitious (or less well-coordinated) agemates. Up until recently, in fact, psychologists have been unable to distinguish a future Nobel prizewinner from a future high school dropout.

Just in the past few years, however, real progress has been made in identifying aspects of infant development that do appear to be relevant to later intelligence. As we said in Chapter 1, the new tests of infant intelligence are based on how quickly a baby gets bored when you repeatedly show her the same picture—in other words, on how quickly she *habituates* to a visual stimulus (see p. 158) and stops paying attention to it. Habituation occurs when the baby decides, "I don't have to look at that picture anymore—I already *know* it!" How long it takes her to make this decision is a measure of the speed with which she learns. After she has gotten bored with one picture the baby might be shown another one, to test her interest in a novel stimulus. If she is more interested in the new one than she was in the old one, she must recognize that it's not the same picture she saw before, so this is a way of testing the baby's memory. Since she has to be able to tell the difference between the old picture and the new one, it's also a test of her ability to notice differences. Thus, simply by showing pictures to a baby and watching where she points her eyes, we can test her ability to learn, to remember, and to discriminate.

Because these abilities are all part of what we mean by "intelligence," a habituation test given to a baby can be considered a rough measure of the baby's intelligence. Such tests, given to babies as young as 3 or 4 months old, can predict, to some extent, how well these babies will do on IQ tests several years later. The infant tests don't predict IQ perfectly, but longitudinal studies have found the correlation with later IQ to be surprisingly high, about .40 to .50 (Bornstein and Sigman, 1986). One study looked at babies who had suffered a variety of medical complications at birth and hence were at greater risk of mental retardation. The babies who continued to stare at the same picture for long periods of time—in other words, who habituated slowly— tended to be the least intelligent at 8 years of age (Sigman, Cohen, Beckwith, and Parmelee, 1986). Another study looked at normal babies and, on the basis of the tests given in infancy, predicted that 29 of them would turn out to be brighter than average. When IQ tests were given to these children three years later, 21 of the 29 proved to be above average (Fagan and Knevel, 1989).

Infant Environment and Later Intelligence

The infant tests are designed to measure the potential that a baby is born with. The tests do not predict later IQ perfectly, for two reasons. First, these tests are not perfectly accurate—many random factors will affect how a baby performs on them. Second, the potential a baby is born with is only one of the factors that determine how intelligent he will turn out to be. His ultimate intelligence will also be determined by what happens to him as he grows up and by the environment in which he lives.

In recent years, there has been a lot of interest in enriching babies' environments. Parents have been led to believe that they can raise their babies' IQs by buying special toys for them or by teaching them to read at an absurdly early age. But it appears that certain subtle aspects of the child's early environment may be more important than fancy mobiles over the crib or blocks shaped like letters of the alphabet. In Chapter 6 we saw how a mother's responsiveness to her baby's signals has an effect on his social and emotional development. It turns out that the mother's responsiveness toward her baby affects his *cognitive* development as well. In fact, a child's social and emotional life appears to be closely intertwined with his cognitive development.

Consider the results of a study of high-risk mothers and their infants, in a clinic in Massachusetts. These were economically deprived mothers—mostly single parents with, at most, a high school education. Some had a history of abusing or neglecting their children; some were depressed. The mothers in this group did not have successful interactions with their babies. They seldom smiled at them; they generally either ignored their babies or acted angry at them. The mothers hardly ever responded to what their babies did—the babies' behavior had little or no effect on the mothers' behavior.

Not surprisingly, these babies looked unhappy much of the time; *they* seldom smiled, either. What's worse, they showed little interest in their surroundings. They were not just uninterested in people—they were also uninterested in objects. The researchers felt that these babies used up so much

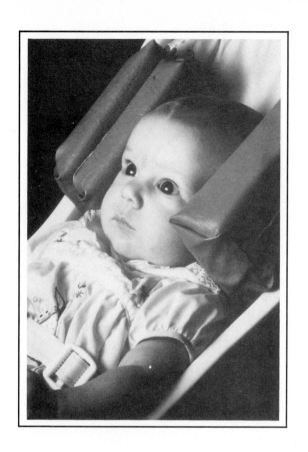

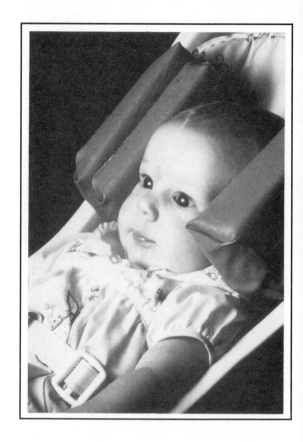

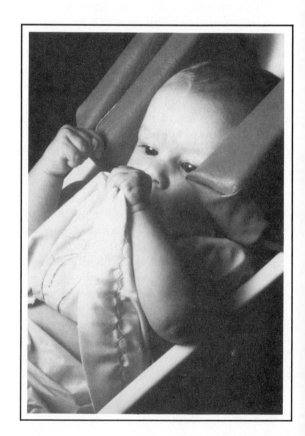

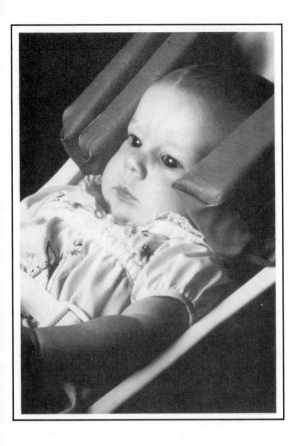

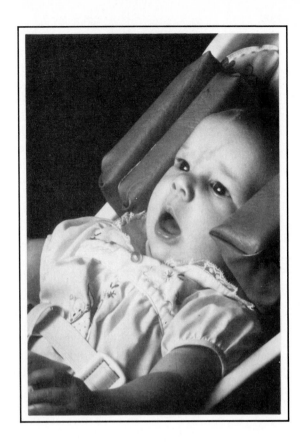

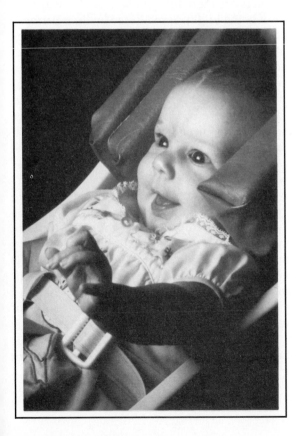

A 3-month-old baby taking a habituation test. In the first picture (upper left), a picture of a face has just appeared on a screen in front of her. She is interested at first, then gradually gets bored (next four pictures). In the last picture (lower right), she reacts with enthusiasm when a new picture appears on the screen. (From Maurer and Maurer, 1988, pp. 128–129.)

energy in coping with their sadness and frustration that they had little left over for exploring their environment. Thus, unsuccessful social relationships can turn off a baby's interest in learning about the world around him, and this has a serious impact on his cognitive development (Cohn and Tronick, 1989).

A contrasting study looked at families on the other end of the socioeconomic scale: a group of well-educated families, each consisting of a married couple and their firstborn child. All these babies were well cared for and given plenty of attention. Nonetheless, the researchers were able to detect differences in the ways these parents behaved with their babies, and these differences had an effect on how the babies did on an intelligence test given later, at 30 months. Some mothers did more to advance their babies' cognitive development than others: they responded to the sounds their babies made (usually by saying something), noticed what their babies were looking at (for example, if the baby looked at a toy the mother made some comment about that toy), and helped their babies' investigations by showing them objects and demonstrating or talking about the features of these objects. The mothers who consistently acted in these ways during their babies' first year had babies who were advanced in cognitive development by their third year. There was no connection between the babies' cognitive development and how the *father* behaved to the baby; evidently, these fathers didn't interact with their babies enough to have a measurable influence (Hunter, McCarthy, MacTurk, and Vietze, 1987).

So far this is straightforward enough: when mothers notice what their babies are interested in and respond in ways that encourage those interests, the babies' cognitive development is enhanced. But now we must complicate matters by telling you that mothers are more likely to behave this way with babies who *already* show signs of being bright, as measured by their performance on infant habituation and novelty tests. A group of babies did very well on a habituation test given when they were 4 months old. When these babies were 12 months old, their mothers were doing more to encourage their cognitive development—by showing them toys, pointing to pictures, naming objects—than the mothers of babies who hadn't done so well on the habituation tests. Evidently, these mothers were *responding* to the brightness, the eagerness to learn, that these babies had been born with. And the mothers' behavior, in turn, led the babies to become brighter still. "The infant and mother," concluded the researcher, "mutually influence one another during their continuing transactions" (Bornstein, 1985, p. 7471).

Thus, the superior intelligence of children who were fast habituators in early infancy doesn't result *entirely* from qualities they were born with: there are transactional effects between the environment and the child's inborn qualities. This means that trying to assess the potential intelligence of very young babies may have some risks. If a habituation test predicts that Alicia is going to be smart and Amanda is going to be dull, we may behave quite differently to these two children. If we think of Alicia as bright, we are likely to act toward her in ways that will increase her brightness. But if we think of Amanda as dull, we are likely to act in ways that will *decrease* her intelligence, in a vicious-circle fashion. Which is all very nice for Alicia, but not very fair to Amanda—especially if she was one of those babies for whom the infant test did not provide an accurate indication of her real abilities.

INTELLIGENCE AND EARLY DEPRIVATION. "Infancy," one knowledgeable researcher said recently, "does not appear to be a critical period for accelerating intellectual development" (Clarke-Stewart, 1989, p. 269). This doesn't mean that intellectual development *can't* be accelerated in infancy: it means that if things don't go well during infancy, all is not lost. What is missed during infancy can be made up later on.

Jerome Kagan, a developmental psychologist at Harvard, has described what infancy is like in an Indian village called San Marcos, in western Guatemala. In this society,

> Infants typically spend their first year confined to a small, dark hut. They are not played with, rarely spoken to, poorly nourished . . . and their health [is] poor.   (Kagan, 1978, p. 70)

As we would expect, this kind of environment has an unfavorable effect on cognitive development:

> When compared to American babies of the same age, the Guatemalan infants are retarded. Some of the major developmental milestones, such as the ability to recall past events, the belief that objects continue to exist when they are out of sight (object permanence), symbolic play, and language appear from two to 12 months later than they do in American infants. . . . American children begin to speak their first words about the middle of the second year; San Marcos children do not begin to speak until the middle or end of their third year.   (pp. 70–71)

If an American toddler were that far behind at age 3, it would be cause for serious concern. But the retardation of these San Marcos children is only temporary. Their lives grow more stimulating after the first year or so, when "they are allowed to wander outside the hut and encounter the rich variety of the world" (p. 71). By adolescence, these children have nearly caught up with their American counterparts and are performing at normal levels on tests of memory and reasoning.

Other information is provided by cases of children who have been the victims of appalling neglect. In 1967, for instance, a pair of 7-year-old twin boys were discovered in a house in a small town in Europe. These boys had spent their preceding years in a small, unheated closet. They had been kept in almost total isolation by their father and stepmother, and had been brutally beaten from time to time. When the twins were rescued they could barely walk and had less language than the average 2-year-old. After weeks of hospitalization they were tested by psychologists. According to the test results, the twins were mentally retarded.

After seven years of such cruel deprivation, could these boys possibly recover? To everyone's surprise, they did. They were adopted by a normal family and were eventually enrolled in a school for normal children. They were several grades behind their agemates at first, but by the age of 14 they were only one grade behind, and their tested IQs were around 100—exactly average (Koluchová, 1972, 1976).

Problems in Development

It seems to be possible to overcome the effects of intellectual deprivation in infancy if the later environment is good. But what about the effects of *nutritional* deprivation? Poor nutrition has been assumed to have its worst effects on intelligence when it occurs very early—before birth or in the first year or two. The reason has to do with the physical development of the brain: the most important period of brain growth occurs during prenatal development and infancy.

A major study of the long-term effects of starvation was performed in Barbados, West Indies, beginning in 1967. In this study, 129 children who had suffered from severe malnutrition in the first year of life were compared with a control group of 129 Barbadian children (matched in age, sex, and socioeconomic level) who had not been malnourished. The malnourished children were hospitalized and given good medical care before they were a year old, so their period of starvation was not prolonged. Afterward, health-care workers kept track of their families and made sure that these children received enough food and medical attention from then on.

By the age of 11, the Barbadian children who were malnourished in infancy had caught up with the control-group children in physical growth. But they were noticeably different in other ways. Their IQ scores averaged 12 points lower than the children in the control group. They did poorly in school, not only because of their intellectual deficits but also because they had trouble paying attention in class. These intellectual and behavioral problems were still present when the children were last seen, at the age of 18 (Galler, 1984).

Thus, malnutrition in infancy appears to have a permanent effect on intelligence. This is not sur-

If this severely undernourished Indonesian child survives, what are the chances that his intelligence will be normal?

prising, in view of the fact that it has a permanent effect on the brain. Children who have been malnourished early in development have smaller heads and smaller brains, containing fewer neurons, than their well-nourished agemates (Lozoff, 1989).

But wait—there are other data to consider. A study was made of a group of undernourished Korean babies who were adopted into middle-class American homes. Several years later, these children were performing at average American levels, both in school and on IQ tests. A second study involved middle-class American children who

Although these boys were almost completely deprived of intellectual stimulation, their emotional and social deprivation was not complete: they had each other. Children seem to be able to recover from early intellectual deprivation if the later environment is stimulating enough, but the failure to form attachments early in life may be impossible to repair. The companionship these twins were able to give each other during those years in the closet made their isolation less severe and undoubtedly aided their recovery.

were malnourished as infants because of medical problems involving their digestive systems. These children, too, were later found to have normal intelligence. Finally, a study was made of Dutch children who had been undernourished before they were born. Their mothers had undergone starvation during pregnancy due to a severe famine in the Netherlands at the end of World War II. These children—the ones who survived—are now adults, and IQ tests have detected no differences between them and their agemates from other parts of the Netherlands where there was no famine. There is no evidence that prenatal starvation lowered their intelligence at all (Winick, 1980).

What is the reason for this apparent contradiction? The answer is that environment makes a big difference. If the environment is good enough, after the initial period of starvation, the intellectual effects can be overcome. In most cases, however, the undernourished children go back to the same environment they came from, the same environment in which they hadn't gotten enough to eat in the first place. They go back to the same parents who had been unable to take good care of them —parents who, in all probability, had suffered from starvation themselves.

A closer look at the families of the undernourished Barbadian children showed that the mothers of many of these children were severely depressed. The feelings of hopelessness expressed by these women were at least partly explained by the hardships of their lives. At the same time, their depression made things worse by undermining their ability to find solutions to their problems. Whatever the cause of their depression, it undoubtedly had a bad effect on their children. A depressed mother is less able to provide adequate care for a baby, so her baby is at greater risk of suffering from malnutrition. And a depressed mother is less able to provide an older child with the kind of stimulation and encouragement that lead to intellectual growth. Thus, the lowered IQs of these Barbadian children wasn't just a function

of their early starvation: it was starvation *plus* growing up with a depressed mother under conditions of severe economic hardship (Salt, Galler, and Ramsey, 1988).

The human brain is remarkable in its capacity to recover from injury, if the injury occurs in infancy or early childhood. Babies born very prematurely often sustain minor damage to their brains, which can lead to permanent intellectual deficits. But premature babies reared in good environments by attentive, responsive mothers almost always recover completely and catch up with their agemates (Beckwith and Parmelee, 1986). Under optimum conditions, the brain can compensate for damaged or missing neurons by assigning their duties to other cells.

The most dramatic evidence of this comes from a study of people with a brain disorder called *hydrocephalus*—"water on the brain." These people have more than the normal amount of fluid in their heads; as a result, there is less room for brain cells. Some of the people in this study had so much fluid in their brains that the cerebral cortex—the "thinking" part of the brain—occupied only one-twentieth of its usual space. Yet most of them were intellectually normal. One, in fact, had a university degree in mathematics and had graduated with highest honors! The researcher who studied these people concluded that we can manage very well with a brain that is "substantially reduced in size, as long as the loss occurs before birth or early in infancy, thus giving the brain a chance to adjust. It appears that the brain has greater plasticity than was previously thought possible" (Lorber, 1981, p. 126).

Neurologists speak of "plasticity"; Piaget calls it "adaptation." What it boils down to is that human babies have an amazing ability to make the best of whatever hand they are dealt. They are fully capable of profiting from a good environment in the first year or two of life. But if things go badly during infancy, all is not lost.

Acquiring Language

In the first year or so, the baby's most noticeable achievements are in the realm of motor development: she learns to turn over, to sit, to crawl, to walk; and she learns to use her hands and fingers to perform increasingly skilled manipulations. But in the second year of life the striking milestones are in the realm of cognitive development: the baby makes impressive gains in knowledge and understanding, and speech begins. The acquisition of language is the most impressive of all these achievements—it is, as one researcher has put it, "the jewel in the crown of cognition" (Pinker, quoted in Kolata, 1987, p. 133).

Learning to Talk

Remember Stephanie, the 4-day-old baby we met at the start of this chapter? She can communicate with the people around her in only one way: by crying when she's unhappy and by not crying when she's not unhappy. It's a simple system, but it works. Soon, however, Stephanie will want to communicate more complicated ideas and make a wider range of sounds.

THE EARLY STAGES. By the time she is 2 or 3 months old, Stephanie will have discovered the sound of her voice and will begin to play with it, producing a variety of "oo," "ah," and "rr" sounds—a typical stage-2 circular reaction. She is also likely to make these sounds during face-to-face interactions with her mother or father, particularly during periods of eye contact. By the age of 3 months, a baby's vocalizations have already begun to take on a communicative function (Keller and Schölmerich, 1987).

In the second half of her first year, Stephanie will be able to produce a large number of different sounds—even some sounds that her parents can't imitate, sounds that she herself will soon lose the ability to produce! This is the period of babbling: ba-ba-ba-ba, ma-ma-ma-ma, assorted goos, and various juicy sounds. The baby can now modify the sounds she makes in response to the sounds she hears. If Stephanie is saying "goo-goo" and her mother says "da-da," Stephanie may switch over to "da-da." Her babbles will be lower in pitch when she's with her father than when she's with her mother (Reich, 1986). She'll also practice her sounds when she's alone in her crib, sometimes for long periods of time.

By her first birthday, Stephanie, if she's an average baby (see Table 7–4), will be using "ma-ma" and "da-da" to refer to her mother and father, and will probably have an additional word or two. A few babies seem to be starting to talk even earlier, at 8 or 9 months, but these early words may be misleading

A young baby can produce a variety of cooing sounds in her early "conversations" with her mother.

—they often disappear as mysteriously as they appeared. Most babies wait until two or three months after their first birthday to begin talking in earnest. Perhaps they're concentrating on learning to walk, and can't devote much attention to language until they've gotten used to that exciting new way of getting from place to place.

In the meantime, many babies engage in what seems to be a pretend kind of speech—they'll come out with what sounds like long, complicated sentences, complete with expression, except that the "words" are totally unintelligible. This kind of pseudospeech is called **expressive jargon.** Some babies continue to produce it for months, even after they've learned to say real words.

True speech begins when the baby can produce about 10 understandable words. This occurs, on the average, at around 16 months; the age range in one study was from 13 to 19 months. At about 18 months the typical baby starts to acquire new words very rapidly; she'll reach the 50-word milestone at around 21 months (range: 14 to 24 months). By 24 months she'll probably know between 25 and 450 words; the average is about 200 words at 2 years (Nelson, 1973).

The baby's ability to understand the speech of the older people around her —her **receptive language**—at every age is greater than her ability to

TABLE 7–4
Milestones of Language Development

AVERAGE AGE IN MONTHS[1]	LANGUAGE ACQUISITION MILESTONE
2	Makes "oo" and "aah" sounds
4	Says "ah-goo"
6	Babbles
8	Says "dada," but not as a name
9	Understands the word "no"
11	Uses "Mama" and "Dada" as names
	Responds to one-step command accompanied by gesture
	Says first word (other than "Mama" or "Dada")
12	Talks in expressive jargon without real words
	Says second word
13	Says third word
14	Responds to one-step command without gesture
15	Says four to six words
17	Talks in expressive jargon with some real words
	Can point to five body parts
	Says 7 to 20 words
19	Forms two-word combinations such as "Daddy chair"
21	Has a 50-word vocabulary
	Forms two-word sentences such as "Daddy sit"
24	Uses "I," "me," and "you," but not correctly
	Has a 200-word vocabulary
30	Uses "I," "me," and "you" correctly
	Forms three-word sentences

[1] Because these are average ages, many children will reach these milestones at earlier ages than those listed, and just as many will reach them later. Children whose language development falls very far behind the ages listed in the table should have their hearing tested.

Source: Capute and others (1986). Clinical Linguistic and Auditory Milestone Scale: Prediction of Cognition in Infancy. DM and CN, 28, 762–771.

express herself in speech—her **productive language.** (This continues to be true all through life. Most people can understand words that they have read or heard but have never used.) Thus, by the end of the first year most babies can understand words such as *doll* and *bottle.* In the second year they can understand sentences that are far more complex than those they can produce.

WHAT'S IN A WORD? Joshua, 17½ months old, sits by his mother's side. They're "reading" a picture book together: Joshua's mother points at a picture of, say, a house and says "house." Joshua tries—more or less successfully—to imitate her. In some cases he can say the word as soon as his mother points to the picture: he knows *dog* ("doh"), *baby* ("ba-ba"), and *car* ("cah"). Joshua's productive vocabulary now contains about 20 words. Not much, actually, when you consider that he said his first word ("Dada") more than six months ago. In the time since then he's acquired only three or four words a month.

But his rate of learning new words is about to increase dramatically. He'll pick up around 15 words a month between 18 and 20 months, and more than 30 a month between 20 months and 2 years. What's the reason for this sudden acceleration?

Apparently, it's due to a leap forward in cognitive development. The toddler starts out by imitating words and learns by imitation when to use them. But at first he has no idea that the word he is saying is the *name* of the object he is pointing to—that it is a symbol, a representation, of the object itself. The realization seems to come to the child suddenly, as a flash of insight, after he's learned a certain number of words. He first learns the words and then realizes that the words are names (McShane, 1980; Acredolo and Goodwyn, 1988).

Once the child has gotten the idea that things have names, he wants to know the name for everything. So the flash of insight must occur just before the dramatic increase in vocabulary, at around 18 months. The timing fits in very well with Piagetian theory. Insight, according to Piaget, is a mental process that isn't possible until stage 6 of the sensorimotor period, which begins at around 18 months.

Is there any evidence, other than the sudden acceleration in learning new words, that this insight actually occurs? Unfortunately, toddlers can't tell us if and when it happens, and later (when their language ability is up to the task) they'll have forgotten. But what if a child were introduced to language at a later age, when she's old enough to retain a memory of her experiences? That happened in the case of Helen Keller, and Keller's memories provide striking evidence for the existence of the flash of insight as a cause of the explosion in vocabulary size.

Helen Keller lost her sight and hearing in infancy, and was without language until she was almost 7 years old. At that point Anne Sullivan became her teacher and began to teach her a new language. The words in this language were tapped into her hand, letter by letter, by her teacher's fingers. Here's Keller's description of how her lessons began:

> The morning after my teacher came she led me into her room and gave me a doll. . . . When I had played with it a little while, Miss Sullivan slowly

spelled into my hand the word "d-o-l-l." I was at once interested in this
finger play and tried to imitate it. When I finally succeeded in making the
letters correctly I was flushed with childish pleasure and pride. Running
downstairs to my mother I held up my hand and made the letters for doll. I
did not know that I was spelling a word or even that words existed; I was
simply making my fingers go in monkey-like imitation. In the days that
followed I learned to spell in this uncomprehending way a great many
words, among them *pin, hat, cup,* and a few verbs like *sit, stand,* and *walk.*
But my teacher had been with me several weeks before I understood that
everything has a name.   (Keller, 1905, p. 22)

Years later, Keller still remembered the excitement of the moment when
she came to that realization:

We walked down the path to the well-house, attracted by the fragrance of
the honeysuckle with which it was covered. Some one was drawing water
and my teacher placed my hand under the spout. As the cool stream
gushed over one hand she spelled into the other the word *water,* first
slowly, then rapidly. I stood still, my whole attention fixed upon the
motions of her fingers. Suddenly . . . the mystery of language was revealed
to me. I knew then that "w-a-t-e-r" meant the wonderful cool something
that was flowing over my hand. That living word awakened my soul, gave
it light, hope, joy, set it free! . . . I left the well-house eager to learn. Everything had a name, and each name gave birth to a new thought. . . . I
learned a great many new words that day.   (pp. 23–24)

For a child who can see and hear, being taught the names of things begins
quite early: parents start to give names to the objects they show a baby when
she's only 3 or 4 months old. By the time she's 10 or 12 months old, if she's
asked "Where's the doll?" or "Where's your blanket?" the child might
respond by looking at, or pointing to, the appropriate object. At about the
same age, she begins pointing at objects herself, in order to draw her parents'
attention to them. There is often some kind of sound effect ("uh-uh-uh!") that
goes along with the gesture. Sometimes she is asking to have something given
to her, but sometimes she just wants to be told its name (Reich, 1986).

Later, when she starts to use words, there is a lengthy period in which she
can say only a single word at a time. During this stage, a single word has to
take the place of a whole sentence. A child who says "Cat!" can mean many
things by that utterance: "There's a cat!" "I want the cat!" "Get that cat away
from me!" and so on. Often it's possible to tell what is meant from the context
and from the child's gestures and facial expression.

Even when toddlers use a word simply to name an object, their use of the
word may not correspond exactly to the way adults use it. Sometimes they use
a word in a narrower way than an adult would; this is called **underextension.** For example, Quentin, the son of a psycholinguist, at first used the word
shoes to refer only to the shoes in his mother's closet. Later, Quentin expanded
his use of the word to include the shoes in his father's closet, and still later he
began to apply the word to the shoes on people's feet (Reich, 1986).

Overextensions are also common during this period. A toddler might call
all four-legged mammals *dog* and anything round a *ball.* Nicholas, the son of

two psycholinguists, once pointed to a bowl of salad and said "Nunu," the name of the family dog. His parents were puzzled until they noticed that the shiny black olive on top of the salad resembled their dog's shiny black nose! (de Villiers and de Villiers, 1979).

Toddlers make many errors in pronunciation. Difficult sounds like *th, l,* and *r* tend to be replaced with easier sounds like *d, y,* and *w. That* becomes *dat, lady* becomes *wady* or *yady, run* becomes *wun.* Combinations of two consonants are particularly difficult, so one consonant is usually omitted, as in *poon* for *spoon.* It's also easier for a toddler to say the same consonant twice than to switch to a different one in the middle of a word, so *doggie* may become *doddie* or *goggie.* The problem is in pronunciation, not in hearing. A child who pronounces *mouse* and *mouth* in exactly the same way will have no trouble pointing to the right picture when you ask him "Where is the mouse?" and "Where is the mouth?" (de Villiers and de Villiers, 1979).

TWO- AND THREE-WORD PHRASES. Children begin to put words together in original combinations at around 19 or 20 months—eight or nine months after they said their first words. Why does it take them so long? It's not because they can't produce more than one syllable at a time: they are capable at an earlier age of saying ready-made phrases such as "What's dat?" or "Don' wanna."

Putting together original phrases is an accomplishment of the mind, not of the tongue. Many cognitive advances occur around the age of 18 to 20 months. This is when the typical child first realizes that everything has a name, which marks the beginning of the great explosion in vocabulary. This is when the child begins to recognize that the image in the mirror is "me," and when (according to Piaget) the child has developed the concept of object permanence and the ability to use mental representations. This is when the child starts to put together other things besides words: to imitate an action consisting of two or three parts, or to perform a series of several actions in symbolic play—for example, hugging a doll, putting it to bed, and covering it with a blanket (Shore, 1986).

All these new achievements rest on the child's ability to combine things in increasingly complex ways. The realization that words are names requires that the child understand the relationship between an object and the word that serves as a symbol for that object. Putting together two words—two symbols—rests on that realization and occurs only a short time later.

But even after children have managed to put two or three words together, they are still not capable of uttering long, complex sentences. A toddler's sentences are short and to the point. Instead of saying "A boy is walking down the street," she'll say "Boy street," or "Boy walk," or "Downa street." Verb endings such as *-ing* are left out, and so are unimportant words such as *the* and *is.* The toddler's language has been described as **telegraphic speech,** because it sounds like the language used in telegrams ("Car broke down. Wallet stolen. Send money quick."). Although toddlers' sentences are strictly no-frills, their words generally appear in the proper order. They say "Billy chair" instead of "Billy's chair"; they don't say "Chair Billy." They say "Hit Mommy" to mean they hit Mommy, and "Mommy hit" to mean Mommy hit them.

Individual Differences in Language Development. One way that psycholinguists measure the development of children's speech is with an index called **mean length of utterance (MLU).** An utterance is a phrase or a sentence said all in one piece. The length of an utterance is calculated by counting the number of words it contains and adding the number of grammatical suffixes such as the verb endings *-ing* and *-ed* and the plural or possessive *-s.* (Thus, in "See the dog," the length of the utterance is 3; in "See the dogs," or "Seeing the dog," it is 4. In "I'm seeing the dog," it is 6, because *I'm* counts as 2.) So the MLU is the average length of a child's recorded utterances at a given age.

Figure 7–2 shows the relationship between MLU and age in three children studied by a group of Harvard psycholinguists. There are two things to note about this graph. First, MLU increases fairly steadily with age. This increase reflects the children's growing vocabularies and their ability to say more words at a time, and also their greater use of grammatical forms as they get older. Second, notice how rapidly Eve's MLU increases relative to Adam's and Sarah's. Eve reaches an MLU of 4 at about 26 months; Adam and Sarah reach that point at 3½ years—more than a year later. Such wide individual differences in speed of language acquisition are not rare. Most children don't use 10-word sentences until they are 3 or 4 years old; yet one young girl we know said things like "Wish we could get a cute little puppy like that" at the age of 24 months. Albert Einstein, on the other hand, was so slow in learning to

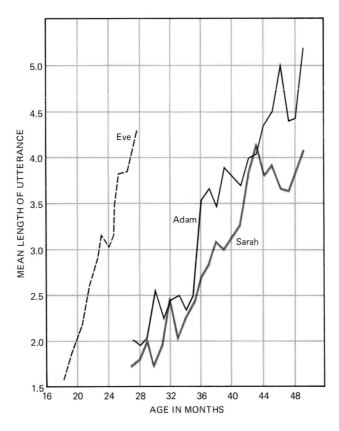

FIGURE 7-2
Children speak in longer and longer utterances as they get older. This graph shows how MLU increased with age for Eve, Adam, and Sarah. (Source: Brown, 1973.)

speak that his worried parents consulted a doctor about it (Loewenberg, 1988). More often than not, the children whose language development is unusually advanced are girls, like Eve and the little girl who wanted a puppy. The children who progress more slowly tend to be boys, like young Einstein. On the average, girls are a little ahead of boys in acquiring language (Acredolo and Goodwyn, 1988).

Both heredity and environment play a role in individual differences in language development. Firstborn children tend to advance more rapidly than their later-born siblings, and this is clearly due to differences in environment: later-borns must compete with their older siblings for their parents' attention, and thus they have fewer opportunities for verbal interactions with an adult (Wellen, 1985). For a similar reason, twins are delayed in language relative to singletons (single-born children). Although mothers of twins speak to their children as much as mothers of singletons do, each individual twin receives less speech directed specifically to him. In particular, each twin has fewer experiences in which he and his mother both focus their attention on the same object or activity, and she talks to him about it (Tomasello, Mannle, and Kruger, 1986).

Mother–toddler interactions in which both have their attention focused on the same thing play a uniquely important role in the toddler's language development. These periods of mutually focused attention—for example, when the toddler and his mother are playing together with the same toy—have been found to advance a child's language development: the more time mother and child spend in this type of activity, the faster the child progresses. Interestingly enough, the child learns more in this situation if *he* is the one who makes the decision about what to pay attention to. If the mother notices what her child is looking at and tells the child the name of that object, he is likely to add that word to his vocabulary. If the mother tries to redirect the child's attention to what *she* is looking at, he is less likely to learn anything new (Tomasello and Farrar, 1986).

How Adults Speak to Toddlers

Here's a typical dialog between a 2-year-old and his mother:

ADAM: See truck, Mommy. See truck.
MOTHER: Did you see the truck?
ADAM: No I see truck.
MOTHER: No, you didn't see it? There goes one.
ADAM: There go one.
MOTHER: Yes, there goes one.
ADAM: See a truck. See truck, Mommy. See truck. Truck. Put truck, Mommy.
MOTHER: Put the truck where?
ADAM: Put truck window.
MOTHER: I think that one's too large to go in the window.
         (Brown and Bellugi, 1964, p. 135)

Notice that the mother speaks in a characteristic way—different from the way she would speak to another adult. It's not only mothers who do this. Researchers have found that other adults, and even children as young as 4, modify their speech appropriately when they are talking to a toddler. Adults speaking to toddlers use short, clear, simple sentences, and they say the words

Verbal interactions with an adult—especially one-to-one interactions in which both adult and child have their attention focused on the same thing— advance a child's language development.

distinctly and with greater than usual stress and expression. They pause between sentences. Many of their sentences are repetitions of all or part of their previous sentence, or they may correct or expand on the child's previous sentence. Many more questions are used than in speech directed at another adult.

The *content* of adults' speech also differs when they are talking to a toddler. Their conversation is generally focused on the here and now, rather than on the past or the future. It concerns concrete objects, animals, or people, rather than abstract ideas. The objects and animals tend to be named at an intermediate level of specificity: flower, not plant or rose; dog, not animal or collie (de Villiers and de Villiers, 1979).

Adults generally avoid using words that toddlers find hard to say and substitute words better suited to the toddler's pronunciation ability. Thus, Mommy, Daddy, and Nana are used instead of Mother, Father, and Grandmother. This special language—which has been called **motherese**—also includes words like *choo-choo, boo-boo, wee-wee, tick-tock,* and *bow-wow.*

If parents "talk down" to their children in these ways, what makes the child's vocabulary, pronunciation, and grammar continue to improve? Not through attempts by the parents to correct their child's speech: such efforts usually prove futile. Here is one father's attempt to improve his son's pronunciation of the word "turtle":

FATHER: Say *tur.*
NICHOLAS: *Tur.*
FATHER: Say *till.*
NICHOLAS: *Till.*
FATHER: Say *turtle.*
NICHOLAS: *Kurka.*
            (de Villiers and de Villiers, 1979, pp. 109–110)

The Child in Society

**Box 7-3
Learning to Take
Turns in
Conversation**

A parent's speech to a toddler has two functions—communication and language teaching. Both of these functions are better served if the parent's speech is simple enough that the child can easily understand it, so it's not surprising that parents speak in a special way to toddlers.

What *is* surprising is that parents speak in the same manner even to very young babies—babies who are nowhere near being able to understand speech, much less produce it. Mothers speaking to 3-month-old babies use the same kinds of simple sentences and just as many repetitions and questions as mothers speaking to toddlers. Why do they do this? Evidently, the mother's goal, right from the beginning, is to teach the child to be a partner in a conversational game that involves taking turns.

The process starts in early infancy. Here's a "conversation" between Ann, a 3-month-old baby girl, and her mother:

ANN: (smiles)
MOTHER: Oh what a nice little smile! Yes, isn't that nice? There. There's a nice little smile.
ANN: (burps)
MOTHER: What a nice wind as well! Yes, that's better, isn't it? Yes. Yes.

ANN: (vocalizes)
MOTHER: Yes! There's a nice noise. (Snow, 1977, p. 12)

Despite Ann's inadequacies as a partner in the conversation, Ann's mother attempts to keep the dialog going. She indicates to the baby that it's *Ann's* turn now, by asking a question or by pausing. Then, almost anything Ann does is interpreted as a conversational response—a turn. Ann can coo, smile, burp, cough, or look attentively at something, and her mother will accept that response as an attempt to communicate. If Ann does nothing at all, her mother will take Ann's part too—she'll fill in the gap in order to keep the conversation going.

MOTHER: Oh you are a funny little one, aren't you, hmmm? Aren't you a funny little one? Yes. (p. 13)

Gradually, as the baby gets older, the mother gets more particular about what she will accept as a response in the conversation. At 7 months, Ann plays imitation games with her mother, and her mother clearly expects her to play by the rules:

MOTHER: Ghhhhh ghhhhh ghhhhh ghhhhh. Grrrrr grrrrr grrrrr grrrrr.
ANN: (whines)
MOTHER: Oh, you don't feel like it, do you?
ANN: Aaaaa aaaaa aaaaa.

Children do not need to have their pronunciation and grammar corrected by their parents in order to learn to speak correctly—all the parents have to do is speak correctly themselves, at a level the child can understand. When a child uses incorrect grammar, such as "There go one," most mothers do not say "No, there *goes* one": they acknowledge the factual correctness of the child's statement at the same time they improve on his grammar: "Yes, there goes one" (Penner, 1987).

As children grow older and more verbal, their parents' style of speech gradually changes—the sentences grow longer and more complex and are spoken more rapidly. The speech of the parent is closely related to the child's level of verbal development but is always at a higher level than the child's (Reich, 1986).

Is Language Innate?

The same four-legged animal would be called *un chien* in France, *un perro* in Mexico, *ein Hund* in Austria, and *a dog* in the United States. That makes it seem ridiculous to ask whether language is innate. But it's clear that *something* about language is innate. Babies appear to be "tuned in" to speech right from

MOTHER: No, I wasn't making that noise. I wasn't going aaaaa aaaaa.
ANN: Aaaaa aaaaa.
MOTHER: Yes, that's right. (p. 16)

Notice that these conversational partners are already taking turns: Ann vocalizes, then her mother says something, then Ann vocalizes again. But in the early months it is primarily the *mother* who maintains this pattern of alternation, by letting Ann vocalize whenever she wants to and then taking her turn whenever Ann stops (Rutter and Durkin, 1987).

By the time babies are 9 months old, however, they have begun to participate in the process of taking turns. Some researchers recorded the sounds made by 9-month-old babies and their mothers during periods of playful interaction. The researchers concluded that infants of this age, who have not yet learned to speak, are nonetheless able to participate in "vocal exchanges" in which the partners alternate: one says something and then the other responds. The pauses between turns are brief, and there are relatively few occasions in which the turns overlap and both partners say something at the same time (Jasnow and Feldstein, 1986).

By 18 months, children can engage in true conversations with adults:

ANN: Hot.
MOTHER: Hot, hot.

ANN: Tea.
MOTHER: No, it's not tea, it's coffee.
ANN: Coffee. (Snow, 1977, p. 18)

In conversations between adults, turn-taking is partly coordinated by nonverbal signals that indicate when one person has finished speaking and the other can begin. These signals consist chiefly of patterns of eye contact. Typically, in adult conversations, the speaker will look away from the listener as she begins her turn, glance at him from time to time while she is talking, and fix her eyes on him as she gets to the end of her turn, to signal that it's now time for him to respond. The listener, meanwhile, has been gazing at the speaker to indicate attention and to watch for the signal that it's his turn to speak. Toddlers begin to conform to this pattern by the time they are a year old: a 12-month-old will gaze at his mother while she is talking, and wait his turn. By 24 months, he is behaving much as an adult does, looking up at his mother as he finishes his turn, and watching for her signal that she has finished with hers (Rutter and Durkin, 1987).

By using the language known as "motherese" long before it serves a true communicative function, the mother trains her baby in the art of conversation. Both the mother and the baby are entirely unaware that she is teaching him something and that he is learning it. But then, that is true of most of the teaching and learning that go on between parent and child.

the start. They can detect subtle differences in speech sounds, such as the difference between "pah" and "bah" (see p. 165). At a very early age they prefer to listen to speech or to songs sung by a human voice, rather than to instrumental music (Butterfield and Siperstein, 1974).

The development of language follows a relatively fixed, universal pattern. The baby progresses from crying to cooing to babbling. The first words generally appear when she is about a year old. Later, her utterances become longer and more complicated. The child does not need lessons in learning to speak —in fact, formal training is usually of little use. She does not need to be particularly intelligent—only the most severely retarded or brain-damaged children are entirely without language. If she is totally deaf she will work out a system of communicating by means of gestures, even if she is given no training in sign language (Goldin-Meadow and Feldman, 1975). All in all, the normal course of language acquisition is much like the normal course of learning to walk. At a given level of maturation the behavior appears. It can be speeded up or slowed down a little, but not very much.

If a child must reach a certain level of maturation before she can learn to speak, what happens if she passes that level without having learned it? Can she be too old to learn a language? Some psycholinguists believe that learning a language becomes more difficult once childhood has ended. A person who learns a second language after early adolescence seldom learns to speak it like a native. Can a person who has never learned a *first* language learn one after early adolescence?

The best answer we can give to this question is that the ability to acquire language may decline as a child reaches maturity, but it probably doesn't disappear completely. An illustration of this is provided by the tragic case of Genie. In 1970, a 13½-year-old girl in shocking condition came to the attention of California authorities. Genie could not speak, nor stand erect, nor control bowel or bladder, nor eat solid foods. She weighed only 59 pounds (27 kg). It turned out that Genie had been confined in a small room since infancy, harnessed by day to a potty chair and by night to her crib. No one ever spoke to her. Her mentally disturbed father used to bark or snarl at her like a dog; he beat her whenever she made a sound. (He was charged with child abuse, but on the day he was to appear in court he shot himself.) Genie's mother was partially blind and terrified of her husband.

Genie was hospitalized for several months and then went to live with a foster family. She learned to say many words, and eventually she learned to combine them into seven- and eight-word phrases. But her language development was slower than that of a young child, and her speech never became entirely normal. She never learned to ask questions or to use pronouns such as *I* and *you* correctly. Her language retained many of the characteristics of "telegraphic speech" (Curtiss, 1977; Pines, 1981).

Even so, her progress came as a surprise. No one thought that a child that old could still acquire a first language. Genie's condition when she was found was assumed to be comparable to the well-known case of Victor, the "wild boy of Aveyron." Victor was captured by hunters in a forest in France in 1799. A young French doctor named Jean Itard tried to teach him to speak, starting when Victor was about 12 years old. But Victor never learned to say more than a few simple words. It's possible, however, that Victor was brain-damaged or retarded—perhaps that's why he was abandoned in the first place (Lane, 1976).

Genie, too, may have been brain-damaged, perhaps as a result of her father's beatings. The cases in which children are deprived of language for many years are fortunately very rare, and it's never possible to tell for sure whether their later abnormalities resulted from their period of deprivation or were present from the start. We do know that a child with any kind of handicap is far more likely than a normal child to be abused, neglected, or abandoned. Thus, children who recover completely from a period of severe deprivation (like the twins we mentioned earlier in the chapter) provide us with valuable information. When children *don't* recover completely, we never really know why.

CAN CHIMPANZEES LEARN A LANGUAGE? Putting all the evidence together, many psychologists, psycholinguists, and biologists have concluded that the ability to learn language is a built-in human trait—a species-specific characteristic. But is the human species *alone* in its language-learning ability? Obviously, parrots don't really learn language—they just learn to imitate a sequence of sounds without any understanding of what they mean. But dogs can learn to follow dozens of different spoken commands. Chimpanzees are much more intelligent than dogs—why don't they learn to speak?

One reason is that their mouths and vocal cords don't seem to be designed for it. However, their hands are quite nimble. A pair of researchers at the University of Nevada were the first to teach a chimp American Sign Language, the gestural language used by many deaf people in the United States (Gardner and Gardner, 1971).

The chimp, whose name was Washoe, was a year old when she started to learn sign language. Within three years she had learned the signs for 130 words, including *fruit, toothbrush, gimme,* and *tickle.* She also used combinations of signs, such as *"gimme tickle"* and *"more fruit."* There was one problem, though. It wasn't clear whether Washoe was combining signs in a specific order, the way children do at the two-word stage. Was Washoe as likely to say *"tickle gimme"* as *"gimme tickle"?*

To look into that question, a researcher at Columbia University taught sign language to a chimp named Nim. Nim learned his first sign (*drink*) when he was only 4 months old. He learned his 125th sign (*peach*) 3½ years later, just before the experiment ended. Nim was also able to combine signs—he produced combinations of two, three, four, and even more signs (Terrace, 1979).

In some ways, Nim's use of language was much like that of a human child's. He was clearly capable of using sign-language "words." Nim used signs such as *dog, cat, bird, apple, red,* and *play* at appropriate times—for instance, he would see a picture of a cat and sign *cat.* But the chimp's "phrases" were not like those of a normal child. Some of Nim's two-, three-, and four-word phrases are shown in Table 7–5. The two-word combinations seem pretty reasonable, but the three- and four-word phrases don't look at all like what a child would say. They look more like random strings of words. There are many repetitions. Nim's longest utterance was 16 words long. It went, "Give orange me give eat orange me eat orange give me eat orange give me you" (Terrace, 1979, p. 210).

Chimps and human children also differ in the way they learn new words. Chimps learn new signs with difficulty, after a great deal of training. Children

Nim is being taught to make the sign for "house."

TABLE 7–5
Sign-Language Phrases Used by Nim, a Chimpanzee

TWO-WORD PHRASES	THREE-WORD PHRASES	FOUR-WORD PHRASES
play me	play me Nim	play me Nim play
me Nim	eat me Nim	me Nim eat me
eat Nim	eat Nim eat	Nim eat Nim eat
Nim eat	banana Nim eat	banana me eat banana
drink Nim	banana eat Nim	banana eat me Nim
tickle me	tickle me Nim	eat drink eat drink
more tickle	tickle me tickle	tickle me Nim play
sorry hug	hug me Nim	banana me Nim me

From *Nim* by Herbert S. Terrace. Copyright © 1979 by Herbert S. Terrace. Adapted by permission of Alfred A. Knopf, Inc.

pick up new words readily, with no special training at all. Chimps produce their signs mainly in order to obtain a reward such as food or tickling. If the trainer wants a chimp to sign *banana,* he generally has to hold up a banana and keep it out of reach until the chimp makes the sign. In contrast, a human child will often say a word simply to direct her parent's attention to an object or to show the parent that she has seen the object. According to Nim's trainer,

> Noticeably absent from an infant ape's reaction to an object is the sheer delight a human infant expresses in contemplating the object and sharing it perceptually with the parent. . . . There is no evidence that suggests that the infant ape seeks to communicate, either to another ape or to its human surrogate parent, the fact that it has simply noticed an object. (Terrace, 1985, p. 1022)

The ape uses words at the level of the infant who has not yet had the insight that "everything has a name." Apes don't seem to take pleasure in learning new words or in using them simply to convey information, as human children do. And most of all, they don't learn to combine words into original sentences, according to rules of grammar. It seems unlikely that an ape could ever figure out the rules of a grammar—the rules that young children use when they combine words to form phrases.

FIGURING OUT THE RULES. For that matter, it seems unlikely that *children* could ever figure out the rules of a grammar from the huge assortment of sounds they hear. How do you know that "I have hurt myself" is a grammatical English sentence and "He has hurt myself" isn't? Can you explain the rule for deciding which is correct: "Where is Mommy?" or "Where Mommy is?"?

But children don't have to know the rules, you may be thinking. They just have to imitate what they hear other people say. That turns out not to be true, though. Children don't learn just by imitation. For one thing, they don't seem to be able to acquire a new language from passively listening to radio or TV shows (de Villiers and de Villiers, 1979). For another, young children routinely come out with utterances that they've never heard anyone else say, such as "Two feets," "Daddy goed 'way," "Dat's mines," and even "Put on a clo" (instead of "some clothes").

What's interesting about these examples is that all of them are incorrect applications of general rules. What's more interesting is that a child might say *feet, went,* and *mine* before he's 2 years old, and then a few months later switch to *feets, goed,* and *mines.* At some point he notices that most past tenses end in *-ed* and most plurals and possessives end in *-s,* and he tries to apply this rule consistently. Still later he'll learn the exceptions to the rule.

Learning the rules of grammar is really something that preschoolers do, and we'll discuss it in more detail in Chapter 9. Right now we just want to point out that young children do seem to be willing and able to notice patterns in the speech they hear, and to make guesses about the rules that underlie the patterns. Sometimes their guesses are right, sometimes they're wrong. The wrong rules eventually get replaced with better ones. It's rather like an experimental science. The main difference is that the children aren't consciously aware of what they're doing and couldn't actually tell you the theories they're testing at the moment. But the comparison between the toddler and the scientist is a valid one: remember Laurent doing experiments on the behavior of falling objects, and Jacqueline studying the properties of water?

Human babies are born helpless and ignorant. But they come equipped with the most valuable equipment in the world: a thirst for knowledge and understanding, and the ability to acquire them.

Summary

1. Cognitive development is the growth of intelligence, understanding, reasoning, and knowledge. Piaget believes that cognitive development progresses in stages—each child must go through the same stages in the same order, though the rate of progress may vary.

2. According to Piaget, children's interactions with the environment result in **adaptation;** adaptation leads to cognitive development. The two ways in which children adapt are through **assimilation,** which involves applying previously acquired abilities or ideas to new situations, and **accommodation,** which involves modifying previously acquired abilities or ideas to suit new situations.

3. Piaget calls the first major period of development (roughly the first two years) the **sensorimotor period.** This period is divided into six stages. In stage 1 (the first month of life), the baby uses inborn **schemes** such as sucking, rooting, and looking at things.

4. In stage 2 (1 to 4 months), babies acquire new schemes by means of **circular reactions.** In stage 3 (4 to 8 months), they become interested in the effects they can produce on their environment. In stage 4 (8 to 12 months), babies can search for an appropriate method to achieve a goal; they apply previously acquired schemes to new objects as a means of systematically exploring their possibilities. In stage 5 (12 to 18 months), toddlers may

perform series of experiments just to see what will happen; they approach problems in a flexible, sometimes even inventive way.

5. In stage 6 (18 to 24 months), problems may be solved not only by trial and error but also by insight. Children in this stage can think out possibilities and plan ahead by means of mental **representations.** According to Piaget, such representations make **deferred imitation** possible.

6. Piaget believes that the concept of **object permanence** is acquired gradually during the sensorimotor period. The stage-1 baby has no understanding of the permanent existence of objects or people. The first signs of object permanence appear in stage 3: if the baby sees her father drop a toy, she'll look for the toy on the floor. However, if an object is completely hidden, the baby will immediately lose interest in it.

7. Separation distress, which begins early in stage 4, demonstrates the baby's realization that his mother still exists even if he can't see her. "Person permanence" occurs a little before object permanence.

8. Stage-4 babies will search for a completely hidden object, but they will often search in the place where they previously found it, even if they see it being put somewhere else. In stage 5, toddlers will search for an object in the place where they saw it hidden, but they cannot yet use mental representations to take account of movements they didn't actually see. This ability appears in stage 6.

9. Play involves exploration, experimentation, and practice—activities that are necessary to advance a child's cognitive development. The earliest kind of play is called **sensorimotor play** or **mastery play.** The second kind is **pretend play** or **symbolic play.** True symbolic play, according to Piaget, doesn't begin until mental representations are possible, around 18 months. At this point, the toddler might pretend to drink from an imaginary cup.

10. The newborn baby has no concept of self and cannot distinguish between "me" and "not me." The concept of self develops gradually during infancy. The realization that the baby in the mirror is "me" generally appears between 18 and 21 months.

11. Piaget appears to have underestimated the baby's ability to imitate. Babies only a week old can imitate facial expressions, and deferred imitation has been reported in infants only 9 months old.

12. Piaget's theories of object permanence have also been called into question. There is evidence that 4-month-old babies have already formed some expectations about the permanence and solidity of objects.

13. The **stage-4 error** (when babies search in an old hiding place instead of where they saw an object hidden) is less likely to occur if babies are permitted to search for the object immediately. This error is also less likely to be committed by babies who have had experience crawling or moving around in a walker.

14. During the first two years of life the baby gradually becomes able to keep track of more and more actions, objects, or ideas at the same time and to combine them in increasingly complex ways.

15. Newborn babies are capable of only two emotions, distress and pleasure. Later, these are differentiated into more complex emotions on the basis of cognitive advances.

16. Babies who are quick at learning to reach for things or to crawl do not turn out to be more intelligent, on the average, than babies who do these things later. The only kind of infant test that has been shown to have predictive value for later intelligence is based on how quickly a baby habituates to a visual stimulus. Habituation tests measure a baby's ability to learn, to remember, and to discriminate.

17. A mother's responsiveness to her child can affect his cognitive development. The brightest babies tend to have mothers who notice what their babies are interested in and who respond in ways that encourage those interests. Mothers are more likely to act this way to babies who *already* show signs of being bright.

18. Babies who spend their first year or two in an environment that doesn't advance their cognitive development can catch up later if their environment becomes more stimulating.

19. A period of severe malnutrition during infancy has a permanent effect on brain size, but if the later environment is good enough the child's intelligence is likely to be normal. Starvation in infancy *plus* an impoverished environment and a depressed mother lead to lowered intelligence.

20. Most babies can say a word or two at 12 months, but true speech doesn't usually appear until around 16 months, when the average baby can produce 10 words. In the meantime, some babies use **expressive jargon,** which sounds like speech but is unintelligible.

21. The average baby can produce 50 words at around 21 months and around 200 words at 24 months. At every age, **receptive language** is ahead of **productive language.**

22. The productive vocabulary begins to increase dramatically at around 18 months. This increase appears to be due to the child's sudden insight that words are names—symbols or representations of the things they stand for.

23. A toddler may use a single word to take the place of a whole sentence. His use of a word may not correspond to the way adults use it: in **underextension** the toddler uses a word in a narrower way, and in **overextension** he uses it in a wider way—for example, he might call anything round a ball.

24. The average child begins to combine words at 19 or 20 months. This is an accomplishment of the mind, not of the tongue.

25. Toddlers are not capable of uttering long, complex sentences; they leave out verb endings and unimportant words. The remaining words appear in the proper order. This type of language is called **telegraphic speech.**

26. One way that psycholinguists measure the development of children's speech is in terms of **mean length of utterance (MLU).** MLU increases fairly steadily with age, but there are large individual differences. On the average, girls progress a little more rapidly than boys.

27. Both heredity and environment affect verbal development. Later-born children don't progress as rapidly as first-borns, apparently because they have fewer opportunities for verbal interactions with an adult. Periods of mutually focused attention, when a mother pays attention to and talks about whatever her child is looking at, are particularly important.

28. Adults speak in a characteristic way to a toddler: they use short, clear, simple sentences, with many repetitions and questions, and they avoid using words that toddlers find hard to say. This kind of speech has been called **motherese.**

29. Mothers apparently try, right from the beginning, to teach their babies to take turns in conversation. At first almost anything the baby does is interpreted as a conversational response; later the rules get stricter. By 24 months a toddler will gaze at his mother to watch for her signal that it's his turn to talk and to indicate when he is done talking.

30. Babies appear to be "tuned in" to speech right from the start. All but the most severely retarded or brain-damaged children learn to speak without any special training.

31. The ability to acquire a first language may decline as a child reaches maturity, but it probably doesn't disappear completely.

32. Chimpanzees have been taught to communicate in sign language; one chimp learned to make 125 signs and could combine them into phrases. However, these phrases appeared to be strings of words arranged in random order.

33. Children do not learn a language simply by imitating what they have heard. Some of their speech errors are incorrect applications of general rules—evidence that they have noticed patterns in the speech they hear and have made reasonable guesses about the rules that underlie these patterns.

Key Terms

cognitive development
adaptation
assimilation
accommodation
scheme
sensorimotor period
circular reaction
representations

deferred imitation
object permanence
sensorimotor play
mastery play
pretend play
symbolic play
stage-4 error
expressive jargon

receptive language
productive language
underextension
overextension
telegraphic speech
mean length of utterance (MLU)
motherese

8

The Preschool Child

At age 2½, children no longer toddle—they walk and even run steadily. Toddlerhood is over and what is called the **preschool period** has begun. Of course, not all children attend a preschool during this period. The term **preschooler** means only that the child is too young to enter elementary school.

Many changes—in size, shape, motor skills, intellectual abilities, and so on—will come about before the 2½-year-old will be ready to enter first grade. But many important changes have already taken place.

You've Come a Long Way, Baby!

At 2½, Neil is a sturdy-looking little boy, with short, chubby arms and a rounded body. He has lost that fragile, helpless look that he had for the first few months of his life and the cherubic look that came after it. But, if anything, he's more appealing than ever. Neil still has the high forehead, the big eyes, and the round cheeks that made him so irresistible in infancy. His skin is still soft and smooth. But in infancy he was virtually bald—now he has a full head of shiny curls. In infancy he was toothless—now he has a complete set of 20 baby teeth, white and even. In infancy his head was set squarely on his shoulders—now a short but slender neck holds his head erect.

In behavior as well as appearance, Neil has come a long way since infancy. He has been talking for barely a year, but he can already communicate a wide range of ideas and information to anyone he happens to meet. Twenty months ago Neil could only crawl; now he can run and jump, walk up and down the stairs, and even climb a short ladder (using the same foot for each upward step and then bringing the other foot up to that rung). He has recently begun to use the potty occasionally, though he continues to wear disposable diapers most of the time. He can eat with a fork or spoon and drink from a cup he holds himself. He's not too good at putting on his shoes or clothes (buttons and shoelaces are still beyond him), but he's quite capable of taking them off. He can build a tower of blocks, knock it down with enthusiasm, and build it up again. He can even sing "Row, row, row your boat"—well, it sounds *something* like "Row, row, row your boat"!

Physical Growth

At 2½, Neil is exactly 3 feet tall (91 cm), which is just a shade above the mean for boys his age. If we were to try to predict his eventual adult height at this point, our best guess would be 5'10" (177 cm), or 1.94 times his present height (Tanner, 1978). But the correlation between height in early childhood and height in adulthood is not perfect: our estimate has about a 5 percent chance of being off by 3 inches (7½ cm) or more.

Neil's growth depends on many things. He will end up shorter if he is undernourished or if his health is poor. His body must produce the right hormones for growth. He needs at least a minimum amount of exercise: children who are confined to bed do not grow as much as other children (Teeple, 1978).

Neil weighs 32 pounds (14½ kg)—again, slightly above the mean for 2½-year-old boys. Note that Neil has now attained more than 50 percent of his adult height but only about 20 percent of his adult weight. Moreover, the different parts of his body have not all grown at the same rate. Neil's brain growth is more than 75 percent complete; by the time he's 5 it will be 90 percent complete (Tanner, 1978). His bulging abdomen attests to the fact that his internal organs are closer to their adult size than is the rest of his torso. His legs have the most growing to do, because preschoolers are proportionately short-legged, relative to adults.

Growth during the preschool period is considerably slower than growth during infancy. Neil grew 16 inches (41 cm) in the first 2½ years of his life; he'll grow only 7 inches (18 cm) between 2½ and 5 years. A similar trend exists in weight gain: Neil gained 24 pounds (11 kg) in the first 2½ years; he'll gain only 10 pounds (4½ kg) in the second 2½ years. Considered in proportion to total body size, the slowdown in growth is even more apparent: Neil's weight tripled during infancy and toddlerhood, but it will increase by only 30 percent during the preschool period.

Despite the fact that growth during the preschool years is comparatively slow, there are noticeable changes in proportions and in overall appearance. By the time he is ready to begin elementary school, Neil will look less like a baby and more like an adult. His limbs will be longer relative to his body. His body will have grown more than his head, so he will be less top-heavy in appearance. Due to the lengthening of his torso and the development of his abdominal muscles, Neil's stomach will gradually stop protruding and will be fairly flat by the end of the preschool period.

Preschool boys are slightly taller and heavier than girls of the same age. The differences are small—they amount to less than an inch, and no more than a pound, between the heights and weights of the average boy and the average girl. Despite the fact that they are slightly heavier, boys have less fat on their bodies than girls do—boys lose their baby fat more quickly. Girls, however, are physically ahead in other ways: for example, they will begin to lose their baby teeth and get in their permanent teeth at an earlier age than boys.

The Role of Nutrition

At around 6 months of age, babies begin to increase their intake of solid foods. The reliance on solid foods increases in toddlerhood; toddlers take great pleasure in feeding themselves "finger foods" such as Cheerios or bits of meat or vegetables. At this point they are still willing to eat almost anything

Although preschoolers tend to be picky eaters, they eat enough to meet their nutritional needs. Forcing them or bribing them to eat is not a good idea.

that is offered to them. But their openness to new eating experiences is only a brief stage: by the preschool period, most children have developed very definite likes and dislikes. High on the list of things that preschoolers dislike is anything new. The preschooler is likely to turn down any food he hasn't encountered before (Birch, 1987). Trying to get a preschooler to like a food by insisting that he take "just one bite" is often a futile endeavor, or worse than futile. Consider the case of the mother who told her son that he couldn't leave the table until he ate at least one bite of beets:

> After a tearful battle of wills his mother picked up the spoon and forced a beet into the boy's mouth. He sat there with the beet in his cheek for nearly an hour before chewing and swallowing it. That was 15 years ago. Now, as an adult, he cannot bring himself to eat beets, even though he says he would probably enjoy the taste. (Boston Children's Hospital, 1986, p. 135)

Simply presenting the child with a small amount of the new food from time to time, without urging him to eat it, is one technique that often works. But by far the most successful method for getting a preschooler to try a new food is to sit him at a table with a couple of other children who eat it with obvious enjoyment (Birch, 1987). As the social learning theorists would put it, we are providing the child with *models* for the desired behavior.

HOW MUCH SHOULD A PRESCHOOLER EAT? Because preschoolers grow at a slower rate than infants or toddlers, they need less food—they are less hungry. This decrease in appetite, plus their tendency to stick to a small number of preferred and familiar foods, have earned preschoolers a well-deserved reputation as "picky eaters." But it is unwise for adults to try to persuade a preschooler to eat more than he wants to. By urging a child to continue to eat after his appetite has been satisfied ("Finish what's on your plate"), we are asking him to ignore his own feelings of when he's had enough—the signals supplied by the body that tell the child he has consumed enough calories to meet his nutritional needs. By teaching him to ignore these signals, we are increasing the risk of later eating problems such as obesity, anorexia, or bulimia. As a group of researchers from the University of Illinois put it, "Parents who apply heavy external pressure to regulate their child's eating behavior may impede the development of adequate self-controls" (Birch and others, 1987, p. 304).

When allowed to decide on their own how much they want to eat, even young infants are capable of regulating their own caloric intake. Breast-fed babies are less likely to become obese than bottle-fed ones, and one probable reason is that a mother who is breast-feeding her baby can't see how much milk he has "left over," so she is less likely to urge him to take more than he wants (Lansky, 1988).

However picky they may be, virtually all preschoolers like sweet foods and drinks. But it is a mistake to engage in food bargaining such as "Eat your broccoli and then you can have some cake." This is likely to *decrease* the chances that the child will like broccoli. As an experiment, some preschoolers were promised rewards for drinking a glass of a certain kind of juice. By the end of the experiment, most of the children had stopped liking that kind of juice, or liked it less than they had before the experiment (Birch, 1987). Giving the child the cake *before* the broccoli doesn't work either. Children who are given a sweet snack before dinner will eat less dinner, and the food they are most likely to leave on their dinner plate is the food they like the least—the broccoli, in all probability. The trouble with sweets is that they satisfy the child's appetite without meeting his nutritional needs (Birch, McPhee, and Sullivan, 1989).

EATING THE RIGHT STUFF. Despite parents' fears that their preschoolers aren't getting enough to eat or aren't eating the right foods, the great majority of American children appear to be well nourished (in some cases, *too* well nourished—we will discuss childhood obesity in Chapter 11). We eat more processed foods today than people did 30 or 40 years ago, but there is no evidence that this has had any bad effects on children—in fact, today's preschoolers are taller than children of the same age were 30 or 40 years ago. There is also no reason to think that preschoolers' fussy eating habits prevent them from taking in an adequate amount of basic nutrients such as protein.

Protein deficiencies are likely to occur only when a child's parents, because of severe economic deprivation or misguided theories about diet, fail to provide enough of the appropriate foods. The children of vegetarian parents are at risk of protein deficiency unless the parents permit some form of animal protein, such as eggs, milk, or cheese, in their children's diet. It is difficult to meet a child's nutritional needs with vegetable proteins alone, because vegetable proteins are not complete—they lack some of the amino acids (proteins are composed of amino acids) that are essential for growth.

Children also require a certain amount of fat in their diets. Low-fat diets may be healthy for adults but they are not recommended for young children. (Note that human breast milk is not low in fat; nor is it low in cholesterol.) Fat is required for the normal development of the nervous system and for the utilization of vitamins A, D, and E (Boston Children's Hospital, 1986).

There is one group of children, however, for whom the benefits of dietary fat must be carefully balanced against the health risks that might be involved for them. These are the children who have inherited a tendency to have high levels of blood cholesterol—a tendency that can be detected in tests given as early as 6 months of age. For children with this condition, intake of saturated fat and cholesterol (found in dairy products, egg yolks, and red meat) must be kept to a minimum, because these children are at risk of developing heart disease and cholesterol-clogged arteries at an early age. Fat is necessary for growth, so it should never be eliminated entirely from a child's diet; but other kinds of fat, such as corn oil and olive oil, can be substituted for the saturated kind.

Although the diet of the American child is more likely to contain too much of everything than too little of anything, there is one dietary shortage that is still fairly common: a deficiency of iron. According to a recent estimate, more than 20 percent of the world's children are anemic (have too few red blood cells) due to iron deficiency—it is the most widespread nutritional disorder in the world. Although it is found most often among the disadvantaged, iron deficiency may occur at any socioeconomic level. When the deficiency is severe enough to produce anemia, it can interfere with a child's normal development. Iron-deficient children score lower on tests of intellectual and motor development, and show behavioral problems such as increased fearfulness and irritability and shortened attention span (Lozoff, 1989). Iron is present in many foods: red meats, egg yolks, green leafy vegetables, beans, and whole and enriched grains. But the iron found in these foods will not be absorbed properly unless the child's diet also includes an adequate amount of vitamin C (found in most fruits and many vegetables).

Health and Safety

In past generations, the major threats to a child's health were infectious diseases and malnutrition. But medical science has learned to prevent or cure almost all the childhood diseases that took so many lives in the past (although no cure has yet been found for AIDS; see Box 8–1). Deaths from malnutrition have also been greatly reduced, at least in the industrialized nations. Now the greatest threat to a child's life is injury due to accidents. In fact, about half of all deaths in young children result from accidents (Christophersen, 1989).

ACCIDENTS. For both fatal and nonfatal injuries, boys are at significantly higher risk than girls. There are also certain personality characteristics associated with "accident-prone" children—notably a high activity level and a tendency to be impulsive. Children from homes where there is a high level of noise, confusion, and clutter are at greater risk from household accidents such as falls, poisonings, and being scalded by hot water (Matheny, 1987).

Many accidental deaths of young children are preventable, and organized efforts at prevention are proving to be worth the trouble. All 50 states now have laws requiring the use of restraining devices for children in automobiles; the result has been a significant decrease in the number of children who die in motor vehicle accidents. (Roughly half of all accidental deaths to children involve motor vehicles.) Similarly, legislation mandating the use of childproof caps on medical bottles has reduced the number of poisonings from aspirin and other drugs. A New York City law requiring window guards in high-rise apartment buildings has reduced by 50 percent the children who are killed in that city by falling out of windows (Christophersen, 1989).

LEAD POISONING. Urban life has other, less visible dangers that threaten the life and health of young children:

> When Ray Spells was two, his mother took him to a clinic in New Orleans' St. Thomas public-housing development for a checkup. The result was routine for St. Thomas preschoolers: like two of his three siblings, Ray had lead poisoning. He has since been hospitalized 19 times for therapy that helps his body excrete lead.   (Pollack, 1989, p. 22)

Lead paint covers an estimated 60 to 75 percent of the housing in New Orleans. Over the whole United States, there is something like 3 million tons of lead in paint accessible to children, distributed over 25 to 40 million housing units. The children don't have to chew on these surfaces in order to be poisoned by the lead: old paint flakes off and forms dust, and the dust settles on food and toys. It is taken in through the mouth and through the lungs.

Problems in Development

A little girl—we'll call her Krystal—sits in her mother's lap in the Newark health clinic. Her hair is neatly plaited into eight braids, each tipped with a barrette of a different color. She doesn't look unhappy—she doesn't even look sick—but at age 3½ she is the size of a 15-month-old. Krystal's small size is the only outward sign that she is a child with **acquired immune deficiency syndrome,** or **AIDS.**

Krystal was infected with the **HIV virus,** the virus that causes AIDS, either in her mother's uterus or while she was being born. Krystal's mother tests positive for the virus, although as yet she has no symptoms of the disease. She thinks she got the AIDS infection from "a guy I was going with a long time ago," a guy who was "doing drugs." She didn't know she had been infected with the virus until Krystal was diagnosed, at the age of 1½ (Klass, 1989, p. 35).

As of November 1988, 1230 cases of AIDS in children under the age of 13 had been diagnosed and reported to the Centers for Disease Control. Although this is only 2 percent of all AIDS cases in the United States, the number is increasing rapidly. The National Academy of Sciences predicts that by 1991 an additional 10,000 children will be infected with the HIV virus (Task Force on Pediatric AIDS, 1989).

About 20 percent of the children diagnosed as having AIDS were infected with the HIV virus through a contaminated blood transfusion; most are children with blood diseases such as hemophilia, who received the transfusion before testing of donated blood became routine. A far greater number—78 percent of the cases—were, like Krystal, exposed to the virus during prenatal development or birth: the virus was transmitted to them from their AIDS-infected mothers. Most of the infected children come from minority racial and cultural groups: 54 percent are black, 23 percent are Hispanic. Almost half of these children are from three states: New York, New Jersey, and Florida. But the geographical spread of the disease is widening. Cases have now been reported in 43 of the 50 states (Task Force on Pediatric AIDS, 1989).

Krystal's mother didn't know she had been exposed to AIDS, so she didn't know her baby had been infected with the virus. She thought at first that Krystal was just one of those babies who are always sick. Bad colds, asthma, digestive difficulties, fevers with convulsions—it was one thing after another. And Krystal wasn't growing, wasn't gaining weight. This combination of frequent infections and the failure to gain weight, typical of babies with AIDS, was what led a doctor to test her for the HIV virus. Now Krystal is being maintained on antibiotics and monthly injections of gamma globulin (to boost her immune system), and she is holding her own—but just barely. She is way behind her agemates in physical, motor, and cognitive development. Krystal is fortunate in only one thing: her

Once it is in the child's body it can inflict irreversible damage on the nervous system. Medical treatment can reduce the amount of lead in the child's body, but the harm it did to the child's brain may have permanent effects.

As with other causes of unintentional injury, legislation has helped. Lead paint was banned by the U.S. government in 1977, and in 1986 they banned the use of lead pipe and solder in plumbing that supplies drinking water. Lead in gasoline has also been greatly reduced. Such measures, combined with testing and increased public awareness, have dramatically reduced the incidence of lead poisoning in children: according to the Centers for Disease Control, the proportion of children affected went from 6 or 8 percent in the 1970s to only 1 or 2 percent in the mid-80s (Pollack, 1989).

OTHER HEALTH PROBLEMS. Most preschoolers in this country do not have lead poisoning, AIDS, dietary deficiencies, or any other serious health problems. But this period is, nonetheless, not a very healthy time of life. The early preschool period tends to be plagued by a constant series of minor illnesses —colds, ear infections, and digestive upsets. Children who go to day-care centers or nursery schools seem to get sick more often than those who stay at

mother is still well, still able to take care of her. "The question," says a Newark social worker who deals with AIDS-infected children and their AIDS-infected mothers, "is always, who is going to die first?" (Klass, 1989, p. 35).

It is still unclear how the virus is passed from the mother to the child: does the virus cross the placenta during prenatal development, or is the infection spread from the mother to the baby during delivery? If the virus can cross the placenta, as seems likely, why don't all babies of AIDS-infected mothers get AIDS? The risk appears to be well below 100 percent: somewhere between 20 to 65 percent of these babies will be infected with the AIDS virus (Schwarcz and Rutherford, 1989).

There have been 12 sets of twins born to mothers who were known or assumed to be infected with the AIDS virus, and in four of these cases, only one twin got the infection. Tyesha and Ieshia are identical twins—formed by the same genes, grown in the same uterus, delivered within a few minutes of each other. But Tyesha is a normal, healthy child, and Ieshia has AIDS. The disease was diagnosed when the twins were 2 years old. Now, at 9, Ieshia has survived twice as long as most children with AIDS. She has had several close shaves with death, including a near-fatal bout of pneumonia. Both her body and her brain have been attacked by the virus. She is almost a foot shorter than her healthy twin and two years behind her in school, where she attends a class for neuro-logically impaired children (Esper, 1989).

Some parents worry about sending their children to school with a classmate who has AIDS. But Ieshia and Tyesha have shared everything—they shared a uterus, and since they were born they have shared toys, bottles, clothing, and playpen. In spite of all this close contact with her infected twin, Tyesha continues to test negative for the AIDS virus. Close contact with a person with AIDS, in the home or in a schoolroom, is not how the disease is transmitted. There are only three known ways of getting AIDS: through sexual contact with an infected person, through contact with infected blood (from a contaminated transfusion or from a needle shared by intravenous drug users), or from an infected mother to her child before or during delivery. If Tyesha hasn't caught AIDS from Ieshia, Ieshia's classmates aren't going to catch it from her, either.

Tyesha worries about her twin: "Is my sister going to the hospital today?" Krystal's mother tries not to think about her child's future: "I'm living day by day," she says. Many of the children who are diagnosed with AIDS by the age of 2 die within a year, so Krystal and Ieshia have already beaten the odds—Ieshia by quite a large margin. Although AIDS is still considered to be invariably fatal, there are now several drugs in use or being tested that hold out some hope for the blameless victims of this terrible disease (Esper, 1989, p. A1; Klass, 1989, p. 35).

home. However, this may be beneficial for them in the long run, because by the time they enter first grade they will have built up a resistance to whatever "bugs" they have already encountered. Children whose parents smoke at home also get sick more often, but this is clearly *not* beneficial for them. The children of smokers have significantly higher rates of bronchitis, pneumonia, and ear infections, and they run a greater risk of developing chronic lung problems (U.S. Environmental Protection Agency, 1989).

Health tends to improve during the preschool period: by the end of this period, children are getting sick less often. When they do get sick, they are less likely to run a high fever (Lowrey, 1978).

Other physical changes also take place during this period. For instance, breathing becomes slower and deeper, and the heart rate decreases; these changes result from the increase in the size of the organs. The preschooler doesn't need as much sleep as the toddler; the afternoon nap is generally given up by the end of the preschool period. The preschooler also has better control over bladder and bowels, and doesn't have to urinate as often. By the

Physical Changes

age of 6, 85 percent of children can make it through the night without wetting the bed (Houts and Liebert, 1984).

The preschooler no longer sits in a high chair and eats baby food; he has taken his place at the family dining table and can take part in family conversations. He can now participate in the society of which he is a member. The experiences that come from this participation will contribute to his cognitive and social development.

Motor Development

Neil spends his waking hours in almost constant activity—in his mother's words, "He's never still for a moment." Preschool children don't have to be reminded to practice their running, jumping, and tricycle riding, or to polish their block-building skills: they have ample motivation to do these things on their own.

When not asleep or watching TV, most preschoolers are in almost continuous motion. Their ability to go for longer times without eating, sleeping, or using the toilet, plus their increased muscular strength and the development of the motor areas of the brain, enable them to engage in vigorous, sustained physical activity. The games that preschoolers like to play are action games —games like Follow the Leader or Hide and Seek. It is during this period that children begin to engage in physical competition with each other—to race each other across the yard or to see who can build the highest tower of blocks. Such activities not only aid in the further development of motor skills, but also give children new opportunities for interactions with their agemates.

Using the Body Skillfully

By the time he is 3 years old, Neil will be able to climb up a flight of stairs in the adult fashion, so that both his feet don't end up on the same step. (He won't have mastered the trick of alternating feet going down the stairs, however.) The 3-year-old can jump a short distance into the air, walk on tiptoe, and ride a tricycle. His manual skills include the ability to pour milk from a pitcher, to unbutton buttons, to put on his shoes, and to draw an approximation of a circle or a straight line.

At age 4, Neil will be able to climb down a flight of stairs without putting both feet on the same step. The 4-year-old can hop on one foot, catch a large ball, and dress himself. He can draw designs (and perhaps even letters) and can cut on a line with a pair of scissors. By age 5, Neil will be able to run smoothly, skip, fasten the buttons on his shirt, and maybe even tie a bow in his shoelaces.

As these examples suggest, there are significant advances in motor control during the preschool period. These advances depend both on physical maturation of brain and body systems, and on the increasing skill that comes through practice. They involve both the large muscles (such as those that are used in running, jumping, and climbing) and the small muscles (such as those that are used in drawing, cutting with scissors, and tying a bow).

Three important factors are involved in the development of motor skills

during the early years of life. The first is the transition from the reflex behavior of the newborn to the voluntary actions of the preschooler. When the newborn baby grasps an object that is pressed into her palm, the movement of her hand is controlled by a reflex and not by her desire to hang on to the object. Reflexes give way to voluntary actions gradually, during infancy and toddlerhood. During the preschool period, the child becomes the master of the movements of her body. The exercise of this mastery—the ability to get her body to do exactly what she wants it to do, or to produce a certain effect on the physical world—becomes a motivation in itself. The preschooler performs a variety of activities, over and over again, just for the pleasure that comes from getting better at them. Building on the cognitive advances that occurred during the second year of life, she can now set up specific goals for herself, judge how well she did in terms of standards of performance, and take great satisfaction in meeting her goals (Bullock and Lütkenhaus, 1988).

The second factor in the development of motor skills is the preschooler's increasingly accurate awareness of her own body—of its size and shape, and of the positions of its parts. When a child is blindfolded, touched lightly on her hand or arm, and asked to point to the exact spot where she was touched, a 5-year-old can perform with almost perfect accuracy. A 4-year-old is much less accurate (Williams, 1983). During infancy, the child's body is growing so rapidly that it may be difficult for her to develop a realistic body image. The slower growth during the preschool period makes it possible for the child to acquire an accurate picture of her body and its parts. This knowledge of the body's size, shape, and position is an essential component of skillful motor performance.

The final factor involves **bilateral coordination**—the coordination of the right and left sides of the body. Virtually every motor skill requires some sort of cooperation between the two sides of the body: walking involves using the two feet in alternation; jumping up into the air involves using the two feet together; tying a bow involves a highly complex interaction of the two hands. Harriet Williams, a specialist in motor development in children, has this to say about the importance of bilateral coordination:

> In some manipulative tasks both hands/arms must move simultaneously; however in most tasks they must move in some kind of alternately timed relationship to one another. To use the example of cutting, if the child is cutting a picture out of a book or from a piece of paper, the hands must work together in a coordinated alternating fashion. One hand leads in the sense of holding the scissors and performing the cutting action; the other hand assists by holding the paper, maintaining its proper orientation, and moving the paper when and if it is necessary to accommodate the cutting action of the lead hand. (1983, p. 182)

With the help of these three factors—the achievement of voluntary control over the various parts of the body, the acquisition of an accurate body image, and the establishment of bilateral coordination—the preschooler makes impressive advances in motor development. Both the speed and the accuracy of movements increase during this period. In addition, reaction time—the time it takes to react to a stimulus such as a bell or a light—gets shorter, which means that the child reacts more quickly. Researchers tested reaction time in preschoolers by having them touch a little light on a board in front of them whenever the light went on. Reaction time, defined as the amount of time between when the light went on and when the child's hand began to move, declined from about one second at age 2 to half a second at age 5 (Brown, Sepehr, Ettlinger, and Skreczek, 1986).

Large-Muscle Skills in the Preschooler

The term **large-muscle** (or *gross-muscle)* **skills** refers to a wide variety of motor activities that involve the whole body: walking, running, jumping, skipping, throwing a ball, and so on. Children first learn to perform such activities and then learn, more gradually, to perform them skillfully and smoothly. Walking, for example, is awkward at first—the toddler walks with her feet far apart and she falls down easily. As toddlerhood ends and the preschool years begin, walking becomes more skillful. The stride lengthens, speed increases, balance is more stable, and the child is able to walk for longer periods of time without resting. By the age of 4, the movements the child makes in walking are essentially the same as the adult's.

The changes that take place in running patterns are more noticeable than those involved in walking and take a little longer to master, but they are similar in nature. Figure 8–1 shows the difference in running style between an 18-month-old toddler and a 3-year-old preschooler.

FIGURE 8-1
The running pattern of an 18-month-old toddler (top) versus that of a 3-year-old preschooler (bottom). (Adapted from Ridenour, 1978.)

THROWING A BALL. In some cases, the development of a motor skill involves the gradual integration of already existing movements—what start out as separate actions are eventually combined into a smooth, continuous pattern. In other cases, new movements must be acquired. Learning to throw a ball skillfully is an example of an activity that involves both of these components: integrating existing movements and acquiring new ones.

At 2 or 3 years of age, the child merely swings his arm while holding his trunk steady. There is no rotation of the trunk, and the feet are fixed (see Figure 8–2). Next, horizontal movements of the arm and body begin to occur, producing some rotation of the body. Although the child is now rotating his trunk to compensate for the greater power of his arm movement, his feet still remain fixed in one place.

Around the age of 4 or 4½, the child will begin to take a step forward with his right leg (assuming he throws with his right hand). The rotational movement of his hips gradually increases, leading to greater power and accuracy.

The final phase doesn't occur until the end of the preschool period. Now the child moves his weight forward from his right to his left leg during the throw. Rotation of the trunk is a little ahead of the swing of the arm, and the throwing movement is smooth and well controlled.

Manual Skills

The term *large-muscle skills* covers a wide variety of activities. In contrast, the term **small-muscle** (or *fine-muscle) **skills** is used almost exclusively to refer to manual skills—the use of the hands and fingers to manipulate objects. We have also referred to this skill (in Chapter 5) as eye–hand coordination. As Williams puts it,

Fine motor control has been previously defined as the ability to coordinate or regulate the use of the eyes and the hands together in efficient, precise,

FIGURE 8-2
Throwing a ball: the
development of this skill
during the preschool period.
(From Williams, 1983, p. 235.)

and adaptive movement patterns. These movement patterns can manifest themselves in a myriad of forms ranging from writing, drawing, and coloring to cutting, pasting, and manipulation of small objects and/or instruments. More universally, these movement patterns are referred to as eye–hand coordination skills. Development of fine motor control or eye–hand coordination skills represents an important and integral part of the total motor development of the young child.   (1983, p. 171.)

Just as the baby learned to reach successfully for toys by watching her hand movements, the preschooler learns to manipulate objects by watching her hands as they perform the task. She sees the results of her movements, and this visual feedback tells her whether her hands are doing what she wants them to, or whether she must modify her movements in some way. A child who lacks this visual feedback (a blind child, for instance) must rely on other types of feedback, generally the sense of touch, to tell her whether she is succeeding at the task. But feedback by means of touch is slow and inefficient compared to visual feedback. The blind child is generally very delayed in motor development (Fraiberg, 1977).

The preschool period is an important time for the development of manipulation skills. This increasing manual dexterity is applied both to play activities (cutting, pasting, coloring, and so on) and to practical things such as using a

This 3-year-old girl can put on her shoes, but the complex movements involved in tying a bow are still too difficult for her.

toothbrush and helping with family chores. The manual skills acquired during the preschool period enable children to deal successfully with the many paper-and-pencil activities of kindergarten and first grade.

Individual differences in motor development are striking—some children are better coordinated, stronger, or more athletic than others. They can run faster or jump farther than their agemates, or they learn to catch a ball or do cartwheels at an earlier age. These individual differences tend to persist throughout the lifespan. What is the source of such differences? Genetic factors unquestionably play an important role—there is evidence that identical twins are more alike than fraternal twins in their performance of motor skills during the preschool years. What's inherited may be a certain physique (perhaps a more muscular body), a talent for coordinated movements, or even a tendency to be very active and thus to devote more time to practicing motor skills.

    Nutrition, which we have already discussed, is also important. Children

Variability in Motor Development

who have been undernourished for long periods of time are likely to be retarded in their motor development. It may take them many years to catch up with their better nourished agemates, or (if the undernutrition went on too long or was too severe) they may never catch up.

We should mention in passing that there are difficulties involved in the assessment of preschoolers' motor development. For one thing, day-to-day variations in performance are much greater in preschoolers than in older children, due partly to changes in motivation and in willingness to cooperate. For another thing, no test of motor abilities has been accepted as the established standard, the way the Apgar test has been accepted as the standard for assessing the physical condition of the neonate. The tests that do exist are of questionable value and correlate poorly with one another (Galahue, 1983). Thus, work in the area of motor development has remained focused on establishing norms—that is, on determining the average ages at which various motor skills are acquired. But the age at which a child first becomes able to do something is a very poor indicator of how skillful she will eventually be at it. A child who learns to walk and run unusually early will not necessarily turn into a track star.

GENDER DIFFERENCES. In infancy, there are no consistent differences between boys and girls in motor development: the average girl sits up, crawls, and walks at virtually the same age as the average boy. By the preschool period, however, some differences have emerged. Boys, on the average, have larger muscles than girls do. Partly for this reason, they can run faster, jump farther, climb higher, and throw a ball harder. Girls are ahead in other aspects of motor development, particularly in manipulation skills such as using scissors and fastening buttons. They're also a little ahead in large-muscle activities that require coordination rather than strength—for instance, skipping, hopping, and balancing on one foot (Cratty, 1979).

These differences are not particularly surprising, since many factors combine to produce them. Boys are physically more muscular than girls; girls are physically more mature. Boys spend more time than girls do in large-muscle activities such as running, jumping, and climbing; girls spend more time in activities that involve manipulation and precise coordination. A study of preschoolers in a California nursery school showed that the boys spent more of their time in vigorous outdoor play, whereas the girls spent more time indoors. Perhaps these children were yielding to social pressures to do "boy things" and "girl things," but the investigators thought not—they saw no evidence that the differences in behavior resulted from anything other than the children's own preferences:

> We found little evidence that the behavior of the nursery school staff, the expressed concerns or the overt practices of the children's parents, or the nature of the available apparatus could account for the observed sex differences in behavior. (Harper and Sanders, 1978, p. 48)

The investigators concluded that the different styles of play reflected, at least in part, biological differences. They point out that in most species of mammals the males explore over a wider territory and engage in more vigorous forms of activity than the females.

Development of the Brain

Growth of the head and brain occurs early in the life of the human—brain growth, in fact, is most rapid in the period just preceding birth. By age 2, brain growth has slowed considerably. It has not ended, however—the neurons in the brain continue to increase in size, and there will be a small increase in the number of glial cells. Myelination (see p. 176) also contributes to brain growth. But the development of the brain consists not only of growth: excess neurons and unused connections continue to be pared away all through childhood. The process has been compared to the way a sculptor works: more clay is added here and there, and then the unwanted portions are carved away (Kolb, 1989).

The human brain appears to be symmetrical—its two wrinkled hemispheres are almost perfect mirror images of each other. But although they look very similar, the two hemispheres are not, in fact, identical. It has been known for over a century that the part of the brain that enables us to speak and understand language is located in the left hemisphere in most people. The left side of the brain is also in charge of the right hand and foot: each side of the body is controlled by the brain hemisphere on the opposite side.

Because the left hemisphere controls both verbal ability and the right hand—the dominant hand in most people—it used to be called the "dominant side" of the brain. It is dominant, however, only in the particular things that it does best. *Both* sides of the brain serve important functions, but the two hemispheres are used in somewhat different ways. The left hemisphere specializes in producing and understanding speech and in reading and writing. The right hemisphere specializes in nonverbal things such as spatial ability, perception of patterns and melodies, and the expression and recognition of emotions. The left hemisphere seems to be involved in processing any infor-

The Two Sides of the Brain

The human brain.

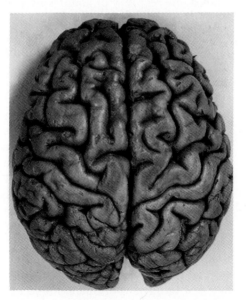

mation in which the *order* of the individual items is important—in reading, for example, letters must be read in the appropriate order. The right hemisphere predominates in tasks in which things are taken as a unified whole—the spatial arrangement of a room, the perception of a face (Witelson, 1987).

The discovery of hemispheric specialization gave rise to the theory that some people and some kinds of activities are "left-brained" and other people and activities are "right-brained." But people actually use both sides of their brains at once, whatever they happen to be doing. As one researcher put it, "The two hemispheres do not function independently . . . each hemisphere contributes its special capacities to all cognitive activities" (Levy, 1985, p. 44).

THE LEFT HEMISPHERE AND LANGUAGE ACQUISITION. The early information on hemispheric differences came from observing what happened when someone sustained an injury to one hemisphere or the other, due to a stroke (a blood clot or hemorrhage in the brain) or an accident. An adult who suffers an injury to the left side of the brain might lose the ability to speak or to understand what someone is saying. But what happens when damage to the left hemisphere occurs early in life? The answer is that damage in infancy seldom leads to a serious language disability. The right hemisphere takes over some of the language functions that would normally have been served by the left, and the child learns to speak. However, depending on the extent of the injury, the child's IQ might be permanently lowered and there may be motor problems as well (Kolb, 1989).

If the damage to the left hemisphere occurs after the child has learned to speak, she could lose this ability temporarily. Then, depending on how old she is when the injury occurs, undamaged parts of the brain may gradually take over the functions of the damaged parts and the ability to speak will be regained. The older the child is at the time of the injury, the less likely it is that there will be full recovery of language and other cognitive functions. But the brain's plasticity—its ability to reassign functions to different areas when something goes wrong—is never lost completely. Even adults are likely to show some recovery of abilities they lose due to a stroke or an accident.

If the right hemisphere can take over the left hemisphere's job of handling language, does that mean that the two hemispheres are basically the same? Earlier researchers assumed that **lateralization** of the brain—the tendency for the two sides to serve different functions—happens gradually during development and that there are no important differences between the hemispheres at first. But evidence from a variety of studies indicates that the two hemispheres *aren't* the same, even in newborn babies. From the very start, most babies appear to process speech sounds in the left hemisphere and music in the right. The lateralization of the brain is present from birth (Hahn, 1987).

The existence of this built-in specialization makes the plasticity of the human brain all the more remarkable. The ability of a young child to acquire (or reacquire) speech after left-hemisphere damage shows that parts of the brain not originally destined for language functions can take over those functions if necessary (Witelson, 1987).

RIGHT- AND LEFT-HANDEDNESS. Like the two sides of the brain, the two sides of the body also have their own specialties. It was noticed many years ago that most newborn babies tend to keep their heads turned to the right.

This tendency was found to be related to handedness: the few babies who keep their heads turned to the left generally prove to be left-handed (Gesell and Ames, 1947). Although young infants show no preference for reaching with one hand rather than the other, most are able to hold a rattle for a longer time in the right hand than in the left (Caplan and Kinsbourne, 1976).

By 18 months, around 65 percent of toddlers have established a clear preference for using the right hand to hold a crayon or a spoon. About 10 percent favor the left, and the remaining 25 percent show no consistent preference. The percentages are about the same at age 2½, but between 18 months and 2½ years many children switch from one category to another—a child who consistently favored his right hand at 18 months might be inconsistent at 2½ years, or one who was inconsistent at 18 months might be favoring her left hand at 2½ (Archer, Campbell, and Segalowitz, 1988).

Most children have made up their minds by age 4. In a study of hand preference in 4-year-olds, 88 percent of the children were clearly right-handed and 8 percent were left-handed. Only 4 percent were ambidextrous or had not yet established a dominant hand (Tan, 1985). Longitudinal data show that almost all children who are right-handed at age 5 remain right-handed. A 5-year-old who doesn't have a strong preference is also likely to end up right-handed. Social pressures favor right-handedness: it's inconvenient to be left-handed in a right-handed world (Fennell, Satz, and Morris, 1983).

But right-handedness is not just a cultural convention. In every human society, the majority of people are right-handed. Archeological evidence suggests that right-handedness has prevailed since the dawn of our species. Thus, the tendency toward right-handedness appears to be an innate human characteristic. And yet, almost a tenth of the people in our society are left-handed. Left-handedness is somewhat more common in males than in females; it is also more common in twins. It is most common in children whose parents are left-handed: the probability that a child will be left-handed is 20 percent if one parent is left-handed and 50 percent if both are (Corballis and Beale, 1976; Longstreth, 1980).

Right-handed people almost invariably use the left side of their brain for language. The situation is considerably more variable in lefties: some process language in the left hemisphere, some in the right, and some use both sides. Left-handed people tend to be less lateralized (less one-sided, more bilateral) than right-handed ones. This means that they are better at using their non-dominant hand: it is easier for a lefty to use his right hand than it is for a righty to use his left. A left-handed person who sustains a brain injury is more likely to regain the functions she lost—better able to switch over to the other side of her brain—than a right-handed person.

In what other ways do lefties and righties differ? There are other differences, but they tend to be small and variable enough so that they show up only when large groups of children are tested. Despite the fact that lefties and righties have equal IQs on the average, higher than usual proportions of lefties (and children who have mixed or inconsistent dominance) are found in certain groups: among learning-disabled, mentally retarded, and autistic children, and among stutterers. However, there is also a higher percentage of lefties among children who are exceptionally gifted in math, in music, or even in verbal ability (Benbow, 1988; Hassler and Birbaumer, 1989).

In other words, the children who are not clearly right-handed are a mixed bunch: some of them do better than righties and some of them do worse. A plausible explanation for the ones who do better is that these children may be able to use *both* sides of their brain for mathematical and verbal reasoning tasks, rather than having the left hemisphere do most of the work. Lefties are less lateralized than righties, not only in how they use their hands but also in how they use their brains (Benbow, 1988).

What about those lefties who do *worse* than righties? In some cases, a child might become left-handed because the left side of his brain (the side that controls the right hand) was damaged at birth. The proportion of lefties is higher among children who were born prematurely or whose mothers suffered complications of childbirth. Brain damage to the left hemisphere could lead to mental retardation or a learning disability, and it could also account for a tendency to favor the left hand (Searleman, Porac, and Coren, 1989).

Other cases appear to have a genetic basis. Learning disabilities and stuttering tend to run in families—and they tend to run in the *same* families that have a higher than usual proportion of lefties. Perhaps there are inherited differences in the structure of the brain or in the way it develops, and these differences increase the likelihood of both left-handedness and learning disabilities (Geschwind and Behan, 1982).

Although left-handed adults have been found to have more accidents than right-handed ones (Hilts, 1989), left-handed children do not appear to be clumsier than their right-handed peers. At least during the preschool period, there are no overall differences in motor skills. In a study of manual dexterity in 4-year-olds, right- and left-handed children did equally well on tasks such as lacing beads on a string and putting beans in a bottle as quickly as possible. The children who didn't do so well were those who hadn't yet established a dominant hand—who sometimes used the right hand and sometimes the left (Tan, 1985). Being ambidexterous is not necessarily an advantage—in some respects it can be a handicap. A child who always uses her right hand for skilled tasks gives her right hand a great deal of practice. But if she uses her right hand and her left hand interchangeably, her right hand gets only half as much practice. Thus, the advantage in having a dominant hand is that that hand gets twice as much practice in carrying out skilled tasks. More precisely, each hand gets twice as much practice in its own specialty: the nondominant hand in holding objects, and the dominant hand in manipulating them.

LEFT-RIGHT CONFUSIONS. In an experiment performed more than 50 years ago, young children were given a sheet of paper containing some letters of the alphabet. They were asked to mark all the letters that were exactly like the large sample letter printed on the side of the sheet. The children had little difficulty distinguishing letters such as *b* and *p*, which differ only in up-down orientation. Yet many 5-year-olds confused *b* and *d*. When the sample letter was *b*, they marked all the *d*'s as well as all the *b*'s (Davidson, 1935).

Now consider a different kind of experiment. A researcher shows a young child two boxes, exactly alike. They are placed side by side in front of the child, one to his left and one to his right. The researcher lifts the lid of one of the boxes, puts a treat inside, covers both boxes briefly with a cloth (so the child can't just keep staring at the box that contains the treat), and then lifts the cloth and lets the child choose one box. Even 2-year-olds find this test quite easy, despite the fact that the only difference between the two boxes is that one is on the left and one is on the right (Braine and Eder, 1983).

Why is it that toddlers can easily distinguish between the left box and the right one, but preschoolers can't distinguish between *d* and *b*? The answer is that the first kind of distinction has to do with "real-world" directions and locations. In the real world, the difference between left and right is important: the drawer on the left contains underwear, the one on the right contains toys. Turn left to get to the bathroom, right to get to the kitchen. A child does not need to know how to use the words "left" and "right" in order to know which drawer contains toys or how to get to the kitchen.

On the other hand, the difference between *d* and *b* is a difference between two visual stimuli that are mirror images of each other, and such distinctions are normally of little importance in the real world. The baby sometimes sees his mother's left profile and sometimes her right profile, but he learns early on that these are two views of the same mother. A chair is the same chair, whether the seat is facing right or left. So it's not surprising that a child might consider two visual stimuli that are mirror images of each other to be equivalent (Gibson, 1969).

How and when do children learn to distinguish confusing stimuli such as *d* and *b*? Two studies of 4-year-olds give us some clues. In the first, children were taught to distinguish between two mirror-image stimuli by giving one name to the stimulus that was pointing left and a different name to the one that was pointing right. They learned to do this fairly readily, but it turned out that most of them were relying on landmarks in the room: for example, they would give one name to the snowman that was pointing toward the window and the other name to the snowman that was pointing toward the door (Fisher and Braine, 1981). Thus, they were converting a distinction of the *d*-versus-*b* variety into a distinction of the left-box-versus-right-box variety!

In the other experiment, 4-year-olds were tested on their ability to discriminate mirror-image pairs of simple geometric forms—for example, a triangle with its apex pointing left versus one with its apex pointing right. The children were shown the triangles one at a time and asked to say whether they were "exactly the same" or "different in any way." Only about 40 percent of these 4-year-olds noticed the difference. What was interesting was that the children who passed this test were generally the same ones who tended to name the pictures in a picture book in consistent left-to-right order and to write their names without getting any of the letters backward. Although 82 percent of the 4-year-olds could write their own names, many of the children who had failed the same-different test wrote some letters backward (Casey, 1984).

Then the researcher took the children who had failed the same-different test and gave them training in making left-right distinctions: she taught them to name the pictures in left-right order, and she pointed out that the two triangles "are different because they go different ways." After this training, most of the 4-year-olds were able to tell the triangles apart. It seemed to be mainly a question of bringing the difference to their attention—of making them realize that the left-right distinction is an important one.

But when the researcher tried the same procedure on 3-year-olds, she was far less successful. To begin with, very few of the 3-year-olds spontaneously solved the same-different test or named the pictures in left-to-right order. Even with training, only about a third of the children could pass these tests. So there is more involved in making visual left-right distinctions than simply knowing that they matter.

What is involved is the same ability that enables many 4- and 5-year-olds, but hardly any 3-year-olds, to say which is their left hand and which is their right. The ability to do this seems be connected to the establishment of a dominant hand. Once the child has developed a preference for using one hand for manipulation tasks, and once that hand has become noticeably more skillful at those tasks than the other hand, the two hands are no longer equal. Now the child can tell them apart. A 5- or 6-year-old who is asked, "Which is your right hand?" might make writing motions with her right hand before she can answer that question. People who do not have one hand clearly dominant over the other (that is, ambidextrous people) tend to have difficulty even in adulthood with making quick decisions about left and right.

Once the child can distinguish between the two sides of her body, she can learn to distinguish between visual stimuli such as *b* and *d*. She now has an internal guide and no longer has to rely on landmarks in the room. However, for a while she may still have trouble remembering which is which—which is called *b* and which is called *d*. In the same way, she may have trouble remembering which animal is called "lion" and which is called "tiger," even though she can easily see the difference between them.

Perceptual Development

"Perceptual functioning reaches adultlike or near-adultlike levels remarkably quickly," states one authority in child development. "At birth," he continues, "infants have considerable ability to see, hear, and integrate information from different sensory systems. These abilities develop considerably further in the next 6 months" (Siegler, 1986, p. 174).

If children are almost fully mature, in a perceptual sense, by the time they're 6 months old, what can be left to develop in the preschool period? Not the basic features of perceptual functioning—these are already well established by this time. However, some of the more complex and subtle abilities develop more gradually, and we'll describe them in this section.

Seeing Things as They Really Are

There are two ways to perceive a visual scene: the way you usually see it, and the way it is seen by a camera or by an artist who is making a realistic painting of the scene. You may never have noticed the difference, but there is one. If there are two coffee cups on the table, one on your side and one at the other end, you can easily see that they are the same size. But to the camera and the artist, the one that's farther away looks smaller—it will take up a smaller area of a photograph or a painting of the scene. The rims of the cups are round and they *look* round to you, but in the photo and the painting they come out as ellipses or ovals. The part of the tablecloth that's in the shadow of the cup looks the same color to you as the rest of the tablecloth, but the camera's eye and the artist's eye sees the shadowed part as considerably darker than the rest of the tablecloth.

"But that's just because I know that the two cups *really are* the same size," you say, "and I also know that the rim of the cup is round and that the tablecloth is all the same color. I don't *see* them that way—I just know they *are* that way."

That's exactly what researchers in perception used to think—in fact, they thought that children had to learn through experience to see things the way they "really are." But this theory turned out to be wrong. In fact, children *start out* seeing things the way they "really are," and they actually have to *learn* to see them the way artists and cameras see them. As in the case of the left-right distinctions, the earliest perceptions are based on the "real world."

Adults have a choice: they can judge the size of an apple, for instance, either the way the camera does or the way it "really is." If they choose to see the apple's size in the manner of the camera, the apple takes up less and less of the visual field the farther away it is, so in that sense it looks smaller. This is called the apple's **projective size** (referring to the size of the image that is projected from the apple to the back of the eye, or to the film in the camera). Alternatively, adults can choose to perceive the *objective* (or "real") size of the items in view—for example, if several apples of various sizes are located at different distances, the adult can still judge which is the biggest apple and which is the smallest, without being misled by the inconsistencies in projective size.

Young children, and even babies, are surprisingly good at perceiving "real" size and shape, but they are not good at seeing *projective* size and shape. Some researchers tested the ability of 3- and 4-year-olds to see things the way a camera does. They showed the children figures cut out of cardboard and asked them questions such as: "If I put this way far away over there, will it look big to you or will it look little to you?" and "If I put this right up close to your eyes, will it look big to you or little to you?" The 3-year-olds answered correctly (in terms of projective size) about 70 percent of the time—not much better than if they were guessing, since they would be right 50 percent of the time if they answered at random. The 4-year-olds did much better: they were correct almost 90 percent of the time. The 4-year-olds also knew that in order to make a round disk look "fat" it has to be turned so that its round side is facing them, and in order to make it look "thin" it has to be rotated so that it is at an angle to their line of sight. The 3-year-olds were baffled by this task. The researchers concluded that children do not become aware of projective size and shape—the fact that things "look" smaller when they're farther away and that circles "look" like ellipses when you see them from an angle—until the preschool years. By age 4, most children have noticed these changes and the conditions under which they occur (Pillow and Flavell, 1986, p. 128).

THE VISUAL CONSTANCIES. The 4-year-olds in the study we just described were aware that things may look smaller when they're far away, and circles may look skinnier when you see them at an angle, but that their *real* size and shape remain the same. The perceptual mechanisms that enable us to see things as the correct size and the correct shape, regardless of viewing angle and distance, are called *constancies*. As this term suggests, these mechanisms

FIGURE 8-3
An illusion based on size constancy (Rosinski, 1977, p. 64). Although these children are actually drawn the same size, the one who appears to be farther away looks larger. This illusion is what causes athletes filmed through a telephoto lens to appear too large or too small: through a telephoto lens, two athletes may have almost exactly the same projective size, even though one is farther away. The result is that the one who is farther away appears to be much larger than the closer one.

produce a constant perception despite changes in the actual images that reach your eyes. **Size constancy** keeps things looking roughly the same size regardless of how near or far away they are, and **shape constancy** keeps things looking the same shape even when they're viewed at different angles.

Normally we are completely unaware of these perceptual mechanisms. But their existence can be demonstrated if we arrange things so that, instead of producing accurate perceptions, they produce illusions. The illusion shown in Figure 8–3 is a demonstration of size constancy. When we view a scene, the projective image of an object is smaller when the object is farther away. The constancy mechanism takes distance into account in such a way that the distant object is perceived to be as large as the nearer object. But when something appears to be farther away (like the second child in Figure 8–3), and yet its projective image *isn't* smaller, the constancy mechanism is tricked. The result is that the child who looks farther away appears to be larger. The two children in Figure 8–3 are actually the same size.

As this illusion demonstrates, constancy mechanisms are not based on our knowledge of what size or shape objects ''really'' are—they are automatic and, to some extent, involuntary. Furthermore, they are innate. Babies do not have to learn through experience, by moving around in their environment and touching things, that distant objects are just as big as nearby objects. Two Australian researchers have shown that size constancy is present in babies as young as 4 months of age—too young to have learned anything by moving around and touching things. The same researchers have also found that shape constancy is present in early infancy (Day and McKenzie, 1973, 1981).

On the other hand, the constancy mechanisms are not perfectly accurate at first. A baby doesn't have to learn that the actual size of a faraway object is much greater than its projective size, but what she does have to learn is exactly *how much greater*. Young children do not have very accurate size constancy. Their constancy improves with age. In this case, information obtained from moving around in the environment undoubtedly plays a role. That is why the preschool period, a period of lively and active exploration of the environment, is an important time for the development of accurate size, shape, and distance perception.

Picture Perception

When we see a picture of something—even if it is in black and white (and therefore very different in coloring from the original)—we see it as a replica of the original. We are not fazed by the distortions involved when a three-dimensional scene is reduced to two dimensions. Even an outline drawing of an object—different in so many ways from the object itself—is generally recognized without difficulty. Is our ability to interpret pictures innate, or have we learned it in infancy or early childhood?

In an attempt to answer that question, two experimental psychologists raised their son from infancy without showing him any photographs or drawings, or letting him watch TV. Although he must have seen *some* pictures during infancy, purely by accident, no one ever pointed to a picture and told him what it was. Normally, in our society, parents do quite a lot of picture naming with their infants and toddlers.

When the child was 19 months old and had a sizable vocabulary, his parents finally showed him some pictures. The pictures were of things the child knew—common household objects and familiar toys. He had no difficulty naming these objects, either in photographs or in drawings. Although this classic experiment involved only a single child, the results are clear-cut: recognizing pictures of things does not depend on experience with pictures (Hochberg and Brooks, 1962).

But there's more to seeing pictures than simply knowing what objects they represent. Pictures are two-dimensional, but usually they depict three-dimensional objects or scenes. Although actual depth is absent, there are several ways that a picture can give the viewer an impression of depth: by shadings and shadows, by the relative sizes and positions of pictured objects, and by the way lines converge toward the horizon. Are young children responsive to pictorial depth cues of this sort?

The answer is yes, they are. Experiments have shown that 3-year-olds, and even 2-year-olds, respond appropriately to depth cues such as shading and the convergence of lines in the distance. But experience does appear to play some role in this kind of perception, as shown by the fact that sensitivity to such cues improves with age. Babies under 6 months do not seem to respond to the kinds of depth cues shown in pictures (Yonas, 1979).

Preschool children are capable of deriving some fairly subtle kinds of information from pictures. In one experiment, 4-year-olds were shown photographs of people's faces; the people ranged in age from infancy to over 70. The children were asked, "Which is the oldest person?" Their replies indicated that 4-year-olds are capable of discriminating quite accurately between a picture of a child their own age and a picture of a 7- or 8-year-old, or between an adolescent and a young adult, or between a middle-aged adult and a 70-year-old (Jones and Smith, 1984).

HOW CHILDREN LOOK AT PICTURES. Although the preschooler may be remarkably mature in some of his perceptual abilities, he nevertheless does not necessarily see a picture in the same way as an adult. One reason for this is that preschoolers don't know as much about the world—they lack the extensive store of memories and experiences that adults bring to any situation. But there's another factor involved. Preschoolers see a picture differently than adults partly because they *look* at it differently.

By using special cameras that take photographs of a person's eyes, researchers can tell exactly what part of a picture the person is looking at. Such techniques provide information about the movements of the eyes that occur whenever we look at something. When we look at a picture, we **fixate** (or focus) our eyes on one location, then move them to another location. These eye movements occur about four times a second. During the movement itself the eyes are, in effect, "turned off." Seeing takes place only during the brief periods of fixation between eye movements, when the eyes are momentarily still.

This alternation of eye movements and eye fixations is found in children as well as in adults. The age differences have to do with the *kinds* of eye movements children make, and what parts of the pictures they fixate on. Adults scan systematically. They use long, leaping eye movements to sweep around the picture as a whole, and short eye movements when they are concentrating on particular details of the picture. Young children, on the other hand, tend to get stuck on certain conspicuous details. Their eye movements are much shorter than those of adults, and their fixations tend to be restricted to small areas of the picture, generally near the middle. The outer portions are often ignored. Thus, children tend to miss a lot—they don't get all the information that a picture has to offer (Davidoff, 1975).

The ability to pay attention to what's important is not usually considered a perceptual skill: it's really a cognitive skill. This is an area where cognition and perception overlap, because when the preschooler sees less in a picture

Preschoolers see things differently from adults partly because they don't know as much about the world, and partly because they look at things differently.

than an adult does, the difference is more likely to be an attentional problem than a perceptual one. The child may be unable to focus his attention on the parts of a picture that are relevant, or to keep his attention focused for a long enough time (Flavell, 1985).

THE DRAWINGS OF PRESCHOOL CHILDREN. If looking at a picture involves both perceptual and cognitive abilities, *drawing* a picture requires yet a third ability: motor skills. Because all three of these important domains of development are involved, children's drawings are of special interest to us.

The 2½-year-old holds a crayon in his hand and "writes" on a piece of paper, but what he produces are scribbles. Most 3½- or 4-year-olds, in contrast, can draw recognizable houses, flowers, trees, cars, and people. The human figure they draw is the so-called **tadpole person** of the preschool child. The tadpole person (see Figure 8–4) has no body—only a big head with some sticks for legs.

The transition from drawing scribbles to drawing tadpole people usually occurs between the child's third and fourth birthdays. Increased motor control—better eye–hand coordination—is one of the factors involved in this achievement. A younger preschooler has great difficulty in simply tracing over the outline of a circle or a square. An older preschooler can trace over a

FIGURE 8-4
Tadpole people. These bodyless people are typical of the drawings of 3- and 4-year-olds. (Top row: Goodnow, 1977, p. 54; bottom row: Taylor and Bacharach, 1981, p. 374.)

Close-Up

Box 8-2
The Preschool Artist

With a purple felt-tip pen clutched firmly in her small fist, 2½-year-old Ashley makes a series of curvy lines on a piece of paper and punctuates them with several emphatic dots. She appears to be quite satisfied with her creation in purple and white. "I wanna 'nother paper," she announces.

In the months to follow, Ashley will continue to cover pieces of paper with various samples of abstract art. She'll experiment with scribbles-in-the-middle versus scribbles-in-the-corner. She'll discover certain geometric forms: the straight line, the cross, the rectangle, and the circle. The circle seems to be particularly fascinating to her. She covers whole sheets of paper with roundish forms. Of course, we're using the term *circle* loosely here—few of these forms are perfectly round, and many of them are not even completely closed. Jacqueline Goodnow, an Australian psychologist who has studied children's art, says that the preschooler is plagued with "budget problems": "The difficulty is one of 'making ends meet'" (1977, p. 89).

Somewhere around her third birthday, Ashley will begin to combine forms—circles within circles, crosses within circles, squares filled with dots. Sometimes she'll look at something she's drawn and claim "It's a fish" or "a car" or "a baby." But her identifications are very much after the fact. She didn't plan on making a fish or a car—it just looked that way to her when she was done.

The time will soon come when Ashley will put pen to paper with a definite idea in mind and produce a recognizable picture of whatever she's thinking of. That crucial moment will probably occur during the year she's 3. Her first real drawing is quite likely to be a person—a tadpole person, to be precise. This bodyless person (shown in Figure 8–4) consists of a head and legs. The head usually has eyes; it may also have a nose, mouth, and possibly hair. If there are arms they will emerge horizontally from the head, roughly where the ears would be. If there are ears, there probably won't be arms. The preschooler's motto about such things seems to be "When in doubt, leave it out."

The armless drawings often produced by preschoolers do not mean that they have failed to notice that people have arms. Children who usually produce armless drawings will put on arms if they're asked to draw someone playing ball, for example (Winner, 1986). Some researchers believe that the arms are ordinarily left off because the child feels that the drawing looks better without them (Kellogg, 1969). Others have noted that the arms, when they are included, are usually put on last—more or less as "extras." In many cases the child simply doesn't bother to go back and add them (Goodnow, 1977).

The art of the preschooler is noteworthy for its economy. Goodnow puts it this way:

> Children are thrifty in their use of units. They will use one graphic unit (a particular kind of circle, a particular sun shape, a particular type of human figure) over and over. The same line often doubles as an arm or a leg; the same human figure stands for every member of the family. . . . The repetition of units helps create a sense of charming simplicity or unity. . . . When children do make a change, they are usually conservative. Typically, a change in meaning will be carried, especially among younger children, by varying only one unit (sometimes only by varying the name given to the drawing). (1977, p. 141)

A final characteristic of preschool art is that children like to put only one thing in a given space—they are very reluctant to overlap anything. Thus, in drawings of people, the arms stick straight out, seldom crossing each other or another part of the body. Hair tends to remain well on top of the head, where there's less danger it will intrude on the space given to the arms or the ears. If there's a hat it may even float above the head, so it won't interfere with the border of the head or with the

line even when it involves a wide variety of movements—forward and backward, curves and straight lines (Williams, 1983).

The second transition in drawing generally occurs about a year after the first tadpole person. Somewhere between his fourth and fifth birthdays, the child learns how to draw a complete person (Figure 8–6), with a body as well as a head. Most 5-year-olds draw complete people (Taylor and Bacharach, 1981).

If most 3- and 4-year-olds draw tadpole people, does this indicate a lack of knowledge about human anatomy? No, ignorance does not seem to be the

hair. Goodnow studied this dislike of overlapping by asking preschoolers to finish a drawing of a train by giving it two more wheels. The train already had two wheels that took up all the space underneath it. Only one child out of 99 overlapped the second pair of wheels on top of the first. Figure 8–5 shows some of the ingenious solutions the other children used in order to avoid overlapping.

What if we ask children to draw something that *has* to overlap? A clever researcher asked preschoolers and older children to draw a picture of a "robber" hiding behind a wall—only the wall wasn't high enough, so his head stuck out. Even in this case, fewer than half of the 4-year-olds drew the wall blocking the view of the robber's body, the kind of drawing most of the 6-year-olds produced (Cox, 1981). When 4-year-olds are asked to draw one thing in front of the other, what they usually do is draw the two things side by side, showing each thing in entirety. This is another example of their tendency to see the *objective* view of things, rather than the *projective* view. They draw what they know is "really there," instead of what the camera would see (Light and Foot, 1986).

Although they are not yet capable of viewing a scene in the manner of an adult artist, preschoolers often produce works of art that are pleasing to the eye of the adult beholder. In the opinion of one critic,

> A summit of artistry is achieved at the end of the preschool period. . . . Drawings by youngsters of this age are characteristically colorful, balanced, rhythmic, and expressive, conveying something of the range and the vitality associated with artistic mastery. . . . And the often striking products reinforce a general notion of the child at this age as a young artist—an individual participating in a meaningful way in processes of creation, elaboration, and self-expression. (Gardner, 1980, p. 11)

Preschoolers are vivid, uninhibited people who see the world with fresh eyes. They tend to be

FIGURE 8-5
Children were given a drawing of a "train" with two wheels and were asked to put two more wheels on it. Here are some of the ways the children solved the problem of how to add two more wheels without overlapping them. (From Goodnow, 1977, p. 45.)

pleased with their own drawings, even though the house looks like it will fall over any minute and the man's arms are where his ears should be. They show us their artwork, expecting us to admire it—and we do.

problem. Some 3-, 4-, and 5-year-olds were shown cardboard cutouts of a tadpole person, like those in Figure 8–4, and a person with a body, like those in Figure 8–6. They were asked to point to the one that looked "most like a real man." The youngest preschoolers—children who had not yet begun to draw tadpole people and whose drawings were still only scribbles—picked the person with a body as being most like a real man. So did the oldest preschoolers, who had already begun to draw people with bodies. Only the children whose drawings looked like tadpole people tended to say that the tadpole person—the one without a body—looked most like a man. So evidently child-

FIGURE 8-6
Complete people. Most 5-year-olds draw people with bodies. (From Taylor and Bacharach, 1981, p. 374.)

ren know at an earlier age what a "real man" looks like, and then later change their minds when they start drawing tadpole people. The experimenters concluded that there's an interaction between children's concepts about things and the way they draw those things. Not only do their concepts influence their drawings; their drawings also influence their concepts (Taylor and Bacharach, 1981).

In general, children's understanding of the world is ahead of their ability to depict it. Nonetheless, when given a choice of drawings done "their way" and drawings done "the correct way," children often prefer the ones drawn in their own style. For example, preschoolers were shown simple line drawings of houses done in two ways: a house with just the front showing—this is how preschoolers always draw houses—and a more realistic view that correctly depicted the front plus part of one side (see Figure 8–7). When asked, "Which do you think is the best drawing of a house?" the children usually picked the house drawn the way they would draw it, with only a front (Moore, 1986).

The preschool child does not look at the world in exactly the same way an adult does; nor does she draw it in the same way. Her drawings are not sophisticated, but that doesn't mean they are not artistic. The preschooler's art is like the preschooler herself: full of life and delightful to look at.

FIGURE 8-7
Four- and 5-year-old children generally pointed to the house on the left—drawn the way *they* draw houses—when asked "Which do you think is the best drawing of a house?" (From Moore, 1986, p. 191.)

Summary

1. At age 2½, toddlerhood is over and the **preschool period** has begun. The **preschooler** is noticeably more advanced than the toddler in appearance, in behavior, and in the ability to communicate.

2. A 2½-year-old boy has achieved more than 50 percent of his adult height but only about 20 percent of his adult weight. His brain growth is more than 75 percent complete. Preschoolers are proportionately short-legged, compared to adults.

3. Toddlers will eat almost anything that is offered to them, but this stage of openness to new eating experiences is brief. Preschoolers tend to dislike any food they haven't eaten before.

4. Preschoolers need less food than toddlers because they aren't growing as fast. Urging a child to eat more than he really wants is teaching him to ignore his own feelings of when he's had enough, which can increase the risk of later problems such as obesity.

5. Most American preschoolers are well nourished. Protein deficiency is likely to occur only in cases of severe economic deprivation or when the parents are vegetarians who do not permit their children any form of animal protein. Children also require an adequate amount of fat in their diet.

6. The greatest threat to a child's life is no longer infectious diseases or malnutrition: it is accidental injury. About half of all deaths of young children result from accidents.

7. The number of children with **AIDS** is increasing rapidly in the United States. Most of these children were infected with the **HIV virus** before or during birth. Not all the babies born to infected mothers are infected with the AIDS virus; it's even possible for one twin to have AIDS and the other to be free of the virus. Such cases demonstrate that AIDS is not spread merely through close contact.

8. Lead poisoning can do irreversible damage to a child's nervous system.

9. Preschoolers tend to get one minor illness after another. Illnesses are most frequent in children who attend day-care centers or nursery schools (but this may be beneficial in the long run) and in those whose parents smoke (this is clearly *not* beneficial). By the end of the preschool period, most children have built up some resistance to common infections.

10. Significant advances in motor skills occur during the preschool period. These advances depend both on practice and on the maturation of brain and body systems. They involve both **large-muscle** and **small-muscle skills.**

11. Three factors involved in the development of motor skills are (1) the establishment of voluntary control, as the preschooler becomes better at directing her movements; (2) the preschooler's increasingly accurate awareness of the size, shape, and position of the parts of her body; and (3) the development of **bilateral coordination**—the coordination of the two sides of the body.

12. The toddler can walk and run, but her gait is slow and awkward. Walking and running become skilled activities during the preschool period.

13. Using the hands and fingers to manipulate objects is a small-muscle skill; it requires eye–hand coordination. The child learns to manipulate objects skillfully by means of visual feedback.

14. Individual differences in motor development are noticeable in the preschool period; they tend to persist throughout life. Genetic factors play a role in such differences.

15. The average preschool boy can outrun, outjump, and outclimb the average preschool girl. Girls are ahead in manipulation skills and also in skipping, hopping, and balancing. Such differences are due to a combination of factors, including the tendency of preschool boys to engage in more active and vigorous play than preschool girls.

16. Although brain growth has slowed considerably by age 2, neurons continue to increase in size and the process of myelination is still going on. Excess neurons and unused connections continue to be pared away.

17. The two hemispheres of the brain look alike but serve different functions. The left side of the brain, which controls the right hand and foot, is generally used for language. The right side specializes in nonverbal skills such as spatial ability, perception of patterns and melodies, and the expression and recognition of emotions.

18. An injury to the speech area on the left side of a young child's brain seldom produces a permanent language disability, the way it would in an adult. When damage to the left side occurs early in life, the right side can apparently take over language functions.

19. Earlier researchers assumed that brain **lateralization**—the tendency for the two hemispheres to serve different functions—develops gradually during infancy and childhood. But recent research indicates that the two hemispheres are different right from the start.

20. Infants show no strong tendency to use one hand rather than the other, but by the preschool period most children favor the right hand. The tendency to be right-handed is a built-in characteristic of the human species.

21. Left-handedness is more common in children whose parents are left-handed; it's somewhat more common in males and in twins. Left-handed people may process language on the left, right, or both sides of their brain; they are less lateralized than right-handed people.

22. Left- and right-handed children do not differ in intelligence on the average, but there are more lefties among retarded and learning-disabled children, and also among children who are gifted in music or math.

23. Children who have not yet established a dominant hand do not perform as well as right- or left-handed children on tests of manual dexterity. The advantage in having a dominant hand is that that hand gets all the practice (instead of only half the practice) in manipulating objects.

24. Although even 2-year-olds can distinguish between two identical objects, one on the left and one on the right, preschoolers have difficulty distinguishing between two visual stimuli that are mirror images of each other, such as *d* and *b*. The first kind of distinction has to do with "real-world" directions and locations; the second is normally of little importance in the real world.

25. Many 4- and 5-year-olds can say which is their right hand and which is their left. This ability seems to be connected to the establishment of a dominant hand. Once a child can distinguish between the two sides of her body, she can distinguish between mirror-image stimuli without relying on landmarks in the room.

26. Basic perceptual abilities—the ability to see, hear, and integrate sensory information—are well established by the preschool period.

27. Adults can see a visual scene in two ways: the usual way (the way things "really are") and the way an artist or a camera sees it. Formerly it was believed that infants have to learn to see things the way they "really are," but they actually *start out* seeing them that way and have to learn to see them the way artists and cameras do. Children become aware of **projective size** and shape during the preschool period.

28. The perceptual mechanisms that enable us to see things as the correct shape and size, regardless of viewing angle or distance, are called **shape constancy** and **size constancy.** The constancies are not based on experience —they are automatic and innate. However, the *accuracy* of the constancies increases during development, as a function of experience.

29. It is not necessary to have had experience with pictures in order to recognize a picture of a familiar object. However, experience does play a role in sensitivity to pictured depth cues such as shading, convergence of lines toward the horizon, and relative size.

30. One reason that children don't always see pictures the way adults do is that they don't look at them the same way. Adults scan a picture systematically, whereas young children do not. The ability to pay attention to what's important in a picture is a cognitive skill, rather than a perceptual skill.

31. The first recognizable drawing that children produce is usually a **tadpole person**—a head with legs attached. This milestone generally occurs when the child is 3 or 3½. About a year later the child begins to draw people with bodies.

32. Preschoolers' art is noteworthy for its economy: their motto seems to be, "When in doubt, leave it out." They avoid overlapping—they prefer to put only one thing in a given space. They draw what they know is "really there," rather than what the camera would see.

Key Terms

preschool period
preschooler
acquired immune deficiency
　　syndrome (AIDS)

HIV virus
bilateral coordination
large-muscle skills
small-muscle skills
lateralization

projective size
size constancy
shape constancy
fixate
tadpole person

9

Preschoolers Think and Communicate

At the beginning of Chapter 7 we described a 4-day-old baby named Stephanie. Although Stephanie could do hardly anything and appeared to be completely clueless, we predicted a bright future for her: we said she was "one of the most efficient learning machines on the face of the earth." Now Stephanie is 3 years old and it's time to justify that statement. Let's see how the 3-year-old child compares with a different type of learning machine—a computer.

Getting computers to think and learn like people is the goal of a field called *artificial intelligence*. Marvin Minsky, a professor at M.I.T., is known as "the father of artificial intelligence." Minsky has described one of his early efforts to get a computer to think and learn: he attempted to teach a computer to build a tower of blocks. The computer was equipped with a mechanical arm for picking up the blocks and a television camera to see with. It was programmed to look at a tower of blocks that was already built, figure out how it was constructed, and build one like it.

The figuring-out part it did quite well. . . . The building part, however, proved problematic. After the computer had figured out what it wanted to build, it stubbornly insisted on trying to stack its blocks from the top down, repeatedly releasing each one in midair. While the flaw in such a construction strategy seems obvious to us, the computer had every reason to be confused: no one had ever taught it the concept of gravity. (Minsky, 1989, pp. 55–56)

No one ever taught the 3-year-old, either, yet Stephanie knows enough to start her tower from the bottom. She learned about gravity through her experiments in stage 5 of the sensorimotor period, beginning at around 12 months of age (see Chapter 7).

Minsky also describes efforts to teach computers to understand language. This is what would be involved if we wanted a computer to understand the sentence, "The man is drinking from a cup":

The computer would have to be taught, for example, what "cup" is. The explanation would have to include everything from the size, shape, and purpose of a typical cup, to the fact that the open end must always point up or gravity will make the fluid inside fall out. If the computer were also taught what "man" is and what "drinking" is, it could comprehend the sentence without any further help. (p. 56)

Minsky estimates that a program containing the kind of everyday information that would enable the computer to understand simple sentences and build towers from the bottom up would require "a few million computer entries." *A few million computer entries* to learn what every 3-year-old knows! That means that Stephanie has acquired the equivalent of roughly 4000 computer-entries worth of knowledge for every day she has been alive, or more than 5 for each minute she has been awake!

But some see the cup as half full, others as half empty. Not all child development specialists are impressed with how clever and knowledgeable the preschool child is: some are more impressed with how much she *doesn't* know.

The Cognitive Capacities of the Preschool Child

In Chapter 7 we discussed Piaget's theory of cognitive development in the sensorimotor period, starting with a newborn infant who possessed only a few built-in schemes and progressing to a 2-year-old who could use mental representations to make plans, understand the permanence of objects, and imitate actions that had occurred several days earlier. Despite all these achievements of infancy and toddlerhood, Piaget does not have a very high opinion of the preschooler's cognitive abilities. Current theorists feel that Piaget might have been a bit unfair to the young child. We will see how some of the findings that Piaget used to demonstrate the limitations of preschool thought have been reinterpreted in the light of later research.

In Piagetian terms, preschoolers are in the **preoperational period.** According to Piaget, preoperational children can't **decenter**—they can't consider more than one aspect of a situation at a time. Their thought is **egocentric**—they can't see something from another person's point of view. It isn't that preoperational children simply think less well or less clearly than older children and adults, or that they simply possess less information about the world: Piaget believes that their thought processes are *qualitatively different* from those of older people. This assertion deserves careful consideration.

As we explained in Chapter 3, when Piaget uses the term *egocentric* to describe preschoolers' thought, he is not accusing them of being selfish or conceited. He means that children of this age judge everything from their own perspective: "The child experiences the greatest difficulty in entering into anyone else's point of view" (Piaget, 1928, p. 215).

For evidence of this inability to take another's point of view, Piaget points to the results of his well-known "three mountains" experiment. In this experiment, children were shown a three-dimensional model of three mountains, varying in size and color (see Figure 9–1). The setup also included a small doll, facing the mountains. The children were asked to show (by means of cardboard cutouts of the mountains) what the mountains would look like from the doll's point of view, which was different from their own. Children were unable to do this before the age of 7 or 8—the age, according to Piaget, that marks the beginning of the next stage, the period of concrete operations. The younger, preoperational children depicted their *own* view of the mountains, instead of the doll's view (Piaget and Inhelder, 1956). In later experiments, other researchers have made the task a little easier by supplying pictures of the various views of the scene, but preschool children still tend to choose their own point of view in preference to the doll's.

Is Preschool Thought Always Egocentric?

FIGURE 9-1
Piaget's three mountains experiment. The child's task is to show how the mountains would look from the doll's point of view.

This seems like undeniable evidence of egocentric thought: apparently, the child imagines that everyone sees things in the same way that *he* sees them. But later researchers showed that egocentricism was not the problem: the same errors may occur when the child is asked to indicate his *own* point of view. If three blocks are put down in front of a preschooler and he is asked to pick the picture that shows his own view of them, he is likely to pick one that shows all three blocks—even if two of them are not visible from his position because a larger block is in front of them (Liben and Belknap, 1981). So this is another example of the preschooler's tendency to see the *objective* view—what he knows is "really there," rather than the *projective* view—what the camera would see. (We discussed this in Chapter 8; see pp. 279 and 285.)

The preschooler's dislike of overlapping in pictures also plays a role in this situation. In a study similar to the three mountains experiment, researchers asked 4- and 5-year-olds to judge "what the doll would be able to see." Each child was seated at a table with just two objects on it, a bottle and a jar. The doll was in another chair, facing the table from a different angle. The child was shown various photographs of the bottle and the jar, and was told to choose the one that showed the objects from the doll's point of view. When the child had a "good view" of the two objects (he saw them side by side), and the doll had a "bad view" (one of the objects was in front of the other, partly blocking it), the child chose the photo representing his own point of view instead of the doll's. But when the *doll* had the "good view" and the *child* had the "bad view," he correctly chose the photo that showed the doll's point of view. In other words, regardless of points of view, the child chose the photo that showed the objects the way he would draw them, side by side and not overlapping (Light and Nix, 1983). Piaget loaded the deck against the preschool child by making the doll's view of the three mountains better than the child's view.

According to John Flavell of Stanford University, the child's ability to understand how something will look from another person's viewpoint develops in two stages, which he calls *levels.* Children reach the first stage of understanding, level 1, by age 2 or 3: at this point they have realized that even though *they* can see something, it doesn't mean that someone *else* can see it. For instance, a 2½-year-old knows that if she wants to show a picture to someone seated across from her, she can't just hold it up—she has to turn it around so that the back of the picture is facing her and the front is facing the other person.

What the level-1 child *can't* do is to judge how the picture will look to the other person. A researcher showed some children a picture of a turtle that could either be standing on its feet (right side up) or lying on its back (the same picture upside down); the turtle's two positions were demonstrated several times. Then the picture was placed flat on the table between the child and the researcher, who were seated on opposite sides of the table. Thus, if the turtle was right side up for the child, it was upside down for the researcher. When 3-year-olds were asked whether the researcher saw the turtle standing up or lying down, more than half of them gave the wrong ("egocentric") answer. But almost all the 4- and 5-year-olds were able to solve this problem. The 4- and 5-year-olds had reached level 2, where the child can consider not just *whether* another person can see something, but also *what* the other person sees (Flavell, 1985).

Although a 4-year-old may realize that the other person doesn't have the same view that she does, it may take her several more years to figure out, in complicated situations, exactly what the other person does see. The two levels of understanding might sound like Piagetian stages but they are not, because the child's understanding of another person's point of view develops gradually and depends very much on the complexity of the situation.

The understanding of what another person *knows* (rather than what the other person *sees*) takes longer to achieve. Researchers showed children a picture of an animal and then blocked off all but a little piece of the picture—a very uninformative piece. Four- and 5-year-olds believed (incorrectly) that another person, seeing just that little, uninformative piece of the picture, would still be able to tell what kind of animal it was. However, these children were well aware that the other person might not necessarily know *everything* that they knew about the picture: they knew that the other person wouldn't be able to tell, just from looking at the little bit of a picture, that the giraffe's name was George, or that the deer liked to listen to music. The preschooler's ability to understand exactly what another person knows will go on developing all through childhood—perhaps all through life. Even adults sometimes have trouble making allowances for a person who is less knowledgeable than they are (Taylor, 1988).

Preschoolers are also capable of making nonegocentric judgments about other people's likes and dislikes. When some 3- and 5-year-olds were asked to pick a picture that their mother would like, and one that their little brother would like, they picked different pictures—different, also, from the ones they said that *they* liked best. Moreover, these young children were able to give plausible reasons for why they thought that their mother or their younger sibling would prefer one particular picture over another (Hart and Goldin-Meadow, 1984).

THE INVISIBLE PRESCHOOLER. If you ask a 2½- or 3-year-old to cover her eyes with her hands and then ask, "Can I see you?" she is likely to say "No." This well-known observation has been used as further evidence for the preschooler's alleged egocentricity. But research has shown that when the child says no, you can't see her, it's not simply because she thinks that *you* can't see if *she* has her eyes covered. She will answer correctly if you ask her whether you can see the chair, or whether you can see her arm (Flavell, Shipstead, and Croft, 1980).

The researchers figured out that children are taught to use the words "you" and "me" in a special way in contexts that involve looking and seeing. When an adult says to a child, "Look at me when I'm talking to you!" he doesn't mean "Look at my arm." He means "Look at my face—look at my eyes." Thus, children draw the logical conclusion that, in this context, "me" means "the eye area of my face." So if I cover up my eyes, you can't see me!

Piaget claimed that preschoolers lack an understanding of many concepts that adults and older children take for granted. He attributed this lack of understanding to their inability to decenter—to consider more than one aspect of a situation at a time. As an illustration of this inability he used his famous experiment on the conservation of liquid volume (described in

Does the preschooler think that you can't see her if she covers her eyes?

The Preschooler's Understanding of Complex Concepts

Chapter 3): when liquid is poured from an ordinary glass into a tall, skinny beaker, the preschooler says that the quantity has increased, because she **centers** (or focuses her attention) on the height of the liquid and ignores everything else. But her error may be due, not to a failure to decenter, but to a failure to distinguish clearly between appearance and reality.

DISTINGUISHING BETWEEN APPEARANCE AND REALITY. We have been telling you, in the last part of Chapter 8 and in the previous section of this chapter, that preschoolers tend to see and depict things in terms of what is "really there," instead of how they appear to their eyes (or to a camera). This tendency to respond in terms of reality when they are asked to respond in terms of appearances has been called **intellectual realism.** We've already given several examples of this; here's another: preschoolers were shown a candy box that turned out to contain pencils, not candy. After they were shown the contents of the box, most of the 3-year-olds and many of the 4-year-olds insisted that the box *looked* as though it contained pencils, not candy (Gopnik and Astington, 1988).

Intellectual realism in a preschooler is a little surprising, because we tend to think of young children as easily mislead by appearances. Well, they *are* easily mislead by appearances. These two tendencies coexist in preschoolers —sometimes they're more impressed by reality and ignore appearances, and sometimes they're more impressed by appearances and ignore reality. The second tendency is called **phenomenism.** If we show a preschooler a white egg and then let her look at it through a blue filter that makes it look blue, she is likely to maintain that the egg "really is" blue. If she sees the egg through a magnifying glass that makes it look big, she will say it "really is" big. These replies are examples of phenomenism. But if we show the same preschooler what looks exactly like an egg but turns out to be a piece of stone, shaped and painted to look like an egg, she will maintain with equal certainty that the object *looks* like a stone and not like an egg—this is intellectual realism (Flavell, 1986).

Although it's sometimes hard to predict whether a preschooler will respond according to realism or phenomenism, as a general rule of thumb she is more likely to respond in terms of appearances (phenomenism) when asked about characteristics such as shape, color, or size. She is more likely to respond in terms of reality (realism) when she's asked about something's identity or existence. Thus, she draws three blocks even though she can see only one, because she knows that there really are three blocks there. She says the box looks as though it contains pencils because she knows that it *does* contain pencils. Her knowledge of the existence of the blocks and pencils outweighs what her eyes tell her. But when it comes to a quality such as size, color, or amount, she relies on what her eyes tell her. This is why the child in Piaget's conservation experiment says that there is more liquid in the tall, skinny beaker than there is in the glass. Preschoolers are in the process of clarifying their ideas on appearance versus reality, and Piaget's experiment on the conservation of liquid volume catches them in one of the areas they are still uncertain about (Flavell, 1985).

But preschoolers who are fuzzy about the distinction between appearance and reality are likely to be much clearer about the distinction between *pretend*

These sponges look very much like chunks of rock. But once a preschooler has discovered that they're actually made of sponge, he will insist that they don't look *like rocks—they look like sponges. This is intellectual realism. (Source: Flavell, 1986.)*

and reality. They've been pretending about things since they were about a year old, and by age 3 they've become quite good at it. And it's the *identity* or *existence* of objects that they pretend about—they pretend that a block of wood is a car or that an imaginary friend is sitting next to them. It's odd that children who mix up appearance and reality are able to deal so well with the pretend–reality distinction. A 3-year-old can't accept the idea that an object *really is* a stone but it *looks* like an egg; yet he has no trouble grasping the idea that it *really is* a stone but we can *pretend* it's an egg. The fact that pretense occurs so early (and so universally) in development suggests that it plays an important role: by practicing on the distinction between pretense and reality, children eventually learn to distinguish between appearance and reality (Flavell, Flavell, and Green, 1987).

NUMBERS AND COUNTING. Preschoolers fail the Piagetian test on the conservation of liquid volume because when qualities such as size or amount are involved they tend to be swayed by appearances. For the same reason, they fail the Piagetian test on the conservation of number. Take eight or nine pennies and the same number of jellybeans and put them in two rows of equal length, one jellybean under each penny. Preschoolers will say correctly that there are the same number of jellybeans and pennies. But if you then spread out the jellybeans so that the row of candies is longer than the rows of coins, they are likely to claim that there are now more jellybeans than pennies. According to Piaget (1965), they center on the length of the row of jellybeans because they lack the concept of number. Piaget believes that concepts such as conservation of volume and number aren't acquired until the child reaches the period of concrete operations, at around age 7.

Rochel Gelman and her colleagues at the University of Pennsylvania have done a series of studies on preschoolers' understanding of the concept of number. She believes that preschoolers understand a lot more than Piaget gave them credit for, as long as the numbers involved are small enough for them to feel comfortable with—numbers no bigger than four. In some of her experiments she shows 4- and 5-year-olds a small set of objects (two, three, or four), and then makes one object "magically" disappear or an extra one appear. The children are quick to notice the change in number:

> They not only recognize the resulting change; they tell us what must have happened, i.e. that somehow an item was either removed or added. On the other hand, when the experimenter surreptitiously lengthens or shortens a row or changes the color or identity of items in a row, the children notice the changes but say that they are irrelevant to number.   (Gelman, 1978, p. 301)

This is just what Piaget claims preschoolers can't do. Indeed, they generally can't, if you overload their capabilities by giving them eight or ten objects at a time instead of three or four.

In other contexts, however, preschoolers are capable of coping with larger numbers of objects. Perhaps because of Sesame Street or educational preschool experiences, most present-day 4-year-olds are capable of correctly counting a row of eight or ten objects (Briars and Siegler, 1984). This may not seem like a big deal to you, but counting actually involves some fairly sophisticated underlying principles (Gelman and Gallistel, 1978).

First, the child has to understand that each number word is assigned to one object and that each object gets one number word; this is known as the **one-to-one correspondence rule.** Preschoolers sometimes have difficulty coordinating their counting with their pointing, but that doesn't mean they're unaware of the principle. Gelman (1982) says that even 3-year-olds will often stop and correct themselves when they deviate from the one-to-one rule.

Another principle involved in counting is called the **cardinality rule:** it involves knowing that the last number word spoken is the answer to the "how many?" question. If you say "one, two, three, four," and then run out of objects to count, the number of objects is four, the last word you spoke. Preschoolers show their awareness of this rule by saying the last number with special emphasis when they are counting.

The most abstract of the principles involved in counting is called the **order-irrelevance principle;** it says that the order in which you count the objects doesn't matter—the number will still be the same. Piaget (1964) describes an incident in which a 4-year-old boy arranged some pebbles in a row and counted them. There were ten pebbles. Then he counted them in the other direction, starting with the pebble at the end of the row. The result was again ten. Being quite intrigued with this result, the boy then arranged the pebbles in a circle and counted them once more. Again, the answer was ten. Not every child, certainly, would find this result so fascinating: this particular boy grew up to become a mathematician! In fact, not many preschoolers have reached this level of mathematical sophistication: an understanding of the

Preschoolers are capable of understanding some basic concepts of numbers and counting.

order-irrelevance principle comes later in development than the other two principles we've mentioned (Briars and Siegler, 1984).

How and when do young children acquire the principles of cardinality and one-to-one correspondence? Recent research indicates that an understanding of these principles is achieved between the ages of 2½ and 3½ in most middle-class children. When 2½-, 3-, and 3½-year-olds were asked to give a Big Bird puppet a certain number of toy dinosaurs (from one to six) from a pile of toy dinosaurs, most of the older children carefully counted them out. But, whenever the number asked for was more than two, the younger children just grabbed a handful of dinosaurs and plopped them down in front of Big Bird. It wasn't that these children were unable to count higher than two: in other situations, almost all these children could count correctly to four or five. But they seemed to have only a partial grasp of the cardinality principle. One little girl gave two dinosaurs when asked for five; when she was asked to count them she said "Five, five!" The responses of another child indicated that he thought that the last number spoken was, in some sense, the *name* of the item rather than its number. He counted three dinosaurs as "One, two, five!" When the researcher pointed to the three dinosaurs and asked, "So there's five here?" the child replied, "No, *that's* five," pointing to the last dinosaur he had counted (Wynn, 1990, p. 178).

The researcher concluded that, although 2½- and 3-year-olds are aware of the cardinality *rule* (that the last number word you say is the answer to "how many?"), they do not yet understand the **cardinality principle**—that the last number spoken represents some property of the entire set and is not simply a name for the last thing you counted. Children achieve an understanding of this principle at around the age of 3½. It appears to be based on their earlier

Close-Up

Box 9-1
Metacognition and Memory

One thinks of the mind of the pre-schooler as fresh and open, ready to soak up knowledge like a sponge. It's a little surprising, therefore, to find that preschoolers actually learn most things *less* readily than older children. In just about any test of memory or learning, preschoolers don't do as well as older children. The age differences are greatest when children are memorizing things on purpose: school-age children do much better than pre-schoolers on memory tasks assigned to them by researchers ("I'm going to show you some toys and later I will ask you to remember what toys I showed you"). The age differences are smaller when children are asked about things they didn't purposely try to remember ("Tell me what you did yesterday on your trip to the museum"). This doesn't mean that young children remember things better if they aren't trying to remember them—it just means that older children do *much* better than younger ones in deliberate memory tasks, and only a little better in nondeliberate ones (Jones, Swift, and Johnson, 1988).

There's nothing the matter with preschoolers' minds. The cognitive apparatus they have inside their heads is an excellent one, even if there still is a small amount of physical development to be completed. The main reason for their lack of profi-ciency in learning and memorizing is that they haven't mastered all the tricks of *using* their cognitive apparatus. One might say that their equipment hasn't been fully programmed yet. It can do the basic things, but it still can't handle the fancy stuff. Getting all the necessary programs written and running smoothly takes some time.

"Learning how to operate the memory" is how some theorists describe one of the skills that preschoolers are in the process of acquiring. But there's more to it than that. In a classic experiment, preschoolers and school-age children were shown pictures of a small number of objects and asked to remember those objects. As usual, the preschoolers remembered fewer of the objects than the school-age children. But what was more interesting was that the younger children *thought* they had memorized the objects when in fact they hadn't. The children were asked to look at the pictures of the objects until they felt that they could remember all of them. The preschoolers and the school-age children both studied the pictures for a while and then said they were ready. The older children *were* ready—they remembered all of the objects. The younger children thought they could remember all of the objects but they could not (Flavell, Friedrichs, and Hoyt, 1970).

So it wasn't just that the preschoolers didn't know "how to operate the memory"—they didn't even *know* that they didn't know how to operate it. These findings, which have been supported by

---

understanding of the numbers *one, two,* and *three,* which children achieve very early because they can see these quantities directly, without having to count them. A toddler can see at once that there are two dinosaurs or two cookies and learns to use the word *two* appropriately. A little later he learns to do this for *three* as well. By around the age of 3½, most middle-class children have figured out that the higher number words are used in the same way as *one, two,* and *three*—to represent an abstract concept of numerosity (Wynn, 1990). And by the age of 4, many of these children are able to answer questions such as, "If I put two cookies in the bag and then put in two more, how many cookies are there in the bag?" (Ginsburg and others, 1989).

Children do not acquire their concepts in a vacuum: environment unques-tionably has an effect. Preschoolers in middle-class homes are encouraged to participate in activities and games involving numbers, and these activities help them to develop number concepts. In working-class homes, the number activities and games tend to be at a lower level of complexity, and the child-ren's concepts develop somewhat more slowly (Saxe, Guberman, and Gear-hart, 1987).

the results of a number of other studies, show that preschool children are quite inaccurate when it comes to judging their own cognitive abilities. What they lack is not exactly a cognitive skill—it's a *metacognitive* skill. **Metacognition** is the ability to understand, to think about, and to keep track of the progress of one's own cognitive processes.

Metacognition includes such things as an awareness of whether you're paying attention to something or are letting your mind wander, and an awareness of whether you understand something or are confused about it. It also includes knowledge about what factors are likely to interfere with paying attention and what factors help you to understand something. Perhaps the most important type of metacognitive skill is the one that involves knowledge and understanding about one's own learning and memory processes. "Learning how to learn" is a metacognitive task.

Preschoolers know very little about learning and memory. If first graders are given a list of words to memorize, they are likely to say them over and over to themselves; this is called **rehearsal.** Third graders may also use a technique called **categorization,** which means grouping the words into categories like "animals," "tools," or "furniture." Eighth graders will often use more elaborate strategies to help themselves remember, such as making up stories, poems, or mental images that serve to link the words together. But preschool children do not, on their own, even use rehearsal. They think that memorization is easy. Many preschoolers will deny that they *ever* forget anything (Kreutzer, Leonard, and Flavell, 1975).

It is possible to teach metacognitive skills to young children, but it's an uphill battle. For example, preschoolers can be taught to use rehearsal in order to remember a set of objects—we can instruct them to say the names of the objects over and over to themselves. If the children do this, they will be able to remember more of the objects. The trouble is that as soon as we stop reminding them to rehearse, they stop rehearsing. And when they stop rehearsing, they remember less (Flavell, 1985). Preschoolers are more likely to continue to use rehearsal and other strategies for improving their memory if the memory strategy makes a big difference in how well they do on the memory test, and if they have some idea as to *why* the strategy helps them remember (Whittaker, 1988; Fabricius and Cavalier, 1989).

At the beginning of this chapter we compared the mind of a 3-year-old to a computer; in this box, we've made that comparison again. But please don't take the analogy too seriously—in most ways, the child's mind is very different from a computer. Here's one difference: a computer is not more likely to run a certain program if we explain to it *why* that particular program works.

Obviously, the cognitive abilities of preschool children are more advanced than those of younger children and less advanced than those of older children. But was Piaget right in claiming that their thought is *qualitatively different* from that of babies and toddlers, and from that of school-age children and adolescents?

To the first part of the question, we believe that the answer is yes. Representational thought—especially the ability to think in abstract symbols such as words—makes preschoolers' mental abilities a clear step above those of infants and toddlers. It's not like the difference between crawling and walking—it's more like the difference between crawling and flying.

On the other hand, the case for a qualitative change between preschool thought and later thought is much less persuasive. Yes, older children and adults can perform most cognitive tasks better than preschoolers, but this may be due simply to their greater knowledge and experience.

What *is* clear is that the cognitive advances still to come are not going to be as dramatic or impressive as those that have already occurred. Cognitive development from here on in will be a more gradual and continuous process.

Preschool Thought: Conclusions

Intelligence

By the beginning of the preschool period, variations in cognitive abilities and in the rate of cognitive development have become apparent. Some children come much earlier than others to the understanding of principles such as cardinality and conservation of liquid volume. Some are speaking in long, complicated sentences when others are using only a few words. Some can put together a puzzle in record time or figure out how to unlatch a cabinet, while others are stumped. Of course, these different abilities don't necessarily go together—one child may be way ahead verbally but no good at puzzles, another might be just the opposite. Nonetheless, parents and teachers feel that they can tell whether a particular child has an unusually high amount, or an unusually low amount, of that quality we call *intelligence.* IQ tests are a convenient way of turning those overall impressions into a single number—a number that is only a score on a given test, taken on a given day. It is not a magic number to be engraved on the child's forehead for the rest of his or her life.

IQ Tests
Although intelligence testing doesn't usually begin until the school years, it is possible (and increasingly common, in this highly competitive era) to give IQ tests to preschoolers. What do these tests measure? And how well do they measure it?

Psychologists have been working for a long time on the question of exactly what characteristics an "intelligent" person has that an "unintelligent" person lacks. The answers they have come up with are very much in accord with what nonpsychologists think of when they are asked to define "intelligence." The characteristics that are usually mentioned include the ability to learn quickly, to reason logically, to use and understand language competently, and to solve problems insightfully (Weinberg, 1989).

IQ tests are designed to measure all of these abilities. When we speak of a child's *IQ* we are referring to how well he does on an IQ test. When we speak of *intelligence* we are speaking of the quality (or qualities) that IQ tests are supposed to measure. But if the child being tested is tired, ill, frightened, or uncooperative, or if the language of the test is not his native language, then his test performance might be a very poor measure of his actual intelligence. A test might also be a poor measure of intelligence just by being a poor test. A good test is one that succeeds in measuring what it's supposed to measure. Such a test is said to have **validity.**

HOW THEY BEGAN. The idea of testing children's intelligence started in France around 1900. The Paris school system wanted a way of identifying those children who would have problems in school and would need extra help. They asked a psychologist named Alfred Binet to help with this task. Binet and his co-worker, Théophile Simon, devised the first successful IQ test. It was successful because it produced results that agreed pretty well with teachers' opinions of their students' intelligence. It also did a fairly good job of predicting how well the students would do in school. These two criteria are still used in judging the validity of an IQ test. The IQ tests used today correlate about .60 with grades in elementary school (Jensen, 1981). They don't correlate perfectly, partly because grades depend on many other factors in addition to intelligence.

The Binet-Simon test was based on the concept of **mental age.** Binet decided that an intelligent child of 5 might be the intellectual equal of an average child of 6. That meant that the bright 5-year-old could answer as many questions or solve as many problems as the average 6-year-old. Then this 5-year-old would have the mental age of 6. Binet and Simon spent a lot of time finding test items (questions or problems) that most 6-year-olds could answer but most 5-year-olds couldn't, items that most 7-year-olds could answer but most 6-year-olds couldn't, and so on. A child who could answer all of the test items for 5-year-olds, most of the items for 6-year-olds, and a few of the items for 7-year-olds would have a mental age of 6.

Later researchers found a convenient way to express the relationship between mental age and chronological (actual) age. They divided the mental age by the chronological age to get what they called the **intelligence quotient,** or IQ for short. A 5-year-old with a mental age of 6 would have an intelligence quotient of 6 ÷ 5, or 1.20. For convenience the score was multiplied by 100, so the decimal point was eliminated and the child's IQ was expressed as 120. A 5-year-old with a mental age of 5 (or any child whose mental age and chronological age were the same) would have an IQ of 100. A 5-year-old with a mental age of 4½, and a 10-year-old with a mental age of 9, would both have IQs of 90.

The problem with this way of expressing intelligence was that it was difficult to apply it to older teenagers and adults. A brilliant 5-year-old might have a mental age of 7 (IQ = 140), but it's meaningless to say that a brilliant 25-year-old has a mental age of 35. So nowadays IQ scores are defined entirely in terms of how well a person does compared to others of the same age. A person who scores exactly at the mean will have an IQ of 100. The other IQ scores are distributed in such a way that IQs close to 100 are very common and IQs much higher or lower than 100 are relatively rare (see Figure 9–2). About 50 percent of people have IQs between 90 and 110, but only 0.4 percent—fewer than 1 in 200—have IQs of 140 or more.

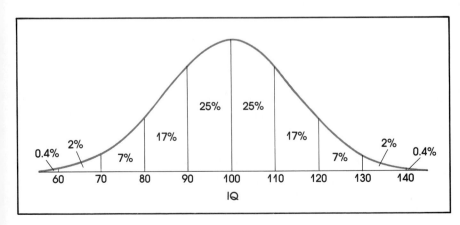

FIGURE 9-2
The distribution of IQs, showing the approximate percentage of the population that falls into each range of IQs. About 50 percent of people have IQs between 90 and 110. This is a theoretical curve; the actual distribution is very similar except that there is a greater percentage of people with IQs under 60, due to genetic or chromosomal forms of retardation. (Source: Jensen, 1969, p. 24.)

MODERN TESTS. The Binet–Simon IQ test was, of course, written in the French language. An English translation of that test attracted the attention of Lewis Terman, a professor at Stanford University. Terman and his colleagues at Stanford revised the test so that it would be more suitable for American children. The new test, called the **Stanford–Binet,** first appeared in 1916 and has been updated several times since then. It is designed to be administered individually and can be used with children from age 2 on up. The Stanford–Binet consists of a wide variety of test items, with some items used mostly for younger children and others for older ones. A young child might be shown a picture of a common object and asked to say what it is, or shown a square and asked to copy it. An older child might be asked to define a vocabulary word or to discover what is missing in a picture of a familiar object.

Another popular IQ test is the Wechsler, which is also meant to be administered individually. There are three versions of this test. The one for school-age children is called the **WISC-R** (the Wechsler Intelligence Scale for Children, Revised edition). The one for younger children, ages 4 to 6, is called the **WPPSI** (the Wechsler Preschool and Primary Scale of Intelligence). The third version, the WAIS, is used for adults. The Wechsler tests consist of several different subtests, designed to measure two different kinds of ability. The verbal subtests measure language ability and general knowledge; the performance subtests are for nonverbal abilities such as assembling puzzles or copying patterns with colored blocks. A child who takes the WISC-R or the WPPSI receives a verbal IQ score, a performance IQ score, and a full-scale score that is a combination of the other two.

We said earlier that a child may be advanced verbally but no good at things like puzzles, or vice versa. It's certainly *possible* for a child to be ahead in one thing and behind in something else, but the fact is that the various intellectual abilities tend to go together: a child who is way ahead verbally is likely to be above average in puzzle assembly, too. To put it another way, the scores on the various subtests of the Wechsler are correlated with each other.

This tendency for children who do well (or poorly) on one kind of test to also do well (or poorly) on others has been interpreted in two different ways. Some theorists assume that intelligence is made up of a number of separate abilities, but that whatever genetic and environmental factors cause a child to be high in one ability are likely to cause him to be high in others as well. The alternative interpretation is that all the different kinds of tests are different ways of getting at one underlying characteristic, which has been called *g* (for the *general factor* in intelligence). None of the tests measures *g* perfectly, but all of them measure it to some extent. To the extent that they measure it, the scores will be correlated. In other words, a child who is high in *g* will tend to do better at all kinds of intelligence tests than a child who is low in *g*.

It is not necessary—and it may not be possible—to decide whether intelligence is made up of a bunch of separate abilities or whether it all boils down to an elusive quality called *g*. Even if neither theory can be proved, they are both useful ways of thinking about intelligence.

STABILITY OF IQ. A question that is often asked about IQ scores is: Are they likely to change as a child gets older, or do they remain stable? Does a 3-year-old with a measured IQ of 110 become a 10-year-old with an IQ of 110 and eventually an adult with an IQ of 110? One way of answering this ques-

There is a positive correlation between scores on verbal and nonverbal IQ subtests. This means that a child who is a whiz at puzzles is also likely to be above average in verbal ability and general knowledge.

tion is to say that IQ scores obtained in middle to late childhood correlate quite well (about .75) with adult IQ. For scores obtained in the preschool period, the correlations are lower (about .50), but even preschool scores give us some idea of adult IQ.

The reasonably good correlations between IQ scores in childhood and adulthood don't mean that IQ can't change, though. It is possible for a child's IQ score to change dramatically. In one long-term study, a group of children were tested many times over the course of 14½ years. Each child was given a total of 17 IQ tests, starting at age 2½ and ending at age 17. About half the children stayed pretty much the same, but the other half varied considerably. Some IQs went steadily up, some went up for a while and then down, and so on. In one out of three children, the difference between the lowest and the highest of the 17 scores was 30 points or more. One child's IQ went up 74 points! This study shows how unwise it is to pigeonhole a child on the basis of a single IQ score (McCall, Appelbaum, and Hogarty, 1973).

What could be the cause of such major changes in IQ scores? In some cases, the change in scores probably reflected a real increase or decrease in the child's rate of intellectual development, relative to others of the same age. Some children start out slowly but turn out to be "late bloomers"; others show early promise but fail to maintain their lead. Drastic changes in a child's environment—her parents lost their jobs or got divorced, or she was transferred to a better school—can also affect a child's intellectual development and therefore her performance on an IQ test.

In other cases, however, the changes in IQ scores were probably due, not to actual changes in intelligence, but to **error of measurement.** Even when a test is measuring what it's supposed to, it may not measure it perfectly. All sorts of things can interfere: the test-giver may be in a grumpy mood, or make a mistake in presenting an item or in scoring it. The child being tested may

The Child in Society

Box 9-2
Preschool Enrichment Programs

Young children growing up in economically disadvantaged homes, whose parents are employed in low-paying jobs, or are unemployed, or are absent, tend to miss out on much of the intellectual stimulation available in middle-class homes. One consequence of this deprivation is that the disadvantaged children are more likely to do poorly in school. They run a greater risk of being held back or placed in special classes for slow learners, and of eventually dropping out of school. Their IQs may be as much as 15 or 20 points below the middle-class average.

Starting in 1965, efforts have been made to improve the outlook for these children through preschool enrichment programs. The idea was to provide the children growing up in inner-city ghettos with some of the advantages that middle-class children take for granted. The first and best known of these efforts is Head Start, but there have been several similar programs, all based on the idea of teaching disadvantaged preschoolers some of the cognitive and verbal skills they will need in primary school. Most of the programs also provide health services for the children, and some provide counseling for their mothers.

The initial effects of these programs were extremely encouraging. Preschoolers' IQ scores often shot up by 10 points within their first year in the programs. But the early enthusiasm was soon followed by disappointment: when the children graduated from the enrichment programs, their IQ scores gradually declined. After two or three years in public school, the children who had participated in the enrichment programs were scoring no higher on IQ tests than their agemates from similar homes who had not participated. Some educators took these results to mean that the

A Head Start classroom.

enrichment programs were pointless; others maintained that the programs had benefits that weren't easily translated into numbers.

Now, 25 years later, we have more data about the long-term effects of preschool enrichment programs. A number of the participating children have been followed right through their school years. How much effect did their participation in Head Start, or in other preschool enrichment programs, have on them in the long run?

have a bad cold, or may have missed lunch, or may not feel like cooperating that day (or, for that matter, that *year*). And luck comes into it too—perhaps a vocabulary word happens to be one that the child just encountered (and learned) yesterday; or perhaps it's a word he won't encounter till tomorrow. Perhaps he guesses, and he's right (or wrong).

All these random factors, and many others, contribute to error of measurement. Error of measurement lowers what is called a test's **reliability.** A perfectly reliable test is one that would, theoretically, give a child the same score if he took the test twice, a week or a month apart. But we can't actually check

As far as Head Start itself is concerned, the answer still seems to be: not a lot. Although large initial gains in IQ scores and school readiness tests are consistently found, a few years later the Head Start children are indistinguishable from control groups of children from the same neighborhoods (Haskins, 1989). However, some recent evidence suggests that the children who are accepted into Head Start programs may come from the very poorest environments of all and start off at an even greater disadvantage than the children with whom they are compared. Thus, if they end up doing no worse than the other children, Head Start might have helped them after all (Lee, Brooks-Gunn, and Schnur, 1988).

Stronger evidence of favorable long-term results comes from the Consortium for Longitudinal Studies (1983), a group that has studied the effects of several "model" preschool programs over a period of many years. The Consortium programs have served a much smaller number of children than Head Start, but these programs were richly funded, carefully planned, and staffed by talented and well-trained educators. Rather than relying solely on enrichment in a group setting, some of the programs had teachers going to the children's homes for an hour or so a day, and working on a one-to-one basis with the children and their mothers.

For these model programs, long-term positive effects were found: the Consortium students were less likely to have been left back in grade school and more likely to have graduated from high school than the students in the control group. The differences between the Consortium students and the control group were not large, but they were statistically significant. There were also significant differences in other aspects of their lives: the graduates of one of the best programs had less delinquency, fewer teenage pregnancies, and were more likely to have jobs than their agemates from similar homes (Haskins, 1989).

We should not be surprised by the relative lack of success of Head Start—a program that serves a large number of children but that has limited funds to spend on each of them—and the greater success of the programs that serve a smaller number of children but serve them very well (and very expensively). A year or two in a classroom, where a teacher reads stories to a group of preschoolers and teaches them the alphabet, is not likely to insulate a child against all the environmental shortcomings of the next 12 years. It's probably going to take more than that to make a long-term impact on a child's life. Nonetheless, a program like Head Start is better than nothing, and may help the children from the very poorest backgrounds to begin kindergarten with a little less of a disadvantage.

What about enrichment programs for preschoolers who are *not* disadvantaged? In a recent study, middle-class children in "accelerated" preschools—where they were instructed in letters, numbers, computer literacy, and even in foreign languages—were compared with middle-class children in preschools where they just played. Although the children in the accelerated preschools did test higher at age 4, their advantage disappeared by the time they were in kindergarten. A more worrisome finding was that the children in the "accelerated" group were more anxious, less creative, and had less positive attitudes about school (Hirsh-Pasek, Hyson, Rescorla, and Cone, 1989).

For preschoolers from homes where there are no books, no trips to the zoo, and no one who has the time or energy to talk to them, a good preschool enrichment program can open a new door. But for preschoolers who already have all those advantages, there is no point in forcing them through that door before they're ready to go.

on a test's reliability this way, because the child would remember the test items and his responses to them. So reliability is usually assessed in one of two ways. Some tests have two alternate forms, containing different items that have been chosen to be equivalent in difficulty. The correlation between children's scores on the two forms is one way of measuring reliability. The second, more common way is to correlate the scores on half of the items on a single test (all the odd-numbered items, say) with scores on the other half (the even-numbered ones). This method takes into account only the kinds of unreliability that would make a child do better on some items than others—

for instance, lucky guesses and lucky recent encounters with test items. It leaves out things such as whether the test-giver and the child being tested are feeling grumpy, uncooperative, or ill.

With this second method of checking reliability, the reliability of individually given IQ tests is generally found to be between .85 and .95; it's lower for preschoolers than for older children. A reliability in the neighborhood of .90 means that a child who receives an IQ score of 105 is likely to have a "true" IQ (what we'd get if we measured him again and again and averaged all the scores) between 100 and 110. However, there's a one-in-three chance of his obtained score being more than 5 points off the "true" score (Anastasi, 1976).

In light of all this, a 30-point spread between the highest and lowest of 17 IQ scores, collected over 14½ years, doesn't sound like so much. And when you also take into account the fact that the first IQ test was given at age 2½, it is even less surprising. Preschoolers may not be as difficult to test as infants and toddlers, but testing them does require their cooperation—and their cooperation isn't always forthcoming. Some are stubborn or negative, some are uninterested, and some are simply more inclined to chat with the test-giver than to answer questions or draw squares (Harris, 1982).

In recent years there has been much controversy over the use of IQ tests as a means of assessing children's abilities. We will return to this topic in Chapter 12.

Language Development

Among the achievements of the preschool period, surely the most impressive is in the realm of language development. The average 2-year-old has a vocabulary of 200 or 300 words; she is likely to be talking mostly in short, simple phrases: "Fall down." "All-gone milk." The 3-year-old preschooler, in contrast, speaks in complex sentences that show a sophisticated grasp of the rules of the language, as well as a sizable vocabulary: "We went to see Uncle Walter and he was sitting on the sofa. And he gave me some chocolate lollipops. They were in a red box. And he pulled me in the wagon."

By the time she is ready to enter first grade, the average child will have a productive vocabulary—the words she uses in her speech—of about 2500 words. Her receptive vocabulary—the words she can understand—may be as high as 14,000 words (Carey, 1978). That means she has learned nine new words a day, every day since she started to talk! The rapid pace of learning does not slow down when the preschool period is over; in fact, it gets even more rapid once the child learns to read. The average 17-year-old has a reading vocabulary of about 80,000 words, which means she has acquired an average of 13 words a day (Miller and Gildea, 1987).

How do children learn words so quickly? Linguists use the term *fast mapping* to describe the way young children add new words to their vocabulary.

Learning What Words Mean

Fast mapping is a method that children use for quickly homing in on a word's meaning. For example, an adult may say to a child, "Bring me the chartreuse one. No, not the red one—the chartreuse one." This is enough to enable the child to figure out that *chartreuse* is not an action, not an object, not a shape or a size, but a color—a color other than red. Hearing the new word contrasted with a familiar one provides the child with a great deal of information. Children are extraordinarily good at picking up and retaining this kind of information (Heibeck and Markman, 1987).

When young children hear someone use a word they don't know, they form a rough idea about its meaning, often on their very first exposure to that word. One of the ways they narrow down the possible meanings of the word is by assuming that words are used in a mutually exclusive way. This means that if they hear a new word they assume that it must apply to something they don't already have a word for. Some 3- and 4-year-olds were shown pairs of objects—a familiar object such as a plate, and an unfamiliar one such as a cherry pitter—and asked by a researcher to "show me the vab" (or "the zil" or "the jum"). The children assumed, reasonably enough, that if the researcher had wanted the plate she would have asked for the plate, so they handed her the unfamiliar object. In a second experiment, the researcher showed some preschoolers a metal cup and told them, "This is pewter." Then the children were shown a pottery cup and asked "Is this pewter?" The children said no—they had correctly interpreted "pewter" as meaning something *other* than "cup." But when the researcher showed another group of children a pair of metal tongs (an unfamiliar object for which the children had no name) and told them, "This is pewter," more than half of the children assumed that "pewter" meant the tongs and that a pair of *wooden* tongs could also be called "pewter" (Markman and Wachtel, 1988).

Fast mapping narrows down the possibilities for what a given word might mean, but more work is required to learn its precise meaning. When a child first learns a word such as "dog" he has no way of knowing whether the word applies just to Spot, or to all furry, four-legged things that wag their tails, or to anything with four legs that can move by itself. This is why overextensions and underextensions occur so commonly during toddlerhood and the early preschool period. A child who has no word for *rabbit* or *goat* might refer to those animals as "doggies," but once he has a name for them he no longer makes that error.

CLASS INCLUSION PROBLEMS. Because children start out by assuming that each kind of thing has one and only one name, they have trouble at first when they encounter multiple names for the same thing. For example, a dog can also be referred to as "an animal," which causes some children to protest, "It's not an animal, it's a dog!" Piaget found that preschoolers are confused by what he called **class inclusion problems:** if you show them a bouquet of seven roses and three lilies and ask, "Are there more roses or more flowers?" they are likely to say that there are more roses. Later researchers found that preschoolers can reply correctly to questions such as "Would you have more wood if you chopped down the oak trees or if you chopped down the forest?" Young children can understand words like "forest," which apply to *collections* of things, more easily than they can understand that the *same thing* can be referred to by more than one name. A young preschooler might be perfectly willing to use the word "toys" for an assortment of his belongings strewn on the floor, but he might deny that any one item in the collection could be called "a toy." To use the word "toy" for a ball or a teddy bear would violate his rule about not having two words that apply to the same thing. Although this rule does get him into trouble with class inclusion problems, it greatly simplifies the task of learning which of the thousands of words he hears apply to which of the thousands of things he sees (Markman and Wachtel, 1988).

By the end of the preschool period, most children have come to understand that words can belong to subordinate and superordinate categories, and that the same thing can be called by two different names—"food" and "meat," for example. A 5-year-old can define *food* as "something what I eat," and then name some of the things that fit into that class. Here's how a 5½-year-old girl responded when asked to name some kinds of foods:

> There's cinnamon crackers. There is meat. Yuck. Spinach. Yuck. There is noodles. There is chocolate bars. There is turkey. There is chicken. There is rice. There's Chinese food. There is eggplant. Yuck.   (Anglin, 1977, p. 216)

THE NAMES OF THINGS. Some of the characteristics of children's speech are reflections of the way adults speak to children, rather than an indication of the maturity of the children's thought processes. A child will deny that a tree is a plant, or that a caterpillar is an animal, simply because he's never heard anyone refer to a tree as a plant or a caterpillar as an animal. Adults use different words when they're naming things for a child than when they're talking to another adult. When mothers were asked to identify some pictures for their 2-year-olds, they used the word *dog* for a picture of a collie, but they used the word *collie* when they were talking to another adult. Similarly, they labeled pictures *shoe, money,* and *bird* for their children; to an adult they called these pictures *sandal, dime,* and *pigeon.* And when a group of preschoolers were shown these same pictures, they used the same words that the mothers had used with the 2-year-olds: *dog, shoe, money, bird*—not *collie, sandal, dime,* or *pigeon* (Anglin, 1977).

Notice that it's not always the more general term, or even the shorter one, that parents teach their children. For instance, mothers gave their 2-year-olds the words *pineapple, typewriter,* and *butterfly,* rather than *fruit, machine,* and *insect.* Parents choose words that convey useful information by distinguishing between things that are responded to in different ways. A butterfly is admired, a cockroach is not. To call them both *insects* would be throwing away a lot of information. On the other hand, a collie and a chihuahua are both called *dogs,* even though they look quite different, because you behave in similar ways to both of them: they can both be patted, they may (or may not) come when you call them, they may (or may not) bite (Anglin, 1977; Rosch and Mervis, 1978).

Parents' choices of words to teach their children are also influenced by whether something is or isn't a typical member of its class. If the thing is *not* a typical member of its class, and if a more specific name is readily available, parents use (and children learn) the more specific name. For example, one researcher noticed that mothers used the word *bird* when showing their preschoolers pictures of robins or bluejays, but they used the word *turkey*—not the word *bird*—for a picture of a turkey. When these preschoolers were later shown a picture of a turkey and asked, "Is this a bird?", most of them said no (White, 1982).

Thus, preschoolers' use of names does not necessarily tell us anything about their cognitive development or their understanding of subordinate and superordinate categories. It may merely reflect the way adults label things when they're talking to children.

Learning a language does not just consist of learning a lot of words: children must also learn how to combine these words into phrases and sentences. They must learn verb forms, possessives, plurals, and definite and indefinite articles. Think of all the rules involved in speaking the English language! Think of all the *exceptions* to the rules!

To appreciate the kinds of problems that face young learners of English, and the ways they deal with these problems, consider the following dialog. The speakers are a developmental psycholinguist named Peter de Villiers and a 2½-year-old named Katie. They've been making things out of Play-Doh and their conversation concerns the ownership of some disputed pieces.

> KATIE: Don't crush mines up!
> DE VILLIERS: What was yours? What was it? Had you made it into something?
> KATIE: Dis is mines.

Katie has probably never heard anyone refer to anything as "mines." But she has heard words like *yours, ours, theirs,* and *hers,* and from these examples she has apparently generalized a rule: possessive pronouns should end in *s.*

> KATIE: Dat's yours.
> DE VILLIERS: That's mine. OK. I'll keep that. Is that as well? I have lots of pieces now, don't I?
> KATIE: Dis is mine.

Now Katie has noticed that de Villiers says *mine,* not *mines,* and she follows suit. She seems to have decided that her previous rule is incorrect, so she comes up with a new one:

> DE VILLIERS: Did you steal some more? You stole some more! Keep stealing all mine, don't you?
> KATIE: I keep stealing all your.
>   (de Villiers and de Villiers, 1979, p. 111)

Not all children are as quick to change their minds about a rule as Katie was. Here is perhaps a more typical example:

> CHILD: My teacher holded the baby rabbits and we patted them.
> ADULT: Did you say the teacher held the baby rabbits?
> CHILD: Yes.
> ADULT: What did you say she did?
> CHILD: She holded the baby rabbits and we patted them.
> ADULT: Did you say she held them tightly?
> CHILD: No, she holded them loosely.
>   (Gleason, 1967)

Learning the Rules of a Language

It is possible that this child, at an earlier age, used the word *held.* It is probable that Katie, at an earlier age, used the word *mine.* In English the exceptions to the rules usually involve the most common words, and some of these are learned in the early phases of language acquisition. But then, at a later point in time, a child who previously used *mine, held, went,* or *feet,* begins to use *mines, holded, goed,* or *feets* (we've mentioned this before, in Chapter 7). To the casual observer, it appears that the child is progressing backward. That is far from the truth, however. On the contrary: she has apparently worked out some of the general rules of the English language—a remarkable achievement, when you think about it. A child who says *holded* must be following a rule that goes, To form the past tense of a verb, add *-ed.* Yet she's not consciously aware that she's following a rule, and it's hard to believe that she possesses the concept of a verb! What's more, she's somehow managed to come up with this generalization despite the sizable proportion of common English verbs that don't follow the rule (such as *bring–brought, ring–rang, eat–ate, go–went, get–got,* and so on).

At a later time—usually before they enter first grade—most children learn the correct use of the common irregular verbs (such as *held*), plurals (*feet*), and possessives (*mine*). Thus, they have figured out both the rules and the exceptions. We know that they do use rules (and haven't just memorized each verb form, plural, and possessive individually) because they can apply them to words they've never seen before. This was demonstrated in a classic experiment carried out in the 1950s. The researcher made up nonsense words such as *wug* and *zib,* and used pictures to teach children these words—"This is a wug," or "This is a man who knows how to zib." A child who was shown a picture of a wug, for instance, would then be shown a second picture containing two of the birdlike creatures (see Figure 9–3), and the researcher would say, "Now there are two of them. There are two __." If the child said "wugs," it had to be because she knew the rule for forming plurals, since she's not likely to have heard the word *wugs* before. In answering questions of this sort, children between the ages of 4 and 7 proved that they knew how to form plurals, past tenses such as *zibbed,* and present progressives such as *zibbing* (Berko, 1958).

ACQUIRING GRAMMATICAL MORPHEMES. When children first start putting words together they speak in "telegraphic" phrases: "Kick truck." "Daddy chair." Later they speak in longer, fully formed sentences: "I kicked the truck." "That's Daddy's chair." The older child can express more complex ideas partly because he can use words such as *in, on, is, are,* and *the,* and suffixes such as *-ing, -ed,* and *-s.* Linguists call these **grammatical morphemes.** (A morpheme is defined as the smallest unit of meaning—a word or any detachable part of a word, such as a prefix or suffix).

The grammatical morphemes tend to appear in a fairly consistent order in the language of English-speaking children. The first to appear is usually the *-ing* ending on verbs, which is used at first without the auxiliary verbs *is* or *are,* as in "Mommy sitting." At about the same time the child begins to use the prepositions *in* and *on,* and the plural *-s.* Next come the possessive *-'s,* the articles *a* and *the,* some irregular past tenses such as *went* and *ate,* and some forms of the verb *to be,* used not as auxiliaries but as verbs in themselves (as in "Here

This is a wug.

Now there is another one.
There are two of them.
There are two _____ .

FIGURE 9-3
When 4- and 5-year-olds are given this test (it is read aloud to them), they can give the correct response, "wugs." This shows that they know the rule for forming plural nouns. (From Berko, 1958.)

I am," and "What is it?"). The regular past-tense ending *-ed* appears after children have started to use the irregular forms such as *went*.

Another group of morphemes appears relatively late: they are the *-s* that goes on the third person singular of English verbs ("He runs") and the forms of *to be* used as an auxiliary ("Mommy is sitting," "The dogs were running") and as a contractible verb ("I'm here," "They're nice"). These forms don't usually appear until children are between 3 and 4 years old (Brown, 1973).

Why do the grammatical morphemes appear in this particular order? It doesn't depend on the frequency with which these morphemes are used in adult speech; rather, the order of appearance of grammatical morphemes seems to be determined chiefly by the difficulty or complexity of the rules governing their use. The forms of the verb *to be* are more complex than morphemes like *-ing* and *on* because the child must take into account both the subject of the verb *(I am, you are, she is . . .)* and the tense *(I am, I was . . .)*. Because other languages make some distinctions that English doesn't, and fail to make some distinctions that English does, the order of acquisition will differ in other languages. For example, the concepts conveyed by *in* and *on* in English are conveyed quite differently in Serbo-Croatian, the language of Yugoslavia. In Serbo-Croatian these concepts require a preposition plus a special ending on the noun they go with, and the ending differs according to the way the noun is used in the sentence. For this reason, it takes children more time to learn to use these morphemes correctly if they are learning Serbo-Croatian than if they are learning English (de Villiers and de Villiers, 1979).

NEGATIVES. Children begin to express negative ideas as soon as they begin to combine words—"No bath!" they might say, or "No wet!" (pointing to a dry diaper). At this stage, negative statements are constructed simply by adding *no* or *not* in front of (or occasionally after) a word or phrase. "All-gone," used as one word, or "bye-bye," as in "bye-bye bird," may also be used to express the nonexistence or disappearance of something. The ability to express these ideas, interestingly enough, first appears at about the time children develop the concept of object permanence (see Chapter 7). So they are able to *talk* about an object that is no longer present at about the same age that they are able to *think* about it (Gopnik and Meltzoff, 1987).

Full and correct use of negatives takes a long time to achieve in English. A 2-year-old might use *no* as an all-purpose negative in sentences such as "He no bite you." A 3- or 4-year-old might say "I didn't did it," and even a school-age child might say "I can't see nothing" (de Villiers and de Villiers, 1979).

QUESTIONS. The first questions, like the first negatives, appear quite early. They are recognizable as questions only by the rising intonation of the child's voice: "More cookie?" "Daddy come home?" At about the same time, some *wh-* words (such as *who, what, where,* and *why*) begin to be used: "What's dat?" "Where doggie go?"

Even after children have acquired most of the important grammatical morphemes, they may still be having trouble with the word order in questions. Young preschoolers often use constructions such as "Why kitty can't stand up?" or "What he can ride in?" There is also the problem of putting both the verb and the auxiliary into the proper tense: in "Did I caught it?" the child has put both verbs into the past tense—reasonable, but (as it happens) incorrect (Clark and Clark, 1977).

The complexities of learning the English language are well illustrated by what linguists call **tag questions.** In "Barbara plays tennis, doesn't she?" and "You can't do it, can you?" the tag questions are "doesn't she?" and "can you?". To produce such questions, the speaker must perform three separate operations on the first part of the sentence: (1) if the subject is a noun, turn it into a pronoun; (2) turn a negative construction into a positive one, or vice versa; and (3) invert the word order to form a question. Adults who learn English as a second language may find tag questions so difficult that they don't even attempt them—they simply use a general-purpose "Right?" or "True?" But, by the time they enter first grade, most English-speaking children understand the basic principles of tag questions and are able to produce them correctly in at least some contexts. Complete mastery of the tag question takes several more years, however (Dennis, Sugar, and Whitaker, 1982).

Environment and Language

Obviously, children will not learn a language if they are never exposed to it. But one of the remarkable things about human language is the way it develops in virtually every child—in all but the most severely retarded or brain-damaged—under an incredibly wide range of environmental conditions. In the three-year period between 12 months and 4 years, just about every child has acquired some sort of language. A totally deaf child who hears no spoken language, even if given no training in sign language, will develop some simple gestural language of his own in order to communicate with the people around him. As one pair of psycholinguists put it,

> Normal human children all acquire their native tongue at a high level of proficiency by the age of four or five years. The learning is much the same for Greek and Chinese as it is for English or Hungarian; as true for dull children as for wiser ones; as true for children of kind and talkative mothers as for children of nasty or taciturn ones; and as true for children from intellectually primitive backgrounds as for those from more sophisti-

cated ones. In sum, we find for language learning a uniform and early success with a complex task, despite differences in the learners, their motivations, their environments, and the languages they have to learn. . . . It seems that, for all its complexity, language is an irrepressible human activity.   (Gleitman and Gleitman, 1981, p. 383)

Naturally there is a catch. Within an incredibly wide range, the environment has no effect on whether or not a child will develop language. But the environment will inevitably have an effect on what kind of language the child acquires and on how well he acquires it. A child cannot learn words he never hears. He *will* learn words he does hear, even if those words are ones his parents would prefer he didn't learn. He learns from his playmates and acquaintances as well as from his parents: if his friends are native speakers of English he will learn to speak English without an accent, even if his parents cannot.

Preschoolers pick up words everywhere. Although they can't learn a language from scratch just by watching TV shows (see p. 254), they can learn individual *words* by hearing them used on a TV show geared to their level of understanding (Rice and Woodsmall, 1988). However, children learn better and more quickly if they can take an active role in the conversation and if the person they are talking to is responsive to their interests. In a recent study, English-speaking preschoolers were taught to use Spanish words to ask for ten desirable toys that were kept on shelves out of their reach. For some children, the researcher told them the Spanish name for a toy every time they expressed an interest in that particular toy. For another group of children, the researcher told them the Spanish names for the toys just as often, but at random times during the training sessions. The children in the first group—the ones who had been told the new words at the times they were paying attention to those particular toys—learned an average of six Spanish words. The children in the second group learned an average of only three. Thus, an adult who simply throws words at a child is a far less effective language teacher than one who responds to what the child is interested in (Valdez-Menchaca and Whitehurst, 1988).

Another factor that affects a child's language development is the ability of his parents and teachers to tailor their conversation to the level of his understanding. We have mentioned several times that people talk differently to very young children than to older children or adults. To do this is so natural, so compelling, that even young children themselves "talk down" to still younger children. When we're speaking to a 2- or 3-year-old, we don't use long, complicated sentences and we don't talk about philosophy, politics, or parthenogenesis. Both the words and the topics are different from what they would be if we were talking to an adult.

Studies of mothers' conversations with their children show that most mothers are very good at adjusting their speech to their children's level of verbal development. A mother's speech is closely related to her child's MLU (mean length of utterance—see p. 247). As the child's MLU increases, so does the length and complexity of his mother's utterances to him. The mother's utterances are longer and more complex than the child's, but still within his capacity to understand. By remaining always a little ahead of her child, the mother stimulates the child to make continual progress (Reich, 1986).

Fathers also adjust their speech to their child's level of verbal development, but they seem to do this a little less well (or less consistently) than mothers do. Whereas mothers tend to restrict their vocabulary to common, familiar words when talking to a toddler or preschooler, fathers are more likely to throw in an unusual word here and there: in one study, some fathers were heard to use terms such as "domesticated animal" and "ratchet wrench" to 2-year-olds (Ratner, 1988). There is no reason to think that this does the children any harm; perhaps it even serves as a sort of challenge to them. And mothers sometimes err in the other direction—by labeling a leopard a "kitty cat," for instance. Overall, though, mothers generally do seem to be more attuned than fathers to the child's verbal ability. Evidence suggests that preschoolers advance in language more quickly when their caregivers are knowledgeable about, and sensitive to, their level of language development (Lane and Bergan, 1988).

It's not only parents who influence children's ability to use and understand language: now that so many young children attend day-care centers or preschools, researchers have wondered whether the quality of care at those facilities has an effect on the children's verbal development. A study in Bermuda (where a large proportion of preschoolers go to day-care centers) showed that it does. The researcher found a clear correlation between the quality of a day-care center and the verbal skills of the children attending that center. The children's language development was related as closely to the quality of their day-care center as to the socioeconomic background of their family.

What aspects of the children's experiences at the center were responsible for this surprisingly strong effect on their verbal ability? One factor proved to be very important: how much time the children spent talking to adult caregivers, versus how much time they spent talking to each other. Those centers at which the caregivers spent a lot of time conversing with the children (especially when their speech involved giving information, rather than just telling a child what to do) produced children who were relatively advanced in their verbal development. Those centers at which children conversed mainly with each other produced children whose verbal development was relatively slow (McCartney, 1984).

A well-established fact of language development is that the firstborn child

Parents tailor their speech to the level of their children's understanding. If Daddy occasionally drops in a word like bivalve *or* mollusk, *children don't seem to mind.*

in a family is likely to be the most verbal; the younger siblings tend to score a little lower on verbal tests. Since genetic factors cannot account for this difference between biological siblings, it is clearly an effect of environment. The Bermuda study lends support to the traditional explanation for the first child's verbal superiority: the first child in the family is the one who gets the most verbal interaction with the parents. The younger children get the most verbal interaction with each other.

A researcher who was studying preschoolers' understanding of words tried to find out how much they knew by interviewing them. Here's the conversation that was recorded when a child named Sharon, age 4½, was asked to define the word *dog:*

The Preschooler's Conversational Skills

RESEARCHER: Tell me, what's a dog?
SHARON: I don't know, it has soggy ears that go, that hang down.
RESEARCHER: Mm hm, and?
SHARON: Um, it chases cats.
RESEARCHER: Mm hm.
SHARON: Guess what?
RESEARCHER: What?
SHARON: My cat got bit by a dog.
RESEARCHER: Really.
SHARON: Yeah.
RESEARCHER: Where did the dog bite him?
SHARON: On both sides.
RESEARCHER: Really.
SHARON: He got bit on both sides.
RESEARCHER: Aaa, that's too bad.
SHARON: And his dog is the animal doctor.
RESEARCHER: Uh huh. OK, do you know what kind of dogs there are?
SHARON: Yeah, um, there are plain doggies, and let's see, there are, um, there are igloos doggies, and let's see, there are scouts doggies, um, there are, there are minuteman doggies.
RESEARCHER: Minuteman doggies? What kinds of doggies do minutemen have?
SHARON: They have ones that um that's, that can get, that go, that is that stay, they um, that go in, that get in the house, that that man, minuteman doggies are ones, minuteman has, has a doggie in the house.
RESEARCHER: Uh huh.
(Anglin, 1977, p. 205)

This conversation is a good illustration of some of the preschooler's shortcomings as a conversationalist. For example, Sharon concluded her story about how her cat got bitten by a dog by telling the researcher, "And his dog is the animal doctor." Did she mean "It was the animal doctor's dog"? Whatever she meant, she failed to communicate it to the listener. Moreover, she failed to *notice* that she had failed to communicate it. As Piaget pointed out, preschoolers' conversations often give the impression that they're speaking more for their own pleasure than to convey any information to their listener. The preschooler appears to be both unconcerned and unable to judge whether her listener has understood her. For example, one preschooler trying to

Close-Up

Box 9-3
Private Speech

■ Omar sits down at the art table and says to himself, "I want to draw something. Let's see. I need a big piece of paper. I want to draw my cat."

■ Paula is given a new box of crayons and says to no one in particular, "Wow! Neat!"

■ Peter wanders around the room, repeating in a sing-song manner, "Put the mushroom on your head, put the mushroom in your pocket, put the mushroom on your nose." (Berk, 1986, p. 39)

These children are talking to themselves, a form of utterance known as **private speech.** Piaget (1926) was the first researcher to take note of this phenomenon: he named it "egocentric speech." According to Piaget, a great deal of preschoolers' speech is spoken with no regard at all for the listener. There is no concern about whether the listener is interested or is able to understand what is being said—or even, for that matter, is listening. Piaget concluded that this type of speech is yet another indication of preschoolers' egocentrism—of their inability to put themselves in the place of the other person. He felt that private speech gradually disappears as children get older because

social pressures cause their speech to become more communicative.

A very different interpretation was offered by the Russian psychologist Lev Vygotsky. Vygotsky (1962) proposed that private speech was children's way of regulating their own behavior. Very young children say the words out loud, and this helps to direct their actions and to focus their attention on what they are doing. As children grow older this speech does not disappear—it simply goes underground and becomes verbal thought. Private speech, then, is simply "thinking out loud."

Support for Vygotsky's interpretation was provided by a study done some years ago. The researchers found that children of average intelligence actually increase their output of private speech during the preschool years, until they are about 5 or 6. Then the output declines, disappearing entirely by the time the child is about 9. But in very bright children this increase and decline occur more quickly: the bright preschoolers reach their maximum output of private speech at around age 4 (Kohlberg, Yaeger, and Hjertholm, 1968).

The fact that the decline of private speech is related to intelligence and not to social skills suggests that Vygotsky is right—that this speech goes underground not because of social disapproval

describe something to another child said it "looks like Mommy's hat," a description that conveyed nothing meaningful to the second child (Glucksberg, Krauss, and Weisberg, 1966).

Although this seems to be a perfectly clear case of the preschooler's egocentricity—her failure to take into account the other person's point of view —it turns out not to be so clear after all. When a preschooler is talking to someone, trying to communicate some information, and the listener doesn't understand it, the preschooler blames the listener for failing to understand. But if someone is talking to the preschooler—so that the preschooler *is* the listener—she blames any failures of communication on *herself* (Speer, 1984). She assumes that it was *her* fault if she didn't understand what the other child meant by the description "looks like Mommy's hat." Since she *was* the listener in this case, the problem can't possibly consist of her inability to adopt the listener's point of view!

Preschoolers are so ignorant of the factors that determine their own (as well as other people's) comprehension that they don't even realize that the reason for taking turns in a conversation is that it's hard to understand something if two people are talking at once. A researcher played the beginning of a tape-recorded story to some 3-year-olds and then asked them how they wanted to hear the rest of it. Part of the story was narrated by a clown and part by a sailor, and the children were asked: "Do you want the clown and the sailor to talk at the same time, or do you want them to take turns talking?"

but because it turns into thought. In fact, later research showed that very sociable children use more private speech than less sociable ones: "The children who talked to others the most also talked to themselves the most" (Berk, 1986, p. 38).

There has also been support for Vygotsky's notion that private speech gradually turns into verbal thought. In another study, preschoolers ranging in age from 3½ to 6 were given some tough problems to work on and were told that it was okay if they wanted to talk out loud while they were doing them (Frauenglass and Diaz, 1985). The preschoolers in this study put out quite a lot of private speech. But it was generally the younger children who actually spoke out loud. The older children mostly confined themselves to muttering or whispering to themselves—private speech caught in the act of going underground!

Does talking out loud to themselves help children solve problems? The answer appears to be yes, at least in some cases. First graders of average intelligence who talked out loud while they were working on math problems did better than those who remained silent. The results were a little different for the brighter children in the class, who were further along in the process of internalizing their speech: the bright children who talked out loud didn't do quite as well as those who only mut-

tered or whispered to themselves. Also, the content of the private speech made a difference: children whose speech was unrelated to the task at hand did a lot of squirming around in their seats, playing with their pencils, and so on. The children who used private speech that *was* relevant to the task at hand were much more focused. The children who were most attentive of all, and who wiggled around the least, were those whose private speech had become nearly inaudible. Their ability to convert their words into thoughts went hand in hand with their ability to focus their energies on what they were supposed to be doing (Berk, 1986).

Vygotsky said that private speech has an important function in helping children to regulate their own behavior, by bringing their actions under the control of their thoughts. A researcher recently recorded children in the process of doing just that. A preschool-age boy, sitting in the bathtub and talking to himself, told himself sternly, "Be quiet and grow up." And a girl of about the same age, who had just made a rude sound, reprimanded herself: "Don't do that, Jenny." Then she paused and, in a babyish voice, said, "I'm sorry" (Becker, 1988, p. 463).

The majority of these children replied, "At the same time." Before playing the tapes the researcher asked them, "When the clown and the sailor both talk at the same time, is it easy to understand or is it hard to understand?" Only half of the 3-year-olds said that it would be hard to understand two tape-recorded stories being played simultaneously (Pillow, 1988, p. 41).

On the other hand, preschoolers give evidence of having absorbed many of our society's rules of conversation. Young children know that when the other person stops talking that's their cue to start talking, and when the other person asks a question they're supposed to give an answer. They also have a good idea of what form the answer should take: for example, a question that starts with "When" or "What" has to be answered with a statement containing appropriate information, whereas a question that starts with "Can you" or "Do you" can be answered with yes or no. Children as young as 2½ or 3 show their awareness of conversational rules by making comments about other people's failure to follow them—"I said *hi* to him and he didn't said *hi* to me"; about their own role in the conversation—"I was talking to Mommy, I wasn't talking to you"; and even about their own *inability* to participate in a conversation—"I can't talk, I'm dead" (Becker, 1988, pp. 461–464).

If preschool children sometimes fail to communicate, either because they don't make themselves clear, like Sharon, or because at the moment they happen to be "dead," they nonetheless make entertaining conversational partners.

Summary

1. To program a computer with enough information to enable it to understand the things that any 3-year-old child can understand would require a few million computer entries. This implies that a 3-year-old child has acquired the equivalent of 4000 computer-entries worth of knowledge each day since she was born.

2. According to Piaget, preschoolers are in the **preoperational period.** He believes that preschooler's thought is qualitively different from that of older children—that it is **egocentric,** which means preschoolers judge everything from their own point of view. For example, in the three mountains experiment, preschoolers depict their own point of view when they're asked to give the doll's.

3. Other researchers attribute preschoolers' responses in the three mountains experiment to their tendency to see the *objective* view (what they know is really there), rather than the *projective* view (what a camera would see). Their dislike of overlapping also plays a role: they choose the "good view" (the view that doesn't overlap), not necessarily the doll's view.

4. According to Flavell, children's ability to understand another person's point of view progresses in two levels. In level 1 (reached by age 2 or 3) they realize that another person might not be able to see everything they see. In level 2 (age 4 or 5) they also realize that the other person might not have the same view that they have.

5. Preschoolers sometimes respond in terms of reality when they're asked to judge appearances; this is called **intellectual realism.** At other times they respond in terms of appearances when they're asked about reality; this is called **phenomenism.** Realism is more likely to occur when the judgment involves identity or existence; phenomenism is more likely when qualities such as color, size, or amount are involved, as in Piaget's conservation experiments.

6. Although young children have problems distinguishing between appearance and reality, they have no trouble with the distinction between *pretend* and reality.

7. In Piaget's experiment on the conservation of number, preschoolers say that a spread-out row of jellybeans contains more candy than a closely spaced row. However, if the numbers involved are small enough—no more than four—older preschoolers (ages 4 and 5) appear to understand the conservation of number.

8. Most 4- and 5-year-olds can correctly count a row of ten objects. Counting involves at least three underlying principles: (1) the rule of **one-to-one correspondence** between objects and number names; (2) the **cardinality**

rule—the last number word spoken equals the number of objects; and (3) the **order-irrelevance principle**—the order in which you count things doesn't matter. Preschoolers generally acquire the first two concepts by age 2½ or 3, but the third one takes longer to achieve.

9. Preschoolers are not as good at learning and memory tasks as older children. One reason for this is their lack of metacognitive skills. **Metacognition** is the ability to understand, to think about, and to monitor the progress of one's own cognitive processes.

10. Preschoolers' thought is qualitatively different from that of babies and toddlers, because preschoolers are capable of representational thought. The evidence for a qualitative change between preschool thinking and that of older children is much less persuasive.

11. IQ tests are designed to measure the qualities that characterize people we consider "intelligent." A test that measures what it's supposed to measure is said to have **validity.** Evidence for the validity of IQ tests is the fact that the results agree fairly well with other ways of judging children's intelligence, such as how well they do in school.

12. An IQ score is a number that represents how well a given child did on a given test, taken on a given day. Under some circumstances, it may not be a good measure of a child's actual intelligence.

13. IQ, or **intelligence quotient,** originally meant **mental age** divided by chronological age (times 100). Nowadays IQ is defined in terms of how well a child does compared with other children of the same age. Children who score at the mean have IQs of 100.

14. Childhood IQ scores correlate reasonably well with adult IQ scores, but some children show large changes in IQ scores. Such changes may reflect actual increases or decreases in the rate of cognitive development, or may result from **error of measurement.** Tests vary in their **reliability**—a reliable test is one that (theoretically, at least) would yield similar scores if the child took it twice within a month. If a test is reliable, a child's obtained score is likely to be fairly close to his "true" score.

15. Preschool enrichment programs such as Head Start are designed to provide children from disadvantaged homes with intellectual and verbal stimulation. Such programs often produce sizable gains in IQ and school readiness scores, but these gains tend to be temporary. However, some "model" programs have produced significant long-term benefits.

16. The average 2-year-old has a vocabulary of 200 or 300 words and speaks mostly in short, simple phrases. By the time she is ready to enter first grade, she will be speaking in complex sentences and have a productive vocabulary of around 2500 words and a receptive vocabulary that may be as high as 14,000 words.

17. Fast mapping is a method children use to form a quick, approximate idea of the meaning of a new word. Hearing the new word contrasted with an old one is one way they can do this.

18. Children start out by assuming that each thing has one and only one name, so they have trouble when they encounter multiple names for the same thing—for example, *dog* and *animal.* By the end of the preschool period, children understand that the same thing can be called by more than one name, and that words can belong to subordinate and superordinate categories.

19. Some of the characteristics of children's speech are reflections of the way adults speak to children. Adults use different words when they're naming things for a child than when they're talking to another adult.

20. A child who uses words such as *mine, held,* and *feet* may later switch to *mines, holded,* and *feets.* Although this appears to be backward progress, it shows that the child has worked out some of the general rules of the English language.

21. Prepositions such as *in* and *on,* and suffixes such as *-ing* and *-ed,* are **grammatical morphemes.** Children's acquisition of grammatical morphemes follows a fairly orderly sequence, which depends on the complexity of the rules governing their use, rather than on their frequency in adult speech.

22. Children at first express negative ideas by putting *no* or *not* in front of a word or phase, or with phrases such as *bye-bye* and *all-gone.* The ability to talk about an object that is no longer present appears at about the same time as the ability to *think* about an object that is no longer present.

23. The first questions may be recognizable as such only by the child's intonation; some *wh-* words begin to be used at about the same time. Young preschoolers are likely to have trouble with the word order in questions and with putting the verb and the auxiliary into the proper tenses.

24. Language develops in virtually every child—all but the most severely retarded or brain-damaged—under an incredibly wide range of environmental conditions. Although preschoolers can pick up words anywhere, they learn language most readily if they can take an active role in conversations, and if the person they talk to is responsive to their interests and their level of understanding.

25. Preschoolers are not always successful at communicating information. When there's a failure to communicate, the preschooler's tendency is to blame the listener, rather than the speaker—even when the preschooler *is* the listener. Three-year-olds are ignorant about the factors that affect their own comprehension of what they hear.

26. Young children often talk out loud to themselves; this is called **private speech.** According to Vygotsky, children use this form of speech as a way of regulating their own behavior—it helps to focus their attention and direct their actions. Later, private speech goes underground and becomes verbal thought.

Key Terms

preoperational period
decenter
egocentric
center
intellectual realism
phenomenism
one-to-one correspondence rule
cardinality rule
order-irrelevance principle

cardinality principle
metacognition
rehearsal
categorization
validity
mental age
intelligence quotient
Stanford–Binet
WISC-R

WPPSI
error of measurement
reliability
fast mapping
class inclusion problem
grammatical morphemes
tag question
private speech

10
Becoming a Member of Society

J ulia, age 2½, is alone in the kitchen; her mother has gone to run an errand in another part of the house. Julia sees an open carton of eggs on the table. She reaches for them, then hesitates as she realizes that her mother wouldn't approve. There's a brief period of indecision and then Julia makes up her mind. When her mother returns, she finds Julia cheerfully making "scrambled eggs" on the kitchen floor: plopping the eggs down, one by one, and scolding herself for each plop, "NoNoNo. Mustn't dood it. NoNoNo. Mustn't dood it!" (Fraiberg, 1959, p. 135).

This story illustrates three important points about young preschoolers. First, they may use private speech (see Chapter 9) in an attempt to regulate their own behavior, but it doesn't always work. Second, even though they misbehave at times, they at least have some knowledge of what they should and shouldn't do. Julia, age 2½, made scrambled eggs *despite* the fact that she knew she shouldn't. We can consider this progress of a sort. At 1½, Julia might have done the same thing, but in complete innocence. At that age she would have been genuinely surprised when her mother failed to share her enthusiasm about the results. Now she knows better. She looks embarrassed and guilty when her mother returns and catches her egg-handed.

The third point this story illustrates is the preschooler's growing independence from her mother. When Julia was 1½ her mother might not have left her alone in the kitchen, or if she did, Julia might have toddled out after her. Toddlers and their parents, while at home and awake, spend almost all of their time in the same room with each other. Preschoolers spend less time in close proximity to their caregivers.

Other important changes in parent–child relationships also take place during toddlerhood and the early preschool period. Mother and child look at each other and speak to each other less often as the child gets older. Conversation between mother and child reaches a peak at 2 years and then declines. Physical contact between mother and child also tends to decline as the child gets older. This is especially true of children who were judged securely attached at age 12 months (see Chapter 6). Some of the children who were insecurely attached as infants are still physically clinging to their mothers at age 2½ (Clarke-Stewart and Hevey, 1981).

The securely attached child appears to have acquired in infancy what Erik Erikson (see Chapter 3) calls *basic trust*. This child has come to believe that the world in general, and her parents in particular, will not let her down. In toddlerhood she moved on to develop a sense of autonomy—a sense of confidence and pride in her ability to do things on her own. She no longer feels the need to check on the whereabouts of her parents every few minutes, and she is no longer willing to have everything done for her. She wants to do things on her own, and this might include making scrambled eggs on the kitchen floor. The relationship between the child and her parents has undergone some important changes in the last year.

Socialization in the Preschool Period

In order to become an acceptable member of society, it's not enough for a child to learn what kinds of behavior are approved of and what kinds aren't. He or she must also develop the ability to *act* according to those rules, even if no adults are around.

Much of this development takes place during the preschool period. Selma Fraiberg, the child psychologist who described the incident with Julia and the eggs, says that what has to happen is that the "policeman outside" (in other words, the child's parents) has to become "the policeman inside"—the child's conscience. The child has to **internalize** her parent's rules and standards of behavior—they have to become a part of her, something she believes in, rather than something imposed on her by others. When we overheard Julia telling herself, "Mustn't dood it!" we were listening to one of the steps in the process of the "policeman outside" becoming the "policeman inside" (Fraiberg, 1959, p. 138).

Before a child can learn to follow the rules of her society, she must first learn to follow the rules of her own family. Thus, socialization has its beginnings within the family, with the parents playing a major role. Why do some parents seem to be more successful at this job than others?

Problems in Development

Most preschoolers are deeply attached to their parents and feel affection for a number of the people in their lives. But there are some children who withdraw almost completely from human interactions and seem to have little affection for anyone. These children have a disorder called **infantile autism.**

As the word *infantile* suggests, this disorder appears very early in development, usually in infancy, although the diagnosis is ordinarily not made until the child is a preschooler. However, the parents are likely to have noticed signs of trouble much earlier. Babies who will later be diagnosed as **autistic** generally fail to make eye contact with their parents in infancy—or, for that matter, later in childhood. They tend not to lift up their arms in anticipation of being picked up, as normal babies do.

Most telling of all, they fail to develop normal attachments. One mother of an autistic child realized that there was something wrong with her daughter when, at the age of 2, the child walked away from her on a crowded beach. The mother ran after her, of course, but the child just kept walking, passing within inches of other children but never looking at them, and without a backward glance to see where her mother was. "She might have walked straight ahead forever," her mother said, "so little did she need of human contact" (Park, 1967, p. 5).

If an autistic child does develop an attachment, it's more likely to be to an object than to a person. One autistic child spent hours every day looking at a water heater. He even loved to look at *pictures* of water heaters. Another symptom of autism is an intense desire for sameness in the environment. Typically, autistic children become upset if there's any change in the position of the furniture in their house or even of the objects in a room. Some autistic children rock back and forth or twiddle their fingers for hours on end; some hit or bite themselves (Rimland, 1964; Kanner, 1951).

Almost all autistic children have speech and language problems. About half do develop some speech, but they tend to use it in unusual ways. An autistic child may simply echo samples of speech that he's heard—TV commercials, for instance. A question such as "Do you want some milk?" may be answered with "Do you want some milk?" Normal children generally learn to refer to themselves as *I* or *me* by the age of 2½. An autistic child may go on calling himself *you* for many years (Carr, Pridal, and Dores, 1984; Rutter, 1978).

The long-term outlook for these children is bleak. Although about half can eventually lead some sort of independent existence, very few are able to hold jobs. Behavior therapy, using rein-

Patterns of Parenting

Developmental psychologist Diana Baumrind, of the University of California at Berkeley, has been studying the effects of various methods of childrearing since 1960. On the basis of her work with preschoolers, Baumrind (1967, 1975) distinguished three major patterns of childrearing.

The first childrearing style is called **authoritarian**—old-fashioned strictness. Authoritarian parents follow the "traditional" viewpoint: obedience is viewed as a virtue, and conflicts between child and parent are met with punishment and force. Children are expected to do what they're told without argument, and that includes helping with household chores. The children of authoritarian parents are not given much freedom or independence.

Baumrind has named the second childrearing style **authoritative.** Authoritative parents, like authoritarian ones, believe in firm enforcement of family rules, but there's a difference: authoritative parents give their children the reasons behind their decisions and permit verbal give-and-take. They listen to their children's objections and take them into consideration, but the final decision belongs to the parents. On the other hand, their children are not hemmed in by restrictions and they are encouraged—even pushed—to be independent.

The third parenting style is called **permissive.** Permissive parents behave in a kind, accepting way toward their children and demand very little. Their

forcement and punishment, can help to improve the behavior of autistic children, but the dramatic successes generally involve only the less serious cases and require thousands of hours of one-on-one training. Drug therapy is being tested, but so far the results have been disappointing. Fortunately, autism is a rare disorder: only four or five children per 10,000 are autistic. Boys are four times more likely to be affected than girls (Clarke and Clarke, 1988; Gillberg, 1988).

What causes autism? Psychiatrists originally blamed it on the parents, who were accused of being cold and unresponsive to the child. But now it is recognized that the parents' behavior is a result of the child's failure to respond in normal ways to *them*. Most psychiatrists and psychologists today believe that autism is the result of a physical abnormality in the child's brain. The brain defect may result from several different causes, such as injury or disease. A genetic factor must also be involved: if one member of a pair of identical twins is autistic, the chances are better than 90 percent that the other twin will be autistic too (Gillberg, 1988; Steffenburg and others, 1989).

The brain abnormality that causes autism is a curious one, because it affects some parts of the brain so severely, while other parts seem to be unaffected, or even—in some cases—to work *better* than usual. In the majority of autistic children and adults, there is one special ability that has been spared: the individual functions normally in that respect and very poorly in everything else. In a much smaller number of autistic people, 10 percent at most, this special ability functions way *above* normal levels—it may even amount to genius (Gillberg, 1988). The result is someone like Raymond, the character played by Dustin Hoffman in the movie "Rain Man." Some of these people (they used to be called *idiot savants*) can multiply and divide multidigit numbers in their heads. Others can give you the day of the week for any date you name. Still others possess extraordinary artistic or musical talent. All these abilities are, in normal people, processed in the *right* hemisphere of the brain (see Chapter 8). Thus, some researchers believe that autism must involve a malfunctioning of the *left* hemisphere—the hemisphere that normally controls language and reasoning (Treffert, 1988).

But it is not only language and reasoning that are disrupted in autism: emotional and social functioning are affected just as severely. And that somehow seems even sadder, especially when we think of that little girl walking on the beach, walking past normal children who are playing with each other and calling out to their parents, "Look at me!" She will never smile at these children or make friends with them. Perhaps she will never even see them, except as obstacles in her path.

children are given as much freedom as possible (short of endangering their health or safety). These parents see their role as helping or serving their children, rather than the opposite.

What Baumrind discovered about these three major patterns of childrearing was unexpected. She found few differences between the children of authoritarian parents and the children of permissive parents. Both groups of children were less motivated to achieve and less independent than the children of authoritative parents. Both groups tended to be discontented, distrustful, self-centered, and (in the case of boys) hostile. Authoritative parents, in contrast, produced the most successful children. Their children were responsible, assertive, self-reliant, and friendly.

One interesting finding that emerged from these studies is that unconditional love or acceptance—expressions of tenderness and warmth given without regard to the child's behavior—did not produce its expected results. Children who received unconditional love (given most commonly by permissive parents) were not especially independent, cooperative, friendly, or assertive. According to Baumrind, these desirable traits were more likely to be found in children from homes in which all was not serene—homes in which there was some tension between the children and their parents. Baumrind believes that unconditional love has been much overrated: she says that

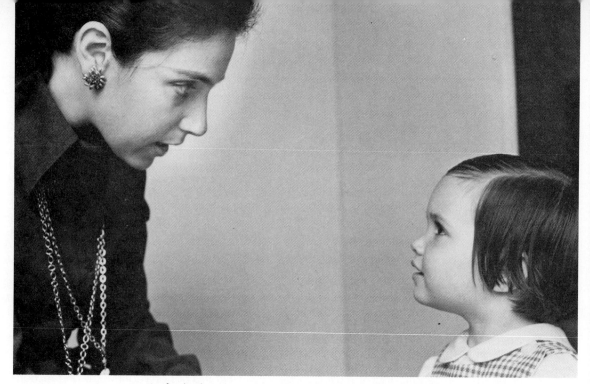

Authoritative parents give their children the reasons behind their decisions and permit verbal give-and-take.

"unconditional acceptance of a child's misbehavior is a psychological impossibility over the long haul for any parent," and that attempts to achieve this impossible goal have "deterred many parents from fulfilling important parental functions" (1975, p. 20).

Baumrind comes out strongly in favor of firm but reasonable parental control, enforced by punishment when necessary. She believes that parents should listen to the child's point of view, but they shouldn't feel they have to accept it. Reasons should be given for rules and restrictions; when rules or restrictions are not needed they shouldn't be used.

In the years since Baumrind first described the three parenting styles, much additional information has been obtained. Although there is still no evidence for the view that young children require *unconditional* acceptance or love, it is clear that children whose parents generally like and accept them are better off than ones whose parents dislike and reject them. However, parents do not necessarily have to show their affection by means of hugs and kisses. What may matter more is the parents' responsiveness to the child—their sensitivity to the child's needs and interests—and whether the majority of their interactions are positive or negative in tone. A child whose parents take an interest in what he is doing and talk to him in a friendly and informative way is likely to do well, both socially and intellectually. A child whose parents seldom pay attention to him except to yell at him or punish him is, as we will see, far more likely to become a problem to his family and to society (Pettit and Bates, 1989; Roberts, 1987).

When researchers have looked at the long-term effects of various childrearing styles, their findings have generally been in agreement with Baumrind's theories. Adolescents and young adults whose parents used an authoritative childrearing style make better grades in high school and have higher self-esteem than those reared by authoritarian or permissive parents (Buri and others, 1988; Dornbusch and others, 1987).

A TRANSACTIONAL REINTERPRETATION. Baumrind took it for granted that the children's characteristics she observed *resulted* from the childrearing patterns she identified. But the cause-and-effect relationship is not at all clear. Perhaps the parents' childrearing style was, at least in part, a *reaction* to their children's characteristics. Surely a cooperative, competent child is more likely to be treated in an authoritative manner than a disagreeable or impulsive one. A child who shows that she is capable of handling responsibility will probably be allowed more independence than an irresponsible child. A child who is receptive to reasoning might be given the reasons for his parents' decisions, whereas a child who objects to everything his parents tell him might be given the traditional authoritarian explanation: "Because I said so, that's why!"

The transactional view is becoming more widely accepted by child development researchers, and evidence is mounting for the two-way nature of adult–child interactions. A lot of this evidence is based on experimental situations in which adults are asked to deal with children who are strangers to them. The way the adults act in such a situation depends on the behavior of the child. Adults give more advice and commands to a child who acts helpless and dependent than to one who acts capable and independent. With a child who acts disagreeable and uncooperative, adults react by being bossy and critical or by ignoring the child. A child who acts shy and anxious is given encouragement and verbal rewards (Bell and Chapman, 1986).

One interesting finding that has come out of these studies is that, after an adult has had a chance to deal with a particular child for a while, she comes to expect the child to act in a certain way. Then she begins to react according to her expectations, as well as to the child's actual behavior. In the study where children acted uncooperative and disagreeable (these were normal children trained to act this way for the purpose of the experiment), occasionally a child slipped out of his role and did what the adult asked him to do. But the adult tended not to notice that the child had, for once, listened to her, and she continued to dish out commands or criticism. Thus, the child who is most in need of a kind word may be the least likely to receive it, because his occasional moments of cooperativeness may be overlooked (Bell and Chapman, 1986).

TODAY'S PARENTS. Baumrind developed her theory of the three major kinds of parenting styles based on observations made in the 1960s. Nowadays, neither authoritarian nor permissive childrearing practices seem to be very popular, at least in middle-class homes. In a recent study of preschoolers interacting at home with their mothers and older siblings, almost all the mothers used what the researchers called "justifications" in explaining to their children why they should or shouldn't do something. These were explanations based on principles such as rules of ownership ("That doesn't belong to you") or consideration of the consequences of their actions ("You'll break it if you do that"). By the age of 3, most of the children were using similar forms of reasoning in talking to their mother or siblings—for example, in explaining why they didn't want to do something, or why they wanted their sibling to *stop* doing something (Dunn and Munn, 1987, p. 793).

Clearly, the middle-class mothers in this study—each of whom had exactly two children—were participating in quite a lot of verbal give-and-take. There was no sign of the "children should be seen but not heard" attitude that goes with an authoritarian parenting style, and no indication that these mothers were overly permissive, either.

TROUBLED FAMILIES, TROUBLESOME CHILDREN. The authoritative pattern of childrearing is least likely to be seen in families under stress: economically deprived families, families where there are many children, where the parents are getting along poorly, where there is only one parent, or where there is a problem of drug abuse, alcoholism, or mental illness. In such families, the parents may not have the physical or emotional energy it takes to reason with children and to be responsive to their needs. They may not have the energy it takes to set limits on their children's behavior and to see that those limits are enforced. Thus, their children, at preschool age, might still be defying their parents' orders and failing to follow family rules.

According to Gerald Patterson and his associates at the Oregon Social Learning Center, young children who haven't learned to comply with their parents' rules and requests, or whose parents have been unable to get them to comply, are at risk for a variety of serious problems later on. These children —the majority of whom are boys—may be shunned by their peers, do poorly in school, and become juvenile delinquents or adult lawbreakers (Patterson, DeBaryshe, and Ramsey, 1989).

Often, the trouble lies in the parents' inability to handle one particular child—in most of these families there are other children whose behavior is within normal limits. But for the "problem" child, a vicious circle is in effect that causes things to go from bad to worse:

> The process begins with the toddler having difficulties learning normal levels of compliance to parental house rules and requests. It may be that the child's temperament makes him or her more difficult than most to train; but the fact is that the parents fail to respond effectively. Scolding and explosive, irritable, and inconsistent discipline produce a child who becomes increasingly noncompliant. . . .
>
> Instead of clear commands to stop, the parent makes vague threats; then, without backing up these threats, the parent scolds and lectures. In the face of this nattering, the problem child is significantly more likely to continue noncompliant behavior than is the normal child faced with similar parental reactions.
>
> Why is it that in some families parental efforts to intervene actually make things worse? Normal families tend to set specific consequences for misbehavior and follow through with punishments when appropriate. In families with [unsuccessful] parenting styles, however, the child learns that threats to punish do not imply a parental willingness to follow through.   (Patterson and Bank, 1989, pp. 170, 178)

Patterson believes that parents with unsuccessful childrearing styles can benefit from training in family management skills. These parents need to learn how to react to their children's behavior in an appropriate and effective way—by giving attention of a positive sort when the child is being cooperative, and by dealing with misbehavior promptly and firmly, before it has a chance to escalate.

Punishment

How do ordinary parents—parents whose children are not unusually trouble-some—deal with misbehavior? The parents' response is very much determined by the nature of the child's transgression. For some types of misbehaviors, the parents will use reasoning: they will tell the child that she shouldn't have done whatever she did, and explain why. For other types of misbehaviors, the parent will use punishment, either to make the child stop what she is doing or to make it less likely that she will do it again. The punishment may consist of isolation (sending or carrying the child to her room) or the withdrawal of privileges ("No TV tonight!"), or it may be verbal ("You're a bad girl!") or physical (spanking).

Physical punishment is still used in the overwhelming majority of homes: only 3 percent of American children make it through childhood without ever having received physical punishment from a parent (Straus, 1983). Is there a difference between parents who occasionally administer a spanking and parents who physically abuse their children? Researchers questioned two groups of parents about what methods of discipline they used with their children, ages 4 to 11. One group consisted of parents who had been reported for child abuse; the second was a control group of normal parents. Eighty percent of the child-abusing parents and 65 percent of the normal parents admitted to having used physical punishment within the previous five days. That's a surprisingly small difference. However, the child-abusing parents used all types of punishment, including isolation, more often than the normal parents. They also used more severe forms of physical punishment, such as striking the child in the face or with an object (Trickett and Kuczynski, 1986).

Even when mild forms of physical punishment are used, it boils down to a large person inflicting pain upon a small one. Is this fair? Oddly enough, children seem to think so. Researchers in Australia read some stories about misbehaving children and their fathers to a group of 6- and 8-year-olds, and then asked their subjects to evaluate the discipline techniques used by the fathers in the stories. The discipline techniques consisted of reasoning, physical punishment, withdrawal of love, and no punishment at all (permissiveness). The children expressed greater approval for reasoning and punishment than for the other two techniques, and punishment was rated just as highly as reasoning (Siegal and Barclay, 1985).

Of course, children don't necessarily know what's good for them. Punishment may be effective in the short run in getting a child to comply, but reasoning seems to produce better results in the long run because it's a more effective way of getting children to internalize their parents' standards. Moreover, punishment—especially when it's severe—has some unfortunate side effects. In the study of the child-abusing and normal parents, the abused children were found to be more aggressive and less compliant than the children who hadn't been abused (Trickett and Kuczynski, 1986).

Aggression

Researchers have observed many times that children who are subjected to harsh physical punishment are likely to be unusually aggressive. There are at least three separate reasons for this. First, when aggressive parents have aggressive children, we have to suspect that heredity may be involved—in fact, genetic factors have been shown to play a role in aggressiveness (Ghodsian-Carpey and Baker, 1987). Second, child-abusing parents tend to have very poor parenting skills. It's not just that they punish too often and too severely—they also fail to provide the positive things that children need from their parents, such as attention and approval.

The third reason is probably the most important one, because it applies not just to child-abusing parents but to all parents who use physical punishment in disciplining their children: physical punishment is likely to increase a child's aggressiveness. Children learn a good deal of their behavior from observing and imitating models, and a parent who is dishing out physical punishment is providing a very clear model of aggressive behavior. The parent is saying, in effect, "The best way to get people to do what you want is by hurting them."

When parents use physical punishment in an attempt to control their child's aggressiveness, a vicious circle of escalating violence may be set up, because physical punishment tends to produce the very behavior it is designed to stop. Most people realize that hitting a child for crying doesn't work, because crying is the child's natural reaction to being hurt—the child will cry more, not less. Similarly, hitting a child for *hitting* doesn't work, because aggression is a natural response to pain. If two white rats are put into a cage and given painful electric shocks, they will attack each other. A monkey whose tail is pinched will bite the experimenter or anything else that

The parent who resorts to harsh physical punishment is providing a clear model of aggressive behavior. Children treated in this manner are likely to be unusually aggressive.

happens to be handy. Of course, it is possible to suppress aggressive behavior (or any behavior) if the punishment is severe enough. But the aggression is likely to be inhibited only in the presence of the punishing adult and to get worse when that adult isn't around (Eron, 1987).

This doesn't mean that aggressiveness is "stored up," however. It used to be thought that people stored up aggression as though it were water in a tank, and that if you prevented it from coming out at one time or place, it would simply force its way out at another time or place. But there is no evidence for this theory. If anything, "letting out" aggression—for instance, by encouraging children to use aggressive language—makes it *more* likely that they will hit or push another child (Slaby, 1975).

Children's tendency to behave aggressively can also be increased (experimentally) by the use of reinforcement—by rewarding aggressive behavior with gifts or nods of approval. Some of the children in one study were given marbles when they punched a life-sized doll made of inflated plastic. Later, the researchers observed them while they played group games. The children who had received the marbles were significantly more aggressive with other children than the ones who had not been rewarded for punching the doll. The experimenters also found that rewarding children only when they punched the doll very hard made them even more aggressive with other children (Walters and Brown, 1963, 1964).

Studies like these have important implications. Some parents buy their sons punching bags or boxing gloves, in the hope that hitting a punching bag will serve as a harmless outlet for some of their child's aggressive impulses. But the evidence suggests that the opposite outcome is more probable—the child will become more aggressive, not less.

On the other hand, some parents refuse to buy their children war toys for fear that these toys will make their children more prone to violence. It is

Will letting a child play with guns turn him into a little killer?

unlikely that playing with toy guns and tanks will turn little boys into little killers—or even into little hitters. However, children clearly do become more aggressive in the presence of adults who have a permissive attitude toward aggression (Sutton-Smith, 1988). So perhaps it is better for parents to avoid buying guns for their children, rather than risk giving their children the impression that they approve of violence.

A child's aggression is usually directed against other children, rather than adults. The way these other children respond to the aggression has a powerful effect. If a child launches an attack on another child and the second child fights back, the aggressor is less likely to tackle that particular victim in the future. On the other hand, if the victim reacts by crying or running away, the aggressor feels that the attack has "succeeded" and is likely to attack that child (or other children) again. For this reason, the neighborhood bully is usually a strong, muscular child whose aggressive attacks on other children are often successful. Later, such children are more likely to become teenage delinquents than those without a history of successful aggression (Patterson, Littman, and Bricker, 1967; Glueck and Glueck, 1950).

Aggressiveness is definitely increased by seeing someone else behave aggressively. In Chapter 3 we mentioned an experiment in which children were shown a movie of an adult attacking a large "Bobo" doll (the kind that bounces back when it is knocked down). These children were far more likely to punch or kick the doll than children who had not seen that film (Bandura, 1965). Critics pointed out that the fact that the children behaved aggressively to a doll doesn't mean they would do the same to a person. This objection was met by a later study involving 4- and 5-year-old boys. Half of the children in this study saw a movie in which an adult was shown hitting and insulting a person dressed as a clown. Later, the children were put in a room with an adult dressed in the same clown costume. Some of the children who had seen the movie behaved quite aggressively toward the clown—one even hit the clown's arm hard enough to leave a bruise. None of the children who hadn't seen the movie behaved in this way (Hanratty, Liebert, Morris, and Fernandez, 1969).

Watching aggressive and violent TV shows appears to have similar effects. In one major long-term study, there were highly significant correlations between how much TV children watched at home and how aggressive they were with their nursery school classmates (Singer and Singer, 1981). In particular, watching action and adventure shows was associated with greater aggressiveness than watching "Sesame Street" and "Mr. Rogers." It is worth noting that the 3- and 4-year-olds involved in this study spent an average of 23 hours a week watching television. One child watched 72 hours a week!

DEALING WITH THE AGGRESSIVE CHILD. How should aggression be handled? Although physical punishment creates more problems than it solves, milder forms of punishment may be effective—for example, isolating a child for a short period. Isolation is a particularly sensible punishment, in fact, because there are indications that the attention paid to a child who speaks or acts aggressively may serve as a reinforcer for such behavior. Of course, we can't simply ignore aggressive behavior. What we *can* do, however, is to reinforce other kinds of behavior—behavior that is incompatible with aggres-

sion. When the teachers in a nursery school began to reinforce their pupils for sharing and for playing cooperatively, physical and verbal aggression decreased (Brown and Elliot, 1965).

An aggressive child is a problem to himself, to his family, and to society. A number of factors are involved in aggressiveness; thus, there are a number of ways that aggressiveness can be decreased. Improving a child's relationship with his parents—perhaps by coaching them in better parenting techniques—is the first. Second, since aggression often results from frustration, we should avoid putting children into situations where frustration is extreme or prolonged. Third, we should make sure they are not rewarded for being aggressive, and that any rewards that are given out (verbal or otherwise) reinforce the kinds of behavior we want to encourage. And fourth, we can try to provide them with models—in real life and in the entertainment media—who behave responsibly and considerately, rather than ones who behave cruelly or impulsively.

Self-Control

As children get older, they are expected to gain control over their own behavior—to refrain from behaving in ways our society deems inappropriate. This means, among other things, that they must learn to keep their emotions under control, at least in public. Adults who jump up and down and clap their hands when things go well, or who burst into tears or burst out in anger when they don't, are not likely to be successful in life. Uninhibited displays of emotions are expected to be confined to the home.

Nowadays, children must learn to control their emotions at an early age, because day-care centers and nursery schools are public places. According to a Scandinavian sociologist, modern societies put a lot of emphasis on self-control:

> People have learnt to control their feelings and exercise restraint in all kinds of situations. . . . Children seem to learn this control at a very early age. When still toddlers at the day-care center, they make their appearance in the public arena where it is just this ability for self-control which is considered to be a sign of adaptability.   (Dencik, 1989, pp. 165).

Although freer displays of emotion are permitted in the privacy of the home than in public, training in self-control begins at home. As children get older, they are expected to learn to master their distress and anger: a preschooler who is asked to wait for a snack until his mother finishes her telephone conversation, and then wails loudly the whole time she is on the phone, is not living up to expectations. At some point, most mothers stop being tolerant about this sort of thing and begin to demand that the child exercise more control over his emotions. Language is a very powerful tool for this training, because once children can talk they can be given "verbal feedback about the appropriateness of their emotions," and they can "think about ways to manage them" (Kopp, 1989, p. 349).

Some children fail to learn these lessons, either because their parents aren't good at teaching them or because they have unusually emotional temperaments. Their lack of emotional control is likely to create problems for them. Preschoolers who cry too often are generally unpopular with their peers (Kopp, 1989). A failure to control anger is far more serious in the long run. In a longitudinal study, researchers followed a group of children who were still having "temper tantrums" at the age of 10. These children did poorly in life: as adults, they had trouble getting and keeping jobs, they had high divorce rates, and they were not well liked even by their own children (Caspi, Elder, and Bem, 1987).

DELAY OF GRATIFICATION. Which would you rather have, a single jellybean right now or a whole bag of them tomorrow? A dollar today or ten dollars next year? Most adults would choose to wait and receive the larger reward; they can tolerate what is called **delay of gratification.** This is one of the things that young children are not good at and that we want them to acquire —the ability to withstand the temptation of immediate gratification for greater benefits in the long run.

A preschooler's ability to exert this kind of self-control is related to how well he or she will get along later in life. In two separate studies, researchers have tested 4-year-olds on their ability to delay gratification and to resist temptation, and then observed these same children again when they were in elementary or high school. The preschoolers who had shown the most self-control at age 4 developed into school-age children and adolescents who were more responsible, competent, socially adept, and better able to cope with frustration than their classmates (Funder, Block, and Block, 1983; Mischel, Shoda, and Rodriguez, 1989).

How can we help young children to develop self-control? A number of experiments on this question, involving children of various ages, have been carried out by social learning theorist Walter Mischel and his colleagues.

These experiments have shown that children are very much influenced by the choices they see other people make. A child who hears an older person say, "No, I don't want that piece of candy—I'll wait till tomorrow and get a whole bag of candy," becomes more likely to make that decision herself when faced with a similar choice (Mischel, 1974).

But it's not always necessary for children to see others model the desired behavior—in some situations verbal instructions are quite effective. Preschoolers can be helped to wait longer for gratification by the simple procedure of telling them to say to themselves, "It is good if I wait" (Toner and Smith, 1977).

Prosocial behavior is the opposite of aggressive behavior: aggression is intended to harm someone else, whereas prosocial behavior is intended to help. The more aggressive a child is, the less likely he or she is to behave in a prosocial manner (Eron, 1987).

Prosocial Behavior

Prosocial behavior appears very early in development. Toddlers of 1½ or 2 years take great delight in feeding bites of their cookie to their parents, and they will readily run errands and help with household chores. Expressions of concern for another person's distress also appear very early—perhaps even before the first birthday. By age 2, children may try to comfort the sufferer with toys, hugs, or words of sympathy (Radke-Yarrow, Zahn-Waxler, and Chapman, 1983).

Helpful and sympathetic behavior is frequently observed in preschool children. In a recent study of children in a university nursery school, 85 percent of the children attempted to help or comfort a crying classmate on at least one occasion during the 30 hours of observation. Nonetheless, because crying is so common in a preschool group, a crying child had only one chance in five of being comforted by a peer. The children who cried most often were the ones most likely to be ignored (Caplan and Hay, 1989).

One of the best ways to encourage prosocial behavior in young children is by setting a good example: they can learn desirable behavior from models who behave prosocially just as readily as they learn undesirable behavior from models who behave aggressively. Researchers have found that mothers who are helpful and sympathetic toward their children (and toward other people in the presence of their children) tend to have helpful and sympathetic children (Zahn-Waxler, Radke-Yarrow, and King, 1979). Of course, such similarities between mothers and their children could have genetic causes as well as environmental ones. However, a similar result has been observed when the caregiver was not related to the children being studied. A group of children were cared for by an adult who treated them in a helpful and considerate way, while a second group of children spent the same amount of time (a total of five hours) with an adult who ignored or criticized them. By the end of this period, the children with the kind caregiver were acting significantly more helpful and sympathetic than the children with the unkind caregiver (Yarrow, Scott, and Waxler, 1973).

Because prosocial behavior is so common in children of all ages, the role played by adult models is still unclear. Assuming that all children have both aggressive and prosocial impulses, then the model's role might only be to teach them when and how to display these behaviors.

Sex-Role Development

By the preschool years one can usually tell at a glance—and not just by clothes or hairstyle—whether a child is male or female. Let a group of young children into a roomful of toys and most of the girls will head for the kitchen corner, the dolls, or the dress-up stuff. Most of the boys will go for the tricycles, the toy trucks and fire engines, or the blocks. The girls are likely to seek out other girls to play with; the boys show a similar preference for members of their own sex. Ask a little boy what he wants to be when he grows up and he might say "a fireman" or "an astronaut." A little girl might reply "a ballet dancer" or "a mommy." This is true even of children whose mothers work in professions that were formerly dominated by men. A 4-year-old girl whose own mother was a physician insisted that only boys could become doctors—girls have to be nurses (Maccoby and Jacklin, 1974).

Cognitive Aspects of Sex-Role Development

These preschoolers know that they're girls, and they have acquired some sex-role knowledge about how girls and women are supposed to act.

Sex-role development can be loosely divided into a cognitive side and a behavioral side. The cognitive part begins very early, before the age of 2, when children begin to label people according to gender: girls and boys, men and women, mommies and daddies, his and hers. They also learn which of the two categories, male or female, they themselves fall into—they learn to say "I'm a girl" or "I'm a boy." The ability to classify themselves and other people according to gender is called **gender identity.** By the age of 2, most children know their own gender; by 2½ or 3 they can correctly make the distinction for others, including people they don't know (Thompson, 1975).

At the same time that children are learning how to distinguish between males and females, they are also picking up information about these two types of people; this is called **sex-role knowledge. Sex roles** are the attitudes, behaviors, and psychological characteristics a society expects from males and females: for example, in our society women are expected to be concerned about their appearance, to be warm and caring, and to be good at taking care of babies. Men are expected to be strong, competent, not too emotional, and good at taking care of cars. Sex-role knowledge consists of this sort of information. When sex roles are defined too rigidly, they become **sex stereotypes.** The little girl who thought that only men can be doctors and women have to be nurses had absorbed a sex stereotype, perhaps from watching TV or looking at picture books.

Although most young preschoolers can tell girls from boys and men from women, they are often unclear on the nature of the difference. They might believe that the distinction is based on clothing or hairstyle, and that a girl can become a boy simply by having a haircut. They may also be unaware that little girls become women and little boys turn into men—that boys can't become mommies, even if they want to. The understanding that gender depends on differences in genitals and is (under ordinary conditions) permanent has been labeled **sex constancy** by the followers of Piaget. Their idea is that children have to acquire the concept of the "conservation of sex"—the understanding that a person's sex stays the same, despite changes in clothing or hairstyles—just the way they come to understand that the volume of water stays the same even when it's poured into different containers. Thus, Piagetian theory predicts that children won't acquire the concept of sex constancy until the end of the preoperational period, around age 6 or 7.

But the limitations Piaget put on preoperational thought have been crumbling, one by one, and the achievement of sex constancy is no exception. Recent research shows evidence of sex constancy in children much younger than 6 or 7. One study involved preschoolers between the ages of 3 and 5. The preschoolers were shown full-length photos of naked toddlers, one plainly male and the other plainly female. Neither of these toddlers had much hair, so the genitals were the *only* indication of their sex. A preschooler would be shown one of the photos of the toddlers and the researcher would tell her, "This is Gaw. What does Gaw look like—a girl or a boy?" (Gaw was the name the researcher gave to the photo of the male toddler; the female toddler was called Kwan.) If the preschooler said, correctly, that Gaw was a boy, the researcher asked how she knew that. Then the researcher showed her another photo of Gaw, with long hair and a frilly blouse, and told the child that this was another picture of the same toddler, taken "one day when Gaw was playing silly dress-up games and got all dressed up in a girl's wig and a girl's blouse." The child was asked, "What does Gaw look like—a boy or a girl?" (Gaw looked like a girl in this picture.) After the child replied to this question, she was asked, "What is Gaw really—a boy or a girl?" Similar questions were asked about the photos of Kwan, the girl toddler, who was shown wearing a boy's shirt and holding a football (Bem, 1989, p. 654).

Overall, 40 percent of the preschoolers gave the right answer to the "What is Gaw really?" question, showing that these children (average age, 4¼) knew that someone's sex does not change just because they are wearing different clothes or hairstyles. But sex constancy was shown *only* by those children who knew the answer to the earlier questions, "Is Gaw a girl or a boy? How do you know?" Some of the children, especially the younger ones, had no idea that someone's "real" sex is defined by their genitals.

Come to think of it, how *would* children know that it's the genitals that matter? Their parents are constantly referring to various people as men or women, girls or boys, even though the genitals of the people in question are not on public display. The parents base their judgment on clues like clothing, hairstyle, or names, so how are the children supposed to figure out that these are not the crucial things? Obviously, they *can't* figure it out—they have to be told this information. Some parents mention it sooner, others later, so children learn it at various ages. Sandra Bem, the researcher who did the "Gaw" experiment, tells about her son Jeremy's experiences with a nursery school classmate who evidently came by this knowledge at a later age than Jeremy. One day Jeremy decided to put barrettes in his hair and to wear them to nursery school. The classmate—who no doubt came from a less liberated home than the Bems'—gave Jeremy a hard time about his new hairstyle:

> Several times that day, another little boy insisted that Jeremy must be a girl because "only girls wear barrettes." After repeatedly asserting that "wearing barrettes doesn't matter; being a boy means having a penis and testicles," Jeremy finally pulled down his pants as a way of making his point more convincingly. The boy was not impressed. He simply said, "Everybody has a penis; only girls wear barrettes." (Bem, 1989, p. 662)

Close-Up

Box 10-2
The Case of the Opposite-Sex Identical Twins

The parents were a young couple from a rural background, with only a grade-school education. Their children were identical twins, grown from a single fertilized egg. They were both born normal boys. But at the age of 7 months, one twin suffered a tragic accident in which his entire penis was destroyed.

Doctors explained to the parents that there was no satisfactory way of replacing a penis. They recommended raising the child as a girl, and said that reconstructive surgery could produce the outward appearance of female genitals (though, of course, there would be no ovaries or uterus). With hormone treatments, the child would develop breasts and all the other feminine characteristics that appear during puberty.

For several months the parents agonized over the decision. Finally, when the child was 17 months old, they decided to follow the doctors' advice. The child was given a girl's name. Surgery was performed a short time later. The little boy became a little girl.

The child was treated at the Johns Hopkins Hospital. Two psychologists there, John Money and Anke Ehrhardt, counseled the parents on how to handle a situation for which their own experiences had given them little preparation. Money and Ehrhardt continued to see the family from time to time, up until the children were 7 years old. Their published report quotes the comments the mother made to them on the progress of her new daughter.

For a first step, the mother said, "I started dressing her not in dresses but, you know, in little pink slacks and frilly blouses . . . and letting her hair grow." By the preschool period, her daughter preferred dresses to slacks and took pride in her long hair. "She just loves to have her hair set; she could sit under the dryer all day long to have her hair set" (Money and Ehrhardt, 1972, pp. 119–120).

At 4½, the mother reported, the girl liked to be neat and clean, whereas her brother preferred being dirty. "She seems to be daintier. Maybe it's because I encourage it. . . . I've never seen a little girl so neat and tidy as she can be when she wants to be" (p. 119).

It was also during the preschool period that the parents' "double standard," for what behavior is acceptable in a boy and not in a girl, became evident. "In the summer time, one time I caught him —he went out and he took a leak in my flower garden in the front yard, you know. He was quite happy with himself. And I just didn't say anything. I just couldn't. I started laughing and I told daddy about it." She was asked whether the girl ever did anything like that. She replied, "I've never had a problem with her. She did once when she was little, she took off her panties and threw them over the fence. And she didn't have no panties on. But I just, I gave her a little swat on the rear, and I told her that nice little girls didn't do that, and she should keep her pants on. . . . And she didn't take them off after that" (p. 120).

Sex-Typed Behavior

The other side of sex-role development has to do with behavior. **Sex-typed behavior** is behavior that our society considers appropriate for boys (but not girls), or appropriate for girls (but not boys). Wearing barrettes in one's hair is an example: it's all right for girls to do it, but not for boys. Our society is much more permissive about the kinds of behavior that are acceptable in girls: girls who act "tomboyish" do not get nearly as much teasing (from their peers) or disapproval (from adults) as boys who act like girls or "sissies."

Behavioral differences between girls and boys start to appear very early in development—before the age of 2. Although gender identity and sex-role knowledge also begin this early, the two kinds of development do not appear to depend on each other. In fact, researchers have found little or no relationship between how sex-typed a child's behavior is and how much the child knows about sex roles and gender (Serbin and Sprafkin, 1986). But this research involved preschoolers, and it's important to bear in mind that, by the time they are preschoolers, *all* children know whether they are girls or boys.

What are the origins of sex-typed behavior? They are numerous, and they

"One thing that amazes me," said this woman about her daughter, "is that she is so feminine." Nevertheless, there seemed to be certain aspects of her personality that Money and Ehrhardt describe as "tomboyish":

> The girl had many tomboyish traits, such as abundant physical energy, a high level of activity, stubbornness, and being often the dominant one in a girls' group. Her mother had tried to modify her tomboyishness: "Of course, I've tried to teach her not to be rough . . . she doesn't seem to be as rough as him . . . of course, I discouraged that. I teach her more to be polite and quiet." (p. 122)

Despite her tomboyish traits, this child had established a firm gender identity as female—she thought of herself as a girl. She was able to do this, according to Money and Ehrhardt, because her parents treated her consistently as a girl and because the change of sex was made before 18 months. After the age of 18 months it may be impossible to change children's gender identity, because they have already begun to think of themselves as a boy or as a girl.

The case of the baby boy who became a girl tells us two important things about sex-role development. First, social influences and learning are very important in the establishment of a gender identity: if people consistently treat you like a girl, you will probably become a girl. Second, there is a limit to how much social influences and learning can accomplish. Despite all the pressure on this child to act "ladylike," her boyishness sometimes peeked out around the edges.

On rare occasions, children will fail to develop a secure gender identity even when social influences and biological sex are all pointing in the same direction. A small number of little boys begin at an early age to express a wish that they had been born female. The writer Jan Morris, born James Morris, was such a child. Morris has described what it's like to feel that one has been assigned the wrong gender:

> I was three or perhaps four years old when I realized that I had been born into the wrong body, and should really be a girl. I remember the moment well, and it is the earliest memory of my life. (Morris, 1974, p. 3)

No one knows why some little boys reject their male identity and are drawn, at an early age, to female interests and behavior. These children like to dress up in women's clothing; they show no interest in playing with boys or with the things that most boys like. Their characteristics are not the result of their parents having "wanted a girl"; in fact, parents—especially fathers—generally show strong disapproval of this kind of behavior in their sons. One current theory is that some hormonal malfunction during prenatal development caused a female brain to form, instead of a male brain, but there is no proof of this. All we can do at present, according to a psychiatrist who works with such children, is to reassure the parents by making it clear that they are not responsible for their child's behavior, and to help them accept their child the way he is (Zuger, 1988).

begin at birth, from the moment the announcement is made, "It's a girl!" or "It's a boy!" The baby is given a girl's name or a boy's name, and is referred to as "her" or "him." Most children are kept in clothing and hairstyles that clearly indicate their gender, so everyone a child meets knows right away whether the child is a girl or a boy. If they *don't* know, it makes people feel uncomfortable, because they are unsure how to act toward a child until they know the child's gender. Once they know the child's gender, this knowledge affects their interpretation of everything the child does. In an experiment, some adults were shown a movie of a 9-month-old baby who was identified either as Dana, a girl, or David, a boy. The adults made different comments about the baby, depending on whether they thought they were seeing a girl or a boy. For instance, they tended to interpret a certain facial expression as fear if they thought they were seeing a girl, but as anger if they thought they were seeing a boy (Condry and Condry, 1976).

People act differently toward girls and boys. They tend to respond to and reinforce different kinds of behavior in girls and in boys. For example, the adults in charge of a play group for 1-year-olds paid attention to the boys when they acted in an assertive or demanding way (taking a toy away from another child or pulling at an adult's leg), or when they whined or cried. The adults tended to ignore girls when they behaved in these ways. On the other hand, girls got more attention when they made any attempt at verbal communication. At the beginning of the study, the rates of all these kinds of behavior were the same for the male and female toddlers. By the time they were 2 years old, however, the boys were acting demanding and assertive significantly more often than the girls, and they were also whining and crying more than the girls. The girls were talking significantly more than the boys (Fagot, Hagan, Leinbach, and Kronsberg, 1985).

The traditional explanation for sex-typed behavior is imitation: little boys imitate their fathers and little girls imitate their mothers. Although this is certainly true, it is not enough to account for the differences in boys' and girls' behavior. For one thing, much of children's sex-typed behavior is not based on their parents' behavior. Young boys play with cars and trucks, though they may see their mothers driving the family car more often than their fathers. They tend to play in all-male groups, though their fathers do not shun the company of women. Similarly, young girls are unlikely to have seen their mothers playing jacks or hopscotch (Maccoby and Jacklin, 1974). Moreover, boys reared in fatherless homes are not noticeably less masculine than boys reared in two-parent homes: the boys reared without fathers are slightly less sex-typed in the preschool period and slightly more sex-typed later on, but these differences are very small (Stevenson and Black, 1988).

GENDER DIFFERENCES. Even in homes like Jeremy's, where little boys are allowed to wear barrettes in their hair and encouraged to play with dolls, and where little girls wear jeans and Reeboks and are given toy trucks, boys and girls do not act the same. In fact, as one authority states, "Parents are

Doonesbury   **by G. B. Trudeau**

observed to treat their young girls and young boys similarly, yet the children show a great deal of sex-stereotyped knowledge and behavior" (Jacklin, 1989, p. 130). If you give a doll to a little girl, she is likely to dress it up or give it a bottle. Little boys often treat dolls quite differently, "treading on them or beating them like hammers against pieces of furniture" (Goshen-Gottstein, 1981, p. 1261).

Although adults may approve of and reinforce certain behaviors in girls and different behaviors in boys, the boys and girls themselves may react in different ways to adult approval and reinforcement. In another study of nursery school teachers and 2-year-old children, the girls were found to respond to reinforcements given out by other girls and by teachers of either sex—they responded by continuing to do whatever it was they were reinforced for. But the boys' behavior was quite unaffected by the approval or reinforcements given out by the teachers; they responded only to reinforcements given by other little boys (Fagot, 1985).

It is a universal fact of childhood that, from the preschool period through middle childhood, girls and boys prefer to play with children of their own sex and avoid (at least to some extent) children of the opposite sex. This tendency to seek out members of their own sex is quite apparent by the age of 3. It is not based on imitation of adults' behavior: adults segregate themselves by sex much less than children do. It is not based on how adults think children ought to behave: in fact, children are more likely to play in mixed-sex groups when they are under the direct influence of adults than when their play is unsupervised. Nor is it based on unfamiliarity with the opposite sex: the more contact preschoolers have had with members of the opposite sex, the less they want to play with them (Maccoby and Jacklin, 1987).

Eleanor Maccoby and Carol Jacklin, leading researchers in the field of sex-role development, believe that there are three reasons why children avoid those of the opposite sex. First is a gender difference in activity level and style of play. On the average, boys are only a little more active than girls, but their play tends to be a great deal more "rough-and-tumble" than girls' play (DiPietro, 1981). Boys' play is more physical and more intense. Preschool girls are, on the average, slightly more timid than preschool boys, and perhaps they tend to be put off by the males' boisterousness.

Second, boys and girls have different ways of interacting with their playmates. There is a tendency, starting in preschool and becoming more noticeable as children get older, for girls to try to influence the behavior of other children by making polite suggestions, and for boys to become increasingly less responsive to polite suggestions. Boys are more likely to use blunt demands and physical force (or the threat of physical force) to try to influence their playmates.

The third reason involves what happens if you put girls and boys together. Maccoby and Jacklin observed the interactions of unacquainted pairs of children, both age 2½. When the children were both girls and one girl told the other girl not to do something, the second girl stopped doing it. The same thing happened when the children were both boys. But with a mixed-sex pair of children, the boy didn't pay any attention to the girl—if she told him to stop doing something, he just kept on doing it. The girl, however, stopped what she was doing if the boy told her to. So in mixed-sex interactions, even at this very early age, girls tend to be dominated by boys. This is probably one of the reasons why girls start preferring same-sex playmates at an earlier age than boys do (Maccoby and Jacklin, 1987).

It is possible that all three of these motivations for sex segregation boil down to a single underlying factor: a gender difference in aggressiveness. The tendency for boys to be more aggressive than girls is the largest and most consistent gender difference in behavior, and is quite clear by the age of 2 or 2½. According to Maccoby and Jacklin, neither social reinforcement and punishment nor imitation of models can account for this difference. It is not restricted to our own culture or even to our own species: male chimpanzees, young or old, are more aggressive than female chimpanzees. Maccoby and Jacklin feel that the gender difference in aggressiveness is at least partly biological in origin, and that one of its sources is the male hormones (androgens) produced by the testes before birth and all through the lifespan (Maccoby and Jacklin, 1974, 1980).

GENDER SIMILARITIES. Many differences between boys and girls are detectable by the preschool period, but most of these differences are small (the difference in aggressiveness is the chief exception). Although it is fairly easy to find gender differences that are statistically significant, the differences between one girl and another girl, or between one boy and another boy, are far greater than the average difference between the sexes. Thus, even though boys are, on the average, more active than girls, an active girl is more often in motion than an inactive boy. There are timid boys and brave girls; there are boys who make polite suggestions to their friends, and girls who demand obedience from their playmates and threaten to hit them. Differences in group averages may be real, but we shouldn't allow them to blind us to the characteristics of the individual child.

Girls and boys are similar in many more ways than they are different. In the preschool period there are no important differences in cognitive development, for example, or in sociability, or in self-esteem (Maccoby and Jacklin, 1974).

Children today are growing up in a society where boys and girls are treated much more similarly than they used to be—where boys can wear barrettes in their hair, girls are given names like Taylor and Whitney, and children of both sexes wear the same clothes. Their role models are mothers who work as doctors and lawyers, and fathers who help with the housework and childcare. Will males and females become more alike? Yes, they probably will, but the differences are unlikely to disappear completely. As the case of the opposite-sex identical twins illustrates, sex-typed behavior isn't entirely a function of how a child is reared: nature plays a role in it, too.

Play and Imagination

The scene is a day-care center for preschool children aged 2½ to 5. Ryan and Kyle sit at the clay table side by side. Ryan is using his index finger to poke holes in a roundish lump of clay; Kyle is banging his into a "pancake." Carletta sits by herself at another table, stringing brightly colored wooden beads on a long shoelace. In the kitchen corner, Michelle and Rashida are pretending to make dinner for Jeannie and Caitlin. Jeannie, the ''baby,'' is indicating her impatience by waving her arms and whimpering. David is watching them with interest but making no attempt to join in their game. Eric and Casey, meanwhile, are galloping loudly through the large room, pretending to ride horses—or perhaps to *be* horses.

With minor variations, scenes like this can be found all over the world and all through history. We call such activities *play,* and we distinguish them from what we consider the important business of life, which we call *work.* But anyone who has observed the intensity and seriousness that young children devote to their play probably realizes that it is important business to a child.

One way of classifying children's play is according to how much interaction with other children is involved. Five categories of play can be distinguished in this way (Parten, 1932). Examples of these types of play can be found in the day-care center we just described.

THE AMOUNT OF INTERACTION WITH OTHER CHILDREN. The first type is called **solitary play.** Carletta provides the example. A frequent activity of infants and young toddlers, solitary play involves no interaction at all with other children. As preschoolers grow older, they are less and less likely to

Categories of Play

Cooperative pretend play: going for a ride in the car.

engage in solitary play when other children are present (McLoyd, Thomas, and Warren, 1984).

Onlooker behavior, shown by David, is the second type. The onlooker simply watches other children play, perhaps asking a question or making a comment occasionally. This is often the first stage of a young preschooler's interaction with other children.

Ryan and Kyle exemplify **parallel play.** Children often play side by side at the same activity, without seeming to take much notice of each other. Again, this is common in the early part of the preschool period.

Associative play is shown by Eric and Casey. In the slightly older preschooler, play becomes interactive to a certain extent. Two or more children will take part in the same activity, all doing basically the same thing, but there is still no attempt to organize the activity or to take turns.

Michelle, Rashida, Jeannie, and Caitlin are engaged in **cooperative play.** This type of play involves organized activity in which the individual children cooperate to achieve some sort of group goal—for instance, by taking different roles in an imaginative game.

As children mature they become more able and more eager to participate in the social forms of play, but solitary play does not ever disappear. Most people—children and adults—are capable of amusing themselves if a companion is not available. Onlooker behavior, too, persists into adulthood. When people attend football games or watch soap operas on TV, they are engaging in the type of play called onlooker behavior.

THE LEVEL OF COGNITIVE DEVELOPMENT. Piaget (1962) was very interested in children's play because of its connection with cognitive development. In Piagetian terms, the earliest kind of play is called *sensorimotor play.* This involves moving the body and, usually, manipulating things: a baby bats at a toy hung above her crib; a preschooler pounds on a lump of clay or strings wooden beads on a shoelace.

At around 12 months a new form of play appears: pretend play. In its earliest form it is very simple—a toddler may pretend to go to sleep or to drink out of an empty cup. Play becomes more sophisticated when children become capable of representational thought, at around 18 months. Now they can use one object to symbolize another: they may pretend to drink from a seashell or from a round block, or use a stick to represent a spoon or a sword. Soon they will begin to share such fantasies with their playmates (Howes, 1985).

By 18 months, children are also capable of deferred imitation. They can pretend to cook a meal or to drive a car, using memories of what they've seen adults do. Deferred imitation is particularly important in what Piaget called **sociodramatic play,** now more often referred to as **social** (or cooperative) **pretend play.** In this form of play, which first appears around the age of 2½, two or more children engage in mutual fantasy games such as "I'm the mommy, you're the baby," or "I'm the bus driver (vroom, vroom), where do you want to go?" (Howes, 1987).

An interesting aspect of social pretend play is the way the children involved in it talk to each other about what they're doing, slipping into and out of their assigned roles with remarkable ease. When a child says "I'll be the mommy, you be the baby," she is speaking as herself, but when she says "Eat your dinner, baby," she is speaking as the mommy—in fact, she is likely

Calvin and Hobbes   by Bill Watterson

to use a different voice when she's in the mommy role. Piaget was not impressed with the cognitive abilities of preschool children; yet, in their fantasy games, these children manage to keep track of two levels of reality at the same time.

Children are not always successful in persuading their playmates to accept their fantasies. Consider this exchange:

FIRST CHILD: I have to call the wedding man. Who is going to marry me?
SECOND CHILD: Nobody is going to marry you, you're just on a dance. (Göncü and Kessel, 1988, p. 334)

Both solitary and social forms of pretend play reach a peak around age 5 and then decline. School-age children are more likely to engage in a different kind of play with their friends: cooperative play involving games with rules (Fein, 1981).

The Functions of Play

An adult considers play to be, almost by definition, unproductive. But for a child, the time spent in play is extremely productive. When a kitten plays by pouncing on a leaf and shaking it, it's plain that she is rehearsing movements that later may be used on real prey. In humans, too, play enables the young to practice many of the skills they will need as they grow older. Social, cognitive, language, and motor skills all benefit from the practice that children get while they are having fun.

In play, children are able to experiment with the environment in ways that do not have serious consequences. It's trial and error with no penalty for error. In cooperative play, the child can learn about the nature of social interactions, about what is permitted and what is not. The rules for social behavior are far more lenient in a play situation. Preschool boys sometimes play quite roughly with each other, but it's accepted as fun rather than fighting if the participants are smiling or laughing. In the same way, older children and adults say "I'm only kidding," and get away with insults that would otherwise not be tolerated (Sutton-Smith, 1985).

Play also permits children to act out in fantasy what they cannot achieve in reality. A child may pretend to be an astronaut, a doctor, a king, or a queen. Many psychologists and educators believe that this kind of fantasy has a wish-fulfillment function. Although in reality young children are weak and powerless, in fantasy they can be Batman or She-Ra.

Finally, play gives children a way of dealing with their anxieties and fears. A mother described how her 4-year-old daughter Skye plays a game called "Stranger" with her younger brother Daniel. The game starts with Skye driving up to Daniel in a pedal-powered fire engine:

> "Get into my car, little boy," she hissed. "I have candy for you." Offering pebbles with one hand, she placed the other eloquently on his thigh. Daniel . . . recognized the game and squealed in mock horror, scattering the pebbles and running into the house. "You're bad! I'll tell my daddy and he'll call the policeman." (Compton, 1989, p. 30)

The rest of the game involves Skye's arrest (a teddy bear is the arresting officer), conviction, and execution (by Daniel, using a bubble pistol). Thus do Skye and Daniel rid their world of sex abusers.

FANTASY AND FEAR. Although fantasy is often used by children to make scary things seem less scary, sometimes it seems to have the opposite effect —contributing to fears instead of taming them. The fears of the infant and toddler usually concern real things: loud noises, the dark, being dropped, strangers. But by the age of 3, many of a child's fears are of imagined terrors. A 5-year-old is afraid, not so much of the dark itself, but of the imaginary monsters with which he populates it.

All children seem to have frightening fantasies of this sort, even those whose parents have tried hard to keep them away from scary TV shows and comic books. Such fears have sometimes been interpreted as having symbolic meaning. For instance, according to one theory, the witch in fantasies and fairy tales represents the angry, punishing aspect of the child's mother (Bettelheim, 1976).

The parent or caregiver is less concerned about what these fantasy fears represent than about how to handle them. Some experts suggest having the child draw a picture of whatever is frightening him, the idea being that once the imaginary monster is outside the child's mind and down on paper, it is less threatening (Kutner, 1988). But such methods are, at best, only partially successful. Time is the only sure cure for childhood fears: eventually, no matter how they're handled, most children simply outgrow them.

It is discouraging to think that we can't do much to help young children banish the imaginary creatures that haunt their closets and lie in wait for them under their beds. It might help, however, to realize that such fears may actually be of *benefit* to the child in the long run. Biologists have found that laboratory animals that are allowed to grow up peacefully in their cages do not develop as well as those that are subjected to some stress early in their lives. Baby rats that are made to experience fear (for example, by being handled occasionally) are better able to withstand stress when they are adults. As adults they are sturdier and less excitable than rats that had been left in peace in their infancy (Meaney, 1988).

We try very hard to protect children against anything that might frighten them. But the history of the human race suggests that we were designed for a pretty rough environment. Perhaps, in order to develop properly, the human brain requires the stimulation of a certain amount of fear. And perhaps, if the environment does not provide enough of it, children provide it for themselves with their imaginary monsters.

Lying

Not all of children's fantasies can be taken at face value: sometimes they cross the line between imagination and deceit. Lori, age 3½, used her new crayons to scribble on the bedroom wall. When her mother angrily confronted Lori with the evidence, the child denied having done it. "It wasn't me, Mommy," she said. "It was a ghost" (Ekman, 1989, p. 64).

According to Paul Ekman of the University of California, Lori wasn't confusing fantasy and reality: she was deliberately attempting to mislead her mother in order to avoid the punishment she sensed was coming. Although it was formerly believed that children of this age are not capable of telling deliberate lies, this view of preschool innocence is changing. Preschoolers do attempt to deceive—they're just not very good at it. Several more years of practice are required before they can lie convincingly (Hyman, 1989).

Most children know by the age of 4 that lying is bad. But they're still fuzzy on *why* it's bad. They are likely to think that the reason it's bad to lie is that you're bound to be found out and punished. "You should never tell a lie," said one 5-year-old, "because the brains inside grownups' heads are so smart they always find out" (Ekman, 1989, p. 65).

Preschoolers are also not clear on the difference between lying and making an honest mistake, or between lying and breaking a promise. A child whose father promises to bring home a new toy for her may accuse him of lying if he comes home empty-handed, even if he explains that the toy store was closed.

Are children less likely to lie as they get older, or does lying increase with age? This is another question on which opinion is changing. Older research seemed to indicate that the frequency of lying hits a peak around the age of 5 and then declines (Macfarlane, Allen, and Honzik, 1954). But it may be that children just become better and better at getting away with their deceptions.

Ekman feels that children should be educated about the importance of telling the truth as soon as they become capable of deception, around the age of 3 or 4. The parent should explain to the child why lying is harmful: not because the liar might be found out and punished, but because people need to be able to trust each other.

Imaginary Playmates

One of the nicer fantasies of the preschool period is the imaginary playmate. These persistent and occasionally annoying characters are quite common, especially among firstborn and only children. It has been estimated that from 15 to 30 percent of children engage in this kind of fantasy for at least some portion of their preschool years. Although the fantasy fades as the child grows older, many people of college age can still remember having an invisible playmate. Such people tend, on the average, to be higher in creativity than their classmates (Schaefer, 1969).

Although imaginary playmates are especially common among children who do not have siblings, there is no evidence that these children are shy or maladjusted. On the contrary: a child who has an imaginary companion is likely to be better than average in adjusting to nursery school and in cooperating with other children and adults. This is another example of how the rich fantasy life of children permits them to profit from a wider variety of experiences than their "real life" provides for them (Singer and Singer, 1981).

Making Friends

Three-year-olds tend to pick playmates who are similar to themselves in age and gender, and who like to play in similar ways.

The fact that a preschooler without playmates will sometimes invent an imaginary one shows how important it is for a child to have the companionship of other children. Getting along with one's peers is a skill that can't be acquired just through playful interactions with parents or siblings. Interactions with parents are almost too easy for a child: unlike agemates, parents generally tailor their play to the child's interests and abilities, and are unlikely to misinterpret her attempts at communication or to take offense if she monopolizes the toys. As for sibling interactions, they tend to be dominated by the older sibling (Eckerman and Didow, 1988).

Children show an interest in socializing with their peers even before they possess any skills for doing so. A 10-month-old might offer a toy to another baby, but she doesn't seem to be aware that the other baby must be looking at her in order for the gift to be accepted: she might offer the toy to the other baby's back. By the time she is 1½, the child will have gained enough social sophistication that she will either wait until the other child is paying attention to her or she will make some sound to attract his attention.

Between 1½ and 2, toddlers begin to interact with each other by engaging in parallel play. A pair of 1½-year-olds will show their awareness of each other by playing side by side with the same toys. This will lead, around the age of 2, to a kind of game based on imitation: one child hits the wall or runs across the room or licks the table, and then the other child does the same thing. Then the first child either repeats the action or does something else, in which case it becomes a game of Follow the Leader. Thus, even at an age when there is little verbal communication between children, a cooperative game is possible—and, though it tends to be brief, the players appear to enjoy it tremendously (Eckerman, Davis, and Didow, 1989).

At around the age of 2½, as toddlers are turning into preschoolers, they begin to participate in longer-lasting and more complex forms of social interaction with their agemates. This social development rests on a base of cognitive development, because now children can use language to communicate with each other, and they can think about more complicated combinations of actions and ideas (see Chapter 7). These cognitive achievements make social pretend play possible. The ability to communicate also enables the preschooler to play with a wider variety of playmates, so preschoolers have more friends than toddlers (Hartup, 1989; Howes, 1987).

When they are around 3, children first show their awareness of the characteristics of individual children in their nursery school or neighborhood play group: they will make comments such as "Steven likes to play train," or "Jacob hits," or "Angela cries too much." At this point, children begin to notice that they like some of their playmates better than others, and they start to differentiate between friends and nonfriends (Howes, 1987). They are likely to pick friends who are similar to themselves in age, gender, and preferred style of play.

Even in the preschool period, some children are consistently more popular with their peers than others. Friendly, physically attractive preschoolers who are good at cooperative play and who respond favorably to the words and actions of their playmates tend to be popular. Preschoolers who have not learned to control their temper and who argue a lot or act aggressively tend to be unpopular (Masters and Furman, 1981; Ladd, Price, and Hart, 1988).

Although preschoolers—like older children and adults—tend to avoid people who are disagreeable or aggressive, in life it is impossible to avoid all conflict. In fact, children have more conflicts with their friends than with their nonfriends, since they spend more time with them. But conflicts with friends tend to be resolved with less animosity and a greater degree of fairness, and after they are resolved the participants usually go on playing with each other (Hartup, 1989). Learning ways of resolving conflict—or, better still, of preventing it—is one of the essential social skills that children acquire through interactions with their peers. Children learn social skills from interactions with their parents, too, but parents don't provide the same kind of feedback: if a child takes a block from his mother when she is building a tower of blocks, she is unlikely to yell "Mine!" and knock him over (Eckerman and Didow, 1988).

We began this chapter with a section on preschoolers' relationships with their parents; we end it with a section on their relationships with their peers. This is an accurate reflection of the social development in the preschool period itself: the social world of 2½-year-olds revolves around their parents, but 5½-year-olds are entering a wider world, where they will have to meet stiffer standards and where friends and agemates will become increasingly important.

Summary

1. Preschoolers spend less time in close proximity to their mothers than toddlers do. There's less conversation and less physical contact between mother and child than there was in infancy and toddlerhood.

2. Autism is characterized by an almost complete withdrawal from human interactions. Infants who will later be diagnosed as **autistic** fail to make eye contact with their parents and fail to develop normal attachments. Other symptoms are language difficulties and an intense desire for sameness. Autism appears to be caused by some kind of brain abnormality.

3. Although preschoolers have some knowledge of what they should and shouldn't do, they sometimes misbehave.

Socialization consists not only of learning what kinds of behavior are acceptable or unacceptable in our society: the child must also learn to *act* according to those rules.

4. Baumrind distinguishes three major styles of childrearing: (1) **Authoritarian** parents expect their children to do what they're told without argument. (2) **Authoritative** parents believe in firm enforcement of rules but give reasons for the rules and listen to their children's objections; their children are encouraged to be independent. (3) **Permissive** parents behave in a kind, accepting way toward their children and demand very little. The children of authoritative parents have been found to be the most responsible, assertive, self-reliant, and friendly.

5. Although there is no evidence that children require *unconditional* acceptance or love, children whose parents like and accept them are better off than those whose parents constantly criticize or ignore them.

6. Parents' childrearing style may be, at least in part, a *reaction* to their child's characteristics. The transactional view is supported by research showing that an adult's behavior toward a child is influenced by how the child behaves.

7. Certain children may be unusually difficult to manage; if, in addition, the parents' childrearing methods are ineffective, this may set up a vicious circle in which the child's behavior gets worse and worse.

8. Physical punishment is still used in the overwhelming majority of American homes. Child-abusing parents use all kinds of punishment more often than nonabusive parents, and they use more severe forms of physical punishment.

9. Children who are subjected to harsh physical punishment are likely to be unusually aggressive. One reason for this is that a parent who uses physical punishment is providing a model of aggressive behavior.

10. There is no evidence that aggressiveness can be "stored up" or "let out" like water in a tank. Encouraging children to "let out" their aggression makes them more aggressive, not less.

11. In order to get along in our society, children must learn how to keep their emotions under control. Children who do not learn to manage their distress and anger early in life may be unpopular with their peers in childhood and have a variety of problems in adulthood.

12. Children also need to learn how to tolerate **delay of gratification.** Verbal instructions and modeling are both effective ways of teaching children to wait longer for gratification.

13. Prosocial behavior is behavior that is intended to help someone else; it appears very early in development. Preschoolers will often try to help or comfort a crying playmate. They are more likely to behave in a helpful and sympathetic way if their caregivers act that way to them.

14. Sex roles are the attitudes, behaviors, and psychological characteristics a society expects from males and females; when these are defined too rigidly, they become **sex stereotypes.**

15. The cognitive aspect of **sex-role development** begins before the age of 2, when children begin to classify people (including themselves) according to gender; this is called **gender identity.** Most children know their own gender by the age of 2 and can make the distinction for others by 2½ or 3.

16. Young preschoolers might not know that the distinction between males and females is based on differences in genitals. This is information that someone has to tell them, not something they can figure out on their own.

17. Sex-typed behavior is behavior our society considers appropriate for one sex but not for the other. Behavioral differences between girls and boys appear before the age of 2; these differences do not appear to depend on the acquisition of **sex-role knowledge,** although it might depend in part on the acquisition of gender identity.

18. People behave differently to girls and boys; they will interpret a child's behavior differently, depending on whether they think the child is a girl or a boy.

19. The case of the opposite-sex identical twins shows that a child who is born male can be successfully given a female gender identity if the child is treated consistently as a girl and if the change is made early enough. However, despite all the social pressure to act "ladylike," this child was a "tomboyish" girl.

20. Neither imitation of parental models nor parental reinforcement of different behaviors in boys and girls can account for all the gender differences among preschoolers. Even when parents treat their sons and daughters alike, girls and boys don't act the same.

21. Preschool and school-age girls and boys prefer to play with children of their own sex. Three factors involved in this sex segregation are: (1) the style of play differs—boys play more roughly than girls; (2) the style of interaction differs; and (3) boys tend to dominate girls.

22. The largest and most consistent gender difference is the difference in aggressiveness: males are more aggressive than females. This male aggressiveness, which is also found in other cultures and other species, is thought to be partly biological in origin.

23. Five categories of play, varying in the amount of social interaction they involve, are **solitary play, onlooker behavior, parallel play, associative play,** and **cooperative play.** As children mature they become more able and eager to participate in social forms of play.

24. The Piagetian categories of preschool play are sensorimotor play, pretend play, and **sociodramatic play** (now called **social pretend play**). Solitary pretend play appears at around 12 months of age, social pretend play at around 2½. Both forms of pretend play reach a peak around age 5 and then decline.

25. Play enables children to practice many of the skills they will need later on, to experiment with the environment in ways that do not have serious consequences, and to act out in fantasy what they cannot achieve in reality.

26. Playing out their fears in fantasy form may give children a way of dealing with them; on the other hand, fantasies often seem to contribute to their fears.

27. Preschool children are capable of telling deliberate lies—but they just aren't very good at it. Most children know by the age of 4 that lying is bad, but they're not clear on why it's bad.

28. From 15 to 30 percent of children invent imaginary playmates; they are most common among firstborn and only children. Children with imaginary playmates are better than average at getting along with other children and adults.

29. Babies show an interest in socializing with other babies even before they possess any skills for doing so. Between 1½ and 2, toddlers begin to interact with each other by engaging in parallel play. At around age 2, they begin to imitate each other. At around 2½, children begin to participate in longer-lasting and more complex forms of social interaction, based on language and other cognitive achievements.

30. Even in the preschool period, some children are consistently more popular with their peers than others. Popular children tend to be friendly, physically attractive, and good at cooperative play. Aggressive or argumentative preschoolers are likely to be unpopular.

31. Children have more conflicts with their friends than with their nonfriends, but conflicts with friends are likely to be resolved with less animosity and more fairness. Learning ways to resolve or avoid conflicts is one of the social skills that children can gain from interactions with their peers.

Key Terms

infantile autism
autistic
internalize
authoritarian
authoritative
permissive
delay of gratification
prosocial behavior

sex-role development
gender identity
sex roles
sex-role knowledge
sex stereotypes
sex constancy
sex-typed behavior
solitary play

onlooker behavior
parallel play
associative play
cooperative play
sociodramatic play
social pretend play

11

The School-Age Child

We call the years from 6 to 12 the years of **middle childhood.** They could also be called the years of primary school: typically, the years from 6 through 12 correspond to school grades first through seventh.

Although these are important years in a child's life, they are relatively calm ones. Behind us is the rapid physical growth of infancy and toddlerhood; the rapid physical growth of early adolescence is still to come. The dramatic acquisitions in motor development, cognitive development, and language development are also in the past. But some crucial changes occur during middle childhood. There is a gradual but sizable increase in the child's intellectual competence and in the ease with which he makes use of that superb piece of biological engineering, his brain. There is a similar increase in the fund of knowledge his brain holds. And there is a noteworthy change in his relationships with others. When children enter middle childhood, they are dependent on their parents and on other adults —not just for food and shelter, but also for emotional support and companionship. By the end of middle childhood, adults are no longer the central figures in their lives. Their social and emotional needs are filled

to a large extent (though, in most cases, not entirely) by their friends and agemates—their **peer group.**

Children enter middle childhood looking and acting much more similar to one another than they do when they leave it. Differences in size, shape, facial features, intellectual ability, talents, and inclinations are not as evident in the early school years as in the later ones. It is really in middle childhood, more than at any time since birth, that the child becomes a unique individual.

Physical Changes and Physical Skills

Erika is 9 years old; she's in the fourth grade. She is 49 inches (125 cm) tall and weighs 50 pounds (23 kg)—well below the means for her age in both height and weight. She's a full head shorter than the tallest girl in her class, Danielle. Because of her small size, Erika is less powerful and can't run as fast as the other children, and this places her at a considerable disadvantage in team sports, though she's pretty good in gymnastics. Her classmates, and even the teacher, tend to treat her like a second grader; this has led to a lowering of her self-esteem and a tendency to act younger than her years. It isn't easy being different, in any way, from other children. Danielle, the tall girl, gets teased because she's so large and pudgy (see Box 11–1), and because she is already starting to develop breasts.

Although Danielle is now considerably taller than Erika, they will eventually both be average-size adults, with only a couple of inches difference in height between them. The difference that is so evident now is due mainly to the fact that Danielle is maturing at a faster rate than most of her classmates, and Erika is maturing at a slower rate. Danielle will stop growing at an earlier age than the others, and Erika will keep growing for a longer time, and this will even up most of the difference. Meanwhile, since girls tend to mature more rapidly than boys, Danielle is already a bit taller than the tallest boy in her class.

Even small, slow-maturing 9-year-olds like Erika are noticeably different in size and shape from preschool children. School-age children are, in general, leaner—they have less fat and more muscle. Their proportions are more like those of an adult: their legs are longer, relative to their height, than those of younger children. The proportions of the head and face have also changed. The brain and skull do most of their growing in the first few years after conception; later, the lower part of the face fills out, so Erika no longer has the high forehead and proportionately big eyes that made her so appealing as a toddler and a preschooler. The pads of fat that used to round out her cheeks have also decreased; as a result, her nose now looks more prominent. Although school-age children are attractive people, they are no longer appealing in a babyish way. The final blow to Erika's baby cuteness came when her first set of front teeth fell out. The permanent teeth that replaced them seem much too big for her face, and her smile—which formerly revealed an even row of perfect baby teeth—now shows a pair of large incisors with serrated edges, uneven in size because one is still growing in. They

Problems in Development

Box 11-1
Childhood
Obesity

Fat Albert is a figure of fun to everyone but himself. Other children tease him and make jokes about him, and he has to laugh and pretend not to mind. He can't run as fast as they can, and his mother has to buy him special clothes designed for "husky" kids. If he is still fat as a teenager, girls won't want to go out with him. If he remains fat into adulthood, companies will be reluctant to hire him and insurance companies will be reluctant to insure him, because he will be at significantly greater risk for a variety of health problems. No, being fat is not much fun.

Despite all the emphasis on health and fitness, obesity has become increasingly common among American children. Between 1963 and 1980, moderate obesity increased by over 50 percent and severe obesity nearly doubled among 6- to 11-year-olds. About a quarter of school-age children are now somewhat overweight, and 12 percent are very overweight. Most of these pudgy children will become pudgy adults: about 40 percent of obese 7-year-olds, and close to 70 percent of obese 10- to 13-year-olds, will still be obese when they reach adulthood (Gortmaker and others, 1987; Epstein and Wing, 1987).

What causes obesity? Heredity plays an important role. A study of adopted children showed that how fat or thin they were as adults was related to the fatness or thinness of their biological parents, not to that of their adoptive parents (Stunkard, 1988). In biologically related families, a child has a 40 percent chance of becoming obese if one parent is obese and an 80 percent chance if both are (Rosenthal, 1990). There is evidence that babies destined to become obese are born with slower metabolisms than other babies: their bodies use up less energy, so they gain more weight even when

their caloric intake is the same. By the age of 2, they are already fatter than their agemates (Roberts and others, 1988).

But genetic factors can't account for the rapid increase in childhood obesity in the past 30 years —people's genes haven't changed. One thing that *has* changed, however, is how much TV children watch: the average child today watches 23 hours of TV a week, and the fat child watches more than the thin one. We are raising a generation of couch potatoes, who sit in front of a TV set instead of playing kickball or jump-rope. They must also be munching while they sit, because an increase in TV viewing alone isn't enough to account for the increase in childhood obesity—

will soon even up, but it will take a few more years for the sawtooth edges to wear off and for the teeth to stop looking too big for Erika's face.

School-age children always seem to be losing teeth. The first two (the bottom front teeth) usually fall out around age 6; the last of the 20 baby teeth (the canines, or "eye teeth") fall out around age 12. Middle childhood is the period that keeps the Tooth Fairy busy.

In the past, middle childhood was also the period that kept the doctor busy. So many diseases used to be prevalent at this age: measles, mumps, chicken pox, rubella, polio, rheumatic fever, scarlet fever, diphtheria, whooping cough, and chronic ear and mastoid infections. But today almost all of these diseases are curable, through the use of antibiotics, or preventable, through

some change in eating habits must be involved as well (Dietz, 1987).

Obesity runs in families; and yet environmental factors are clearly involved. We discussed similar findings in Chapter 2, and what we concluded there—and this conclusion applies equally well to obesity—is that the child inherits, not the trait or the disorder itself, but an increased vulnerability to it. Environmental conditions will determine whether or not the vulnerable child actually develops the disorder, and how severely he or she will be affected.

In the past few years, researchers have come to a much better understanding of obesity and have learned why it's so difficult for overweight children and adults to get thin. Many researchers now believe that everyone's body has a certain weight, a certain level of fatness, that it is programmed to maintain. Trying to change this level is fighting an uphill battle against nature. This preferred weight or level of fatness is called a **set point,** because it's like a setting on a thermostat: if a child has less fat on her body than her set-point level dictates, her appetite increases and she eats more; if her body fat goes above the set-point level, her appetite decreases and she eats less (Stunkard, 1988).

For children who are not obese, this mechanism serves to maintain an appropriate amount of body fat despite fluctuations in growth rate. But a child who has inherited a tendency to obesity may have a higher than normal set point. People who don't want to be as heavy as their set point dictates, and who diet to lose weight, run into the problem that their body tries very hard to counteract their efforts and to defend its set-point weight. The less they eat, the more efficient their body becomes at making use of the calories it gets: their metabolism goes down and energy expenditure decreases, so the dieter (especially the person who goes on repeated diets) may not lose weight even if she eats less than other people. The same thing happens to teenage boys who were never obese but who went through repeated cycles of weight loss in order to participate in high school wrestling matches. These boys have a slower metabolism—they burn up fewer calories—than other boys who hadn't undergone these cycles of lost and regained weight (Steen, Oppliger, and Brownell, 1988).

Because of all the problems that obesity causes —not just social problems, but also health problems such as high blood cholesterol, high blood pressure, diabetes, and bone and joint disorders —it's important for overweight children to thin down. To do this, they must become more active and they must cut down on their caloric intake, especially their intake of fatty foods. Although we said in Chapter 8 that a low-fat diet is inadvisable for normal preschoolers, this statement does not apply to overweight school-age children: cutting down on dietary fat is essential for such children, both to help them look better and to reduce the health risks associated with obesity. The most successful weight-loss programs for children are long-term group programs in which the participants are taught to modify their eating habits and to get more exercise, and are reinforced for making these changes by winning the approval of the group. Chances of success are higher if the child's parents—who may also be obese—participate in the program (Epstein and Wing, 1987).

If close to 70 percent of obese 10- to 13-year-olds become obese adults, this means that 30 percent do *not* remain obese. When scientists find out how these children differ from the others, perhaps obesity will become as curable as ear infections or as preventable as mumps.

inoculations. (An inoculation for chicken pox, the last of the childhood diseases to be vanquished, is currently being tested.) The danger now is that parents have stopped worrying about these diseases and sometimes neglect to bring their children to the pediatrician for inoculations or medical tests. One result is a recent upsurge in the number of measles cases. Measles can be serious or even fatal—it occasionally leads to a dangerous brain infection called encephalitis. Another disease that may be making a comeback is rheumatic heart disease, a life-threatening complication of strep throat (a sore throat caused by streptococcus bacteria). Strep throat must be diagnosed by a physician and treated with antibiotics in order to prevent the infection from spreading to the heart.

From the beginning to the end of middle childhood, baby teeth are falling out and permanent teeth are growing in.

Even though a few diseases we thought had been conquered reappear from time to time, children are healthier today than at any time in history. Now the most frequent threat to a child's life is from accidents, particularly car accidents. The most frequent threat to a child's health is the common cold. But school-age children don't get nearly as many colds as preschoolers (Parmelee, 1986).

Many preschoolers still wear diapers at night, but most school-age children can retain their urine till morning. For some, however, this achievement takes longer: bed-wetting occurs in 15 to 20 percent of 5-year-olds, 5 percent of 10-year-olds, and 2 percent of 12- to 14-year-olds. Psychological problems are no longer believed to be a major cause of bed-wetting: in a minority of children, physical abnormalities may be at fault, but most bed-wetters are simply having trouble learning to control the muscles involved in urination (just as others may have trouble learning to control the muscles involved in jumping rope or drawing circles). The most effective treatment involves the use of an alarm that wakes the child up if he begins to urinate during sleep (Walker, Milling, and Bonner, 1988).

Size, Strength, and Athletic Ability

Growth in middle childhood is relatively slow: less than 2½ inches (6.3 cm) and 8 pounds (3.6 kg) per year. In contrast, growth during the first year of life averaged 10 inches (25 cm) and 14 pounds (6.4 kg). During the growth spurt of early adolescence, a boy might add as much as 6 inches (15 cm) to his height in a year.

Because the gain in weight consists more of muscle than of fat, strength increases considerably during middle childhood. The average 10-year-old can throw a ball twice as far as the average 7-year-old (Keogh, 1973). Muscle development is also partly responsible for the disappearance of the bulging stomach that characterized the preschooler. The other reason for the school-age child's flatter contour is the fact that his larger trunk provides more room for the internal organs.

GENDER DIFFERENCES. Gender differences in height and weight at age 6 are negligible. The average 6-year-old boy is slightly taller and heavier than the average 6-year-old girl. But by the end of middle childhood, that will have changed. Girls begin their adolescent growth spurt a full two years earlier, on the average, than boys. Thus, at age 11 or 12, the average girl is taller and heavier than the average boy.

Despite girls' advantage in physical maturity (and, by the end of middle childhood, their advantage in size) they persistently lag behind boys in most measures of athletic ability and strength. Take running speed, for example. Between 6 and 11 years of age, running speed increases by approximately 1 foot (30 cm) per second each year; but all through this period, boys run about 1/3 foot per second faster than girls. After age 11 the difference becomes greater, because boys' performance continues to improve, whereas girls' levels off or even declines (Herkowitz, 1978).

Many other measures of physical ability follow a similar pattern. There is a slow but steady increase in grip strength, long jumps, and sit-ups during middle childhood; boys are a little ahead of girls all through this period. Then, in early adolescence, girls' performance levels off and boys' improves dramatically. By mid-adolescence, boys are so far ahead of girls in running, jumping, grip strength, and sit-ups that the average boy is likely to outdo all but the most athletic girls.

The biggest gender differences in athletic ability involve catching and throwing. In both skills, boys' performance is better than girls' all through childhood. The differences are not slight but sizable, and they increase with age. In catching there is no gender difference at age 5, but from that age on the difference becomes more and more noticeable. In throwing speed there is a difference even in the preschool period: 3-year-old boys can throw a ball significantly harder than 3-year-old girls, and the difference widens steadily. By age 12, fewer than one girl in a thousand can throw a ball as hard as the average boy (Thomas and French, 1985).

There are some exceptions to this pattern, however. Girls are slightly better than boys in certain skills, especially those requiring fine eye–hand coordination, balance, or flexibility. Girls are also better in hopping. They learn to hop earlier than boys do; in middle childhood the average girl can hop farther and faster than the average boy (Williams, 1983).

Why are boys better than girls in most measures of athletic ability? One obvious factor is the amount of practice they get in these activities: compared with girls, boys in our culture spend considerably more time throwing and catching balls, running, and jumping. From the preschool period on, boys spend more time in active outdoor play (Harper and Sanders, 1978). In addition, boys are more likely to compete with their friends than girls are—to pit themselves against each other in strength, speed, or agility (Stoneman, Brody, and MacKinnon, 1984). Perhaps the only outdoor activity that girls are likely to engage in more than boys is hopping, and this is one of the few large-muscle skills in which girls outdo boys.

A second factor is the physical difference between the sexes. Even in mid-

Boys do better at sports partly because they tend to be more competitive and more muscular, and partly because girls are often unwilling to compete with them.

dle childhood, boys are more muscular than girls. Boys' arms are longer and have larger muscles, and their shoulders are broader. These gender differences in muscularity and body structure increase greatly during early adolescence and are probably responsible for the sudden widening of the gender differences in strength and speed at that time. In middle childhood, however, the physical differences are not great enough to account for boys' superiority in athletic ability (Clark and Phillips, 1986).

A third possible source of the difference in ability is a somewhat puzzling one: in mixed-sex situations, girls seem to be unwilling to compete with boys. An informative study looked at 12-year-old girls and boys who were playing dodge ball, a game that involves (among other things) competition for the possession of the ball. Since the children in this study had played the game only in school, girls and boys had had equal experience with it. (However, the boys had probably had more practice with ball games in general.)

The researchers divided the children into four groups: high-skill and low-skill girls, and high-skill and low-skill boys. They found that although the boys were in general better at the game than the girls, the high-skill girls were noticeably better at it than the low-skill boys—that is, they were better at it when they were playing against other girls. But in mixed-sex games the boys always won—even when low-skill boys played against high-skill girls, and even though the girls were taller and heavier than the boys. These results were found in two different cultural groups: a group of middle-class African-American children in Chicago and a group of Hopi Indian children from a reservation in Arizona (Weisfeld, Weisfeld, and Callaghan, 1982).

Why did these highly skilled girls lose? Analysis of movie films of the games made the answer clear: most of the girls were much less competitive when they were playing against boys than when they were playing against other girls. The girls stood in an alert, ready-to-go posture when they were playing against other girls. Playing against boys, the Hopi girls tended to stand with their legs crossed, their arms folded. The black girls stopped paying attention to the game when boys were present—they talked to each other, teased the other players, or ate potato chips. Yet the girls in both groups were completely unaware of these striking changes in their behavior. In fact, the girls' explanation for why the boys always won was that the boys "cheated." But the boys hadn't cheated.

We should mention that similar results have been found in other age groups (especially adolescents) and in a variety of situations. Many—though not all—females seem to be unwilling to compete against males. They compete more vigorously against other females. And, in general, they are unaware of this tendency.

Cognitive Advances in the Transition to Middle Childhood

Between the ages of 5 and 7, some important advances occur in cognitive development. It is no coincidence that these advances take place at just about the age when children begin their formal education: over the generations, educators have found that this is a good age to begin schooling. Progress that has already occurred makes the 6-year-old ready for school; what he or she learns in school leads to further progress. In countries where not all children go to school, the schooled children are found to be more advanced in cognitive development than the unschooled ones (Greenfield, 1966). It's not simply that the schooled children are more verbal or better at arithmetic—they also do better on Piagetian tests such as the conservation of liquid volume.

The Period of Concrete Operations

In the Piagetian view, the preoperational period gives way to the **period of concrete operations** around the age of 7. The transition is gradual, rather than sudden. With regard to the concept of conservation, for instance, the child does not wake up one morning thinking, "Ah ha, now I see it! How could I have been so foolish?"

Instead, the changeover is less dramatic. A child who at 5 says with assurance that the tall skinny glass holds more juice than the short fat one, at 6 or 7 is no longer so sure. She looks back and forth from one glass to the other, perhaps because she is teetering between the equally strong pulls of appearance and reality (see Chapter 9). By age 8 this child has become certain again and reality has won: "They're just the same. All you did was pour the juice from one glass to the other."

LOOKS CAN BE DECEIVING. In Chapter 9 we discussed Piaget's claim that preschoolers lack the ability to decenter—to consider more than one aspect of a situation at the same time. However, as we showed in that chapter, preschoolers can decenter if the situation is a simple or familiar one. The ability to decenter is not something children either have or don't have. With increasing maturity the child gradually becomes better at thinking about two or more things at the same time; he can do this with greater ease and in a growing variety of contexts. He can notice that one glass *looks* as though it contains more juice, but at the same time he can consider other information he has about the situation.

The school-age child is also able to think about things that happened in the past or that might happen in the future, whereas preschoolers focus almost exclusively on the present. The preschooler sees the juice in the two glasses and compares them directly. The school-age child notes that "all you did is pour it," a reference to the past. He may also anticipate the future: "If you pour it back into the other glass it will be the same again." He is not as likely to be confused about the difference between appearance and reality because he can take into account both what he perceives and what he knows. Unlike preschoolers, most school-age children understand the difference between "looks bigger" and "really is bigger" (Flavell, 1985).

A group of third graders served as subjects in an experiment in which their understanding of this difference was put to an exceptionally severe test. The researchers began with a traditional Piagetian situation: they showed the children two identical glasses filled equally full of a colored liquid, and asked them what would happen if the contents of one of the glasses was poured into a much wider glass container. Almost all (90 percent) of the children predicted that the level of the liquid would be lower in the wider container.

Then the researchers played a dirty trick on these children: by means of a tube connected to a hidden container of extra liquid, they secretly added more liquid to the wider container while they were pouring in the contents of the glass, so that the wider container actually filled up to a higher level than the narrower one.

As you can imagine, many of these third graders looked quite surprised when the liquid level in the wide container ended up even higher than the level in the glass. While they sat there, gazing in perplexity at the containers of liquid, the researchers asked them a tough question: Is there the same amount of water in the two containers? A little more than half of the children said that there was now more liquid in the wider container than there was in the narrow glass (which, in fact, was true). The rest of the children—about 42 percent—insisted that the amount of liquid was still the same, despite all appearances to the contrary. Some even attempted to explain away the apparent contradiction by saying, in effect, that appearances can be deceiving: "It just looks like there's more in the big glass 'cause that's a special kind of glass that makes things look big" (Lindsay and Creedon, 1985, p. 346).

THE OTHER PERSON'S POINT OF VIEW. Another charge that Piaget laid against preschoolers was that they are egocentric and cannot consider something from another person's point of view—he used the three mountains experiment (see p. 291) to support his claim. But, as we showed in Chapter 9, the preschooler doesn't necessarily choose her *own* point of view in this situation: she chooses what she considers the *best* point of view—the view in which nothing overlaps. Preschoolers are also unable to draw pictures that show things overlapping. Children learn to do this around the time they enter first grade. First graders can, with some difficulty, draw scenes that show one object partially blocking their view of a second object (Radkey and Enns, 1987).

The ability to adopt another person's point of view depends on the complexity of the situation: preschoolers are capable of understanding what another person can see if the situation is simple enough. It is harder to figure out what the other person *knows,* so this ability takes longer to acquire. Four- and 5-year-olds are poor at judging how much knowledge other people have:

for example, they think that someone who sees only a little piece of a picture can tell that it's a picture of a giraffe, just because *they* know it's a giraffe (see p. 293). Judgments of this sort are difficult even for first graders. When 6-year-olds were asked to guess whether another person would know what kind of animal was depicted in a picture where only a little bit of the animal was showing, they weren't sure: only 56 percent of them got it right (they said the other person wouldn't know). But when 9-year-olds were asked the same question, almost all of them realized that the other person wouldn't be able to tell the identity of the animal from the little, uninformative piece that was visible (Olson and Astington, 1987).

During middle childhood, there is a gradual improvement in the ability to judge how much information other people have and how much they need to be given. A researcher tested some first and fourth graders (average ages 6½ and 9½) on their ability to communicate information to a friend. Each child was asked to imagine that she and the friend were playing in the kitchen of her house, and that she wanted the friend to get a particular toy from her bedroom. The job was to describe the toy to the friend so that the friend would know which toy to get. Both the first graders and fourth graders gave more information to an imaginary friend who had never been to their house before than to an imaginary friend who had played there often. But the fourth graders were much better at giving precise information about the toy—information that would enable a friend who had never been there before to pick it out from a bunch of other toys (Sonnenschein, 1988).

Advances in Knowledge and Understanding

During middle childhood, children acquire a great deal of knowledge and understanding about the world and what is in it. They also learn about what *isn't* in it—what is imaginary, or a product of their own minds. Piaget found that most preschoolers think that their dreams are "real"—that a dream is actually there in the room so anyone can see it. By age 7 or 8, most children realize that another person can't see their dreams, but they may still localize the dream as being "in the room." It isn't until they're 9 or 10, according to Piaget (1929), that they localize dreams "in the head."

ANIMISM. At what age do children come to understand the distinction between living things and nonliving things? Piaget claimed that preschoolers and younger school-age children are *animistic*. **Animism** is the belief that inanimate things such as a fire or a rolling ball are alive. The young children Piaget interviewed told him that a ball rolled down a hill because "it wanted to" or because "it knew you were there." They ascribed human feelings and motivations to objects, plants, and animals, and they believed that if something moves without anyone having moved it, it must be alive. According to Piaget (1926, 1929), children go on thinking this way until they are 7 or 8 years old.

Present-day American children appear to be considerably more knowledgeable than the Swiss children Piaget questioned in the 1920s: today, even 3- and 4-year-olds appear to have at least a partial understanding of the difference between living things and inanimate objects. A researcher showed children between the ages of 3 and 5 some videotapes of people, animals, and objects in motion—for example, a live rabbit, a wooden block that was

How do children decide whether something is or isn't alive? The most important criterion is whether it can move on its own.

moved by an invisible wire, and a plastic wind-up toy worm. After seeing each one, the children were asked, "Is it alive?" The 5-year-olds gave the correct answer to this question 98 percent of the time, and even the 3-year-olds were right almost 80 percent of the time (Bullock, 1985). In another study, a researcher asked children what various objects and animals have inside of them, and most 4- and 5-year-olds (as well as almost all 7- and 8-year-olds) knew that teddy bears contain things like feathers and polyester, whereas spiders and snakes have "liquidy stuff" and bones inside. One remarkably knowledgeable 5-year-old boy explained that "A snake has . . . lots of teeny bones, right? So it can wiggle. 'Cause if it was one long bone, it would just have to slide" (Gelman, 1989, p. 69).

Despite this impressive fund of biological knowledge, children are still confused at times about the question of what is alive and what isn't. But this question can be a difficult one for people of any age: even a physician might have trouble deciding, for example, whether a brain-dead person being maintained on a respirator is alive or dead. To take a simpler example, is a plant alive? Is a carrot in your refrigerator alive? Is it alive after you cut it up? After you cook it?

Researchers have found that most children under the age of 7 are not willing to say that plants are alive. And even for 8- to 11-year-olds, the most important criterion for deciding whether something is alive or not alive is whether it can move on its own (something plants do not do very well). However, as the researchers point out, this is not too surprising: "How many people have inferred that chipmunks are alive from observing them breathe, grow, or have babies? The way in which they dart across a forest trail seems much more persuasive evidence that they are living beings" (Richards and Siegler, 1986, p. 20). Similarly, if you find a little black thing in your breakfast cereal, the first thing you will probably want to know is: Is it moving?

AN UNDERSTANDING OF DEATH. Understanding the distinction between living things and inanimate objects does not necessarily mean that children understand the concept of death: a full understanding of this concept comes a little later than the understanding of the animate–inanimate distinction. Preschool children know something about death, but they are likely to think of it as a temporary state:

> These young children tend to see death as sleep (from which you wake up) or like a trip (from which you return). In addition, the fact that a large number of children mention medical intervention (e.g., going to a hospital, getting a shot) as a method for reversing death also suggests that some children see death as similar to being sick. (Speece and Brent, 1984, p. 1673)

Rebecca, age 5½, thought (or hoped) that burying a dead mouse would make it come to life again. All summer long she kept digging up the little corpse to see if her "cure" had worked. By the end of the summer there was not much left to dig up, and Rebecca finally had to accept the fact that the mouse was gone forever.

But understanding the concept of death requires more than an awareness of its permanence. It also involves the realization that dead people or animals do not think or have feelings, and that all living creatures eventually die. In the late preschool period or the early part of middle childhood, there is an interval of uncertainty about the implications of death. Children may realize that death means a cessation of breathing before they understand that thinking and feeling also cease. They may realize that all animals eventually die before they understand that this is also true of people. They are likely to accept the idea that other people will die before they accept the idea that their parents will, or that they themselves will.

A full understanding of all these aspects of death—that it is permanent, that it involves a cessation of all functions, and that it comes eventually to everyone—occurs at around the same time, around the age of 6 or 7. Since this is roughly the age Piaget gave for the transition from preoperational to operational thought, it is tempting to assume that there is a connection. But efforts to link an understanding of death to the level of cognitive development of the individual child have not been successful. What seems to matter more is the child's own experiences—his contact with the actual deaths of relatives or pets, and what his parents or other people have said to him on the topic (Speece and Brent, 1984).

UNDERSTANDING SICKNESS AND INJURY. Most young children have not had personal experience with death, and most parents don't bring up the topic unless there is a specific reason to do so. Thus, children's knowledge about death may lag behind their knowledge of other topics.

In contrast, most young children have had considerable experience with sickness and minor injuries, and their ideas on these topics seem to be pretty clear. In a recent study carried out in Australia, some 5-year-olds and 8-year-olds watched videotaped stories in which puppets were shown to be suffering from a cold or a toothache; the puppets gave various explanations of how they got these ailments. Afterward the children were asked questions such as "Can children get a toothache by playing with a friend who has a toothache?" and "Can children get a cold by being naughty?" Almost all the children (including 93 percent of the 5-year-olds) knew you could get a cold by playing with someone who has a cold, and most of the children (including

73 percent of the 5-year-olds) knew you couldn't get a cold by being naughty. But toothaches are no longer very common among children, and the 5-year-olds weren't at all sure about them: around half thought you could catch a toothache, and more than 60 percent thought you could get one by being naughty. The 8-year-olds, however, knew that toothaches are not contagious and are not caused by being bad. The importance of experience became clearer when the researcher did a second experiment in which, instead of toothaches, the children were asked about skinned knees. This time even the 5-year-olds got it right: they knew that you can't catch a skinned knee from a friend (Siegal, 1988).

THE CONCEPT OF TIME. Piaget used a pair of toy trains, running on two separate tracks, to test children's concept of time. He found that if he asked 4- or 5-year-olds "Which train traveled for the longer time?" they would judge simply by the stopping place: whichever train stopped farther down the track would be picked as the one that had traveled for the longer time. Children under the age of 7 or 8 would ignore the fact that the trains might have started at different times and traveled at different speeds (Piaget, 1969).

Other researchers have confirmed Piaget's finding that before the age of 7 children have difficulty in judging time durations according to when they began; they tend to notice only when they ended. For example, children were asked to say which of two "sleeping" dolls had been asleep longer. Up to the age of 7, the children picked the doll that was "woken up" later—they tended not to take into account the difference in the times the dolls were put to bed (Levin, 1982).

During middle childhood, children gradually improve in their ability to estimate durations of time—to judge, for example, which of two spans of time is longer (Levin, Wilkening, and Dembo, 1984). They also become better at locating themselves within the week and within the year. Most second graders can name the days of the week; most third graders can name the months of the year. At first they can tell you which day or month comes next only by running through the series from the beginning ("Sunday, Monday . . ." or "January, February . . ."). By fourth or fifth grade they can start from any point in time and tell you which day or month it will be three days or three months from now. But it is not until tenth grade that they can start from any day or month and count *backward* with reasonable accuracy (Friedman, 1986).

In middle-class homes, time is very important and people's lives tend to be dominated by the clock: the clock tells them when to get up, when to leave for school, when to eat dinner, and when to go to bed. When middle-class children begin school, they already know that the day is cut up into arbitrary pieces of time and that certain activities are performed at certain times of day. But children who grow up in poverty do not necessarily know these things. In homes where no one leaves for work at a regular time and no one tells them when to eat dinner or when to go to bed, children may fail to acquire an adequate understanding of time. When they begin school they may feel bewildered by the way the school day is divided into segments: instructions such as "Now it's time to put away our crayons and take out our workbooks" may make no sense to a child who has never been told that it's time to do anything. Some researchers feel that such children need to learn more about time before they can be expected to conform to the rigidly structured agenda of the school day (Taylor, 1989).

HUMOR. Four-year-old Matthew laughed when he heard the joke about the elephant sitting on the fence:

> What time is it when an elephant sits on your fence?
> Time to get a new fence.

But when he retold it to his mother, here's how it went:

> What time is it when a monkey sits on your house?
> Time to get a new monkey.
> (Buscell, 1987, p. B15)

For a preschooler, a joke consists mainly of silliness—elephants sitting on a fence are silly, and monkeys are even sillier. They don't *get* verbal humor, unless it involves funny sounds, rhyming words, or calling people or things by wrong names.

But school-age children can appreciate jokes like the elephant sitting on the fence; they enjoy verbal humor that turns on double meanings or on words that sound the same but mean different things. Consider the knock-knock joke, long a favorite among 6- to 8-year-olds:

> Knock, knock.
> Who's there?
> Banana.
> Banana who?
> Knock, knock.
> Who's there?
> Banana.

This goes on for as long as the joke teller has the patience to repeat it. Then:

> Knock, knock.
> Who's there?
> Orange.
> Orange who?
> Orange you glad that I didn't say banana?
> (Honig, 1988, p. 61)

Of course, toilet humor and jokes about sex are eternally popular among school-age children. Seven-year-old Naeesha whispered to her friends on the school playground, "Bobby and Tiara got married—again!" She waited until she had their full attention and then announced, "And they did the nasty!" Everyone giggled (Giegerich and Moslock, 1989, p. AA1).

The changes that occur in children's humor as they get older are closely related to their cognitive development. As they acquire new cognitive abilities, children can appreciate jokes that not long ago were over their heads, and these are usually the ones they like best (Masten, 1986). Thus, in the

Close-Up

Box 11-2 "Where Do Babies Come From?"

At the age of 3 years, 3 months, Piaget's daughter Jacqueline asked her father "her first question about birth." Referring to her sister Lucienne, she asked, "Daddy, where did you find the little baby in a cradle?" "My reply," said Piaget, "was simply that mummy and daddy had given her a little sister." He was describing something that occurred in 1928, the year that Lucienne was born.

Two years later Jacqueline still didn't know where babies came from, and her parents gave her a pair of guinea pigs "to help her discover the true solution." "Where do little guinea pigs come from?" she asked her father. Piaget continued to evade the question. "What do you think?" he asked. "From a factory," the child replied (Piaget, 1962, pp. 246–247).

Modern parents are unlikely to be as close-mouthed on the subject as parents were back in the early part of the century. Nonetheless, notions such as Jacqueline's—that babies are made in factories—are still to be found in preschoolers today. Piaget calls this kind of thinking **artificialism.** Young children's explanations of natural phenomena often contain artificialisms. For example, many preschoolers think that lakes and rivers were dug out by hand and supplied with water from hoses or watering cans, and perhaps even that the sun and the moon are products of human construction.

How sophisticated are modern children when it comes to knowledge about making babies? Researchers Ronald and Juliette Goldman interviewed 838 children from Australia, England, Sweden, and North America (the United States and

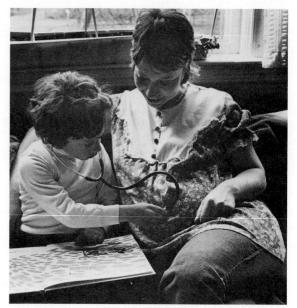

It is possible to advance a child's understanding of reproduction if the information is given in a suitable form.

Canada) to determine their views on this question. The children ranged in age from 5 to 15. The Goldmans found that, despite the fact that modern parents are considerably more informative than Piaget and his contemporaries, an understanding about conception and birth develops slowly. Moreover, it develops in much the way that Piaget would have predicted, starting with artificialisms and similar oversimplifications, and gradually becoming increasingly abstract.

To be specific, the 5- to 7-year-olds in the Gold-

school-age period they enjoy jokes that capitalize on their increasing skill in using (and playing with) language, or their growing storehouse of knowledge about the world—what they've learned about sex, for instance (see Box 11–2).

The popularity of toilet and sex jokes also reflects a general human tendency to use humor as a way of dealing with things that we are uncomfortable about. This was one of the functions that fantasy play served during the preschool period.

Just as older children laugh at more sophisticated jokes than younger children, more intelligent children laugh at more sophisticated forms of

mans' sample said things like this in answer to the question, ''How are babies made?'':

A 5-YEAR-OLD NORTH AMERICAN GIRL: I don't know, I never saw. Jesus makes them in a factory.
A 7-YEAR-OLD AUSTRALIAN BOY: The father does it. He buys the seed from the seed shop and puts it into the mummy.
A 7-YEAR-OLD ENGLISH BOY: By eating good food. She swallows it and it grows into a baby, if it's good food.   (Goldman and Goldman, 1982, p. 494)

In middle childhood, many children think that a miniature baby is present in the egg or, alternatively, in the sperm (see the medieval notion of preformationism, p. 79):

A 7-YEAR-OLD ENGLISH BOY: Sperm hits the egg and sets it off. The baby's in the egg.
AN 11-YEAR-OLD ENGLISH GIRL: By an egg of the man. It turns into a baby inside the mother's stomach.   (p. 495)

The explanations of 9- to 11-year-olds are generally a little more sophisticated than those of 5- to 7-year-olds. Most of the older children have figured out that both a mother and a father are essential, but they're still not sure exactly *why* they're essential. A third party—the doctor—is also thought to be very important.

A 9-YEAR-OLD NORTH AMERICAN BOY: When the lady likes a man they get an egg in their stomach, and then it goes into a baby. He has to be by her side to help her.
A 9-YEAR-OLD ENGLISH GIRL: The doctor gives an injection and that starts it to grow. . . . It's a kind of tube that grows and grows until it becomes a baby.
AN 11-YEAR-OLD NORTH AMERICAN BOY: The baby just grows from the food mother eats. Father warms her tummy in bed and it grows.   (p. 494)

Although nowadays most children hear the basic facts at least by middle childhood, they seldom understand them completely at this stage. It's generally not until early adolescence, at around age 12, that they get the idea of two things—an egg and a sperm—uniting to form one thing, the beginning of a baby.

A 13-YEAR-OLD ENGLISH GIRL: When the man and woman have sex, the sperm from his penis goes into the vagina and fertilizes the egg. It goes inside and joins it. It forms a cell which then goes into two, then four, then eight, and so on and forms a baby. (p. 495)

But it's a mistake to think that children's understanding of reproduction depends solely on their age or their level of cognitive development, and that giving them the information won't work until they're ready for it. Their understanding *can* be speeded up, if the information is given in a suitable form. The Goldmans found that, in middle childhood, the Swedish children were about two years ahead of the English-speaking children in their understanding of reproduction. Swedish children receive sex education in public school, starting at age 8. Their society tends to be frank and open on the subject of sex. (Only 5 percent of Swedish parents refused to give the Goldmans permission to interview their children. The refusal rate averaged 20 percent in the other countries.)

Piaget wouldn't have been surprised to hear that education can hasten understanding. His daughter Jacqueline didn't figure out until she was 5½ that baby guinea pigs come out of the mother's ''tummy.'' But Lucienne, Piaget's second daughter, achieved this level of understanding a full two years earlier. How did she figure it out at such an early age? She didn't: Jacqueline told her.

humor than less intelligent ones. In fact, children with high IQs tend to laugh more at any kind of joke than children with lower IQs. Regardless of their IQs, children with a good sense of humor tend to be more popular with their peers and are considered to be better students by their teachers. Finally, boys are more likely than girls to laugh out loud at a joke (Masten, 1986, 1989).

Joke-telling declines toward the end of middle childhood. Older school-age children still appreciate clever puns and ''absurdity riddles'' (How do you fit six elephants into a Volkswagen? Three in front and three in the back), but adolescents prefer spontaneous forms of humor such as anecdotes or witty comebacks (Honig, 1988; Yalisove, 1976).

School-age children appreciate verbal humor.

CAN WE SPEED UP COGNITIVE DEVELOPMENT? In 1967, Jean Piaget gave some lectures in the United States. In one of these lectures he raised what has become known as "the American question":

> If we accept the fact that there are stages of development, another question arises which I call "the American question," and I am asked it every time I come here. If there are stages that children reach at given norms of age, can we accelerate the stages? Do we have to go through each one of these stages, or can't we speed it up a bit?   (Quoted in Elkind, 1973, p. 172)

Although the studies that have been carried out to answer this question have yielded a variety of results, at least some of them have succeeded in teaching cognitive skills at an earlier age than they usually appear. For example, a group of 4-year-olds were given extensive training in the conservation of number (the number of candies stays the same, whether they're strung out in a long line or all bunched together) and length (if two sticks are the same length when they're right next to each other, they're still the same length when one is moved ahead of the other). The children not only learned these concepts—they also showed an advanced understanding of the conservation of liquid volume, which they *hadn't* been trained on (Field, 1981).

It's also possible to teach school-age children concepts that aren't ordinarily learned until early adolescence. According to Piaget, children can't deal with tasks such as the pendulum problem (see p. 100) until they reach the period of formal operations, at around age 12. Indeed, only a small fraction of 10- and 11-year-olds who were tested in one study were able to determine the length of time it takes for a pendulum to complete its swing. But the researchers took a second group of 10- and 11-year-olds and put them through an instructional procedure that trained them in the use of scientific methods. About 70 percent of these children were then able to solve the pendulum problem (Siegler, Liebert, and Liebert, 1973).

Piaget himself admitted that acceleration is possible, just as he had previously acknowledged that the speed of children's cognitive development will be affected by their intelligence and by their social and cultural environments. What can't be changed, according to Piagetian theory, is the *order* of the stages—they can be neither reversed nor skipped entirely.

Whether or not it's a good idea to speed up cognitive development is another question—one that is still unanswered. Many American psychologists seem to feel that "the sooner the better," but Piaget remained skeptical. He pointed out that human babies take nine months or more to develop the first four stages of object permanence, whereas kittens do it in three months.

Is this an advantage or isn't it? We can certainly see our answer in one sense. The kitten is not going to go much further. The child has taken longer, but he is capable of going further so it seems to me that the nine months were not for nothing. . . . It is probably possible to accelerate, but maximal acceleration is not desirable. There seems to be an optimal time. What this optimal time is will surely depend upon each individual and on the subject matter. We still need a great deal of research to know what the optimal time would be.   (Quoted in Elkind, 1973, p. 172)

The Growth of Metacognitive Skills

As children grow older they become more skilled in a wide variety of cognitive tasks, reflecting their growing competence at using their mental machinery in efficient and effective ways. A major reason for this growth in cognitive competence is the development of metacognitive skills. And one source of this development is the school-age child's increasing ability to use words and symbols to serve a variety of metacognitive functions. As we will see in Chapter 12, children who lag behind their agemates in this ability are likely to have trouble keeping up in school.

Verbal Mediation

In our discussion of private speech (Box 9–3), we suggested that some tasks are easier if you can "talk to yourself" about them. Harold Stevenson, a specialist in children's learning, believes that private speech (either spoken out loud or in the form of verbal thought) plays a central role in cognitive development:

When the child's experiences can be summarized or coded by means of words, learning can occur with greater rapidity, effectiveness, and generality. Words enable the child to form rules. They become a dominant factor in thinking. Concepts gain firmness and durability when they can be put in the form of words. Before the child can use words to govern his behavior, he must act in order to know. Later [around the age of 6 or 7], he may use words to short-circuit action; behavior may be guided by the application of rules, concepts, or other components of the inner world of thought. (Stevenson, 1972, p. 57)

Stevenson describes the following experiment. A number of geometric figures are drawn, each on a separate card. There's a small circle, a large circle, and a middle-sized circle; a small square, a large square, and a middle-sized square; and so on. One set of cards—let's say the squares—is placed in front of a child. He is told, "See these cards? One of these is a lucky card. If you point to the lucky card you will win a penny." The child points to a card and is told whether or not that was the "lucky" one. Then the three cards are rearranged (so that the correct card can't be chosen simply on the basis of position), and a new trial begins. Eventually the child learns that the middle-sized square is always the "lucky" one. Then these cards are put away and three new figures—triangles, perhaps—are introduced. Again the child is reinforced only for responding to the middle-sized figure.

This kind of problem—psychologists call it a **discrimination task**—is learned very slowly by 3-year-olds. But a 6-year-old learns it very rapidly. By the time the third or fourth set of figures is produced, he is choosing correctly on the first try. As he gathers up his pile of pennies, we ask him how he knew which card to pick. "Well," he replies, "it was always the middle-sized picture" (Stevenson, 1972, p. 56).

In all probability, explains Stevenson, the child started saying that to himself—"It's always the middle-sized picture"—during the experiment, and that was why he was soon able to choose the correct card on every trial. The words served as what are called **verbal mediators**—they directed the child's responses. A verbal mediator comes between a stimulus and a response: the stimulus sets off the verbal mediator and the verbal mediator controls the response. But children cannot use verbal mediators unless their vocabularies contain the appropriate word or phrase: children whose vocabularies lack the term "middle-sized" or "medium-sized" have great difficulty in solving the problem of the middle-size squares and triangles (Spiker, Gerjuoy, and Shepard, 1956).

Metacognitive Memory Strategies

Children who don't know a term for "intermediate in size" may be unable to solve the problem of the middle-size squares. But just *knowing* a term is not necessarily enough—what matters is whether the child *uses* it in an appropriate context. The evidence suggests that most school-age children do use verbal mediators when using them would be helpful. Most preschoolers, on the other hand, do not. The use of verbal mediators to learn or remember something is an example of a **metacognitive strategy** (see Box 9–1). School-age children tend to be way ahead of preschoolers in their use of such strategies.

REHEARSAL. Verbal mediators can be extremely helpful when it's necessary to remember something for a period of time. A well-known study of verbal mediation involved 5- and 8-year-olds who had to remember three or four common objects in a specific order. Each child was shown a set of pictures of various objects. A researcher pointed to three or four of the pictures, one at a time. Then the child's eyes were covered for 15 seconds and the pictures were rearranged. After the blindfold was removed, the child was supposed to point to the same pictures that the researcher had pointed to, in the same order. The easiest way for the children to remember the pictures would be to say the names of the objects to themselves, over and over again: "Flag, cup, wagon . . . flag, cup, wagon . . . flag, cup, wagon." This kind of verbal mediation is called *rehearsal.*

Because children usually move their lips when they talk to themselves, it's possible to tell whether or not they are using rehearsal. During the 15-second interval when the children's eyes were covered, the researchers watched their lips carefully, to see whether they were repeating to themselves the names of the objects they had to remember. Most of the 8-year-olds did do this, but only 10 percent of the 5-year-olds used rehearsal to help them remember the pictures (Flavell, Beach, and Chinsky, 1966).

Adults use rehearsal spontaneously in a variety of situations. For example, if you look up an unfamiliar phone number and then have to go into another room to use the phone, you will probably repeat the number to yourself several times on your way to make the call. If your rehearsal is interrupted—say, if someone asks you a question—you will probably forget the number and have to go back and look it up again.

Like adults, most school-age children above the age of 8 know that repeating something to themselves is a good way to keep from forgetting it. Most 5-year-olds either lack this bit of metacognitive knowledge or do not make use of it. Among 7-year-olds, some will use rehearsal and some will not, and the ones who use it do better on memory tasks such as remembering which pictures were pointed to (Keeney, Cannizzo, and Flavell, 1967).

Recently it has been discovered that one reason younger children do not tend to use rehearsal to remember pictures is that younger children are more

Rehearsing a phone number (repeating it over and over to yourself so you won't forget it) is a metacognitive memory strategy.

likely to use *visual* memory in such situations, whereas older children are more likely to remember things in the form of words. Researchers in England tested 5-year-olds and 11-year-olds on a picture-remembering task. They found that the 5-year-olds tended to confuse pictures that *looked* alike—for example, two long, thin things such as a pen and a tie. The 11-year-olds, on the other hand, tended to confuse things that *sounded* alike, such as "cap" and "cat" (Hitch, Woodin, and Baker, 1989).

In almost every memory task you can think of, older children remember more than younger children. The only exceptions to this rule involve tasks that are purely visual, where words spoken in the mind are of no help at all. Researchers tested children of various ages by showing them picture books containing 40 color photographs of common objects and animals. There were four pictures on each page, two on top and two on the bottom. The children were asked to name the object or animal shown in each picture, but this was simply to draw their attention to the picture. Afterward, they were tested by being shown a second copy of each picture and asked to indicate where on the page—top or bottom, left or right—the first copy of the picture had appeared. This proved to be a surprisingly easy task: many of the 3- and 4-year-olds were quite good at it, and the 5- and 6-year-olds did just as well as college students. From the age of 5 on, age made no difference in how accurately a child remembered—by means of *visual* memory—the locations of the pictures (Ellis, Katz, and Williams, 1987).

Thus, not all kinds of memory continue to improve as children get older. But performance on most memory tasks does improve, and this improvement appears to be closely related to the development of the ability to think in words: older children are much better than younger children at using words to help them remember.

CATEGORIZATION AND ELABORATION. Older children can use words even to help them remember the locations of things. Experimenters in Germany tested some 4- and 6-year-olds with a "game" where pictures of people (a policeman, a ballet dancer, a king, and so on) were hidden in little toy houses. The houses were all identical except that some of them were decorated with pictures of objects such as a police car, a crown, and a comb. Each child was asked to hide the people-pictures in the houses in such a way that it would be easy to find them again. When all the people-pictures were hidden, there was a short intermission (during which the child did something else) and then he was shown an identical set of people-pictures and asked to find the "twin" of each of them.

Compared to the 4-year-olds, the 6-year-olds did a better job of hiding the pictures and a better job of finding them. The older children generally hid the people-pictures in the houses with the appropriate object-picture (for instance, they hid the king in the house marked with the crown), whereas the younger ones did this only part of the time. And for the people-pictures that had no obviously matching object-picture, the 6-year-olds made up stories to help them remember which house they put that person in: for example, the ballet dancer went into the house marked with a comb, because "she needs to comb her hair very often" (Schneider and Sodian, 1988, p. 217).

This experiment illustrates two of the metacognitive memory strategies used by many school-age children but not by preschoolers: categorization and

TABLE 11–1
How Categorization Makes It Easier
to Remember a List of Things

UNCATEGORIZED LIST	CATEGORIZED LIST
oranges	apples
broom	oranges
eggs	bananas
detergent	
milk	milk
apples	eggs
sponge	cheese
bananas	broom
cheese	detergent
	sponge

elaboration. Categorization means grouping together words that go together, such as "king" and "crown." If you had to memorize a list of things—for example, a shopping list—it would be easier to remember all the items if you grouped them the way they are shown on the right side of Table 11–1 than if they were in the random order shown on the left side. The reason for this is that by grouping the words into categories you can use one item to remind you of the next one: "apples" reminds you of "oranges," the same way "crown" reminds you of "king."

Categorization does help: children who group words into categories remember more of them than children who don't use this strategy. Moreover, if you time children to see how long it takes them to come up with each item on the list, they will say "oranges" more quickly if they just said "apples" than if they just said "milk." But (except in carefully devised situations such as the people-pictures experiment), children seldom use categorization on their own before they are about 9 years old (Bjorklund, 1988).

The second strategy, **elaboration,** generally appears even later in development, and yet it was used by the 6-year-old in the people-pictures experiment who said that the ballet dancer "needs to comb her hair very often"—thus forging a link in his mind between "ballet dancer" and "comb." That experiment was purposely designed to encourage the children to link together two unrelated (or not very closely related) things in their memory, by creating a little story or mental picture that combines them. In ordinary learning situations where the task is to remember pairs of things (such as a French word and its English translation), even 8- to 10-year-olds seldom use elaboration to help them form the connection. The use of this strategy is still developing well into adolescence. What increases with age is not only the tendency to use it at all, but also the ability to use it well. The visual or verbal elaborations thought up by older children are likely to be more vivid and more memorable than those used by younger children (Siegler, 1986).

Why do younger school-age children so seldom use categorization and elaboration to help them learn, even though (as the people-picture experiment demonstrated) they are capable of doing so under certain conditions? It may be simply a matter of the amount of mental effort involved. A first or second grader can be trained to use these strategies, but she will use them less effectively than an older child and will tend to *stop* using them as soon as she's free to do so. Because any kind of mental activity is more difficult for a younger child than for an older one, giving her an additional task may just be too much of a load in terms of mental effort (Bjorklund and Harnishfeger, 1987).

Increases in Other Kinds of Metacognitive Understanding

Metacognitive knowledge consists of knowledge about how one's mind works—for example, what makes it easier to learn something and what makes it harder. Children's understanding of the various factors that enable them to pay attention to a task comes under this heading. Older school-age children are more likely than younger ones to realize that it's easier to pay attention to something if you're highly motivated, and harder to pay attention if there are distracting sights or noises (Miller and Weiss, 1982).

Children's ability to judge how accurately they are performing a cognitive task is another kind of metacognitive understanding that increases with age. For example, some children were shown a beaker containing about 30 beans and asked to "count" them—without taking the beans out of the beaker. Five-year-olds gave an answer and then confidently asserted that they were sure their judgments were correct. Seven- and 9-year-olds recognized that their judgments were unlikely to be exactly right (Saxe and Sicilian, 1981). The ability to monitor one's own accuracy is also relevant to taking tests in school: older children are better than younger children at judging how well they did on a multiple-choice exam (Pressley, Levin, Ghatala, and Ahmad, 1987).

METACOGNITIVE COMMUNICATION SKILLS. Knowing whether you're successfully communicating an idea to another person, or whether you're understanding what another person is saying to you, also falls into the realm of metacognition. The fact that the speech of young children sometimes conveys very little to their listeners has often been noted; so has the fact that the children themselves are usually unaware of their failure to communicate. The ability to transmit ideas in an understandable way gradually improves with age. Piaget (1926) believed that this is because older children are less egocentric—thus, they can take on the point of view of the listener.

But, as we explained in Chapter 9, there's more to it than that: young children are as poor at monitoring the quality of the communications they *receive* as they are at monitoring their own efforts at communication. John Flavell and his associates at Stanford University did an experiment in which kindergartners and second graders were asked to build a "house" out of different colored blocks, according to the tape-recorded instructions spoken by a 12-year-old named Kiersten. Kiersten's instructions were purposely ambiguous—for example, she would say something like "Then put the next block on top," with no indication of which of several different blocks she meant. But the kindergartners (5- and 6-year-olds) didn't realize that Kiersten's instructions were unclear: they would just arbitrarily pick a block and then state with assurance that their house was "exactly like Kiersten's" (Flavell, Speer, Green, and August, 1981).

One reason that these children assumed that Kiersten's instructions must be all right is that Kiersten was older than they were. Research has shown that 6-year-olds are unlikely to be critical of the communications of older people: they assume that the older person is wise and that therefore her communications must be okay. Another factor is that it's particularly hard for them to detect ambiguity in a message—it's much easier for them to notice out-and-out contradictions, such as "Put the blue block on top" when there *isn't* any blue block (Sonnenschein, 1986).

When children fail to notice that a communication is ambiguous, it's usually due to their tendency to confuse what the speaker *meant* with what the speaker actually *said.* If they think they know what the speaker meant, they are unlikely to notice that it didn't correspond exactly to what she said (Beal, 1987). Children begin to monitor the quality of the communications they receive around the age of 7: some 7-year-olds can do this, others cannot. In a recent study, a researcher tested a group of 7-year-olds and found that about half of them were "good monitors" and the other half were "poor monitors." The poor monitors didn't notice the ambiguities in the messages they got: they assumed they knew what the speaker meant, and then they assumed that that was what the speaker had actually *said.* In other words, they weren't listening closely to the speaker's words—they jumped to conclusions. As the researcher pointed out, this tendency puts these children at a disadvantage in school, where it's important to follow instructions precisely and to do what the teacher *says,* not what you *think* she says (Bonitatibus, 1988).

Information-Processing Views of Cognitive Development

In Chapter 3 we described a relatively new way of looking at cognitive development: the information-processing approach. Information-processing theorists see their views as a contrast to the traditional Piagetian view of cognitive development. They tend to interpret human cognitive activities as being, in certain ways, akin to what goes on inside a computer. The mind is depicted as a set of components that function more or less independently and that work by following a set of instructions, like a computer program. The various components send outputs to each other and receive inputs from each other or from the outside world.

Memory

Memory was the first aspect of human cognition to be given an information-processing interpretation. According to this interpretation, memory consists of hardware—the built-in structural components—and software—the programs for operating those components. Two main hardware components have been defined: **short-term memory** and **long-term memory.**

SHORT-TERM MEMORY. That telephone number that you look up and will forget if someone interrupts your rehearsal—it's in short-term memory. Short-term memory has a very limited storage capacity. An adult can generally hold six or seven items in short-term memory—the seven digits of a phone number, for instance. However, although the capacity is severely limited, the nature of the item is not. Adults can remember a list of six or seven letters of the alphabet, whether someone says them out loud or they appear briefly on a screen. Adults can also remember six or seven words, even though each word is composed of several letters. If the words form a meaningful sentence, more than seven are likely to be remembered—the sentence provides a structure for remembering the words, just as the words provide a structure for remembering the letters.

The number of items that can be held in short-term memory is called the **memory span.** Memory span increases during childhood, and this increase is not due solely to the use of metacognitive strategies such as rehearsal. A 3-year-old can hold about three items in short-term memory, a 6-year-old can hold four or five, and 8- to 12-year-olds can hold five or six (Case, Kurland, and Goldberg, 1982).

Why does memory span increase? There are probably several reasons, but a major one seems to be a gradual improvement in the speed and efficiency of information processing. The term **information processing** applies specifically to the very complex things that go on inside the brain when a person sees or hears a stimulus. The sensation produced by the stimulus can last only for a second or so after the stimulus is gone. Then it will ordinarily be lost forever unless it is "processed" and "stored." What this means is that when we see or hear a word, for example, we are unlikely to remember it unless we have first *encoded* it (see p. 103). **Encoding** means noticing a stimulus, taking it in. In the case of a letter or a word, it also involves identifying it—recognizing it for the particular letter or word it is. It is the encoded version of a word that is stored in short-term memory. And both the encoding and the storing are evidently done with increasingly greater efficiency as children get older. Less and less mental effort is required to perform these tasks, and thus more is left over for other things, such as metacognitive memory strategies (Case, 1985; Bjorklund, 1987).

Skill at information processing depends on practice with that specific kind of information. Children who are expert chess players have a larger memory span for the locations of chess pieces than adults who can play chess but are not good at it.

This improvement in processing information seems mainly to be a result of practice: older children have had more experience at it than younger ones, and as a result their information-processing systems are running smoothly and automatically. But the practice can be quite specific in nature—children can become "experts" at processing particular kinds of information. Ten-year-old children who are expert chess players actually have a larger memory span for the location of chess pieces than adults who know the game but aren't good at it (Chi, 1978). And poor students who know a lot about soccer remember more details from a story about a soccer player than good students who don't play soccer (Schneider, Körkel, and Weinert, 1989).

The increased efficiency in information processing during middle childhood may not result entirely from improvements in the software of the system. There may also be changes in hardware—physical changes in the brain. Myelination (see p. 176) is still going on, and other kinds of brain maturation may also be occurring (Case, Kurland, and Goldberg, 1982).

LONG-TERM MEMORY. Things stored in short-term memory are lost almost at once unless they are rehearsed. If we want to retain a bit of information for more than a few minutes, it must be put into long-term memory. Everything that is stored in long-term memory has first been in short-term memory. The reverse, however, is not true. That telephone number, for instance, will probably never enter long-term storage if it's an unimportant number—one that is used only on a single occasion. Most people have to make a special effort to commit a number to long-term storage.

On the other hand, our long-term memory undoubtedly contains more things than we can get out of it at any given time. Information-processing theorists speak of memory storage and memory **retrieval.** Storing a memory is like putting it in a file cabinet; retrieving it is like finding it in the file and getting it out. A memory that is stored is not necessarily one that can readily be retrieved. We often have trouble retrieving a memory that we know we possess—a person's name, for instance. "It's right on the tip of my tongue," we moan.

Though we might not be able to think of that name ourselves, we will instantly recognize it if someone else says it. Researchers use two different kinds of memory tests in studying long-term memory: **recall** tests and **recognition** tests. In recall, the subjects have to get the memory out of storage—for example, by remembering a name or a number. In recognition, all they have to do is decide whether a given name or number is or is not the correct one. It's much harder to answer the question, "What was that person's name?" than the question, "Was it Merrill?"

Recognition is a simple sort of memory. It is present even in very young babies, as shown by the preferential-looking technique described in Chapter 5. A baby who looks at a new picture in preference to one he's seen before shows us that he remembers—or, to be precise, recognizes—the familiar picture. Older children do better on recognition tests than younger ones. Researchers showed children of various ages some drawings of faces; later the children were asked to say which of two very similar drawings was among the ones they had seen earlier. There was no improvement during the preschool years, but first graders did considerably better than preschoolers, and college students did better than school-age children (Sophian and Stigler,

1981). These results may mean that recognition memory improves during childhood, but it is also possible that the change is due solely to an improvement in encoding efficiency: older children may be able to encode more details than younger ones.

Recognizing something requires only that the item be stored in memory; recalling it requires both storage and retrieval. Although it is not clear whether recognition memory gets better during childhood, there is no question about recall: recall memory improves steadily throughout childhood and adolescence. This improvement is due partly to the use of metacognitive strategies such as categorization and elaboration, and partly to better storage and better retrieval. The increase in retrieval skills appears to be a more important factor than the increase in storage skills. It seems that each time an item gets retrieved from memory it gets easier and easier to get it out (Brainerd, Howe, Kingma, and Brainerd, 1984; Bjorklund, 1987).

SCRIPTS. We have compared long-term memory to a file cabinet in which memories are stored and from which they are later retrieved. That makes it seem odd that older children and adolescents, who have more years' worth of memories to store, are better at retrieving things than younger children. With real file cabinets, the more stuff you have in them, the harder it is to find any particular item. One reason for the increase in retrieval efficiency as children get older is, as we've said, practice. But there may be another reason: a gradual improvement in memory *organization.* Memory researchers have come up with an interesting notion about how certain types of long-term memories may be organized: the concept of **scripts.**

A script is a way of organizing memories to take advantage of the fact that many of the things that happen to people happen over and over again. Take, for example, going to a fast-food restaurant. Each time you go to one, there are certain things that always occur: you go into the restaurant, get on line, arrive at the counter, place your order, pay your bill, get your food, take it away from the counter, and eat it.

Instead of remembering each trip to a restaurant separately and individually, these memories can be stored in the form of a "restaurant script." This would consist of a standard sequence of events like the one we just described, plus "slots" to be filled in with variable items such as the person who took your order, the people who accompanied you, what you ordered, and where you ate it. It might take several visits to a fast-food restaurant to build up the script, but after that, all you have to do for each new visit is to fill in the slots.

There is good evidence that children and adults do, in fact, remember routine sequences of events in the form of scripts. Even preschoolers can give clear and correct answers to questions like "What happens when you go to a restaurant?" Their reply to such questions consists of a sequence of typical events, arranged in the proper order (Nelson and Gruendel, 1981).

Since school-age children have had a wider variety of experiences than preschool children, they have a wider variety of scripts in memory storage. In addition, the scripts of older children appear to be richer in detail. Some preschoolers and school-age children were told a story that began, "Sarah and Billy decided to go out to eat." The children were later asked to recall the story. All the children recalled the events of the story in the proper order, but the school-age children were more likely than the preschoolers to add details that were not actually in the original story—details that came out of the restaurant script in their memory. For example, the original story contained no mention of what Sarah and Billy ate, but one first grader reported, "Sarah had a hamburger" (Slackman and Nelson, 1984, p. 337).

Selective Attention

There's a close link between memory and attention: we are most likely to remember things that we pay attention to. The ability to focus attention on something—**selective attention**—is yet another cognitive skill that increases during childhood. Selective attention can be thought of as a sort of spotlight that lights up one particular thing and leaves everything else in the dark. Older children are better than younger ones at deciding what they want their spotlight to shine on and better at keeping it fixed on that spot (Enns and Girgus, 1985).

Studies of selective attention show that younger children are less able than older ones to ignore irrelevant stimuli and to concentrate on what's important. This is true in a variety of situations. For example, second graders have more trouble than sixth graders in concentrating on a task while music is playing (Higgins and Turnure, 1984). When the task is to sort a pack of cards into two piles depending on whether the square in the middle of each card is large or small, first graders are slowed down more than fifth graders by the presence of other geometric figures printed on the cards (Lorch and Horn, 1986). And when the task is to memorize one of three words printed on a card (whichever one the researcher calls out), school-age children are bothered more than college students when one of the words—not necessarily the one they are supposed to remember—is printed in red (Ackerman, 1987).

Problem Solving

The 5-year-old looks at two containers of water—one narrow and filled to the top, and one wide and filled only half as high—and says that the narrow container holds more water. Piaget's explanation was that the 5-year-old centers on only one dimension, the height of the water. Older children, he said, answer correctly because they can decenter—they can consider more than one dimension at a time.

Information-processing theorists, such as Robert Siegler of Carnegie–Mellon University, describe this scene somewhat differently. According to Siegler, the 5-year-old has failed to *encode* the width of the containers and has encoded only their height. The width simply hasn't registered, so naturally the child can't take it into account when deciding which container holds more water.

How does Siegler's view differ from Piaget's? What's the difference between "centering" on one dimension and "failing to encode" the other? The main difference is that Piaget proposed an inability to decenter as a general characteristic of all children under the age of about 7, whereas Siegler allows children to differ widely in how much they will encode, depending on their individual characteristics and on their familiarity with the situation. As Siegler points out, young children are capable of keeping track of several dimensions at once in situations that are very familiar to them. In speaking, for example, they routinely take into account pronunciation, grammar, the meaning they wish to convey, and how loudly they must talk in order to be heard, all at the same time (Siegler, 1986).

When Siegler uses the term *encoding,* he is also talking about selective attention. *Encoding* refers to what gets taken in, whereas the term *selective attention* puts more emphasis on what gets left out or ignored (irrelevant things are ignored). As children get older, they become increasingly skillful at determining what is and isn't relevant, and at encoding the important things and ignoring the unimportant ones. Their ability to encode relevant aspects of a situation plays an important role in their ability to solve problems: older children (and more intelligent children) may spend more time encoding a word problem on a math exam, but then they are able to solve the problem more quickly and accurately than those who spent less time on encoding (Siegler, 1989).

According to Siegler, older children are also able to use more efficient problem-solving strategies than younger children. Siegler believes that children solve problems by means of strategies or rules, which are comparable to computer programs. For example, in solving an addition problem such as 3 + 2, a first grader must choose between two strategies: she can retrieve the answer from her memory, or she can use what Siegler calls a "backup strategy." In reading, the backup strategy would consist of sounding out a word letter by letter; in the case of the addition problem, the backup strategy would be counting: "three, four, five." The backup strategy is slower but, in cases where the child isn't sure of the answer, it's more likely to produce the correct result. So the child relies on retrieval (memory) for the easy problems and answers them quickly; for the harder problems she falls back on counting. As she gets more certain of the answers she retrieves from her memory, she comes to rely more and more on the quicker retrieval strategy.

Siegler (1989) sees cognitive development as a kind of competition, similar to the competition between species that leads to evolution. Different ways of encoding the features of the environment are competing for the child's attention, and the most successful forms of encoding win out in the long run. More efficient rules and strategies eventually take the place of less efficient ones. The result of this competition, just as in Piaget's theory, is the child's adaptation to the environment.

Siegler uses the word *competition* to refer to what goes on inside an individual child during cognitive development. But the word is used more often to describe what goes on *between* children, in settings such as the school. In this chapter our emphasis has been on the "typical" or "average" school-age child, and on those aspects of development that are common to all children during this period. But in the next chapter we will look at what happens in school, where competition between children is a fact of life and where individual differences between one child and another are crucial.

Summary

1. Middle childhood (ages 6 to 12 years) is an important period in the child's life. Although physical growth is relatively slow, there are striking changes in intellectual competence and in relationships with others. Individual differences (in appearance, intellectual abilities, talents and inclinations, and so on) show up clearly during this period.

2. School-age children differ from one another in their rate of physical maturation. A child who is smaller than her agemates may just be maturing at a slower rate and may eventually catch up with them.

3. School-age children are taller and more muscular than preschoolers. The proportions of face and body are closer to those of adults. Middle childhood is the period when baby teeth fall out and permanent teeth appear. Most of the diseases that used to threaten the lives of school-age children are now preventable or curable; accidents are now the major threat to life.

4. Obesity runs in families; babies destined to become obese gain weight even if they eat no more than other babies. Environment also plays a role, as shown by the fact that obesity has become increasingly common among American children. Many researchers believe that the body has a **set-point weight** it is programmed to maintain. When a person goes on repeated diets, his body cuts down on energy expenditure in an effort to defend its set-point weight.

5. Although girls are physically more mature than boys, boys surpass them in most measures of athletic ability and strength. Two reasons for the gender difference in athletic ability are the physical differences between the sexes and the difference in the amount of practice they get (boys spend more time in active, competitive play). In addition, many girls seem to be unwilling to compete with boys—their performance is poorer when boys are present. The girls are unaware of this tendency.

6. Important advances in cognitive development that occur between the ages of 5 and 7 make children ready for first grade; what they learn in school leads to further cognitive development.

7. According to Piaget, the preoperational period gives way to the **period of concrete operations** around the age of 7; he claimed that younger children lack the ability to decenter. But the ability to decenter is not something children either have or don't have: with increasing maturity they gradually get better at thinking about two or more things at the same time.

8. The preschooler focuses on the present, but the school-age child is able to think about the past and the future. School-age children are less likely to be confused about the difference between appearance and reality because they know that appearances can be deceiving.

9. The ability to adopt another person's point of view depends on the complexity of the situation. Unlike preschoolers, school-age children realize that other people don't always know everything that *they* know. During middle childhood there is a gradual increase in the ability to judge how much information other people have and how much they need to be given.

10. Piaget claimed that children under the age of 7 or 8 are **animistic,** but today even 3- and 4-year-olds have at least a partial understanding of the difference between living things and inanimate objects. Although young children don't think wind-up toys are alive, their most important criterion for deciding whether something is alive is whether it moves on its own. Thus, children under the age of 7 don't think plants are alive.

11. An understanding of the concept of death develops gradually; most children achieve a full understanding around age 6 or 7. The timing appears to depend on what children have heard and experienced, and not on their level of cognitive development.

12. Children's understanding of sickness and injury develops earlier than their understanding of death, because they have had more experience with sickness and injury.

13. During middle childhood there is a gradual improvement in children's ability to estimate the duration of a period of time; they also get better at locating themselves within the week and within the year. Children who grow up in poverty may not be aware, when they enter school, that the day is cut up into arbitrary pieces of time and that certain activities are performed at certain times of the day.

14. For a preschooler, a joke consists mainly of silliness, but school-age children appreciate verbal humor. As children acquire new cognitive abilities and new knowledge, they can appreciate jokes that previously went over their heads, and these are the jokes they like the best. The popularity of toilet and sex jokes also reflects the tendency to laugh about things we feel uncomfortable about.

15. Preschool children may say that babies are made in factories; older children know that a mother and a father are essential, but they're not exactly sure why. Although American children seldom have a complete understanding of reproduction until they're around 12, it is possible to accelerate this understanding if the information is given in a suitable form.

16. With special training, children as young as 4 can acquire conservation concepts and school-age children can be taught to use some of the techniques of formal operational thought. Piaget admitted that it's possible to accelerate cognitive development; he was not convinced, however, that it's a good idea.

17. During middle childhood, there is a steady increase in the ability to use words and symbols for metacognitive functions. Being able to verbalize a concept such as "middle-sized" will determine whether or not a child can make a discrimination based on this concept. Words serve as **verbal mediators:** the stimulus sets off the verbal mediator, which then directs the child's response.

18. The use of verbal mediators to learn or remember something is a **metacognitive strategy.** Preschoolers tend not to use verbal mediators, even when they know the words that would help them to solve a problem or perform a memory task. They tend to remember things visually, rather than in words. Visual memory is the only kind of memory that doesn't improve during middle childhood.

19. Three metacognitive memory stretches are rehearsal, categorization, and **elaboration;** they appear during development in that order. Children who use these strategies do better on memory tests than those who don't use them.

20. Younger children are not only worse than older ones at knowing when they've failed to communicate something to another person—they're also poor at knowing when another person has failed to communicate something to *them.* Young school-age children have trouble detecting ambiguities in a message because they tend to confuse what the speaker *meant* with what she actually *said.*

21. Information-processing theorists interpret human cognitive activities as being akin to what goes on inside a computer. The mind is depicted as a set of components that function more or less independently and that work by following a set of instructions, like a computer program.

22. Short-term memory can hold only a few items at a time, and only for as long as they are rehearsed. The **memory span** (the number of items that can be held in short-term memory) increases gradually from about three items at age 3 to six or seven items in adulthood. This increase is primarily due to an increase in the speed and efficiency of information processing. As children get older they become more efficient at **encoding** and storing information, largely due to practice.

23. Items in **long-term memory** have always been in short-term memory first, but not all items in short-term memory enter long-term storage. **Recall** memory depends on **memory retrieval** as well as on memory storage; **recognition** is easier because it does not require retrieval. Recognition memory improves during development, but there is much more improvement in recall memory.

24. Some kinds of memories appear to be organized in the form of **scripts**—standard sequences of events (such as what happens when you go to a restaurant) with "slots" to be filled in with variable items.

25. Selective attention—the ability to focus attention on a specific thing—improves during middle childhood. Older children are less distracted by irrelevant stimuli than younger children.

26. According to Siegler, as children get older they get better at encoding relevant aspects of a situation and ignoring irrelevant ones. They also develop more efficient strategies for solving problems. Siegler sees cognitive development as a kind of competition, in which different ways of encoding the environment are competing for the child's attention, and more successful rules or strategies eventually win out over less successful ones.

Key Terms

middle childhood
peer group
set-point weight
period of concrete operations
animism
artificialism
discrimination task

verbal mediator
metacognitive strategy
elaboration
short-term memory
long-term memory
memory span
information processing

encoding
memory retrieval
recall
recognition
scripts
selective attention

The Child in School

I t's a sunny morning early in September, in a small town or a big city somewhere in North America. Children are waking up early, with a touch of butterflies in the stomach. This is the big day: the day school starts! For weeks they have been anticipating this day—some with eagerness, some with dread, most with a mixture of the two. They've been told by older children that first grade (or whatever grade they're going into) is "really hard." Perhaps they've also been told that the teacher is "mean" or "dumb" or "weird."

The children dress and comb their hair with greater care than usual. They assemble pencils, pens, rulers, and notebooks. There are tears and smiles, skimpy breakfasts and extra trips to the bathroom. All too soon it's time to go. The younger children permit their mothers or fathers to walk with them; some children (and some parents) are reluctant to let go at the door to the classroom. The older children refuse to be accompanied. They say goodbye to their parents with exaggerated casualness.

For the parents, too, there may be a touch of butterflies in the stomach. They know—better than their children—how much hinges on what

happens in that school building. They know how much depends on whether their child does well or poorly in school.

Going to school is the job, the career, of middle childhood. It is likely to be a challenging job, at times an anxiety-producing one. It's a job at which one can succeed brilliantly or fail miserably, in which one is judged and possibly found wanting. For those children who do poorly at it, their school years may be by far the most difficult period of their entire lives. For those who succeed at it, there are long-term benefits that become cumulative over the years. A child who does well in first grade, especially one who learns to read rapidly and easily, will have a head start in second grade. By early adolescence, the good student is likely to be on a different "track" from the poor student—a track consisting of advanced courses, leading directly to college. The child who does well in school will probably end up in a very different kind of career, and in a very different kind of adult life, than the child who does poorly.

What are the factors that determine whether a child will do well or poorly in school? There are many, and in this chapter we'll tell you what is known about them.

Ability and Achievement

In Chapter 11 we discussed some of the cognitive advances that prepare 6-year-olds to meet the challenges of first grade. Although there does not appear to be any sudden, qualitative change at this time, a lot of smaller advances do occur around the age of 5 to 6. These are not only cognitive advances—they also involve increases in attention span and self-control, in fine motor control, in willingness to comply with rules, and in the desire to be liked and respected by others. All these advances combine to make the age of 6 a good time to begin formal instruction. But not all children are ready for reading, writing, and 'rithmetic when the calendar says they're 6 years old.

Age, School Readiness, and Grade Retention

Because schools take in a new class of first graders only once a year, the oldest child in the class will be about a year older than the youngest child. A year of age may not matter much at 15 or 16, but it makes a big difference to a 5- or 6-year-old. Studies have shown that the children whose birthdays fall in the first three months of school eligibility (the oldest children in the class) do significantly better in first grade than the children whose birthdays fall in the last three months (the youngest children). Being among the youngest is particularly likely to cause problems for boys. However, even for boys, the disadvantage of being younger is only a temporary one: by fourth or fifth grade they will have caught up with their classmates (Teltsch and Breznitz, 1988; Charlesworth, 1989).

What about those children who are old enough in chronological age but lag behind their agemates in "readiness" for first grade? There are various theories of what to do about such children, but the first problem is to identify them. Unfortunately, the tests designed to do this job do not do it very well.

When the calendar says it's time to go to school, not all children are ready to meet the challenges of first grade.

Moreover, some educators question the whole idea of using a single test to assess all the qualities and abilities that affect how well the child will do in school. A child who is behind in one way may be ahead in other ways.

Even if there were a test that succeeded in identifying the children who are "not ready" for kindergarten or first grade, are schools justified in shutting these children out? As educational psychologist Rosalind Charlesworth asks, "What does 'not ready' mean? Isn't it our job to help each child progress from wherever she or he is?" In most school systems, a child judged "not ready" for kindergarten is sent home to wait another year. But as Charlesworth points out, this means that "many of the children who need optimal experiences *most,* often because their home environment is lacking in intellectual stimulation, find themselves at home getting farther behind" (1989, pp. 6, 8).

Charlesworth feels that a better solution is to put these children into a special prekindergarten class. Since some of them may catch up with their age-mates during the course of the year, they should be given the chance to switch into a regular kindergarten class, or to go right into first grade the following year, if their teachers think they are ready for it.

Controversy also surrounds the practice of "grade retention" for older children—making them repeat a grade if they do poorly in it. In a survey of over 1800 school-age children in six different countries, the children rated "Being kept in the same grade next year" as the third most upsetting thing that could possibly happen to them, right after "Losing my mother or father" and "Going blind." Yet there is little evidence that repeating a grade solves the problem of low academic achievement (Byrnes and Yamamoto, 1986; Yamamoto, Soliman, Parsons, and Davies, 1987).

Some educators feel that the problem lies not in the children—after all, why should we expect all children to do equally well?—but in the whole concept of grades. Charlesworth believes that a better solution (though far more difficult to carry out) would be an ungraded system in which children

Problems in Development

Eddie was the second child of a 16-year-old mother who had dropped out of high school, used drugs, alcohol, and tobacco during her pregnancies, and received no prenatal care until she went into labor. Eddie went home to a barren apartment in an inner-city slum where the air was polluted with lead and carbon monoxide. His mother didn't pay much attention to him, especially after her third baby was born, followed later by a fourth. Eddie's father didn't live with them, and his grandfather died when he was 3. There were no books in Eddie's home, and the only places his mother ever took him were to her sister's apartment and the supermarket. His diet consisted mostly of potato chips and soda. When he started school, Eddie didn't know the alphabet and could count only up to three. He spent two years in kindergarten and then was placed in a class for the **educable mentally retarded.** He eventually learned to read, but his reading never progressed much beyond the second-grade level. Eddie's IQ was measured at 63.

Zachary was born to a couple in their late thirties who had two older daughters, 9 and 12, and a nice home in a pleasant suburb. When he was ten minutes old the doctor told his mother that her baby had Down syndrome and that she should "take him home and love him." She obeyed this prescription, and so did Zachary's father and sisters. Starting when he was 6 months old, Zachary went with his mother to a special class in which parents were taught to give their Down syndrome

children the extra stimulation they need. When he was older, his sisters took him for walks in the neighborhood and defended him against the teasing of other children, who eventually came to accept him. Zachary went to a private nursery school and kindergarten, but by second grade he was in a regular public school—in a class for the educable mentally retarded. He eventually learned to read, but his reading never progressed much beyond the second-grade level. Zachary's IQ was measured at 63.

For Eddie, just about everything that could go wrong with an environment—before birth and afterward—did go wrong. For Zachary, only one thing went wrong: the fertilized egg from which he developed happened to have 47 chromosomes instead of 46.

Eddie and Zachary are examples of the two major types of mentally retarded children. Zachary's retardation is classified as **organic**—it is caused by something physically wrong with the brain. Organic retardation can result from genetic or chromosomal defects such as Down or fragile X syndrome (see Chapter 2), or from brain injuries or infections. Organic retardation may be mild or severe; severe retardation is virtually always due to organic causes.

Eddie is a victim of the other type of mental retardation, called **cultural-familial.** No specific physical cause is known: it is presumed to result from an unfavorable combination of genetic and environmental factors. The genetic factors determined a range of possible IQs for Eddie, and Eddie's environment put him at the bottom of that range. Cultural-familial retardation is almost always mild; as its name suggests, it tends to run in

are not divided up by ages at all, but are allowed to progress through the school curriculum at their own rates.

The IQ Score   People who do well in school tend to do well in life. One reason for this is that many of the qualities that lead to high achievement in school are also extremely useful outside of school. These qualities include the ability to concentrate on a task in the face of difficulties or distractions, the motivation to do well, confidence in one's ability to succeed, and intelligence. Intelligence is measured with IQ tests, but all those other factors—ability to concentrate, motivation, and so on—will also affect a child's performance on an IQ test. Thus, it is not surprising that there is a fairly high correlation (around .60) between IQ scores and school grades.

Although intelligence, as estimated by the IQ score, is the best predictor we have of how well a child will do in school, it is far from being a perfect pre-

families. About 75 percent of cases of mental retardation are of the cultural-familial type (Scott and Carran, 1987).

In the past, the diagnosis of mental retardation was based solely on the child's IQ: children with IQs between 55 and 69 were classified as mildly retarded (the educable mentally retarded), and those whose IQs fell in the 40 to 54 range were classified as moderately retarded (the trainable mentally retarded). The problem with this method of categorization was that many children who fell into the retarded range on an IQ test didn't seem particularly retarded in other ways—they were all right outside of school, it was just schoolwork they couldn't manage. Eddie is this kind of child: when he's on the street, playing kickball and joking with his friends, there is nothing to mark him as different from other children his age. The existence of children like Eddie gave rise to the phrase "the six-hour retarded child"—the child who is retarded only during school hours. One could also speak of the "ten-year retarded child"—the child who is considered normal as a preschooler, classified as retarded when he enters school at age 6, and keeps that label until he leaves school at age 16. Only 0.2 percent of 5-year-olds are considered retarded; the proportion rises to 2 percent at age 15 and then declines to 0.5 percent at age 30 (Baumeister, 1987).

Today the diagnosis of **mental retardation** is based not just on IQ scores but on the presence of other problems as well: even if a child has an IQ below 70, he is not labeled as retarded if he is capable of adaptive behavior outside the classroom (Landesman and Ramey, 1989).

Zachary, the child with Down syndrome, would be categorized as retarded under any diagnostic system. But many children like Zachary now grow up to lead satisfying, nearly normal lives. Chris Burke, the actor who plays Corky on the TV show "Life Goes On," has Down syndrome. So does Myles Levy, of Point Pleasant Beach, New Jersey. Myles, who is 21, has a job at a bank, where he files checks: "I love my job," he says. He lives with his parents and he doesn't have a driver's license, but he leads a semi-independent existence. He even has a girlfriend. Myles's mother is proud of her son's accomplishments: "Functionally, he is hardly retarded anymore" (Moslock, 1989, p. D7).

In an enriched and supportive environment, even the effects of organic retardation can be minimized. And cultural-familial retardation can often be prevented, if an enriched and supportive environment is substituted for an impoverished one and the change is made early enough. An experimental day-care program provided intensive enrichment, starting in infancy, for a group of children whose mothers had IQs below 70. These children would ordinarily run a high risk of being mildly retarded, like their mothers. But at age 4½, their IQs exceeded their mothers' by an average of 31 points, putting them well into the normal range (Landesman and Ramey, 1989).

About 90 percent of mentally retarded children fall into the mildly retarded category; unless there are behavioral or emotional problems as well, these children do not require institutional care. Although they may never become the president of the bank, most are capable of leading fulfilling lives and performing useful roles in our society.

dictor. Intelligence is not the only characteristic that affects school performance; nor is an IQ test a perfect measure of intelligence. However, when IQ score and school performance differ considerably, it is likely to be in the case of a high-IQ child who does very poorly in school. The low-IQ child who does very well is rare indeed. High intelligence does not guarantee high achievement, but low intelligence makes it exceedingly difficult to attain (see Box 12–1).

IQ, or intelligence quotient, means mental age divided by chronological age (we discussed this in Chapter 9). Thus, an IQ below 100 implies that a child's mental age—cognitive age—is less than his chronological age: in other words, the child has not yet acquired the cognitive skills and knowledge that the average child of that age possesses. Conversely, a 6-year-old with an IQ *above* 100 might have the cognitive skills and knowledge of an average 7-year-old, or even of an average 10-year-old.

The intellectually gifted child tends to excel in a wide variety of school subjects; he is also likely to be above average in physical and social development.

THE INTELLECTUALLY GIFTED CHILD. Todd learned to read at the age of 2½. At 4 he knew the names of dozens of different dinosaurs and could tell you what each one looked like, what it ate, and which other dinosaurs it was related to. At 6 he was studying college math. At 10 he became a chess master, routinely beating adults in national competitions. He graduated from high school at 15, from college at 18, and earned a Ph.D. at 21. Todd's IQ was estimated to be 180.

What do you think Todd was like as a child? Do you picture a nerdy kid wearing glasses, no good in sports and no good at making friends? Many people do have unfavorable stereotypes of children with exceptionally high IQs: such children are thought to be "odd" and "loners" (Halpern and Luria, 1989). But the popular conception of the gifted child is correct in only one respect: he is likely to be nearsighted and hence to need glasses (Benbow, 1988).

The best known study of gifted children is a large, longitudinal one begun in California in the 1920s. Stanford Professor Lewis Terman and his associates selected a group of almost 1500 schoolchildren on the basis of their very high IQs. The IQs in this group ranged from 140 to 200; the mean was around 150. The children were repeatedly examined over the course of their lives.

In middle childhood these children measured roughly an inch (2½ cm) taller than their agemates. They were superior in physical development and in health, and above average in social skills and psychological adjustment. On achievement tests they ranked far ahead of their agemates—not just in one or two areas, but in a wide variety of school subjects.

The record of high achievement and good adjustment continued into adulthood. Close to 90 percent attended college. Many of the men became doctors, lawyers, college professors, and writers. The women in the group generally became housewives. (But remember, these women were born in the 1910s. In their day, women weren't expected to have careers.) As a group, these people exhibited far lower than average rates of alcoholism, insanity, ill health, criminality, and even divorce (Terman, 1954a).

Recent studies have supported Terman's conclusions: as a group, gifted children are either equal or slightly superior to their average classmates in all measures of social and emotional adjustment (Olszewski-Kubilius, Kulieke, and Krasney, 1988). They tend to have more perseverance and a higher drive to achieve and excel, but they are *less* hostile and aggressive than their agemates (Stamps and Clark, 1987). There is some evidence that *extremely* gifted children—those who are years ahead of their agemates and who have little in common with other children of any age—may have more adjustment problems than the moderately gifted (Feldhusen, 1989). However, it is hard to confirm these reports because there are so few children with IQs that high.

School textbooks and teaching methods are geared to the average—or below-average—child. Thus, gifted children are likely to find the pace too slow and the material boring (Reis, 1989). School systems have tried many techniques for keeping these children occupied and interested: having them spend part of their school day in "enrichment groups" with other gifted children, accelerating (skipping) them, or just giving them extra work—the least successful technique, since it makes gifted children feel that they're being punished for being bright. Enrichment groups are successful or unsuccessful depending on how well the program is carried out and, especially, on who teaches them: only a bright and talented teacher can keep a step ahead of these bright and talented students.

Acceleration is the most controversial method for dealing with gifted children. Many parents are opposed to having their children skipped, out of fear that they will encounter social problems as a result of being younger than their classmates. However, studies of children who were accelerated have generally found them to do as well socially, and better academically, than similarly gifted children who were not accelerated (Brody and Benbow, 1987).

Group Differences

Whenever we divide people into groups on the basis of race, gender, national origin, or the way they eat corn on the cob, we are likely to find some differences between the groups. These differences may be statistically significant, but this doesn't mean that they are important or even that they are large (see Chapter 1). Nor does the existence of a group difference enable us to draw conclusions about particular individuals within the groups. There is a significant and sizable difference in height between men and women, but a tall woman is taller than a short man. Group differences are most noticeable at the extreme ends of the distribution. *Extremely* tall people are almost always men.

Predictably, group differences are found when large groups of children are given IQ tests, or when their aptitude for various school subjects is measured. There are also group differences in academic achievement. In a society in which everyone is supposed to start off equal, these differences have been the source of a great deal of concern.

AFRICAN AMERICANS. Although there are many examples of group differences in IQ scores, the one that worries people most is the black–white difference. On the average, black children and adults score about 15 points lower than white children and adults. Controlling for socioeconomic class (by taking into account average socioeconomic level) reduces the difference to 11 or 12 IQ points. Just for comparison, the average IQ difference between two siblings in the same family is about 12 points.

The racial differences in performance on IQ tests are often blamed on the tests themselves. It has been claimed that IQ tests are biased against black culture and in favor of white culture. But the original purpose of IQ tests was to predict school achievement, and they perform this function as accurately for black children as for white ones. Children who get low scores on IQ tests, whatever their color, are more likely to have problems in school. They are more likely to drop out of high school, less likely to go to college, and less likely to hold high-paying jobs in adulthood (Elliott, 1988). In other words, children who get higher scores on IQ tests devised by white psychologists also make higher grades in a system of schooling designed by white educators. These children are better equipped to succeed in a predominantly white society.

Since racial differences in IQ scores are visible as early as the preschool period, researchers have asked whether black–white differences in childrearing styles play any role. One way to answer this question is by looking at adopted children. Elsie Moore, of Arizona State University, studied a group of 46 black children who were adopted in infancy by middle-class, largely college-educated parents. Half of the adoptive parents were black, half were white. When the children were around 8½ years old they were given IQ tests. The black children adopted by black parents had a mean IQ score of 104; the black children adopted by white parents had a mean IQ of 117—well above average.

Moore didn't stop there; she also looked at the way these 46 children responded to the challenge of being tested, and at the way the mothers of these children—black and white—acted when their children were given a difficult problem to solve. She found that the children reared by white mothers showed more confidence in their problem-solving ability: "Their styles of responding . . . suggest that they felt comfortable in such problem-solving situations and that they may actually enjoy the process." As a result, they were more successful problem solvers than the children reared by black parents. Moore attributes their success to the "supportive" way in which their white mothers encouraged them to solve problems, in part by indicating to them that "It's okay to be wrong as long as you are trying." She believes that middle-class black mothers may unconsciously give their children the message that it's *not* okay to be wrong, and that it's better to say nothing rather than to guess at an answer and risk making a mistake (Moore, 1986, p. 325).

Black children and white children grow up in different environments, and the differences are not confined to the home and the family. Only black children have the experience of growing up in a white society as members of a minority group that is often stereotyped in an unfavorable way. If being "typecast" in a certain way by one's family has profound effects on how a child turns out (see p. 71), what effects might there be from being typecast in a certain way by an entire society?

ASIAN AMERICANS. Chau Pham, with her parents and brother, escaped from Vietnam in 1980 in an overcrowded fishing boat. They made their way to Indonesia, then to Singapore, and finally reached the United States. When Chau arrived in America at the age of 10, the only English word she knew was "hello." But now, at 17, she is valedictorian of her high school class. She has won a scholarship to Vanderbilt University, where she will be a pre-med student. She spends her time on schoolwork, chess games with her father, and playing the organ at her church; she doesn't plan to start dating until she is 21. Her parents expect her to work hard and to do well. "It's up to me and my brother to fulfill their dreams," Chau says (Brand, 1987, p. 51).

Asian Americans have been the success story of the decade. Children of Chinese, Japanese, Korean, Vietnamese, and Cambodian origin have done remarkably well on American tests and in American schools. Although only about 2 percent of the U.S. population belongs to this minority group, Asian Americans made up 17 percent of the 1989 freshman class at Harvard and more than 25 percent at the University of California at Berkeley (Buderi, 1989).

The academic success of Asian Americans is generally attributed to a cultural ethic that emphasizes hard work and devotion to one's parents; these children work hard not just for themselves, but in order to bring honor to their families. However, their high motivation to achieve has a negative side to it: feelings of stress, anxiety, and—if they don't live up to their parents' expectations—guilt (Dion and Toner, 1988).

Asian students do especially well in math and science. We will return to this topic under the heading "Learning Mathematics."

GENDER DIFFERENCES. Here's what is known at present about the differences between girls and boys in ability and achievement:

- There is no overall difference in IQ scores between girls and boys, but that is because IQ tests are *designed* to yield equal scores for girls and boys. However, boys' scores vary over a wider range: there are probably more boys than girls with extremely high IQs, and there are certainly more boys than girls with extremely low IQs.

- Girls do better than boys in school. They make better grades all through elementary school, high school, and college (Maccoby and Jacklin, 1974; Kimball, 1989).

- Girls do a little better than boys on tests of verbal ability, verbal fluency (how quickly they can think of words), and reading. This is mainly due to the fact that there are more boys than girls who are verbally handicapped or reading disabled (Halpern, 1989; Sincoff and Sternberg, 1988).

- Boys do better than girls on tests of **visual–spatial ability,** the ability to deal with mental representations of shapes and directions. For example, one test involves judging whether two patterns, shown in different orientations, are the same—a judgment that requires mentally rotating one of the patterns. The gender difference is small in the early school grades but gets larger over the years; by high school, there is a sizable difference (Johnson and Meade, 1987).

- Even though girls get better grades in math from first grade through college, boys score higher than girls on most tests of math aptitude. This difference first appears toward the end of middle childhood; it widens in high school. It shows up mainly on tests of problem solving or abstract reasoning in math—on tests of computational skills, girls usually do better. Like the difference in height, the difference in math aptitude is most noticeable at the extreme end of the distribution. Among a small group of exceptionally gifted 12-year-olds who scored above 700 in math on the Scholastic Aptitude Tests (SATs), boys outnumbered girls by almost 13 to 1 (Kimball, 1989; Benbow, 1988).

The gender difference that has been the cause of the most concern and controversy involves the SAT scores obtained by high school seniors. These exams are taken only by college-bound adolescents—the upper half of the class. Adolescents who have problems with reading or language are unlikely to take them. Because a disproportionate number of verbally handicapped students are male, eliminating them eliminates the female superiority in verbal ability. For this reason, girls do no better than boys on the verbal SATs. On the other hand, boys do considerably better than girls on the math SATs, because a disproportionate number of the students who are extremely talented in math are male. Thus, boys' SAT scores are higher overall, and awards or scholarships based on SATs go more often to boys than to girls, which many people feel is unfair—especially in view of girls' superiority in grades. But despite their proven ability to do well in high school and college courses (including math), young college women are less likely than their male classmates to major in math, physics, or engineering, and far less likely to get Ph.D.s in those fields. This is why researchers are most anxious to explain the gender difference in abstract reasoning ability in math.

Some researchers believe that biological causes are involved, and that boys' superiority in math is closely related to their superiority in visual–spatial ability: both seem to be localized mainly in the right hemisphere of the brain. Verbal ability is localized mainly in the left hemisphere, so boys appear to do better in right-hemisphere things and girls in left-hemisphere things. It has been proposed that there are male–female differences in the way the brain is organized, due to the influence of male and female hormones during prenatal development (Benbow, 1988; Jacklin, 1989).

Other researchers look for explanations in the fact that girls and boys have different environments and different experiences. For example, boys engage in more active, outdoor play than girls do; perhaps this is one reason their spatial ability is better. But this may boil down to another sort of biological explanation, since prenatal sex hormones also seem to play a role in styles of play (Krasnoff, Walker, and Howard, 1989; Geary, 1989).

Girls and boys also have different experiences in school. Boys tend to take more math courses in high school, and perhaps that is one reason why they do better on the math SAT. But the difference shows up even in girls and boys who have taken the exact same math courses, given by the same teachers (Ducey, 1989). Perhaps the teachers were "favoring" the boys: many studies have shown that teachers (both male and female) tend to pay more attention to boys in the classroom—girls are more likely to be ignored (Kelly, 1988). Although this form of discrimination definitely exists and may have long-term effects on girls' self-confidence and motivation, girls nonetheless get higher grades in school.

Perhaps parents are more likely to encourage their sons to achieve in math, and more likely to encourage their daughters to achieve in other subjects. But there is no convincing evidence for this. One study compared the attitudes toward math achievement in parents of girls with those of parents of boys. The girls' parents did expect their children to have to work harder in math, but their ratings of their daughters' mathematical ability were no lower than the ratings given by the parents of boys (Parsons, Adler, and Kaczala, 1982). Another study found no difference in how much encouragement mathematically talented girls and boys said they had received from their parents. Parents gave more encouragement to more talented children and less to less talented ones, but the differences weren't related to the children's gender (Raymond and Benbow, 1986).

The most intriguing theory of male–female differences in math and science has to do with the type of motivation girls and boys bring to intellectual tasks, and the ways they react to successes and failures. We'll discuss this theory in a later section of this chapter.

It's important to keep in mind that the differences we have been discussing in this section—differences between children of different races or genders—are differences between means (averages). The "*average* girl" may be a little more verbal and a little less talented in math than the *"average* boy." But the differences between one girl and another girl, or between one boy and another boy, are likely to be far greater than those between the "average girl" and the "average boy"; the same is true for differences between the "average European-American child," the "average African-American child," and the "average Asian-American child." Children are individuals, not just members of groups. As one researcher summed it up, "Our efforts are best spent encouraging all individuals to develop their cognitive talents and let group norms fall where they may" (Halpern, 1989, p. 1157).

Other Factors Affecting Achievement

Children who have high aptitude for math, or high IQ scores, do not necessarily do well in school. In Terman's study of gifted children, for example, not all of the children turned out to be high achievers. Terman (1954b) looked at factors such as personality and family background in an effort to explain the differences in achievement. Later researchers carried on the effort, enlarging on Terman's work. In this section we will look at the factors they have studied.

Home and Family Influences

A child's achievement in school will depend, in part, on his home and family. Terman found, and many later researchers have confirmed, that children who grow up in one-parent families don't do as well in school as children who have two parents. Since the likelihood of living in a one-parent family is greater for black children than for white children (see p. 38), this may contribute to the racial differences in school achievement. A parent who is rearing her children without assistance simply doesn't have much leftover time and energy for carrying on conversations with them, or reading stories. The presence of another adult in the household—a partner, sibling, or grandparent —makes life a little easier for the single parent and improves the school achievement of her children (Thompson, Alexander, and Entwisle, 1988).

The socioeconomic status of the family influences every aspect of the lives of its members, and school achievement is no exception. Even in stable, two-parent families, lower socioeconomic status is associated with lower achievement in school. This is true for adopted children as well as those reared by their biological parents, so it can't be due solely to genetic factors (Duyme, 1988).

In Chapter 9 we discussed patterns of parenting and described the authoritative, authoritarian, and permissive childrearing styles. Many studies have shown that authoritative parents, who use firm but reasonable control and encourage independence, have children who are likely to do well in school. However, this finding seems to apply only to white and Hispanic families. The relationship between authoritative parenting and achievement in children is less clear for black families and doesn't seem to hold for Asians at all. Many Asian parents use an authoritarian parenting style—demanding unquestioning obedience rather than independence—and yet their children do very well in school. Thus, the effects of parenting style on achievement will depend on the cultural context in which it occurs (Mounts, Lamborn, and Steinberg, 1989).

Creativity Whereas achievement in school is closely related to IQ, achievement outside of school is not. That is, intelligence plays a role in determining what kind of occupation you will have, but not in how well you do at it. Success in a given profession depends more on other characteristics, such as creativity.

How many things can you think of that are round? How many different uses can you think of for a brick? Researchers use questions such as these to assess children's creativity. Children who come up with unusual answers to these questions are said to be good at **divergent thinking**—thinking that is off the beaten track.

Because verbal tests of creativity are also a measure of what we previously called "verbal fluency" (see p. 389), children with high IQs generally do better on them than children with low IQs, and girls do a little better than boys (Harrington, Block, and Block, 1983). When tests of creativity are based on nonverbal, visual things—drawings, designs, and so on—children with higher or lower IQs do about equally well, but girls still score a little higher than boys (Kershner and Ledger, 1985).

One of the ways children develop creativity is through being encouraged to think for themselves. Mothers were asked at what age they allowed their children to do things on their own—making decisions about spending money, going to bed without being told, and so on. The children whose mothers allowed them independence at a relatively early age were more creative (Albert and Runco, 1989). However, mothers also allow more independence to brighter children, so it's possible that the relationship between independence and creativity is simply a reflection of the relationship between

Creativity can be expressed either in words or in nonverbal ways such as drawing pictures.

IQ and creativity. Also, these results probably can't be generalized to cultural groups such as Asians, in which independence may have a very different meaning.

There are a number of other personal characteristics that can be measured in childhood and that are related to achievement in school and in adult life. In this section we will discuss several of the nonintellectual characteristics that researchers have looked at.

Differences in Personality, Motivation, and Cognitive Style

IMPULSIVE AND REFLECTIVE CHILDREN. Figure 12–1 shows a sample problem from the Matching Familiar Figures Test, devised by developmental psychologist Jerome Kagan and his associates (Kagan and others, 1964). The task in this test is to find the picture that exactly matches the one on the top.

When the test is given to school-age children, it is found that some of them respond quickly, without checking carefully to see if their answer is correct. As a result, they tend to make many errors. These children are said to be **impulsive. Reflective** children, on the other hand, examine each picture carefully, respond more slowly, and make fewer errors.

Kagan (1965) believes that reflectiveness or impulsiveness is an enduring characteristic of a child's "cognitive style" or "cognitive tempo," although all

FIGURE 12-1
A sample problem from the Matching Familiar Figures Test (Kagan, Rosman, Day, Albert, and Phillips, 1964). The children's task is to find the picture that exactly matches the one on top. Both their speed and their accuracy are measured.

Children with a reflective cognitive style spend enough time and effort to make sure that their answers are correct.

children tend to become more reflective as they grow older. He found that reflective children do better in school than impulsive children. This is not surprising, especially in view of the fact that reflective children tend to have higher IQs (Pellegrini, Masten, Garmezy, and Ferrarese, 1987).

Later researchers have criticized the concept of impulsiveness–reflectiveness. First, some children respond slowly yet nevertheless make a lot of errors; there are also some that respond rapidly, yet accurately. Second, impulsiveness as measured by the Matching Familiar Figures Test does not correspond to what we usually think of as impulsive behavior. Children who are impulsive in the sense that they behave in a disruptive manner in the classroom or can't tolerate a delay of gratification do not necessarily qualify as "impulsive" on the matching test. Such children do tend to make a lot of errors, but they don't respond any more rapidly than the accurate children (Victor, Halverson, and Montague, 1985).

Although the children who respond inaccurately *and* rapidly are not necessarily impulsive in their behavior, they do have a distinctive cognitive style —one that is likely to lead to poor achievement in school. Perhaps these children have difficulty keeping their attention focused, or perhaps they put too little effort into their cognitive activities (Smith and Nelson, 1988). Children with an impulsive cognitive style can be trained to become more careful and analytical in their thinking, but it is not clear whether such training has any lasting effects (Cohen, Schleser, and Meyers, 1981).

INTRINSIC VERSUS EXTRINSIC MOTIVATION. A term that was popular among psychologists and educators in the 1950s was **achievement motivation:** the drive to succeed. Since then it has been increasingly clear that there are many different kinds of achievement motivation and that describing them all by a single term is an oversimplification. For example, a child may be motivated to do well in school because she wants to uphold her family's honor, or because she feels guilty if she doesn't do what her parents or teachers expect of her, or because she enjoys learning new things, or because her parents promised her a reward if she gets good grades, or because her parents promised her a spanking if she doesn't. Although any of these motivations may be sufficient to make her do her schoolwork, they do not necessarily operate in similar ways.

Motivations can be either **intrinsic** or **extrinsic.** When 10-year-old Cynthia reads a book because she's interested in it, that's intrinsic motivation; when she reads it because her mother promised her a dollar for each chapter she finishes, that's extrinsic motivation.

Researchers have discovered that introducing an extrinsic motivator, such as money, may reduce a child's intrinsic motivation. If Cynthia reads the first four chapters of a book because her mother is paying her to do so, she is very likely to stop reading as soon as her mother stops dishing out dollars. She feels that she is reading the book only because of the reward, so there's no point in continuing once the reward is no longer forthcoming. The reward makes her think, "This can't be a very interesting book if I have to be paid to read it" (Lepper, Greene, and Nisbett, 1973).

Activities themselves can be used as rewards for other activities, but this may have unforeseen effects on intrinsic motivation. When children are told, "If you finish reading your book you can play the piano," it makes them feel that reading the book must be less fun than playing the piano. Then, when they are later allowed to choose between the two activities, they are likely to choose the piano in preference to the book. If they hear, "If you play the piano for a while you can finish reading your book," reading the book becomes more appealing and playing the piano less so (Boggiano and Main, 1986). You may recall from Chapter 8 that something very similar happens with preschoolers when they are told, "Eat your broccoli and then you can have some cake."

Introducing an extrinsic motivator can't reduce intrinsic motivation if there isn't much of it to begin with. In some of the "open classrooms" of the '70s, children were allowed to decide what they would do and when they would do it. The theory was that being told what to do decreases children's intrinsic motivation to learn: we should just provide them with the proper materials and leave them alone, and they'll educate themselves (see the discussion of Jean-Jacques Rousseau in Chapter 3). What actually happened was that the children in those classrooms wasted a good deal of time talking to each other and moving aimlessly around the room. As a result, they learned significantly less than children in traditional classrooms (Bennett, 1976). Learning to do math problems or studying spelling and grammar holds little intrinsic interest for most children. When intrinsic motivation is lacking, it may be necessary to supply some extrinsic motivation (Lepper, 1988).

It may not be necessary, however, to continue supplying it indefinitely. There appears to be a third type of motivation, in addition to intrinsic and extrinsic: internalized. The child who works hard in school to uphold her family's honor, or because she would feel guilty if she didn't do what her parents and teachers expected of her, has acquired internalized motivation. Young children won't do tasks they dislike unless there is some sort of extrinsic motivation, but as they get older they become less dependent on extrinsic motivation and better at making themselves do something simply because they feel they ought to (Chandler and Connell, 1987).

PERFORMANCE GOALS VERSUS LEARNING GOALS. When extrinsic motivators are used as a way of getting children to do their schoolwork, they are not usually given in the form of tangible rewards and punishments: they normally consist of things like grades and verbal praise or criticism. These motivators have different effects than the purely extrinsic ones, because children are less likely to see them as goals in themselves and more likely to take them as indications of how well they are doing.

According to Carol Dweck of the University of Illinois, the effects of motivators such as grades and praise will depend, in part, on whether the child is oriented toward a **performance goal** or a **learning goal.** For children with a performance-goal orientation, grades and praise are important motivators: these children want others to think well of their abilities. Children with a learning-goal orientation, on the other hand, are motivated to become more competent and to understand or master a challenging subject. They appear to enjoy the process of getting better at something, and grades or praise are consequently less important (Dweck, 1986).

Most children are capable of adopting either kind of goal, depending on the situation. For example, it is possible to nudge a child from a learning goal to a performance goal simply by telling him, "This is a test. Let's see if you can do as well on this test as other children your age." One unfortunate effect of this shift in orientation is that it makes children less willing to take on challenges: if children know that they are going to be judged on their performance, they tend not to attempt something unless they are sure they can do well at it. In a classic study, 11-year-olds were asked to solve anagrams (sets of letters that can be unscrambled to make words). The anagrams varied in difficulty from easy ones of three letters to hard ones of six, and the children were allowed to choose the level of difficulty they wanted to work on. Some of the children were told that this was a game; others were told that they would be graded on their performance. The "grades" children chose easier problems to work on than the "game" children (Harter, 1978).

A typical school classroom will contain some children who are oriented more to learning goals and others who are oriented more to performance goals. Although these types of children do not differ in intelligence, they differ in the way they react when they meet an obstacle or experience a setback. When children with a learning goal are faced with an obstacle—say, a new subject that they have trouble understanding at first—they rise to the challenge and respond by working harder. But, according to Dweck, the reaction of children with a performance goal will depend on how much confidence they have in their own abilities. If they have a lot of confidence, they will respond to obstacles by working harder; if their self-confidence is low, they will give up. The differences between performance-goal-oriented and learning-goal-oriented children are summarized in Table 12–1.

Why do some children adopt learning goals while others—in the same situation and with just as much ability—adopt performance goals? Dweck (1986) believes it is a result of the children's differing "theories" about ability and achievement. Learning-goal children think that ability is mainly a matter of how hard you work, so if they have trouble learning something, the solution is obvious: just work harder. Performance-goal children, in contrast, think that their ability is fixed and that there is nothing they can do to change it. If their confidence in their ability is high, a temporary setback is not likely

TABLE 12–1
Performance Goals versus Learning Goals:
What Happens When a Child Encounters Difficulties
in a Learning Situation?

GOAL ORIENTATION	THE EFFECTS OF HIGH OR LOW CONFIDENCE IN ONE'S ABILITY
Performance Goal The goal is to win positive evaluations and avoid negative evaluations from others.	Children who have *high* confidence in their own ability will seek challenge and persist in their efforts.
	Children who have *low* confidence in their own ability will avoid challenge and give up easily.
Learning Goal The goal is to increase competence and gain mastery.	Children whose confidence in their own ability is either *high* or *low* will seek challenge and persist in their efforts.

Source: Based on Dweck, 1986.

to bother them much. But if their confidence in their ability is low and they have trouble learning something, they take it as just another indication that they're not intelligent enough. There's no point trying any harder—might as well give up.

The academic self-confidence of children with a performance-goal orientation also affects their willingness to have their abilities evaluated. Those who have high confidence in their abilities will look for situations in which they can demonstrate their superiority and win positive evaluations. But those who have low confidence will either avoid such situations altogether or choose tasks that conceal their ability. They may choose tasks that are too easy for them and on which they are sure they cannot fail, or they may choose tasks that are too difficult in order to give themselves a good excuse for failing (Dweck, 1986).

ATTRIBUTIONS FOR SUCCESS AND FAILURE. In the past few years, it has become clear that children differ considerably in how they react to successes and failures. It is also clear that their reactions have an important influence on their willingness to take on new challenges and, consequently, on how much they will achieve.

Children's explanations for their own successes and failures vary along three dimensions. The first is *stability*. In the previous section, we said that children with learning goals tend to think of ability as something that can be changed—it can be improved by working harder. Children with performance goals, however, see ability as something unchangeable or *stable*. Some see their ability as stable and high, and that's all right, but some see their ability as stable and low, and that's not so good. A child who thinks of himself as "dumb" is likely to avoid challenges and is easily discouraged when he encounters an obstacle.

The second dimension has to do with whether explanations for successes or failures are *global* or *specific*. An explanation (or attribution) is global when children think their ability is high or low in *everything* they do. It is specific if they can say to themselves, "I may be dumb in this subject, but I'm good in lots of other things."

The third dimension is called *locus of control.* A child who feels that he is responsible for his own successes—either because he has worked hard or because he has high ability—has an **internal locus of control.** One who feels that he has little control over the events in his life, and who attributes his successes and failures to things outside of himself, such as luck or the actions of other people, has an **external locus of control.**

Children do not necessarily react in a consistent way to their successes and failures. Some children attribute their successes to luck and feel that, just because they did all right today, there is no reason to think they will do all right tomorrow. So they have unstable, specific, and external attributions for success. But, at the same time, they may have stable, global, and internal attributions for failure. Even a small setback may make them feel, "I'm no good—I'll never be any good at anything." This reaction has been termed *learned helplessness,* because it is thought to result from repeated experiences of being miserable and powerless. For example, a baby whose cries are usually ignored, or an older child who is unable to get any reaction out of her depressed mother, or whose father abuses her every time he gets drunk, no matter how quiet and obedient she is, may come to feel that she is powerless to have any effect on what happens to her (Seligman, 1975).

It's a reasonable theory, but it has never been proved: the *causes* of the "learned helplessness" pattern of attributions are still unknown. However, much is known about its *consequences.* Children who fit this pattern—who take minor failures as a sign that they are "dumb" or "no good" and will always be that way—are at much greater risk of suffering from depression when they get older. Furthermore, the school achievement of these children is significantly lower than that of the children who have changeable and nonglobal attributions for failure and who feel that they have some control over their lives (Nolen-Hoeksema, Girgus, and Seligman, 1986).

Children who have the "helpless" pattern of attributions for success and failure will say, if they do well on a test, that it was just luck or it was an easy test; if they do poorly on a test, they will say it's because they're "dumb." So these are the same children we previously described as performance-goal oriented and with low confidence in their own ability. These are the children who tend to give up when they encounter obstacles. Because they don't expect themselves to succeed at academic tasks, they don't set high achievement goals for themselves, and their school achievement is likely to fall below their actual ability.

"Helpless" children can be contrasted with **mastery-oriented** children, who react to failure by trying harder. Mastery-oriented children are likely to be learning-goal oriented; if they are performance-goal oriented they have confidence in their own ability. When confronted with difficulty, these children don't dwell on the fact that they are having trouble: instead they concentrate on solving the problem (Licht and Dweck, 1984).

Clearly, it is important for children to have self-confidence in their own ability to succeed—the quality that has been called **self-efficacy** (Bandura, 1989). How can we help them to gain this kind of confidence in their own ability? By letting them have plenty of experiences with success and guarding them against failure, right?

A mastery-oriented child has confidence in his own ability. If he meets an obstacle, he reacts by concentrating on the problem and trying harder.

Strangely enough, that does not seem to be the solution. Despite repeated academic successes, some highly capable children feel that they lack the ability to succeed. A researcher examined third and fifth graders who were in the top third of their classes and who had done very well on national achievement tests. More than 20 percent of these highly competent children seriously underestimated their own abilities (Phillips, 1987).

GENDER DIFFERENCES REVISITED. For unknown reasons, girls appear to be more likely than boys to underestimate their own abilities and to attribute their successes to luck and their failures to being incompetent. As a result of this maladaptive pattern of attributions, girls are more likely than boys to have an "I can't do it" reaction when they're faced with something they have trouble understanding. Boys are more likely to take an "I'll have to try harder" approach. Thus, if the introduction of a new subject at school—algebra, for example—starts out by seeming confusing and difficult, girls are more likely to feel incompetent and to give up.

What's particularly interesting about this gender difference in academic self-confidence is that it's most noticeable among the very brightest students. Researchers gave some fifth-grade students a test that was purposely designed to be confusing. Experiencing this confusion caused many of the children to perform more poorly on a learning task they were given immediately afterward. And the ones whose performance suffered the most were the brightest girls in the class, not the average or below-average ones. With the boys, the results were just the opposite: the brightest boys were *least* bothered by their previous experience of being confused (Licht and Dweck, 1984).

Girls seem to be more likely than boys to believe that ability is fixed and there is nothing they can do to change it. Yet, even for highly competent girls, knowledge of their past successes does nothing to inoculate them against fear of failure in the future. Even if they are bright enough to get excellent marks all through grade school and high school, in the long run their lack of confidence in their own abilities may cause them to avoid situations that hold the threat of failure. This may be the explanation of why college women are less likely than their male classmates to major in challenging subjects such as math, physics, or engineering, and less likely to go on to graduate school in those fields (Dweck, 1986).

The maladaptive pattern of attributions that is so common in bright girls may also contribute to the puzzling gender differences found on tests of mathematical ability. The question is: Why do girls get better grades in math classes and yet get lower scores on tests such as the math section of the SATs? An answer that has recently been proposed is that people who lack self-confidence generally do all right in familiar situations, but may have the "I can't do it" reaction as soon as they're faced with novel and difficult material such as the harder problems on the math SAT exam. Because boys have greater confidence in their ability (especially in math) and are more mastery oriented than girls, they are more likely to consider the math SAT an interesting challenge (Kimball, 1989).

How can we give children—especially girls—more confidence in their own abilities and arm them against the fear of failure? Obviously, just letting them succeed doesn't do it; in fact, making things too easy for children may backfire, because having too *few* experiences with failure may be just as bad as having too many. Researchers are currently studying ways of training children to think in mastery-oriented ways ("I love a challenge") and to worry less about performance goals. It's also important for parents and teachers to convey to children—especially to girls—their confidence in the child's ability. It has been found that a child's self-confidence is more closely related to how well her parents expect she will do in the future than to how well she has actually done in the past (Boggiano, Main, and Katz, 1988; Phillips, 1987).

But it may be less important to make children feel that their ability is high than to make them feel that it is changeable—that they can improve it by working harder. Many Asians and Asian Americans have this "theory" of ability and achievement: they imbue their children with the attitude that they can do anything if they try hard enough. This attitude has paid off handsomely in terms of academic achievement.

The School's Influence on Achievement

When children do poorly in school, often it is not they who are blamed, or even their parents. Instead, the school is held responsible. How much influence do schools and teachers have on children's achievement?

Quite a lot, according to a number of studies that have looked at children's academic progress as a function of what school they attend. Although children differ coming *into* a school, even schools with comparable student bodies (comparable when they entered) vary considerably in how well the students do. In one study of "successful" and "unsuccessful" schools, children at the most successful school who measured in the bottom 25 percent in verbal ability did as well on standardized achievement tests as students at the least successful school who were in the *top* 25 percent in verbal ability. Successful schools also tend to have lower rates of absences and delinquency (Rutter, 1983).

What makes a school successful? Not a fancy building, not a lot of fancy books in the library, not even a lot of teachers with fancy degrees. It's more a matter of the school's *climate,* its spirit, the attitudes and values of its students, teachers, and administrators—things that are hard to measure or even to specify. Good schools seem to foster a feeling of "We're all in this together and we know we can succeed."

How does a school accomplish this? Here are some of the factors that have been found to make a difference (Good and Weinstein, 1986; Linney and Seidman, 1989):

- A principal who is clearly committed to quality teaching and academic excellence, who can provide leadership in attaining these goals, and who is able to engender enthusiasm and cooperation among his staff.

- Teachers who spend a high proportion of their time actually teaching, and who convey to their students the expectation that all of them will achieve at least a minimum mastery of the material.

- A safe, orderly school atmosphere in which discipline is maintained without resort to harsh punishments. A school is unlikely to be successful if discipline is a constant problem and if students and teachers fear for their safety. In a recent nationwide poll, 22 percent of 10- to 16-year-olds said they don't feel safe in their schools. Many of these children mentioned classmates with guns and knives—even in elementary school (Werner, 1989).

- Other factors include public recognition for students' academic achievement, student participation in school activities (this tends to be higher in smaller schools), parents' involvement and support of the school, and a curriculum that focuses on academics rather than offering a wide range of exotic electives.

DEALING WITH INDIVIDUAL DIFFERENCES. One fact of life that schools have to deal with is that children differ tremendously in knowledge and skills, right from the start, and these differences do not narrow over the years. Some children enter first grade reading fourth-grade books; others haven't learned the alphabet. The school's job is not an easy one: to educate its least able students as well as its most able, all to the highest level of their ability, and to reward high academic achievement without demeaning those who aren't capable of it. Ever since the beginning of public schooling, schools have been torn between its two goals: to promote equality and to promote excellence (Labaree, 1987).

One way of dealing with wide disparities in cognitive ability and academic skills is to divide students into relatively homogeneous groups. This can be done either on a between-class basis—an entire classroom would then consist of children who were matched in ability—or on a within-class basis, as with reading groups. In either case, the teacher's job becomes easier because the content of the lesson can be adjusted to the group's ability.

Although between-class ability grouping is still used in some school systems, numerous studies have shown that it is not effective. There is little or no benefit for the brighter students and possibly some harmful effects for the slower ones (Slavin, 1987). Students of any level of ability seem to do better in a school or a classroom in which there are a fair number of highly able children, so siphoning off these highly able children lowers the achievement of those who remain (Rutter, 1983). What seems to happen in a classroom consisting only of "slow learners" is that teachers lean over backward in their effort to enable these children to succeed at academic tasks. The children are given work that is too easy, and they end up with "an illusion of intelligence" instead of intellectual growth (Dweck, 1986, p. 1046).

Within-classroom ability grouping, on the other hand, seems to have benefits for students at all levels. The important thing seems to be that the students are grouped only for certain subjects, usually reading and math, and remain together for everything else (Slavin, 1987). The main concern about this procedure is the fear that children might be locked into high or low educational "tracks" on the basis of their first-grade reading group assignment. However, research has shown that teachers do not automatically reassign children to the same group they were in the previous year—they take the child's achievement into account (Gamoran, 1989).

CULTURAL DIVERSITY. The view of the United States as a giant "melting pot," in which ingredients that are different when they go into the pot come out looking all the same, is outmoded. The new view is of a country in which cultural diversity is preserved and valued, so that each culture can contribute its own unique flavor to the society as a whole. This change in attitudes has made the school's job even harder: now it's expected to promote equality, promote excellence, and maintain diversity, all at the same time!

Children from certain cultural backgrounds—such as European-American and Asian-American—tend to do well in school, partly because their cultures emphasize values and behaviors that are well suited to the school environment. Children from other cultural backgrounds—such as native American, African-American, and Hawaiian-American—tend to do less well, partly because their cultures' values and behaviors are not in harmony with those of the school. For example, black parents seldom ask their children a question unless they are genuinely seeking information; but in school, black children are expected to respond to the teacher's question even though she already knows the answer (Heath, 1989).

Efforts to make schools and teachers more sensitive to their students' cultural backgrounds are now under way. One such effort is taking place in Hawaii. Children from native Hawaiian families do not learn much in classrooms where the seats are arranged in rigid rows and the teacher stands in front and lectures them. In that setting, Hawaiian children tend to pay little attention to the teacher or their schoolwork, and spend most of their time talking to each other. In Hawaiian culture, children do things in groups, cooperatively, not by themselves. These children learn much more when classes are divided up into small groups and the teacher moves from one group to another for brief but intense periods of instruction (Tharp, 1989).

Navajo children in Arizona, in contrast to the Hawaiians, are quite self-sufficient: if left to their own devices, they will sometimes wander off and spend the rest of the day playing outside, all by themselves. Within the classroom, these children withdraw if teachers are too forceful in their attempts to control the students' behavior: Navajo culture stresses individuality, and efforts to manipulate others are seen as a violation of cultural values. Another cultural value is wholeness—Navajos don't like to take things apart and examine the parts. Navajo children want to hear a story through to the end before they start to discuss it (Tharp, 1989).

Teachers can gear their instructional methods to their students' cultural backgrounds when they're teaching a class of Hawaiian students or a class of Navajos. However, it is very difficult for them to do this when they're faced with a classroom of students from all different cultural backgrounds.

BILINGUAL EDUCATION. With as many as 25 percent of children in some states coming from homes in which a language other than English is spoken, the question of bilingual education has assumed new importance. When children are not proficient in English when they enter school, should we instruct them in English right from the start? Or should we instruct them at first in their native language, thus making the transition easier for them but delaying their entry into an English-speaking society?

Unfortunately, we don't have enough information at present to answer that question, because well-designed and well-controlled studies have not yet been carried out. This is partly due to a lack of agreement on what the criterion should be. Is the question: Which method leads to quicker learning of English? Then the answer is probably to instruct the children in English right from the start. But maybe the question should be: Which leads to better long-term academic success and lower rates of dropping out? In this case, bilingual education might be preferable.

In any event, being bilingual is not, in itself, harmful to a child's cognitive development. Two researchers—one Japanese American and one Mexican American—who have studied this question have come to the following conclusions:

> In the process of second-language acquisition, the native language does not interfere in any significant way with the development of the second language.... There does not appear to be competition over mental resources by the two languages, and there are even possible cognitive advantages to bilingualism.   (Hakuta and Garcia, 1989, pp. 375–376)

These researchers also point out the inconsistency of an educational system that labors mightily to convert children from minority language backgrounds into monolingual speakers of English, and then wonders why American students have such a tough time learning foreign languages!

COMPUTERS IN THE CLASSROOM. In 1953, B. F. Skinner (see Chapter 3) visited his daughter's fourth-grade classroom and discovered two major faults in the teaching of arithmetic: all the children were forced to proceed at the same pace, and they didn't find out until the next day whether their answers were right or wrong. Skinner went home and invented a "teaching machine" for tutoring students in arithmetic: each child could proceed at her own pace and would get immediate feedback (Benjamin, 1988). Skinner's machine was not a computer—in those days, computers consisted of whole rooms full of equipment, cost millions of dollars, were hardly any quicker at addition than a fourth grader, and were so far from being "user friendly" that "user hostile" would be an understatement.

Computers have now become considerably smaller, cheaper, quicker, and friendlier. But they have not—as some people predicted they would—taken over the classroom and made human teachers superfluous. It's not clear whether they ever will, or whether they ever should.

Close-Up

Box 12-2
An Apple for
Miss A

The time was the 1940s. The setting was an old, fortress-like school located in a poor section of a large city in northeastern North America, surrounded by factories and crowded tenements. A brothel stood across the street from the school's front entrance; behind it lay a junkyard. The asphalt playground of the school was enclosed by a chain-link fence. Iron bars protected the first-floor windows.

Of the 400 to 500 children attending this elementary school on a given day within this period, about two-thirds were white, one-third were black, and all were poor. Only a minority of these children would ever graduate from high school, much less go to college. Fights and behavior problems were common in the school. Unruly children were strapped; there were about 500 strappings a year.

In the early 1950s a graduate of this school—one of the few who made good—returned to the school as a teacher. His name was Eigil Pedersen. Pedersen remained at the school for a number of years. During this time he began to look into the records of the children who had been students there in the 1940s. Eventually, he and his associates located a number of these ex-students—now adults—and interviewed them. The results of this research were reported in the *Harvard Educational Review* (Pedersen, Faucher, and Eaton, 1978).

Pedersen began his research in an attempt to find out why such a small proportion of the students ever finished high school. But somewhere along the way that purpose was abandoned. He came across something that interested him much more: the effects on her students of a particular first-grade teacher, whom Pedersen called "Miss A."

The school still had the records of all its former students—their marks in each grade, teachers' comments, and so on. Pedersen noticed that Miss A's students got higher grades in first grade than the students of the other first-grade teachers, although the school always made an effort to give each teacher an equal selection of children. At first he figured that Miss A was just an "easy marker." But then he noticed that Miss A's students did pretty well in second grade, too, even though her class was split up among several different second-grade teachers. Regardless of which second-grade teacher they had, Miss A's former students got significantly better marks in second grade than children from other first-grade classes. The same was true in third grade, in fourth, and in fifth. The difference was still detectable in seventh grade! The differences weren't small, either. In second grade, 64 percent of Miss A's ex-pupils got average marks of A or B+. Only 28 percent of the former students of the other first-grade teachers did that well.

Then Pedersen and his colleagues interviewed some graduates of the school and rated them on their adult socioeconomic status. The ratings were based on such factors as number of years of schooling completed, occupational level, and quality of housing. It turned out that Miss A's former students were *still* doing significantly better

When computers are used in the classroom today, they are used in two different ways: as an end in themselves, in order to make students "computer literate"; and as a means of teaching something else, such as math or spelling. Potentially, computers could become a powerful tool for increasing children's writing skills, because they make it so easy to create prose and to revise it. However, this is easy only for those who know how to type, and most school-age children are not good typists. At present, it is mainly seventh to twelfth graders who are carrying out writing assignments on the computer. Their response, by and large, has been favorable, so it is likely that the use of computers for this purpose will continue to gain in popularity (Bracey, 1989).

In the long run, the benefits of having computers in the classroom will depend very much on the specific purposes they are used for and on the software programs that are developed to serve those purposes (Lepper and Gurtner, 1989). In the short run, the main danger is that computers will widen the gap between students who vary in ability or in degree of "com-

than the former students of the other first-grade teachers.

Clearly, Miss A had had a lasting impact on the lives of her pupils. And they hadn't forgotten her. During the interviews, people were asked to recall their first-grade teachers of 25 years earlier.

> Many of the subjects could not remember the names of their teachers, and sometimes their memories were actually wrong, as we discovered when comparing their recollections with information on the permanent record cards. Despite the general difficulty of remembering every teacher, not a single subject who had been in Miss A's class failed to recall that fact correctly. Of those who had not been Miss A's pupils in first grade, 31 percent had no recollection of who their teacher had been, fewer than half identified their first-grade teacher correctly, and four subjects incorrectly named Miss A as their teacher. Memory seems to have been influenced by wishful thinking! (Pedersen, Faucher, and Eaton, 1978, p. 19)

One reason Miss A's students cared so much about her is that she cared so much about *them.* Twenty years after they graduated from her class, she could still remember them by name. Every one of her students learned to read, regardless of background or aptitude—she devoted many of her after-school hours to the children who were having trouble. If children forgot their lunches, she'd share her own lunch with them. She never lost her temper: she kept control of the class by the power of her personality and the obvious affection she had for them.

Most of all, Miss A believed in her students.

Pedersen's report sums it up this way:

> If children are lucky enough to have a first-grade teacher who has high expectations for their achievement, they will be more likely to develop positive academic self-concepts and to be more successful in school. (p. 22)

Out of school, too. It was a vicious circle, working in an exceptionally nonvicious way. Miss A expected her students to do well, and they did do well. What they learned in first grade, plus their heightened self-esteem and motivation, gave them an advantage in second grade. This led their second-grade teacher to expect good things from them, too. And so it went.

Miss A isn't unique: there are other teachers who care very deeply about their students and who can imbue them with the desire to do well and the feeling that they can. Some of these teachers, such as Jaime Escalante, the real-life hero of "Stand Up and Deliver," have had books and movies made about them. But no one ever wrote a book or made a movie about Miss A. It's possible that she never even realized what a remarkable effect she had had on her students' lives. Eigil Pedersen never got to tell Miss A about his findings. By the time he was ready to, it was too late: she was in the hospital, dying of cancer.

Miss A would not, in any case, have remembered Pedersen's name. Despite the fact that he was one of the most successful graduates of that school, Pedersen had not been one of the lucky ones. His first-grade teacher was Miss B.

puter anxiety." When computers were used to teach math to elementary school students in Israel, what happened was that the high-achieving students benefited more than the low-achieving ones, so the difference between them became greater (Hativa, 1988). Computers may also widen the gap between girls and boys, because many boys take to computers like a duck to water, a reaction that, for some reason, is rare in girls. In 1988, only 10 percent of the Ph.D.s awarded in computer science went to women (Markoff, 1989).

THE ROLE OF THE TEACHER. Computers have not made teachers superfluous. According to one authority, "Students achieve more in classes where they spend most of their time being taught or supervised by their teachers rather than working on their own or not working at all" (Brophy, 1986, p. 1070).

No school can be successful unless the teachers within that school are successful. Teachers determine the amount of time students spend on academic

Although computers are now being used in some classrooms, they haven't made human teachers obsolete.

tasks. They also provide their students with information in an appropriate form, help them relate new material to what they already know, keep track of their progress, and provide them with feedback. How well a teacher performs these functions will determine, to a large extent, how much the students will learn that year.

The amount of time students spend on academic tasks will depend on how good the teacher is at classroom management. A good teacher has the ability to organize the classroom into an efficiently run environment for learning, where a minimum of time is wasted in going from one activity to another or in dealing with disciplinary problems. "Time on task" has proved to be a reliable predictor of children's achievement in the classroom (Brophy, 1986; Rutter, 1983).

Good teachers expect their students to work hard and to do well. But, because they are realists, they don't expect all their students to do equally well: they expect certain students to achieve more than others, and those students do, in fact, tend to achieve more than the others. Generally, the teachers have good reasons for expecting (or predicting) that certain students will excel, and they tend to be correct in these predictions (Jussim, 1989). But the "teacher expectancy effect" also works when the teacher *doesn't* have a good reason for the expectancy. In a famous experiment done many years ago, researchers told some elementary-school teachers that certain children in their classes were "spurters" who were likely to show sudden, rapid growth in intellectual ability. Actually, the names of the "spurters" were simply chosen at random. But at the end of the school year, those children showed significantly larger gains in IQ scores than the other children in the same classes. The teachers expected these particular children to show increases in intelligence, and they *did* show increases in intelligence. This effect is called a **self-fulfilling prophecy**—a prediction that comes true because people believe that it will (Rosenthal and Jacobson, 1968).

Recent research indicates that the way teachers' expectancies influence students' achievement is by increasing their self-confidence in their own ability (Jussim, 1989). The same thing happens when parents have high expectancies for their children. But researchers have not discovered how these expectancies are conveyed to children. One report concluded, "It is primarily what the teacher does in the classroom, rather than personality characteristics of the teacher, that affects student achievement" (Linney and Seidman, 1989, p. 337). But distinctions like that break down when it comes to expectancies, because no one knows what teachers are actually *doing* in order to convey their expectancies. And everyone knows that there are teachers whose personalities are so potent, and whose expectancies for their students are so high and so compelling, that their students achieve more than they ever thought they were capable of, and they remember that teacher all the rest of their lives (see Box 12–2).

Learning Mathematics

Today the average child in the United States comes into kindergarten knowing how to count up to 29, and can count at least as high as 39 by the time he or she enters first grade (there are no gender differences in the early use of numbers). Most kindergartners can also solve simple problems in addition and subtraction, such as "If we put five pennies in this box and then put in two more, how many pennies are in the box?" Many 4-year-olds can solve such problems too, but they have to do it by counting all the pennies (or their fingers), starting at one: "One, two, three, four, five . . . six, seven" (Ginsburg and others, 1989). But kindergartners can solve such problems by a method called "counting on"—starting at five and counting "five, six, seven." Their ability to start in the middle of the series like this is not a mark of their cognitive maturity but simply a matter of how much practice they've had at it: it's not until fourth or fifth grade that children can run through the days of the week or the months of the year without starting from the beginning (see p. 362).

By the time they are in first grade, most children solve problems such as 2 + 5 by inverting the numbers and counting on from the larger number. They don't have to be taught to do this: children realize on their own, a year or two after they start adding, that numbers can be added in any order. By third or fourth grade, children can perform subtraction problems such as 8 − 2 by counting down from 8, and problems such as 8 − 6 by counting *up* from 6. They'll choose whichever procedure requires fewer counts (Resnick, 1989).

Most kindergartners solve addition and subtraction problems by counting on their fingers. But many first graders have reached the point where the number words themselves have become representations of the objects to be counted, and the children can count them off mentally instead of physically. Furthermore, as children get more and more practice with addition and subtraction, more and more solutions can simply be retrieved from memory, rather than counted out. Thus, the answer to a problem such as 2 + 2 comes instantly—it is remembered, rather than calculated (Resnick, 1989; Siegler, 1989).

Older children are faster and more accurate in math than younger ones,

In the early stages of learning to add and subtract, children rely on the time-honored method of counting on their fingers.

and they're also less likely to count on their fingers. Perhaps teachers assume that there is a causal connection between these two signs of progress, and that is why they often try to stop their younger students from using their fingers. But researchers have found that finger-counting is beneficial in the early stages of learning math. Children are more likely to give the wrong answer if they are prevented from counting on their fingers, and giving wrong answers delays the time when they can reliably retrieve the right answer from memory (Siegler and Shrager, 1984).

Addition and subtraction with regrouping (borrowing and carrying) are usually introduced in the latter half of second grade in American schools. Many children have trouble with the idea that a digit's meaning depends on its position (or *place value*) within a multidigit numeral. They make errors, and many of these errors have been found to be predictable on the basis of the erroneous rules the children are following—"bugs" in their "programs" for performing arithmetic calculations. For example, a child might subtract 34 from 71 and get 43, because she's followed the rule "Always subtract the smaller number from the larger one." Or, in subtracting from a number such as 504, she may borrow 100 from the hundreds column but return only 10 to the units column. When decimals are introduced, in fifth or sixth grade, many children think at first that .413 must be more than .5, because it has more digits (a rule that worked fine with nondecimal numbers). After they achieve a partial understanding of decimals, they may develop another wrong rule and state that .613 is *less* than .5, their reasoning being that "tenths are bigger than thousandths, so the number that has only tenths must be larger" (Nesher, 1986).

Clearly, it is not enough that children learn to calculate—they must also understand what they are doing. What is less clear, and becoming increasingly controversial, is how much practice children have to have in calculating in order to understand what they are doing. This brings us back to the use of computers (or calculators) in the classroom. Is it necessary, now that there are machines that can do it so much better, to know how to add, subtract, multiply, and divide? There are two views on this issue. The first is that children must have a firm foundation in basic number facts in order to gain a real understanding of the principles of mathematics. The second is that we are wasting too much of our children's time in drilling them in basic number facts—we could better spend this time by teaching them to think mathematically (Resnick, 1989). As one educator has put it, "Computers now compute, so students should learn to think. More important, students need to learn at every grade level when to use their heads and when to use their machines" (Steen, 1987, p. 302).

Why Are American Children So Poor at Math?

American children lag behind children from many other countries—especially Asian countries—in their understanding of the principles of mathematics. The differences are detectable by first grade: in a study of U.S., Chinese, and Japanese first graders, only 15 of the highest scoring 100 students were American. By fifth grade the difference has widened: only one of the top 100 fifth graders was from the U.S.; the other 99 were from China and Japan. The *average* twelfth-grade student in Japan outperforms 95 percent of U.S. twelfth graders in mathematics (Steen, 1987).

These are not negligible differences, and they have sobering implications for the future: if its citizens can't do math, the United States cannot expect to compete in a world where science and technology play increasingly important roles.

There seem to be a number of reasons, all operating together, for the American deficit in math achievement. First is how much time school children spend studying this subject. Fifth graders in Japan and Taiwan are in school an average of 235 days a year and 40 hours a week, as opposed to 174 days and 30 hours for U.S. children. When they are in school, Japanese and Taiwanese fifth graders spend about 26 percent of their time being instructed in math, versus only 17 percent in the U.S. While they are being instructed in math, the Asian fifth graders are working "on task" 90 percent of the time, as opposed to 83 percent for U.S. children. Researchers also report that grade-school teachers in Japan and Taiwan are more enthusiastic about math than their American counterparts: "Chinese and Japanese teachers appear to be better prepared for teaching mathematics and endow their classes with a liveliness and variety that typically are missing in American elementary school classes in mathematics" (Stigler, Lee, and Stevenson, 1987, p. 1284).

So it is not surprising that children in Asian countries learn more math than American children. But wait—how do we account for the fact that Asian-American children *learning math in U.S. schools* outperform European-American, African-American, and Hispanic-American children learning math in those same schools? The proportion of Asian-American twelfth graders who score above 650 on the math SAT is twice as high as that of other Americans (Steen, 1987). A remarkably high proportion of U.S. students who win competitions in math or science are Asian Americans (McLeod, 1986).

Some of the explanation for this high achievement undoubtedly involves the cultural emphasis on hard work and the belief that ability is changeable —not something you're born with and stuck with forever. But cultural differences tend to fade after a couple of generations in this country: third- and fourth-generation Asian Americans are hardly any better in math than their classmates from other racial or cultural groups. The children who outperform their classmates by such a wide margin are almost always those who were born in Asia or whose parents came here as immigrants. These children come from homes in which English is not the preferred language; they are bilingual. But being bilingual does not, in itself, lead to high achievement in math: children who are bilingual in Spanish and English perform below the national average on tests of math achievement (Miura and Okamoto, 1989).

Irene Miura of San Jose State University, and Yukari Okamoto of Stanford, have proposed an intriguing explanation for why children whose first language is Japanese, Chinese, or Korean do better in math than those who speak only English. It seems that these Asian languages all use the same number system, and it's a far more sensible system than the one we have in English (or in other Western languages). English-speaking children have to learn an irregular pattern of number names that, for numbers under 20, give no clue to the underlying base-10 structure of the number system. For numbers under 20 there is no correspondence between the spoken form of the numbers and the written form in Arabic numerals.

Arabic numerals are also used in Asian countries, but the spoken forms of these numbers are quite different. The system of number names used in most

Asian languages is logical and easy to learn. For example, 12 in Japanese is spoken as "ten-two," 20 as "two-tens." Whereas English confuses things by putting the "seven" in first place both in "seventeen" and in "seventy," Asian languages say "ten-seven" for the first and "seven-tens" for the second, thus conveying the concept of place values in a natural way.

Miura and Okamoto believe that this difference in spoken language accounts for the Asian child's earlier and deeper grasp of the base-10 number system. They did a study of first graders in the U.S. and Japan, testing what they called the children's "cognitive representation of number." They used a set of blocks that are sometimes used in the U.S. to teach the concept of place value. These blocks are constructed in such a way that ten "unit-blocks" equal one "ten-block": the ten-block is marked off in segments that each correspond to one unit-block. The Japanese and American children were asked to use these blocks to depict various numbers such as 13, 28, and 42. There are two ways of depicting the number 42: with four ten-blocks and two unit-blocks (the solution used by most of the Japanese children), or with 42 unit blocks. The American children were much more likely to use 42 unit blocks and to look blank when they were asked, "Can you think of another way to show the number?" (Miura and Okamoto, 1989).

As Miura and Okamoto point out, a child who does not have a firm grasp of the concept of place value is going to have trouble with things like carrying, borrowing, and decimals. They do not suggest that U.S. children be taught to count in Japanese (though that might not be such a bad idea), but they do feel that American children need extra help in developing the necessary concepts. In other words, American children should be spending *more* time learning math than Asian children, not *less* time.

Learning to Read

Of all the skills a child acquires in school, the ability to read is the most important. Reading is the skill that most later learning is based upon. Children who have not learned to read "do not have a tool to open the chest where the tools are kept" (Tharp, 1989, p. 355).

In Chapter 9 we pointed out that virtually every child—all but the most severely retarded or brain-damaged—develops some sort of language. To communicate in words (or, for the totally deaf, in gestures) seems to be an ability that is built into the human species. But this is not the case with reading. Reading is a cultural invention, not a built-in biological legacy. Speech develops in almost all children between the ages of 1 and 3; if it hasn't been acquired by adolescence, it probably never will be. Reading, on the other hand, is much more variable and unreliable in its appearance. It is seldom acquired before the age of 2½, but there is no upper age limit. Some people learn to read in adulthood. Some never do. Estimates of the proportion of adults in our society who, for all practical purposes, are illiterate range as high as 10 percent.

Because so much later learning depends on the ability to read, reading is the most important skill a child acquires in school.

Given the variability of this skill, it isn't surprising that so much attention has focused on the issue of how to teach children to read. And given the importance of reading, it isn't surprising that this subject has generated some strong feelings. In 1955 a book by Rudolf Flesch, called *Why Johnny Can't Read,* became a nationwide best seller. Flesch argued in his book that the reason some children didn't learn how to read (he called them the ''remedial reading cases'') was that they were taught by the wrong method. His prose was vivid, inflammatory, and often sarcastic. Here's a sample:

> And how do the educators explain all the thousands and thousands of remedial reading cases? This is what really got me mad. To them, failure in reading is never caused by poor teaching. Lord no, perish the thought. Reading failure is due to poor eyesight, or a nervous stomach, or poor posture, or heredity, or a broken home, or undernourishment, or a wicked stepmother, or an Oedipus complex, or sibling rivalry, or God knows what. The teacher or the school are never at fault. As to the textbook or the method taught to the teacher at her teachers' college—well, that idea has never yet entered the mind of anyone in the world of education. (Flesch, 1955, p. 18)

The method of teaching reading that Flesch objected to so vehemently is called the **sight-reading** or **whole-word method.** With this method, children are taught to recognize words as wholes, by their overall shape, rather than sounding them out letter by letter. Flesch thought that this was a ridiculous procedure. He believed in teaching children **phonics**—the correspondences between letters and speech sounds—right from the beginning. And he felt that if they weren't taught this way, they were quite likely never to learn to read at all.

In that last belief at least, Flesch was overly pessimistic. The fact is that the great majority of children do learn to read, regardless of the method used to teach them. American children are able to recognize by sight a great many words—just as Chinese children learning the traditional Chinese characters have done for centuries. But American children have an advantage in that

411

their written language is phonetic. Once they have learned to recognize a certain number of English words, many children are able to figure out for themselves the correspondences between letters and sounds. Proof that they have done this is their ability to read words they've never seen before—something that a child who simply recognizes words by their overall shape cannot do.

Perhaps you feel that figuring out the "code" of English phonics is an impossible task—that English spelling is too irregular. But, although English spelling and pronunciation are full of exceptions, they are exceptions to the *rules.* That there *are* rules is clear. People are quite able to offer pronunciations for nonwords like "snurb" and "flape," and there is usually good agreement on the pronunciation of such nonwords. As for the exceptions, they exist in spoken language, too—remember (from Chapter 9) "mines," "holded," "goed," and "feets"? Toddlers make such errors, showing that they have learned the rules despite the irregularities of spoken English. They soon learn the exceptions to the rules as well. Both in written and in spoken English, the exceptions often involve the most commonly used words, which means that children get plenty of practice in learning them.

Why Can't Johnny Read?

Many children can work out the phonic code on their own, even if no one teaches it to them. But not all children do this. Children with higher than average intelligence, and those who are strongly motivated to learn to read, are more likely to do it than children who lack these assets. The brighter, well-motivated ones tend to become good readers regardless of the teaching method used. But what about the others? Is Flesch right in believing that many children can't learn to read with the sight-reading method and that these children *can* learn with the phonic method?

Although Flesch undoubtedly overstated the case, the evidence from thousands of studies carried out since the publication of *Why Johnny Can't Read* has supported his basic premise. Children who are taught phonics— taught to *decode* written words—are better off. They're more likely to become good readers, less likely to become Flesch's "remedial reading cases," than children taught by the sight-reading method (Chall, 1967).

But children don't have to be taught phonics all at once, from the very beginning. Today, teachers generally use a mixed approach, starting with a few words learned by the sight-reading method and introducing phonics gradually. Because children can, at first, acquire new words more quickly by the sight-reading method, this enables them to start reading "real books" right away, and their early success gives them the motivation to embark on the harder job of learning phonics (Ellis and Large, 1988).

Not all words are readily decodable by phonics: many very common words—such as *of, one, sure,* and *though*—are highly irregular. Most children use the sight-reading method for familiar words (especially irregular ones), and use phonic decoding for new or longer words. However, there are children who stick to just one of these methods and who use it almost all the time. The children who stick to a letter-by-letter decoding process tend to be very slow at first—some teachers refer to them as "plodders." But in the long run, the plodders win the race. Although these children do not read as well in second grade as the children who rely on sight-reading or those who use a mixed strategy, by third grade their reading comprehension is equal to that of the mixed readers and well above that of the sight readers. At higher reading levels, a knowledge of phonics is essential (Freebody and Byrne, 1988).

WHAT DOES IT TAKE TO LEARN HOW TO READ? Nowadays most children enter kindergarten knowing the alphabet—that is, they can identify most or all of the capital letters. Some know the lower-case letters as well. But others cannot identify a single letter, and these children are at greater risk of doing poorly in school. Children who cannot identify upper- and lower-case letters quickly and accurately by the middle of their kindergarten year are likely to have trouble learning to read in first grade (Walsh, Price, and Gillingham, 1988).

The other major predictor of later reading achievement is the child's ability to break up words into their component sounds. Most children can tell you, by the beginning of first grade, that "pig" sounds like "ig" if you take off the sound at the beginning, and that "get" and "sit" both have the same sound ("t") at the end. Children who cannot do this are at a considerable disadvantage in learning to read (Ellis and Large, 1988).

Both the lack of knowledge of the alphabet and the lack of ability to divide up words into their component sounds can be remedied: a child can be taught these things. But this teaching takes time, and meanwhile the other children, who already know them, are learning how to read. Moreover, the very fact that the child doesn't know what other children of the same age already know may be a symptom of a deeper problem, not so easily remedied. For example, it could be a sign that the child's environment is intellectually impoverished, which in itself is likely to lead to lower achievement in school. Homes in which economic deprivation is severe contain little or no reading material; no one reads bedtime stories to the children before they go to sleep. No one recites nursery rhymes to them. Word-play with rhyming words is one way that children learn to take words apart and put them together again (Warren-Leubecker and Carter, 1988; Bradley, 1988).

The children who become good readers are more likely to come from middle-class homes where books are plentiful and the parents enjoy reading. These children are likely to have better than average vocabularies and to do well on IQ tests, especially on tests of verbal ability (Scarborough, 1989).

Some children learn to read even before they get to kindergarten. Although these children tend to be bright, not all highly intelligent children learn to read early, and not all early readers are highly intelligent. The distinguishing characteristic of the early readers is a strong interest in reading. Most of them learn to read because of their intrinsic motivation to do so, and not because of parental pressure or any special kind of training. These children generally do very well in school (Jackson, 1988).

GOOD READERS VERSUS POOR READERS. The children who have difficulty in "hearing" the separate sounds that words are composed of do not have a hearing problem—there is nothing wrong with their ears. And the children who have trouble identifying the letters of the alphabet do not have a problem with visual perception—they can *see* the letters as well as their agemates, they just can't name them as accurately or as quickly (Wagner and Torgerson, 1987).

To show that reading difficulties do not result from problems in visual perception, some researchers did an experiment with a group of second graders who had been unable to learn to read: they taught these children to read Chinese characters. The traditional Chinese characters are abstract symbols of the words they represent—they stand for ideas, rather than sounds. The nonreaders were taught 30 Chinese characters—for example, the characters for *mother, good,* and *car* (see Figure 12–2). With only three to six hours of instruction, the children could read and understand simple stories written in these Chinese characters. So their failure to learn to read English could not lie in an inability to discriminate and remember the 26 letters of the alphabet: they had readily learned to discriminate and remember 30 Chinese characters (Rozin, Poritsky, and Sotsky, 1971).

If children with reading problems are able to interpret nonphonetic word symbols, it would seem that they'd be better off learning to read English with a sight-reading approach. Why teach them phonics if that's exactly what they're having trouble with? Three reasons. First, even at interpreting nonphonetic symbols, they do not do as well as good readers. In an experiment, children were asked to associate arbitrary words with irregularly shaped black blobs, so that they could give the right word for each shape. Poor readers had more trouble with this task than good readers (Swanson, 1984).

Second, if children don't know how to decode written English words—how to analyze them phonetically—they will never be able to read a word they haven't seen before, even if it's a word they frequently use in speech.

Third, there seems to be a rather severe limit on how many words can be remembered purely by sight. The average high school student in the U.S. can read approximately 50,000 written English words. An adult Chinese scholar, on the other hand, can identify only about 4000 characters. And Chinese characters are more distinctive in appearance than written English words: many of the characters have some pictorial value that reminds the reader of their meaning. It's much harder to recognize English words purely by sight. As a matter of fact, adult nonreaders in our society—the so-called functional

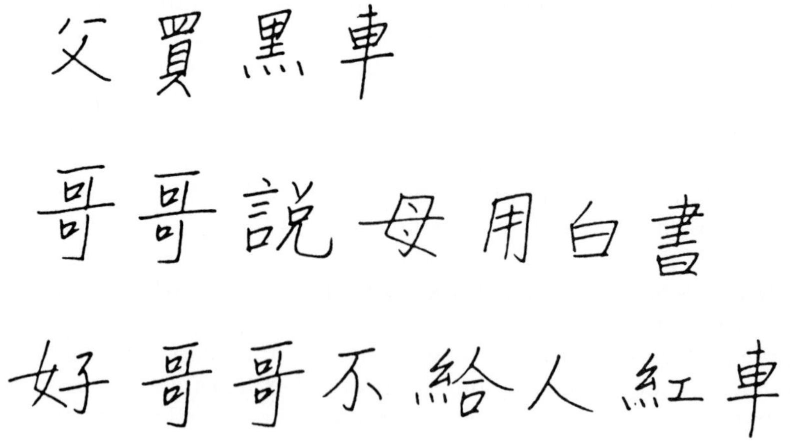

FIGURE 12-2
Three sentences written in Chinese characters, read successfully by American children who couldn't read English (Rozin, Poritzky, and Sotsky, 1971). The top sentence, read from left to right, means "Father buys (a) black car." The middle one means "Older brother says Mother uses (the) white book." The last one says "Good older brother (would) not give (the) man (a) red car."

父買黑車

哥哥說母用白書

好哥哥不給人紅車

illiterates—generally can recognize a certain number of common words by sight. Most of them have acquired a reading vocabulary of a few hundred words but have failed to progress beyond that point (Rozin and Gleitman, 1977).

If the difference between good readers and poor ones does not reside in their visual or auditory systems, where does it come from? How do poor readers differ from good ones? The answer seems to be that poor readers differ from good ones in their ability to use words to serve a variety of cognitive functions. In the section on The Growth of Metacognitive Skills, in Chapter 11, we said that older children are better than younger children at using verbal mediators to solve problems, and better at using words for metacognitive purposes. We said that older children have better memories because they can remember things in the form of words, whereas younger ones are more likely to use visual images. In all these uses of language, poor readers are more like younger children and good readers are more like older ones.

The difference shows up on a wide variety of tests. For example, poor readers are not only slower than good readers at naming letters and words, they are also slower at naming objects and colors (Wagner and Torgerson, 1987). It seems to take them longer to retrieve any kind of verbal information from long-term memory. They have problems with short-term memory as well: poor readers can hold fewer words in short-term memory than good readers, whether the words to be remembered are presented in written form or spoken aloud (Das and Siu, 1989). Children who are poor readers also lag behind their agemates in the quality of their spoken language—their vocabulary and sentence structure is comparable to that of good readers a year or two younger in age (Feagans and Short, 1984).

When the information-processing task does not involve a verbal component, poor readers generally do as well as good readers. For example, in the experiment where children were supposed to learn to associate arbitrary words with irregularly shaped black blobs, the poor readers did not do well. But the poor readers did as well as the good readers when the task was to remember which of five face-down cards had exactly the same blob as the card in the experimenter's hand (Swanson, 1984). On IQ tests, poor readers generally score lower than good readers on verbal items, but they may do very well on nonverbal items, and thus their IQ scores may be average or above. These children are considered to be **dyslexic** (see Box 12–3). Poor readers who don't do well on either verbal or nonverbal items, and whose IQ scores are therefore below average, are not considered dyslexic—they are sometimes referred to as "garden-variety poor readers" (Stanovich, 1988).

Some researchers believe that good readers and poor readers differ in brain organization: good readers are better at left-hemisphere tasks, poor readers at right-hemisphere tasks. This would fit in with the fact that boys are far more likely to have reading difficulties than girls. It would also fit in with the fact that heredity plays a role in reading problems. A child with a parent or a sibling who reads poorly runs a greatly increased risk of becoming a poor reader (Scarborough, 1989).

But environmental factors also play a role in reading problems. A child from a home at a low socioeconomic level is more likely to be a poor reader than one from an upper socioeconomic level, even if the two children have

Problems in Development

Box 12-3
Learning Disabilities

Here's 10-year-old Laura looking at the word *reverence* and trying to sound it out:

Rever . . . renay . . . never . . . r . . . never . . . r . . . never . . . r . . . never . . . in . . . cent . . . er . . . er . . . ev . . . er . . . eve . . . er . . . ence . . . er . . . ev . . . ence . . . ent. (Farnham-Diggory, 1984, p. 67)

If listening to this halting rendition is uncomfortable for us, just think how painful it must be for Laura. Laura spent a total of 51 seconds in her unsuccessful attempt to sound out the word *reverence*—a word that most other fifth graders can read.

Laura has a **learning disability,** which means that her achievement in school—her achievement in reading, in this case—is far below what it should be, given her IQ score, her family background, and her good physical and emotional health. An estimated 10 percent of American children are classified as learning disabled; about 80 percent are boys (Vogel and Walsh, 1987). Most learning-disabled children fall into two categories: those with a reading disability, or **dyslexia,** like Laura, and those who have **attention deficit disorder with hyperactivity.**

Because the problems of children with dyslexia resemble those of adults with certain kinds of brain injuries, their disability is believed to result from something wrong with their brains. The brain abnormality is assumed to be an inherited one, because dyslexia is known to run in families (Scarborough, 1989). According to one theory, the problem is due to abnormalities in brain lateralization—to a failure to localize speech and reading functions firmly on the left side of the brain, where they are in most people (see Chapter 8). It is true

A class for learning-disabled children.

that dyslexic children are somewhat more likely than other children to be left-handed or to have close relatives who are left-handed, and some of them do seem to have less lateralized brains. However, the majority of children who process speech and reading in both hemispheres are not handicapped in any way, and the majority of dyslexics are right-handed (Hiscock and Kinsbourne, 1987).

Thus, the lateralization theory, at least in its simplest form, has not been upheld. Researchers are currently looking for more subtle abnormalities in brain organization or structure in an effort to explain dyslexia. But their search is complicated by new evidence that dyslexia is not a single disorder: there are different types of dyslexics, with different patterns of abilities and disabilities, and each might have a different cause (Bonnet, 1989).

the same IQ (Bow, 1988). And notice that, for the child whose parent is a poor reader, there may be environmental causes as well as genetic causes for his tendency to follow in his parent's footsteps. Early experiences with language and with books are bound to have an effect on how well the child learns to read.

How well the child learns to read will, in turn, have a domino effect on many other aspects of his school achievement and his life outside of school. Good readers and poor readers grow up in different environments partly because, as they get older, they choose different environments for themselves. Children who are good readers enjoy reading and are more likely to

Many people still think that dyslexic children can't read because they "see things backward," but this theory has long been discredited. Most dyslexics are average or above average in visual and spatial ability, and even those who aren't do not see things backward. Problems with writing letters backward, or reading them in the wrong direction, are common in beginning readers. Dyslexics remain at that stage longer than other children because their rate of progress in reading is abnormally slow (Vogel, 1989).

The other major group of learning-disabled children are classified as having **ADD-H**: attention deficit disorder with hyperactivity. Again, most of these children are boys. These are the children who can't sit still, who can't keep quiet, and who can't focus their attention on anything long enough to learn it. Their school achievement is poor, and the main reason seems to be that they are "off task" most of the time.

Although subtle brain abnormalities are also thought to be to blame for ADD-H, they are not necessarily due to heredity: prenatal or postnatal exposure to certain toxic substances, such as lead, alcohol, or cocaine, can affect the child's developing brain. The mothers of children with ADD-H have been found to consume more alcohol than mothers of normal children, and if they started drinking before the child was born, this might have caused or contributed to the child's disorder. But it's also possible that their drinking is a *reaction* to the stress of having a child with ADD-H (Cunningham, Benness, and Siegel, 1988). Living with such a child is not easy. These children evoke unfavorable reactions not only from parents, but also from teachers and peers. In addition to their hyperactivity, many of these children also suffer from conduct disorder (see Box 2–4), which means that they may be aggressive and defiant, in addi-

tion to being overly active. Such children tend to be disliked by other children (Hinshaw, 1987).

ADD-H is often treated with drugs, most often with methylphenidate (trade name: Ritalin). The drug helps the majority of hyperactive children to calm down and sit still, and this usually has a beneficial effect on their schoolwork and on their relationships with adults and other children (Campbell and Spencer, 1988).

What happens to learning-disabled children when they grow up? For those with ADD-H, it depends on whether the child is *just* hyperactive or is conduct disordered as well. Of the ones who also have conduct disorder, many will jeopardize their future by getting into trouble with drugs, alcohol, and delinquency. The outlook is better for those who only have ADD-H: they may never be brilliant students, but they usually do all right once they're out of school (Hinshaw, 1987; Mannuzza and others, 1988).

With regard to dyslexia, much depends on what kind of help the child gets and how soon she gets it. The outcome is much better for children whose families can afford to have them tutored or to send them to special schools: most of these children end up going to college. But of a group of lower- to middle-class children who attended special classes in public schools, 62 percent dropped out without finishing high school (Bruck, 1987).

Learning disabilities never seem to go away entirely; what happens instead is that many children eventually learn how to deal with their problems and are able to compensate for them. These children may emerge from the struggle with renewed self-confidence and a great determination to succeed. Many highly successful people, including Thomas Edison, Winston Churchill, and the actor Tom Cruise, were learning disabled as children.

read books for pleasure—thus, good readers get more reading practice and more exposure to sources of knowledge, and their advantage over poor readers widens over the years. Good readers are also likely to become good writers: the correlation between reading ability and writing ability gets stronger with each grade in school (Bracey, 1989; Stanovich, 1988).

Because they watch so much television, children today don't read as much as they did a generation or two ago. But reading and writing are not likely to become obsolete skills. Although it is possible nowadays to operate computers by using a "mouse" to move a pointer to a picture, only low-level computer tasks can be done that way. Most interactions between people and computers take place in the English language. That may be the one real advantage we have over Japan and China: a language that can be written with only 26 characters plus a few punctuation marks—almost as though it was designed to fit neatly onto a computer keyboard.

Summary

1. A number of advances in cognitive, motor, and social development combine to make most 6-year-olds ready to start school. The younger children in the class are at a disadvantage at first, but catch up after a few years. Other children lag behind in "readiness" for first grade. Making such children wait at home for another year is not likely to do them any good.

2. Intelligence, as measured by the IQ score, is the best predictor of how well a child will do in school, but many other factors affect school achievement. When IQ score and achievement differ greatly, it is usually in the case of a high-IQ child who does poorly.

3. Mental retardation consists of a low IQ (below 70) *plus* other indications—children who are capable of adaptive behavior are no longer labeled retarded. The two kinds of retardation are **organic,** due to brain injury or genetic defects, and **cultural-familial,** due to an unfavorable combination of heredity and environment.

4. The intellectually gifted children studied by Terman were superior to their agemates in physical development, social skills, and psychological adjustment, and were ahead of their agemates in a wide variety of school subjects.

5. There are many examples of group differences in IQ scores, but the one that worries people most is the black–white difference. Although it is claimed that IQ tests are culturally biased, they predict school achievement as accurately for black children as for white children. Black–white differences in childrearing styles may play a role in differences in performance on IQ tests and in school achievement.

6. Children of Asian origin do remarkably well on American tests and in American schools. This is attributed to a cultural ethic that emphasizes hard work and devotion to one's parents.

7. There are no overall differences in IQ between girls and boys, but girls do better than boys in school and on tests of reading and verbal ability. Boys are considerably more likely than girls to have verbal handicaps such as reading disabilities.

8. Boys do better on tests of **visual–spatial ability** and of mathematical reasoning. The majority of children who are exceptionally talented in math are male. Since SAT exams are generally not taken by students who are verbally disabled (most of whom are male), boys do as well as girls on the verbal part of the exam and considerably better on the math part.

9. Why do girls make better grades in math than boys, but get lower scores on tests of math aptitude? One theory is that there are biological differences in brain organization. Other possibilities are differences in styles of play, experiences in school, parental encouragement, and motivational factors.

10. The home and family affect a child's school achievement. Children who grow up in one-parent homes or at a low socioeconomic level don't do as well.

11. Children who come up with unusual answers on tests of creativity are said to be capable of **divergent thinking.** Girls, and children with higher IQs, do better on verbal tests of creativity. Girls also do somewhat better on nonverbal tests of creativity.

12. Children who are **impulsive** in their "cognitive style" respond quickly on the Matching Familiar Figures Test and make many errors; **reflective** children respond more slowly and make fewer errors. Children who are scored as impulsive on the MFF test are not necessarily impulsive in the sense that they can't control their own behavior.

13. A child who has **intrinsic motivation** to read a book is reading it because she's interested in it; if she reads it to earn a reward such as money, that's **extrinsic motivation.** Providing an extrinsic motivator may lead to a decline in intrinsic motivation, but it may be necessary if no intrinsic motivation exists. Eventually, motivation may become internalized.

14. Children with a **performance goal** are motivated to get praise and good grades; those with a **learning goal** are motivated to understand and master a challenging subject. Most children are capable of adopting either type of goal.

15. When children with a learning-goal orientation meet an obstacle, they try harder. Children with a performance-goal orientation will try harder only if they have confidence in their own ability; if they don't, they will give up. A child who thinks that ability is mainly a matter of working hard is more likely to be learning-goal oriented; one who thinks that ability is fixed and unchangeable is more likely to be performance-goal oriented.

16. Attributions for successes and failures vary along three dimensions: stable vs. changeable, global vs. specific, and external vs. internal. The internal vs. external dimension is called **locus of control.** Some children have changeable, specific, external attributions for success ("I was lucky this time"), but stable, global, internal attributions for failure ("I'm no good at anything"). This pattern of attributions for failure is called *learned helplessness.*

17. "Helpless" children give up when confronted with obstacles; **mastery-oriented** children work harder. Girls are more likely than boys to underestimate their own ability and to have the "helpless" reaction to failure. Thus, if they find something confusing, girls are more likely to give up.

18. There are "successful schools" and "unsuccessful schools," judged by students' achievement scores, absence rates, and so on. Successful schools are likely to have (1) a principal who is committed to academic excellence and who provides leadership, (2) teachers who have high expectations for their students and who spend a high proportion of their time "on task," and (3) a safe, orderly atmosphere.

19. Children from some cultural backgrounds may have trouble because their values and behaviors are not in harmony with those of the school. Schools are becoming more sensitive to the issue of cultural diversity.

20. Being bilingual is not, in itself, harmful to a child's cognitive development. The question of whether children who do not know English when they enter school should be taught in English or in their native language has not yet been answered.

21. Computers are used in the classroom either as a way of making children "computer literate" or as a means of teaching them other things. In the long run, the benefits of having computers in the classroom will depend on the purposes they are used for. In the short run, the danger is that computers may widen the gap between students who vary in ability or in degree of "computer anxiety."

22. If a teacher is good at classroom management, the students will spend more time "on task" and will learn more. Good teachers expect their students to work hard and to do well. The teacher's expectancy that a child will do well may become a **self-fulfilling prophecy,** because it increases the child's academic self-confidence.

23. The average kindergartner can count up to 29 and can do simple problems in addition and subtraction. Four-year-olds do problems such as 5 + 2 by counting from 1, but kindergartners can use a method called "counting on"—starting from 5.

24. Most kindergartners solve addition and subtraction problems by counting on their fingers, but most first graders can count in their heads. Eventually, they don't even need to count—they can retrieve the answer from memory. Preventing younger children from counting on their fingers causes them to make more mistakes and delays the time when they can retrieve the answer from memory.

25. American children often have trouble with the idea that a digit's meaning depends on its position (place value). Asian children are way ahead of American children in learning math, and one reason may be that their number system gives them a better grasp of place value.

26. Reading is the most important skill that the child learns in school. Although the ability to use language is built into the human species, the ability to read is not.

27. Much controversy has surrounded the teaching of reading—particularly the issue of teaching **phonics** versus teaching by the **sight-reading method.** The great majority of children learn to read regardless of the method used; however, children who are taught to "decode" written words are more likely to become good readers.

28. Children who cannot name the letters of the alphabet quickly and accurately, or who cannot break up spoken words into their separate sounds, are likely to have trouble learning to read. Good readers tend to have a strong interest in reading and to come from homes where books are plentiful.

29. Poor readers differ from good ones in their ability to use words and language. In nonverbal tests, poor readers may do as well as good readers.

30. **Learning disabilities** include **dyslexia** and **attention deficit disorder with hyperactivity (ADD-H).** Dyslexia is thought to result from some subtle kind of brain abnormality; it is evidently inherited. Children with dyslexia do not "see things backward."

31. Children with ADD-H can't sit still and can't keep their attention focused on anything long enough to learn it. Drug therapy helps many children with this disorder to calm down and sit still.

Key Terms

educable mentally retarded
organic retardation
cultural-familial retardation
mental retardation
visual–spatial ability
divergent thinking
impulsive
reflective
achievement motivation

intrinsic motivation
extrinsic motivation
performance goal
learning goal
internal locus of control
external locus of control
mastery oriented
self-efficacy
self-fulfilling prophecy

sight-reading method
whole-word method
phonics
dyslexic
learning disability
dyslexia
attention deficit disorder
  with hyperactivity
  (ADD-H)

Getting Along with Oneself and with Others

Although in our society we no longer expect 8-year-old children to take care of infants or to work in the fields or the factories, that doesn't mean their lives are free of responsibility and stress. School-age children are expected to behave properly in a wide variety of situations and to get along with a wide variety of people. They are enmeshed in a complex network of relationships, with parents, teachers, siblings, and agemates. Children's lives can be very miserable indeed if these relationships go badly, because they are stuck with them. Adults can get divorced, or move to a different town, or find another job, but children don't have these options.

What determines whether children's relationships with other people will be successful or unsuccessful? What determines whether they will become responsible, caring, and self-assured members of society? These are some of the questions we will try to answer in this chapter.

Social Cognition

In Chapter 2 we told you about the 4-year-old Inuit girl who smiled when her aunt asked her, "Don't you want to die? Do die, then I can have your shirt." We used that incident to illustrate the effects of cultural differences, and the fact that a child growing up in Inuit (Eskimo) society, where that type of teasing is common, will have a different reaction to those words than a child growing up in American society. But the child's reaction was not based solely on her cultural experiences. She had other reasons for believing that her aunt was teasing her, based both on her previous experiences with her aunt and on her interpretation of her aunt's tone of voice and facial expression. Even a 4-year-old can usually tell when a person is "just kidding." She can also tell when a person is sad, happy, angry, or in pain. This type of understanding is one aspect of what is called *social cognition.*

Social cognition refers to knowledge and understanding about people's thoughts and feelings, and about the way they behave and their interactions with each other. The subject of this knowledge can be oneself, as well as someone else. It involves understanding that other people (as well as oneself) *have* thoughts and feelings, and it also involves understanding what those thoughts and feelings are. Because this is knowledge and understanding about mental processes, it is a type of metacognition.

Social cognition develops along with other types of cognition: children learn, as they grow older, about the physical characteristics of the objects in their world, and they also learn about the psychological characteristics of the people in their world, including themselves. Thus, social cognition includes self-knowledge and self-concepts, and it also includes the kinds of knowledge that are involved in social relationships.

Responding to Other People's Emotions

Even very young babies are responsive to the emotions displayed by others. We saw in Chapter 6 that a 3-month-old baby will respond in appropriate ways if his mother pretends to be happy, sad, or angry. By 12 months, he will glance at his mother's face (or at the face of another friendly adult) for information about how to react in an unfamiliar situation; this is called *social referencing.* If his mother looks fearful or angry, a toddler won't cross a visual cliff or touch a scary toy; if she looks calm or pleased, he will be reassured that it's okay. A toddler who sees someone crying may react by becoming distressed or even by offering comfort.

Facial and vocal expressions of emotions are universal: all over the world, people smile and laugh when they are happy, and frown or cry when they are sad or in pain. These responses do not have to be learned; even blind babies smile and frown. But it is quite possible for people to portray these emotions without actually feeling them. The findings we referred to in the previous paragraph came mostly from experiments in which adults *pretended* to be happy, sad, or angry. And the babies fell for it. There is a popular myth that dogs and young children have some kind of second sense that enables them to detect the "real" person under the facade. The truth is, however, that it is pretty easy to fool a dog (a juicy bit of steak is usually quite persuasive), and it is extremely easy to fool a young child. As one prominent researcher put it,

> The young child can read the big, obvious signs of gaiety in another, but she will require additional social-cognitive growth before she can also pick up the little, nonobvious signs that indicate that this individual's gaiety is forced and false. Seeing through social facades is not the long suit of young children. (Flavell, 1985, p. 123)

It is not until they're about 8 or 9 that children begin to detect falsity in facial expressions. In an experiment in which school-age boys (average age 9 to 10) interacted with unfamiliar women, the women smiled at the boys even if the boys weren't being very nice. But these forced smiles were abrupt and faded quickly from the women's faces. Many of the boys were evidently able to detect the falsity of these abrupt smiles: they acted friendlier to women whose smiles began and ended in a slower, more natural manner (Bugental, 1986).

EXPRESSING, CONCEALING, AND FEIGNING EMOTIONS. It's odd that it takes children 8 or 9 years before they can detect false displays of emotions, because they are aware at a much earlier age that emotions can be feigned. Children begin to feign emotions themselves as early as age 2; in social pretend play in the preschool period, they may take on roles such as "I'm the baby and I'm crying because I want my dinner," or "I'm the daddy and I'm mad at you for breaking my car." Not many preschoolers can portray emotions in a manner that can fool an adult (which is probably why they are unable to lie convincingly), but they get better at it as they get older. A 7-year-old girl pretended to cry and held her hand as though she had hurt it, and when her mother fell for it the child laughed and said "I just wanted to see how you'd react" (Bretherton, Fritz, Zahn-Waxler, and Ridgeway, 1986, p. 541).

As children get older, they also get better at *covering up* their emotions, but their ability to conceal genuine feelings—especially when they're strong feelings—develops much more slowly than their ability to act out emotions that they don't feel. We pointed out in Chapter 9 that children have to learn to keep their emotions under control if they are to become acceptable members of society, and that preschoolers who are prone to outbursts of distress or anger are likely to be unpopular with adults and agemates. By the time they enter elementary school, children are also expected to regulate their *verbal* expressions of feelings. School-age children are expected to know that it isn't "polite" to tell someone that you don't like her or that she smells bad. They are expected to say "thank you" for a gift even if they think it's yucky.

Still later in development comes the ability to regulate one's *facial* expressions of negative feelings. Social pressure to regulate one's words is firmer and more direct than the pressure to regulate one's facial expressions, so it is not surprising that children learn the verbal forms of politeness before they are able to use the facial expressions that go with them. They can *say* "thank you" for a yucky gift several years before they are able to do a convincing job of *looking* thankful. Researchers asked children in different grades what kind of facial expression they thought a child their age would have if a relative gave her a gift of an ugly sweater. First graders said the child would look disappointed, but about half of the fifth graders thought that she would succeed in concealing her disappointment. However, even in fifth grade, only a minority of children thought that a child their age would be able to put on a show of indifference if she were being teased or if she lost a contest and everyone was applauding the winner (Gnepp and Hess, 1986).

Perhaps because they are so poor at covering up their feelings, children seem to concentrate more on trying to make their negative feelings go away. Researchers questioned some school-age children about how they cope with unpleasant things such as the pain of an inoculation. Half the 6-year-olds and three-quarters of the 12-year-olds suggested a strategy such as "thinking happy thoughts" as a way of distracting themselves from pain (Band and Weisz, 1988). More surprisingly, children also suggest such strategies to their elders. Because adults' displays of emotions are often upsetting to children, children sometimes try to influence their parents to tone them down. A 7-year-old boy whose mother missed a flight connection told her, "I don't think you should think about it. If you don't think about it, it'll get better." Another child of about the same age told his father, who had come home shouting that he hates his job, "Take it easy, Dad. Calm down. It'll be all right." And, of course, children often try to get their parents to stop fighting with each other (Bretherton and others, 1986, pp. 540–541).

Becoming Aware of Other People's Psychological Characteristics

Preschool children understand that other people have feelings; they can even predict, under some circumstances, what these feelings will be: "If I hit Freddy he will be sad, if I give Jeannie a present she will be happy." However, this understanding does not go very deep. A 4-year-old does not realize that Jeannie might not be happy if you give her a puppy and she is afraid of dogs, or if you give her a box of chocolates and she is allergic to chocolate. In particular, preschoolers are unable to appreciate that Jeannie might have two emotions at the same time—happiness and fear, or happiness and sadness. The understanding that emotional reactions can be complex and ambivalent develops gradually during middle childhood (Gnepp, McKee, and Domanic, 1987).

School-age children also come to understand that people differ in their reactions to situations. Preschoolers are not very good at recognizing that people have individual psychological characteristics. It is not until they are about 8 years old that children come to realize that the consistencies in people's behavior (which they started noticing much earlier) represent stable psychological traits of those people. Researchers told kindergartners, second graders, and fourth graders stories about children their own age; one story, for example, was about a boy named Tommy, who "helps old people down the stairs . . . shows new kids around the school . . . [and] sets the table for his mom whenever he can." Then the child who was being tested was asked what Tommy would do, and how he would feel, when Tommy's mother asked him to help his little sister clean her room. The kindergartners tended to base their answers on how *they* would feel if they were asked to do that chore, but most of the older children drew reasonable conclusions about Tommy's reaction from the information they had about his personality. The older the children were, the more importance they placed on Tommy's own characteristics, and the less likely they were to assume that Tommy would respond the same way as other people (Gnepp and Chilamkurti, 1988, p. 746).

This growing ability to notice that people are different *inside,* as well as outside, also shows up in other contexts. In a classic study carried out in England, children aged 7 to 15 were asked to give detailed descriptions of someone they knew. The researchers told the children that they wanted to know what the person was really like and what they thought of him or her. Nonetheless, the 7-year-olds tended to base their descriptions on superficial things such as physical appearance, clothing, and family statistics. But, with increasing age, the children put more and more emphasis on psychological characteristics. Here is the often-quoted description given by a child who is going on 10:

> He smells very much and is very nasty. He has no sense of humor and is very dull. He is always fighting and he is cruel. He does silly things and is very stupid. He has brown hair and cruel eyes. He is sulky and 11 years old and has lots of sisters. I think he is the most horrible boy in the class. He has a croaky voice and always chews his pencil and picks his teeth and I think he is disgusting.   (Livesley and Bromley, 1973, p. 217)

Notice that this description is 100 percent negative: this 10-year-old can't think of a single nice thing to say about the subject of her scrutiny. It takes children 7 or 8 years to figure out the *consistencies* in people's behavior; then they have to learn to accept the fact that most people are *not* 100 percent consistent. The truth is, almost everyone has some good traits and some bad ones. School-age children—along with many adolescents and adults—tend to believe that a person is either all one way or all the other. They have difficulty in reconciling contradictory information about the same individual, just as younger children have trouble understanding that a person might experience two contradictory emotions at the same time. What do they do when they have some information that doesn't fit? They throw it out! When 8-year-olds were told a story about a doctor who became a thief, most of them denied that he was still a doctor (Donaldson and Westerman, 1986). In a child's world, doctors are helpful and thieves are harmful, so how could one person be both?

Children (and adolescents and adults) are more likely to accept the fact that someone has both good and bad characteristics if they know that person well. The trouble is that if they have a stereotype of someone as all bad, they are unlikely ever to get to know that person.

The Development of Self-Knowledge

It might surprise you (it surprised us) to learn that the development of self-knowledge proceeds no faster than the development of knowledge about other people, and in some ways it proceeds more slowly. This is true right from the start: it takes babies about 18 months to recognize themselves in the mirror (see Box 7–1)—far longer than it takes them to recognize their mothers. At 21 months, children are about equally good at identifying photos of themselves and photos of their mothers.

Who am I? By the end of middle childhood, most young people have developed some understanding of their own psychological characteristics.

In middle childhood, children's descriptions of themselves are similar in nature to their descriptions of other people. In reply to the question "Who am I?" younger school-age children tend to concentrate on their physical characteristics, their activities, and their possessions, whereas older children are more likely to mention psychological attributes. Older children are also more likely to admit that not all of their attributes are good. Here's a self-description from an 11½-year-old:

> My name is A. I'm a human being. I'm a girl. I'm a truthful person. I'm not pretty. I do so-so in my studies. I'm a very good cellist. . . . I try to be helpful. I'm always ready to be friends with anybody. Mostly I'm good, but I lose my temper. I'm not well-liked by some girls. I don't know if I'm liked by boys or not.   (Montemayor and Eisen, 1977, pp. 317–318)

One way that self-concepts lag behind concepts of other people is in giving explanations for behavior. Children are more likely to attribute their own behavior to an external cause—something outside of themselves—and more likely to attribute someone else's behavior to a internal cause, a stable personality characteristic. For example, if they picked some flowers they will explain that they did it because the flowers were pretty, but if Chris picks some flowers they'll say it's because Chris loves flowers. Attributing behavior to temporary, external causes rather than to stable, internal characteristics is more common in younger children than in older ones, so the external kind of explanation is considered less mature. And yet people of all ages—adults included—are more likely to attribute their own behavior to external causes and other people's behavior to internal causes (Miller and Aloise, 1989). For example, if you kick someone in the shins your explanation is likely to be something like "He insulted me" or "He grabbed my book," whereas if someone else kicks him in the shins you might say about the kicker, "She's a very aggressive person" or "She's been having a bad time of it this semester." At least in this respect, children and adults seem to be better at understanding others than they are at understanding themselves.

In Chapter 12 we discussed children's attributions for their academic successes and failures, and we said that these attributions varied along three dimensions: stable versus changeable, global versus specific, and internal versus external. Now we're talking about children's attributions for their own and other people's behavior, and the same three dimensions turn up again. As children get older, they tend to see people (including themselves) as having stable rather than changeable psychological characteristics, as having a number of specific characteristics rather than one global one, and as being controlled more by internal factors and less by external forces. What may seem confusing is that in Chapter 12 we said that children who believe that their academic ability is changeable, not stable, are better off in some ways. However, this is true only for children whose estimation of their own academic ability is low. Children who have a high estimation of their own ability are likely to do well, regardless of whether they think it is changeable or stable.

SELF-ESTEEM. Middle childhood is when children begin to form ideas about their own abilities, not just in respect to academic achievement but in many other areas as well. At around 7 or 8 years of age, children begin to compare themselves to their agemates and to use these comparisons to learn about their own characteristics. They become aware of what they're good at and what they're not so good at.

Research has shown that third through sixth graders are able to give consistent and fairly accurate judgments of their own competence in three different areas: academic, athletic, and social. The children's judgments of how good they are in school, or at sports, or at making friends, agree pretty well with independent ratings (made by teachers and classmates) of how good they are in these areas. Moreover, there is a steady increase, as children get older, in the accuracy of their self-judgments. During the elementary school years, children develop a self-image that corresponds ever more closely to reality (Harter, 1982). This doesn't mean that older school-age children are perfectly accurate in assessing their own abilities (as we mentioned in Chapter 12, some very good students seriously underestimate their own academic ability), but that there is a reasonably good correlation between self-judgment and ability. Even when children underestimate themselves, they are likely to be in the right ballpark.

It would be nice to live in a world where "all the children are above average," but in the real world that is not possible. Fortunately, children who are below average in one thing (or who *think* they are) may be well above average in something else. Thus, children's feelings of self-worth need not depend solely on how they do in school. Although there is a significant correlation between academic self-esteem and overall feelings of self-worth, the correlation is far from perfect (Alpert-Gillis and Connell, 1989). Children who do poorly in school are likely to place more importance on things they *are* good at.

At any rate, a large majority of American children appear to have high confidence in their own ability to succeed in life. In a study of almost 600 fourth, fifth, and sixth graders, the children were asked to agree or disagree with statements such as "In the future I expect that I will be able to handle myself well in whatever situation I'm in," and "I expect that I will succeed at most things I try." Agreement with such statements was considered to be a sign of optimism about the future. The highest possible optimism score on this test was 16, and these children got an average score of 14! In fact, a large number of children scored a perfect 16, implying that they had no doubts at all that their future would be rosy (Fischer and Leitenberg, 1986).

As children get older they recognize that they can't be good at everything. But most children are able to compensate for their failures in one area by concentrating on their successes in other areas, and thus keep their self-esteem intact.

Sex-Role Development

"My name is A. I'm a human being. I'm a girl." If you ask a child to answer the question "Who am I?" the statement "I'm a girl" or "I'm a boy" is likely to appear as soon as the child is old enough to understand the question. Gender is one of the basic components of our self-concepts and of our concepts of other people. A British writer named Sarah Caudwell writes mystery books in which the detective, an Oxford professor named Hilary Tamar, has no identifiable gender at all. It's curious how unsettling it is to read these books. One is constantly looking for clues about Hilary's sex—clues that the writer has purposely withheld. It makes the reader realize how much our interpretations of people's words and actions depend on our concepts of maleness and femaleness.

At a very early age, children begin to develop sex-role concepts and stereotypes about how males and females are supposed to look and act. These stereotypes are often quite rigid in preschoolers and younger school-age children, but they tend to become more flexible over the years. Older school-age children have more complex, less global concepts of people's psychological characteristics, at least for people they know well. Thus, they are more likely to understand that females may have some characteristics they think of as male, and that males may have some characteristics they think of as female (Berndt and Heller, 1986).

In a recent study, children between the ages of 4 and 10 heard stories about a girl named Susie and a boy named Tommy. Here is how Susie was described: "Susie's best friend is a boy, and Susie likes to play with airplanes." The description of Tommy said that his best friend is a girl and that he likes to play with his toy iron and ironing board. After hearing these descriptions, the children were asked to guess what *other* toys Tommy and Susie would like to play with. The younger children (ages 4 to 6) ignored the information about Tommy and Susie's personal preferences and based their decisions solely on gender stereotypes: most of them said that Tommy would like cars and trains and that Susie would like dolls and toy sewing machines. But many of the older children (ages 7 to 10) guessed that if Tommy likes toy irons he might also like dolls, and that if Susie likes airplanes she might also like trains (Martin, 1989).

ANDROGYNY AND SELF-ESTEEM. It's possible that Susie likes trains *and* dolls. Nowadays, in Western society, many parents and teachers lean over backward not to pressure children to conform to gender stereotypes. It's not just a question of toys or hairstyles—it goes deeper than that. Girls are encouraged to strive for achievement and independence; boys are less likely to be shamed for expressing tenderness, fear, or pain. The gender stereotypes are becoming more similar to each other, so that the very feminine female and the very masculine male now seem somewhat out of date. The new ideal is for a person to have the positive attributes of both genders—both independence and assertiveness (traditional masculine attributes) plus warmth and expressiveness (traditional feminine attributes). People who have characteristics of both genders are called **androgynous.** Some researchers believe that androgynous people are better off psychologically than those who adhere more closely to the traditional gender stereotypes (Bem, 1974; Spence and Helmreich, 1978).

Most of the previous research involved adolescents and adults, but recently androgyny has been studied in school-age children as well. Fourth-, fifth-, and sixth-grade children were asked to agree or disagree with statements such as "I am often the leader among my friends" (a "masculine" statement) or "I am a very considerate person" (a "feminine" statement). On the basis of their replies, the children were divided into four different categories:

■ Masculine (these children scored high on masculine characteristics, low on feminine characteristics).

■ Feminine (high on feminine characteristics, low on masculine characteristics).

■ Androgynous (high on both masculine and feminine characteristics).

■ Undifferentiated (low on both masculine and feminine characteristics).

A generation ago, a boy who showed an interest in sewing might have been mocked by his peers and worried over by his parents. Today the gender stereotypes are not so rigid, and androgyny—even for boys—is more acceptable.

The researchers also gave the children a test that measured their overall self-esteem. In line with previous results on adults and adolescents, androgynous children were found to have higher self-esteem than feminine and undifferentiated children. However (also in line with work on adults and adolescents), masculine children had just about as much self-esteem as androgynous children (Alpert-Gillis and Connell, 1989). In other words, the characteristics that were associated with high self-esteem were the masculine characteristics, such as assertiveness, independence, and leadership ability. The feminine characteristics, such as warmth, expressiveness, and gentleness, didn't have much effect on self-esteem. This doesn't mean that these traits have no value—it's just that they don't seem to contribute to people's feelings of self-worth.

On the other hand, it may be the case that our society values "masculine" traits more than "feminine" ones. Perhaps that is the reason why boys are still under a certain amount of pressure to be masculine, whereas much less pressure is put on girls to be feminine.

Relationships with Other Children

Theoretically, girls could learn about being assertive and independent by associating with boys, and boys could learn about being expressive and considerate by associating with girls. But school-age boys and girls, unless they are siblings, don't have much opportunity to learn from each other. They are too busy avoiding each other.

Girls and Boys Together?

At no time in their lives are girls and boys farther apart than in middle childhood. In the preschool period, girls and boys sometimes play together, although mixed-sex friendships are less common than same-sex friendships even then. In adolescence, of course, the sexes get back together again. But school-age children segregate themselves rigidly by sex. A researcher who spent some time observing preadolescents in an urban middle school reported that virtually no sixth or seventh graders sat at lunch with a member of the opposite sex. At one point in a science class, a teacher was forming groups of three for doing an experiment. He told a sixth grader named Juan to join "Diane's group" of two girls. Juan refused. The teacher became angry when he was unable to make Juan give in and ended by sending him out of the room. Juan accepted this punishment as preferable to joining the girls' group (Schofield, 1981). Perhaps Juan was less afraid of his teacher's wrath than of the taunts of the other children: "Juan and Diane, sitting in a tree, K-I-S-S-I-N-G!"

According to Sigmund Freud, middle childhood is a period of latency—a period in which nothing much happens. But Freud may have been misled. According to Eleanor Maccoby and Carol Jacklin, prominent researchers in the area of sex-role development,

> In middle childhood, sex segregation is fueled in part by avoidance of implications of sexuality. This period could hardly be considered a "latency" period in Freud's sense, in that the two sexes are intensely aware of each other and excited by each other. Yet something akin to a taboo appears to be operating. The gender of other children is both salient [vividly perceived] and emotionally charged. Children know that members of the opposite sex are their future romantic partners, but also know that they are not ready for dating. Strong group norms are formed, and the teasing that can result from violating them can be intense. (Maccoby and Jacklin, 1987, p. 244)

Maccoby and Jacklin quote an 11-year-old girl who told them that if she dared to be friendly with boys, "People would not be my friends. They would scorn me." Sitting next to a boy, she said, would be the equivalent of "peeing in your pants"—"You would be teased for *months*."

GENDER DIFFERENCES IN STYLES OF INTERACTION. There is a second reason for sex segregation in middle childhood. In Chapter 10 we described Maccoby

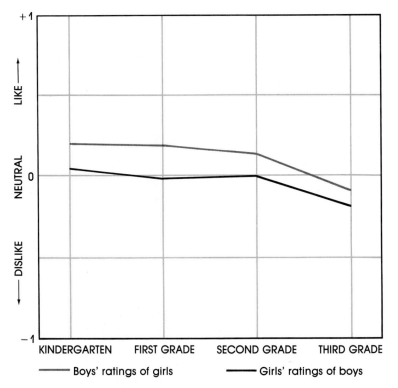

FIGURE 13-1
Girls' and boys' opinions of each other across four years of coeducation.
The black line shows girls' ratings of how much they like their male
classmates; the colored line shows boys' ratings of how much they like
their female classmates. (Source: Hayden-Thomson, Rubin, and Hymel,
1987.)

and Jacklin's findings on preschool children. They discovered that the more
contact girls and boys have had with each other, the more they avoid each
other. The same thing has been found in middle childhood (see Figure 13–1).
Children who are made to work in mixed-sex groups in school become less
willing, not more willing, to participate in such groups again. This is especially true for girls: the more experience girls have had in collaborating with
boys, the stronger are their negative stereotypes about boys (Lockheed and
Harris, 1984). In middle childhood, familiarity breeds avoidance.

Eleanor Maccoby feels that a major factor in this avoidance is a gender difference in styles of interaction. Although girls and boys are not very different
from each other when they are observed or tested individually, there are big
differences in the way they behave in all-girl or all-boy groups. Boys' groups
are oriented around issues of competition and dominance; in their conversations, boys interrupt each other and use commands, threats, and boasts. Girls'

The Child in Society

Box 13-1 Desegregation and Race Relationships

Children tend to make friends with children they perceive as similar to themselves. This was true in nursery school, it is even more true in elementary school, and it is still more true as children approach adolescence.

In a school where there are children of different races and both sexes, friendships tend to be formed between children of the same sex and the same race. Of these two factors, race is less important than sex in determining relationships between preadolescents (Whitley, Schofield, and Snyder, 1984). In the incident in which Juan was asked to join Diane's group of two girls, both Juan and the girls were black. Had Juan been asked to join a group of two white boys, he probably would have obeyed. In the cafeteria of Juan's school, it is unusual for black students to sit next to white ones, but it is virtually unheard of for a boy to sit next to a girl.

Juan's school is located in a large city in the northeastern United States. About half the students are African American. The administration and faculty are biracial. Both the blacks and the whites on the staff are openly committed to furthering good relationships between the black students and the white ones. But the black students and the white ones eye each other with wary mistrust. Both races perceive the black children as being aggressive and tough and the whites as soft, unable to defend themselves (Schofield, 1981).

One problem at this school is that the white students, who are mostly from middle- and upper-middle-class homes, do much better academically than the black students, who are mostly from lower-class homes. Understandably, this produces a lot of resentment among the black students. They think of the white children as "conceited," as "goody goody two-shoes." If a higher-achieving white student offers to help a lower-achieving

The chances that a child will have a friend of another race decline steadily from fourth grade through seventh. As children get older, they show an increasing tendency to choose friends who are similar to themselves.

black student in a school subject, the black student is likely to interpret the offer as just another indication of the white's feelings of superiority. The white student, in turn, is puzzled and angry when an offer made in a spirit of helpfulness is rejected.

There is a good deal of social pressure on the black students in this school to avoid friendships with whites. If a black student is nice to a white student, her actions are likely to be interpreted by her fellow blacks as disloyalty to her race. Similarly, when black students show any signs of doing well academically, they may be pressured by other blacks not to work so hard. Doing well in school is seen as another kind of disloyalty.

groups are oriented more towards cooperation and the avoidance of conflict; girls make polite suggestions, express agreement, and pause to give someone else a turn to talk (Maccoby, 1990).

These different styles of interaction lead to difficulties when girls and boys interact with each other. School-age girls find that they are unable to influence their male agemates: when girls make polite suggestions, boys generally

All in all, the attempt to foster good white-black relationships through desegregation seems to have failed at this school. What went wrong?

The biggest problem is that most of these children came from elementary schools that were overwhelmingly white or overwhelmingly black. It wasn't until sixth grade that they were thrown together, and by then it was too late: children of different races are much less likely to become friends with each other in sixth grade than in earlier grades. Two sociologists did a study of race relationships in a town in California where the elementary schools were about 50 percent black. They found that the chances that a child will have a friend of another race decline steadily from fourth grade through seventh. The researchers concluded:

> As students approach adolescence, their friendships become more exclusive and the importance of similarity as a basis for friendships becomes more pronounced. Students often establish norms about the undesirability of forming friendships with dissimilar classmates, and peer pressure can be difficult to resist. (Hallinan and Teixeira, 1987, p. 566)

By sixth grade, children have also formed stereotypes about people—people of different races, of different genders, of different professions, and so on. When people are thrown together with a large number of people they don't know and who are different from themselves, it's all too easy to think of the other group in terms of stereotypes. Both the black students and the white students in Juan's school used this kind of thinking: the whites were seen as weak and conceited, the blacks as aggressive and low achievers. Once people have a stereotyped view of a person or a group of people, they tend to interpret any new information in terms of that stereotype and throw out any information that doesn't fit. As we said before, school-age children (along with many adolescents and adults) have difficulty in dealing with contradictory information about people, especially about people they don't know very well.

Is there a solution? As the California study showed, it is not enough to integrate schools from kindergarten on: the races get further apart as time goes on, not closer together. The same thing happens between boys and girls in middle childhood, and for a similar reason: association with members of the opposite sex strengthens the negative stereotypes each group holds about each other.

But there is an interesting fact about sex segregation that is relevant here. Girls and boys seldom play together in school, but they are much more likely to do so in their neighborhood, especially if there are not many children in that neighborhood. Children who associate with each other in small, mixed-age groups, as they do in some small village societies in Africa, are much more likely to have friends of the opposite sex than children who have access to a greater number of agemates (Maccoby and Jacklin, 1987). When there are only a few of the other kind of people, we are much more likely to see them as individuals and less likely to lump them together as a group.

This is true for race as well as gender. The sociologists in California found a connection between class size and mixed-race friendships: children in smaller classes were more likely to have friends of another race. The chances of children having friends of another race were also higher if they associated with each other in any activities involving smaller groups, such as reading groups or extracurriculars. In this respect, self-segregation by race differs from self-segregation by sex: black and white children who work together in small groups seem to like each more, but girls and boys forced to work together in small groups seem to like each other less. Perhaps it's partly the public nature of such groups that makes girls and boys so reluctant to work together.

Educators are now beginning to group elementary school students into small, mixed-race "learning teams" as a way of fostering better relationships between children of different races. So far, the results have been very promising (Goleman, 1989).

ignore them. Maccoby believes that girls find it unpleasant "to try to interact with someone who is unresponsive" and that consequently they learn to avoid boys (1990, p. 515). Perhaps a greater motivation for their avoidance of boys is the gender difference in styles of settling disagreements. Researchers studying conflict resolution in mixed-sex groups of 5- to 7-year-olds found that the girls generally tried to resolve conflicts with diplomacy or compro-

Girls and boys have different styles of play and different styles of interaction. These differences tend to keep them apart in middle childhood.

mise. The boys were more likely to resort to "heavy-handed persuasion"—force or the threat of force. Not surprisingly, the girls behaved more aggressively when they were interacting with boys. What *is* surprising is that the boys did not moderate their aggressiveness when they were interacting with girls—if anything, they were more aggressive with girls than with other boys (Miller, Danaher, and Forbes, 1986).

Because boys tend to dominate girls in mixed-sex groups, they tend to be dominant in the mixed-sex environment of the school. Boys get more of the teacher's attention. They are more likely to speak out of turn in class—to call out answers if the teacher doesn't call on them. And in mixed-sex work groups, boys do more of the talking than girls (Morgan and Dunn, 1988; Kelly, 1988).

Maccoby (1990) doesn't believe that boys and girls learn their different styles of interaction at home, by observing their parents. She admits that we just don't know why, for example, little girls respond to polite suggestions but little boys do not. If these gender differences are partly biological in origin, they may never disappear completely, even in a society that values androgyny.

Friendship   Like preschoolers, school-age children tend to choose friends who are similar to themselves in age, sex, and race (see Box 13–1). Although this reduces their chances of learning about people who are different from themselves, children's friendships serve many other important functions. For example, friends may serve as substitutes when, for some reason, parents are unable to meet a child's need for emotional support. Other children can also act as corrective influences for a child who has been overindulged or undersocialized at home.

Children are influenced in a variety of ways by the actions and attitudes of their peers. In one study, children were asked what they would do in ten different social situations if friends and parents gave contradictory advice. The tendency to choose the friends' advice rather than the parents' advice increased steadily between the ages of 8 and 12, but even the 8-year-olds chose the friends' advice a little more often than the parents' (Utech and Hoving, 1969).

School-age children appear to be more afraid of the disapproval of their peers than of the disapproval of their parents. We said earlier that school-age boys, when forced to associate in mixed-sex groups, tend to be more aggressive with their female agemates than with males. One likely reason for this is that boys don't anticipate much disapproval from other boys for aggression directed against girls. Although they anticipate plenty of disapproval from *parents* for aggression against girls, that apparently doesn't worry them as much (Perry, Perry, and Weiss, 1989).

PLAY AND GAMES IN MIDDLE CHILDHOOD. The cooperative play of preschoolers generally involves imagination ("You be the mommy and I'll be the baby") and/or lots of action—the kind of activity known as "rough-and-tumble play." Both of these activities decline in frequency as children get older; in fact, games based on imagination disappear entirely by the end of middle childhood (Baumeister and Senders, 1989).

Rough-and-tumble play does not disappear entirely, but it takes up only about 10 percent of the playground time of school-age children. Boys engage in this kind of activity more than girls do, and boys' rough-and-tumble is rougher and involves more tumbles. Girls might chase each other around but they seldom wrestle with each other (Humphreys and Smith, 1987).

School-age children spend most of their playground time playing games with rules. Whereas preschoolers like to take on fixed roles (such as "mommy" or "bus driver") in games of pretend, 8- to 10-year-olds favor games that involve switching back and forth between different roles. In tag, for instance, the alternate roles are the chaser and the ones who are chased; in jump-rope they are the jumper and the rope turners. According to Piaget, this kind of role-switching helps children develop the ability to view a situation from another person's point of view. Taking on multiple roles is also a way of experimenting with one's identity and hence may contribute to the development of a self-concept (Baumeister and Senders, 1989).

Starting around the age of 10, the games of American children become quite competitive. Games like jump-rope and tag have no definite ending—they are over when recess is, or whenever children get tired of playing them. But competitive games—games like baseball and checkers—have a definite ending: they end when someone wins and someone else loses. In organized team sports a great deal of emphasis is placed on winning; this is as true of the Little League as it is of the major leagues. In informal neighborhood play, children are not as concerned about winning. But competitiveness on the school playground is almost as high as in organized team sports—as if the competitive nature of the classroom had spilled out onto the playground (Greer and Stewart, 1989).

WHAT IS A FRIEND? A friend is someone you like to be with and who likes to be with you, someone who is similar to you and who understands you, someone you can tell secrets to, someone who cooperates and shares with you, someone who is loyal to you and helps you if you need help.

In middle childhood, friends are also people you have conflicts with—in fact, school-age children have more conflicts with their friends than with agemates who are not their friends, no doubt because they have more interactions with their friends. Although conflicts between friends involve as much aggression as conflicts between nonfriends, those between friends are more likely to result in a ''fair'' outcome, and afterward the participants are much more likely to remain together (Hartup, 1989).

In middle childhood, friends are also people you compete with—in fact, school-age children compete more with their friends than with agemates who are not their friends. Researchers tested fourth graders in a situation in which they were motivated (by the promise of rewards) to make as many geometric designs as possible in a given period of time. To do this they were supposed to use a special ''tracer'' (an artist's template). But the children were tested in pairs, and there was only one tracer. It turned out that children were less willing to share the tracer with a friend than with a nonfriend. These children were apparently worried that if they got fewer rewards than their friend they might appear inferior (Berndt, Hawkins, and Hoyle, 1986).

DEVELOPING CONCEPTS OF FRIENDSHIP. We said earlier that children below the age of 8 generally fail to recognize that people have stable psychological characteristics. This is one reason that friendships between younger children, below the age of 8, are often short-lived: these friendships tend to be based on superficial factors, rather than on compatible personalities. Researchers showed some 7- and 9-year-old boys a videotape of a boy their age; the boy was called Robby. Some of the children were told that Robby was ''real nice''; others were told that he had a new game. Then the children were asked if they wanted to play with Robby. The 7-year-olds were more likely to want to play with Robby if they were told that he had a new game, but the 9-year-olds were more likely to want to play with him if they heard that he was nice (Boggiano, Klinger, and Main, 1986).

Children's expectations about friendship deepen as they get older. Friends can tell each other things about themselves they wouldn't tell to acquaintances, and this is true even in kindergarten. But as children get older, they become more discriminating about the personal information they reveal to their agemates: older school-age children reveal less of themselves to acquaintances and more to friends (Rotenberg and Sliz, 1988).

Robert Selman, of Harvard University, has proposed that children's concepts of friendship proceeds in four stages (see Table 13–1). According to Selman (1981), friendships become more stable and longer lasting during middle childhood, as the child develops an awareness of the two-way nature of relationships and is better able to see things from the other's point of view.

Other researchers have disagreed with some of Selman's conclusions. Although a child's ''best friend'' might become her ''second-best friend'' (or worse still, an ex-friend) before recess is over, even first and second graders show a fair amount of stability in their friendships. After third grade (age 8 to 9), there is little or no change in stability: fourth graders' friendships last as

TABLE 13-1
Selman's Stages of Friendship

STAGE	APPROXIMATE TIME PERIOD	DESCRIPTION
Playmateship	Preschool period	A friend is someone who lives nearby and whom one happens to be playing with at the moment.
One-way assistance	Early school years	A friend is important because he or she does specific things that the child wants done. A close friend is someone who is known better than other people, where "known" means being aware of the other person's likes and dislikes.
Fair-weather cooperation	Later school years	There is a new awareness of the reciprocal nature of friendship and a new willingness to adjust to the likes and dislikes of the other person. But there is no long-term continuity—arguments are seen as a cause for breaking off the relationship.
Intimate and mutually shared relationships	Beginning in late childhood or early adolescence	There is a closer bond between friends and a new awareness of the continuity of the relationship. Friendship is not seen merely as a way to avoid being bored or lonely but as a basic means of developing intimacy and mutual support. Friends share intimate problems. Conflicts do not necessarily bring an end to the relationship.

Source: Selman, 1981.

long as those of eighth graders. In both fourth and eighth grades, more than two-thirds of those who are friends in the fall are still friends the following spring (Berndt, Hawkins, and Hoyle, 1986).

Selman may have underestimated another aspect of friendship in younger school-age children. First and second graders can't give sophisticated replies when they are asked questions about their concepts of friendship, but their behavior reveals a deeper understanding than their words. Researchers studying first graders observed that the interactions of friends often involved sharing, helping, loyalty, confiding, showing recognition of the other's accomplishments, and an awareness of similarity. Moreover, if a child's friend *failed* to live up to these standards—for example, by not sharing or not

Boys tend to play in groups; their friendships are less close and less exclusive than girls', and focus more on issues of competition and dominance.

being loyal—it often led to a dispute between them: "The children appeared to initiate disputes with their friends in an effort to improve their relationship." The researchers concluded that, although first graders may not be able to express their concepts of friendship in words, they recognize that a friend is not simply someone to play with, and that friendships require effort to develop and maintain (Rizzo and Corsaro, 1988, p. 231).

GIRLS' FRIENDSHIPS AND BOYS' FRIENDSHIPS. All over the world, the same difference can be seen: boys are more likely to play in groups, girls are more likely to play in pairs. Closeness and the sharing of personal concerns are more apt to occur in a one-to-one relationship, and girls' friendships are generally more intimate than boys'. Boys reveal less of themselves to their friends than girls do. This may be partly because of boys' concern for dominance— they are reluctant to show their weaknesses to other boys (Maccoby, 1990).

Zick Rubin, a developmental psychologist who has studied children's friendships, points out another difference between girls' and boys' friendships:

Along with their greater concern with intimacy, girls have been found to be more exclusive than boys, in the sense that they are less likely to expand their two-person friendships to include a third person. Girls appear to have a more acute appreciation than boys of the fragility of intimate relationships and of the ways in which one friendship may sometimes threaten another. Eleven-year-old Sarah reports: "Joan's now trying to hang around the older kids so as to be admitted into their gang so she has no time to be with Liz who therefore tries to be friends with Christine which doesn't please Sally." Boys . . . are typically less sensitive to such dilemmas of intimacy. And because of girls' greater concern with intimacy, jealousy

Girls tend to play in pairs; they form close, one-to-one friendships in which secrets are exchanged and outsiders are excluded.

seems more likely to arise in girls' than in boys' groups.   (Rubin, 1980, p. 108)

Girls' groups are "nicer" than boys' groups in the sense that there is less aggression, less competition, and more emphasis on taking turns. But girls' style of friendship also has its drawbacks: there is more jealousy, more attempts to exclude third parties, and more hurt feelings (Maccoby and Jacklin, 1987).

Children Whose Agemates Don't Like Them

A third grader named Ted was interviewed by a developmental psychologist who was doing a study on children's friendships. She kept asking him questions and Ted kept saying "I don't know." Finally, she asked him how he felt when he was playing with a friend. "I don't know," admitted Ted; "I don't *have* any friends" (Chance, 1989, p. 30).

Children without friends—children whose classmates don't like them—are at greater risk of a variety of problems later on. They are more likely to drop out of school, to become delinquent, and to require psychiatric care. But not all unpopular children run these risks— only a certain type of unpopular child: the *rejected* child.

Psychologists and sociologists who study popularity in children usually begin by asking all the children in a class to make ratings of how much they like their classmates. The children may be asked to name the three children they like most and the three they like least. Or they may be asked to rate each of their classmates according to how much they like to play with them, with ratings ranging from "Like to a lot" to "Don't like to." In either case, the researchers can categorize all the children in the class on the basis of how many of their classmates say they like them a lot and how many say they dislike them. Five types of children have been defined on the basis of such ratings:

- Popular children—these are the children who get many positive ratings and few negative ones. These children tend to be friendly, pleasant, and physically attractive.
- Average children—children who get a moderate number of positive and negative ratings.
- **Rejected** children—these are the ones who get many negative ratings and few positive ones.
- **Neglected** children—they get few positive *or* negative ratings. These are the "invisible" children whom nobody notices.
- Controversial children—some children like them a lot, others can't stand them.

Figure 13–2 shows the proportion of children who fell into each of these categories in a recent study of 1446 second through fifth graders (Kupersmidt, 1989).

FIGURE 13-2
The proportion of elementary school children (second through fifth graders) who were classified as popular, average, rejected, neglected, and controversial, on the basis of ratings made by their classmates. (Source: Kupersmidt, 1989.)

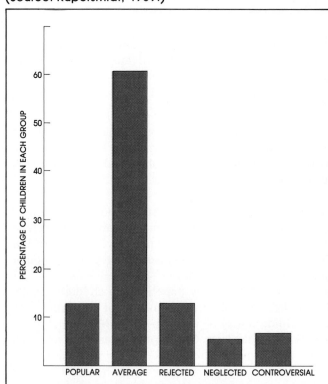

NEGLECTED CHILDREN. Ted, the third grader who doesn't have any friends, could be either a neglected child or a rejected one. If he is a neglected child, no one likes him very much, but no one dislikes him, either. The problem is that no one pays any attention to him at all.

Some neglected children are shy and lonely; others are introverts who aren't particularly troubled by their lack of friends. Aside from their lack of popularity, neglected children aren't very different from children with average ratings. They do as well in their schoolwork and they are no more likely to drop out or become delinquent. Whether they are at greater risk of developing a psychiatric disorder is still unclear, but in any event the risk is low. Even in terms of self-esteem, they are not measurably different from the average child. And being neglected may be only a temporary setback in their lives: at a later time or in another place, these children may be more popular. A child who is neglected by his classmates may have friends in his neighborhood or in summer camp (Parker and Asher, 1987; Boivin and Bégin, 1989).

REJECTED CHILDREN. Ted is in far more trouble if he is a rejected child—a child whose classmates actively dislike him. Children who are rejected in one grade are also likely to be rejected in the next; they're likely to be unpopular wherever they go. On the average, they make lower grades in school than their classmates and are more likely to drop out. They are at greater risk for a variety of problems, including depression (Parker and Asher, 1987; Kennedy, Spence, and Hensley, 1989).

Children have various reasons for disliking a classmate, but the most obvious one is that he is aggressive—he is a bully. About half of rejected children are aggressive, and these are the ones who are at greatest risk for all sorts of problems later on, including criminal behavior. But aggressiveness alone does not cause a child to be rejected. Most of the children in the controversial group are also quite aggressive, but evidently they have positive qualities as well. Thus, controversial children are liked by some of their classmates in spite of their aggressiveness (French, 1988; Coie and Dodge, 1988).

A few years ago, the leading theory about rejected children was that their classmates didn't like them because they were lacking in social skills and social cognitive understanding. Researchers noticed that these children were inept at conversing with other children and that they didn't seem to know how to blend into a group—their behavior made them stick out like a sore thumb (Putallaz and Gottman, 1981). Researchers also reported that rejected children tended to interpret an accident—for example, getting hit in the back with a ball—as an act of aggression on the part of whoever threw the ball (Dodge and Frame, 1982). Thinking that anything a person does must have been done on purpose is preschool-level social cognition.

But in the field of child development, causes and effects are often very difficult to disentangle. The inept conversational and social skills seen in rejected children could be a *result* of being unpopular and having fewer opportunities to practice these skills. As for the rejected child who assumes that getting hit in the back with a ball is an aggressive act by a classmate, he may well be right. Rejected children are often victims or scapegoats, picked on by their classmates. Most victims come from the nonaggressive group of rejected children, but there is a small group of children who are victimized and who are *also* aggressive. These children have been called "provocative victims." Evidently they provoke their classmates into picking on them and then retaliate with more aggression (Kupersmidt, 1989).

Children whose agemates don't like them have fewer opportunities to practice their social skills; thus, they may be inept at conversing with other children or at blending into a group.

Rejected children have social problems, but they do not necessarily have problems in social cognition. When accepted, rejected, and neglected children were questioned on their concepts of friendship, no differences in the maturity of their concepts were found between the three groups (Bichard, Alden, Walker, and McMahon, 1988). But there are certainly differences in their behavior. When videotapes of accepted, rejected, and neglected children in action were shown to other children who had never met them, the other children gave the rejected children significantly lower ratings in likability than they gave the other two groups. However, it can't be *just* their behavior: children also gave lower likability ratings to still photographs of rejected children they had never met (Kennedy, 1989).

Does this mean that rejected children are rejected because of their *looks?* Yes, in some cases, a child might be rejected because she looks odd or isn't pretty. Children who are different in any way from their classmates are more likely to be rejected (remember the story of Rudolph the red-nose reindeer?). But being homely does not inevitably lead to rejection; nor is being beautiful a guarantee of popularity.

There is no simple answer to why children are rejected, because rejection happens for a variety of reasons. But once it happens, the problem tends to perpetuate itself. Some children are rejected because they are aggressive, but aggression can also be a *reaction* to the pain of being rejected, and the result is a vicious circle worthy of the name. Being rejected also lessens a child's social self-confidence and her opportunities to practice social skills, so that even if she enters a new group of children she may not know how to behave. Perhaps her uncertainty shows on her face and makes her less appealing to other children, even in photographs.

When problems in social cognition are involved in rejection, they are more likely to be in the heads of the rejectors than the rejectees. Remember the description of the nasty boy who smells very much and has cruel eyes and no sense of humor? School-age children tend to have global concepts of other children's attributes: they tend to think of someone, like the nasty boy with cruel eyes, as being all good or all bad. (Adults are by no means immune to this pattern of thought.) Thus, whatever a "bad" child does is interpreted as bad; whatever a popular child does is interpreted as good. A rejected child develops a reputation for being "cruel" or "weird" or "out of it," and once the label is pinned on him it is very difficult for him to overcome that negative stereotype. At the same time, the rejected child himself develops the expectation that other children will act in a hostile manner toward him, and he is likely to interpret whatever they do in terms of that expectation (Hymel, 1986; Waas, 1988).

What can we do to help rejected children overcome their social disabilities? It is not easy to break out of this cycle; that is one reason why so many rejected children end up dropping out of school. Intervention programs in which adults coach rejected children in social skills have had mixed results: even in the most successful of these programs, only about half the children become more popular as a result of the coaching (French, 1988).

The most successful intervention programs generally involve pairing a rejected child with one or two of her more popular classmates, letting her interact with them for an hour or two a week over a period of months, and giving her coaching and pep-talks on the side. The period of interaction with her popular classmates may be more important than anything the adult coaches can teach her. For one thing, she gets a chance to practice her social skills with her peers—practice she sorely needs. For another, the classmates with whom she's paired have an opportunity to get to know her better and to realize that, like everybody else, she has good characteristics as well as bad ones. Perhaps they will even grow to like her. If they do decide that she's not so "cruel" or "weird" or "out of it" after all, they may be willing to associate with her at other times, or to stand up for her when their classmates pick on her (Waas, 1988). If not, just the fact that she goes off for a couple of hours a week to these mysterious sessions with her popular classmates may improve her reputation with the rest of the class.

It is unfortunate that children often accept or reject their classmates on the basis of such superficial characteristics as looks, athletic ability, and how well they do in school (doing too well or too poorly can both count as negatives). But perhaps it is unrealistic to expect school-age children to be more open-minded than the rest of us.

Family Relationships

Children who are not popular with their classmates may nonetheless lead reasonably satisfactory lives if they have good relationships at home. In particular, sibling companionship can do much to compensate for a lack of friends. An unpopular child who has a close relationship with a sibling is much less likely to experience the feelings of loneliness and the loss of self-esteem that commonly go along with being unpopular (East, 1989). Even the family dog can provide a child with companionship. One researcher found that many school-age children have "intimate talks" with their pets (Bryant, 1985).

The family can also be the source of much misery. When the parents are unhappy—either because their marriage is going poorly or because of other problems—the children are also likely to be unhappy. Trouble at home can spill over and have a negative effect on the child's relationships with peers, outside the home. Children who are playing together are more likely to get into arguments if they have recently heard adults arguing with each other (Bishop and Ingersoll, 1989; Daniels and Moos, 1988; Cummings, 1987).

Trouble within the family has a more serious effect on younger school-age children than on older ones. There are two reasons for this. First, older children are less dependent on their parents and have more resources outside the home. The second reason has to do with social cognition. Younger children are less aware of what goes on inside other people's minds, and their inability to consider several sources of information at one time leads to an oversimplified view of human relationships. Thus, when Mom is angry, a younger child is more likely to assume that *he* was the cause of that anger. When 5- and 6-year-olds were asked to imagine reasons for why their mothers might be mad, more than half of their reasons had to do with themselves. About 40 percent of the reasons given by 7- to 9-year-olds, and 30 percent of those given by 10- to 15-year-olds, attributed their mothers' anger to themselves. Children under the age of 7 are particularly poor at understanding that anger can be displaced. When they hear a story in which a father yells at a mother and then (after the father leaves) the mother yells at the child, they assume it was the child's fault (Covell and Abramovitch, 1987, 1988).

Parental Influences on Children

Parents influence their children's behavior and feelings in a number of ways: through the quality of their relationships with other family members and with the child, through modeling, through reinforcement and punishment, through direct instruction (mostly in words), and through heredity. Let us look at these influences one by one.

THE QUALITY OF THE PARENT–CHILD RELATIONSHIP. The quality of the parents' relationship with each other is important, but it's not as important as the quality of the parents' relationship with the child. Even in a home where there is much marital discord, some parents are able to keep from directing their anger at their children and to maintain warm parent–child relationships. Mothers seem to be better at doing this than fathers. Researchers have found that fathers whose marriages are unhappy give their children less praise and approval than happily married fathers. In contrast, mothers in unhappy marriages give *more* praise and approval than other mothers (Brody, Pillegrini, and Sigel, 1986).

Children's relationships with their parents have repercussions on how well they function in a variety of situations. A child who feels secure in his relationship with his mother, and who feels that she will continue to accept him despite his flaws, is likely to have high self-esteem and to get along better in school, both socially and academically (Cassidy, 1988; Rothbaum, 1988).

PARENTAL MODELING. Children who come from homes in which the parents are always fighting are likely to have poorer relationships with their peers than those who come from more serene homes. One reason for this is children's tendency to imitate their parents' behavior. A researcher watched mothers and their first-grade children interacting together, and then watched how these children interacted with unfamiliar agemates. The children's behavior with their peers was a reflection of how their mothers behaved with them: "Positive, agreeable mothers had positive, agreeable children; mothers who focused on feelings had children who focused on feelings; and disagreeable mothers had disagreeable children." Although it is often possible to interpret a mother's behavior with her child as partly a *reaction* to her child's behavior and personality, that explanation will not suffice in this case: these mothers tended to act in the same way with other people as well (Putallaz, 1987, p. 336).

Sex-role development and sex-typed behavior are often attributed to modeling—the child is presumed to imitate the behavior of the same-sex parent. Although this no doubt occurs, it is hard to demonstrate. Children are less likely to imitate their same-sex parent if that parent is doing something unusual—something adults of that sex don't ordinarily do (Jacklin, 1989). This makes it hard to tell whether children are imitating their parents' behavior or just the typical behavior of a person of that sex in our society.

REINFORCEMENT AND PUNISHMENT. The other way that parents influence their children's sex-typed behavior is through selectively encouraging and discouraging different behaviors in girls and boys. This does happen, but the influences are subtle—on the whole, parents (especially mothers) act pretty much the same to sons and daughters. However, parents do seem to respond more favorably when girls talk about feelings and emotions than when boys do. Parents tend to have a negative response to sons who talk about their emotions (especially sadness) or who act dependent. They are also more likely to punish sons for misbehavior—if a daughter does the same thing they might just ignore her (Fuchs and Thelen, 1988; Russell and Russell, 1987).

Perhaps parents react more forcefully to a son's disobedience because they expect sons to be more disobedient: from early childhood, boys are less likely than girls to comply with parental orders and requests. This tendency, coupled with the greater parental pressure on boys to be independent, results in a decrease in the parents' (or at least the mothers') influence over their sons by the end of middle childhood. Eleven- to 15-year-old boys are far more likely than girls of that age to *tell* their mothers what they are going to do, rather than *ask* them; girls are more likely to plead with their mothers to let them do something (Cowan and Avants, 1988).

Parents are able to control the behavior of younger school-age children by the use of reinforcement and punishment, including physical punishment or the threat of physical punishment. The use of punishment and threats to control behavior is called **power-assertive discipline.** This method of discipline has its drawbacks (see Chapter 10), especially with school-age children. Firm parental control may be necessary for preschoolers, but when used with school-age children it may lessen the chances that the children will internalize their families' standards and adhere to them when their parents aren't around (Crouch and Neilson, 1989). The reason has to do with intrinsic versus extrinsic motivation, which we discussed in Chapter 12. If a child feels that he is obeying only because of extrinsic motivators such as the threat of punishment, there may be a decline in his intrinsic motivation to obey (Miller and Aloise, 1989).

DIRECT INSTRUCTION. Parental control generally consists either of power-assertive discipline or of **induction.** Induction means explaining to a child the reasons and justifications for behaving in a certain way, or for *not* behaving in a certain way. This is teaching based on cognitive processes—knowledge transmitted from one generation to another in the form of words, a parental practice found only in the human species. In spite of its short evolutionary history, it works remarkably well. School-age children are more likely to comply with a parental request when it is accompanied by an explanation than when it is not (Davies, McMahon, Flessati, and Tiedemann, 1984).

Children do not soak up their parents' beliefs and attitudes through their skin; if they don't know what their parents believe about something, they can't be influenced by their beliefs. The likelihood that children will be influenced by their parents' attitudes on topics such as educational goals, politics, and religion is a function of how accurately the children perceive their parents' beliefs (Alessandri and Wozniak, 1987). Although some nonverbal teaching no doubt occurs, abstract ideas are conveyed most clearly when they're put into words.

Sometimes parents assume that their children understand things even though they *haven't* put them into words, or at least not in words that the children can understand. In an Australian study of the chores that parents expect their children to do around the house, mothers were amazed to discover that their third graders thought it would be perfectly reasonable to be given money for making their own beds. The mothers hadn't *said* that the child shouldn't expect a reward for cleaning up his own room; they had simply taken it for granted that the child knew that. Similarly, a younger school-age child may be baffled when her mother makes a statement such as "I'm not your servant," or "This isn't a hotel." Nonetheless, even first graders know that the main reason they are given jobs to do is that they are expected to make some contribution to the general good of the family. Mothers convey this idea by saying things like "Everybody does something around here," or "You have to give as well as take" (Goodnow and Warton, 1990).

Bear in mind that all messages from the environment, both verbal and nonverbal, have to be interpreted. A child's interpretation of a message will depend, in part, on his past experiences with the sender of that message. A child who has been picked on by his classmates may interpret a pat on the back as a slap, or a question about the homework as a criticism. In the same way, his interpretation of a message from his parents will depend on the nature of his relationship with them. If a parent administers a spanking or says "You idiot!" the effect of these messages will depend on whether the parent is ordinarily kind and gentle or is frequently harsh and rejecting.

Children also interpret messages from parents and other adults on the basis of cultural norms, like the Inuit child who knew her aunt didn't really want her to die. This is why the effects of parental childrearing styles will depend on the family's cultural background—why, for example, an authoritarian childrearing style apparently has different effects on European-American children than on Asian-American children (see p. 391).

GENETIC FACTORS AND TRANSACTIONAL EFFECTS. Remember our long discussion in Chapter 2 of the interactions between heredity and environment, and on the ways that genetic effects sometimes pass themselves off as environmental effects? Correlations between parents' behavior and children's behavior can come about in many ways, and one of the ways is heredity. Thus, if parents who are always fighting with each other have children who also fight a lot, modeling is not the only possible explanation: perhaps quarrelsomeness runs in the family, passed down genetically. Genetic factors may also be involved when "positive, agreeable mothers" have "positive, agreeable children." And if children who have warm, accepting relationships with their parents function better in a variety of circumstances, it could be because these children were born with the ability to evoke favorable responses from other people, including their parents. The transactional nature of human relationships means that two children reared in the same family and going to the same schools can grow up in very different environments, because of the different reactions they evoke from their parents, teachers, siblings, and peers.

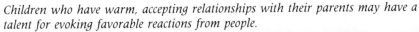

Children who have warm, accepting relationships with their parents may have a talent for evoking favorable reactions from people.

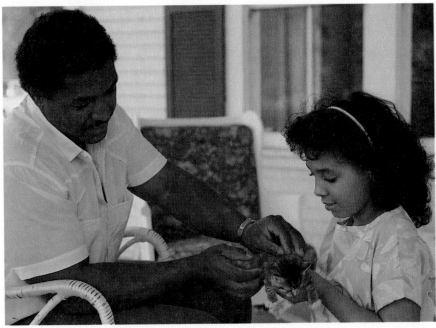

Altruism and Morality

The development of social cognition involves, among other things, an increase in children's ability to see things from another person's point of view—to "walk a mile in their moccasins." This is called **role-taking ability,** and it's closely linked to empathy. Role-taking involves being aware of another person's feelings; empathy means actually sharing—vicariously experiencing—these feelings. When we get pleasure from someone else's happiness, or when we wince when someone else's finger gets pinched in the door, we're empathizing.

There is also a link between empathy and prosocial behavior. Prosocial behavior means doing something that is beneficial to others. When the beneficial act is done without an apparent selfish motive, the act is said to be *altruistic.*

The Development of Altruism

Altruism means doing something for someone else despite cost, inconvenience, or even danger to oneself. Although the classic example is the person who risks his or her own life to rescue another person, altruistic behavior is not really all that rare. It is found in other species (porpoises, for example) and in very young human beings:

> Michael, aged 15 months, and his friend Paul were fighting over a toy and Paul started to cry. Michael appeared disturbed and let go, but Paul still cried. Michael paused, then brought his teddy bear to Paul but to no avail. Michael paused again, and then finally succeeded in stopping Paul's crying by fetching Paul's security blanket from an adjoining room. (Hoffman, 1975, p. 612)

Although Michael showed altruistic concern for another at a very early age, not all toddlers will do this, and Michael himself may not always respond in the same way. A toddler might get upset when he hears another child crying, but it's difficult to predict how he will react: he may respond by fetching his bottle and giving it to the other child, by covering his ears, or even by attacking the other child (Radke-Yarrow, Zahn-Waxler, and Chapman, 1983).

Why would a toddler get upset when he hears another child cry? The fact that this response appears so early suggests that "empathic distress"—the tendency to become distressed by the sight or sound of someone else's misery—may be an innate, involuntary response in human beings. Such a response would provide a motivation for altruistic acts: by helping to relieve the other person's misery, one's own distress is relieved as well.

EMPATHY, HELPING, AND SOCIAL COGNITION. True empathy depends on role-taking ability, because if we don't know what another person is experiencing, how can we share it? Since toddlers and preschoolers are not very good at role-taking, they can empathize only when the other person's distress is particularly obvious. As children grow older, social cognitive development leads to an increase in role-taking ability, and this leads in turn to an increased tendency to behave in altruistic ways (Carroll and Steward, 1984).

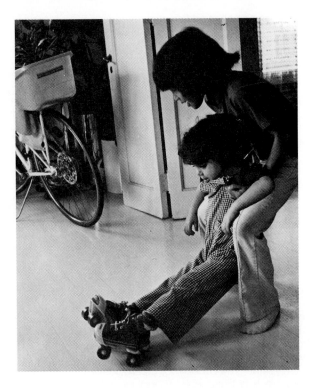

A child who is high in role-taking ability is more likely to behave in an altruistic way toward a younger child.

Role-taking ability is also related to intelligence. Intelligent children are better at role-taking than those who are less intelligent; they are also more altruistic and less aggressive. A child who can empathize with other people's pain is less likely to want to hurt them (Krebs and Gillmore, 1982; Huesmann, Eron, and Yarmel, 1987).

In a typical study of role-taking ability and altruism, the researchers began by asking a group of second graders questions about the intentions, thoughts, and feelings of people shown in videotaped enactments. On the basis of their responses to these questions, the children were classified as high or low in role-taking ability. Then, in the second part of the experiment, these children were asked to do an arts and crafts project with some kindergartners. The high role-takers were kinder and more helpful to the kindergartners—they answered questions, gave encouragement, and assisted the younger children when they were having trouble. The low role-takers often failed to answer the younger children's questions or else gave inadequate answers, and they didn't offer much assistance (Hudson, Forman, and Brion-Meisels, 1982).

Presumably, high role-takers help more because they are more empathic than low role-takers. But efforts to measure children's empathy directly have not always produced the expected results. That is, children who appear to be empathic in one situation (for example, they smile in response to another person's happiness) are not necessarily empathic in another (they may not respond to the other person's distress). Even children who are empathic under a variety of circumstances may not go to the aid of someone who is in need of assistance. It depends not only on the child, but on the situation as well. If the child has reason to feel that her efforts to help may not be successful, she is less likely to make the attempt (Eisenberg and Miller, 1987).

Problems in Development

Box 13-2
Antisocial
Behavior

Antisocial behavior means behavior that violates society's rules or norms. It includes lying, stealing, truancy, drug and alcohol abuse, vandalism, and aggression. The children who do these things were referred to, in Box 2–4, as *conduct disordered*, which is the term that psychiatrists use. Conduct-disordered children may be aggressive or nonaggressive. It is the aggressive conduct-disordered child who is the biggest problem to society and to himself.

We have met this child several times before, starting with that box in Chapter 2. He (most of these children are male) showed up again in Chapter 10, in a section titled "Troubled Families, Troublesome Children." He didn't appear in Chapter 12 because he spent most of his time in the principal's office, but he turned up again in this chapter, first in the description of the nasty boy with cruel eyes who is always fighting, and then under the heading "Rejected Children." The other children don't like him because he is a bully. His teachers don't like him because he doesn't do his schoolwork and he behaves disruptively in class. Even his parents find it difficult to like him.

Antisocial behavior is not always a sign of a long-term problem. In one study of school-age boys who had been diagnosed (by a psychiatrist) as aggressive conduct-disordered, about half got better: two years later, their behavior was within normal bounds (Stewart and Kelso, 1987). Maybe these boys had just been going through a bad patch in their lives, or maybe it was a question of getting older and wiser.

Unfortunately, not all antisocial children get wiser with age. In a study in Sweden, almost half of a group of boys who had been unusually aggressive at age 10 had been convicted of a crime by age 26 (Goleman, 1990b). As we have said else-

where, these boys also run a much greater than average risk of a variety of other problems, including academic failure and rejection by peers in childhood, depression and drug or alcohol abuse in adolescence, and marital problems in adulthood.

There are a remarkable number of vicious circles at work here. We already mentioned one of them: the tendency for children who are rejected by their agemates for being too aggressive to become more aggressive. A second is what happens at home. Many of these children seem to have been born with "difficult" temperaments that make them particularly hard to deal with. By the preschool period, such a child may be failing to comply with his parents' requests and orders, and getting his way by making their lives so unpleasant that they end up giving in to him—or perhaps giving up on him. He gets his way by being obnoxious, so he becomes more obnoxious

Whether a child will offer help also depends on her feelings of responsibility. It has been shown in experiments with adults that people are less likely to offer help if they don't feel it's their responsibility to do so. For example, an adult who witnesses an accident is less likely to help the victim if there are many other people present, because the responsibility for offering help is divided up among all the bystanders and does not weigh heavily on any one individual (Darley and Latané, 1968). Feeling responsible varies from person to person, as well as from situation to situation, and some adults and children feel a stronger sense of responsibility than others. Children who feel a sense of responsibility for people in need, and who would feel guilty if they failed to

(Ghodsian-Carpey and Baker, 1987; Patterson and Bank, 1989).

A third vicious circle involves intelligence. There is a connection between aggressiveness and intelligence: less intelligent children tend to be more aggressive. What makes it a circle is that the IQs of aggressive children tend to go down as they get older, apparently because they behave badly in school and don't learn as much (Huesmann, Eron, and Yarmel, 1987; Patterson, DeBaryshe, and Ramsey, 1989).

A fourth vicious circle involves television watching. Aggressive children like to watch violent TV shows, and it appears that watching violent TV shows makes children more aggressive; this is presumably due to their exposure to aggressive models (Eron, 1987).

The final vicious circle involves the peer group. We have said that children choose friends who are similar to themselves. Thus, nonaggressive children have nonaggressive friends, and aggressive children (if they have friends at all) have aggressive friends. This has been called the "birds of a feather" phenomenon, and it becomes even more noticeable during the adolescent period of development. Adolescents tend to sort themselves out into different "subcultures": the jocks, the brains, the popular group, the delinquent group, and so on. An aggressive, conduct-disordered adolescent will naturally gravitate toward others like himself, and he will find them in the delinquent group. Its members serve each other both as models and as reinforcers of increasingly antisocial behavior (Cairns, 1989).

With all these negative factors operating together, we should be encouraged by the fact that about half the children with aggressive conduct disorder are apparently able to overcome their problems. But what can we do to keep the others from wrecking their own lives and the lives of others?

One thing that is clear is that intervention should come early, before all these vicious circles pick up momentum. Gerald Patterson and his associates at the Oregon Social Learning Center feel that the best place to start is in the home, where the parents of difficult children may unwittingly provide "basic training" in antisocial behavior by reinforcing them for being obnoxious. Patterson has been teaching such parents to use the techniques of operant conditioning (see Chapter 3): they learn to reinforce their children for good behavior and to provide immediate, consistent punishment (reprimands or isolation) for bad behavior. This method has had some notable successes—dramatic improvements in the children's behavior. When improvement occurs, it can be the start of a whole new circle: a *nonvicious* one, in which the parent suddenly finds she likes her child better and is able to give him more of the things he needs, such as warmth, acceptance, and companionship, and this leads to further improvements in the child's behavior (Patterson and others, 1989).

There are limitations, however, to this method of dealing with antisocial children. For one thing, it requires a great deal of cooperation from the parents—cooperation they may be unable or unwilling to give. Second, its effects may not be long-lasting. In many cases, the child will revert back to antisocial behavior as soon as the environment stops providing the right kind of reinforcements and punishments. But a researcher who has looked at the effectiveness of various kinds of treatments has concluded that it's unrealistic to hope for a permanent "cure" for antisocial behavior. He feels that it might be more helpful to think of this disorder as a kind of chronic disease, like diabetes, which doesn't ever get cured but that can be treated very successfully, so that the child who has it can lead a normal life—and maybe even a happy and successful one (Kazdin, 1987).

---

do something, are more likely to offer assistance. Older school-age children generally have stronger feelings of responsibility than younger ones and thus are more likely to help (Chapman, Zahn-Waxler, Cooperman, and Iannotti, 1987).

A feeling of responsibility for others falls into the realm of morality. In Chapter 3 we discussed Lawrence Kohlberg's theory of moral development (preconventional, conventional, and postconventional), and Carol Gilligan's theory (justice orientation versus caring orientation).

Moral Reasoning and Moral Behavior

A third point of view has recently been proposed by Nancy Eisenberg, of Arizona State University. According to Eisenberg (1989a, 1989b), Kohlberg's error was not in placing too much emphasis on justice, but in making his stages too rigid. For Kohlberg, a child is at a fixed level of moral reasoning at a given point in his development. From there he can only move forward, never backward, and only by one step at a time.

Eisenberg believes that children's moral reasoning is much less predictable than that. A child might reason on one level today, a lower level tomorrow. He might reason on one level when he's explaining why he would help someone, and on a lower level when he's explaining why he wouldn't. He might reason at a higher (or lower) level for himself than for other people, he might skip a level, and he might even use two or three different levels of reasoning at the same time.

Table 13–2 shows Eisenberg's classification of the different forms of moral reasoning. This is not a strict developmental sequence—a child may use any or all of these at a given point in time. But the higher forms of reasoning are found only in older children. Younger children just aren't capable of the abstract thinking needed for the higher forms of reasoning. However, older children, even though they may be capable of abstract thought, do not necessarily use it. Thus, a child who is feeling insecure or angry might revert back to a lower form of reasoning. Personality characteristics such as a tendency to be concerned about material possessions or about the approval of others will also affect the form of reasoning that is used.

Kohlberg claimed that the development of moral reasoning is universal—that it follows the same sequence all over the world. His theory ran into trouble when it was discovered that in some non-Western societies there are *no* people who reason on what he defined as the highest level (Snarey, 1985). Eisenberg (1989b) believes that patterns of moral reasoning vary from society to society and that they reflect the values and concerns of that society.

Within a given society, some children will reason on a higher level than others of the same age. Those who are relatively advanced in social cognitive development—intelligent children and children who are good role-takers—are more likely to use the higher forms of moral reasoning (Krebs and Gillmore, 1982).

What about gender differences? Kohlberg was criticized because his theory seemed to favor males. Gilligan's theory was designed to give equal value to what she saw as male (justice-oriented) and female (caring-oriented) forms of reasoning. Eisenberg (1989a) has found that older school-age girls do, indeed, tend to be more caring oriented than boys of the same age; they are also better at role-taking and their moral reasoning is at a higher level. However, she thinks this is mainly due to a difference in rate of maturation —girls mature more rapidly than boys, but by late adolescence boys have caught up. Thus, Eisenberg finds few gender differences in moral reasoning in older adolescents, although girls remain somewhat better at role-taking.

RESISTING TEMPTATION. There are many temptations out there in the world —temptations to lie, to steal, to cheat. What determines whether a given child, in a given situation, will yield to these temptations? Do children who give "better" answers on tests of moral reasoning also behave "better" in real-life situations?

TABLE 13–2
Eisenberg's Six Levels of Moral Reasoning

1. **Self-centered reasoning.** The individual is concerned with the consequences to himself or herself, rather than moral considerations. Reasons for assisting (or not assisting) another are (a) personal benefit (or loss); (b) the expectation of reciprocity—getting "paid back"; or (c) because one needs or likes (or dislikes) the other. This is the predominant mode of reasoning among preschoolers and younger school-age children.

2. **Needs-oriented reasoning.** The individual expresses concern for the needs of others even though they may conflict with his or her own needs. The concern is expressed in simple terms, without clear evidence of role-taking or empathy. This is a common mode of reasoning for some preschoolers and many school-age children.

3. **Stereotyped and/or approval-oriented reasoning.** Stereotyped ideas of good and bad people and good and bad behavior, often coupled with a desire to win the approval of others. This is a common mode among some school-age children and adolescents.

4. **Empathic reasoning.** The individual shows evidence of role-taking and empathy, and recognition of the other's humanness. There may also be awareness of the emotional consequences of helping (feeling good) or not helping (feeling guilty). This is the predominant mode for a few older school-age children and many adolescents.

5. **Partly internalized principles.** Justifications for helping or not helping involve internalized values such as concern for the rights of others and/or feelings of responsibility. However, these ideas are not clearly thought out or strongly stated. This is a predominant mode for a minority of adolescents and adults.

6. **Strongly internalized principles.** Justifications for helping or not helping are based on strongly felt internalized values, such as the desire to improve the condition of society or the belief in the dignity and equality of all people. Emotional consequences of helping relate to the maintenance of self-respect and the feeling that one must live up to one's own values. This form of reasoning is rare, even in adolescents and adults.

Source: Eisenberg, 1989a, 1989b.

There is a correlation, though it isn't strong, between level of moral reasoning and some forms of moral (or immoral) behavior: higher levels of moral reasoning are associated with more prosocial behavior and less aggression (Bear, 1989). But when it comes to honesty—resisting temptations to steal, lie, or cheat—there is little or no connection with moral reasoning. In other words, there is no consistent tendency for children who are capable of higher-level moral reasoning to be better at resisting temptation. And, although some children are more honest than others in a variety of situations, these differences are small. Honesty depends more on the situation than on the child. Under some conditions a child who is normally quite honest may cheat. She is more likely to do so when the stakes are high, when the chances of being caught are low, and when "everyone is doing it" (Humphrey, 1984; Burton, 1976).

Seeing someone else doing it definitely increases children's tendency to cheat, especially if the perpetrators go unpunished for their behavior. In one study, children 8 to 12 years old were asked to perform a boring task while a cartoon film was being shown. To do the task, they had to resist the tempta-

Children who are capable of higher-level moral reasoning are not necessarily any better at resisting temptation.

tion to look at the cartoon. Before they started, some of the children saw an adult model yield to temptation and watch the film. Others saw the model resist the temptation and stick conscientiously to the task. The children who had seen the adult yield to temptation were more likely to yield to temptation themselves—to quit working in order to watch the cartoon (Rosenkoetter, 1973). Other studies have shown that children who yield to temptation feel much less guilty about it if they know that other children in the same situation have acted in the same way (Perry and others, 1980).

Thus, children's own characteristics appear to have little effect on the likelihood that they will behave honestly in a variety of situations. What matters more is what they see other people doing in those situations.

In Chapter 10 we discussed the socialization of preschool children; that chapter was entitled "Becoming a Member of Society." School-age children *are* members of society; their ideas and behavior reflect those of the society as a whole, not just those of their parents. This makes perfect sense: socialization, after all, means adapting your ideas and behavior to those of the society in which you find yourself. A society consists of people—models, if you wish to call them that. Children base their ideas and behavior on those of the models they are exposed to, the other members of their society. Their models are not just their parents but also their siblings, their classmates and teachers, the people they read about in books and magazines, and the people they see on TV and in movies. All these people, real and fictitious, are part of the child's society, and what they say and do sets the standards that the child will live by.

Summary

1. Social cognition is knowledge and understanding about people's thoughts and feelings (including the knowledge that other people *have* thoughts and feelings), and about the way people behave and their interactions with each other. It includes self-knowledge and self-concepts.

2. Young babies respond to the emotions displayed by others; a toddler gets information from reading the emotions in his mother's face (social referencing). Children begin to act out "pretend" emotions as early as age 2. Yet it isn't until they're 8 or 9 that children begin to detect the difference between genuine and feigned emotions in others.

3. The ability to feign emotions develops earlier than the ability to cover up genuine emotions; the ability to regulate verbal expressions of feelings develops earlier than the ability to regulate facial expressions of feelings.

4. The understanding that people can feel two emotions at the same time, and that different people might have different emotional reactions to the same situation, develops during middle childhood.

5. It takes children 7 or 8 years to realize that the consistencies in people's behavior represent stable psychological traits. It takes them far longer to realize that no one is 100 percent consistent and everyone has good traits and bad ones.

6. The development of self-knowledge proceeds no faster than knowledge about other people. Younger school-age children tend to think of themselves in terms of physical characteristics and possessions; older ones are more likely to mention psychological characteristics and to recognize that not all of their characteristics are good.

7. As children get older, they tend to see people as having stable, specific characteristics and as being controlled by internal factors rather than by external events. However, children (and adults) are more likely to attribute their own behavior to an external cause and other people's behavior to an internal one.

8. At around 7 or 8, children begin to compare themselves to their agemates and in this way learn about their own characteristics. Their assessments of their own abilities become more accurate as they get older. Children who are not good in one area can usually keep their self-esteem intact by concentrating on their successes in other areas.

9. Gender is one of the basic components of our self-concepts and our concepts of other people. Sex-role stereotypes are less rigid in older children than in younger ones, because older children have more complex, less global concepts of other people's characteristics.

10. A person who has both "masculine" characteristics and "feminine" characteristics is **androgynous.** Androgynous and masculine children have higher self-esteem than children who lack "masculine" characteristics such as assertiveness, independence, and leadership ability.

11. School-age children segregate themselves rigidly by sex. But this rigid sex segregation masks a great interest, by both boys and girls, in the opposite sex.

12. Though boys and girls are not very different when they're tested individually, there are big differences in their behavior in all-boy and all-girl groups. Boys' groups are oriented around competition and dominance; girls' groups emphasize cooperation and avoidance of conflict. The different styles of interaction lead to difficulties when girls and boys are together.

13. Desegregated schools do not necessarily make black and white children like each other better: they may have the opposite effect, especially if the children are from different socioeconomic levels, if their introduction to each other comes late in childhood, and if the classes are large. In smaller groups, children of different races are more likely to get to know each other as individuals, rather than stereotypes.

14. In middle childhood, children are influenced as much or more by their peers as by their parents.

15. Play during middle childhood generally involves games with rules. Younger school-age children like games such as tag and jump-rope, in which they switch back and forth between alternate roles. Older children like competitive games that end when someone wins.

16. The friendships of younger children (up to third or fourth grade) tend to be short-lived, perhaps because they are based on superficial factors rather than compatible personalities. Researchers found no change in the stability of friendships between fourth and eighth grade.

17. Girls are more likely to have close, intimate, and exclusive friendships; boys usually play in groups. Jealousy arises more often in girls' friendships; boys tend to be more competitive and more aggressive with their friends.

18. Children whose agemates don't like them may either be **neglected** or **rejected.** Neglected children are not liked, but they're not disliked. A child who is neglected in one place or time may have friends in another place or time.

19. Rejected children are disliked by their peers. A child who is rejected in one place or time is likely to meet continued rejection and runs a greater risk of a variety of problems later on. Rejected children tend to have poor social skills and may interpret accidents as acts of hostility by their classmates. However, it is hard to tell whether these are causes or effects of rejection. Some rejected children are aggressive, some are victims, and some are aggressive *and* victims.

20. Trouble at home has a negative effect on children's lives and on their relationships with peers. The effects of the parents' unhappiness or marital discord are likely to be more serious for younger children, partly because younger children tend to think that when Mom is angry, she must be angry at *them.*

21. Since parents serve as models for their children, a parent who acts in a positive and agreeable way with others is likely to have a child who also acts in that way. It is harder to tell if modeling is a factor in sex-role development, since children tend not to imitate a parent who does something that people of that sex don't usually do.

22. Although in most ways parents act about the same to sons and daughters, they are less likely to reinforce sons for talking about feelings or for acting dependent. Boys also get punished more. By the end of middle childhood, parents (especially mothers) have less influence over sons than over daughters.

23. The use of punishment and threats to control behavior is called **power-assertive discipline.** Using this method with school-age children may decrease a child's intrinsic motivation to obey—the child is less likely to internalize the parents' standards.

24. Induction means giving children the reasons for why they should or shouldn't do something. Sometimes parents assume that a child understands something even though they've never put it into words that the child can understand.

25. Because of the transactional nature of human relationships, the quality of a child's relationships with parents, teachers, and peers will depend in part on the child's inborn characteristics.

26. Role-taking ability is the ability to see things from other people's point of view and to understand what they are feeling; **altruism** is doing something beneficial for others without a selfish motive. Older children (and more intelligent children) are better at role-taking and tend to behave more altruistically.

27. Antisocial behavior violates society's rules or norms. Aggressive conduct-disordered children are most likely to engage in antisocial behavior. Several vicious circles tend to make an aggressive child become more aggressive; yet, half of these children get better as they get older. Successful intervention programs involve training the child's parents to reinforce good behavior and to provide immediate, consistent punishment for bad behavior.

25. According to Eisenberg, Kohlberg's theory of the development of moral reasoning is too rigid. Eisenberg feels that the level of a child's moral reasoning tends to increase with age, but that it will vary according to the situation, the child's mood, the child's characteristics, and the culture in which the child is reared.

29. Higher levels of moral reasoning are associated with more prosocial behavior and less aggression. But there is little relationship between moral reasoning and honesty. A child's ability to resist temptations to cheat depends mostly on the situation and on the behavior of the models to whom the child is exposed.

Key Terms

social cognition
androgynous
rejected children

neglected children
power-assertive discipline
induction

role-taking ability
altruism
antisocial behavior

Childhood's End

Research in child development has generally focused on the younger child—infants, preschoolers, and school-age children. In comparison, adolescents have been neglected. This, you may be thinking, is not too surprising: after all, a 14-year-old is almost as uncooperative as a 2-year-old and nowhere near as cute.

But there are other reasons why researchers have tended to avoid adolescents. First is their greater diversity: adolescents seem to come in a wider range of varieties than younger children, and it's harder to make general statements about them. Second is the greater difficulty of demonstrating the effects of the environment on their development. One of the traditional goals of research in this field was to show how the parents' behavior influences the children's behavior, but such influences turned out to be harder to demonstrate in adolescence than in earlier stages of life. As we mentioned in Chapter 2, the effect of the home environment seems to decline over the years. Children become less similar to their

parents in personality and intelligence as they reach maturity. They also become less similar to their siblings. Fraternal twins get less and less alike as they grow older (McCartney, Harris, and Bernieri, 1990).

Genetic and transactional effects underlie these trends. The genetic plan, preprogrammed in the genes of every baby, unfolds itself gradually; it is revealed in full only at childhood's end. Transactional effects—especially active effects (see Chapter 2)—tend to exaggerate genetic differences as children get older and as they become more and more capable of determining their own environments. In addition, the decisions the children have made in the past, about whom to associate with and how to spend their time, have effects that are cumulative over the years. Thus, as children become adolescents, they become less and less like their parents and more and more like—themselves.

We said that showing how the environment affects development was one of the *traditional* goals of research in child development. Now that researchers have begun to realize that development is a transactional process to which the child makes an important contribution, there is a growing interest in adolescence. It is at childhood's end when the individual's contribution to his or her development becomes most evident.

Adolescence can be divided into two subperiods. Early adolescence is the period of physical change, usually marked by a sizable spurt in growth. At the start of this period, the individual still looks and acts like a child; at its end, physical maturation is essentially complete. In late adolescence, the individual begins to confront the concerns of adult life—education, occupation, love and marriage. This chapter will look mainly at development in early adolescence, though we'll follow a few topics through college age. In the final chapter of this book, we'll concentrate on late adolescence and entry into adulthood.

Early Adolescence: A Time of Rapid Change

Think of all the things that are going on between the ages of, let's say, 12 and 16. We start with a child and end with an adolescent. The physical changes are the most noticeable, but they're only a small part of it. There is the transition from elementary school to middle school or junior high, and then a second transition to high school. During the first of these transitions, grades go down (as teachers become stricter in their grading policies) and dissatisfaction with school increases tremendously, even among high-achieving students (Hirsch and Rapkin, 1987).

Other changes involve relationships with parents and peers. The peer group becomes overwhelming in its importance and its demands for conformity. Friendships, which used to be confined to members of the same sex, now expand to include the opposite sex, and this leads to all sorts of complications. Relationships with parents also become extremely complicated, as teenagers struggle to free themselves from their dependence on their families and yet do not feel ready to accept the burdens of adulthood.

The freedom that teenagers struggle to attain brings with it many risks, many opportunities to make decisions—for better or worse—that may prove to be irrevocable. "It is during adolescence," a recent report concludes, "that individuals adopt self-damaging behavior that can sometimes shorten their lives or diminish their prospects for the future" (Hamburg and Takanishi, 1989, p. 826). When they were children, their parents watched over them: saw that they took baths and brushed their teeth, gave them medicine when they were sick, told them when to go to bed, selected their food and drinks, checked that they had done their homework. But teenagers do not want their parents to watch over them that closely, and most parents do not want it either. So teenagers are making many of their own choices for the first time, and "beginner's luck" does not prevent them from making mistakes. There are so many dangers that they now have access to: alcohol and drugs, automobiles, guns and knives, sex. They have adult decisions to make, but they do not yet have an adult's cognitive capacities or experience.

In the past, adolescence was regarded as a time of turmoil, of storm and stress. Some investigators, such as Anna Freud (Sigmund's daughter), went so far as to say that the *absence* of turmoil was a sign of trouble: "To be normal during the adolescent period is by itself abnormal" (1958, p. 275). But research has failed to support this view. "Normal" adolescents generally grow up to be "normal" adults. Troubled adolescents are the ones who are most likely to have problems in adulthood. Furthermore, the likelihood that a person will experience serious psychological or emotional problems is no higher in adolescence than in adulthood (Petersen, 1988; Powers, Hauser, and Kilner, 1989).

On the other hand, adolescents do tend to have more serious psychological problems than younger children, because the major psychiatric disorders generally make their first appearance around this time. Schizophrenia, for example, affects about 1 percent of the adult population, and most schizophrenics first start to show signs of the disorder in adolescence (see Box 2–4). Depressive disorders also tend to appear for the first time in adolescence, and so do alcoholism and drug abuse. Finally, when aggressive, conduct-disordered children turn into aggressive, conduct-disordered adolescents (as, unfortunately, they often do), their behavior is likely to become much more dangerous.

It is estimated that about 20 percent of teenagers suffer from more or less serious psychological disturbances; the other 80 percent are reasonably well adjusted and get along all right—most of the time—with themselves, their peers, and their parents. For the 20 percent who have problems, the nature of the problem tends to vary by gender. Troubled teenage girls are more likely to experience "inwardly directed" psychiatric symptoms such as depression, anxiety, and psychosomatic disturbances like headaches and digestive difficulties. Troubled teenage boys are more likely to engage in **acting-out behavior**—aggression, rule-breaking at home or in school, and substance abuse (Ostrov, Offer, and Howard, 1989).

Gender differences in self-esteem and self-concepts also increase during adolescence. Although there are no important differences in overall self-esteem, which remains fairly stable through early adolescence, girls and boys

How Much Storm and Stress Is Normal?

differ in what aspects of themselves they like and dislike. Teenage girls tend to have higher regard for their own ability to handle relationships with others; they may have problems with body image, however (see Box 14–1). Teenage boys tend to have a better body image and a better view of their own ability to achieve (Hirsch and Rapkin, 1987; Ostrov and others, 1989).

Adolescents have the reputation of being prone to emotional ups and downs, and indeed there is some evidence that moodiness is more common during this period than in adulthood. Mood swings seem to be somewhat more pronounced in teenage girls than in teenage boys (Petersen, 1988).

Physical Changes and Their Effects

Physical growth during middle childhood was relatively calm. In contrast, adolescence starts off with a burst of rapid physical growth followed by a dramatic series of changes in the body, leading to sexual maturity. These changes are triggered by increased secretions of various hormones. Under the direction of the pituitary gland (located at the base of the brain), endocrine glands in other parts of the body start to put out greater quantities of sex hormones. These hormones are secreted by the ovaries in girls, the testes in boys, and the adrenal glands in both sexes. Feminizing hormones (estrogens) and masculinizing hormones (androgens, especially **testosterone**) are present in both girls and boys, but girls' bodies contain more estrogen and boys' bodies contain more testosterone. The difference in the relative amounts of the two kinds of hormones increases during adolescence—at the beginning, girls and boys have fairly similar proportions of estrogen and testosterone in their bodies, but by the time they reach adulthood the differences are considerable.

The Growth Spurt of Early Adolescence

The growth spurt occurs over a period of about four years. It starts and ends about two years earlier in girls than in boys—the fastest growth occurs, on the average, at age 12 in girls and at age 14 in boys (see Figure 14–1). Although girls don't grow as much as boys during this period, their two-year head start means that they will be taller and heavier than the boys for a year or so. By age 13 the two sexes are approximately equal in height again, and by age 14 the boys are taller.

The increase in height goes along with an increase in weight. For both sexes, there is an increase in body fat at the beginning of the growth spurt. In girls the change is permanent—most of this fat will still be there when the growth spurt ends. But boys have a tendency to put on extra body fat just before the growth spurt and then to lose it during the period of maximum growth. The fat is used for energy during this period, or is converted to muscle and bone. Thus, boys are likely to end up looking thinner at the end of the growth spurt than they did at the beginning of it—despite the fact that they may be consuming as many as 6000 calories a day during this period (Haviland and Scarborough, 1981).

Growth during early adolescence does not occur at the same time and at the same rate in all parts of the body. Perhaps you recall that we described

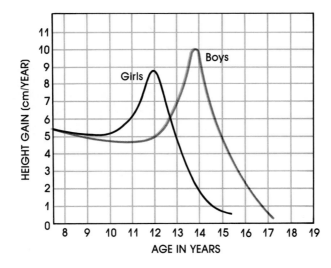

Figure 14-1
Growth rate (in height gain per year) of girls and boys between the ages of 8 and 17. (Adapted from Tanner, 1978.)

growth in the fetus (Chapter 4) as cephalocaudal—starting at the head and working its way downward, and proximodistal—starting in the center of the body and working its way outward. Well, growth in the young adolescent is virtually the opposite. The brain has already reached its adult size before adolescence begins, so there is little or no change in head size during this period. But substantial changes do occur elsewhere in the body. This growth begins with the outer parts of the body and proceeds inward. The hands and feet grow first, then the legs and arms. The trunk is the last part of the body to reach adult size.

Although the brain is no longer increasing in size, important changes in brain organization are believed to occur in late childhood and early adolescence. One sign of these changes is that the plasticity of the brain decreases —if there is a brain injury in adolescence, it is no longer so easy to reassign functions such as speech to undamaged areas. Probably as a result of this loss of plasticity, learning to speak a new language or to play a musical instrument becomes more difficult. But, in compensation, there is a great increase in problem-solving skills and in the ability to think abstractly. The adolescent's brain seems to work more efficiently than the child's. It takes less energy to keep it running (the metabolic rate of the brain is high in childhood and declines to adult levels by age 13 or 14) and it doesn't require as much sleep. Between the ages of 11 to 14, the time spent in deep sleep decreases by about two hours (Blakeslee, 1986).

Other parts of the body also show major changes during adolescence. The muscles, heart, lungs, digestive system, and reproductive system all increase in size. The tonsils and adenoids, which are part of the immune system, get smaller. There are changes in the proportions of the face: the forehead gets higher and wider, the chin becomes more prominent, the lips get fuller, and —of course—the nose gets larger. To top it off, glands near the surface of the skin begin to secrete increased amounts of a substance called sebum, and the teenager's skin breaks out in zits. Other skin glands begin to secrete increased amounts of sweat with a new, stronger odor. Mother Nature seems to love to torment adolescents.

Problems in Development

Box 14-1
Eating Disorders in Adolescent Girls

At the age of 15, Tammy won a beauty contest in the small suburban town in which she lived. No one was surprised, because Tammy was outstandingly good-looking. She had long blonde hair, big green eyes, and a shapely figure. People thought she looked like a model or a movie star. But three years later, Tammy's appearance had undergone a startling change:

> Anyone meeting Tammy today for the first time would not believe that she had ever once been capable of winning a beauty contest.... In the past year, Tammy's weight has dropped from one hundred eighteen to eighty-four pounds. She gives the appearance of a skeleton; her arms and legs seem to dangle from her body like wooden sticks. . . . Much of Tammy's full blonde hair has either fallen out or broken off. Whatever strands are left appear brittle and dry and hang from her head in stringy tufts. . . . Her eyes seem to stare hauntingly out of her head from deeply recessed sockets.   (Landau, 1983, p. 2)

Tammy is suffering from **anorexia nervosa,** a disorder that strikes an estimated 1 to 2 percent of adolescents. Almost all of these **anorectics** (or anorexics) are girls. Somewhere between 5 and 15 percent will eventually die of the long-term effects of chronic starvation (Garfinkel, Garner, and Goldbloom, 1987).

Anorexia is not a new disorder: it was defined and given a name in the 1870s, and there are descriptions of similar cases dating from the Middle Ages. However, it is a disorder that has become increasingly common in the past two decades. What's more, it is a disorder that is found mainly in North America and Western Europe: it is rare in Russia and unknown in nontechnological societies. In places where food is scarce, girls don't starve themselves to death. Within our own society, anorexia is most common in white girls from

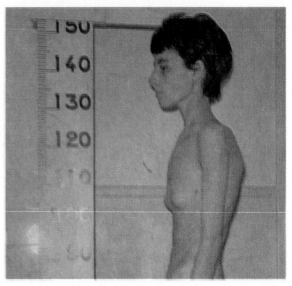

Anorexia is notoriously difficult to treat. Even though she may be starving herself to death, the anorectic may still see herself as "fat."

middle- or upper-middle-class homes (Brumberg, 1988).

Anorexia typically begins when a teenage girl decides that she's "too fat"—many anorectics were somewhat pudgy in childhood. She goes on a diet in order to lose a few pounds. But instead of resuming a normal food intake when that goal has been met, she continues or even increases her efforts to lose weight, often adding a heavy load of exercise to her regimen. She may refuse treatment and give irrational justifications for her behavior. Her perception of her own body does not correspond to reality: she may see herself as fat even when she is dying of starvation. Although she gives the impression that she doesn't care about food, she is actually obsessed with it—she thinks about food all the time.

Puberty   The word **puberty** is used in two ways: sometimes it refers to the entire period of sexual maturation in early adolescence, and sometimes it refers specifically to the point in time when the adolescent becomes theoretically capable of having offspring. By the second definition, puberty occurs in girls when they reach **menarche,** the first menstrual period, and in boys when they first begin to produce live sperm. But notice that we said *theoretically* capable of having offspring. Many (but not all) girls are unable to conceive a child for a year or so after menarche. In boys, the first live sperm are usually too few in

The causes of anorexia are complex. Twin and family studies make it clear that there must be some genetic predisposition for the disorder. But heredity can't explain why anorexia is so much more common now than it was 50 years ago, or why it is found mostly in the upper classes of economically advanced countries. Cultural factors must play a role. They play a role by dictating how young women are supposed to look. They're supposed to be slim: flat stomachs, thin thighs, size 7 jeans. Girls who don't look like this—or who *think* they don't—despair. They become depressed. They go on diets. American girls start dieting as early as the fourth grade. In a 1984 survey by *Glamour* magazine, 75 percent of the women who responded said they thought they were fat, although only 25 percent were actually overweight (Brumberg, 1988; Freedman, 1986).

Once a girl has started to lose weight, a number of factors may make her continue. She may relish the attention and concern her behavior evokes from family and friends. If she had worries about growing up and facing the responsibilities of adulthood, she might be relieved when her breasts disappear and her periods cease as the result of the loss of body fat. If, on the other hand, she was struggling to become independent, she may use self-starvation as a way of proving to her parents or her doctors that they can't make her do something if she doesn't want to do it: they can't make her eat.

And they *can't* make her eat—the anorectic is notoriously difficult to treat. If she is pressured into consuming food, she may vomit it up again as soon as she is alone. When hospitalized, she may conceal food and pretend to have eaten it, or drink lots of water before she is weighed. What has happened, apparently, is that she has become addicted to dieting—she has become dependent on the physical and psychological effects of starvation, the same way an alcoholic becomes addicted to the physical and psychological effects of drinking. Alcoholics, too, tend to resist treatment and deny that they have a problem.

Interestingly, alcoholism and anorexia are often found in the same families—there appears to be a genetic connection between these disorders (Brumberg, 1988; Garfinkel and others, 1987).

We mentioned that anorectics will sometimes use vomiting as a way of ridding themselves of unwanted food; they may also use laxatives for this purpose. Some anorectics occasionally go on eating binges and then purge themselves afterward; this is called the **binge-purge syndrome.** The binge-purge syndrome, however, is more often associated with another eating disorder: **bulimia.**

Although at times they behave in similar ways, the bulimic can be distinguished from the anorectic in that she maintains a normal weight—she may be thin, but she is not emaciated. She also tends to be in better shape psychologically; her disorder is easier to treat. Many bulimics, including those who show no signs of depression, have been treated successfully with antidepressive drugs. This suggests that some biochemical abnormality may be involved in the disorder (Walsh, 1988).

Whereas an anorectic may subsist for months on a food intake of 400 calories a day, a bulimic may take in as many as 8000 calories in a single binge. But everyone overeats from time to time, and one or two episodes of self-induced vomiting do not make a person a bulimic. It's hard to say where normal behavior ends and bulimia begins, because purging has become very common in some high school and college populations. Depending on how bulimia is defined, estimates of its prevalence range from 1 percent to 10 percent (Patton, 1988; Gross and Rosen, 1988). Though not as life-threatening as anorexia, bulimia has health risks of its own: frequent vomiting can irritate or erode the stomach, esophagus, salivary glands, and teeth.

Why are so many young women purging themselves or starving themselves? Maybe our society's emphasis on looking good and being thin has gone too far.

number to make them capable of becoming fathers. In both sexes, fertility increases over a period of time. So the ability to reproduce does not begin all at once—there's a period, early on, in which reproduction is possible but unlikely. The ability to have intercourse occurs long before the ability to reproduce. The male is capable of having an erection even in infancy.

During sexual development the physical differences between males and females increase—the boy's voice deepens and his facial hair begins to grow, the girl develops breasts. Such signs of manhood or womanhood are called

secondary sex characteristics, because they distinguish males from females but are not directly related to reproduction. **Primary sex characteristics** are the reproductive organs themselves—the penis and testes in males, the ovaries, uterus, and vagina in females.

SEXUAL DEVELOPMENT IN GIRLS. For girls in the United States, menarche occurs, on the average, between the ages of 12½ and 13—more precisely, 12.8 years for white girls and 12.5 for African Americans (Powers and others, 1989). But menarche is not the first sign of puberty: the process begins about two years earlier, with a slight swelling of the nipple area of the breasts and the appearance of some downy hair in the pubic area (see Table 14–1). These early changes are followed by a noticeable increase in the rate of growth. Both height and weight increase rapidly during this period, and in girls a large part of the weight gain consists of an increase in body fat. Much of the fat is distributed on the breasts, hips, and thighs. As a result, the girl's body changes in shape and her waist becomes more clearly defined.

Menarche generally does not occur until a girl's body weight is over some minimum, around 100 pounds in a girl of average height. The girls who reach that weight early will menstruate at an earlier age than girls who put on weight more slowly. The timing of menarche depends on having a certain amount of body fat, so well-nourished girls will reach that milestone at an earlier age than poorly nourished ones. Better nutrition (and better health in general) is believed to be the reason why the average age of menarche in American girls has declined steadily over the past 200 years: it was 15½ years in the 1800s and has now leveled off at around 12½ years. This speed-up in maturation has mainly been confined to North America and Western Europe: Czechoslovakian girls have their first period, on the average, at age 14; for the Kikuyu of Kenya the average age is 16; and for the Bindi of New Guinea it is 18 (Frisch, 1988; Powers and others, 1989).

Because the onset of menstruation depends on having a minimum amount of body fat, not muscle, a girl can weigh well over 100 pounds and still not have a period. Many female athletes stop menstruating while they are in training. Female swimmers and runners who begin training in childhood do not reach menarche until age 15, on the average. If they are still competing in these sports in college, fewer than one in five will have regular periods. Ovulation—the release of an egg from the ovary—ceases if the body does not contain enough fat to meet the needs of reproduction (Frisch, 1988).

With the onset of menstruation comes a marked decline in the rate of a girl's growth in height; within two years after menarche she will have essentially reached her adult height. Thus, girls who have an early menarche stop growing sooner than those who develop more slowly. But early developers also tend to grow more rapidly during their growth spurt than later developers, so there are no important differences in height between the two groups (Faust, 1977). There may be differences in proportions, though: late developers tend to have longer legs, as a result of their prolonged period of growth. The fact that boys reach puberty two years later than girls—and thus have two extra years of growth—is one of the reasons why men end up taller than women and have longer legs. The other reason, as you can see in Figure 14–1, is that boys grow faster than girls during their growth spurt (Petersen, 1988; Weisfeld and Billings, 1988).

TABLE 14–1
The Typical Sequence of Physical Development in Adolescence

GIRLS	BOYS
Initial enlargement of the breasts occurs (breast bud stage).	Growth of the testes and scrotum begins.
Straight, lightly pigmented pubic hair appears.	Straight, lightly pigmented pubic hair appears.
Maximum growth rate is attained.	Growth of the penis begins.
	Early changes in the voice occur.
Pubic hair becomes adult in type but covers a smaller area than in adult.	First ejaculation of semen occurs.
Breast enlargement continues; the nipple and the area around it now project above the level of the breast.	Pubic hair becomes adult in type but covers a smaller area than in adult.
	Maximum growth rate is attained.
Menarche occurs.	Underarm hair appears; the sweat glands under the arms increase in size.
Underarm hair appears; the sweat glands under the arms increase in size.	The voice deepens noticeably.
	Growth of mustache and beard hair begins. Pubic hair reaches adult state.
Breasts and pubic hair reach adult stage.	

Sources: The Committee on Adolescence, Group for the Advancement of Psychiatry, 1968; Tanner, 1978.

SEXUAL DEVELOPMENT IN BOYS. In boys, the first sign of approaching puberty is an increase in size in the testes (or testicles), which begins, on the average, at about age 12. This is followed by the appearance of some pubic hair and then an increase in the size of the penis. Underarm hair begins to appear next; some mustache hair may begin to show at about the same time. The growth of beard and body hair is generally not complete until late adolescence.

The boy's first ejaculation of semen occurs, on the average, at about age 14. It may happen during masturbation, or during sleep in a **nocturnal emission.** The great majority of adolescent males have nocturnal emissions from time to time.

The change in pitch of the voice is one of the later changes of male development. It is accompanied by a noticeable growth of the Adam's apple. The voice change is usually gradual, but in some boys it happens abruptly. There may be a period in which the voice shifts suddenly (and embarrassingly) from high to low and back again.

Another possible source of embarrassment for boys is a slight enlargement of the breasts, which sometimes occurs midway through adolescence. About 25 percent of boys experience this temporary swelling, which is caused by the estrogens that are present in small amounts in all normal males. The swelling goes away by itself (Conger and Petersen, 1984).

Teenagers are acutely aware of the changes that are taking place in their bodies. The psychological repercussions of these changes differ for girls and boys.

Psychological Aspects of Puberty

A Girl's Feelings about Menarche. The onset of puberty in a girl is marked by a noteworthy event, her first menstrual period. Thus, for a girl the entry into adolescence is an abrupt one. How does she feel about this sudden change in her life?

In a major study of the emotional aspects of menarche, almost 700 girls, from fifth through twelfth grade, were interviewed or asked to fill out questionnaires. These girls reported their feelings about their first period, if they had had one. Not surprisingly, they had both positive and negative feelings about the event. Their positive feelings were related to their interpretation of menarche as a sign of maturity—as an aspect of becoming a woman and being able to have children. Some also expressed pleasure at being like their friends. The girls' negative feelings were related to the "hassle" of menstruating—the messiness, the nuisance of having to carry supplies. Many also mentioned physical discomfort as a negative aspect—fully half of the girls reported experiencing some unpleasant symptom, usually cramps or nausea, during their first period.

Almost 90 percent of the girls had told their mothers about it when they discovered they had begun to menstruate. They were at first very secretive about it with other people, however. This self-consciousness gradually disappeared, and after a few months the subject was freely discussed with female friends (Ruble and Brooks-Gunn, 1982).

Gender Differences in Body-Image Satisfaction. Adolescents of both sexes spend a great deal of time examining themselves and comparing the various parts of their own bodies to those of their peers or—worse still—to those of movie stars and models. A longitudinal study of adolescents from 11 to 18 showed that body-image satisfaction was lowest at age 13 for girls and at 15 for boys. For both sexes, it went up steadily after that. But at every age, girls were significantly less satisfied with their own bodies than boys were (Rauste-von Wright, 1989).

Girls seem to be especially likely to dwell on their real or imagined physical flaws and to have an unrealistic idea of what a proper female body should look like (Damhorst, Littrell, and Littrell, 1988). Perhaps girls worry more about their appearance than boys do because they know that they will be judged on that basis by their potential mates. As we will see in Chapter 15, it is the male, not the female, who is more likely to choose a mate on the basis of physical attractiveness.

The Effects of Maturing Earlier than Usual. Although on the average girls enter adolescence about two years earlier than boys, there is considerable variation among individuals. Normal American girls may begin to menstruate as early as 9½ or as late as 16½. The rate of maturation is equally variable in boys. The photo on the next page shows three young teenagers of the same age who are at three different stages of physical maturation.

A girl who reaches puberty unusually early is not only ahead of most of the girls in her class: she is ahead of *everyone* in her class. She is developing breasts when everyone else is as flat as a pancake, and she can't easily remain inconspicuous because she is also likely to be tall for her age. Although she may have temporary problems with being teased and feeling embarrassed, in the

These boys are all 13 years old.

long run her early maturation may be to her advantage. In fact, it conveys advantages even in elementary school: one study found that breast development and tallness in 9- to 11-year-old girls was associated with a better body image and better general adjustment (Brooks-Gunn and Warren, 1988). Looking older results in higher social status for children; even adults have a tendency to regard a taller child as more competent than a shorter child of the same age (Brackbill and Nevill, 1981).

Although growing taller seems to have a positive effect on social status and self-image, growing fatter does not. Because of the relationship between body fat and menarche, a plump girl tends to mature more rapidly than a thin one. The growth spurt of early puberty adds additional fat to her body, and this can cause serious body-image problems in a girl who is already somewhat overweight. Early maturing girls who are very dissatisfied with their own bodies have been found to run a significantly increased risk of depression (Savola, 1989).

For males, there are no disadvantages to maturing early: everything seems to favor the individual who is beginning to look like a man while his agemates still look like boys. They are sought after by their female agemates and accepted as a leader by their fellow males. Early maturing boys are likely to be more muscular than average and tend to be good in sports. These characteristics, as well as their greater physical maturity, contribute to their ability to assume a dominant role in relationships with their agemates. Nor is this likely to be a new experience for them: typically, an early maturing adolescent boy was advanced in physical maturity all through childhood. He is likely to have been a dominant member of his group of friends ever since he started elementary school (Weisfeld and Billings, 1988).

Cognitive Development

There is no question that adolescents are better thinkers and better learners than younger children. Piaget had much to say about the superiority of adolescent cognition: in Piagetian theory, early adolescence marks the entry into the highest stage of cognitive development, the **period of formal operations.**

Formal Operational Thought

According to Piaget, adolescents differ from children in that they are able to solve problems in a logical and creative way, by thinking up alternative solutions and testing them systematically. They can distinguish between what is real and what is possible, and they can use imagination not only for fantasy and play, but also to perform mental experiments and to make logical deductions.

David Elkind, a professor at Tufts University, provided support for Piaget's views in a classic study done in 1968. Elkind tested the problem-solving abilities of a group of children, ages 8 to 9, and a group of adolescents, ages 13 to 14. The subjects were shown 72 pairs of pictured objects, one pair at a time, and asked to choose one picture from each pair. If they chose the picture of the "right" object, a light would go on. Their job was to figure out what made the objects "right" or "wrong," so they could make the light go on every time.

The answer to the problem was that objects with wheels were always right and objects without wheels were always wrong. All the 13- and 14-year-olds solved this problem, some in as few as ten trials. But only half of the 7- and 8-year-olds discovered the solution, and those who did required almost all of the 72 trials in order to do so.

The adolescents solved the problem by thinking up possible solutions ("Maybe it's tools," or "Maybe it's vehicles") and then testing out these theories in a systematic way. They were willing to discard a theory as soon as they obtained evidence that it was wrong. The younger children, on the other hand, had difficulty giving up a theory once they had thought of it, even when evidence from later pairs of pictures went against it. According to Elkind (1968), the child appeared to be unaware that her theory was just a theory and not reality—once she had come up with an idea, she seemed to accept it as true, despite all evidence to the contrary. So the adolescents were more flexible, more systematic, and better able to distinguish between their own theories and proven facts.

This ability to distinguish the possible from the actual also enables adolescents to dream up alternate realities, which they know don't exist, and to

Box 14-2
Adolescent Egocentrism: The Imaginary Audience and the Personal Fable

According to Piaget, it's not only preschoolers who have a tendency to be egocentric. He believes that when adolescents enter the stage of formal operations they may become egocentric again in a whole new way. They may get overconfident about the value of intellectual solutions to problems and overvalue the importance of their own mental processes. They may, as a consequence, fail to distinguish clearly between their own thoughts and those of others. Piaget calls this the "egocentrism of formal operations." The adolescent who has come to hold a particular belief may find it hard to accept the fact that others do not share it. She may become self-righteous or intolerant of opposing opinions.

Theorist David Elkind has applied Piaget's notion of adolescent egocentrism to teenagers' apparent preoccupation with themselves. According to Elkind (1967, 1978), young adolescents' newfound capacity for abstract thought, plus their focus on their own rapidly changing bodies, combine to produce a distorted view of reality: they feel that they are being observed by an **imaginary audience.** Teenagers labor under the delusion that other people are just as concerned about how they look and act, and about their feelings and thoughts, as they themselves are. The result is a heightened self-consciousness and a feeling that one is continually being evaluated by others—one is constantly "on stage." This feeling is at the root of many adolescent behaviors—for example, the loudness and showing off and the distinctive clothing and hairstyles that are so characteristic of this stage of development (Buis and Thompson, 1989; Gray and Hudson, 1984).

The other aspect of adolescent egocentrism, according to Elkind, is a belief in what he calls the **personal fable.** This involves a conviction that one is different from everybody else—a feeling that "I am unique, and therefore I am terribly important and not subject to the risks and limitations of ordinary mortals." Adolescents tend to think they are invulnerable. They don't believe they will ever die, or even grow old.

Although not all researchers agree with Piaget and Elkind about the causes of adolescent self-consciousness and egocentrism, most agree that the imaginary audience and the personal fable are very good descriptions of the adolescent's style of thinking. In fact, the teenager's idea that there is an audience watching her all the time may not be entirely a delusion: teenagers are extremely aware of—and critical of—the appearance and behavior of their peers. It's not unreasonable for them to assume that if they're so aware of the way their agemates look and act, then their agemates must be equally aware of how *they* look and act (de Rosenroll, 1987).

But it is the personal fable—the feeling of being special and invulnerable—that is most likely to get teenagers into trouble. They don't avoid risks because they don't really believe that anything bad will ever happen to them. They don't take care of their health because they take health for granted. Even adolescents who *aren't* healthy fail to follow doctors' orders: for example, one study found that only 40 percent of teenagers with cancer were taking their anticancer medication. Asthmatic and diabetic teenagers often fail to follow the regimens prescribed by their physicians; those with scoliosis don't do their exercises and won't wear their back braces. Compliance with medical advice is believed to be lower in early adolescence than at any other time of life (Cromer and Tarnowski, 1989).

Every year, thousands of teenage girls have babies because they didn't think that just a little sex would make them pregnant. Every year, thousands of teenagers start smoking cigarettes in the erroneous belief that they can quit any time they want to. Adolescents do risky things because of their desire to show that they are tough and independent, and because of their delusion that "it can't happen to me."

contemplate what might happen if they *did* exist. Sometimes these ideas are projected far into the future. Thus, reading science fiction becomes popular during this period. At about the same time, adolescents start to mull over alternative ways of organizing the world—*better* ways. The result is that the young person begins, for the first time, to think deep thoughts about questions of truth, morality, and justice (Siegler, 1986).

In general, then, Piagetian theorists characterize formal thought as being relatively free from the constraints of time, place, and reality—that is, it is abstract. Adolescents can take into account the future and the past; they can distinguish between what *is* true, what *could be* true, and what might happen if something *were* true.

Current Views of Adolescent Cognition

Piaget's views on adolescent thought have been criticized as having two major failings. First, the kind of abstract, systematic thinking that is supposed to appear at this time is not universal. Formal operational thought is far more likely to be used in technologically advanced societies than in other parts of the world; it isn't found at all in some preindustrial societies. Thus, the educational and cultural environment are clearly involved in the acquisition of this kind of thinking. Further proof of the importance of education is the fact that even school-age children can be taught to use formal operational procedures for solving problems, simply by giving them careful training in the scientific method (Byrnes, 1988; Siegler and Liebert, 1975).

Second, even in our own society, the use of formal operational thought is not universal. It is more likely to be used by individuals with a high IQ (Orr, Brack, and Ingersoll, 1988). It is more likely to be used for reasoning about familiar things than about unfamiliar things. For example, people are likely to reason correctly when they are asked to judge the logical truth or falseness of a statement such as "If it is raining, then the grass is wet." They are likely to have a lot more trouble with statements such as "If this card is blue, then there are two hearts on the other side" (Byrnes, 1988).

So the use of formal thought depends on the individual's general intelligence, on his cultural background and education, and on his experience with the particular subject matter. A person who has never seen grass or rain but who has had a lot of experience with cards might do a better job with the card question than with the rain question. Emotional factors also play a role: it is rare to see formal thought applied in its purest form to an adolescent's personal or social life.

No one quarrels with Piaget's conclusions that adolescents are, in general, capable of more abstract forms of reasoning than younger children. What is at issue is whether this happens because the adolescent has entered a new stage of development. It appears to us that formal or abstract thought emerges in a gradual and unpredictable fashion, rather than as a giant leap forward. Although the change may depend, to some extent, on the brain reorganization we mentioned earlier, it seems to result primarily from adolescents' greater experience with the world and from the greater amount of practice they've had in using their brains.

METACOGNITIVE ADVANCES. Probably as a result of this kind of practice, adolescents have a deeper understanding of their own learning and memory processes than do younger children. In memorization tests they use more sophisticated strategies of rehearsal or elaboration; as a result, they perform better on such tests than preadolescents. They know that taking notes is a valuable learning and memory aid—younger children don't seem to realize that it's a good idea to keep a written record of something they want to

As children get older, they gain a better understanding of their own cognitive processes. Young adolescents know that taking notes is a valuable aid to learning and memory.

remember. Adolescents are also better at knowing what to write down—at picking out the important points of what they are reading, for example (Suzuki-Slakter, 1988; Haviland and Scarborough, 1981).

An interesting characteristic of adolescents is their metacognitive ability to think about thinking—that is, their ability to reflect about the thought process itself. Adolescents are capable of understanding and using statements such as "I wonder what he thinks I think he is thinking about me," and "I was thinking about my future, and then I began to think about why I was thinking about why I was thinking about my future" (Miller, Kessel, and Flavell, 1970; Siegler, 1986).

SOCIAL COGNITION IN ADOLESCENCE. The cognitive advances that occur during late childhood and early adolescence permit increasingly complex concepts of other people, and also of oneself. Descriptions of self and of others become deeper and less concrete—that is, they dwell less on physical attributes or other objective facts. Especially when it comes to other people, descriptions given by older teens tend to be more "psychological" than those given by younger teens: in other words, older teens are more likely to mention personality characteristics. Older teens are also more likely to organize their descriptions by using phrases that qualify or elaborate on their statements: for example, "She is smart but at times she can be very silly," "She is rather upset right now because her parents have just split up," or "She appears friendly but this is really an act." Girls seem to be better at doing this sort of thing than boys: throughout the teen years, girls' descriptions of people (including themselves) are at a higher level of social cognition than boys' (O'Mahony, 1986, 1989).

Advances in social cognition during adolescence will naturally affect relationships with others. Older teens (and girls) tend to suggest more mature ways of resolving interpersonal conflicts than younger teens (and boys). The more advanced solutions involve taking into account the other person's point of view as well as one's own, and considering the long-term effects on the relationship (Selman and others, 1986).

Parents, Peers, and the Struggle for Independence

Young children look to their parents for guidance, information, and emotional support; parents and family remain influential all through middle childhood. But adolescents seek to put some distance between themselves and their parents. We rejected the notion that adolescent thinking represents a new stage of cognitive development, qualitatively different from what came before. But adolescent relationships, particularly with their parents, do seem to be qualitatively different from what came before. Adolescents have entered a new stage of relating to the people in their lives.

Sociobiologists and ethologists have pointed out that changes in parent–child relationships around the time of puberty are by no means unique to our species. In some species of monkeys and apes, the parents become aggressive toward their maturing offspring: fathers may attack sons, mothers may attack daughters. The purpose, evidently, is to drive away the offspring in order to lessen the chances of an incestuous mating and to reduce the strain on the local food supply. In humans, the offspring are dependent on the parents for a much longer time than in other species. This prolonged period of childhood and adolescence permits young humans first to learn what their parents can teach them about adult roles, and then to form strong bonds with the members of their peer group. Humans are a social species, and the ability to cooperate with the other members of one's own generation is of crucial importance (Weisfeld and Billings, 1988).

The Growing Distance between Parents and Offspring

In a typical study, researchers asked some sixth, ninth, and twelfth graders to put little wooden figures, representing themselves and their parents, on a chessboard. The subjects were asked to position the pieces according to how close the members of the family felt to one another. The sixth graders put the figures representing themselves and their parents fairly close together, the ninth graders put them farther apart, and the twelfth graders put them still farther apart (Feldman and Gehring, 1988).

The growing distance between parents and offspring is not solely a function of age: the physical maturation of the adolescent also plays a role. Physically mature teenagers feel more emotional distance between themselves and

Adolescents question their parents' authority over them; they realize (in fact, are acutely aware) that their parents don't know everything and aren't perfect.

their parents than less mature teenagers of the same age. Physical maturation is also related to the amount of conflict between adolescents and their parents: the most arguing occurs around the midpoint of puberty (Steinberg, 1987a, 1988).

Children see their parents as all-powerful and all-knowing. This perception changes dramatically in adolescence. Even in families where there is no overt conflict between parents and teenagers, the teenagers are likely to realize that their parents do not know everything and that they have flaws. In a recent study, researchers questioned subjects between the ages of 9 and 23 about their feelings about their parents. The 9- to 11-year-olds didn't question their parents' authority over them. Here are some of their comments:

Your mother is your mother. She knows what to do better.

Obey her, because you might do the wrong thing and she'll tell you the right thing. It's for your own good.

The father likes doing things with you but he disciplines you so that you'll be a good man when you grow up.

Here, in contrast, are some comments from the 15- to 16-year-olds about their parents:

Before I used to do whatever she asked. I thought she was always right. Now I state my case.

I thought he could do no wrong but then I started to get my own ideas.

He's not idealized now.

I don't see him as this father-figure anymore. He doesn't have as much power over me.

What happens next is interesting. We have pointed out a number of times that mothers and fathers do not have equal roles in childrearing or equal relationships with their children. This is still true in adolescence and it probably remains true throughout the lifespan. By late adolescence, young people of both sexes have come to see Mom as a person in her own right and to establish a new kind of relationship with her. Here are some comments by 18- to 23-year-olds about their mothers:

I now understand her. I realize she's a person, too—not just a mother, but a person. I know I can do a lot to help her now.

Before, I just had a mother-role for her. . . . Now I see her as more complex than before.

We can disagree now and we don't get mad.

I now know things about her, her qualities. I think highly of her for them.

(Smollar and Youniss, 1989, pp. 75–80)

The same thing does not happen with the father—at least, not by the age of 23. The subjects in this study felt that Dad was interested in their welfare, but that he was mainly concerned about things like school grades, career choices, and enforcing family rules. Mom, on the other hand, was perceived as being more interested in their day-to-day lives and their personal problems. So the relationship with the mother is warmer and closer. The relationship with the father may be more problematic for teens partly because the father has always been better able to command their respect and obedience, and they no longer want to be dominated by a parent.

CONFLICTS BETWEEN ADOLESCENTS AND THEIR PARENTS. One reason that conflicts between parents and adolescents occur is because the parents are looking backward, toward the time when the child respected and obeyed them without question. The adolescent, in contrast, is looking forward, toward the time when he or she will be an autonomous adult. Thus, conflicts between adolescents and their elders are probably inevitable; they have always occurred. Socrates complained about the disrepectful behavior of the youth of ancient Greece.

What do teenagers and their parents argue about? Oddly enough, most of the arguments are about relatively unimportant things. The really important

The Child in Society

Box 14-3
Homeless Youth

In recent years there has been much in the news about homelessness in general and about homeless youth in particular. But this is not a new phenomenon. As Paul Shane, of Rutgers University, points out,

> Homeless and runaway children and adolescents are not peculiar to our era. Dickens wrote about them in *Oliver Twist*. Emile Zola wrote about similar situations in late nineteenth century France. Many immigrants to America were homeless or runaway youth, some taken from jails and workhouses, others coming on their own, often as indentured servants. Many of the pioneers settling the hinterlands of the country were such young people. Nor are homeless and runaway young people in our time unique to the United States. The World Health Organization has published material and sponsored conferences on homeless and runaway youth as a world-wide phenomenon. (Shane, 1989, p. 208)

The difference between homeless youth and runaways is simple: runaways have a home that they can return to. In the late 1960s there was an increase in the number of runaways; many of these young people identified themselves with the "flower children." Now the majority of homeless youth are truly homeless: they haven't left their homes and families—their homes and families have left them. Some have been kicked out; these youths are often referred to as "throwaways." Sometimes the decision to leave was a mutual one. Sometimes the whole family was homeless or in deep trouble; the adolescent may have been removed from the home by legal action, or the parents may be temporarily or permanently unable to care for their children. And sometimes the family has fallen apart—the parents split up and went their separate ways, and the home and the family no longer exist. Robert Frost said, "Home is the place where, when you have to go there, they have to take you in." But what if "they" aren't there anymore, and you're not even sure where "there" is?

Although homeless youth are found at all socioeconomic levels, they are more likely to come from a background of poverty. Many are from mother-headed or stepfather-headed homes; perhaps the family consisted of a mixture of siblings, stepsiblings, and half-siblings. Multiple problems, such as parental fighting and alcoholism, are common in the families (or ex-families) of homeless adolescents. Many suffered years of neglect or abuse—verbal, physical, and/or sexual—before they left or were thrown out.

In a recent sample of homeless youth, about a third were runaways, a fifth were "throwaways," another fifth had left the home by mutual consent, and a fifth were without a home because of their family's inability to care for them or removal by authorities. The remainder were homeless for miscellaneous or undetermined reasons.

There is little point in trying to determine who is to blame for the situation—the parents, the adolescent, or society. The important thing is to provide these young people with food, shelter, medical care, and education. As Shane explains,

> Whether they are called homeless or runaway, only a minority (36%) go back home. The society's remedies for the plight of runaway and homeless youth are not plausible for the majority—they are not going home again. (1989, p. 212)

—and potentially most explosive—issues seldom get discussed. Researchers recently gave some 12- to 15-year-olds a list of topics and asked them which topics they argued about with their parents and which were never discussed. The topics that were most likely to be argued about were fighting with siblings, cleaning up one's room, talking back to parents, and doing household chores. Topics that were seldom, if ever, discussed were sex, dating, using drugs or alcohol, and smoking (Tesser, Forehand, Brody, and Long, 1989).

Although some amount of disagreement between teenagers and parents is normal and may even be healthy, a high level of conflict is often a sign of trouble. Adolescents whose relationships with their parents are particularly stormy are more likely to engage in problem behavior such as drug use, early sexual activity, dropping out of school, and running away (Hall, 1987). Each year, 10 percent of adolescents hit their parents, and 3 percent assault them seriously enough to cause injuries (Agnew and Huguley, 1989). Parents, of course, also hit their children: about 15 percent of cases of serious child abuse involve teenagers, with girls twice as likely to be injured as boys (Rosenthal, 1988).

Parent–adolescent conflict is more common in families where the parents are getting along poorly with each other (Hall, 1987). As we have seen before, a tendency to be argumentative or aggressive often runs in families—due both to genetic and environmental influences. Things are likely to get worse in such families when the sons become teenagers, because boys' aggressiveness has been found to increase during adolescence as a result of the increased production of male hormones. For girls, there doesn't seem to be any connection between hormone levels and aggressive behavior (Susman and others, 1987).

Turning toward the Peer Group

When relationships with parents go poorly, adolescents have an alternative: they can turn to their friends for emotional support, guidance, and, in some cases, even a place to live. But most adolescents remain with their parents and continue to feel strong emotional ties to them, even if they argue with them a lot.

At the same time that they are bickering with their parents about family rules and regulations, adolescents are typically conforming quite closely to the expectations and demands of their group of friends. Thus, most teenagers do not gain true independence—that will not come until later in development. What they do instead is to draw away from their parents and move closer to their peer group, as the first step in the larger process. The family had its chance to socialize the child; now it's the peer group's turn (Tedesco and Gaier, 1988).

FRIENDSHIPS IN ADOLESCENCE. Like children and adults, adolescents choose friends whom they see as being similar to themselves. If two adolescents are good friends, they are likely to have many attitudes and preferences in common. They will probably have similar attitudes toward school and similar academic ambitions; they will probably be fairly well matched in academic achievement, too. They are also likely to share similar tastes in music, clothing, and recreational activities, and to have similar views on drinking, smoking, and drug use (Berndt, 1982).

Not all these similarities are due to the way young people select their friends. There is evidence that the behaviors and attitudes of friends become more alike over the course of their friendship because of the influence the friends have on each other (Fisher and Bauman, 1988).

One way that friendships in adolescence differ from friendships in younger children is in closeness and intimacy. Between seventh grade and eleventh grade, there is a steady increase in how strongly young people agree with statements such as "I feel free to talk with my friend about almost anything," and "I know how my friend feels about things without his/her telling me." This increase in reported intimacy occurs both in boys' friendships with boys and in girls' friendships with girls. In fact, somewhat surprisingly, boys' and girls' responses to the two statements we just quoted did not differ significantly, although other studies have shown girls' friendships to be more intimate than those of boys. It's also interesting to note that the rise of close friendships between young people of the opposite sex does not seem to interfere with same-sex friendships. Opposite-sex friendships show a sharp rise in reported intimacy, starting in seventh grade for girls and in ninth grade for boys. The reported closeness of same-sex friendships continues to increase despite the development of close opposite-sex relationships (Sharabany, Gershoni, and Hofman, 1981).

Few adolescents have just a single close friend. Most are members of groups, usually informal cliques or "crowds." These peer groups provide support for the adolescent, but often at the expense of being petty, intolerant, or even cruel. Erik Erikson (1963) explains that such behavior serves to help the group members protect themselves against what he calls **identity confusion.** By rejecting others who are different from themselves in race, religion, social class, abilities, or appearance (including clothing), adolescents are able to derive a sense of identity from the particular group to which they belong. Erikson suggests that parents should try to understand the motivations behind this kind of intolerance, though they needn't approve of it.

The peer group may even have its own language. It is common for each generation of adolescents to create a special slang vocabulary or **argot.** This special language serves to distinguish them from younger and older people and to strengthen their identification with their agemates. But many of the slang words invented by teenagers eventually work their way into the vocabulary of children and adults, and then the teens must make up new words because the old ones no longer serve their purpose.

PEER GROUP INFLUENCES. Adolescent peer groups are not merely an older version of childhood groups of friends: their influence is far more potent. Preadolescents tend to describe "groups of kids who hang around together" on the basis of common activities ("They ride bikes") and social behavior ("They act tough"); they perceive the group's influence on its members as being restricted to those activities and behaviors. But adolescents perceive peer-group influences as being much more pervasive and far-reaching, affecting not just activities and social behavior but also the style of dress of its

An adolescent peer group has a pervasive influence on the behavior and values of its members. Such influences can be positive, as well as negative.

members, the likelihood that they will break rules, and their overall attitudes and values (O'Brien and Bierman, 1988).

An adolescent peer group can be viewed as a kind of subculture, consisting of a group of teenagers of roughly the same age who share values and experiences. One study of high school peer groups identified six distinct "crowds":

- The jocks—athletes, cheerleaders, and their girl- and boyfriends.
- The populars—well-known students who are leaders in social activities and school government.
- The brains—academically oriented students.
- The normals—the middle-of-the road types who make up the largest proportion of the high school population.
- The druggies and toughs—these students have a reputation for using drugs and engaging in delinquent behavior.
- The nobodies—low in social skills, academic ability, or both.

The researchers found that the adolescents' self-esteem was related to the social status of the group to which they belonged. The jocks and the populars had the highest social status and the highest self-esteem, and the nobodies had the lowest (Brown and Lohr, 1987).

Within every adolescent group, there is pressure to conform to the group's standards and to do whatever the other group members do. When adolescents break rules or take risks—when they drink, use drugs, have sex, skip school, or cheat on a test—peer pressure is often at the bottom of it. At least, that's how they perceive it. Adolescents who report feeling the most peer pressure are the same ones who report doing the largest number of antisocial acts. On the other hand, peer pressure is not always antisocial: peers can *discourage* antisocial behavior as well as encourage it. In fact, teens are more likely to yield to peer pressure when it is *not* antisocial than when it is (Brown, Clasen, and Eicher, 1986).

What kind of teen is most likely to yield to peer pressure to do something wrong or unwise? Boys are more likely to yield to this kind of pressure than girls, and adolescents in single-parent or stepparent homes are more likely to do so than those in intact, two-parent homes. Teens who receive less parental supervision—latchkey kids, for example—are also more likely to succumb to antisocial peer pressure (Brown and others, 1986; Steinberg, 1986, 1987b).

Delinquency

Delinquency is a term applied only to juvenile lawbreakers—those under 16 or 18 years old (the exact age depends on the laws of the state). Older people who break laws are not called delinquents—they are called criminals. Although some acts, such as drinking or running away from home, are illegal only for minors, the fact remains that adolescents are responsible for a disproportionate share of real crime. People under the age of 18 commit more than 50 percent of the serious crimes occurring in the United States, though that age group makes up only 38 percent of the population (Garbarino, Sebes, and Schellenbach, 1984).

According to James Wilson and Richard Herrnstein of Harvard University,

Crime is an activity disproportionately carried out by young men living in large cities. There are old criminals, and female ones, and rural and small-town ones, but, to a much greater degree than would be expected by chance, criminals are young urban males. This is true, insofar as we can tell, in every society that keeps any reasonable criminal statistics. (Wilson and Herrnstein, 1985, p. 26).

Aside from gender (males are responsible for 90 percent of violent crime and 80 percent of property crime), a number of other factors have been found to be associated with delinquent behavior. The young men who commit crimes are likely to have a history of antisocial behavior dating from childhood. They tend to be muscular in build and to have done poorly in school. The chances of serious or repeated brushes with the law are more than twice as high for teenagers in mother-headed households as for teenagers living with two biological parents, and this is true at higher socioeconomic levels as well as at lower ones. A teenager with a stepfather is just as likely to get into trouble as one living only with a mother (Wilson and Herrnstein, 1985; Steinberg, 1987b).

Delinquency is more common among adolescents from economically disadvantaged backgrounds. The fact that so many black youths live in mother-headed homes in poverty-ridden urban environments may explain why a disproportionate number of delinquents are black (Mauer, 1990).

There is a relationship between intelligence and criminal behavior that can't be accounted for by socioeconomic status, race, or neighborhood. Delinquents are likely to be lower in IQ than nondelinquents from the same background—an average of eight IQ points lower. Certain types of cognitive deficits, such as poor verbal skills and poor memory, are especially prevalent in delinquent youths. Because of their limitations, most of the socially approved pathways to achievement or economic success are closed to them (Moffitt and Silva, 1988a, 1988b).

A number of personality traits have been associated with delinquency. Delinquents are more likely than nondelinquents to be impulsive, unconventional, interested in excitement and instant gratification, and—of course—aggressive. An adolescent who engages in criminal behavior is also more likely to engage in other kinds of problem behavior, such as drinking, drug use, gambling, and early sexual activity (Binder, 1988; Donovan, Jessor, and Costa, 1988).

Heredity plays a role in criminal behavior. A Danish adoption study showed that the likelihood of an adopted child becoming a criminal depended more on his biological parents than on the parents who reared him. The biological children of chronic criminals had three times the normal risk of becoming chronic criminals themselves. In contrast, having an adoptive parent who was convicted of a crime had only a slight effect (Mednick, Gabrielli, and Hutchings, 1984).

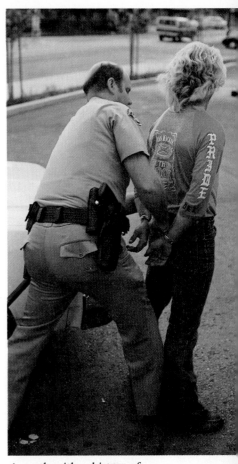

A youth with a history of antisocial behavior may, by mid-adolescence, be getting into more serious trouble.

THE ROLE OF THE FAMILY. Why does a teenager (particularly a boy) without a father tend to get into trouble? One explanation is that a single mother is less able to exert control over her offspring's behavior. Even in intact families, teenagers who are allowed to go where they wish and do what they wish, without parental supervision or monitoring, are at far greater risk of becoming delinquent. One study found that almost three-quarters of seriously delinquent youths, and half of moderately delinquent youths, were poorly monitored by their parents. Only a fifth of nondelinquent youths were found to be poorly monitored. The researchers concluded,

> It seems that parents of delinquents are indifferent trackers of their sons' whereabouts, the kind of companions they keep, or the type of activities in which they engage. . . . Given that rule-breaking behaviors occur, our clinical experience suggests that such parents are less likely to provide a punishment such as a loss of privilege, work detail, or loss of allowance. If they react to such information at all, it is more likely to be with a lecture, a scolding, or a threat; in any case, these abrasive overtures are not backed by an effective consequence. (Patterson and Stouthamer-Loeber, 1984, p. 1305)

But this makes it sound as though delinquency is entirely the parents' fault—a conclusion that is unlikely to be true, in view of the adoption study that we just mentioned. The relationship between teenage delinquency and a lack of parental supervision is likely to be one of those two-way transactions that work in a vicious-circle fashion: the parents become frustrated or indifferent after repeated attempts to supervise an adolescent who defies or outwits them. Eventually, they give up trying, and then the adolescent is free to get into more serious trouble.

CAN DELINQUENCY BE CURED? The discouraging news is that most treatment programs for juvenile offenders do not work. While some programs are capable of producing short-term improvements in the behavior of the delinquent, there is no evidence as yet of long-term benefits to society. That is, there is no evidence that the treated delinquent is less likely to commit another crime than the untreated delinquent (Lab and Whitehead, 1988).

The best cure for criminal behavior seems to be time: most criminals eventually outgrow their antisocial tendencies. Although there are old criminals, as Wilson and Herrnstein pointed out, most criminals are young. Sooner or later most delinquents turn to safer ways of amusing themselves, or easier ways of earning a living.

Substance Use and Abuse   The highest rates of substance use (use of drugs, alcohol, and tobacco) occur during adolescence. Adolescents consume more alcohol and more drugs, both legal and illegal, than adults. If they're using these substances in an effort to look like adults, they're overdoing it (Engel, Nordlohne, Hurrelmann, and Holler, 1987).

The use of various substances tends to go together: adolescents who drink heavily, for example, are also more likely to smoke cigarettes and use marijuana. Furthermore, substance abuse tends to be combined with other problems—that is, the adolescents who abuse alcohol and other drugs are likely to be the same adolescents who have problems at school, problems with their parents, and maybe problems with their peers. Or, to look at it another way, these are the same adolescents who are likely to *be* a problem to the school, to their parents, and maybe to their peers. Substance abuse is often associated with antisocial behavior, and sometimes with serious psychiatric disorders (Osgood, Johnston, O'Malley, and Bachman, 1988; Brown, 1989).

The which-came-first-the-chicken-or-the-egg question is especially perplexing here, because teenagers' substance abuse may be both a cause and an effect of their other difficulties. A history of psychiatric problems—of almost any type—makes it more likely that an adolescent will use alcohol or drugs, perhaps as a way of trying to control the unpleasant thoughts and feelings associated with the disorder. But alcohol and drug use makes the disorder worse, not better: as one research report concluded, "Using drugs adds to the tendency to have psychiatric symptoms" (Friedman, Utada, Glickman, and Morrissey, 1987, p. 242).

Because the topic is so much in the news today, it might surprise you to learn that the use of illegal drugs appears to be declining in the United States. Fewer people are using substances such as marijuana, stimulants ("uppers"), and barbiturates ("downers"). The casual use of cocaine has also begun to decline. However, the amount of cocaine used by people addicted to this drug, particularly in the form of "crack," continues to climb (Bailey, 1989; "Casual drug use," 1989).

The use of illegal drugs by teenagers is usually preceded by the use of legal drugs, most often alcohol (in the form of beer or wine) or cigarettes. Another possible gateway to drugs is through the use of mind-altering inhalants. Preadolescents sometimes experiment with breathing gases such as toluene (found in glues and paint thinners), halogenated hydrocarbons (solvents, typewriter correction fluid), and nitrous oxide (sometimes used as a propellant for whipped cream). Occasionally they make a mistake: children have died from breathing in toxic substances in an attempt to get high. In any event, inhalants are seldom used for more than a year or two; adolescents move on to other substances.

There is a tendency for substance abuse to proceed from legal drugs to illegal drugs, and from less serious to more serious substances (Kandel, 1980). This "stage theory" of substance use is somewhat controversial, because its critics have interpreted it as meaning that someone who starts at stage 1 is compelled to progress through all the stages. This, of course, is not what happens: not all adolescents who drink beer go on to vodka, and only a fraction of those who use marijuana go on to cocaine. At each stage, there are fewer participants than at the previous stage. But the fact remains that it is rare for a person to drink vodka without having first tried beer or wine, or to use crack without having tried marijuana (Bailey, 1989; Newcomb, Fahy, and Skager, 1988).

What determines how far and how fast a teenager will proceed along the sequence of substance use? Aside from the individual's personality characteristics, four environmental factors have been identified:

- The quality of family relationships. Adolescents who get along well with their parents, and whose parents get along well with each other, are less likely to use drugs (Brook, Whiteman, Gordon, and Cohen, 1986).
- The use—or nonuse—of alcohol and drugs by the adolescent's parents (Brown, 1989).

- The use—or nonuse—by the adolescent's friends (Swaim, Oetting, Edwards, and Beauvais, 1989).
- The amount of supervision the adolescent gets. Latchkey kids are more likely to get into trouble with alcohol and drugs (Richardson and others, 1989).

ALCOHOL. So many adolescents use alcohol—about 94 percent of high school seniors have tried it—that drinking is considered normal in this age group. Experimenting with alcohol is seldom frowned on at the beginning, even by parents. Many children have their first drink in their own home, perhaps by being offered a sip of their father's beer (Newcomb and Bentler, 1989).

Drinking by parents and drinking by offspring are, as we said, highly correlated. This parent-to-child influence operates in at least three ways. First, parents serve as models for what is seen as an appropriate and acceptable pattern of alcohol use. Second, if the parents' lives are going poorly and family relationships are full of conflict, adolescents might turn to alcohol as a way of dealing with their own stress and anxiety. Third, offspring may inherit a tendency to use or abuse alcohol from their parents. There may also be a fourth, transactional factor: if adolescents make their parents' lives miserable enough, the parents may use alcohol in an attempt to relieve their own stress (Thompson and Wilsnack, 1987).

Genetic factors clearly play an important role in alcohol abuse, though not, perhaps, in alcohol use. That is, alcoholism appears to be largely genetic, whereas the moderate use of alcohol is controlled primarily by environmental factors such as how much one's friends drink. Data from adoption studies indicate that the biological children of alcoholics have four times the normal risk of becoming alcoholics, even if they are adopted by families that don't drink (Holden, 1985; Marlatt, Baer, Donovan, and Kivlahan, 1988).

The genetic transmission of alcoholism seems to be mainly from father to son. This is only partly because alcoholism is more common in males than in females. For unknown reasons, having an alcoholic biological mother is less of a risk than having an alcoholic biological father. The children (especially the sons) of alcoholic fathers have been found to have physical and psychological characteristics that may put them at risk for alcoholism even before they've had their first drink. There are subtle differences in brain functioning that show up in brain-wave measurements (EEGs) and in tests of intellectual abilities. The sons of alcoholics also respond differently to experimental doses of alcohol: on the average, they are less affected by moderate doses, indicating a greater tolerance. Alcoholics who have a family history of alcoholism start to drink at an earlier age and are more severely affected than alcoholics without such a family history (Marlatt and others, 1988; Pollock, Schneider, Gabrielli, and Goodwin, 1987).

The gender differences in alcohol use and abuse are considerable. Teenage boys consume more beer, wine, and liquor than teenage girls; they start drinking at an earlier age, drink more frequently, and have more problems with alcohol. Boys are more likely to drink and drive than girls: 28 percent of high school boys in one survey admitted driving a car while they were drunk, versus 17 percent of girls. Adolescent boys are more likely than girls to think that drinking is "cool" and to consider themselves mature people who can handle the risks of drinking and driving (Beck and Summons, 1987; Barnes and Welte, 1988).

They probably think that they can handle the other risks of drinking, too, and some of them can. But for those who can't, the future is not bright. Heavy drinkers are much more likely than other adolescents to flunk out or drop out of high school or college. However, some of these young people were doing poorly in school long before they started drinking (Conger and Petersen, 1984; Engel and others, 1987).

Adolescence is an age of experimentation. Almost all adolescents experiment with alcohol, and the majority also try cigarettes and marijuana. But, as we said, substance use decreases after adolescence. Most people find, in the long run, that their minds work better when they're sober.

TOBACCO. Because cigarettes are so easy to obtain, smoking is likely to be a child's first experience with drug use. We were startled to read recently that "A substantial portion of children at least experiment with puffing cigarettes by age nine, and in a new and disturbing trend, a small but significant portion (13% of third-grade boys in one Oklahoma survey) use smokeless tobacco." Currently, about a fifth of high school seniors are daily cigarette smokers, with the rate being higher among girls than boys. Because nicotine is highly addictive, tobacco is likely to be the first drug that adolescents become dependent on, and there is some evidence that it may be the biggest health risk for them in the long run (Newcomb and Bentler, 1989, p. 243).

Whether an adolescent will smoke is influenced by the same factors that influence the use of alcohol and other drugs. The teens who are most likely to become smokers are those whose parents and/or friends smoke, those who are poor students, and those who have a rebellious or risk-taking personality (Ary and Biglan, 1988; Collins and others, 1987; Hover and Gaffney, 1988).

Telling teenagers that smoking is bad for them is useless: their personal fable makes them think that they are invulnerable and that they will live forever. Telling them that smart kids don't smoke is also useless: who wants to be a nerd? In our opinion, the best way to discourage smoking is to tell kids that it's gross. Tell them about phlegm. Tell them that no one wants to kiss a smoker. Such efforts are now being made in a new campaign being carried out in California, financed by a 25-cent tax on each pack of cigarettes (Castro, 1990).

MARIJUANA. Marijuana use among adolescents reached a maximum in the 1970s; it has been declining fairly steadily since then. Only 24 percent of current 11- to 17-year-olds have ever used marijuana (Newcomb and Bentler, 1989). Although this drug has been tried by about half of college students, only 3 percent now agree with statements such as "Marijuana is perfectly healthy and should be legalized" (Sommer, 1988). In 1973, 24 percent agreed with that statement (see Figure 14–2).

High school students who smoke marijuana are, as we've said, likely to be the same ones who use cigarettes and alcohol. Daily users of marijuana tend to come from single-parent homes and to have parents who use drugs or alcohol; their friends are also likely to be substance users or abusers. Marijuana smokers make lower grades in school than nonusers, are truant from school more often, and are more likely than nonusers to break rules or commit

Smoking cigarettes is likely to be a teenager's first experience with an addictive drug.

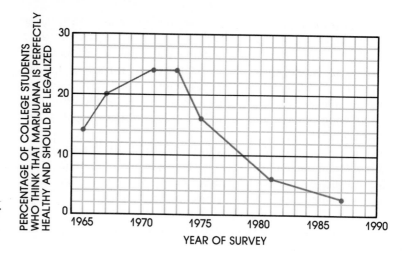

Figure 14-2
How college students'
attitudes toward the use of
marijuana has changed over
the past 25 years. (Based on
data from Sommer, 1988.)

crimes. Boys are twice as likely to use marijuana as girls (Kleinman and others, 1988).

Because almost all users of marijuana also use alcohol and other drugs, it is virtually impossible to tell what long-term effects marijuana has on the people who use it. In a study of adult users of marijuana, almost every one had at one time or another used other drugs (92 percent, for example, had tried cocaine), and the majority were still using other drugs (44 percent were currently using cocaine). More than half of these adults, whose average age was 27, reported problems that they thought were due to their use of marijuana—lack of motivation and lack of energy were the most common. But there was no way of knowing if their problems were due to marijuana use itself, since there were so few subjects who used only marijuana (Rainone, Deren, Kleinman, and Wish, 1987).

AMPHETAMINES. These drugs are stimulants: they produce a feeling of exhilaration and abundant energy, followed by a depression known as "crashing." Like other illegal drugs, the use of amphetamines has declined; only 6 percent of current 12- to 17-year-olds have ever used them (Newcomb and Bentler, 1989; Marcos and Bahr, 1988).

Amphetamines differ from other drugs in that users tend to take them occasionally, rather than on a regular basis. Nonetheless, amphetamine use among adolescents is considered a serious problem, both because overdosing is easy and quite dangerous ("Speed kills") and because those who become dependent may experience severe depression when they try to stop.

COCAINE. Perhaps because of the bad publicity it has gotten for causing the deaths of some prominent college athletes, cocaine has lost favor among adolescents. Only 15 percent of current high school seniors have ever tried cocaine, and only 5½ percent have used it in the form of crack. Almost half of these adolescents perceive cocaine as a risky drug, and 97 percent disapprove of using it on a regular basis. Addiction to crack is a serious problem, but crack addicts are more likely to be young adults than adolescents. Most are members of minority racial or cultural groups and live in big cities (Newcomb and Bentler, 1989; "Casual drug use," 1989).

Adolescents who do use cocaine almost always use other drugs as well. Thus, we have already described them. The results of their cocaine use—except in the case of sudden death—cannot be distinguished from the results of the other substances they use or abuse (Newcomb, Fahy, and Skager, 1988).

HEROIN. The use of heroin is not common in most adolescent populations: only about 1 percent of current high school seniors have tried it. One reason this rate is so low is that it doesn't include high school dropouts. In some inner-city minority groups, 15 percent of the adolescent boys have used heroin (Brooks-Gunn, Boyer, and Hein, 1988).

This drug is highly addictive and very expensive. To support their habit, adolescent heroin addicts usually have to turn to theft, prostitution, or selling drugs to others. They are at risk of death from an overdose or from AIDS, contracted from an infected needle.

STEROIDS. Teenage girls envy the flat stomachs and thin thighs they see on female movie stars and models. Teenage boys envy the big muscles they see on male movie stars and athletes. Girls go on diets in an attempt to achieve the body they dream of. Boys do exercises and pump iron, and if that doesn't work, sometimes they try anabolic steroids.

Steroids are synthetic male hormones; when used in conjunction with exercise, they stimulate the production of muscle tissue. A recent survey of male high school seniors found that 6½ percent were using steroids. The majority of these boys were involved in school-sponsored sports, especially football (Buckley and others, 1988).

Steroids have some serious side effects. When used by young adolescents (some start before they are 15), these drugs can curtail growth by causing the leg bones to harden prematurely. They can also cause the testicles to shrink, resulting in impotence or sterility. Psychological effects are common; they include depression, irritability, and increased aggressiveness—the extreme form of which is known as a "roid rage" (Buckley and others, 1988; Toufexis, 1989).

Although not addictive in the usual sense, steroids create their own special brand of dependence. As one recent report put it, "Bulging biceps and hamhock thighs do a fast fade when the chemicals are halted. So do the feelings of being powerful and manly. Almost every user ends up back on the drugs" (Toufexis, 1989, p. 78).

Awakening of Sexual Interests

School-age boys sneer at school-age girls; the girls think the boys are "gross." In adolescence, both sides change their minds. Thoughts and feelings are changed, over a relatively short period of time, by the powerful hormonal and physical changes taking place in the body.

The experience of sexual awakening is quite different for boys and girls. When a boy begins to have nocturnal emissions at around the age of 14, the

Falling in love is an essential part of the adolescent experience.

release of semen may be accompanied by vivid sexual dreams. Sometimes these dreams contain elements of homosexuality or incest, and these may be a source of anxiety for the boy. Even during his waking hours, unbidden fantasies may come to mind. He may worry about having erections at embarrassing times. His sexual desire is compelling, and it is centered in his genitals.

For girls, although the entrance into puberty is clearly marked by menarche, sexual desire does not increase nearly as suddenly or as urgently as it does in boys. Whereas desire in adolescent boys is erotic or sexual, girls long for romance (Turner and Helms, 1979).

Romance is a firmly embedded part of Western culture: in our society, young people are expected to fall in love and to feel all the emotions that are supposed to accompany that state. Movies, TV shows, novels, and magazines all emphasize romance. The young adolescent is led to interpret certain feelings and experiences as being ''madly in love.'' And the feeling of being madly in love is considered by many teenage girls to be an adequate reason for having sex. For a teenage boy, on the other hand, having sex may be an adequate reason for falling in love.

Effects on Parent–Child Relationships

Psychoanalysts, starting with Anna Freud, have had a great deal to say about adolescence. They believe that this period brings with it a resurgence of Oedipal feelings. According to this view, a teenage boy may begin once again to idolize his mother. He may feel (perhaps correctly) that she cares about him more than his father does, or that she understands him better. A girl may have similar feelings about her closeness to her father.

Parents react in various ways to their children's emerging sexuality. There may be jealousy in the same-sex parent and feelings of discomfort in the parent of the opposite sex. A small minority of fathers might actually engage in incestual sexual relationships with their teenage daughters (see Box 2–1). More commonly, a father will react to the attraction he feels for his developing daughter by unconsciously drawing away from her. The daughter, who does not understand the motivations behind this withdrawal, may feel rejected. This, in turn, may cause her to become uneasy about her relationships with other males.

On the other hand, a teenage girl may vie with her mother for her father's attention. Or the mother may be openly flirtatious with her daughter's boyfriends. A father, for his part, may show strong disapproval of any young man his daughter happens to show an interest in, or set impossibly high standards for his daughter's boyfriends.

Sexual Behavior

Young adolescents' first expressions of romantic and sexual interest typically occur at parties—the group setting permits them to experiment with kissing, hugging, and light petting on a relatively safe basis. By mid-adolescence, most have started to have at least occasional individual dates. Only about 5 percent have not dated at all by the end of high school (Haviland and Scarborough, 1981).

If a girlfriend–boyfriend relationship goes on for any length of time, it is almost certain to involve some sort of sexual activity. Among 18-year-olds who are no longer virgins, 60 percent of the females and 40 percent of the males report that their first experience of sexual intercourse took place within a steady girlfriend–boyfriend relationship. Adolescent sexual behavior typically begins with kissing, moves on to breast fondling, and then to manual contact with the partner's genitals. The next step is usually to sexual intercourse, although in college populations intercourse may be preceded by oral contact with the partner's genitals (Jessor, Costa, Jessor, and Donovan, 1983; Williams and Jacoby, 1989).

The age at which adolescents first have intercourse varies considerably. Many factors have been found to influence the age when sexual activity begins. Here are some of them:

- Gender. Boys reach sexual maturity later than girls but they have sex earlier: 60 percent of white males have had sex by age 18, and 60 percent of white females have had sex by age 19.
- Racial and cultural background. The corresponding statistics for African Americans: 60 percent of black males have had sex by age 16, and 60 percent of black females have had sex by age 18 (Brooks-Gunn and others, 1988).
- Rate of maturation. Girls who reach menarche early tend to have sex at an earlier age than those who mature more slowly. In boys, higher levels of male hormones are associated with earlier sexual activity (Brooks-Gunn and Furstenburg, 1989).
- Parental supervision and monitoring. Adolescents whose parents are extremely permissive have intercourse earliest, followed by those whose parents are extremely strict. Those whose parents are moderately strict tend to be last to lose their virginity (Miller, McCoy, Olson, and Wallace, 1986).
- Home and family. Girls reared in single-parent homes are more likely to engage in early sexual activity (Miller and Bingham, 1989).
- Education aspirations and achievement. Adolescents who do well in high school and who plan to go to college are less likely to engage in early sexual activity (Miller and Sneesby, 1988).

The Child in Society

Box 14-4
When Children
Have Babies

Lisa was a pretty and popular teenager who started dating at the age of 14. She had sex with her boyfriend when she was 15, became pregnant at 16, and became a mother three days before her 17th birthday. By then her boyfriend had vanished; Lisa had dropped out of high school but was still living in her parents' home. Before her baby girl was a year old, Lisa had a new boyfriend. She married him when, at age 18, she became pregnant again. The marriage lasted three years. Now 21, Lisa is divorced and unemployed. She lives in a small apartment with her two children. Her childhood is over, and whatever happened to all the fun she was supposed to have?

There are more than 1 million pregnancies a year among teenage girls in the United States. The rate of teenage pregnancy is substantially higher than in countries such as England, Sweden, and the Netherlands. It is not simply because American teenagers have sex at an early age: the teenagers in other countries also have sex at an early age. The difference is that in the U.S. they get pregnant (Hechtman, 1989).

Not all become parents, however. About 40 percent of teenage pregnancies end in abortion, 10 percent in miscarriage, and 50 percent in live births. Almost all these babies—93 percent—are reared by their mothers, a large majority of whom are unmarried (Sonenstein, 1987; Miller and Jorgensen, 1988).

The cost of teenage pregnancy is high, both to the mother and to her baby. The mother, if she is under 15, runs an increased risk of dying from the complications of pregnancy and childbirth. If she is over 15, the risks are no higher than for older women as long as she takes good care of herself. But since pregnant teenagers are less likely to be well nourished and to receive prenatal care, and

more likely to smoke and use drugs, complications of pregnancy and childbirth are more common in this age group. Both the mother and the baby are affected by these risks (Giblin, Poland, Waller, and Ager, 1989; Hechtman, 1989).

The risks don't end when mother and child come home from the hospital. Someone once said that a girl who has a baby at 16 has most of her life's script written out for her (Cambell, 1968). Although this statement is less true today than in the past, the prospects are still poor for an adolescent who has taken on the task of rearing a child. She is less likely to complete high school and less likely to get married than a young woman without children. If she does marry, her marriage is more likely to end in divorce. As an adult, her standard of living will be significantly lower than that of a

- Drug use and delinquency. These activities are associated with earlier sexual activity (Donovan, Jessor, and Costa, 1988).

- Birth order. Younger siblings in a family tend to have sex at an earlier age than their older siblings. Perhaps the younger siblings are influenced by their older sibling's behavior when the older ones become sexually active (Rodgers and Rowe, 1988).

- Peer-group factors. Adolescents whose friends are "doing it" are likely to do it too (Udry and Billy, 1987).

- Religion. Adolescents who don't go to church are more likely to engage in early sexual activity than churchgoers (Thornton and Camburn, 1989).

woman from a similar background who put off pregnancy until a later age (Hechtman, 1989; Furstenberg, Brooks-Gunn, and Chase-Lansdale, 1989).

The baby also pays a stiff penalty. A teenager is unlikely to provide the kind of responsive, sensitive mothering that is associated with good emotional and cognitive development in children. She may neglect or abuse her children. On the average, they will have lower IQs and do less well in school than the children of older mothers. The boys may be conduct disordered; the girls are likely to follow in their mother's footsteps and become pregnant themselves at an early age (Brooks-Gunn and Furstenberg, 1986).

What about the baby's father? He tends to be somewhat older than the mother; about half are over 20. More often than not, he gets away scot-free: in many cases, he either doesn't know or denies that he fathered a child. Even if he acknowledges parenthood, he is unlikely to marry the mother of his child. But whether or not he marries, he is more likely to drop out of high school than a male adolescent who hasn't fathered a child. Or, to put it the other way, male adolescents who do poorly in school and who eventually drop out are more likely to father a child than male adolescents who are good students (Furstenberg and others, 1989).

Low achievement in school is associated with a higher rate of teenage pregnancy in girls, too. Other factors that are related to teenage parenthood are race (black teens are about twice as likely to have a baby as white teens), poverty, growing up in a single-parent home, and personality factors such as low self-esteem and depression (Sonenstein, 1987; Abrahamse, Morrison, and Waite, 1988).

Few teenagers actually want to become parents, so why do so many girls become pregnant? There are three major reasons. First is ignorance about reproduction—they know that intercourse makes babies, but they don't know much more than that. Countries such as England, the Netherlands, and Sweden have earlier and more extensive programs of sex education, and much lower rates of teen pregnancy. There is no evidence that sex education classes increase the rate of sexual activity in teens (Sonenstein, 1987).

The second reason is the American emphasis on love and romance, and an ethic that says that sex is okay only if you're swept away, unexpectedly, by passions beyond your control. American teenagers seldom *plan* to lose their virginity—it "just happens" (Brooks-Gunn and Furstenberg, 1989).

Third is the adolescent's feeling of invulnerability—the feeling that "it can't happen to me." Even college-age people fall prey to this delusion. In a recent study, sexually active college women were asked to estimate the chances that they would become pregnant within the next year, and also to estimate the chances of pregnancy for a typical college woman of their age. Their estimate for the typical college woman was 27 percent, but they thought that they themselves had only a 9 percent chance of becoming pregnant—even though most of them were not using reliable methods of birth control (Burger and Burns, 1988).

Partly as a consequence of the AIDS epidemic, teenagers are now less ignorant about birth control and about the dangers of impulsive and indiscriminate sex. Not all teenagers seek danger, and this tendency declines after early adolescence. Adult values and behavior are changing in our society, and these changes are starting to have an effect on adolescent values and behavior. Virginity has become acceptable again. The use of condoms among teenage boys has doubled in the past ten years (Stark, 1989).

The rate of teenage pregnancy began to decline in the early '80s (Furstenberg and others, 1989). Given the current trends, it will probably continue to decline. Perhaps Lisa's daughter will not follow in her mother's footsteps after all.

CHANGES IN ATTITUDES. For a long time, sexual activity became more and more prevalent among American teens, and it began at an earlier and earlier age. Now there are signs that this trend has at last begun to reverse. Sexual activity among adolescents has recently decreased somewhat. Although the rate of teenage pregnancy is still disturbingly high in the United States (see Box 14–4), it has been slowly declining for several years. The number of births to *unmarried* teen mothers has not declined, but that is because pregnancy is no longer considered a sufficient reason to get married—thus, there are fewer teenage marriages now (Furstenberg and others, 1989; Murstein, Chalpin, Heard, and Vyse, 1989).

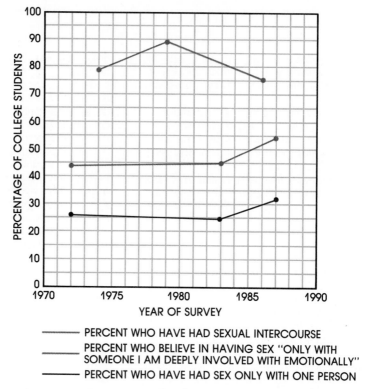

Figure 14-3
Changes in college students
sexual behavior and
attitudes over the past 20
years. (Top line based on
data from Murstein, Chalpin,
Heard, and Vyse, 1989; lower
two lines based on data from
Abler and Sedlacek, 1989.)

——————— PERCENT WHO HAVE HAD SEXUAL INTERCOURSE
——————— PERCENT WHO BELIEVE IN HAVING SEX "ONLY WITH
              SOMEONE I AM DEEPLY INVOLVED WITH EMOTIONALLY"
——————— PERCENT WHO HAVE HAD SEX ONLY WITH ONE PERSON

Adolescents are becoming a little more conservative in their views about sex. Although they still think that sex is a fine thing, they are no longer as willing to hop into bed with someone they just met and might never see again. They are more likely to say that sex should be part of a close, long-term relationship. College-age men and women both say that they would prefer to marry a virgin (Abler and Sedlacek, 1989; Williams and Jacoby, 1989).

Figure 14–3 shows some results from two different surveys, carried out over the last two decades, of sexual behavior and attitudes in college students.

MASTURBATION. About half of all adolescent girls and three-quarters of adolescent boys admit that they masturbate; the percentage for both sexes tends to increase during the teen years. Somewhat surprisingly, the reported incidence of masturbation is lower among virgins than among nonvirgins (Hass, 1979). Perhaps this reflects differences in sexual drive, or perhaps only differences in frankness—those teens who are willing to admit (privately) that they are no longer virgins are also willing to admit (privately) that they engage in masturbation.

Masturbation is more common among middle-class adolescents than among those at lower socioeconomic levels. Middle-class teens and adults are less likely to say that they strongly disapprove of the practice. People with a working-class background are more likely to consider masturbation abnormal and to believe that intercourse is the only proper outlet for sexual drives.

HOMOSEXUALITY. Adolescence is the age of experimentation, and sex is one of the things with which adolescents experiment. It is fairly common, especially among males, to have a few sexual experiences with the members of the same sex before going on to a heterosexual adulthood. About 20 percent of American men have had at least one homosexual encounter in their lives, but only 6½ percent engage in homosexual activity after the age of 19. The proportion of adult men who are *exclusively* homosexual in their preferences is lower than that—perhaps as low as 2 or 3 percent. The rate of homosexual behavior in females is about half that of males (Fay, Turner, Klassen, and Gagnon, 1989; Ellis, Burke, and Ames, 1987).

Homosexuality is found in virtually all human societies, even those in which efforts to suppress it are very severe. In fact, adult homosexuality is disapproved of in most human populations, although some societies consider homosexual activity in late childhood and adolescence to be harmless or even beneficial (Savin-Williams, 1988). **Homophobia**—the fear or dislike of homosexuals—is quite prevalent in the United States today: a recent survey found that most heterosexual college students, both male and female, would not want to marry someone who had had even a single homosexual experience (Williams and Jacoby, 1989).

Given the amount of social pressure directed against it, why do some people nonetheless fall in love with members of their own gender? Male homosexuality used to be attributed, as most things have been, to the mother—she was accused of being domineering or overprotective of her son, too affectionate or not affectionate enough. But this view has been discredited, and now researchers are looking for biological causes. Studies of twins and siblings suggest that there is a genetic factor in homosexuality. However, simple explanations involving missing or extra chromosomes, or missing or extra hormones, are not the answer. If hormones are involved they must have their effects before birth, during prenatal development. Most homosexual men are not deficient in testosterone (Savin-Williams, 1988; Holden, 1988).

In Chapter 10 (Box 10–2) we described little boys who fail to develop a male gender identity—who act like girls and say they wish they had been born female. These children often display a strong interest in their mothers' clothes, makeup, and hair; they have no desire to play with other boys or to do the things that most boys enjoy. Although many of these children learn during middle childhood that they must pretend to be like other boys, they are likely to be rejected by both their male and female agemates. They tend to be less lonely in adolescence, because by then they can usually find other people like themselves. About three-quarters of these effeminate boys become homosexual or bisexual adults (Green, 1987; Zuger, 1988).

We still don't understand why some little boys show these tendencies so early in life. Nor do we know why a quarter of them become entirely heterosexual adults, or why some very masculine little boys become homosexuals in adolescence or adulthood (Bjorklund and Bjorklund, 1988).

AIDS AND OTHER SEXUALLY TRANSMITTED DISEASES. Most adolescents have never met anyone their age who has AIDS: by the end of 1988, only 977 cases in adolescents—about 1 percent of the total number of cases—had been reported to the U.S. Centers for Disease Control. Many more are believed to be infected with the HIV virus, but since symptoms of AIDS might not appear until 5 to 7 years after infection, these cases are as yet undetected. Meanwhile, infected adolescents spread the disease to their sexual partners (Hein, 1989).

They are certainly spreading other things to their sexual partners: the rates for syphilis, gonorrhea, and chlamydia are highest of all in the 15- to 19-year-old age range. So is the rate of hospitalization for pelvic inflammatory disease, which can produce sterility in teenage girls (Brooks-Gunn and others, 1988).

Sterility is not, of course, the worst thing that can happen to an adolescent who contracts a sexually transmitted disease: AIDS is fatal. But, perhaps because they don't know anyone who has AIDS and thus the disease doesn't have any reality for them, many adolescents—particularly the younger ones—ignore the risks. It may even be worse than that: telling teenagers that something is risky may actually make it seem more attractive to them. In one study, the use of condoms by sexually active teens *declined* after they were given information about AIDS (Flora and Thoresen, 1988).

Adolescence: A Risky Business

Nature must have made adolescents like that on purpose: rebellious and adventurous, heedless of danger or perhaps even attracted by it. Young people need to have courage and initiative in order to move out into the world on their own—to form strong ties with members of their own generation and weaken their ties with the older one. Those who survive the risks will someday become the older generation, and they will have the same complaints and worries that their parents had. They will probably say the same things to their own children: "This room is a pigsty!" "That's enough out of you!" "Turn that down!" Like their parents, they will probably fail to talk to their children about the important things: love and sex, drugs and alcohol, responsibilities to other people and telling the truth.

The truth is that even if parents talked to their children about these things, teenagers probably wouldn't listen. Adolescents, who don't know nearly as much as they think they do, generally prefer to listen to other equally ignorant adolescents, rather than to the wisest of adults. In fact, those who do listen to adults are likely to be unpopular with their peers (Allen, Weissberg, and Hawkins, 1989).

"Just say no," we tell adolescents. No to drugs, no to sex, no to drinking and driving, no to dropping out of school. The problem is that just telling adolescents to just say no just doesn't have much effect. Adolescents don't pay much attention to what they hear adults saying. They are much more influenced by what they see adults doing—on movie and TV screens, in commercials and on billboards, and in real life.

Summary

1. Traditionally, adolescents have not been popular subjects for research in child development, partly because it is harder to show effects of the environment on their development. Due to genetic and transactional effects, as children get older they become less like their parents and siblings, and more like themselves.

2. A lot happens between the ages of 12 and 16: physical changes, the transition to junior high and high school, and changes in relationships with parents and peers. Adolescents are confronted with dangers and have adult decisions to make, without having an adult's cognitive capacities or experience.

3. An absence of "storm and stress" is not abnormal in adolescence; in fact, troubled adolescents are more likely to become troubled adults. The major psychiatric disorders, such as schizophrenia and depression, generally first appear in adolescence. Troubled teenage girls are more likely to have "inwardly directed" symptoms; boys are more likely to engage in **acting-out behavior.**

4. The physical changes of adolescence are triggered by the increased production of sex hormones. These changes begin with a burst of rapid physical growth, which starts about two years earlier in girls than in boys. There is also an increase in body fat; this fat is used up during the growth spurt in boys but not in girls.

5. In **anorexia nervosa,** what typically happens is that a teenage girl starts dieting and then can't stop; she may starve herself to death. Genetic, cultural, and psychological factors are all involved in this disorder. The **anorectic** resists treatment; she has apparently become addicted to the physical and psychological effects of self-starvation.

6. The adolescent with **bulimia** goes on eating binges and then purges herself with laxatives or self-induced vomiting. Unlike the anorectic she maintains a normal weight, and her disorder is easier to treat.

7. The brain does not grow during adolescence, but major changes in brain organization are believed to occur. The brain becomes more efficient and its plasticity decreases.

8. One definition of **puberty** is the attainment of the ability to reproduce, at least theoretically. This milestone is marked in girls by **menarche,** the first menstrual period, and in boys by the first production of live sperm. In both sexes, fertility is low at first and gradually increases.

9. Sexual development in girls begins about two years before menarche with the first appearance of developing breasts and pubic hair. The average age at menarche is 12½ to 13; menstruation does not occur until the girl has put on a minimum amount of body fat.

10. In boys, sexual development begins around age 12 with an increase in size of the testes. The first ejaculation of semen occurs about two years later. The deepening of the voice and the growth of beard and body hair are among the later changes of male development.

11. Body-image satisfaction hits a low at age 13 for girls and 15 for boys; then it goes up. At every age, girls are less satisfied with their own bodies than boys are.

12. Early maturation can be a temporary embarrassment for a girl, but it also has some advantages. For boys, there are no disadvantages to maturing early. The early maturing male tends to dominate his agemates.

13. According to Piaget, adolescence marks the entrance into the **period of formal operations.** Adolescents can solve problems by thinking up possible solutions and testing them systematically. Formal thought is relatively free from the constraints of time and reality—it is abstract.

14. Adolescents' preoccupation with themselves gives rise to two delusions, which Elkind has labeled the **imaginary audience** (the feeling that one is constantly being observed) and the **personal fable** (the conviction that "I am unique, terribly important, and not subject to the limitations of ordinary mortals").

15. Critics of Piaget's views point out that formal or abstract thought is not universal. Its appearance depends on the individual's IQ, cultural background, education, and experience with the particular subject matter. It emerges in a gradual and unpredictable manner, rather than as a giant leap forward.

16. Older adolescents (and girls) give deeper and more complex descriptions of people, including themselves, than do younger adolescents (and boys).

17. Children see their parents as all-powerful and all-knowing, but adolescents don't idealize their parents— they question their authority and recognize their flaws. By late adolescence, most people have come to see Mom (but not Dad) as a person, not just a parent.

18. Conflicts between parents and adolescents are probably inevitable. Oddly enough, most of their arguments are about unimportant things. The important things seldom get discussed.

19. The homeless youth is not a new phenomenon. Runaways have homes they can return to; homeless youth do not. Some (the "throwaways") have been kicked out; in other cases there just isn't a home anymore. Only a minority will ever go home again.

20. If two adolescents are good friends, they are likely to have many attitudes and preferences in common. These similarities are due partly to the way adolescents select their friends and partly to the influence that friends have on each other.

21. Most adolescents are members of cliques or "crowds." Erikson believes that belonging to such groups serves to protect adolescents against what he calls **identity confusion.** The special language (or **argot**) used by teenagers serves to strengthen their identification with their peers.

22. Adolescent peer groups are not merely an older version of childhood groups of friends: their influence is more pervasive and far-reaching. Pressure to conform to the group's standards is intense, but it is not necessarily antisocial: teens are more likely to yield to peer pressure when it is *not* antisocial.

23. Adolescent males who live in big cities are responsible for a disproportionate share of crimes. Characteristics of the typical delinquent are: a history of antisocial behavior dating from childhood, an economically disadvantaged background, and a mother-headed or stepfather-headed home. Teenagers who are poorly monitored by their parents are more likely to be delinquent; this is probably due to two-way transactional effects.

24. The highest rates of substance use occur during adolescence. The use of substances such as alcohol, tobacco, and marijuana tends to go together and to be combined with other problems.

25. Drug use generally starts with legal, less serious substances (such as beer and cigarettes) and proceeds to illegal, more serious ones. How far and how fast teenagers proceed is influenced by their parents and friends.

26. Almost all adolescents experiment with alcohol. Genetic factors play a role in alcohol *abuse,* but alcohol *use* is controlled mainly by environmental factors. Males are more likely to abuse alcohol and to think they can handle the risks involved.

27. About a fifth of high school seniors are daily cigarette smokers. Tobacco is the one drug used more by females than by males.

28. The number of adolescents who use marijuana, or who think it is okay to use it, is declining. Only a small minority of high school and college students use amphetamines, cocaine, heroin, or steroids.

29. Sexual interests awaken around the time of puberty. Boys' sexual desire is centered in their genitals. Sexual desire does not increase as suddenly or urgently in girls: what girls want is romance.

30. The emergence of sexual feelings in adolescents com-plicates their relationships with their parents. Parents may feel jealousy or attraction, may withdraw, and/or may flirt with (or resent) their offspring's girlfriends or boyfriends.

31. Sixty percent of girls and 40 percent of boys have their first sexual experience in a steady girlfriend–boyfriend relationship. The age at first intercourse is affected by factors such as gender, racial and cultural background, rate of maturation, and home and family.

32. Although the rate of teenage pregnancy is declining in the U.S., it is still far higher than in other developed countries, possibly because other countries have better sex education programs. Half a million babies are born to (and reared by) teenage mothers, most of whom are not married.

33. A fifth of men have had at least one homosexual encounter in their lives, but only 6½ percent engage in homosexual activity after age 19. The rate of homosexuality in females is about half that of males. Researchers are now seeking biological explanations of homosexuality, such as the influence of prenatal hormones.

34. The chances of getting a sexually transmitted disease are highest in adolescence. Such diseases can cause problems ranging from sterility to death. Although the number of adolescents with AIDS is still small, it is expected to grow.

35. Adolescence is a risky business. Telling teenagers to "just say no" doesn't work very well. They don't pay attention to what adults say—they are influenced more by what they see adults (real and fictional ones) do.

Key Terms

acting-out behavior
testosterone
anorexia nervosa
anorectic
binge–purge syndrome
bulimia

puberty
menarche
secondary sex characteristics
primary sex characteristics
nocturnal emission
period of formal operations

imaginary audience
personal fable
identity confusion
argot
delinquency
homophobia

15

Becoming an Adult

At the beginning of Chapter 1 we asked you to leaf through your family photo album, looking at pictures of yourself as a baby, a toddler, and a child. Now we ask you instead to look in the mirror. Look in the mirror and you will see the results of all those years of development.

If you are like many of our readers, you are a college student, probably around 20 years old. (If you are older than that, try to imagine yourself as you were at 20.) When you look at yourself, what do you see? Do you see an adult?

Clearly, 20-year-olds are no longer children. But are they adults? In our society, people in their late teens and early twenties are neither here nor there. Especially for those who go to college, adulthood seems to hover somewhere in the indefinite future. In simpler times and in simpler societies, the transition came sooner and was more clearly marked. Now the passageway to adulthood is lengthy and the transition is blurred. In this chapter, the last chapter of the book, we will look at what happens during those years of transition.

Five major hurdles lie ahead on the path: to become fully independent of one's parents, to decide what sort of person one is and what sort one wishes to be, to select a mate, to choose and prepare oneself for an occupation, and to deal with the social and personal issues involved in being a woman or being a man.

Rites of Passage to Adulthood

In the ages-old Jewish ceremony of Bar Mitzvah, a 13-year-old boy is told "Today you are a man," and from then on he has the rights and responsibilities of a full-grown man with regard to religious matters. In what sense is he a man? He has not attained his full growth, he doesn't have a beard, in all likelihood he is still a soprano, and his chances of fathering a child are negligible. But ceremonies around the time of puberty, marking the beginning of adulthood, are found in many cultures.

Long ago it took only 13 years for a child to learn all the things he had to know in order to fill an adult role. It takes far longer today, because there is so much more to learn. Children did not mature earlier in the past—physical maturation is more rapid now than it ever has been before. But the knowledge, skills, and cognitive abilities demanded of adults in our society take longer to acquire. That is why a modern Jewish father might have trouble keeping a straight face when he looks down at his son and says, "Today you are a man."

Leaving Home

For many young people, an important marker of the transition to adulthood comes when they leave home to go to college. But only about half of American youth go to college, and many of them live at home and commute to

The Jewish ceremony of Bar Mitzvah confers on a 13-year-old boy the religious rights and responsibilities of a full-grown man.

classes. Even for those who do move to a college dormitory, the transition is not clear-cut. Typically, there are frequent visits home during the first couple of years, or—if home is far away—frequent phone calls. College students generally spend their summers at home. They still expect their parents to handle things like filling out their income tax forms, making appointments for them at the dentist, and perhaps even doing their laundry. Oh, yes—and paying their college bills. Very few college students are financially independent of their families.

In our society, young people do not take over the responsibilities of adulthood all at once—in most cases it happens gradually, over a long period of time. The various markers of adulthood come at different times and have different degrees of importance. A researcher questioned freshmen and sophomores at a small American university about the factors they felt were involved (or would be involved) in becoming an independent adult. Table 15–1 summarizes the results of this study. The items in this table are listed in order of how important the students perceived them to be (Moore, 1987).

One interesting thing to note about this list is that emotional detachment from parents is regarded as the *least* important factor in establishing oneself as an independent adult. In Chapter 14 we described how adolescents seek to put some distance between themselves and their parents—how, by mid-adolescence, they feel less close. This process does not continue during late adolescence: in fact, it reverses itself. Most college students feel more emotional closeness to their parents than they did when they were in high school (see Figure 15–1). Having left home—and thereby having partly resolved the issue of independence—seems to have helped the relationship. Students who go away to college report more affection for their parents and better communication than those who commute to college (Pipp and others, 1985; Moore, 1987).

At what age should young people establish permanent, separate residences

---

TABLE 15–1
Eight Factors Involved in the Transition to Adulthood, in Order of Importance, as Judged by College Students

1. **Self-governance:** Feeling mature, having to do things for myself now, making my own decisions.

2. **Graduation:** Finishing high school and college.

3. **Starting a family:** Getting married, becoming a parent.

4. **Financial independence:** Having a job, no longer receiving financial support from my family.

5. **Disengagement:** Being physically away from home and family, parents no longer telling me what to do.

6. **School affiliation:** Being involved in school, considering school to be my home, feeling that the dorm is the center of my life.

7. **Separate residence:** Not going home as often, moving to an apartment, not spending summers at home.

8. **Emotional detachment:** No longer feeling attached to family, not seeing family very often, feeling of not belonging at home anymore.

Source: Moore, 1987.

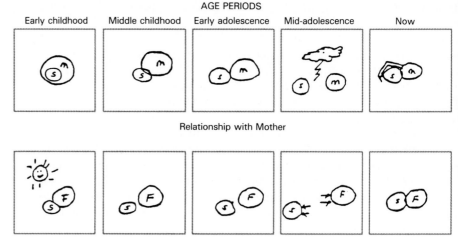

AGE PERIODS

Early childhood | Middle childhood | Early adolescence | Mid-adolescence | Now

Relationship with Mother

Relationship with Father

FIGURE 15-1
This set of diagrams is typical of how college students depict their relationships with their parents at various stages of their lives. *S* stands for *self*, *M* for *mother*, and *F* for *father*. (From Pipp, Shaver, Jennings, Lamborn, and Fischer, 1985, p. 994.)

for themselves? Should offspring continue to live in their parents' home until they get married? As a general rule, parents are more likely to think that their children should remain at home; the offspring are more likely to think that it's time to leave the nest. Parents of sons are more willing to have them establish separate residences than parents of daughters. The parents' willingness to have their children leave home before marriage is also affected by cultural factors (first-generation Americans are more likely to wish their children to remain at home) and socioeconomic factors (at higher socioeconomic levels, there is less disagreement between parents and children over this question). Most important is the type of family: in mother-headed homes, and especially in reconstituted families with stepparents and stepsiblings, both the parents and the offspring wish separate residences to be established at an earlier age (Goldscheider and Goldscheider, 1989).

Finding the Answers to "Who Am I and Where Am I Going?"

In Erikson's theory of psychosocial development, the major crisis of adolescence is identity versus role confusion. According to Erikson, adolescents at first experience uncertainty as their dependence on family and peer group lessens, and as they begin to think about the implications of becoming an adult. To attain a sense of identity, they must decide what sort of people they are and what they want to do with their lives. To fulfill their goals, they must make plans about the future and take steps to carry them out. They must also learn to recognize and accept the various aspects of their own personality, and attempt to reconcile the inconsistencies within themselves.

Identity Formation

Erikson believes that identity formation is a process that goes on all through the lifespan. However, the most important part of this process occurs during late adolescence. Having a sense of identity means being able to see oneself as an individual with certain characteristics—an individual whose important qualities existed in the past and will continue to exist in the future. One is able to view oneself as having a certain place in society; some important decisions have been made in regard to what one believes and what one hopes to accomplish in life.

James Marcia, a professor at Simon Fraser University in Canada, has elaborated on Erikson's theories of identity formation. Marcia (1966, 1976) believes that most young people sooner or later go through a period of **identity crisis,** during which they explore the alternatives that are open to them. They may reach decisions about important matters and they may make commitments to particular choices. The commitments could involve career choices, religious beliefs, or political and ideological positions.

But being committed to a belief or a position does not mean that the young person has necessarily gone through a period of exploration and uncertainty. According to Marcia, some people choose a profession, or adopt a position regarding religion or politics, solely on the basis of what they've been taught to believe by their parents, teachers, or religious leaders. They have accepted these ideas without ever really thinking about them—it's like wearing hand-me-down clothes without checking to see if they fit.

On the basis of whether or not they've gone through the period of exploration and uncertainty, and whether or not they've made a commitment, Marcia defines four levels of what he calls **identity status.**

The first is called **foreclosure.** We've already described foreclosure status: young people in this status are the ones who made their commitments without going through the "crisis" period of exploring alternatives. They tend to be rigid in their beliefs and show little independence from their parents. On the other hand, they experience little anxiety.

Second is **diffusion** status. People in this category have neither made any commitments nor undergone a period of exploration. They are just drifting. Some drop out altogether, perhaps turning to drugs or alcohol as a way of evading adult responsibilities. Others focus on having fun and obtaining immediate gratification, and still others put off making decisions by acting as though life was a giant smorgasbord—for example, they might go to a different church every Sunday (Côté and Levine, 1988).

Young people in the **moratorium** status are currently involved in the identity crisis and are experiencing a period of uncertainty. They are actively engaged in "discovering themselves." In the meantime, there is a moratorium (a period in which no action is taken) on making important personal decisions. Relationships with parents are a little uneasy. There is considerable anxiety associated with this status.

Finally, those who have been through the identity crisis and have made their commitments have reached the status of **identity achievement.** According to Marcia, these people have defined their goals in life and have begun to make progress toward attaining them.

As young people move through college and into the world beyond college, there is generally a progression toward identity achievement status. However, some people take many years to attain a sense of identity (some never do), and progress is not always steady—an identity crisis that is apparently resolved may reappear at a later point in time (Whitbourne and Tesch, 1985; Côté and Levine, 1988).

Young people who have reached identity achievement status tend to be socially at ease with others—they don't feel threatened by other people's differing points of view, because they've already considered the alternatives and have come to a conclusion. Marcia and two of his colleagues interviewed some college men in order to determine their level of identity status. They found that the young men who were relatively far along in achieving identity differed in social behavior from those who had not made much progress:

> High-identity subjects seem more open, more cooperative, and more at ease in discussion of controversial issues, whereas low-identity subjects seem to care less for the feelings and opinions of others, participate less comfortably in the interactions, and, in the case of foreclosures, seem to defend themselves either by antagonistically warding off the opinions of others or by indiscriminately acquiescing to them.   (Slugoski, Marcia, and Koopman, 1984, p. 659)

A similar study of college women yielded comparable results. High-identity women were found to be more willing to express opinions that were contrary to those of the group, and to hold to those positions firmly but without hostility. Women in foreclosure status were more likely to be manipulative or deceptive in their attempts to influence others (Read, Adams, and Dobson, 1984).

Erikson (1959) says that once the identity crisis has been resolved and the individual has established her identity, she can go on to the next stage, which involves the development of close relationships—what Erikson calls **intimacy.** He uses this word to mean a commitment to a particular person, rather than to an idea.

Studies of young adults of college age and beyond have provided support

Once a person has achieved a firm sense of identity, she can go on to develop a close, intimate relationship with a member of the opposite sex.

for Erikson's belief that identity achievement makes a person better able to participate in a close, intimate relationship with someone else—usually a person of the opposite sex. But the findings differ somewhat for men and women. Men who are slow to achieve a strong sense of identity are likely to put off getting married or not marry at all. But women who are slow to achieve a sense of identity are more likely to marry and then get divorced (Kahn, Zimmerman, Csikszentmihalyi, and Getzels, 1985).

INVOLVEMENT IN IDEOLOGY. Political involvement is a favorite arena for trying out new ways of expressing one's identity. For this reason, political causes in every generation have relied on young people on the threshold of adulthood. Youth is a natural time for political activism, though the specific form of activism in a given generation depends on the important political events of that period (see Table 15–2, p. 504).

Trying on various commitments and identities can be done in a variety of ways. Some college-age people become involved with philosophical issues or political points of view. Some identify themselves strongly with a particular hero. Typically, the fervent commitment to philosophical ideas or political beliefs ebbs after a while; it is replaced by personal concerns. Young men and women are idealistic and optimistic, perhaps because they see things as simpler than they really are—they are not yet aware of all the problems and complexities involved in social and political systems. As they become more practical and more realistic, they begin to understand which things can be changed and which must be accepted. A study of student activists 12 years after they graduated from college showed them to be only marginally more active in political and social issues than their classmates (Ellerman, 1988).

Self-Image and Self-Esteem

Adolescents, in general, do not have low self-esteem; in fact, overall self-esteem goes upward, pretty steadily, all during this period. In a longitudinal study of young people between the ages of 13 and 23, the subjects were asked how much they agreed or disagreed with statements such as "I am able to do things as well as most other people," or "Sometimes I think I am no good at all." The results, said the researchers, were "very consistent. . . . They all

Anti-apartheid protesters at the University of Texas.

Problems in Development

Box 15-1
Suicide

"Who am I and where am I going?" When the answers are "no one" and "nowhere," the results can be tragic. On an average day, 14 Americans between the ages of 15 and 25 put an end to their lives. The suicide rate has tripled in this age group since the 1950s. Although the rate has now begun to decline, suicide is still the second most common cause of death among adolescents and young adults (Holinger, Offer, and Zola, 1988).

That doesn't mean it is common, however. Suicide is more common in old people, not young ones. It is extremely rare in childhood, becomes somewhat more frequent in adolescence, and still more frequent in young adulthood. The rate stays about the same during middle adulthood and then goes up again in old age. Males are more than three times as likely to kill themselves as females, and the rate is considerably higher in whites than in blacks (Shaffer and others, 1988).

Here is a portrait of the typical adolescent suicide victim. He is a young white male who has been having problems for a long time. He has been using drugs or alcohol. He may be suffering from a depressive disorder or a conduct disorder. Depression and/or alcoholism run in his family, and his parents are either divorced or are fighting with each other. They're probably not getting along well with him, either. He has done poorly in school for years, and now he's doing worse. Recently he said something about dying and the person he was talking to—a parent or a friend—said "Don't talk like that!" There's a gun in his house and he knows where it is. But it is an impulse, at the end, that makes him pull the trigger. The precipitating cause could be any number of things: he is arrested, he flunks a test, his girlfriend breaks up with him (he hasn't been treating her very well lately), he has a fight with his parents, or he hears or reads about another suicide—one in his town, perhaps, or even one on TV. He is high on drugs or alcohol when he pulls the trigger. With a gun,

What would make a young person choose death over life?

almost all suicide attempts are "successful." And most males commit suicide with a gun.

When a female attempts suicide, she generally uses drugs, and her attempt is generally *not* successful. A rough rule of thumb is that for every death by suicide there are ten attempts. What usually makes the difference between a successful attempt and an unsuccessful one is the method chosen. Young males use guns, hanging, or jumping from heights, and none of these methods offers them a second chance if they change their minds. Some do change their minds. A psychologist questioned four people who had survived after jumping from heights. Two of them said that they had changed their minds in mid-air (Colt, 1983).

Nearly every adolescent thinks about suicide

show significant increases in self-esteem . . . from about age 13 to early adulthood" (O'Malley and Bachman, 1983, p. 261).

The researchers attributed this growth of self-esteem to three factors. First, there is the increase in physical size that occurs for most people during this period. Second, there is the increasing tendency to take on adult roles, responsibilities, and privileges. And third, outwardly imposed standards of success and failure—especially those that are connected with academic

on occasion and many talk about it. A rough rule of thumb is that for every attempt at suicide there are ten who talk about it—thus, out of every 100 talkers there might be ten attempts and one successful suicide. Even though a person who talks about suicide doesn't necessarily do anything about it, he or she is far more likely to make an attempt than one who hasn't said anything. Most suicide victims give some clues in advance. They may not necessarily talk of killing themselves— they may talk of the futility of living, or they may give away some prized possession. Once they've attempted suicide they're more likely to try again, and perhaps succeed the next time, than someone who has never made an attempt (Spirito, Brown, Overholser, and Fritz, 1989).

Not all suicide victims are low achievers—some (the "perfectionists") are high achievers who have a terrible fear of failure. The lives of both the low and the high achievers were probably quite stressful, but many adolescents lead stressful lives and most do not kill themselves. When they do, either substance abuse or mental illness (especially depression) is likely to be involved. The stress in the victim's life may be the result of these problems, rather than (or in addition to) the cause of them (Hoberman and Garfinkel, 1988).

Depression is a danger sign, but it isn't always easy to diagnose depression in adolescents. An adult who is depressed usually acts sad and listless, but a depressed adolescent may be quite active —in fact, he may court death by engaging in dangerous activities (Stivers, 1988).

It's also difficult to find effective treatments for young people at risk for suicide. When they're recommended for psychotherapy, most do not show up for appointments. Antidepressant drugs may help but they can also be dangerous: they can provide the person with enough energy to make a suicide plan and carry it out. Moreover, an overdose of antidepressants can be fatal.

What about prevention? Two methods that have been tried are high-school-based informational programs and telephone hotlines. The high school programs have not proved effective for

two reasons. First, the rate of adolescent suicide is low—a typical high school goes for years without a single death. Second, most adolescents are already aware of the major warning signs of suicide and express sensible attitudes on the topic. With regard to telephone hotlines, most of the callers tend to be female. But most successful suicides are male, and males don't stop to make phone calls before they pull the trigger or jump (Shaffer and others, 1988).

Teenagers often think of the suicide victim as romantic. Beset with problems, the gallant young man decides to end it all. Goodbye, cruel world. And afterward, of course, everyone's sorry. One possible way of preventing adolescent suicide is to de-romanticize it. Depicting the victims as "sickies and druggies" might be harsh, but it also might make suicide seem less appealing.

Young people are often rash and impulsive, and they have a tendency to dramatize themselves. Perhaps the most tragic deaths of all involve those suicides that are carried out on an impulse. Sometimes the victim seems to be saying, "You don't think I'm brave enough to do it, but see—I am!"

A college student (was) having a turbulent affair with a classmate. He said, "If you don't go steady with me, I'll jump off this building." She said, "You don't have the guts." He did. He ran right up the steps to the eighth floor, out on the roof, and jumped off. (Colt, 1983, p. 52)

Unfortunately, we cannot always be there with a safety net. But most impulsive suicides are carried out with guns, and many of those deaths could have been prevented: if the gun hadn't been there, or had been safely locked up, or hadn't been loaded, the victim might still be alive. And maybe he'd have found a better way of dealing with his problems.

As for the young man in the photograph, he made the braver decision. He didn't jump.

achievement—shrink in importance. The result is that, as people progress through their teens and into their early twenties, they are increasingly able to judge themselves by their own personal standards. Most, though not all, judge themselves to be okay (see Box 15–1.)

The ability to judge oneself by one's own personal standards means that one has attained the status of identity achievement. Young people who have achieved a sense of identity no longer feel an urgent need to identify them-

TABLE 15-2
Generations of Youth, the Social and Political Events of That Period, and the Issues That Mattered to Them

TIME PERIOD	IMPORTANT EVENTS	YOUTH MOVEMENTS
1900–1929	World War I Prohibition Women's Suffrage "Roaring Twenties"	Youth culture challenges Victorian social and sexual rules and customs
1930–1940	The Great Depression Roosevelt administration Government welfare and economic programs	Youth join antiwar movement Campus strikes
1941–1949	World War II Roosevelt–Truman years Atomic bomb Formation of the UN	Youth are involved in fighting a war and recovering from it
1950–1959	The Cold War Eisenhower administration McCarthyism Supreme Court school desegregation decision	The "Silent Generation" Rock and roll
1960–1969	Kennedy–Johnson years Peace Corps, poverty programs Vietnam War Assassination of John Kennedy, Robert Kennedy, and Martin Luther King Ghetto riots	The hippies Marijuana and LSD The sexual revolution Black Power Civil rights demonstrations, campus disruption
1970–1979	Nixon–Ford–Carter years Vietnam war ends Watergate Inflation, unemployment Disillusionment and "malaise" Divorce rate rises, mothers enter the workforce	Feminism Concern about the environment Rates of drug use, teen pregnancy, and suicide continue to rise Anti-apartheid movement
1980–1990	Reagan–Bush years Inflation and unemployment decline Homelessness Inner-city violence and crime increase Chinese democracy movement brutally suppressed Iron Curtain crumbles; communism on the wane	Rates of drug use, teen pregnancy, and suicide begin to decline Concern about getting high-paying jobs The yuppies Physical fitness Concern about global warming and the ozone layer

Based in part on Braungart, 1974.

selves with a group. Young adults worry less than adolescents about what their peers might think of them—they are less self-conscious and more resistant to peer pressure (Adams, Abraham, and Markstrom, 1987; Slugoski and others, 1984).

Love and Marriage

College students rank getting married and starting a family as the third most important milestone in the path to adulthood (see Table 15–1, p. 497). If you are surprised that it is not ranked higher, consider that even 14- and 15-year-olds can—and often do—have babies, and that 16-year-olds can get married (with parental consent) in some states. One needn't be an adult to have babies or get married.

Interactions with the opposite sex generally begin with casual acquaintanceships or meeting in groups. The next step is dating, which may progress to a steady boyfriend–girlfriend relationship known as "going out" or "going together"—it used to be called "going steady."

Going Together

What do young men and women want or expect from a romantic relationship? According to Erikson and many other theorists, the answer is intimacy. Erikson (1963) defined an intimate relationship as one that involves trust, openness, sharing, and commitment. A researcher asked some college students about their views—what do *they* think is the difference between an intimate relationship and a nonintimate one? The students agreed with Erikson about the importance of trust, openness, and sharing, but not on commitment—only 8 percent thought that commitment was necessary in order for a relationship to be intimate. In contrast, over 40 percent of the students named something that Erikson hadn't included in his definition: sex. These students didn't think a heterosexual relationship could be intimate without having a sexual aspect. For males, in fact, sex was the most important criterion for an intimate relationship. For females, it was openness (Roscoe, Kennedy, and Pope, 1987).

Some romantic relationships flourish, other fade. What distinguishes the successful ones from the unsuccessful ones? Researchers have found that successful relationships tend to develop very quickly. Some college students who had recently started to date someone were asked to fill out questionnaires about their new relationship. Then they were questioned again 4 months later, by which time some of the couples were no longer seeing each other. The ones who were still dating tended to be those who had initially given a highly favorable evaluation of the new relationship: their relationship was characterized, from the first few dates, by more openness, more feelings of closeness and belongingness, and better communication. The researchers were able to predict fairly accurately, on the basis of how the couples were getting along in the very early stages of their relationship, which ones would stay together and which would break up. A similar finding has been reported for same-sex friendships: people who will become good friends tend to like each other and get along well right from the start (Berg and McQuinn, 1986).

When a romantic relationship doesn't go well, the result is often painful for one or both of the parties involved. Breaking up is hard to do: there may be a good deal of emotional distress on the part of the ex-girlfriend or boyfriend. The distress is greater if the relationship had gone on for a long time and if it had been quite close; the distress is less if the ex-girlfriend or boy-

friend feels that a new romantic partner will be pretty easy to find (or if she or he already has someone else in mind). For a college woman, there is a tendency to be more upset by the breakup of a relationship if she had been having intercourse with her partner (Simpson, 1987).

An intriguing theory of romance links the heterosexual relationships of adulthood to the attachment relationship between mother and child. You may recall from Chapter 6 that all normal babies become attached to their mothers by the time they are 12 months old, but some of these attachments are secure and some are insecure. Babies with insecure attachments may vacillate between clinginess and anger when their mother returns after an absence—these babies are called resistant. Others ignore their mother when she returns—this pattern is called avoidant. Two researchers from the University of Denver have defined "adult attachment types" in a similar fashion. They found that the majority of adults (like the majority of babies) are securely attached to their partners; these people have no problems making commitments and don't worry about being abandoned or about getting too close. A smaller proportion of adults have avoidant relationships: these people feel somewhat uncomfortable about getting close to others or about trusting them completely. And a still smaller proportion were labeled "anxious/ambivalent"; they are ambivalent like the resistant babies. These people worry about whether their partner really loves them; their intense desire for love tends to scare away potential mates (Hazan and Shaver, 1987).

An interesting point about the comparison between romantic love and mother–child attachments is the way these relationships change over time. Both kinds of attachment tend to be most intense in their early stages; babies cling most tightly to their mothers at around 13 months of age. After a while they start to take each other for granted: a 5-year-old is able to spend the better part of the day away from his mother without suffering distress. But the strength of the attachment relationship is revealed when it is threatened or terminated: even a school-age child will become frantic and then desolate if he loses a parent to death or divorce. In a similar way, according to the researchers, the loss of a husband or wife may "reveal the strength of attachment bonds that were previously invisible" (Hazan and Shaver, 1987, p. 523).

FIDELITY. At some point in the development of a romantic relationship, if it is going well, the participants begin to feel that they have a certain amount of commitment to each other. Although there is as yet no promise that the relationship will be a permanent one, the expectation is that neither party will date or have sex with others. Some college students were asked what they would do if they discovered that their romantic partner had been "unfaithful." Their replies were quite similar to responses of married people to the same question, except that the college students were more likely to say that they would simply terminate the relationship. It is not only the lack of legal complications that makes it easier to terminate a dating relationship than a marital relationship: it is also the lower degree of commitment (Roscoe, Cavanaugh, and Kennedy, 1988).

How faithful are dating partners to each other? The indications are that fidelity increases as people get older. Among sexually experienced adolescents, about 40 percent of the males and 15 percent of the females have had three or more sexual partners in the past month. But among sexually experienced young adults (18 to 24 years of age), 40 percent of the males and 15 percent of the females have had three or more partners in the past *year*. Regarding married couples, surveys usually find that around 50 percent of husbands and a somewhat greater percentage of wives have never had an extramarital affair during the entire time they've been married (Brooks-Gunn, Boyer, and Hein, 1988; Roscoe, Cavanaugh, and Kennedy, 1988).

Living Together

It used to be rare for a young man and woman to live together without being married; it is now quite common. In 1950 there were 50,000 unmarried cohabiting couples in the United States, in 1970 there were 500,000, and in 1988 there were 2.6 million. Around 6 percent of all unmarried adults in the U.S. are currently sharing living quarters with a member of the opposite sex. About twice that many will do so at some point in their lives (Glick, 1988, 1989).

When people live together for a while, their relationship changes. Whether they get married, don't get married, or are already married, the passionate emotions they experience in the first year are likely to cool down. Researchers have studied how relationships change over time in four types of childless living-together couples: married couples, heterosexual unmarrieds, homosexual males, and homosexual females. The researchers found that the relationship progressed in a similar way for all these types of couples. The first year, which they called "blending," was characterized by high-intensity romantic love and lots of sex. Years 2 and 3, "nesting," were characterized by homemaking, attempts to find compatibility, ambivalent feelings, and a decline in romantic love. Years 4 and 5, "maintaining," were characterized by a decrease in tension: the couple was learning to deal with conflict and had begun to establish traditions. All four types of couples went through the same stages—the only significant difference among them was that the unmarried heterosexuals experienced more conflict and tension, overall, than the married ones. For all four groups, stress and disillusionment were greatest in the middle stage, years 2 and 3. This is the point, apparently, when many relationships break up (Kurdek and Schmitt, 1986).

Some cohabiting couples don't break up: they get married. Are their marriages any stronger than those of couples who haven't lived together first? The evidence on this point is contradictory. A Canadian study showed that couples who lived together before they were married were more likely to stay married (Grant, 1988), a Swedish study showed that these couples were more likely to get divorced (Hall, 1988), and an American study found no difference (DeMaris and Leslie, 1984).

Getting Married

What makes a couple decide to get married? It's a decision that is now being postponed to a later and later age. The median age at first marriage in 1988 was 26 for men and 23½ for women—two years older, for both sexes, than in 1960 (Glick, 1989).

All through the lifespan, people tend to feel most comfortable with other people who are similar to themselves in the ways that they consider important. They choose their friends this way, and they also choose their husbands and wives this way. Of course, people don't want to marry someone *exactly* like themselves, but there usually have to be some basic similarities in order

for the relationship to work. When there are big differences in age, intelligence, education, or physical attractiveness, there is a much greater chance that the relationship will break up (Simpson, 1987).

The tendency for people to marry other people who are similar to themselves is called **assortative mating.** Husbands and wives are likely to be almost as much alike as brothers and sisters—they tend to be fairly well matched in intelligence, size, socioeconomic status, and even in things such as a predisposition to alcoholism or mental illness (Merikangas, Weissman, Prusoff, and John, 1988). A sociologist has speculated that assortative mating may be one of the reasons people are marrying later: because education can be such a long, slow process nowadays, and because it is harder to tell what qualities might be needed for success in the world of the future, it takes longer to sort people out. It takes longer to decide what kind of person one is and what kind of person one should marry (Oppenheimer, 1988).

This makes it sound almost as though people choose their mates the way they choose a car. What about love? Although men and women have probably been falling in love with each other ever since the dawn of our species, romantic love has not always been regarded as a prerequisite for marriage (Hazan and Shaver, 1987). As recently as 1967, only 24 percent of college-age women, and 65 percent of men, answered "no" to the question, "If a man (woman) had all the other qualities you desired, would you marry this person if you were not in love with him (her)?" As you can see in Table 15–3, two things happened over the next 17 years: a much higher proportion said no, they wouldn't marry someone they didn't love, and gender differences in response to that question virtually disappeared (Simpson, Campbell, and Berscheid, 1986).

Other gender differences regarding love and marriage are still with us. Men and women are not looking for exactly the same things in a mate, and they do not use the same criteria in selecting someone to love or to marry. Women tend to prefer men who are liked by others and who have the qualities that will make them successful in their careers; they want their husband or boyfriend to be an intellectual companion as well as a lover. Men are more concerned about their partner's physical attractiveness and less concerned about her ability to provide intellectual companionship (Kingsbury and Minda, 1988).

Sociobiologists have pointed out that it makes evolutionary sense for the female to be concerned about her mate's earning potential and the male to be

TABLE 15–3
Answers to the question, "If a man (woman) had all the other qualities you desired, would you marry this person if you were not in love with him (her)?"

| | 1967 | | | 1984 | |
	MALE	FEMALE		MALE	FEMALE
No	65	24		86	85
Yes	12	4		2	4
Undecided	24	72		13	12

Source: Simpson, Campbell, and Berscheid, 1986.

concerned about his mate's physical appearance. The idea is that the female's good looks are a sign of youth and health—an indication that she will be able to bear many children. The male's looks are less important, since male fertility is not as much affected by age or ill health. His earning potential, on the other hand, is an indication that he will be a good provider and thus make it more likely that their children will survive (Buss and Barnes, 1986).

THE PATH TO MARRIAGE. As a couple progresses from dating, to going out, to getting engaged, and then to getting married, they are likely to become increasingly caught up in their relationship. They spend more and more time together. More and more activities—both recreational and those involving chores—are done with the other person and fewer are done alone. They spend more time talking to each other about their problems and successes, and showing affection in physical ways (Surra, 1985).

Another thing that happens during this period is that both parties tend, over a period of time, to withdraw from their other friendships and to spend more and more time alone together. The number of friends goes down, especially for men. On the other hand, ties to relatives tend to strengthen, especially for women. Women seem to be better than men at maintaining networks of relationships (Fischer, Sollie, Sorell, and Green, 1989).

MARRYING YOUNG. Although the average age at marriage has been going up, there are still some people who marry before they turn 20. How do these marriages work?

Although some early marriages are successful, the risk that the marriage will end in divorce is far higher for those who marry in their teens than for those who marry in their twenties. In general, the people who marry young lead less successful lives in adulthood: they obtain less education, have lower-status jobs, and earn lower salaries. These statements are true for both men and women, and they're true whether or not early marriage is associated with early childbearing (Teti, Lamb, and Elster, 1987; Teti and Lamb, 1989).

The phrase **lost-adolescence syndrome** has been used to describe the kinds of marital problems experienced by people who marry young, or who marry later but after a long period—sometimes beginning in the early teens —of dating each other exclusively. Such relationships may be quite happy during the early years of the marriage. But later, when there are children to care for and the romance has worn off, these people start to feel trapped. They begin to wish that they had had a chance to get to know a wider variety of members of the opposite sex. They begin to feel that they have missed out on the usual pleasures of adolescence. As their feelings of frustration and unhappiness grow, their attachment to their spouse declines. The usual outcome of this situation is divorce. But divorce cannot give a person a new chance at adolescence—that opportunity comes only once (Jurich and Jurich, 1975).

HAVING KIDS. Childbearing is another decision that tends to get put off nowadays, especially by people in the higher educational brackets. The rate of childbearing by women under 25 has declined slightly in the past decade; the rate for women over 30 is increasing sharply. Some women put it off too long: infertility becomes more prevalent after the age of 30. It has been estimated that one-fourth to one-fifth of the women born between 1950 and 1970 will never have a child (Glick, 1989). Some of these women will remain unmarried, some will be unable to have a child, and some will decide not to. When a couple decides not to have a baby, one of the reasons commonly given is that it will interfere with the wife's career (Neal, Groat, and Wicks, 1989). If any couples have decided not to have a baby because it will interfere with the *husband's* career, we haven't heard about it.

When a couple does have a child, their marital satisfaction tends to go down. Part of this decrease in marital happiness might be a coincidence: many married couples have their first child in the second or third year of marriage, and, as we said in the section called Living Together, stress and disillusionment tend to be greatest in years 2 and 3. The other reason for the decrease in marital satisfaction was discussed in Box 6–1 (p. 185): the husband generally does not live up to the wife's expectations about sharing child-rearing chores, and (we talked about this in Chapter 2) she ends up putting in much longer hours than he does, especially if she also has a full-time job.

MARRIAGE: HIS AND HERS. It has been said that, in any marriage, there are really two marriages, "his" and "hers," and that, in general, "his" is better (Bernard, 1982). Marriage appears to confer more benefits on a man than on a woman. Married men have been found to be happier and healthier, mentally and physically, than unmarried men. In contrast, some studies show no differences between married and unmarried women; others show that unmarried women are actually happier and healthier (Lowe and Smith, 1987).

Although sex-role attitudes have changed dramatically in the past two decades, and many women are embarking on careers that in the past would have been closed to them, these changes have mostly affected life *outside* of marriage. *Inside* marriage it seems to be a case of "the more things change, the more they are the same." True, men know how to change a diaper now, and women know how to change a tire. But these are superficial changes. Keeping the home clean and its inhabitants furnished with food and clothing are still basically the wife's responsibilities; keeping the home and car in repair are still basically the husband's (Lueptow, Guss, and Hyden, 1989).

The longer a couple has been married, the more likely they are to split up tasks in this traditional way. And the more they split up tasks in the traditional way, the less happiness the woman expresses in regard to her marriage. The women who are unhappiest about the division of labor are the ones who least resemble the stereotype of the "feminine" woman. In other words, it is the androgynous woman who is likely to feel the most dissatisfaction with the way things are working out (Belsky, Lang, and Huston, 1986; Antill and Cotton, 1988).

SERIAL MARRIAGE. "So what if my marriage doesn't work out? I can always get divorced and try again with someone else." That attitude has become so prevalent that researchers have coined a term for its consequences: **serial marriage,** defined as three or more marriages by one individual as a result of repeated divorce (Brody, Neubaum, and Forehand, 1988).

Overall, little difference has been found between one's chances of attaining happiness in a remarriage versus one's chances of attaining happiness in a first marriage. Second marriages have one big advantage: the participants might have learned something from the failure of the first. They also have one big disadvantage: they are composed of participants who have already struck out once (Vemer, Coleman, Ganong, and Cooper, 1989).

But there is more to consider than the happiness of the husband and his second or third wife, or the happiness of the wife and her second or third husband, or the happiness of the person who is rearing her children alone because her ex-spouse is now married to someone else. Most marital breakups involve children, and it is they who are most likely to be caught in the cracks of the serial marriage. All through this book we have pointed out the many ways that children from single-parent homes or from stepparent-headed homes are at a disadvantage, compared to children who grow up with their own mother and father.

Making Career Decisions

"What do you want to be when you grow up?" That question is asked of every child, from preschool age on up. But it is not until late adolescence that the question of occupational choice becomes a serious and immediate one.

The development of understanding about occupational choice can be viewed as a series of three stages. In the first stage, which lasts until age 11 or 12, children perceive no limits on what they can potentially do. Children will say during this period that they want to be a fireman, or an actress, or the president of the United States. During the second stage, which ends in mid- or late adolescence, young people show an increasing awareness of their own interests and inclinations; they also begin to realize that jobs require specific talents and training, and that the necessary education may be long and costly. In the third stage, older adolescents or young adults choose a career, after considering job requirements, opportunities for training, and their own talents, abilities, and values (Ginzberg, 1972).

Factors Affecting Career Choices

The kind of temperament and personality one has will affect the kind of job one chooses, and also one's satisfaction with that job. A person who is sociable and physically active, for example, is more likely to decide to be a salesperson or a gym teacher than an accountant or a data processor. If she does decide to become an accountant (perhaps because of parental pressure) she is less likely to be happy in that profession. A person who is introverted and inactive, on the other hand, would probably be happier as an accountant than as a salesperson (Holland, 1985). The aspects of personality that affect occupational choice and job satisfaction are, to a surprisingly large extent, innate. A recent study of identical twins reared apart showed that they not only tended to hold similar jobs in adulthood—they were also likely to report similar degrees of satisfaction with whatever occupations they did choose (Arvey, Bouchard, Segal, and Abraham, 1989).

In early childhood, children develop stereotypes of what males and females are like. In a similar way, though it takes a little longer, children also develop stereotypes of the people in various occupations—stereotypes of

The Child in Society

**Box 15-2
High School
Dropouts**

In 1940, only 38 percent of young American adults, ages 25 to 29, had graduated from high school. Over the next 40 years, as a high school diploma came to be seen as a necessity rather than a luxury, the proportion of high school graduates in the United States rose steadily. In 1980, 84 percent of Americans in the 25-to-29 age range had graduated from high school or obtained an equivalent degree. The other 16 percent are considered dropouts. Since 1980, the proportion of American youth who drop out of high school has stabilized at around 15 to 16 percent (U.S. Bureau of the Census, 1987).

The dropout rate is slightly higher among males than among females: 18 percent versus 14½ percent (Halpern, 1989). It is slightly higher among blacks than among whites, a difference that is due entirely to the higher dropout rate for young black males: black females are as likely to graduate as white females, but black males have a dropout rate of 20 percent. The rate is higher still for Hispanics: 26 percent for both males and females. In some big-city schools, the dropout rate hovers around 50 percent (Rumberger, 1987).

The likelihood that students from a minority background will drop out of school depends very much on what school they attend. There are several reasons for this. One that we discussed in Chapter 12 is the fact that students of any level of ability do better in a classroom in which there is a good proportion of highly able students. Inner-city schools tend not to have such students: either their parents send them to private schools or they are siphoned off into special "magnet" schools, such as the Bronx High School of Science. Second, dropping out, like suicide, can be contagious: if all their friends are dropping out, adolescents may see no point in continuing, even if they're making passing grades (Cairns, 1989). Third, inner-city schools tend to be large and impersonal, with an atmosphere that does not reward academic achievement or encourage participation in school activities. Most of these schools have such large enrollments that an individual has little hope of winning a spot on the school newspaper or the basketball team, much less being named editor-in-chief or team captain. Students in large schools are less likely to participate in school activities, and those who do not participate are more likely to drop out (Linney and Seidman, 1989).

But even in large, impersonal inner-city schools, 50 percent of the students go on to graduate. Why are some students able to make it, while others give up and drop out? In the previous 14 chapters we have touched on many of the problems associated with dropping out of school. They include conduct disorder, low IQ (remember the "ten-year retarded child"?), learning disabilities, having a native language other than English, rejection by classmates, teenage pregnancy, substance abuse, and membership in an antisocial peer group. Others that we haven't mentioned are frequent absences (which could be due to health problems, not only to truancy) and poverty. Many high school dropouts give "wanting to get a job" or "wanting to help out my family" as their primary reason for leaving school (Barber and McClellan, 1987).

"Wanting to get a job" sounds like a pretty poor excuse for dropping out of school, when every-

what doctors are like, or teachers, or accountants, or flight attendants. Finally, they also develop (and this takes considerably longer) an image of what they themselves are like—this is a major aspect of identity formation. When it comes to choosing an occupation, they compare the image they have of themselves with the image they have of the people in various occupations. If the match is poor, they will probably not consider that occupation. They will consider it only if they think the match is good—if they think that people who do that sort of thing are a lot like themselves. Thus, young people might choose an occupation that is wrong for them for either of two reasons: they had an erroneous stereotype of the people who are in it, or they had an erroneous view of themselves. They may also fail to consider certain careers for the same two reasons. This is where gender stereotypes and role models come in: if a girl has never met a female mathematician, she may think of mathematicians as being people "not like me" (Eccles, 1987).

one knows that the unemployment rate is much higher for dropouts—in fact, it's twice as high for young dropouts as for high school graduates of the same age. But this is true mainly for whites. The unemployment rate for young black men and women is so high that it hardly matters whether they've graduated high school: 53 percent of black *high school graduates* under the age of 24 are unemployed. And for Hispanics, although the unemployment rate is lower, a high school diploma also fails to make a lot of difference: 42 percent of Hispanic dropouts are unemployed, versus 34 percent of high school graduates. Hispanic students are particularly likely to mention financial difficulties and wanting to get a job as their reasons for leaving school (Rumberger, 1987).

The main reason, though, for leaving school is low academic achievement. Most of the adolescents who drop out have been doing poorly for years, falling further and further behind. Some are older than their classmates as a result of having been left back. Some cannot read fifth-grade books or do fifth-grade math (Weiss, 1989).

What can be done to help these students? In many cases high school is too late—they're already too far behind. They needed help at an earlier stage. Unfortunately, preschool enrichment programs such as Head Start have had little or no effect on dropout rates (see Box 9–2). Even the more expensive "model" preschool enrichment programs, run by talented educators and serving small numbers of children, have only been able to reduce the dropout rate by a small amount: 65 percent of these children eventually graduated from high school, versus 52 percent in the control groups (Haskins, 1989).

Head Start can only give children from disadvantaged backgrounds a head start—it can't ensure that they will keep on running until they reach the finish line. What happened before a child started school becomes less and less important over the years; what happens *inside* the school matters more and more. In Chapter 12 we mentioned that students from some cultural backgrounds may have academic problems because the values and behaviors of their culture are not in harmony with those of the school. Students whose native language is not English are also handicapped. Some schools have been experimenting with ways of adapting their programs to the cultural and language backgrounds of their students. There is a dropout rate of 95 percent for native American students in Chicago public schools, but at the bicultural, bilingual Little Big Horn High School in Chicago, 89 percent of the students go on to graduate (Hakuta and Garcia, 1989).

Dealing with cultural or language diversity is not going to be a cure-all, however: remember that, in the United States as a whole, the dropout rate is only a little lower for white, English-speaking students than for those from minority groups. This means that the majority of high school dropouts are white, English-speaking Americans. They drop out for many different reasons. Since the problems are diverse, the solutions will also have to be diverse. They will have to include better ways of teaching children to read and to understand mathematical concepts; better ways of helping children with learning disabilities, conduct disorders, and social problems; and better ways of preventing teenage pregnancies and substance abuse.

EDUCATION AND UPWARD MOBILITY. Three related factors that, to a large extent, will determine a person's adult occupation are educational achievement, intelligence, and socioeconomic class. In fact, it is hard to tease these factors apart because they are so closely intertwined. The career options open to young people depend very much on the quantity and quality of the education they receive—especially on whether or not they go to college. Whether or not they go to college is determined, in turn, by how well they do in high school and on their family's socioeconomic status. How well they do in high school is determined by all the factors we discussed in Chapter 12, including intelligence (Willits, 1988).

In general, the status of a person's occupation—how well it pays and how much it is respected in our society—is related quite closely to the socioeconomic class of his or her parents. Although upward mobility is the rule in the United States, only 2 percent of the children of manual laborers become

TABLE 15-4
Upward Mobility in Three Generations of White American Families

SOCIOECONOMIC CLASS	PERCENTAGE OF FATHERS	PERCENTAGE OF SONS	PERCENTAGE OF GRANDSONS
Upper-middle class	—	2	5
Middle class	—	5	10
Lower-middle class	2	18	37
Working class	38	49	44
Lower class	60	26	4

Source: Snarey and Vaillant, 1985.

high-level professionals. The chances are better for their grandchildren. Over the course of 40 years, researchers have studied three generations of white lower- and working-class families in the northeastern U.S. Table 15–4 shows how each generation exceeded the one before it in terms of occupation, income, and education (the determinants of socioeconomic status). A little over 5 percent of the grandsons made it into the ranks of upper-middle-class professionals; IQ was an important factor in this kind of upward jump. It was rare for a son's socioeconomic status to be lower than his father's—in general, this happened only when there was a serious problem such as mental illness, alcoholism, or physical disability (Snarey and Vaillant, 1985).

The families depicted in Table 15–4 are white, though ethnically mixed. What about other racial or cultural groups in our society? Because occupational status is closely associated with education, those groups whose members tend to be low in educational achievement are less likely to show the kind of steady upward mobility we see in Table 15–4. Those groups whose members tend to do very well in school and to go on to college and graduate school move upward in socioeconomic status at a dazzling rate of speed.

Another factor that is involved in upward (or downward) mobility is the composition of the family. Children from mother-headed homes, or from families containing a stepparent and stepsiblings, tend to have lower educational attainment and lower-status occupations as adults. Children from large families, with many siblings, also do less well (McCartin and Meyer, 1988). Since different racial and cultural groups tend to differ in family composition, this is another reason why the offspring of some groups might have a harder time moving upward in socioeconomic level.

OCCUPATION AND GENDER. The researchers who began the 40-year study (Table 15–4) of the sons of lower-class families didn't even bother with the daughters, because in those days they were all expected to become housewives. But even today, daughters are less likely than sons to be upwardly mobile in terms of occupation. There were 73 grandsons over the age of 24 among the families in that study; of these, four ended up as upper-middle-class professionals. But of the 64 granddaughters, none did (Snarey and Vaillant, 1985).

Education is more important now than it has ever been before, because the jobs of the future are going to require much more than the ability to read at a fifth-grade level. The number of jobs that demand only basic literacy is shrinking; growth in the job market is concentrated in those areas that require high-level reasoning ability, communication skills, and mathematical and scientific thinking (Jackson and Hornbeck, 1989).

Although more women are now going into medicine and law, on the average they still get less education than men—even though, as we said in Chapter 12, they make better grades than their male classmates all through elementary school, high school, and college. The trouble is that the high school and college courses they are doing so well in are not quite the same ones that their male classmates are taking: females are less likely to take subjects such as math, engineering, physics, and computer science (Jagacinski, LeBold, and Salvendy, 1988).

Consider a sample of 4000 adolescents, 2000 of each sex. When they graduate (or fail to graduate) from high school, 280 of the males and 220 of the

FIGURE 15-2
The career aspirations of 3949 school children, kindergarten through twelfth grade. (From Eccles, 1987, p. 137.)

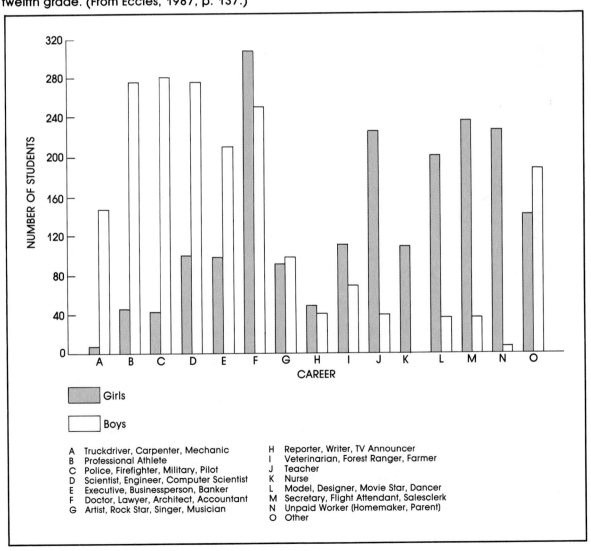

A Truckdriver, Carpenter, Mechanic
B Professional Athlete
C Police, Firefighter, Military, Pilot
D Scientist, Engineer, Computer Scientist
E Executive, Businessperson, Banker
F Doctor, Lawyer, Architect, Accountant
G Artist, Rock Star, Singer, Musician
H Reporter, Writer, TV Announcer
I Veterinarian, Forest Ranger, Farmer
J Teacher
K Nurse
L Model, Designer, Movie Star, Dancer
M Secretary, Flight Attendant, Salesclerk
N Unpaid Worker (Homemaker, Parent)
O Other

females will have enough math to major in science or engineering in college. Of these, 140 of the males and 44 of the females will choose these majors, and 46 of the males and 20 of the females will actually receive B.S. degrees. Of the original 4000 students, five males and *one female* will eventually receive a Ph.D. degree in science or engineering (Widnall, 1988).

"What do you want to be when you grow up?" Researchers asked almost 4000 children in grades kindergarten through twelfth what career they hoped to have as an adult. Figure 15–2 shows the results, with separate bars for girls and boys. Notice that girls are now somewhat more likely than boys to say that they want to become doctors, lawyers, or architects. But they are also a good deal more likely than boys to want to become teachers, nurses, secretaries, or homemakers, and a good deal less likely to want to be scientists, engineers, or business executives (Eccles, 1987).

Gender Roles for the 1990s

The majority of women between the ages of 21 and 65 are now employed outside the home; it is estimated that by 1995 four-fifths of women will be in the workforce. Since 1970, approximately 4 million American women have taken jobs. What jobs are these women filling? Of the 4 million, 3.3 million are employed as secretaries, bookkeepers, cashiers, and other female-dominated service occupations. Women earn an average of $635 for every $1000 a man makes (Gerstein, Lichtman, and Barokas, 1988; Eccles, 1987).

Should Women Be More Like Men?

"Why can't a woman be more like a man?" asks a song in the Broadway show, *My Fair Lady.* Should she be?

Jacquelynne Eccles of the University of Michigan thinks that this is the wrong question. It presumes that males are doing the right things and making the right choices, and that females are doing and making the wrong ones. She asks us to consider the issue from another point of view: *Why* are women making these choices? Might they have very good reasons for making them? Might they be making them on positive grounds—on what they hope to achieve—rather than on negative grounds of fear or avoidance?

People make occupational choices, says Eccles (1987), on the basis of what they think is important, what they think they can succeed at, and how well their stereotypes of various jobs match their image of themselves. Their choices are affected by considerations such as: Will I enjoy doing that kind of work? Will it fit in with my long-term goals? Am I the kind of person who does that sort of thing? Someone who prides herself on being caring and person oriented, and who considers the roles of wife and mother to be important to her, will tend to avoid jobs that don't fit into that picture. She won't want to become a scientist if she sees herself as warm and caring and she sees scientists as cold and ruthless. She won't want to go into professions that she thinks will demand high amounts of time, energy, or travel away from the home, because those jobs are incompatible with some of her goals for the future.

Although women are no longer barred from traditionally male jobs, not many become construction workers. Perhaps it's a lack of role models, or perhaps most women just don't think they'd enjoy that kind of work.

Given her values, her choices make sense. According to Eccles, males and females have different achievement goals because they have different, but equally important, goals for their lives.

Males and females also have different ways of dealing with their various goals. According to Eccles, women worry about reconciling their career and personal goals—they're not sure how they can do everything they want to do. Men, on the other hand, tend to "compartmentalize" their goals: they don't see any conflict between being a husband, a father, and the president of a company. Indeed, there seldom is any conflict—it's only women who are forced to reconcile their conflicting goals, to compromise. A man doesn't say that he isn't sure he wants to have children because it will interfere with his career. Having children *won't* interfere with his career—it will interfere with *hers.* Successful men generally have a single-minded attitude to their work, and this kind of attitude is necessary in order to succeed in male-dominated professions. Most women aren't willing to sacrifice everything else in order to succeed in a male-dominated profession (Eccles, 1987).

This gender difference may be one reason why marital happiness often declines when a couple has a baby. We said in the section on Love and Marriage that women tend to be attracted to men who they think will be successful in adult life—successful in their careers. This means that a young woman is likely to be attracted to a young man who has a single-minded dedication to his work, since this quality is a good predictor of future success. She marries him because (unconsciously) she feels he will work hard at his career, be successful at it, and be a good provider for her children. But then, when the children come along, she is unhappy with him because he continues to have the same single-minded dedication to his work!

DO WOMEN STILL HAVE "FEAR OF SUCCESS"? In 1969, a young experimental psychologist named Matina Horner coined the term **fear of success** to describe a woman's ambivalence about being successful in her academic or

Today, women worry less about the possible negative consequences of being successful, and more about how to reconcile their career goals with their personal goals.

professional endeavors. Women, according to Horner, were worried that if they were too successful, their peers—especially their male peers—wouldn't like them. A bright, achievement-oriented woman is caught in a "double bind": she worries both about failure and about success. If she fails, she doesn't live up to her own standards; if she succeeds, she has violated society's gender stereotypes and may pay a heavy price for it.

Interestingly, Horner herself seemed to have no worries of this sort. When she was offered the job of being president of Radcliffe College (the women's division of Harvard University), she accepted. Moreover, she combined this job (from which she has recently retired) with marriage and childrearing.

Horner's research was carried out over two decades ago. How does she feel about "fear of success" today? A reporter recently asked her that question. Horner replied that women are now "allowed" to be more successful, but they are still "required" to live up to the traditional gender roles of wife and mother—this, in fact, is a good description of her own life. "Really," says Horner, "we went from the 'double bind' to the 'double burden.'" Although women have made remarkable progress in the workplace, they now have the problem of trying to combine the new career with the old one of marriage and childrearing. Many are managing it, but they are finding it very exhausting (McLeod, 1989, p. 8).

Fear of success is not dead; there are still young women who "play dumb" in order to avoid scaring off potential boyfriends. Moreover, Horner never said that *all* women have fear of success in *all* situations. It's most likely to be a problem for a high-achieving, highly motivated young woman, competing in an area that is traditionally male (Piedmont, 1988).

In Chapter 12 we explored some of the reasons why high school girls who do well on math exams in the classroom (where they are competing directly with their male classmates) do less well on tests such as the mathematical section of the SATs. We talked about attributions for success and failure, and the fact that bright girls tend to attribute their successes to luck and their failures to dumbness. Perhaps this is the modern version of "fear of success." Girls no longer refrain from succeeding: what they do instead is to explain away their success by convincing themselves that it was just luck. They don't do this for all their successes, however—just in certain areas such as math. If you ask a woman what *she* thinks she's good at, and then ask her why she is successful in *those* areas, she is likely to attribute her successes to skill or effort, not to luck (Carson, 1988). The things *she* thinks are important are not necessarily the ones society thinks are important, or at least they're not necessarily the ones that will pay well in adult life.

Is Androgyny a Good Thing?

According to the traditional gender stereotypes, females are supposed to be caring and nurturant, quick to express their emotions, easily dominated, and a little helpless. Males are supposed to be tough, assertive, aggressive, unemotional, and very competent.

Do we want women to be more like men? Do we want men to be more like women? In other words, should people be more androgynous?

First, it's important to recognize that not all women fit the female gender stereotype and not all men fit the male one. People don't come in only two kinds—they come in as many kinds as there are people. As we've said before, the differences between one female and another female are likely to be far greater than the difference between an average female and an average male. Gender differences are *statistical* differences—differences between means. There are dominant, aggressive, highly competent females and there are caring, emotional, easily dominated males. However, because statistical differences are most noticeable at the extreme ends of a distribution, someone who is *extremely* aggressive, dominant, and unemotional is most likely to be a male, and someone who is *extremely* nurturant, emotional, and easily dominated is most likely to be a female.

Other gender differences work in similar ways. Intellectual differences between males and females are small, on the average. Much bigger differences show up if you look at the extremes of the distribution. Among adolescents who are outstandingly talented in mathematical reasoning, boys outnumber girls by a considerable margin. Among those who are verbally disabled (dyslexic, for example), boys again outnumber girls. But the differences in math or reading ability between the average boy and the average girl are hardly worth noticing.

Some gender differences, however, are large and important. The differences in height, strength, and aggressiveness are sizable. Of the cognitive differences, the largest is in visual–spatial ability, the ability that's involved, for example, in reading maps. The differences in size, strength, and aggressiveness are biological in origin, and, we think, so is the difference in visual–spatial ability. The males of all mammalian species range over a wider area of territory than females. They have to be able to find their way around. Of course, most species don't do this by reading maps, but they have to be able to figure out how to get from where they are to where they want to go. Male rats are better at finding their way through a maze than female rats (Gadsby, 1990).

Perhaps the same drive to explore the territory is behind little boys' fascination with cars and trains. They also like toys that have anything to do with aggression, such as miniature soldiers and grenade launchers. In every human society, two tasks that are assigned mainly to males are hunting and waging war.

In every human society, caring for babies and young children is a task that is assigned mainly to females. Is it so surprising that they do this job, on the average, a little better than males? Remember that this doesn't mean that *every* woman is better at childrearing than *every* male—it's another statistical difference. There are many couples in which the husband is more nurturant than the wife.

Our society has become more androgynous. Women are now "allowed" to be more assertive, and they are "required" to be less emotional and to work hard at careers outside the home. Men are now "allowed" to be more emotional and are "required" to know how to change a baby's diaper. Clothing and hairstyles are becoming more and more alike. Men are dying their hair and having face-lifts. Women are doing pushups and running in marathons.

Is androgyny a good thing? In many ways it is. It is good for women, because our society values "masculine" traits more than it values "feminine" ones—at any rate, the masculine ones command higher salaries in the workplace. It would be nice if women could become more assertive and less helpless without losing their ability to be caring and nurturant, and if men could become more caring and nurturant without losing their ability to be assertive and competent.

But are gender differences ever likely to disappear entirely, and would we want them to? We have pointed out on several occasions that mothers and fathers play somewhat different roles in childrearing, and that children do best if they have both a mother and a father. If people were entirely androgynous, children might end up with two of the same kind of parent, instead of one of each, and that might not be as good. There is some evidence that androgynous men may have a tendency to be too permissive—too wimpy—

The Child in Society

Box 15-3 Tomorrow's Children

In Chapter 1 we defined **cohort** as "a group of people all born at about the same time." We explained that a cohort of children born in 1986 might not differ much from a cohort born in 1984, but they would probably differ considerably from one born in 1966.

Cohort differences are easiest to see in young people—adolescents and young adults. Look at the changes we've seen in this age group over the past forty years. In the '50s we had the "silent generation," hard-working and earnest. Then, starting around 1965, we had the hippy generation—the flower children. They protested the Viet Nam War, smoked pot, and went in for meditation and Zen Buddhism. In the '80s, the hippie generation gave way to the yuppie generation. The college students of the '80s were more like those of the '50s than like those of the '70s.

It wasn't just their politics (or their lack thereof) that made the students of the '80s seem like something out of the past. Many worrisome trends that kept getting worse all through the '60s and '70s started at last to decline in the '80s. Drug use. Teen pregnancy. Teen suicide.

One of the factors that is thought to be responsible for these trends is the size of the different cohorts—how many young people there are at a given time and what proportion of the population they make up. There have been enormous demographic changes in the United States over the past

Not all of tomorrow's children will know how to speak English when they enter school.

forty years. In 1955 the proportion of the population in the 15-to-24 age range was 3 percent. This proportion gradually went up, all during the '60s and '70s. It reached a high of 9 percent around 1978. Thus, in 1978 there were three times as many young people, relative to the entire population, as there were in 1955. Then the proportion of young people began to decline again. Demographic

in their relationships with their children, and that their children may be less well adjusted as a consequence (Baumrind, 1982).

In 1972, Edmund Muskie of Maine lost the Democratic nomination for president because he broke down and cried when a reporter said something nasty about his wife. In 1988, Michael Dukakis lost the presidential election, partly because he failed to show any emotion at all when a reporter asked him what he would do if someone raped and killed his wife. This has been interpreted as showing how much society has changed in 16 years: now it's okay for men to cry. But we don't think Dukakis would have gained any points by bursting into tears in response to the reporter's question. It's not that cultural sex roles have changed so much: it's just that we don't want (and probably never have wanted) extremes. A "real man" should neither be too soft and vulnerable nor too cold and mechanical. Neither should a "real woman." But that doesn't mean they should be exactly alike.

---

projections indicate that in 1995 it will once more hit 3 percent, and then it will begin another upward climb (Holinger, Offer, and Zola, 1988).

The changes in adolescent suicide rates over this period of time almost precisely mirror the increase in the proportionate size of the cohort. Similar trends have been noted in self-esteem. Adolescents had high self-esteem in the '60s. Their self-esteem went down in the '70s and came back up in the '80s. The adolescents of the '70s were, in general, the least well-adjusted of all these cohorts (Offer, Ostrov, and Howard, 1989).

Why should the size of the cohort (or its relative size, compared to the population) have this effect? Three explanations have been given. The first has to do with the increased competition for jobs, college admissions, places on athletic teams, and so on. Since the number of openings is limited, when there are more adolescents, more of them are deprived of these sources of gratification. A second explanation has been called "social contagion." The idea is that a large cohort of youth has more opportunity to develop its own youth culture, insulated from the influence of an older generation that is shrinking in demographic size and in importance. Third is the fact that the social controls and assistance normally provided by the older generation—by parents, teachers, the police, and so on—are overwhelmed by the sheer numbers of the youth they must deal with (Holinger and others, 1988).

But the size of the cohort is only one aspect of the sweeping changes our society has undergone since the '50s. Many other changes, which may prove to be far more important in the long run, have occurred and are occurring. Consider these facts:

- Of every 100 children born today, 12 will be born to unmarried mothers and 48 to parents who divorce, separate, or die before the child is 18. Only 40 will reach age 18 in an intact family (Otto, 1988).
- The average European-American woman gives birth to 1.7 children over the course of her lifetime. The average African-American woman gives birth to 2.4 children. The average Mexican-American woman gives birth to 2.9 children. By the year 2055, Americans of European descent will be in the minority. The population group that is increasing most rapidly is the Asian Americans—not due to high birth rates, but to immigration (Otto, 1988; Henry, 1990).

Tomorrow's children will not come home to a mother wearing an apron and holding a plate of freshly baked cookies. They will go to a day-care center after school and then home to a family that might consist of just a mother, or just a father, or a mother and a father, or a mother and a stepfather. They might share their home with an assortment of siblings, stepsiblings, and half-siblings. They might speak English, Spanish, or any one of a number of languages. Their mother's face might be white, black, or any shade in between.

What will tomorrow's children be like? We'll have to wait and see.

Summary

1. In simpler times and in simpler societies, the transition to adulthood came sooner and was clearly marked. Now the transition is long and blurry.

2. Going away to college is, for some young people, an important step in the transition to adulthood. But the assumption of full adult responsibilities comes gradually.

3. Emotional closeness to parents decreases during high school and then increases again during the college years. Detachment from parents is not seen as a necessary part of becoming an adult.

4. According to Erikson, the major issue of adolescence is identity versus role confusion. To attain a sense of identity, young people must decide what sort of people they are and what they want to do with their lives.

5. Marcia believes that most people go through an **identity crisis**—a period of exploration and uncertainty. He defines four levels of **identity status**: (1) Young people in **foreclosure** status have made a commitment without going through a period of exploration. (2) Those in **diffusion** status have neither made a commitment nor done any exploring of alternatives. (3) Those in the **moratorium** status are involved in the identity crisis and are experiencing a period of uncertainty. (4) Those who have reached **identity achievement** have been through the period of exploration and have made their commitments.

6. Youth is the time for political activism. As young people mature, their involvement with political or philosophical beliefs typically gives way to personal concerns.

7. Self-esteem goes steadily upward during the years from 13 to 23. Young adults are increasing able to judge themselves by their own personal standards, rather than those of others. They worry less about what their peers might think of them.

8. Suicide is rare in childhood, uncommon in adolescence, and most common in old age. Teenagers who kill themselves are usually white males; substance abuse and/ or depression are often involved. Most suicide victims use guns. Females who attempt suicide usually use drugs; most survive.

9. According to Erikson, what young adults want from a relationship is **intimacy.** College students believe that trust, openness, sharing, and sex are important aspects of intimate relationships.

10. Although a couple who are going together don't have the same degree of commitment as a married couple, infidelity is not permitted. Fidelity tends to increase as people get older.

11. Living together is now quite common. Over the course of five years of living together, a couple's relationship changes. For all types of couples, the most difficult period tends to be years 2 and 3.

12. People are waiting longer to get married now. When they do marry, they usually choose someone who's similar to themselves. This is called **assortative mating.**

13. Women tend to prefer men who they think will be good providers; men tend to prefer women who they think are good-looking. According to the sociobiologists, this makes evolutionary sense.

14. People who marry in their teens are more likely to get divorced and less likely to lead successful adult lives, even if they don't have children. The phrase **lost-adolescence syndrome** is used to describe what happens when someone marries the first person he or she falls in love with.

15. Some couples put off having a child because they fear that childrearing will interfere with the wife's career (not the husband's!). When a couple does have a child, their marital satisfaction tends to decline.

16. Marriage appears to confer more benefits on a man than on a woman. The division of household tasks remains about the same today as it was in the past.

17. Children perceive no limits on their choice of a career. Later they become more realistic.

18. Temperament and personality affect both occupational choice and satisfaction with the chosen occupation. When people consider an occupation, they compare the image they have of themselves with their stereotype of people who hold that job. If the match is poor, they don't consider that job.

19. A person's adult occupation depends on the quantity and quality of his education, which depends on how well he does in high school and on his family's socioeconomic status.

20. About 15 percent of high school students become dropouts; the rate is higher for some minority groups, especially in big-city schools. Low academic achievement is the main reason for dropping out.

21. Although upward mobility is the rule in the U.S., only 2 percent of the sons of manual laborers, and 5 percent of their grandsons, make it into the ranks of upper-middle-class professionals. Upward mobility is harder to attain for women.

22. Women still tend to get less education than men; they are also less likely to major in subjects such as math, engineering, physics, and computer science. Although many girls now say they want to become doctors or lawyers, most still choose female-dominated occupations.

23. A woman may decide not to go into a male-dominated profession because it doesn't fit in with her view of herself or her plans for the future, or because she doesn't think she would enjoy doing that kind of work. Males and females have different, but equally important, goals for their lives.

24. Women worry about reconciling their career and personal goals; men tend to "compartmentalize" them. Successful men usually have a single-minded attitude toward their work—a quality that makes them attractive to women before marriage but that can cause problems later on.

25. Fear of success is Horner's term for a woman's feelings of ambivalence about being successful. A bright woman may be caught in a "double bind"—she doesn't want to fail, but fears that people (especially males) won't like her if she succeeds. Horner says that women are now "allowed" to be more successful, but they are still "required" to live up to the traditional gender roles of wife and mother.

26. The modern version of fear of success: girls no longer refrain from succeeding; instead they explain away their successes by saying they were just due to luck. They do this, however, only in certain areas, such as math.

27. Gender differences tend to be small, except at the extremes of a distribution. However, some gender differences are large: size, strength, aggressiveness, and visual–spatial ability. All these are probably biological in origin.

28. In every human society, hunting and waging war are assigned to males; childrearing is assigned to females.

29. Women and men are becoming more alike—that is, both sexes are becoming more androgynous. Is this a good thing? Yes, in many ways it is. But children seem to do best if they have one female parent and one male parent.

30. The young people of the '70s differed from those of the '50s and the '80s partly because of the size of their **cohort.** During the years when their proportion of the population kept going up, adolescent pregnancy and suicide rates increased and self-esteem went down. Now all these trends have reversed.

31. Tomorrow's children are unlikely to grow up in what used to be thought of as the typical American family.

Key Terms

identity crisis
identity status
foreclosure
diffusion

moratorium
identity achievement
intimacy
assortative mating

lost-adolescence syndrome
serial marriage
fear of success
cohort

Glossary

accommodation. Piaget's term for the kind of adaptation that involves modifying a previously used action or idea to suit a new situation. See also *assimilation*.

achievement motivation. The drive to be successful, to do well, to attain high goals.

achievement status. Same as *identity achievement*.

acquired immune deficiency syndrome. See *AIDS*.

acting-out behavior. Rule-breaking, defiant, or aggressive behavior.

active effects. One of the ways that genetic effects can interact with, or disguise themselves as, environmental effects. Active effects occur because, as children get older, they are increasingly able to choose or modify their own environments according to their own interests and abilities (which are at least partly genetic). These effects usually have a vicious-circle quality, as when a bright child tends to spend his time reading books and an athletic one tends to spend her time engaged in sports. See also *reactive effects, passive effects*.

active sleep. A state of sleep in which the eyes can be seen moving beneath the closed lids, assumed (on the basis of work with adults) to be the state in which dreaming occurs. Also called REM sleep.

adaptation. In Piaget's view, the process of change that results from having to deal with, and adjust to, the environment.

ADD-H. See *attention deficit disorder with hyperactivity*.

adopted child. A child who, through the process of legal adoption, has become a permanent member of his or her adopted family. See also *foster child*.

AFP. See *alpha-fetoprotein test*.

agemates. Children of approximately the same age.

aggression. Physical or verbal acts directed against people, animals, or things, and performed with the intention of hurting, damaging, or destroying.

AIDS. Acquired immune deficiency syndrome. A serious disease caused by a virus, almost invariably fatal once the symptoms appear. It is transmitted through sexual contact, through exposure to infected blood, or from a mother to her child during pregnancy or delivery.

air crib. An enclosed area for a baby to sleep or play in, designed by Skinner. The air crib is provided with warm, filtered air.

alpha-fetoprotein test (AFP). A test done on a sample of a pregnant woman's blood. A high AFP level indicates that there is a possibility that the fetus may have a birth defect such as spina bifida; further tests are then required in order to check on this possibility.

altruism. The willingness to do something for others, possibly at inconvenience or danger to oneself, with no apparent selfish motive.

amblyopia. Poor vision in one eye that is not caused by anything wrong with the eye itself. Also called "lazy eye."

amniocentesis. A method used to check for birth defects in a developing fetus. A needle is inserted into the mother's uterus and some fluid, containing some of the fetus's cells, is withdrawn. The cells are then grown in a culture medium and examined.

amnion. The protective, fluid-filled sac that encloses the developing baby during the prenatal period.

amniotic fluid. The watery fluid contained in the amnion, in which the developing embryo or fetus floats during prenatal development.

anal stage. In Freudian theory, the second stage of development, lasting from around age 1½ to 3. Pleasurable sensations are assumed to be focused on the anus.

androgens. The male sex hormones—a group of several closely related biochemical substances, present in the bodies of males in very small amounts and in the bodies of females in even smaller amounts. The most important of the androgens is testosterone, secreted by the testicles. Testosterone is responsible for male secondary sex characteristics such as beard growth.

androgynous. Having both masculine and feminine characteristics.

androgyny. The state or quality of having both masculine and feminine characteristics.

animism. The belief that inanimate objects (especially anything that moves by itself, such as a fire or a rolling ball) are alive.

anorectic. A person suffering from anorexia nervosa.

anorexia nervosa. An eating disorder (usually just called anorexia) most commonly found in female adolescents and young adults. A person with this disorder restricts her food intake to the point where she may be in danger of starving to death.

anoxia. The physical effects that occur when an organism does not get enough oxygen.

antibodies. Biochemical substances produced by the body's immune system, which attack foreign cells or proteins that enter the body. A woman with Rh negative blood may produce antibodies that attack the red blood cells of her fetus.

antisocial behavior. A term applied to behavior that is contrary to the rules of our society—e.g., harming people or property, lying, stealing, truancy, or drug abuse.

anxiety disorder. Excess nervousness or fearfulness, or symptoms (e.g., refusal to go to school, night terrors, mysterious stomach aches) that are thought to result from nervousness or fearfulness. Anxiety disorders are very common in children; most children outgrow them without treatment.

Apgar test. A test routinely used to assess the physical condition of newborn babies, given one minute and five minutes after birth.

argot. The characteristic vocabulary of slang words used by a particular group of people, such as teenagers, often as a way of excluding outsiders.

artificial insemination. A method of conception in which sperm from a man is injected with a syringe into a woman's cervix.

artificialism. Piaget's term for the belief that certain aspects of the natural environment were manufactured by people. A young child might believe that a river was filled with water from a hose or that babies are made in a factory.

assimilation. Piaget's term for the kind of adaptation that involves applying an already known action or idea to a new object or situation. See also *accommodation*.

associative play. A type of interactive play that involves two or more children doing the same thing and doing it together, but with no attempt to organize the activity or to take turns.

assortative mating. Refers to the fact that the members of the human species do not pair up at random—they tend to marry or have children with someone similar to themselves.

attachment. The bond of affection and dependency felt by a child for another person (usually a parent), which makes the child want to be near that person and turn to her for comfort in times of stress.

attention deficit disorder with hyperactivity (ADD-H). Children with this disorder can't sit still and are highly distractible—they can't keep their attention focused on anything for long.

attributions. The beliefs one holds about one's successes and failures in life. For example, one might attribute one's successes to talent and one's failures to bad luck, or vice versa.

auditory stimulus. Something that can be heard, a sound. See *stimulus*.

authoritarian. Baumrind's term for the parenting style that emphasizes strict enforcement of rules. Authoritarian parents view obedience as a virtue; their children are expected to do as they're told without argument.

authoritative. Baumrind's term for the parenting style that uses firm enforcement of rules but allows verbal give-and-take between parents and children. Authoritative parents listen to their children's objections but retain the right to make the final decision; their children are encouraged to be independent.

autism. A serious psychiatric disorder that is usually detected in late infancy or early childhood but is probably present from birth. Children with this disorder fail to form attachments to people, have speech and language difficulties, and tend to become upset if any change is made in their environment.

autistic. Having or characterized by autism.

automatization. The tendency for mental processes to require less effort and less attention as children get older, and to be carried out more rapidly and efficiently, as a result of practice.

autonomy. Independence, self-determination. The ability to decide for oneself what one is going to do.

avoidant. The way some toddlers react in the Strange Situation:

when the mother returns, the child ignores her. Children who behave in this way are judged insecurely attached to their mothers.

Babinski reflex. One of the reflexes of the newborn baby: when the sole of the foot is stroked, the big toe sticks up and the other toes fan outward.

basic trust. In Erikson's theory, babies in the first 18 months of life develop basic trust if they come to feel that their parents can be relied on to meet their needs.

behavior modification. Using operant conditioning techniques (reinforcement and punishment) to change a person's behavior.

behaviorism. The school of psychology that concerns itself with observable behavior, rather than "inner" things such as thoughts and feelings. Behaviorists stress the importance of the environment (and generally ignore hereditary factors) and study how organisms learn as a result of their experiences.

bell-shaped curve. Same as *normal curve*.

bilateral coordination. The coordinated use of the two sides of the body in some skill—e.g., using the two legs in alternation in walking, or using the two hands together to tie a bow.

binge-purge syndrome. The practice of eating huge quantities of high-calorie food and then using self-induced vomiting or laxatives to get rid of it. This practice is characteristic of bulimia, but it is also found in many anorectics.

binocular cells. Specialized neurons in the brain that receive inputs from both eyes and that are responsible for stereoscopic vision.

biological parents. The man and woman whose genes a child carries. In the case of an adopted child, the biological parents are the woman who gave birth to the child and the man with whom she conceived the child.

biological retardation. Same as *organic retardation*.

birth mother. (1) Same as biological mother. (2) In the case of a child conceived by in vitro fertilization, the term birth mother would refer to the woman in whose uterus the child developed, whether or not it was her egg that was used in the conception.

birthing center. A part of a hospital or a separate facility in which a woman can give birth to her baby in a relaxed, homelike atmosphere.

birthing chair. A chair constructed for use in childbirth, in which a woman can sit more or less upright during labor and delivery.

blastula. The hollow ball of cells formed in the first few days of prenatal development.

bonding. The process by which a mother becomes attached to her baby.

Braxton–Hicks contractions. Irregular contractions of the uterus, usually painless, that occur during the last month or so of pregnancy.

breech birth. The delivery of a baby feet or buttocks first.

bulimia. An eating disorder most commonly found in female adolescents and young adults. The bulimic gorges herself on high-calorie food and then purges herself of it with self-induced vomiting or laxatives.

cardinality principle. The knowledge that, in counting objects, the last number spoken represents some property of the entire set and is not simply a name for the last thing you counted.

cardinality rule. The knowledge that, in counting objects, the last number spoken is the answer to the question, "How many are there?"

carrier. An individual who does not have a particular recessive trait but whose chromosomes carry a gene for that trait. Thus, the carrier can pass on the trait to his or her descendants.

case study. A descriptive study that usually involves only a single subject—often one who is unusual or particularly interesting in some way.

castration. (1) Surgical removal of the testicles from a male animal or human. (2) In psychoanalytic theory, amputation of the penis. Freud said that boys in the phallic stage have an unconscious fear of castration.

categorization. A metacognitive technique for remembering a list of items by grouping the items into categories.

center. To focus one's thought or attention on a single aspect of a situation.

central nervous system. The brain and the spinal cord.

cephalocaudal. Literally, head to tail. Refers to growth or development that begins at the top and works its way down.

cervix. The entrance to the uterus, through which the baby passes during birth.

cesarean. The delivery of a baby through a surgical incision made in the mother's abdominal wall and the wall of the uterus. Also called C-section.

childhood schizophrenia. A serious mental illness that is very rare (the adult form is much more common). The symptoms of childhood schizophrenia are similar to those of the adult form: delusions and hallucinations, peculiar behavior, distorted thinking, and emotional responses that are either inappropriate or absent.

chorionic villus sampling. A method for testing a fetus for birth defects. This method can be performed earlier in pregnancy than amniocentesis and gives quicker results.

chromosomes. Large collections of genes strung together in a particular order. Every normal human cell (with the exception of egg and sperm cells) has 46 chromosomes.

circular reaction. Piaget's term for the repeated performance of an action that was first performed at random. The action is repeated because of the interesting or pleasant results it produces.

class inclusion problem. A question (e.g., "Are there more roses or more flowers?") that cannot be answered correctly without some understanding of the fact that classes of things can include other classes (the class of flowers includes roses). Preschoolers answer such questions incorrectly because they have trouble with the idea that two different words (*flower* and *rose*) can be used for the same thing.

classical conditioning. The linking of a simple, automatic, inborn response to a neutral stimulus, by pairing the neutral stimulus with a stimulus that already evokes the response. The response is conditioned when the neutral stimulus alone is able to evoke the response.

cognition. The use of the mind for activities such as thinking, reasoning, understanding, learning, and remembering.

cognitive development. The development of the capacity to think, to reason, to understand, and so on.

cohort. A group of people all born at about the same time. A cohort of children born in 1985 will differ, in some ways, from a cohort born in 1980, because they were born into different worlds.

conception. The uniting of a sperm with an egg (ovum) to form a fertilized egg, capable of developing into a baby.

concrete operations, period of. In Piagetian theory, the period of cognitive development that begins around age 7 and ends around 11. During this period children can consider several aspects of a situation at once, but their understanding is tied to real (concrete) objects and events.

condition. To use the principles of either classical conditioning or operant conditioning to train an organism to make a particular response. See *classical conditioning, operant conditioning.*

conditioned fear. Fear that can be evoked by a previously neutral stimulus, as a result of that stimulus having been paired with a stimulus that naturally produces fear (a technique of classical conditioning).

conditioning. See *classical conditioning, operant conditioning.*

conduct disorder. Conduct-disordered children break rules (at home and elsewhere), defy adult authority, and constantly get into trouble. Many are aggressive; some are hyperactive. This is a chronic form of *acting-out behavior.*

conservation. The principle that certain qualities, such as the volume of a given amount of liquid or the number of objects in a given set, do not change just because they are put into a different container or arranged differently. According to Piaget, preschoolers lack the concept of conservation; older children have acquired it.

constancy. See *sex constancy, shape constancy, size constancy.*

contingent. Dependent on. For instance, if a parent makes a particular response whenever a child performs a certain action, the parent's response is contingent on the child's action.

contrast effect. The tendency for twins or siblings to become less alike as they get older, due to their own efforts to carve out distinct personalities and to the fact that other family members tend to "typecast" them in contrasting ways.

controlled. A term applied to a factor that is held constant (not varied) in an experiment, so that the effects of another factor, which is varied, can be measured.

conventional moral reasoning. Kohlberg's term for a form of moral reasoning that focuses on upholding society's rules.

cooperative play. A type of interactive play in which two or more children cooperate in an activity—e.g., any kind of game involving rules or taking turns.

cooperative pretend play. Cooperative play based on imagination—e.g., "playing house."

correlated. Two sets of measurements are said to be correlated when our knowledge of one set enables us to predict, with some amount of accuracy, the second set of measurements.

correlation. See *positive correlation, negative correlation.*

correlational study. A study designed to examine the relationship between two (or more) sets of measurements. Often, one set of measurements is presumed to be the "cause" and another set is presumed to be the "effect," but the existence of a correlation actually tells us nothing about causes and effects.

cortex. The outer layer of the brain. In humans, this heavily wrinkled layer controls the functions that distinguish us from other animals—the ability to use language, to think, to make plans, and so on.

critical period. A period during which some aspect of development must occur, if it is to occur at all. See also *sensitive period.*

cross the placenta. To be transmitted from the bloodstream of a pregnant woman to that of her embryo or fetus, by way of the placenta. Many drugs (including alcohol), viruses, and antibodies can be transmitted from mother to unborn child in this way.

cross-sectional study. A method of studying developmental changes by using subjects of different ages. See also *longitudinal study.*

cuddler. A baby or child who likes to be held and hugged.

cultural-familial retardation. A form of retardation, almost always mild, that is not due to brain damage or to genetic or chromosomal defects. It tends to run in families.

culture. The traditions, beliefs, behaviors, values, and language shared by the members of a society.

decenter. To consider more than one aspect of a situation at the same time.

deferred imitation. The imitation of remembered actions—actions seen or heard at some time in the past.

delay of gratification. Waiting for a better reward, instead of going for an immediate but smaller reward. Resisting the temptation of immediate gratification.

delinquency. A term applied to illegal acts committed by juveniles, people under 16 or 18 years of age. The age cutoff varies by state and also may vary depending on the nature of the illegal act.

depression. A period of sadness and, in most cases, listlessness, during which all the joy goes out of life.

depressive disorder. A psychiatric disorder characterized by repeated periods of depression, alternating either with normal periods (unipolar depressive disorder) or with periods of high elation and energy (bipolar depressive disorder, formerly called manic-depressive disorder).

depth perception. The ability to see the world in three dimensions. Stereoscopic vision is one way of doing this, but there are other cues to depth: the projective size of objects, the fact that nearer objects block our view of farther ones, and the visual changes that occur when we move around.

DES. Diethylstilbestrol, a synthetic hormone used in the past to prevent miscarriages, that is now known to produce abnormalities of the reproductive system in young women whose mothers received the drug during pregnancy.

development. The process that turns babies into children, children into adolescents, and adolescents into adults. The physical, mental, and behavioral changes that take place over the course of time and that are more or less irreversible and universal.

differentiation. The process that occurs during prenatal development when the cells of the blastula become specialized and begin developing into different organs and body parts.

diffusion. Marcia's term for the identity status of people who have neither gone through an identity crisis nor made any commitments to goals or beliefs.

dilation. The first stage of labor, involving the widening of the opening of the cervix.

disadvantaged. Families or homes are referred to as disadvantaged when they are headed by individuals who are employed in unskilled, low-paying jobs or who are unemployed.

discipline. See *power-assertive discipline, induction.*

discrimination task. An experimental situation in which the subject must learn to select the "correct" stimulus from two or more stimuli or classes of stimuli.

displaced. In Freudian theory, a displaced drive is one that is repressed because it is socially or psychologically unacceptable, and that reemerges in a different form or directed toward a different target.

displaced aggression. In Freudian theory, an aggressive urge that is directed toward a substitute person or even toward an animal, because its original target was a forbidden one.

divergent thinking. Creative thinking; thinking that is off the beaten track. Children who are good at divergent thinking come up with unusual answers to questions.

dizygotic twins. Twins who developed from two separate eggs, each fertilized by a different sperm. Also known as *fraternal twins.*

DNA. Deoxyribonucleic acid, the protein of which genes are composed.

doctrine of innate ideas. The belief that babies are born with their minds already furnished with the knowledge of such things as Truth, Beauty, and God.

dominant trait. A trait that will show up in an offspring if the offspring inherits a single gene for that trait. Unless it's a mutation, a dominant trait can be inherited only from a parent who has that trait. See also *recessive trait.*

Down syndrome. Also called Down's syndrome; formerly known as mongolism. A birth defect, caused by an extra twenty-first chromosome, that produces mental retardation and a variety of distinctive physical characteristics.

drive. As used by Freud, a powerful instinctive desire.

dyslexia. Reading disability. The inability to learn how to read (or to read well) despite having normal intelligence and normal physical and emotional health. This term is also applied to the *loss* of the ability to read, due to brain damage.

dyslexic. Having or characterized by dyslexia.

educable mentally retarded. A term used to refer to an individual who is mildly retarded (IQ in the 55 to 69 range). The majority of mentally retarded people fall into this category. Most learn to read and write; few are ever institutionalized.

ego. According to Freud, one of the three aspects of the human mind. The ego is the thinking, rational part.

ego growth. In Erikson's theory, the development of the personality, which includes the growth of autonomy, initiative, competence, and so on.

ego integrity. In Erikson's view, what older people have achieved if they can look back on their lives and feel that it was worthwhile and that they did all right.

egocentric. In Piaget's view, a characteristic of the thought of preschool children: the inability to see things from someone else's point of view.

elaboration. A metacognitive technique used to help in remembering something. Verbal ideas or visual images are thought up as memory aids, usually as a way of linking two things together in memory.

Electra conflict. In Freudian theory, the female version of the Oedipal conflict. The phallic-stage girl is assumed to desire her father and have aggressive feelings toward her mother.

embryo. The developing human from two weeks to two months after conception.

empathy. The tendency to feel sad when another person is hurt or distressed, and to feel pleased when another person is happy. The ability to share in other people's feelings.

EMR. Same as *educable mentally retarded.*

encoding. Perceiving, noticing, or identifying something (such as a specific stimulus, a particular aspect of a scene, or a particular word or sentence); taking it into one's thoughts or memories.

environment. Any aspects of the world that a child experiences in any way, or that can affect the child in any way, are part of that child's environment.

error of measurement. The difference between the score a person obtained on a particular test and his or her "true" score. The person's health and state of mind on the day of the test, errors made in administering or scoring the test, and other chance factors all contribute to error of measurement.

estrogens. The female sex hormones—a group of several closely related biochemical substances, present in the bodies of females in very small amounts and in the bodies of males in even smaller amounts. Estrogens are responsible for female secondary sex characteristics such as breast development.

ethological approach. A view that links human behavior to species-specific behavior in animals. For example, attachment in human babies is seen as being similar to imprinting in ducklings; these behaviors are assumed to be inherited because of their survival value.

ethology. A subfield of biology that focuses on the behavior of animals in their natural environment, with particular emphasis on species-specific behavior (instincts).

evocative effects. See *reactive effects*.

experimental method. A method for carrying out research that involves doing something—e.g., treating a group of subjects in a particular way—and observing the results. Typically, that group of subjects is compared with a control group who did not receive the treatment.

expressive jargon. A kind of "pretend speech" that some babies produce shortly before they begin to speak in earnest. It has the rhythms and expressions of real speech but is unintelligible.

external locus of control. The feeling that one has little or no control over the events in one's life. People who have an external locus of control attribute their successes and failures to luck or to the attitudes and actions of other people. See also *internal locus of control*.

extinction. In operant conditioning, the process that occurs when a response is no longer reinforced: it eventually stops being made.

extinguish. To withhold reinforcement, so that a previously reinforced response becomes less and less likely to be made again.

extrinsic motivation. The inclination to do something not because one wants to do it for its own sake, but because of the reward that one will get for doing it or the punishment that will occur if one doesn't. See also *intrinsic motivation*.

extrovert. A person who seeks and enjoys interactions with other people.

eye contact. What occurs when two people look at each other's eyes.

eye–hand coordination. The ability to use information obtained through vision (visual feedback) to guide a sequence of hand movements.

Fallopian tubes. The tubelike structures that extend from the uterus to the ovaries. Conception normally takes place in the Fallopian tubes.

fast mapping. The way young children quickly acquire an approximate understanding of a new word by narrowing down its possible meanings. One way they do this is by assuming that words are used in a mutually exclusive manner, so if they already have a word for an object, they assume that the new word can't refer to that object.

fear of success. Horner's term for the concern of some young women that academic or professional success might lead to unfavorable social or personal consequences.

fetal alcohol syndrome. A group of characteristic physical and mental abnormalities sometimes found in the babies of alcoholic women.

fetus. The developing human from two months after conception to birth.

fine-muscle skills. Same as *small-muscle skills*.

fixate. To point the eyes at something; to look at something without moving the eyes.

fixated. In Freudian theory, if things do not go well during some stage of development, the individual may become fixated, or "stuck," at that stage.

forceps delivery. The use of tongs, shaped to fit around a baby's head, to speed the birth of a baby.

foreclosure. Marcia's term for the identity status of people who have made commitments to goals or beliefs without going through an identity crisis, and thus without really exploring the alternatives.

formal operations, period of. In Piagetian theory, the period of cognitive development that begins around age 11. It is characterized by the ability to reason abstractly, to distinguish between what is real and what is possible, and to test alternative solutions to a problem in a systematic way.

foster child. A child who is living temporarily in a foster home, either because a permanent adoptive home has not yet been found or because the biological parents have not released the child for adoption.

fraternal twins. Twins who developed from two separate eggs, each fertilized by a different sperm. Genetically, they are no more alike than siblings born separately. Also known as *dizygotic twins*.

fussing. One of the states of a newborn baby. The baby whimpers occasionally and there are irritable movements of the face and body. This state usually precedes full-blown crying.

gender difference. A statistically significant difference, found in one study or in many studies, between males' and females' scores on some measurement.

gender identity. A person's knowledge that he is male or that she is female, and the acceptance of that knowledge.

gender roles. Same as *sex roles*.

gender stereotypes. Same as *sex stereotypes*.

genes. The biological units of heredity, composed of DNA.

genetic characteristics. Characteristics carried by the genes. Inherited characteristics.

genital herpes. See *herpes*.

genital stage. In Freudian theory, the stage of development that begins at adolescence and involves the reemergence of sexual feelings.

"gentle birth." Same as *Leboyer method*.

germinal stage. The first two weeks of prenatal development, beginning at conception.

gestation, period of. Same as *prenatal period*.

gestational age. The chronological age of an embryo or fetus, dating from its conception.

glial cell. A kind of cell, not a neuron, that is found in the brain. The function of glial cells is to support and nourish the neurons.

grammatical morphemes. Words such as *in, on, is, are,* or *the,* and suffixes such as *-ing, -ed,* or *-s,* that tie together the other morphemes in a sentence and indicate how they are being used.

grasp reflex. One of the reflexes of the newborn baby: when a narrow object (such as a stick or an adult's finger) is placed in the baby's palm, her fingers close tightly around it.

gross-muscle skills. Same as *large-muscle skills*.

habituate. To cease to respond to a stimulus after repeated or prolonged exposure to it, because it no longer arouses attention or interest.

habituation technique. Used as a method for studying infant perception or intelligence. The baby is habituated to one stimulus. If she then responds to a new stimulus, it is presumed that she can tell the old one and the new one apart.

hand–eye coordination. Same as *eye–hand coordination.*

heredity. A term used to refer to inherited or genetic characteristics, carried by the genes.

heritability. The proportion of the variation of a given trait, within a given population, that can be attributed to genetic factors.

herpes. A family of viruses that are widespread in the human population; most have no serious effects on adults. Two varieties can cause problems for the fetus of an infected mother: genital herpes, a sexually transmitted disease that can infect a baby during its passage through the vagina; and cytomegalovirus, which on rare occasion causes complications during prenatal development.

HIV virus. Short for human immunodeficiency virus, the virus that causes AIDS.

homophobia. Fear or dislike of homosexuals.

hormones. Biochemical substances that are found in the blood in very small amounts and that influence the functioning of various body systems.

hyperactivity. A tendency to be extremely active; the inability to sit still. See *attention deficit disorder with hyperactivity.*

hysterical symptom. One that is due to psychological causes rather than to anything physically wrong.

id. According to Freud, one of the three aspects of the human mind. The id is present from birth and is the home of powerful instinctive desires such as hunger, thirst, and the sexual urge.

identical twins. Twins who developed from a single fertilized eggs, so they have exactly the same genes. Also known as *monozygotic twins.*

identify. To take on another person's values, beliefs, and behaviors. In Freudian theory, when the Oedipal or Electra conflicts are resolved, the child identifies with the same-sex parent.

identity achievement. Marcia's term for the identity status of people who have been through the identity crisis and have made some important decisions regarding their goals in life and what they believe in.

identity confusion. Erikson's term for the feelings of uncertainty and anxiety that the adolescent experiences if he or she has not yet established a firm sense of identity. Also called role confusion.

identity crisis. Erikson's term for the adolescent's search for identity. Marcia uses this expression to refer to a period of uncertainty during which young people engage in an intense exploration of their beliefs and goals.

identity formation. The gradual process, not completed before late adolescence (and sometimes not even then), of developing a firm sense of what sort of person one is and what one wishes to become. The acquisition of self-knowledge and self-understanding.

identity status. Marcia's term for the level of identity formation an adolescent has attained. See *identity achievement, diffusion, foreclosure,* and *moratorium.*

imaginary audience. A term used by Elkind to explain adolescents' self-consciousness, preoccupation with themselves, and tendency to show off. According to this view, adolescents feel that they are constantly being observed and evaluated by other people (the imaginary audience).

imprinting. A quick form of attachment by which birds such as ducklings learn to follow the first moving thing they see after they hatch—in most cases, their mother.

impulsive. Kagan's term for children who respond quickly on the Matching Familiar Figures Test and who make a lot of errors. These children are not necessarily impulsive in the usual sense—that is, they are not necessarily the same children who behave in a disruptive manner or who can't delay gratification. See also *reflective.*

inbred. A term applied to an animal that is the product of a number of generations of inbreeding—that is, of mating animals with their close relatives, such as siblings. Many generations of inbreeding produce animals that are very similar to one another in genetic makeup.

induction. Explaining to a child the reasons and justifications for behaving in a particular way (or for not behaving in a particular way).

infancy. The period of development that starts at birth and ends when the infant becomes a toddler—when he or she begins to use walking as the chief means of getting from one place to another.

infantile autism. Same as *autism.*

information processing. Perceiving, selecting, identifying, and storing information that comes in through the senses. The information generally consists of visual and auditory stimuli.

information-processing approach. A view of cognitive development that depicts the mind as a set of components that work by following a list of rules or instructions, like a computer program. The components send outputs to each other and receive inputs from each other and from the outside world. The inputs from the outside world are the information that must be processed.

insecurely attached. A description of the quality of a toddler's relationship with another person, generally a parent. A child who is insecurely attached to his mother will not greet her enthusiastically after being separated from her in the Strange Situation. See *avoidant, resistant.*

instinct. An inborn pattern of behavior, nowadays more often called species-specific behavior.

intellectual realism. A tendency, often found in preschoolers, to respond on the basis of reality when they're asked to respond in terms of appearance. For example, preschoolers will deny that a rock in the shape and color of an egg looks like an egg—they will insist it looks like a rock. See also *phenomenism.*

intelligence quotient. Mental age divided by chronological (calendar) age, multiplied by 100 to get rid of the decimal point. Same as *IQ.*

intermodal perception. A perceptual linkup between two different senses, usually vision and hearing. The ability to coordinate a certain visual stimulus, for example, with a certain auditory stimulus.

internal locus of control. The feeling of being in control of what happens in one's life. People who have an internal locus of control believe that they are responsible for their own successes and failures. See also *external locus of control.*

internalize. To take on someone else's values or standards of behavior as one's own; to believe in them.

intimacy. Erikson uses this term to mean commitment to a particular person—the development of a close, open, and trusting relationship with that person.

intrinsic motivation. The inclination to do something because one enjoys doing it and finds it interesting or gratifying, and not because of any reward that one will get for doing it. See also *extrinsic motivation.*

introvert. A person who tends to avoid interactions with others and who often prefers to be alone.

in vitro fertilization. Conception in a glass dish. One or more eggs taken surgically from a woman's body are combined in a dish with a man's sperm. A fertilized egg can then be injected into the uterus of the woman from whom the egg was taken, or into that of a different woman.

IQ. An abbreviation of intelligence quotient. Nowadays a child's IQ is calculated, not by dividing mental age by chronological age, but by comparing the child's performance on an IQ test with that of other children of the same age. The IQ score is presumed to be an approximate indication of intellectual ability.

karyotyping. A method used to check for chromosomal abnormalities. A cell nucleus is photographed under a microscope, and the pictures of the individual chromosomes are cut out of the photograph and sorted out.

kinesthesis. The sense that tells us which way the parts of our body are moving, and how fast and how far, even when our eyes are closed.

Lamaze method. A method of "natural childbirth" developed by Fernand Lamaze. The pregnant woman and her husband are trained in breathing and relaxation techniques and use those techniques during labor and delivery.

lanugo. The fine, downy hair often seen on the face or body of newborn babies. It falls out after a few weeks.

large-muscle skills. Motor skills that depend mainly on the use of leg and arm muscles, rather than hand and finger muscles. Examples are running, jumping, and throwing a ball.

latency period. In Freudian theory, a period of development (roughly 5½ to 12 years) during which sexual impulses remain submerged.

lateralization. Specialization of the two sides—e.g., using the right and left sides of the brain, or the right and left hands, for different purposes.

learned helplessness. (1) The tendency for babies to give up hope eventually, if no one ever comes when they cry. They end up feeling that nothing they do makes any difference, so why bother? (2) In older children, a tendency (of unknown origin) to attribute one's successes to luck and one's failures to being "dumb" or "no good." Children with this pattern of attributions tend to give up when they meet obstacles.

learning disability. A disorder that a child is presumed to have if his performance in school is considerably below what you'd expect from his IQ, and if the poor performance is not due to emotional or motivational difficulties, or to serious sensory or motor disabilities.

learning goal. A child with a learning goal is motivated to become more competent and to understand or master something. See also *performance goal*.

Leboyer method. A technique, also known as "gentle birth," designed to make the first moments of life as peaceful and pleasant as possible for the newborn baby.

lightening. A feeling of relief from pressure on the stomach and diaphragm, and of being able to breath more easily, that occurs near the end of pregnancy when the fetus begins its head-first descent into the birth canal.

locus of control. See *internal locus of control, external locus of control*.

longitudinal study. A method of studying developmental changes by observing or testing a group of subjects repeatedly, over a period of time. See also *cross-sectional study*.

long-term memory. "Permanent" memory, capable of retaining information for an indefinite length of time. Information stored in long-term memory must first have been in short-term memory, but not all the information in short-term memory gets put into long-term memory.

lost-adolescence syndrome. A term used to describe the experiences of people who become romantically attached to someone quite early in life, who marry that person, and who later come to feel that they married too soon.

manic-depressive disorder. See *depressive disorder*.

mastery oriented. Tending to deal with difficulties by focusing on solving the problem, rather than worrying about the fact that one is having trouble with it. Mastery-oriented children tend to react to difficulties by working harder or by trying to figure out why they are having trouble, rather than by losing confidence and giving up.

mastery play. Same as *sensorimotor play*. A baby repeats an action she has already performed, for the pleasure of mastering it and of proving to herself that she can do it.

Matching Familiar Figures Test. A test devised by Kagan and his associates, used to classify children as impulsive or reflective. The task is to choose from a set of very similar pictures the one that exactly matches the picture on top.

maturation. Development—often physical or motor development—of a sort that is assumed to result from genetic preprogramming (the gradual carrying out of a plan determined by the genes), rather than from learning or experience.

mean. The average of a group of measurements, determined by adding them up and dividing by the number of measurements.

mean length of utterance (MLU). The average length of a child's utterances, measured at a given age. The length of an utterance is calculated by counting the number of words it contains and adding the number of grammatical suffixes such as *-ing, -ed*, and *-s*.

memory retrieval. The process (or the results of the process) of remembering something that was stored in long-term memory.

memory span. The number of items that can be held in short-term memory. Memory span increases from about three items at age 3 to six or seven items in adulthood.

menarche. A girl's first menstrual period. Pronounced muh-NAR-kee.

mental age. The level of a child's cognitive development in terms of intellectual abilities and knowledge. Children who are developing at an average rate have a mental age that is equal to their chronological age. Children who are intellectually advanced have a mental age that is ahead of their chronological age.

mental representations. See *representations*.

mental retardation. Below-normal intellectual capacity. A score below 70 on an IQ test, plus difficulties in managing the tasks of daily life, are the two criteria now used to define mental retardation.

metacognition. The application of a cognitive process such as thinking to another cognitive process (or the same one). Some examples are thinking about thinking, understanding your own learning processes, and knowing whether you are communicating successfully.

metacognitive strategy. A technique for improving one's performance in some cognitive activity by making use of knowledge or understanding about the cognitive activity itself. For example, rehearsal is a metacognitive strategy for remembering words or numbers.

middle childhood. The years from 6 to 12, which correspond roughly to the first through the seventh grades in school.

MLU. Same as *mean length of utterance*.

model. A person (e.g., an adult) who does something that another person (e.g., a child) might imitate.

modeling. What a model does. An action performed by a person, usually an adult, possibly with the idea that an observer (e.g., a child) may imitate that action. Sometimes this term is also used to refer to the act of imitating.

monozygotic twins. Twins who developed from a single fertilized egg and who have exactly the same genes. Same as *identical twins.*

moratorium. Marcia's term for the identity status of people who are currently involved in an identity crisis and who are in the process of making important decisions about their goals and beliefs. There is a moratorium (a period during which no action is taken) on making personal commitments.

Moro reflex. One of the reflexes of the newborn baby: in response to a loud noise or a sudden loss of support, the baby's arms are flung wildly outward and then quickly brought toward the chest again.

morpheme. The smallest unit of meaning in a spoken or written language. A word with no prefixes or suffixes is one morpheme, a word with a prefix or a suffix is two morphemes.

motherese. A description of the language mothers (and other adults) often use when speaking to toddlers: sentences are short, simple, and repetitive, and easy words are used in place of ones that toddlers find difficult to understand or to pronounce.

motor development. The development of the ability to move and coordinate the parts of the body, as in crawling, walking, and grasping things with the hands.

motor nerve. A nerve that carries neural signals from the brain or spinal cord to the muscles.

mutation. A change occurring in a gene, so that the instructions it contains are different from those it originally contained. Also, a characteristic produced by such a changed gene.

myelin. A fatty substance that coats neurons, acts as an insulator, and speeds the transmission of neural signals.

myelination. The process by which neurons in the nervous system are gradually coated with myelin. Myelination plays an important role in the physical maturation of the brain.

"natural childbirth." A method of childbirth in which the mother receives little or no medication, and uses exercises and breathing techniques to deal with the pain of labor contractions.

nature. When used with *nurture,* nature is another word for heredity.

nature–nurture issue. The debate about whether various characteristics are primarily inherited or primarily the result of environmental influences.

negative correlation. A mathematical relationship between two sets of measurements such that the high measurements in one set tend to be associated with the low measurements in the second set.

neglected children. When contrasted with *rejected children,* this term refers to children who aren't liked by their agemates, but who aren't disliked either. They are the "invisible" children that nobody notices.

neonate. A newborn human or animal baby.

nervous system. The brain, the spinal cord, and the sensory and motor nerves.

neuron. The basic cell of the nervous system, which carries information in the form of very weak electrical pulses.

nocturnal emission. The ejaculation of semen during sleep by a male adolescent or adult. It is often accompanied by a sexually arousing dream.

noncuddler. A baby or child who dislikes being held and hugged.

norm. A mean or average—generally one that is based on a large, representative sample of subjects.

normal curve. A bell-shaped distribution of measurements—a curve of a particular shape and mathematical description. In a normal curve, the majority of measurements are close to the mean; measurements that are much larger or smaller than the mean are rare.

normally distributed. A term applied to measurements that form a normal curve.

nuclear family. A family consisting of a mother, a father, and their biological children.

nurture. A term used to refer to the way a child is reared, or, when contrasted with *nature,* to refer to environment in general.

object permanence. In Piagetian theory, the concept that objects have a permanent existence in the world, even if they are not visible at the moment.

obsessive-compulsive disorder. People who have this psychiatric disorder feel the need to repeat certain actions over and over again—they may wash their hands repeatedly, or touch the doorposts a certain number of times before they feel free to enter a doorway.

Oedipal conflict. In Freudian theory, the struggle going on in the unconscious mind of the phallic-stage boy, between his desire for his mother and his fear of his father's wrath.

one-to-one correspondence rule. A rule that children must know in order to count a row of objects correctly: each number word must be assigned to one and only one object, and each object gets one and only one number word.

onlooker behavior. The child who is engaged in this kind of behavior simply watches other children at play, without participating. The adult equivalent is watching TV or athletic events.

operant conditioning. Skinner's term for the process that occurs when an organism is reinforced for making a particular response. When a response is reinforced, it is more likely to be made again.

oral stage. In Freudian theory, the first stage of development, lasting from birth to age 1 or 1½. Pleasurable sensations are assumed to be focused on the mouth, as in sucking.

order-irrelevance principle. A principle of numbers and counting: the order in which you count objects doesn't matter—the number will still be the same.

organic retardation. Mental retardation caused by something physically wrong with the brain, resulting from an injury or infection, or from a genetic or chromosomal defect such as Down syndrome.

organism. A person or an animal.

ovary. A small organ that contains eggs and produces hormones, found only in females. All normal females have a pair of ovaries; they develop early in the prenatal period.

overextension. The use of a word (usually by a toddler) to refer to a wider category of things than that word is usually used for. The word *moon* might be used for anything round, or *doggy* for any four-legged animal.

ovulate. To release an egg from an ovary. In human females, ovulation occurs about once every 28 days.

ovum. The egg of a mammal—a single cell, lacking a shell, that is just barely large enough to be seen without a magnifying glass.

pairing. In classical conditioning, the presenting of two stimuli simultaneously (or nearly simultaneously). Generally, a neutral stimulus is paired with one to which the organism has a built-in response.

parallel play. When two or more children play side by side at the same activity, paying little or no attention to each other.

partial reinforcement. Reinforcement of some responses but not all of them. A given response may be reinforced on an interval basis (e.g., once every three minutes) or on the basis of the number of responses made (every tenth response is reinforced).

passive effects. One of the ways that genetic effects can interact with, or disguise themselves as, environmental effects. Passive effects are resemblances between the parents' behavior and the child's behavior that appear to be the result of environmental influences but that are actually genetic—the child has inherited these characteristics from the parents. See also *active effects, reactive effects.*

peer group. The group of children of roughly the same age with whom a child interacts at school or elsewhere, and who are presumed to share common values, standards of behavior, and so on.

peers. A child's peers are other children of roughly the same age with whom he or she interacts in some way.

penis envy. In Freudian theory, a little girl's unconscious desire to have a penis.

performance goal. Children with a performance goal are motivated to attain praise or good grades and to avoid negative evaluations. They tend not to take on challenges unless they think they can do well at them. See also *learning goal.*

period of concrete operations. See *concrete operations, period of.*

period of formal operations. See *formal operations, period of.*

period of gestation. Same as *prenatal period.*

permissive. Baumrind's term for the parenting style that uses as few restrictions as possible. Permissive parents behave in a kind, accepting way toward their children and demand very little.

person permanence. The concept that people continue to exist even when they can't be seen or heard.

personal fable. A term used by Elkind to describe adolescents' belief in the uniqueness of their own feelings and their conviction that they are terribly important and therefore not subject to the risks and limitations of ordinary mortals.

phallic stage. In Freudian theory, the third stage of development, lasting from about age 3 to 5½, during which the Oedipal and Electra conflicts occur. Pleasurable sensations are assumed to be focused on the genitals.

phenomenism. A tendency, often found in preschoolers, to respond on the basis of appearance rather than reality. Their response to Piaget's conservation of liquid experiment is an example—the taller container of liquid *looks* as though it holds more, so they say it really does hold more. See also *intellectual realism.*

phobia. An irrational fear of something—a fear strong enough to interfere with one's day-to-day life.

phonics. The correspondences between the spoken sounds and the written letters of English (and of other languages that are written in alphabetic symbols). Children who are taught phonics learn to sound out written words.

PKU. Phenylketonuria, a genetic disorder carried by a recessive gene. PKU results in mental retardation unless the child is kept on a special diet starting in early infancy.

placenta. The organ, also known as the afterbirth, by which the embryo or fetus is attached to the wall of the uterus. Nutrients from the mother are transmitted to the developing child through the placenta.

plasticity. The quality of being flexible, capable of change. Used to refer to the fact that the structure of the nervous system is not entirely determined in advance, but can be influenced by what happens in the first months or years of life.

polygenic trait. A characteristic that is controlled by more than one pair of genes. Most polygenic traits are influenced by environmental factors as well as by heredity.

positive correlation. A mathematical relationship between two sets of measurements such that the high measurements in one set tend to be associated with the high measurements in the second set.

postconventional moral reasoning. Kohlberg's term for a form of moral reasoning that admits the possibility that some principles might be more important than upholding society's rules or laws.

postpartum depression. A period of weepiness and emotional ups-and-downs that affects some women in the first few days after childbirth. Occasionally it becomes a full-blown depression that can last for months.

power-assertive discipline. A form of discipline that consists of enforcing rules of behavior with threats and punishment.

preconventional moral reasoning. Kohlberg's term for a form of moral reasoning concerned only with the likelihood of success or failure, where failure consists of "getting caught."

predisposition. An inborn tendency to develop a certain trait, given the appropriate environmental conditions.

pre-eclampsia. A disorder of pregnancy, formerly called toxemia. Its symptoms are a rise in blood pressure, excess storage of fluids, and protein in the urine. If untreated, this condition can have serious consequences for mother and fetus.

preferential-looking technique. A method for testing infants' visual perception or memory. Two pictures (or other visual stimuli) are placed where the baby can see them, and the researcher records the amount of time the baby spends looking at each picture.

preformationism. The idea that a miniature adult is contained in the egg or sperm—a belief, dating from ancient times, that remained popular until the 1800s.

premature birth. Birth that occurs before prenatal development is complete—generally at least two or three weeks before the due date.

prenatal period. The period that begins at conception and ends at birth. In humans this period averages 266 days (38 weeks).

preoperational period. In Piagetian theory, the second major period of cognitive development—roughly from ages 2 to 7. The preoperational child, according to Piaget, can use mental representations but cannot see things from another's point of view and cannot decenter.

prepared. Having an innate tendency to learn something quickly.

preparedness. The inborn tendency of an organism to learn certain things very readily (e.g., to become afraid of spiders after only one or two mildly scary incidents) and to learn other things much less readily.

preschool period. The period of development that begins around age 2½ and ends when the child enters first grade, usually around age 6.

preschooler. A child who is no longer a toddler but who is too young to enter first grade.

pretend play. Play that involves imagination. A toddler may pretend to be asleep or to drink out of an empty cup; an older child may pretend that pebbles are food or that a carton is a space capsule.

primary sex characteristics. The male and female reproductive organs—the penis and testes in males; the ovaries, uterus, and vagina in females.

private speech. "Thinking out loud," common in the preschool period.

productive language. The words and grammatical constructions that a person uses in his or her speech or writing. See also *receptive language.*

projective size. The size of the image an object makes on the retina (the light-sensitive part of the eye), or the proportion of the visual field that the object takes up. The projective size of an object is smaller when the object is farther away. Its objective size (and, in general, its perceived size) does not change.

proprioception. The sense that keeps us informed of the positions (and locations in space) of the parts of our bodies, even when our eyes are closed.

prosocial behavior. Actions that benefit others—e.g., sharing, helping, or saying something nice to someone.

proximodistal. Literally, near to far. Used to describe growth or development that begins at the center of the body (i.e., the torso) and progresses outward toward the fingers and toes.

psychiatrist. A person who has been through medical school, earned an M.D. degree, and then gone on to study the disorders and disturbances of the human mind and personality. Most psychiatrists see patients and administer psychotherapy and/or drug therapy.

psychoanalysis. A method of psychotherapy devised by Freud and based on his theories. It is still in use today.

psychoanalytic theory. A theory of human personality and development, originated by Sigmund Freud, that stresses the importance of unconscious motivations, particularly those of a sexual nature.

psycholinguist. A person who studies the use or the development of language. Most psycholinguists have Ph.D. degrees.

psychologist. A person who studies human behavior or personality, especially the causes and treatments of psychological problems. Most psychologists have Ph.D. degrees; some administer psychotherapy. People who study the behavior of animals, or who study human development, cognition, or perception, usually use other terms to describe themselves—e.g., experimental psychologist, behaviorist, or developmental psychologist.

psychoprophylactic method. Same as *Lamaze method.*

psychosexual. A term applied to Freudian theory, acknowledging the important role that sexual drives play in this theory.

psychosocial. A term used to describe Erikson's theory (as opposed to Freud's, which is called psychosexual). Erikson puts more emphasis on social interactions, less on sexual matters.

psychotherapy. The treatment of emotional or personality problems by a psychologist or a psychiatrist, generally by means of conversation.

puberty. (1) The attainment of sexual maturity: in girls, menarche; in boys, the first production of live sperm. (2) The entire period of sexual development during early adolescence.

punishment. The administration of something unpleasant, such as a spanking or a reprimand, or the removal of something pleasant, such as the loss of a week's allowance or TV privileges. Punishment following a response usually makes that response less likely to occur again.

quiet alertness. One of the states of the newborn baby. The baby lies quietly but is fully alert, with eyes wide open and usually focused on something.

reaction formation. In Freudian theory, the process that occurs when an unacceptable impulse is repressed and the opposite kind of behavior emerges in its stead.

reactive effects. One of the ways that genetic effects can interact with, or disguise themselves as, environmental effects. Reactive effects occur as a result of the way people respond to a child's characteristics: the way they act toward a given child will be influenced by that child's behavior and appearance. Reactive effects can either increase (in vicious-circle fashion) or decrease a child's inherited characteristics. See also *active effects, passive effects.*

recall. When contrasted with *recognition,* a memory test that involves retrieving an item of information from long-term memory—e.g., remembering someone's name or a telephone number.

receptive language. The words and grammatical constructions that a person can understand when he or she hears them (or sees them) in the speech (or writing) of others. See also *productive language.*

recessive trait. A trait that will not show up in an individual unless he or she inherits two genes for that trait, one from each parent. An individual who inherits only one gene for a recessive trait will not have the trait but will be a carrier.

recognition. When contrasted with *recall,* a memory test that involves only a decision about whether a given stimulus is or isn't the correct one, or whether it has or hasn't been seen (or heard) before.

reflective. Kagan's term for children who respond slowly on the Matching Familiar Figures Test and who make few errors. Reflective children tend to have above-average IQs and to do well in school. See also *impulsive.*

reflex. A simple, automatic response to a stimulus; one that is wired into the nervous system.

rehearsal. A method for remembering something (e.g., a number or a list of words) by saying it over and over to oneself.

reinforce. To reward a particular response.

reinforcement. The presentation of a reinforcer to an organism.

reinforcer. Anything that an organism is willing to work for: food (for a hungry organism), water (for a thirsty one), or a kind word or a pat on the head (for a child or a dog).

rejected children. In contrast to *neglected* children, these are children whose peers actively dislike them.

reliability. A test is said to have reliability when a child who takes it on Friday makes roughly the same score that she would have made if she had taken it on Monday. A reliable test is one that is not very much affected by chance factors or day-to-day variations.

REM sleep. Rapid-eye-movement sleep—the same as *active sleep.*

representational thought. Mental processes that make use of representations.

representations. Mental images of things previously seen, heard, or otherwise experienced; or arbitrary symbols (such as words) used to think about actions or things.

representative sample. A sample of subjects that contains individuals from different racial and ethnic groups, different socioeconomic levels, different geographic locations, and so on, in approximately the same proportions as they occur in the population as a whole.

repressed. In Freudian theory, a repressed thought or desire is one that has been driven down into the unconscious mind.

resistant. The way some toddlers react in the Strange Situation: when the mother returns, the child continues to cry in an angry way and may alternate between clinging to his mother and pushing her away. Children who behave in this way are judged insecurely attached to their mothers.

response. An action—often, an action that occurs after exposure to a stimulus.

retardation. See *mental retardation.*

retina. The membrane at the back of the eye where light is converted into neural signals. The retina of the eye is the equivalent of the film in a camera.

retrieval. See *memory retrieval.*

Rh factor. A nonessential component that is present in the blood of some people (those who are Rh positive) and absent in others (Rh negatives). An Rh negative woman who is pregnant with an Rh positive fetus can form antibodies that destroy the red blood cells of her fetus.

rite of passage. A ceremony or ritual marking a person's transition from childhood to adulthood.

role confusion. Same as *identity confusion.*

role model. An older person filling a particular family, gender, or occupational role, whose behavior can serve as a model for a younger person to follow.

role-taking ability. The ability to imagine or to be aware of another person's thoughts, feelings, and motivations.

rooting. One of the reflexes of the newborn baby: a touch on the cheek causes the baby's head and lips to move in that direction.

rough-and-tumble play. A style of play quite common in preschool-age boys. It involves running, jumping, rolling around, and playful wrestling and shoving.

rubella. A viral disease, also known as German measles, capable of producing severe birth defects if a woman contracts it during the first trimester of pregnancy.

scheme. In Piagetian theory, a simple or complex pattern of action or thought that functions as a unit.

schizophrenia. See *childhood schizophrenia.*

scripts. A way of storing things in long-term memory: by remembering a standard sequence of events plus "slots" to be filled in with variable items. For example, a restaurant script would consist of the sequence of events that usually happens when you go to a restaurant, and the slots would contain details such as what you ordered and where you sat.

secondary sex characteristics. Physical characteristics that distinguish men from women but are not directly related to reproduction—e.g., breast development in females, beard growth and deep voice in males. See *primary sex characteristics.*

securely attached. A description of the quality of a child's relationship with another person, generally a parent. A child who is securely attached to his mother will greet her enthusiastically after having been separated from her in the Strange Situation.

security object. A soft toy or blanket that a baby or toddler (or sometimes an older child, like Charlie Brown's friend Linus) is very attached to. The child carries the blanket or toy around with him and won't go to sleep without it.

security of attachment. The quality of a child's attachment to a particular person, generally assessed in the Strange Situation. See *securely attached, insecurely attached.*

selective attention. The ability to focus attention on a particular stimulus and to shut out, to a certain extent, less important stimuli.

self-efficacy. A feeling of being competent, of having confidence in one's ability to succeed.

self-fulfilling prophecy. A prediction that comes true because people expect it to come true.

sensitive period. A period during which some aspect of development can occur most readily. See also *critical period.*

sensorimotor period. In Piagetian theory, roughly the first two years of life. By the end of this period the child has acquired object permanence and can use mental representations.

sensorimotor play. Piaget's term for the earliest type of play, which involves moving the body and, usually, doing something to an object or objects. Shaking a rattle and building a tower with blocks are examples.

sensory nerve. A nerve that carries neural signals to the brain or spinal cord from the sense organs, the skin, the muscles and joints, or the internal organs.

separation anxiety. Same as *separation distress.*

separation distress. The unhappiness experienced and expressed by a child when a person to whom that child is attached goes away.

serial marriage. A series of three or more marriages by the same individual as a result of repeated divorces.

set-point weight. The weight a person's body attempts to maintain, in the same way a thermostat maintains a certain temperature: by increasing appetite (or decreasing metabolism) if weight falls below that point, and by decreasing appetite if weight goes above it. In growing children it is not weight that is "set"; rather, it is the body's proportion of fat.

sex chromosomes. The pair of chromosomes that determine a person's sex. They are of two types, X and Y. Females have two X chromosomes; males have one X and one Y.

sex constancy. The understanding that maleness and femaleness depend on what kind of genitals a person was born with and not on clothing or hairstyle, and that people stay the same sex all through their lives.

sex difference. Same as *gender difference.*

sex-linked trait. A trait carried on the X chromosome. A boy with such a trait has inherited the gene that's responsible for it from his mother.

sex-role development. The development of a gender identity and the acquisition of understanding about what it means to be male and what it means to be female in our society—what behaviors are accepted and approved, what characteristics the sexes are expected to have, and so on.

sex-role knowledge. The acquisition of knowledge about sex roles.

sex roles. The behaviors, attitudes, and psychological characteristics a society expects from males and from females. Also called gender roles.

sex stereotypes. The ideas that people in a given society tend to hold about the characteristics of males and females. Sex stereotypes are more rigid and exaggerated than sex roles.

sex-typed behavior. Behavior that is considered typical for people of one gender and not for those of the other gender.

SGA. See *small for gestational age.*

shape constancy. The visual mechanism that keeps things looking more or less constant in shape, despite differences in the angle they are viewed from.

shaping. Training an organism to make a new response by reinforcing a response that has some features in common with the desired response, and then gradually increasing the requirements for reinforcement.

short-term memory. Temporary memory, capable of holding a small number of items (such as numbers) for a short period of time, or for as long as they are retained by means of rehearsal. See *long-term memory.*

sibling. A brother or a sister.

SIDS. See *sudden infant death syndrome.*

sight-reading method. A method for teaching children to read that does not involve the teaching of phonics. Children are taught to recognize words as wholes, by their overall shape, rather than to sound them out letter by letter.

significant. A significant result is one that is unlikely (by the laws of mathematical probability) to have occurred by chance or coincidence.

significant difference. A difference between two sets of measurements that is unlikely to be the result of chance variations. To be significant, a difference does not have to be large or important —just reasonably consistent.

size constancy. The visual mechanism that keeps things looking more or less constant in size, despite the fact that a close object has a larger projective image (and takes up more of the visual field) than the same object seen from farther away.

skin senses. The senses that enable us to perceive pressure (or "touch"), heat, cold, and pain. The receptors for all these senses are found in the skin.

Skinner box. A box containing some device with which an animal can make a response (usually a lever for a rat to press or a disk for a pigeon to peck) and another device that dispenses a reinforcer (usually food). Used in operant conditioning.

small for dates. Same as *small for gestational age.*

small for gestational age. A term used to describe a newborn baby or fetus that is smaller than it is expected to be, given the amount of time that has passed since it was conceived.

small-muscle skills. Motor skills that primarily involve the muscles of the hands and fingers. Examples are buttoning buttons, tying bows, and drawing pictures.

social cognition. Knowledge and understanding about people's thoughts and feelings, and about the way they behave and their interactions with each other. The subject of this knowledge can be oneself, as well as other people.

social learning theory. The view that children learn through observing others, as well as through the reinforcements and punishments that they themselves receive. Sometimes called cognitive behaviorism.

social pretend play. Cooperative play in which two or more children adopt imaginary roles and take part in a game of make-believe such as "playing house."

social referencing. Deciding how to react to something by checking first to see how other people are reacting.

socialization. The aspect of development that involves the child's learning to behave according to the rules of his or her society, and acquiring the attitudes, skills, and knowledge needed to get along in that society.

society. A group of people with a common culture.

sociodramatic play. Same as *social pretend play.*

socioeconomic status. The socioeconomic status of a family is determined by the income, occupation, and education of its members.

solitary play. Play that involves no interaction at all with other people.

species-specific behavior. An inherited pattern of behavior. Examples are nest-building in many species of birds, washing the face and paws in cats, and mating rituals in all species of mammals.

stage. A period of development that is assumed to be qualitatively different from the previous or subsequent period. Stages are assumed to occur in a particular order, though their timing can vary.

stage-4 error. The tendency of 8- to 12-month-old babies to look for a hidden object in the place where they found it previously, instead of the place where they most recently saw it hidden.

Stanford–Binet. A frequently used IQ test that can be given to children age 2 or over and that is administered individually.

state. A term used by researchers to describe the various types of sleep and wakefulness seen in newborn babies.

stepping reflex. Same as *walking reflex.*

stereoblind. Lacking stereoscopic vision. An estimated 2 percent of human adults are stereoblind.

stereoscopic vision. Three-dimensional vision that depends on the fact that the left eye's view of the world is a little different from the right eye's view.

stimulus. Anything that can be seen, heard, or otherwise perceived. This term is usually applied to something (e.g., a picture, a sound) that is expected to evoke a response, especially something that is used in an experiment.

Strange Situation. An experimental procedure developed by Ainsworth and her associates, used to assess the quality of a toddler's attachment to his mother. During this procedure the mother twice leaves the child in an unfamiliar room and returns a few minutes later. The first time the child is left with an unfamiliar woman; the second time he is left alone.

strategy. See *metacognitive strategy.*

subculture. A group of people within a culture who associate with each other and who have something in common, such as a common socioeconomic class, a common racial or ethnic background, or (in the case of an adolescent subculture) a common age plus a similar outlook on life.

subject. A person who is observed, interviewed, or tested in any way in a scientific study.

sudden infant death syndrome (SIDS). The death of an infant due to causes that are still not completely understood, usually while he or she is sleeping. It is the leading killer of babies between 1 month and 12 months of age.

superego. According to Freud, one of the three aspects of the human mind. The superego is similar to a conscience; it develops between the ages of 3 and 5½.

surrogate mother. A woman who bears a baby for another couple. She might be the biological mother of the baby, or (if the baby is conceived through in vitro fertilization) another woman might provide the egg and the surrogate mother then gives birth to a baby to whom she is biologically unrelated.

swaddling. Wrapping a baby tightly in a blanket or with strips of cloth.

swimming reflex. One of the reflexes of the newborn baby: when placed on their stomachs, babies sometimes make rhythmic movements of their arms and legs, as though they were swimming.

symbolic play. Same as *pretend play.*

synapse. A junction where a neural message from one neuron is transmitted (by means of a biochemical substance known as a neurotransmitter) to another neuron.

tabula rasa. Literally, a blank slate. According to the philosopher John Locke, the mind of the newborn baby is like a slate with nothing written on it.

tadpole person. A typical drawing produced by a 3-year-old: a head without a body. The legs (and arms, if any) are connected directly to the head.

tag question. A question that is "tagged on" at the end of a sentence, turning a declarative sentence into an interrogative one. In the sentence, "You like candy, don't you?" the tag question is "don't you?"

telegraphic speech. A description of the speech of toddlers, whose utterances are quite limited in length. They tend to leave out verb endings and unimportant words; as a result, their speech resembles the language used in telegrams.

temperament. The persistent aspects of someone's personality —e.g., how adaptable, cheerful, active, and emotional that individual is.

teratogen. Anything that can produce abnormalities in a developing embryo or fetus.

testes. The male sex glands, also called testicles. They produce sperm and hormones. The testes develop early in the prenatal period.

testosterone. A male hormone, one of the androgens, that is chiefly responsible for the development of male secondary sexual characteristics.

thalidomide. A prescription drug, formerly used to quell nausea and vomiting, that produces serious birth defects (e.g., missing arms or legs) when taken in early pregnancy. This drug was never sold in the United States.

toddlerhood. The period of development that starts when the child begins to use walking as his or her chief means of getting from one place to another and that ends around the age of 2½.

tonic neck reflex. One of the reflexes of the newborn baby: when lying on his back the baby generally keeps his head turned to one side, with the arm on that side stretched out and the other arm bent so that his fist is near the back of his head.

toxoplasmosis. A disease sometimes transmitted in cat droppings or raw meat. The microorganism that causes it is capable of crossing the placenta and harming a developing fetus.

trait. A specific characteristic of a person, animal, or plant— usually one that is at least partly genetic. A rabbit's long ears, a child's blue eyes, and an adult's cool temperament are all traits.

transactional view. An approach to child development based on the idea that there is a two-way interaction between the child and the environment. For example, the way parents behave toward a particular child will be influenced by the way the child behaves. The child's behavior will, in turn, be influenced by the way the parents behave.

transition. A relatively brief but painful stage of labor, occurring at the end of the dilation stage, when the cervix is stretched around the baby's head.

traumatic. A term applied to experiences that might have upsetting or even injurious effects.

trimester. A three-month period of pregnancy.

trisomy 21. A fertilized egg with trisomy 21 contains three copies of the twenty-first chromosome (two is the normal number). Trisomy 21 is responsible for Down syndrome.

"true" score. The average score that a person would theoretically make on a test if he or she took the test over and over again, under optimum conditions.

umbilical cord. The ropelike structure, containing blood vessels, that connects the fetus to the placenta.

unconscious mind. In Freudian theory, the part of the mind that contains drives, feelings, memories, and thoughts that we are not aware of, but that nonetheless influence our behavior and our conscious thoughts.

underextension. The use of a word (usually by a toddler) to refer to a smaller class of things than an adult would use that word for. For example, using the word *shoes* to apply only to the shoes in the closet.

uterus. A pear-shaped, hollow organ with muscular walls, located in a woman's abdomen, that houses the fetus during prenatal development. Also known as the womb.

utterance. A single word, phrase, or sentence spoken all in one piece (without pauses).

validity. A test is said to have validity if it accurately measures the quality or characteristic it was designed to measure.

variability. How widely the measurements in a set of measurements differ from each other.

verbal mediators. Words, either thought or spoken aloud, that are used to help oneself make the right response in a learning or memory task. Examples are thinking to oneself, "It's always the middle-sized one," or rehearsing a short list of words so they won't be forgotten.

vernix. A cheesy substance that coats the skin of the fetus and that is present on the skin of a newly born baby.

vicarious punishment. Seeing someone else get punished for something he or she did.

vicarious reinforcement. Seeing someone else receive a reward for something he or she did.

vicious circle. Also called vicious cycle. As used in this book, the tendency for certain characteristics to become increasingly stronger or more exaggerated because of various transactional effects. For example, an aggressive child might become more and more aggressive, due to the physical punishments he receives from his parents and to the fact that he is rejected by his peers. A bright child might become brighter if she chooses to spend her time in the library rather than watching TV.

visual acuity. The sharpness or clarity of vision.

visual cliff. A device for testing depth perception in human or animal babies. It consists of a large table with a glass top. A patterned surface can be seen directly under the glass on one side; on the other, the patterned surface is several feet below the glass.

visual constancies. Perceptual mechanisms that serve to produce a reasonably constant perception despite changes in the pattern of light that falls on the retina. See *shape constancy, size constancy.*

visual feedback. The effects that are seen to occur as an immediate result of making a given movement.

visual–motor skill. An ability that uses information obtained through vision to regulate a pattern of motor responses.

visual–spatial ability. The ability to deal with mental representations of shapes and directions—to visualize relationships among them and the changes that occur when these shapes or directions are moved around or rotated. An example would be visualizing how a diagram would look if it were turned upside down.

visual stimulus. Something that can be seen—a picture, an object, etc. See *stimulus.*

vocalize. To say a word or to make a speechlike sound. A baby's coos and babbles are considered vocalizations.

walking reflex. One of the reflexes of the newborn baby: when held upright with his feet touching a solid surface, the baby will make stepping movements similar to real walking.

whole-word method. Same as *sight-reading method.*

WISC-R. The revised version of the Wechsler Intelligence Scale for Children—an IQ test for school-age children, designed to be administered individually.

WPPSI. The Wechsler Preschool and Primary Scale of Intelligence—an IQ test for 4- to 6-year-olds, designed to be administered individually.

X chromosome. The larger of the two sex chromosomes, shaped roughly like an X. Everyone has at least one X chromosome: females have two, males have one (plus one Y chromosome).

Y chromosome. The smaller of the two sex chromosomes, shaped roughly like a Y. Only males have a Y chromosome; a boy has inherited his Y chromosome from his father.

zygote. A fertilized egg, containing (in the normal human) 46 chromosomes.

References

Abler, R. M., & Sedlacek, W. E. (1989). Freshman sexual attitudes and behaviors over a 15-year-period. *Journal of College Student Development, 30,* 201–209.

Abrahamse, A. F., Morrison, P. A., & Waite, L. J. (1988). Teenagers willing to consider single parenthood: Who is at greatest risk? *Family Planning Perspectives, 20,* 13–18.

Abramovitch, R., Corter, C. Pepler, D. J., & Stanhope, L. (1986). Sibling and peer interaction: A final follow-up and a comparison. *Child Development, 57,* 217–229.

Abravanel, E., & Sigafoos, A. D. (1984). Exploring the presence of imitation during early infancy. *Child Development, 55,* 381–392.

Ackerman, B. P. (1987). Selective attention and distraction in context-interactive situations in children and adults. *Journal of Experimental Child Psychology, 44,* 126–146.

Acredolo, L. P. (1988). From signal to "symbol": The development of landmark knowledge from 9 to 13 months. *British Journal of Developmental Psychology, 6,* 369–372.

Acredolo, L. P., & Goodwyn, S. (1988). Symbolic gesturing in normal infants. *Child Development, 59,* 450–466.

Adams, G. R., Abraham, K. G., & Markstrom, C. A. (1987). The relations among identity development, self-consciousness, and self-focusing during middle and late adolescence. *Developmental Psychology, 23,* 292–297.

Agnew, R., & Huguley, S. (1989). Adolescent violence toward parents. *Journal of Marriage and the Family, 51,* 699–711.

Ainsworth, M. D. S. (1977). Attachment theory and its utility in cross-cultural research. In P. H. Leiderman, S. R. Tulkin, & A. Rosenfield (Eds.), *Culture and infancy: Variations in the human experience.* New York: Academic Press.

Ainsworth, M. D. S., Blehar, M. C., Waters, E., & Wall, S. (1978). *Patterns of attachment.* Hillsdale, N.J.: Erlbaum.

Albert, R. S., & Runco, M. A. (1989). Independence and the creative potential of gifted and exceptionally gifted boys. *Journal of Youth and Adolescence, 18,* 221–230.

Alessandri, S. M., & Wozniak, R. H. (1987). The child's awareness of parental beliefs concerning the child: A developmental study. *Child Development, 58,* 316–322.

Allen, J. P., Weissberg, R. P., & Hawkins, J. A. (1989). The relation between values and social competence in early adolescence. *Developmental Psychology, 25,* 458–464.

Alpert-Gillis, L. J., & Connell, J. P. (1989). Gender and sex-role influences on children's self-esteem. *Journal of Personality, 57,* 97–113.

Alwin, D. F. (1988). From obedience to autonomy: Changes in traits desired in children, 1924–1978. *Public Opinion Quarterly, 52,* 33–52.

American Psychological Association Ad Hoc Committee on Ethical Standards in Psychological Research (1973). *Ethical principles in the conduct of research with human participants.* Washington, D.C.

Anastasi, A. (1976). *Psychological testing* (4th ed.) New York: Macmillan.

Andrews, L. B. (1984). *New conceptions.* New York: St. Martin's Press.

Anglin, J. M. (1977). *Word, object, and conceptual development.* New York: Norton.

Angoff, W. H. (1988). The nature–nurture debate, aptitudes, and group differences. *American Psychologist, 43,* 713–720.

Antell, S. B., & Keating, D. P. (1983). Perception of numerical invariance in neonates. *Child Development, 54,* 695–701.

Antill, J. K., & Cotton, S. (1988). Factors affecting the division of labor in households. *Sex Roles, 18,* 531–553.

Archer, L. A., Campbell, D., & Segalowitz, S. J. (1988). A prospective study of hand preference and language development in 18- to 30-month olds: I. Hand preference. *Developmental Neuropsychology, 4,* 85–92.

Ariès, P. (1962). *Centuries of childhood: A social history of family life* (R. Baldick, trans.). New York: Random House.

Aronson, E., & Rosenbloom, S. (1971). Space perception in early infancy: Perception within a common auditory-visual space. *Science, 172,* 1161–1163.

Arvey, R. D., Bouchard, T. J., Jr., Segal, N. L., & Abraham, L. M. (1989). Job satisfaction: Environmental and genetic components. *Journal of Applied Psychology, 74,* 187–192.

Ary, D. V., & Biglan, A. (1988). Longitudinal changes in adolescent cigarette smoking behavior: Onset and cessation. *Journal of Behavioral Medicine, 11,* 361–382.

Aslin, R. N., & Smith, L. B. (1988). Perceptual development. *Annual Review of Psychology, 39,* 435–473.

Baer, D. M. (1989). A behavior-analytic account of human development. Paper presented at the April meeting of the Society for Research in Child Development, Kansas City.

Bahrick, L. E. (1988). Intermodal learning in infancy: Learning on the basis of two kinds of invariant relations in audible and visible events. *Child Development, 59,* 197–209.

Bailey, G. W. (1989). Current perspectives on substance abuse in youth. *Journal of the American Academy of Child and Adolescent Psychiatry, 28,* 151–162.

Baillargeon, R. (1987). Object permanence in 3½- and 4½-month-old infants. *Developmental Psychology, 23,* 655–664.

Band, E. B., & Weisz, J. R. (1988). How to feel better when it feels bad: Children's perspectives on coping with everyday stress. *Developmental Psychology, 24,* 247–253.

Bandura, A. (1965). Influence of models' reinforcement contingencies on the acquisition of imitative responses. *Journal of Personality and Social Psychology, 1,* 589–595.

Bandura, A. (1986). *Social foundations of thought and action.* Englewood Cliffs, N.J.: Prentice Hall.

Bandura, A. (1989). Human agency in social cognitive theory. *American Psychologist, 44,* 1175–1184.

Banks, M. S., & Salapatek, P. (1983). Infant visual perception. In M. M. Haith & J. J. Campos (Eds.), *Handbook of child psychology* (Vol. 2): *Infancy and development psychobiology* (P. H. Mussen, General Editor). New York: Wiley.

Barber, L. W., & McClellan, M. C. (1987). Looking at America's dropouts: Who are they? *Phi Delta Kappan,* December, pp. 264–267.

Barglow, P., Vaughn, B. E., & Molitor, N. (1987). Effects of maternal absence due to employment on the quality of infant–mother attachment in a low-risk sample. *Child Development, 58,* 945–954.

Barnes, G. M., & Welte, J. W. (1988). Predictors of driving while intoxicated among teenagers. *Journal of Drug Issues, 18*(3), 367–384.

Battelle, P. (1981). The triplets who found each other. *Good Housekeeping,* February, pp. 74–83.

Baumeister, A. A. (1987). Mental retardation: Some conceptions and dilemmas. *American Psychologist, 42,* 796–800.

Baumeister, R. F., & Senders, P. S. (1989). Identity development and the role structure of children's games. *Journal of Genetic Psychology, 150,* 19–37.

Baumrind, D. (1967). Child-care practices anteceding three patterns of preschool behavior. *Genetic Psychology Monographs, 75,* 43–88.

Baumrind, D. (1975). *Early socialization and the discipline controversy.* Morristown, N.J.: General Learning Press.

Baumrind, D. (1982). Are androgynous individuals more effective persons and parents? *Child Development, 53,* 44–75.

Bayley, N. (1969). *Bayley scales of infant development.* New York: Psychological Corporation.

Beal, C. R. (1987). Repairing the message: Children's monitoring and revision skills. *Child Development, 58,* 401–408.

Bear, G. G. (1989). Sociomoral reasoning and antisocial behaviors among normal sixth graders. *Merrill-Palmer Quarterly, 35,* 181–196.

Beck, K. H., & Summons, T. G. (1987). Adolescent gender differences in alcohol beliefs and behaviors. *Journal of Alcohol and Drug Education, 33*(1), 31–44.

Becker, J. A. (1988). ''I can't talk, I'm dead'': Preschoolers' spontaneous metapragmatic comments. *Discourse Processes, 11,* 457–467.

Beckwith, L., & Parmelee, A. H., Jr. (1986). EEG patterns of preterm infants, home environment, and later IQ. *Child Development, 57,* 777–789.

Bell, R. Q., & Chapman, M. (1986). Child effects in studies using experimental or brief longitudinal approaches to socialization. *Developmental Psychology, 22,* 595–603.

Bell, S. M. (1970). The development of the concept of object as related to infant–mother attachment. *Child Development, 41,* 291–311.

Bell, S. M., & Ainsworth, M. D. S. (1972). Infant crying and maternal responsiveness. *Child Development, 43,* 1171–1190.

Belsky, J., Lang, M., & Huston, T. L. (1986). Sex typing and division of labor as determinants of marital change across the transition to parenthood. *Journal of Personality and Social Psychology, 50,* 517–522.

Belsky, J., & Rovine, M. (1987). Temperament and attachment security in the strange situation: An empirical rapprochement. *Child Development, 58,* 787–795.

Belsky, J., Rovine, M., & Taylor, D. G. (1984). The Pennsylvania infant and family development project. III: The origins of individual differences in infant–mother attachment: Maternal and infant contributions. *Child Development, 55,* 718–728.

Bem, S. L. (1974). The measurement of psychological androgyny. *Journal of Consulting and Clinical Psychology, 42,* 155–162.

Bem, S. L. (1989). Genital knowledge and gender constancy in preschool children. *Child Development, 60,* 649–662.

Benbow, C. P. (1988). Sex differences in mathematical reasoning ability in intellectually talented preadolescents: Their nature, effects, and possible causes. *Behavioral and Brain Sciences, 11,* 169–183.

Benjamin, L. T., Jr. (1988). A history of teaching machines. *American Psychologist, 43,* 703–712.

Bennett, N. (1976). *Teaching styles and pupil progress.* Cambridge: Harvard University Press.

Berch, D. B., & Bender, B. G. (1987). Margins of sexuality. *Psychology Today,* December, pp. 54–57.

Berg, J. H., & McQuinn, R. D. (1986). Attraction and exchange in continuing and noncontinuing dating relationships. *Journal of Personality and Social Psychology, 50,* 942–952.

Berg, W. K., Adkinson, C. D., & Strock, B. L. (1973). Duration and periods of alertness in neonates. *Developmental Psychology, 9,* 434.

Berk, L. E. (1986). Private speech: Learning out loud. *Psychology Today,* May, pp. 34–42.

Berko, J. (1958). The child's learning of English morphology. *Word, 14,* 150–177.

Bernard, J. (1982). *The future of marriage.* New Haven: Yale University Press.

Berndt, T. J. (1982). The features and effects of friendship in early adolescence. *Child Development, 53,* 1447–1460.

Berndt, T. J., Hawkins, J. A., & Hoyle, S. G. (1986). Changes in friendship during a school year: Effects on children's and adolescents' impressions of friendship and sharing with friends. *Child Development, 57,* 1284–1297.

Berndt, T. J., & Heller, K. A. (1986). Gender stereotypes and social inferences: A developmental study. *Journal of Personality and Social Psychology, 50,* 889–898.

Berry, D. S., & McArthur, L. Z. (1986). Perceiving character in faces: The impact of age-related craniofacial changes on social perception. *Psychological Bulletin, 100,* 3–18.

Bertenthal, B. I., & Campos, J. J. (1987). New directions in the study of early experience. *Child Development, 58,* 560–567.

Bettelheim, B. (1976). *The uses of enchantment.* New York: Knopf.

Bichard, S. L., Alden, S., Walker, L. J., & McMahon, R. J. (1988). Friendship understanding in socially accepted, rejected, and neglected children. *Merrill-Palmer Quarterly, 34,* 33–46.

Bijou, S. W., & Baer, D. M. (1965). *Child development* (Vol. 2). Englewood Cliffs, N.J.: Prentice Hall.

Binder, A. (1988). Juvenile delinquency. *Annual Review of Psychology, 39,* 253–282.

Bingol, N., Fuchs, M., Diaz, V., Stone, R. K., & Gromisch, D. S.

(1987). Teratogenicity of cocaine in humans. *Journal of Pediatrics, 110,* 93–96.

Birch, L. L. (1987). Children's food preferences: Developmental patterns and environmental influences. *Annals of Child Development, 4,* 171–208.

Birch, L. L., McPhee, L., Shoba, B. C., Steinberg, L., & Krehbiel, R. (1987). "Clean up your plate": Effects of child feeding practices on the conditioning of meal size. *Learning and Motivation, 18,* 301–317.

Birch, L. L., McPhee, L., & Sullivan, S. (1989). Children's food intake following drinks sweetened with sucrose or aspartame: Time course effects. *Physiology and Behavior, 45,* 387–395.

Birnholz, J., & Farrell, E. (1984). Ultrasound images of human fetal development. *American Scientist, 72,* 608–612.

Bishop, J. E. (1986). Genetic omen: Chromosome linked to mental impairment raises abortion issue. *Wall Street Journal,* November 18, pp. 1, 27.

Bishop, S. M., & Ingersoll, G. M. (1989). Effects of marital conflict and family structure on the self-concepts of pre- and early adolescents. *Journal of Youth and Adolescence, 18,* 25–38.

Bjorklund, D. F. (1987a). A note on neonatal imitation. *Developmental Review, 7,* 86–92.

Bjorklund, D. F. (1987b). How age changes in knowledge base contribute to the development of children's memory: An interpretive review. *Developmental Review, 7,* 93–130.

Bjorklund, D. F. (1988). Acquiring a mnemonic: Age and category knowledge effects. *Journal of Experimental Child Psychology, 45,* 71–87.

Bjorklund, D. F., & Bjorklund, B. (1988). Straight or gay? *Parents,* October, pp. 93–98.

Bjorklund, D. F., & Harnishfeger, K. K. (1987). Developmental differences in the mental effort requirements for the use of an organizational strategy in free recall. *Journal of Experimental Child Psychology, 44,* 109–125.

Blake, J. (1989). Number of siblings and educational attainment. *Science, 245,* 32–36.

Blakeslee, S. (1986). Rapid changes seen in young brain. *New York Times,* June 24, pp. C1, C10.

Blakeslee, S. (1989). Crib death: Suspicion turns to the brain. *New York Times,* February 14, pp. C1, C3.

Block, J., Block, J. H., & Gjerde, P. F. (1988). Parental functioning and the home environment in families of divorce: Prospective and concurrent analyses. *Journal of the American Academy of Child and Adolescent Psychiatry, 27,* 207–213.

Blount, R., Jr. (1981). When love is the best gift of all. *Parade,* December 20, pp. 4–6.

Boggiano, A. K., Klinger, C. A., & Main, D. S. (1986). Enhancing interest in peer interaction: A developmental analysis. *Child Development, 57,* 852–861.

Boggiano, A. K., & Main, D. S. (1986). Enhancing children's interest in activities used as rewards: The bonus effect. *Journal of Personality and Social Psychology, 51,* 1116–1126.

Boggiano, A. K., Main, D. S., & Katz, P. A. (1988). Children's preference for challenge: The role of perceived competence and control. *Journal of Personality and Social Psychology, 54,* 134–141.

Boivin, M., & Bégin, G. (1989). Peer status and self-perception among early elementary school children: The case of the rejected children. *Child Development, 60,* 591–596.

Bonitatibus, G. (1988). Comprehension monitoring and the apprehension of literal meaning. *Child Development, 59,* 60–70.

Bonnet, K. A. (1989). Learning disabilities: A neurobiological perspective in humans. *Remedial and Special Education, 10*(3), 8–19.

Boring, E. G. (1950). *A history of experimental psychology.* Englewood Cliffs, N.J.: Prentice Hall.

Bornstein, M. H. (1985). How infant and mother jointly contribute to developing cognitive competence in the child. *Proceedings of the National Academy of Sciences, 82,* 7470–7473.

Bornstein, M. H., Gaughran, J., & Homel, P. (1986). Infant temperament: Theory, tradition, critique, and new assessments. In C. E. Izard & P. B. Read (Eds.), *Measuring emotions in infants and children* (Vol. 2). New York: Cambridge University Press.

Bornstein, M. H., & Sigman, M. D. (1986). Continuity in mental development from infancy. *Child Development, 57,* 251–274.

Boston Children's Hospital (1986). *Parents' guide to nutrition: Healthy eating from birth through adolescence.* Reading, Mass.: Addison-Wesley.

Boswell, J. (1988). *The kindness of strangers.* New York: Pantheon.

Bouchard, T. J., Jr., & McGue, M. (1981). Familial studies of intelligence: A review. *Science, 212,* 1055–1059.

Bow, J. N. (1988). A comparison of intellectually superior male reading achievers and underachievers from a neuropsychological perspective. *Journal of Learning Disabilities, 21*(2), 118–123.

Bower, T. G. R. (1976). Repetitive processes in child development. *Scientific American,* November, pp. 38–47.

Bower, T. G. R. (1977). *A primer of infant development.* San Francisco: W. H. Freeman.

Bowlby, J. (1969). *Attachment and loss.* Vol. 1: *Attachment.* New York: Basic Books.

Bracey, G. W. (1989). Learning to read and write. *Phi Delta Kappan,* March, pp. 559–564.

Brackbill, Y., & Nevill, D. (1981). Parental expectations of achievement as affected by children's height. *Merrill–Palmer Quarterly, 27,* 429–441.

Bradley, L. (1988). Rhyme recognition and reading and spelling in young children. In R. Masland and M. Masland (Eds.), *Preschool prevention of reading failures.* Parkton, Md.: York Press.

Braine, L. G., & Eder, R. A. (1983). Left–right memory in 2-year-old children: A new look at search tasks. *Developmental Psychology, 19,* 45–55.

Brainerd, C. J., Howe, M. L., Kingma, J., & Brainerd, S. H. (1984). On the measurement of storage and retrieval contributions to memory development. *Journal of Experimental Child Psychology, 37,* 478–499.

Brand, D. (1987). The new whiz kids: why Asian Americans are doing so well, and what it costs them. *Time,* August 31, pp. 42–51.

Braungart, R. G. (1974). The sociology of generations and student politics: A comparison of the functionalist and generational unit models. *Journal of Social Issues, 30,* 31–54.

Brazelton, T. B. (1977). Implications of infant development among the Mayan Indians of Mexico. In P. H. Leiderman, S. R. Tulkin, & A. Rosenfeld (Eds.), *Culture and infancy: Variations in the human experience.* New York: Academic Press.

Brazelton, T. B, Koslowski, B., & Main, M. (1974). The origins of reciprocity: The early mother–infant interaction. In M. Lewis & L. A. Rosenblum (Eds.), *The effect of the infant on its caregiver.* New York: Wiley.

Bregman, E. (1934). An attempt to modify the emotional attitude of infants by the conditioned response technique. *Journal of Genetic Psychology, 45,* 169–198.

Breslau, N., Klein, N., & Allen, L. (1988). Very low birthweight: Behavioral sequelae at nine years of age. *Journal of the American Academy of Child and Adolescent Psychiatry, 27,* 605–612.

Bretherton, I. (1980). Young children in stressful situations: The supporting role of attachment figures and unfamiliar caregivers. In G. V. Coelho & P. Ahmed (Eds.), *Uprooting and development.* New York: Plenum Press.

Bretherton, I., Fritz, J., Zahn-Waxler, C., & Ridgeway, D. (1986). Learning to talk about emotions: A functionalist perspective. *Child Development, 57,* 529–548.

Bretherton, I., & Waters, E., Eds. (1985). Growing points of attachment theory and research. *Monographs of the Society for Research in Child Development, 50* (1–2, Serial No. 209).

Breznitz, Z., & Friedman, S. L. (1988). Toddlers' concentration: Does maternal depression make a difference? *Journal of Child Psychology & Psychiatry, 29,* 267–279.

Breznitz, Z., & Sherman, T. (1987). Speech patterning of well and depressed mothers and their young children. *Child Development, 58,* 395–400.

Briars, D., & Siegler, R. S. (1984). A featural analysis of preschoolers' counting knowledge. *Developmental Psychology, 20,* 607–618.

Brody, G. H., Neubaum, E., & Forehand, R. (1988). Serial marriage: A heuristic analysis of an emerging family form. *Psychological Bulletin, 103,* 211–222.

Brody, G. H., Pillegrini, A. D., & Sigel, I. E. (1986). Marital quality and mother–child and father–child interactions with school-age children. *Developmental Psychology, 22,* 291–296.

Brody, G. H., Stoneman, Z., & Burke, M. (1987). Child temperaments, maternal differential behavior, and sibling relationships. *Developmental Psychology, 23,* 354–362.

Brody, J. E. (1988). Cocaine: Litany of fetal risks grows. *New York Times,* September 6, p. C1.

Brody, L. E., & Benbow, C. P. (1987). Accelerative strategies: How effective are they? *Gifted Child Quarterly, 3*(3), 105–110.

Bronshtein, A. I., & Petrova, E. P. (1967). The auditory analyzer in young infants. In Y. Brackbill & G. G. Thompson (Eds.), *Behavior in infancy and early childhood.* New York: Free Press.

Brook, J. S., Whiteman, M., Gordon, A. S., & Cohen, P. (1986). Some models and mechanisms for explaining the impact of maternal and adolescent characteristics on adolescent stage of drug use. *Developmental Psychology, 22,* 460–467.

Brooks, J., & Lewis, M. (1976). Infants' responses to strangers: Midget, adult, and child. *Child Development, 47,* 323–332.

Brooks-Gunn, J., Boyer, C. B., & Hein, K. (1988). Preventing HIV infection and AIDS in children and adolescents. *American Psychologist, 43,* 958–964.

Brooks-Gunn, J., & Furstenberg, F. F., Jr. (1986). The children of adolescent mothers: Physical, academic, and psychological outcomes. *Developmental Review, 6,* 224–251.

Brooks-Gunn, J., & Furstenberg, F. F., Jr. (1989). Adolescent sexual behavior. *American Psychologist, 44,* 249–257.

Brooks-Gunn, J., & Lewis, M. (1984). The development of early visual self-recognition. *Developmental Review, 4,* 215–239.

Brooks-Gunn, J., & Warren, M. P. (1988). The psychological significance of secondary sexual characteristics in nine- to eleven-year-old girls. *Child Development, 59,* 1061–1069.

Brophy, J. (1986). Teacher influences on student achievement. *American Psychologist, 41,* 1069–1077.

Brown, B. B., Clasen, D. R., & Eicher, S. A. (1986). Perceptions of peer pressure, peer conformity dispositions, and self-reported behavior among adolescents. *Developmental Psychology, 22,* 521–530.

Brown, B. B., & Lohr, M. J. (1987). Peer-group affiliation and adolescent self-esteem: An integration of ego-identity and symbolic-interaction theories. *Journal of Personality and Social Psychology, 52,* 47–55.

Brown, J. L. (1964). States in newborn infants. *Merrill–Palmer Quarterly, 10,* 313–327.

Brown, J. V., Sepehr, M. M., Ettlinger, G., & Skreczek, W. (1986). The accuracy of aimed movements to visual targets during development: The role of visual information. *Journal of Experimental Child Psychology, 41,* 443–460.

Brown, P., & Elliott, R. (1965). Control of aggression in a nursery school class. *Journal of Experimental Child Psychology, 2,* 103–107.

Brown, R. (1973). *A first language: The early stages.* Cambridge: Harvard University Press.

Brown, R., & Bellugi, U. (1964). Three processes in the child's acquisition of syntax. In E. H. Lenneberg (Ed.), *New directions in the study of language.* Cambridge: MIT Press.

Brown, S. A. (1989). Life events of adolescents in relation to personal and parental substance abuse. *American Journal of Psychiatry, 146,* 484–489.

Brownell, C. A. (1986). Convergent developments: Cognitive-developmental correlates of growth in infant/toddler peer skills. *Child Development, 57,* 275–286.

Brownell, C. A. (1988). Combinatorial skills: Converging developments over the second year. *Child Development, 59,* 675–685.

Bruck, M. (1987). The adult outcomes of children with learning disabilities. *Annals of Dyslexia, 37,* 252–263.

Brumberg, J. J. (1988). *Fasting girls: The emergence of anorexia nervosa as a modern disease.* Cambridge: Harvard University Press.

Bryant, B. K. (1985). The neighborhood walk: Sources of support in middle childhood. *Monographs of the Society for Research in Child Development, 50* (3, Serial No. 210).

Brunk, M. A., & Henggeler, S. W. (1984). Child influences on adult controls: An experimental investigation. *Developmental Psychology, 20,* 1074–1081.

Buckley, W. E., Yesalis, C. E., Friedl, K. E., Anderson, W. A., Streit, A. L., & Wright, J. E. (1988). Estimated prevalence of anabolic steroid use among male high school seniors. *Journal of the American Medical Association, 260,* 3441–3445.

Buderi, R. (1989). Berkeley's changing student population. *Science, 245,* 694–696.

Bugental, D. B. (1986). Unmasking the "polite smile": Situational and personal determinants of managed affect in adult–child interaction. *Personality and Social Psychology Bulletin, 12,* 7–16.

Buis, J. M., & Thompson, D. N. (1989). Imaginary audience and personal fable: A brief review. *Adolescence, 24,* 773–781.

Bullock, M. (1985). Animism in childhood thinking: A new look at an old question. *Developmental Psychology, 21,* 217–225.

Bullock, M., & Lütkenhaus, P. (1988). The development of volitional behavior in the toddler years. *Child Development, 59,* 664–674.

Burger, J. M., & Burns, L. (1988). The illusion of unique invulnerability and the use of effective contraception. *Personality and Social Psychology Bulletin, 14,* 264–270.

Buri, J. R., Louiselle, P. A., Misukanis, T. M., & Mueller, R. A. (1988). Effects of parental authoritarianism and authoritativeness on self-esteem. *Personality and Social Psychology Bulletin, 14,* 271–282.

Burton, R. V. (1976). Honesty and dishonesty. In T. Lickona (Ed.), *Moral development and behavior.* New York: Holt, Rinehart & Winston.

Buscell, P. (1987). *Child's humor develops with age.* Asbury Park [N.J.] Press, December 6, p. B15.

Buss, D. M., & Barnes, M. (1986). Preferences in human mate selection. *Journal of Personality and Social Psychology, 50,* 559–570.

Butterfield, E. C., & Siperstein, G. N. (1974). Influence of contingent auditory stimulation upon non-nutritional suckle. *Proceedings of the Third Symposium on Oral Sensation and Perception: The Mouth of the Infant.* Springfield, Ill.: Charles C Thomas.

Byrnes, D., & Yamamoto, K. (1986). Views on grade repetition. *Journal of Research and Development in Education, 20,* 14–20.

Byrnes, J. P. (1988). Formal operations: A systematic reformulation. *Developmental Review, 8,* 66–87.

Cairns, R. B. (1989). Social networks, rejection, and aggressive behaviors. Paper presented at the April meeting of the Society for Research in Child Development, Kansas City.

Caldwell, B. M., Bradley, R. H., & Elardo, R. (1975). Early stimulation. In J. Wortis (Ed.), *Mental retardation and developmental disabilities: An annual review.* New York: Brunner/Mazel.

Camara, K. A., & Resnick, G. (1987). Marital and parental subsystems in mother-custody, father-custody, and two-parent households: Effects on children's social development. *Advances in Family Intervention, Assessment, and Theory, 4,* 165–196.

Cambell, A. A. (1968). The role of family planning in the reduction of poverty. *Journal of Marriage and the Family, 30*(2), 236–245.

Campbell, M., & Spencer, E. K. (1988). Psychopharmacology in child and adolescent psychiatry: A review of the past five years. *Journal of the American Academy of Child and Adolescent Psychiatry, 27,* 269–279.

Caplan, M. Z., & Hay, D. F. (1989). Preschoolers' responses to peers' distress and beliefs about bystander intervention. *Journal of Child Psychology and Psychiatry, 30,* 231–242.

Caplan, P. J., & Kinsbourne, M. (1976). Baby drops the rattle: Asymmetry of duration of grasp by infants. *Child Development, 47,* 532–534.

Capron, C., & Duyme, M. (1989). Assessment of effects of socioeconomic status on IQ in a full cross-fostering study. *Nature, 340,* 552–554.

Capute, A. J., Palmer, F. B., Shapiro, B. K., Wachtel, R. C., Schmidt, S., & Ross, A. (1986). Clinical Linguistic and Auditory Milestone Scale: Prediction of cognition in infancy. *Developmental Medicine and Child Neurology, 28,* 762–771.

Carey, S. (1978). The child as word learner. In M. Halle, J. Bresnan, & G. A. Miller (Eds.), *Linguistic theory and psychological reality.* Cambridge: MIT Press.

Carlson, D. E. (1988). Maternal diseases associated with intrauterine growth retardation. *Seminars in Perinatology, 12,* 17–22.

Carmichael, L. (1927). A further study of the development of behavior in vertebrates experimentally removed from the influence of external stimulation. *Psychological Review, 34,* 34–47.

Carpenter, G. (1975). Mother's face and the newborn. In R. Lewin (Ed.), *Child alive.* Garden City, N.Y.: Doubleday.

Carr, E. G., Pridal, C., & Dores, P. A. (1984). Speech versus sign comprehension in autistic children: Analysis and prediction. *Journal of Experimental Child Psychology, 37,* 587–597.

Carroll, J. J., & Steward, M. S. (1984). The role of cognitive development in children's understanding of their own feelings. *Child Development, 55,* 1486–1492.

Carson, R. C. (1988). Personality. *Annual Review of Psychology, 40,* 227–248.

Carver, C. S., & Gaines, J. G. (1987). Optimism, pessimism, and postpartum depression. *Cognitive Therapy and Research, 11,* 449–462.

Case, R. (1985). *Intellectual development: A systematic reinterpretation.* New York: Academic Press.

Case, R., Hayward, S., Lewis, M., & Hurst, P. (1988). Toward a neo-Piagetian theory of cognitive and emotional development. *Developmental Review, 8,* 1–51.

Case, R., Kurland, D. M., & Goldberg, J. (1982). Operational efficiency and the growth of short-term memory span. *Journal of Experimental Child Psychology, 33,* 386–404.

Casey, M. B. (1984). Individual differences in the use of left–right visual cues: A reexamination of mirror-image confusions in preschoolers. *Developmental Psychology, 20,* 551–559.

Caspi, A., Elder, G. H., Jr., & Bem, D. J. (1987). Moving against the world: Life-course patterns of explosive children. *Developmental Psychology, 23,* 308–313.

Cassidy, J. (1986). The ability to negotiate the environment: An aspect of infant competence as related to quality of attachment. *Child Development, 57,* 331–337.

Cassidy, J. (1988). Child–mother attachment and the self in six-year-olds. *Child Development, 59,* 121–134.

Castro, J. (1990). Volunteer vice squad. *Time,* April 23, pp. 60–61.

Casual drug use is sharply down (1989). *New York Times,* August 1, p. A14.

Cernoch, J. M., & Porter, R. H. (1985). Recognition of maternal axillary odors by infants. *Child Development, 56,* 1593–1598.

Chall, J. S. (1967). *Learning to read: The great debate.* New York: McGraw-Hill.

Chance, P. (1989). Kids without friends. *Psychology Today,* January/February, pp. 29–31.

Chandler, C. L., & Connell, J. P. (1987). Children's intrinsic, extrinsic, and internalized motivation: A developmental study of children's reasons for liked and disliked behaviours. *British Journal of Developmental Psychology, 5,* 357–365.

Chapman, M., Zahn-Waxler, C., Cooperman, G., & Iannotti, R. (1987). Empathy and responsibility in the motivation of children's helping. *Developmental Psychology, 23,* 140–145.

Charlesworth, R. (1989). "Behind" before they start? Deciding how to deal with the risk of kindergarten "failure." *Young Children,* March, pp. 5–13.

Chi, M. T. H. (1978). Knowledge structure and memory development. In R. Siegler (Ed.), *Children's thinking: What develops?* Hillsdale, N.J.: Erlbaum.

Chollar, S. (1987). Latchkey kids: Who are they? *Psychology Today,* December, p. 12.

Christophersen, E. R. (1989). Injury control. *American Psychologist, 44,* 237–241.

Clark, H. H., & Clark, E. V. (1977). *Psychology and language.* New York: Harcourt Brace Jovanovich.

Clark, J. E., & Phillips, S. J. (1986). An examination of the contributions of selected anthropometric factors to gender differences in motor skill development. In J. E. Clark & J. H. Humphrey (Eds.), *Advances in motor development research,* Vol. 1. New York: AMS Press.

Clarke, A. M., & Clarke, A. D. B. (1988). The adult outcome of early behavioral abnormalities. *International Journal of Behavioral Development, 11,* 3–19.

Clarke-Stewart, K. A. (1989). Infant day care: Maligned or malignant? *American Psychologist, 44,* 266–273.

Clarke-Stewart, K. A., & Hevey, C. M. (1981). Longitudinal relations in repeated observations of mother–child interaction from 1 to 2½ years. *Developmental Psychology, 17,* 127–145.

Clarkson, P. (1988). Ego state dilemmas of abused children. *Transactional Analysis Journal, 18,* 85–93.

Cohen, P., Velez, C. N., Brook, J., & Smith, J. (1989). Mechanisms of the relation between perinatal problems, early childhood illness, and psychopathology in late childhood and adolescence. *Child Development, 60,* 701–709.

Cohen, R., Schleser, R., & Meyers, A. (1981). Self-instructions: Effect of cognitive level and active rehearsal. *Journal of Experimental Child Psychology, 32,* 65–76.

Cohn, J. F., Matias, R., Tronick, E. Z., Connell, D., & Lyons-Ruth, K. (1986). Face-to-face interactions of depressed mothers and their infants. In E. Z. Tronick & T. Field (Eds.), *Maternal depression and infant disturbance. New Directions for Child Development, No. 34.* San Francisco: Jossey-Bass.

Cohn, J. F., & Tronick, E. Z. (1987). Mother–infant face-to-face interaction: The sequence of dyadic states at 3, 6, and 9 months. *Developmental Psychology, 23,* 68–77.

Cohn, J. F., & Tronick, E. Z. (1989). Specificity of infants' response to mothers' affective behavior. *Journal of the American Academy of Child and Adolescent Psychiatry, 28,* 242–248.

Coie, J. D., & Dodge, K. A. (1988). Multiple sources of data on social behavior and social status in the school: A cross-age comparison. *Child Development, 59,* 815–829.

Collins, L. M., Sussman, S., Rauch, J. M., Dent, C. W., Johnson, C. A., Hansen, W. B., & Flay, B. R. (1987). Psychosocial predictors of young adolescent cigarette smoking: A sixteen-month, three-wave longitudinal study. *Journal of Applied Social Psychology, 17,* 554–573.

Colt, G. H. (1983). The enigma of suicide. *Harvard Magazine,* September–October, pp. 46–66.

Committee on Adolescence, Group for the Advancement of Psychiatry (1968). *Normal adolescence.* New York: Scribner's.

Compton, J. C. (1989). Modern-day monsters. *Psychology Today,* March, pp. 30–31.

Condon, J. T., & Watson, T. L. (1987). The maternity blues: Exploration of a psychological hypothesis. *Acta Psychiatrica Scandinavia, 76,* 164–171.

Condry, J., & Condry, S. (1976). Sex differences: A study of the eye of the beholder. *Child Development, 47,* 812–819.

Conger, J. J., & Petersen, A. C. (1984). *Adolescence and youth: Psychological development in a changing world.* New York: Harper & Row.

Consortium for Longitudinal Studies (1983). *As the twig is bent: Lasting effects of preschool programs.* Hillsdale, N.J.: Erlbaum.

Corballis, M. C., & Beale, I. L. (1976). *The psychology of left and right.* Hillsdale, N.J.: Erlbaum.

Corsaro, W. A. (1981). Friendship in the nursery school: Social organization in a peer environment. In S. R. Asher & J. M. Gottman (Eds.), *The development of children's friendships.* New York: Cambridge University Press.

Côté, J. E., & Levine, C. (1988). A critical examination of the ego identity status paradigm. *Developmental Review, 8,* 147–184.

Covell, K., & Abramovitch, R. (1987). Understanding emotion in the family: Children's and parents' attributions of happiness, sadness, and anger. *Child Development, 58,* 985–991.

Covell, K., & Abramovitch, R. (1988). Children's understanding of maternal anger: Age and sources of anger differences. *Merrill-Palmer Quarterly, 34,* 353–368.

Cowan, G., & Avants, S. K. (1988). Children's influence strategies:

Structure, sex differences, and bilateral mother–child influence. *Child Development, 59,* 1303–1313.

Cowan, W. M. (1979). The development of the brain. *Scientific American,* September, pp. 112–133.

Cox, M. V. (1981). One thing behind another: Problems of representation in children's drawings. *Educational Psychology, 1,* 275–287.

Crain, W. C. (1980). *Theories of development.* Englewood Cliffs, N.J.: Prentice Hall.

Cratty, B. (1979). *Perceptual and motor development in infants and children.* Englewood Cliffs, N.J.: Prentice Hall.

Crawford, C. B., Smith, M. S., & Krebs, D. (1987). *Sociobiology and psychology: Ideas, issues, and applications.* Hillsdale, N.J.: Erlbaum.

Cromer, B. A., & Tarnowski, K. J. (1989). Noncompliance in adolescents: A review. *Journal of Developmental and Behavioral Pediatrics, 10*(4), 207–215.

Crouch, J. G., & Neilson, P. B. (1989). Perceived child-rearing dimensions and assertiveness. *Adolescence, 24,* 179–191.

Cummings, E. M. (1987). Coping with background anger in early childhood. *Child Development, 58,* 976–984.

Cunningham, C. E., Benness, B. B., & Siegel, L. S. (1988). Family functioning, time allocation, and parental depression in the families of normal and ADDH children. *Journal of Clinical Child Psychology, 17,* 169–177.

Curtiss, S. R. (1977). *Genie: A linguistic study of a modern day "wild child."* New York: Academic Press.

Damhorst, M. L., Littrell, J. M., & Littrell, M. A. (1988). Age differences in adolescent body satisfaction. *Journal of Psychology, 121,* 553–562.

Daniels, D., & Moos, R. H. (1988). Exosystem influences on family and child functioning. *Journal of Social Behavior and Personality, 3,* 113–133.

Dannemiller, J. L., & Stephens, B. R. (1988). A critical test of infant pattern preference models. *Child Development, 59,* 210–216.

Darley, J. M., & Latané, B. (1968). Bystander intervention in emergencies: Diffusion of responsibility. *Journal of Personality and Social Psychology, 8,* 377–383.

Das, J. P., & Siu, I. (1989). Good and poor readers' word naming time, memory span, and story recall. *Journal of Experimental Education, 10,* 101–114.

Davidoff, J. B. (1975). *Differences in visual perception: The individual eye.* New York: Academic Press.

Davidson, H. P. (1935). A study of the confusing letters B, D, P, and Q. *Journal of Genetic Psychology, 47,* 458.

Davies, G. R., McMahon, R. J., Flessati, E. W., & Tiedemann, G. L. (1984). Verbal rationales and modeling as adjuncts to a parenting technique for child compliance. *Child Development, 55,* 1290–1298.

Day, R. H., & McKenzie, B. H. (1973). Perceptual shape constancy in early infancy. *Perception, 2,* 315–321.

Day, R. H., & McKenzie, B. H. (1981). Infant perception of the invariant size of approaching and receding objects. *Developmental Psychology, 17,* 670–677.

DeCasper, A. J., & Fifer, W. P. (1980). Of human bonding: Newborns prefer their mother's voice. *Science, 208,* 1174–1176.

DeCasper, A. J., & Spence, M. J. (1986). Prenatal maternal speech influences newborns' perception of speech sounds. *Infant Behavior Development, 9,* 133–150.

DeMaris, A., & Leslie, G. R. (1984). Cohabitation with the future spouse: Its influence upon marital satisfaction and communication. *Journal of Marriage and the Family, 35,* 244–255.

Dencik, L. (1989). Growing up in the post-modern age: On the child's situation in the modern family, and on the position of the family in the modern welfare state. *Acta Sociologica, 32,* 155–180.

Dennis, M., Sugar, J., & Whitaker, H. A. (1982). The acquisition of tag questions. *Child Development, 53,* 1254–1257.

Dennis, W. (1973). *Children of the Crèche.* New York: Meredith Corporation.

Dennis, W., & Dennis, M. G. (1940). The effects of cradling practices upon the onset of walking in Hopi children. *Journal of Genetic Psychology, 56,* 77–86.

de Rosenroll, D. A. (1987). Early adolescent egocentrism: A review of six articles. *Adolescence, 22,* 791–802.

Devillier, P. L., & Forsyth, C. J. (1988). The downward mobility of divorced women with dependent children: A research note. *Sociological Spectrum, 8,* 295–302.

de Villiers, P. A., & de Villiers, J. G. (1979). *Early language.* Cambridge: Harvard University Press.

deVries, M. W., & deVries, M. R. (1977). Cultural relativity of toilet training readiness: A perspective from East Africa. *Pediatrics, 60,* 170–177.

Dick-Read, G. (1944). *Childbirth without fear: The principles and practice of natural childbirth.* New York: Harper & Row.

Dickson, S., & Parke, R. D. (1988). Social referencing in infancy: A glance at fathers and marriage. *Child Development, 59,* 506–511.

Dietz, W. H., Jr. (1987). Childhood obesity. *Annals of the New York Academy of Sciences, 499,* 47–54.

Dion, K. L., & Toner, B. B. (1988). Ethnic differences in test anxiety. *Journal of Social Psychology, 128,* 165–171.

DiPietro, J. A. (1981). Rough and tumble play: A function of gender. *Developmental Psychology, 17,* 50–58.

Dodge, K. A., & Frame, C. L. (1982). Social cognitive biases and deficits in aggressive boys. *Child Development, 53,* 620–635.

Donaldson, S. K., & Westerman, M. A. (1986). Development of children's understanding of ambivalence and causal theories of emotions. *Developmental Psychology, 22,* 655–662.

Donovan, J. E., Jessor, R., & Costa, F. M. (1988). Syndrome of problem behavior in adolescence: A replication. *Journal of Consulting and Clinical Psychology, 56,* 762–765.

Dontas, C., Maratos, O., Fafoutis, M., & Karangelis, A. (1985). Early social development in institutionally reared Greek infants: Attachment and peer interaction. In I. Bretherton & E. Waters (Eds.), Growing points of attachment theory and research. *Monographs of the Society for Research in Child Development, 50* (1–2, Serial No. 209).

Dornbusch, S. M., Ritter, P. L., Leiderman, P. H., Roberts, D. F., & Fraleigh, M. J. (1987). The relation of parenting style to adolescent school performance. *Child Development, 58,* 1244–1257.

Drexler, M. (1989). Nature vs. nurture. *Boston Globe Magazine,* December 3, pp. 16, 38–49.

Ducey, S. J. (1989). Gender differences in mathematics: Beyond descriptions. Paper presented at the April meeting of the Society for Research in Child Development, Kansas City.

Duncan, G. J., & Rodgers, W. L. (1988). Longitudinal aspects of childhood poverty. *Journal of Marriage and the Family, 50,* 1007–1021.

Dunn, J., Bretherton, I., & Munn, P. (1987). Conversations about feeling states between mothers and their young children. *Developmental Psychology, 23,* 132–139.

Dunn, J., & Munn, P. (1987). Development of justification in disputes with mother and sibling. *Developmental Psychology, 23,* 791–798.

Dunn, J., Plomin, R., & Daniels, D. (1986). Consistency and change in mothers' behavior toward young siblings. *Child Development, 57,* 348–356.

Duyme, M. (1988). School success and social class: An adoption study. *Developmental Psychology, 24,* 203–209.

Dweck, C. S. (1986). Motivational processes affecting learning. *American Psychologist, 41,* 1040–1048.

East, P. L. (1989). Missing provisions in peer-withdrawn and aggressive children's social relationships: Do siblings compensate? Paper presented at the April meeting of the Society for Research in Child Development, Kansas City.

Eccles, J. S. (1987). Gender roles and women's achievement-related decisions. *Psychology of Women Quarterly, 11,* 135–172.

Eckerman, C. O., Davis, C. C., & Didow, S. M. (1989). Toddlers' emerging ways of achieving social coordinations with a peer. *Child Development, 60,* 440–453.

Eckerman, C. O., & Didow, S. M. (1988). Lessons drawn from observing young peers together. *Acta Paediatrica Scandinavia, 77,* 55–70.

Eckerman, C. O., Whatley, J. L., & Kutz, S. L. (1975). Growth of social play with peers during the second year of life. *Developmental Psychology, 11,* 42–49.

Edelman, N. H. (1988). Smoking in pregnancy. *New York Times,* October 4, p. A30.

Edwards, M., & Waldorf, M. (1984). *Reclaiming birth: History and heroines of American childbirth reform.* Trumansburg, N.Y.: The Crossing Press.

Egeland, B., & Farber, E. A. (1984). Infant–mother attachment: Factors related to its development and changes over time. *Child Development, 55,* 753–771.

Egeland, B., & Sroufe, L. A. (1981). Attachment and early maltreatment. *Child Development, 52,* 44–52.

Eibl-Eibesfeldt, I. (1975). *Ethology: The biology of behavior* (2nd ed.). New York: Holt, Rinehart, and Winston.

Eimas, P. D. (1975). Speech perception in early infancy. In L. B. Cohen & P. Salapatek (Eds.), *Infant perception: From sensation to cognition* (Vol. 2). New York: Academic Press.

Eisenberg, A., Murkoff, H. E., & Hathaway, S. E. (1988). *What to expect when you're expecting* (2nd ed.). New York: Workman Publishing.

Eisenberg, N. (1989a). The development of prosocial moral reasoning in childhood and mid-adolescence. Paper presented at the April meeting of the Society for Research in Child Development, Kansas City.

Eisenberg, N. (1989b). The development of prosocial values. In N. Eisenberg, J. Reykowski, & E. Staub (Eds.), *Social and moral values: Individual and social perspectives.* Hillsdale, N.J.: Erlbaum.

Eisenberg, N., & Miller, P. A. (1987). The relation of empathy to prosocial and related behaviors. *Psychological Bulletin, 101,* 91–119.

Eisenberg, N., Shell, R., Pasternack, J., Lennon, R., Beller, R., & Mathy, R. M. (1987). Prosocial development in middle childhood: A longitudinal study. *Developmental Psychology, 23,* 712–718.

Ekman, P. (1989). Would a child lie? *Psychology Today,* July–August, pp. 62–65.

Elkind, D. (1967). Egocentrism in adolescence. *Child Development, 38,* 1025–1034.

Elkind, D. (1968). Cognitive development in adolescence. In J. F. Adams (Ed.), *Understanding adolescence.* Boston: Allyn & Bacon.

Elkind, D. (1973). Giant in the nursery—Jean Piaget. In *Annual Editions: Readings in Psychology, '72–'73.* Guilford, Conn.: Dushkin Publishing Group.

Elkind, D. (1978). Understanding the young adolescent. *Adolescence, 13,* 127–134.

Ellerman, D. A. (1988). Student activists 12 years later: Political and personal career paths. *Australian Journal of Psychology, 40,* 251–260.

Elliott, R. (1988). Tests, ability, race, and conflict. *Intelligence, 12,* 333–350.

Ellis, N., Katz, E., & Williams, J. E. (1987). Developmental aspects of memory for spatial location. *Journal of Experimental Child Psychology, 44,* 401–412.

Ellis, L., Burke, D., & Ames, M. A. (1987). Sexual orientation as a continuous variable: A comparison between the sexes. *Archives of Sexual Behavior, 16,* 523–528.

Ellis, N. R., & Large, B. (1988). The early stages of reading: A longitudinal study. *Applied Cognitive Psychology, 2,* 47–76.

Emery, R. E. (1989). Family violence. *American Psychologist, 44,* 321–328.

Engel, U., Nordlohne, E., Hurrelmann, K., & Holler, B. (1987). Educational career and substance use in adolescence. *European Journal of Psychology of Education, 2*(4), 365–374.

English, H. B. (1929). Three cases of the "conditioned fear response." *Journal of Abnormal and Social Psychology, 34,* 221–225.

Enns, J. T., & Girgus, J. S. (1985). Developmental changes in selective and integrative visual attention. *Journal of Experimental Child Psychology, 40,* 319–337.

Entwisle, D. R., & Alexander, K. L. (1987). Long-term effects of cesarean delivery on parents' beliefs and children's schooling. *Developmental Psychology, 23,* 676–682.

Entwisle, D. R., & Doering, S. (1988). The emergent father role. *Sex Roles, 18,* 119–141.

Epstein, L. H., & Wing, R. R. (1987). Behavioral treatment of childhood obesity. *Psychological Bulletin, 101,* 331–342.

Erickson, M. F., Sroufe, L. A., & Egeland, B. (1985). The relationship between quality of attachment and behavior problems in preschool in a high-risk sample. In I. Bretherton & E. Waters (Eds.), Growing points of attachment theory and research. *Monographs of the Society for Research in Child Development, 50* (1–2, Serial No. 209).

Erikson, E. H. (1959). *Identity and the life cycle.* New York: International Universities Press.

Erikson, E. H. (1963). *Childhood and society* (2nd ed.). New York: Norton.

Eron, L. D. (1987). The development of aggressive behavior from the perspective of a developing behaviorism. *American Psychologist, 42,* 435–442.

Eron, L. D., Lefkowitz, M. M., Huesmann, L. R., & Walder, L. O. (1972). Does television violence cause aggression? *American Psychologist, 27,* 253–263.

Esper, G. (1989). Identical twins, but one has AIDS. Asbury Park [N.J.] Press, September 10, pp. A1, A18.

Fabricius, W. V., & Cavalier, L. (1989). The role of causal theories about memory in young children's memory strategy choice. *Child Development, 60,* 298–308.

Fagan, J. F., III, & Knevel, C. R. (1989). The prediction of above-average intelligence from infancy. Paper presented at the April meeting of the Society for Research in Child Development, Kansas City.

Fagot, B. I. (1985). Beyond the reinforcement principle: Another step toward understanding sex-role development. *Developmental Psychology, 21,* 1097–1104.

Fagot, B. I., Hagan, R., Leinbach, M. D., & Kronsberg, S. (1985). Differential reactions to assertive and communicative acts of toddler boys and girls. *Child Development, 56,* 1499–1505.

Falbo, T., & Polit, D. F. (1986). Quantitative review of the only child literature: Research evidence and theory development. *Psychological Bulletin, 100,* 176–189.

Fantz, R. L. (1958). Pattern vision in young infants. *Psychological Record, 8,* 43–47.

Fantz, R. L., Fagan, J. F., & Miranda, S. B. (1975). Early visual selectivity. In L. B. Cohen & P. Salapatek (Eds.), *Infant perception: From sensation to cognition* (Vol. 1). New York: Academic Press.

Farnham-Diggory, S. (1984). Why reading? Because it's there. *Developmental Review, 4,* 62–71.

Faust, M. S. (1977). Somatic development of adolescent girls. *Monographs of the Society for Research in Child Development, 42* (No. 1), 1–90.

Fay, R. E., Turner, C. F., Klassen, A. D., & Gagnon, J. H. (1989). Prevalence and patterns of same-gender sexual contact among men. *Science, 243,* 338–348.

Feagans, L., & Short, E. J. (1984). Developmental differences in the comprehension and production of narratives by reading disabled and normally achieving children. *Child Development, 55,* 1727–1736.

Fein, G. G. (1981). Pretend play in childhood: An integrative review. *Child Development, 52,* 1095–1118.

Feinkind, L., & Minkoff, H. L. (1988). HIV in pregnancy. *Clinics in Perinatology, 15,* 189–201.

Feiring, C., Lewis, M., & Starr, M. D. (1984). Indirect effects and infants' reactions to strangers. *Developmental Psychology, 20,* 485–491.

Feldhusen, J. F. (1989). Synthesis of research on gifted youth. *Educational Leadership,* March, pp. 6–11.

Feldman, S. S., & Gehring, T. M. (1988). Changing perceptions of family cohesion and power across adolescence. *Child Development, 59,* 1034–1045.

Fennell, E. B., Satz, P., & Morris, R. (1983). The development of handedness and dichotic ear listening in relation to school achievement: A longitudinal study. *Journal of Experimental Child Psychology, 35,* 248–262.

Ferleger, N., Glenwick, D. S., Gaines, R. R. W., & Green, A. H. (1988). Identifying correlates of reabuse in maltreating parents. *Child Abuse & Neglect, 12,* 41–49.

Field, D. (1981). Can preschool children really learn to conserve? *Child Development, 52,* 326–334.

Field, T. M. (1977). Effects of early separation, interactive deficits, and experimental manipulations on infant–mother face-to-face interaction. *Child Development, 48,* 763–771.

Field, T. M., Healy, B., Goldstein, S., Perry, S., Bendell, D., Schanberg, S., Zimmerman, E. A., & Kuhn, C. (1988). Infants of depressed mothers show "depressed" behavior even with nondepressed adults. *Child Development, 59,* 1569–1579.

Field, T. M., Woodson, R., Cohen, D., Greenberg, R., Garcia, R., & Collins, K. (1983). Discrimination and imitation of facial expression by term and preterm neonates. *Infant Behavior and Development, 6,* 485–489.

Finkelstein, H. (1988). The long-term effects of early parent death: A review. *Journal of Clinical Psychology, 44,* 3–9.

Finnegan, L. P., & Fehr, K. O. (1980). The effects of opiates, sedative-hypnotics, amphetamines, cannabis, and other psychoactive drugs on the fetus and newborn. In O. J. Kalant (Ed.), *Alcohol and drug problems in women: Research advances in alcohol and drug problems* (Vol. 5). New York: Plenum Press.

Fischer, J. L., Sollie, D. L., Sorell, G. T., & Green, S. K. (1989). Marital status and career stage influences on social networks of young adults. *Journal of Marriage and the Family, 51,* 521–534.

Fischer, K. W. (1987). Relations between brain and cognitive development. *Child Development, 58,* 623–632.

Fischer, M., & Leitenberg, H. (1986). Optimism and pessimism in elementary school-age children. *Child Development, 57,* 241–248.

Fisher, C. B., & Braine, L. G. (1981). Children's left–right concepts: Generalization across figure and location. *Child Development, 52,* 451–456.

Fisher, L. A., & Bauman, K. E. (1988). Influence and selection in the friend–adolescent relationship: Findings from studies of adolescent smoking and drinking. *Journal of Applied Social Psychology, 18,* 289–314.

Fisher, S. E. (1988). Selective fetal malnutrition: The fetal alcohol syndrome. *Journal of the American College of Nutrition, 7,* 101–106.

Flavell, J. H. (1985). *Cognitive development* (2nd ed.). Englewood Cliffs, N.J.: Prentice Hall.

Flavell, J. H. (1986). Really and truly. *Psychology Today,* January, pp. 38–44.

Flavell, J. H., Beach, D. R., & Chinsky, J. M. (1966). Spontaneous verbal rehearsal in memory task as a function of age. *Child Development, 37,* 283–299.

Flavell, J. H., Flavell, E. R., & Green, F. L. (1987). Young children's knowledge about the apparent-real and pretend-real distinctions. *Developmental Psychology, 23,* 816–822.

Flavell, J. H., Friedrichs, A. G., & Hoyt, J. D. (1970). Developmental changes in memorization processes. *Cognitive Psychology, 1,* 324–340.

Flavell, J. H., Shipstead, S. G., & Croft, K. (1980). What young children think you see when their eyes are closed. *Cognition, 8,* 369–387.

Flavell, J. H., Speer, J. R., Green, F. L., & August, D. L. (1981). The development of comprehension monitoring and knowledge about communication. *Monographs of the Society for Research in Child Development, 46* (5, Serial No. 192).

Flesch, R. (1955). *Why Johnny can't read.* New York: Harper & Row.

Flora, J. A., & Thoresen, C. E. (1988). Reducing the risk of AIDS in adolescents. *American Psychologist, 43,* 965–970.

Flynn, J. R. (1987). Massive IQ gains in 14 nations: What IQ tests really measure. *Psychological Bulletin, 101,* 171–191.

Fox, N. A., & Davidson, R. J. (1987). Electroencephalogram asymmetry in response to the approach of a stranger and maternal separation in 10-month-old infants. *Developmental Psychology, 23,* 233–240.

Fraiberg, S. H. (1959). *The magic years.* New York: Scribner's.

Fraiberg, S. H. (1977). *Insights from the blind: Comparative studies of blind and sighted infants.* New York: Basic Books.

Frank, D., & Vogel, M. (1988). *The baby makers.* New York: Carroll & Graf.

Frankenburg, W. K., & Dodds, J. B. (1967). The Denver Developmental Screening Test. *Journal of Pediatrics, 71,* 181–191.

Frauenglass, M. H., & Diaz, R. M. (1985). Self-regulatory functions of children's private speech: A critical analysis of recent challenges to Vygotsky's theory. *Developmental Psychology, 21,* 357–364.

Freebody, P., & Byrne, B. (1988). Word-reading strategies in elementary school children: Relations to comprehension, reading time, and phonemic awareness. *Reading Research Quarterly, 23*(4), 441–453.

Freedman, R. (1986). *Beauty bound.* Lexington, Mass.: Lexington Books.

Freij, B. J., & Sever, J. L. (1988). Herpesvirus infections in pregnancy: Risks to embryo, fetus, and neonate. *Clinics in Perinatology, 15,* 203–231.

Freij, B. J., South, M. A., & Sever, J. L. (1988). Maternal rubella and the congenital rubella syndrome. *Clinics in Perinatology, 15,* 247–257.

French, D. C. (1988). Heterogeneity of peer-rejected boys: Aggressive and nonaggressive subtypes. *Child Development, 59,* 976–985.

Freud, A. (1958). Adolescence. In *Psychoanalytic study of the child* (Vol. 13). New York: International Universities Press.

Freud, A., & Dann, S. (1967). An experiment in group upbringing. In Y. Brackbill & G. G. Thompson (Eds.), *Behavior in infancy and early childhood.* New York: Free Press.

Freud, S. (1938). The history of the psychoanalytic movement. In A. A. Brill (Ed. and Trans.), *The basic writings of Sigmund Freud.* New York: Modern Library.

Freud, S. (1950). The analysis of a phobia in a five-year-old boy. In *Collected Papers* (Vol. 1). London: Hogarth. (Originally published in 1909.)

Freud, S. (1965). *New introductory lectures in psychoanalysis* (J. Strachey, Ed. and Trans.). New York: Norton. (Originally published in 1933.)

Fried, P. A., Watkinson, B., Dillon, R. F., & Dulberg, C. S. (1987). Neonatal neurological status in a low-risk population after prenatal exposure to cigarettes, marijuana, and alcohol. *Developmental and Behavioral Pediatrics, 8,* 318–326.

Friedman, A. S., Utada, A. T., Glickman, N. W., & Morrissey, M. R. (1987). Psychopathology as an antecedent to, and as a "consequence" of, substance use in adolescence. *Journal of Drug Education, 17*(3), 233–243.

Friedman, W. J. (1986). The development of children's knowledge of temporal structure. *Child Development, 57,* 1386–1400.

Friedrich, O. (1983). What do babies know? *Time,* August 15, pp. 52–59.

Frisch, R. E. (1988). Fatness and fertility. *Scientific American,* March, 88–95.

Fry, D. P. (1988). Intercommunity differences in aggression among Zapotec children. *Child Development, 59,* 1008–1019.

Fuchs, D., & Thelen, M. H. (1988). Children's expected interpersonal consequences of communicating their affective state and reported likelihood of expression. *Child Development, 59,* 1314–1322.

Funder, D. C., Block, J. H., & Block, J. (1983). Delay of gratification: Some longitudinal personality correlates. *Journal of Personality and Social Psychology, 44,* 1198–1213.

Furstenberg, F. F., Jr., Brooks-Gunn, J., & Chase-Lansdale, L. (1989). Teenage pregnancy and childbearing. *American Psychologist, 44,* 313–320.

Gadsby, P. (1990). Wanderlust. *Discover,* April, p. 24.

Galahue, D. L. (1983). Assessing motor development in young children. *Studies in Educational Evaluation, 8,* 247–252.

Galkowski, T., Jacunska, M., & Scott, R. (1987). IQ and achievement profiles of disadvantaged children: Polish-American comparisons. *Mankind Quarterly, 28*(1), 13–26.

Galler, J. R. (1984). The behavioral consequences of malnutrition in early life. In J. R. Galler (Ed.), *Nutrition and behavior*. New York: Plenum Press.

Gamoran, A. (1989). Rank, performance, and mobility in elementary school grouping. *Sociological Quarterly, 30,* 109–123.

Garbarino, J., Sebes, J., & Schellenbach, C. (1984). Families at risk for destructive parent–child relations in adolescence. *Child Development, 55,* 174–183.

Gardner, B. T., & Gardner, R. A. (1971). Two-way communication with an infant chimpanzee. In A. M. Schrier & F. Stollnitz (Eds.), *Behavior of nonhuman primates* (Vol. 4). New York: Academic Press.

Gardner, H. (1980). *Artful scribbles: The significance of children's drawings*. New York: Basic Books.

Garfinkel, P. E., Garner, D. M., & Goldbloom, D. S. (1987). Eating disorders: Implications for the 1990's. *Canadian Journal of Psychiatry, 32,* 624–631.

Garrod, A., Beal, C., & Shin, P. (1989). The development of moral orientation in elementary school children. Paper presented at the April meeting of the Society for Research in Child Development, Kansas City.

Garwood, S. G., Phillips, D., Hartman, A., & Zigler, E. F. (1989). As the pendulum swings: Federal agency programs for children. *American Psychologist, 44,* 434–438.

Geary, D. C. (1989). A model for representing gender differences in the pattern of cognitive abilities. *American Psychologist, 44,* 1155–1156.

Gelman, R. (1978). Cognitive development. In L. W. Porter & M. R. Rosenzweig (Eds.), *Annual review of psychology* (Vol. 29). Palo Alto, Calif.: Annual Reviews.

Gelman, R. (1982). Basic numerical abilities. In R. J. Sternberg (Ed.), *Advances in the psychology of human intelligence* (Vol. 1). Hillsdale, N.J.: Erlbaum.

Gelman, R., & Gallistel, C. R. (1978). The child's understanding of number. Cambridge: Harvard University Press.

Gelman, S. A. (1989). Children's use of categories to guide biological inferences. *Human Development, 32,* 65–71.

Gerstein, M., Lichtman, M., & Barokas, J. U. (1988). Occupational plans of adolescent women compared to men: A cross-sectional examination. *Career Development Quarterly, 36,* 222–230.

Gesell, A., & Ames, L. B. (1947). The development of handedness. *Journal of Genetic Psychology, 70,* 155–175.

Gesell, A., & Thompson, H. (1929). Learning and growth in identical infant twins: An experimental study by the method of co-twin control. *Genetic Psychology Monographs, 6,* 1–125.

Geschwind, N., & Behan, P. (1982). Left-handedness: Association with immune disease, migraine, and developmental learning disorder. *Proceedings of the National Academy of Science, 79,* 5097–5100.

Gewirtz, J. L. (1972). Attachment, dependence, and distinction in terms of stimulus control. In J. L. Gewirtz (Ed.), *Attachment and dependency*. Washington, D.C.: Winston & Sons.

Ghodsian-Carpey, J., & Baker, L. A. (1987). Genetic and environmental influences on aggression in 4- to 7-year-old twins. *Aggressive Behavior, 13,* 173–186.

Giblin, P. T., Poland, M. L., Waller, J. B., Jr., & Ager, J. W. (1989). Correlates of neonatal morbidity: Maternal characteristics and family resources. *Journal of Genetic Psychology, 149,* 527–533.

Gibson, E. J. (1969). *Principles of perceptual learning and development*. Englewood Cliffs, N.J.: Prentice Hall.

Gibson, E. J., & Walk, R. D. (1960). The "visual cliff." *Scientific American*, April, pp. 64–71.

Giegerich, S., & Moslock, J. A. (1989). Class of the year 2000: Schoolyard perc. Asbury Park [N.J.] Press, October 29, pp. AA1, AA4.

Gillberg, C. (1988). The neurobiology of infantile autism. *Journal of Child Psychology and Psychiatry, 29,* 257–266.

Gilligan, C. (1982). *In a different voice: Sex differences in the expression of moral judgment*. Cambridge: Harvard University Press.

Gilligan, C., & Attanucci, J. (1988). Two moral orientations: Gender differences and similarities. *Merrill–Palmer Quarterly, 34,* 223–237.

Ginsburg, H., & Opper, S. (1969). *Piaget's theory of intellectual development: An introduction*. Englewood Cliffs, N.J.: Prentice Hall.

Ginsburg, H. P., Lopez, L., Chung, Y. E., and others (1989). Early mathematical thinking: Role of social class, racial, and cultural influences. Paper presented at the April meeting of the Society for Research in Child Development, Kansas City.

Ginzberg, E. (1972). Toward a theory of occupational choice: A restatement. *Vocational Guidance Quarterly, 20,* 169–176.

Gleason, J. B. (1967). Do children imitate? *Proceedings of the International Conference on Oral Education of the Deaf, 2,* 1441–1448.

Gleitman, L. R., & Gleitman, H. (1981). Language. In H. Gleitman, *Psychology*. New York: Norton.

Glick, P. C. (1988). Fifty years of family demography: A record of social change. *Journal of Marriage and the Family, 50,* 861–873.

Glick, P. C. (1989). The family life cycle and social change. *Family Relations, 38,* 123–129.

Glucksberg, S., Krauss, R. M., & Weisberg, R (1966). Referential communication in nursery school children: Method and some preliminary findings. *Journal of Experimental Child Psychology, 3,* 333–342.

Glueck, S., & Glueck, E. (1950). *Unraveling juvenile delinquency*. Cambridge: Harvard University Press.

Gnepp, J., & Chilamkurti, C. (1988). Children's use of personality attributions to predict other people's emotional and behavioral reactions. *Child Development, 59,* 743–754.

Gnepp, J., & Hess, D. L. R. (1986). Children's understanding of verbal and facial display rules. *Developmental Psychology, 22,* 103–108.

Gnepp, J., McKee, E., & Domanic, J. A. (1987). Children's use of situational information to infer emotion: Understanding emotionally equivocal situations. *Developmental Psychology, 23,* 114–123.

Goddard, H. H. (1912). *The Kallikak family*. New York: Macmillan.

Goldberg, S., Blumberg, S. L., & Kriger, A. (1982). Menarche and interest in infants: Biological and social influences. *Child Development, 53,* 1544–1550.

Goldberg, S., Perrotta, M., Minde, K., & Corter, C. (1986). Maternal behavior and attachment in low-birth-weight twins and singletons. *Child Development, 57,* 34–46.

Goldin-Meadow, S., & Feldman, H. (1975). The creation of a communication system: A study of deaf children of hearing parents. *Sign Language Studies, 8,* 225–234.

Goldman, M., & Goldman, M. (1986). Sit down, Ma. *American Health*, January/February, p. 82.

Goldman, R. J., & Goldman, J. D. G. (1982). How children perceive the origin of babies and the roles of mothers and fathers in procreation: A cross-national study. *Child Development, 53,* 491–504.

Goldscheider, F. K., & Goldscheider, C. (1989). Family structure and conflict: Nest-leaving expectations of young adults and their parents. *Journal of Marriage and the Family, 51,* 87–97.

Goldsmith, H. H., & Alansky, J. A. (1987). Maternal and infant temperamental predictors of attachment: A meta-analytic review. *Journal of Consulting and Clinical Psychology, 55,* 805–816.

Goldsmith, H. H., Buss, A. H., Plomin, R., Rothbart, M. K., Thomas, A., Chess, S., Hinde, R. A., & McCall, R. B. (1987). Roundtable: What is temperament? Four approaches. *Child Development, 58,* 505–529.

Goldstein, M. J. (1988). The family and psychopathology. *Annual Review of Psychology, 39,* 283–299.

Goleman, D. (1989). Psychologists find ways to break racism's hold. *New York Times,* September 5, pp. C1, C8.

Goleman, D. (1990a). As a therapist, Freud fell short, scholars find. *New York Times,* March 6, pp. C1, C12.

Goleman, D. (1990b). Taming unruly boys: Old techniques and new approaches. *New York Times,* February 1, p. B10.

Göncü, A., & Kessel, F. (1988). Preschoolers' collaborative construction in planning and maintaining imaginative play. *International Journal of Behavioral Development, 11,* 327–344.

Good, T. L., & Weinstein, R. S. (1986). Schools make a difference: Evidence, criticisms, and new directions. *American Psychologist, 41,* 1090–1097.

Goodnow, J. J. (1977). *Children drawing.* Cambridge: Harvard University Press.

Goodnow, J. J., & Warton, P. M. (1990). The social bases of social cognition: Interactions about work and their implications. *Merrill-Palmer Quarterly,* in press.

Gopnik, A., & Astington, J. W. (1988). Children's understanding of representational change and its relation to the understanding of false belief and the appearance-reality distinction. *Child Development, 59,* 26–37.

Gopnik, A., & Meltzoff, A. (1987). The development of categorization in the second year and its relation to other cognitive and linguistic developments. *Child Development, 58,* 1523–1531.

Gortmaker, S. L., Dietz, W. H., Jr., Sobol, A. M., & Wehler, C. A. (1987). Increasing pediatric obesity in the United States. *American Journal of Diseases of Children, 141,* 535–540.

Goshen-Gottstein, E. R. (1981). Differential maternal socialization of opposite-sexed twins, triplets, and quadruplets. *Child Development, 52,* 1255–1264.

Graham, J. M., Hanson, J. W., Darby, B. L., Barr, H. M., & Streissguth, A. P. (1988). Independent dysmorphology evaluations at birth and 4 years of age for children exposed to varying amounts of alcohol in utero. *Pediatrics, 81,* 772–778.

Granrud, C. E., Yonas, A., & Pettersen, L. (1984). A comparison of monocular and binocular depth perception in 5- and 7-month-old infants. *Journal of Experimental Child Psychology, 38,* 19–32.

Grant, E. (1988). Marriage: Practice makes perfect? *Psychology Today,* March, p. 14.

Gray, W. M., & Hudson, L. M. (1984). Formal operations and the imaginary audience. *Developmental Psychology, 20,* 619–627.

Green, R. (1987). The "sissy boy syndrome" and the development of homosexuality. New Haven: Yale University Press.

Greenfield, P. M. (1966). On culture and conservation. In J. S. Bruner, R. R. Olver, & P. M. Greenfield (Eds.), *Studies in cognitive growth.* New York: Wiley.

Greenough, W. T., Black, J. E., & Wallace, C. S. (1987). Experience and brain development. *Child Development, 58,* 539–559.

Greer, D. L., & Stewart, M. J. (1989). Children's attitudes toward play: An investigation of their context specificity and relationship to organized sport experiences. *Journal of Sport and Exercise Psychology, 11,* 336–342.

Gross, J., & Rosen, J. C. (1988). Bulimia in adolescents: Prevalence and psychosocial correlates. *International Journal of Eating Disorders, 7,* 51–61.

Grossman, F. K., Pollack, W. S., & Golding, E. (1988). Fathers and children: Predicting the quality and quantity of fathering. *Developmental Psychology, 24,* 82–91.

Guisinger, S., Cowan, P. A., & Schuldberg, D. (1989). Changing parent and spouse relations in the first years of remarriage of divorced fathers. *Journal of Marriage and the Family, 51,* 445–456.

Haake, R. J., & Somerville, S. C. (1985). Development of logical search skills in infancy. *Developmental Psychology, 21,* 176–186.

Hagerman, R. J., & Sobesky, W. E. (1989). Psychopathology in fragile X syndrome. *American Journal of Orthopsychiatry, 59,* 142–152.

Hahn, W. K. (1987). Cerebral lateralization of function: From infancy through childhood. *Psychological Bulletin, 101,* 376–392.

Hakuta, K., & Garcia, E. E. (1989). Bilingualism and education. *American Psychologist, 44,* 374–379.

Hall, H. (1988). Marriage: Practice makes imperfect? *Psychology Today,* July/August, p. 15.

Hall, J. A. (1987). Parent–adolescent conflict: An empirical review. *Adolescence, 22,* 767–789.

Hallinan, M. T., & Teixeira, R. A. (1987). Students' interracial friendships: Individual characteristics, structural effects, and racial differences. *American Journal of Education, 95,* 563–583.

Halpern, D. F. (1989). The disappearance of cognitive gender differences: What you see depends on where you look. *American Psychologist, 44,* 1156–1158.

Halpern, J. J., & Luria, Z. (1989). Labels of giftedness and gender-typicality: Effects on adults' judgments of children's traits. *Psychology in the Schools, 26,* 301–310.

Hamburg, D. A., & Takanishi, R. (1989). Preparing for life: The critical transition of adolescence. *American Psychologist, 44,* 825–827.

Hanratty, M. A., Liebert, R. M., Morris, L. W., & Fernandez, L. E. (1969). Imitation of film-mediated aggression against live and inanimate victims. *Proceedings of the 77th Annual Convention of the American Psychological Association, 4,* 457–458 (abstract).

Hapgood, C. C., Elkind, G. S., & Wright, J. J. (1988). Maternity blues: Phenomena and relationship to later postpartum depression. *Australian and New Zealand Journal of Psychiatry, 22,* 299–306.

Hareven, T. (1985). Historical changes in the life course: Implications for child development. In A. B. Smuts & J. W. Hagen (Eds.), History and research in child development. *Monographs of the Society for Research in Child Development, 50* (4–5, Serial No. 211).

Harlow, H. F., & Harlow, M. K. (1965). The affectional systems. In A. M. Schrier, H. F. Harlow, & F. Stollnitz (Eds.), *Behavior of nonhuman primates* (Vol. 2). New York: Academic Press.

Harper, L. V., & Sanders, K. M. (1978). Preschool children's use of space: Sex differences in outdoor play. In M. S. Smart & R. C. Smart (Eds.), *Preschool children: Development and relationships.* New York: Macmillan.

Harrington, D. M., Block, J., & Block, J. H. (1983). Predicting creativity in preadolescence from divergent thinking in early childhood. *Journal of Personality and Social Psychology, 45,* 609–623.

Harris, C. S. (1980). Insight or out of sight? Two examples of perceptual plasticity in the human adult. In C. S. Harris (Ed.), *Visual coding and adaptability.* Hillsdale, N.J.: Erlbaum.

Harris, S. H. (1982). An evaluation of the Snijders–Oomen Nonverbal Intelligence Scale for Young Children. *Journal of Pediatric Psychology, 7,* 239–251.

Hart, L. M., & Goldin-Meadow, S. (1984). The child as a nonegocentric art critic. *Child Development, 55,* 2122–2129.

Harter, S. (1978). Pleasure derived from challenge and the effects of receiving grades on children's difficulty level choices. *Child Development, 49,* 788–799.

Harter, S. (1982). The perceived competence scale for children. *Child Development, 53,* 87–97.

Hartup, W. W. (1989). Social relationships and their developmental significance. *American Psychologist, 44,* 120–126.

Haskins, R. (1989). Beyond metaphor: The efficacy of early childhood education. *American Psychologist, 44,* 274–282.

Hass, A. (1979). *Teenage sexuality.* New York: Macmillan.

Hassler, M., & Birbaumer, N. (1989). Handedness, musical abilities, and dichaptic and dichotic performance in adolescents: A longitudinal study. *Developmental Neuropsychology, 4,* 129–145.

Hativa, N. (1988). Computer-based drill and practice in arithmetic: Widening the gap between high- and low-achieving students. *American Educational Research Journal, 25*(3), 366–397.

Hatwell, Y. (1987). Motor and cognitive functions of the hand in infancy and childhood. *International Journal of Behavioral Development, 10,* 509–526.

Havemann, E., & Lehtinen, M. (1986). *Marriages and families.* Englewood Cliffs, N.J.: Prentice Hall.

Haviland, J. M., & Lelwica, M. (1987). The induced affect response: 10-week-old infants' responses to three emotion expressions. *Developmental Psychology, 23,* 97–104.

Haviland, J. M., & Scarborough, H. S. (1981). *Adolescent development in contemporary society.* New York: Van Nostrand.

Hayden-Thomson, L., Rubin, K. H., & Hymel, S. (1987). Sex preferences in sociometric choices. *Developmental Psychology, 23,* 558–562.

Hazan, C., & Shaver, P. (1987). Romantic love conceptualized as an attachment process. *Journal of Personality and Social Psychology, 52,* 511–524.

Heath, S. B. (1989). Oral and literate traditions among black Americans living in poverty. *American Psychologist, 44,* 367–373.

Hechtman, L. (1989). Teenage mothers and their children: Risks and problems: A review. *Canadian Journal of Psychology, 34,* 569–575.

Heibeck, T. H., & Markman, E. M. (1987). Word learning in children: An examination of fast mapping. *Child Development, 58,* 1021–1034.

Hein, K. (1989). AIDS in adolescence: Exploring the challenge. *Journal of Adolescent Health Care, 10,* 10S-35S.

Helton, A. S., & Snodgrass, F. G. (1987). Battering during pregnancy: Intervention strategies. *Birth, 14,* 142–147.

Henry, W. A., III (1990). Beyond the melting pot. *Time,* April 9, pp. 28-31.

Herkowitz, J. (1978). Sex-role expectations and motor behavior of the young child. In M. V. Ridenour (Ed.), *Motor development: Issues and applications.* Princeton, N.J.: Princeton Book Co.

Hess, E. H. (1970). The ethological approach to socialization. In R. A. Hoppe, G. A. Milton, & E. C. Simmel (Eds.), *Early experiences and the processes of socialization.* New York: Academic Press.

Hetherington, E. M., Stanley-Hagan, M., & Anderson, E. R. (1989). Marital transitions: A child's perspective. *American Psychologist, 44,* 303–312.

Higgins, A. T., & Turnure, J. E. (1984). Distractibility and concentration of attention in children's development. *Child Development, 55,* 1799–1810.

High PCB levels found in Eskimo breast milk (1989). *New York Times,* February 7, p. C9.

Hilts, P. J. (1989). A sinister bias: New studies cite perils for lefties. *New York Times,* August 29, pp. C1, C6.

Hinshaw, S. P. (1987). On the distinction between attentional deficits/hyperactivity and conduct problems/aggression in child psychopathology. *Psychological Bulletin, 101,* 443–463.

Hirsch, B. J., & Rapkin, B. D. (1987). The transition to junior high school: A longitudinal study of self-esteem, psychological symptomatology, school life, and social support. *Child Development, 58,* 1234–1243.

Hirsh-Pasek, K., Hyson, M., Rescorla, L., & Cone, J. (1989). Hurrying children: How does it affect their academic, social, creative, and emotional development? Paper presented at the April meeting of the Society for Research in Child Development, Kansas City.

Hiscock, M., & Kinsbourne, M. (1987). Specialization of the cerebral hemispheres: Implications for learning. *Journal of Learning Disabilities, 20,* 130–142.

Hitch, G. J., Woodin, M. E., & Baker, S. (1989). Visual and phonological components of working memory in children. *Memory and Cognition, 17,* 175–185.

Ho, D. Y. F. (1989). Continuity and variation in Chinese patterns of socialization. *Journal of Marriage and the Family, 51,* 149–163.

Hoberman, H. M., & Garfinkel, B. D. (1988). Completed suicide in children and adolescents. *Journal of the American Academy of Child and Adolescent Psychiatry, 27,* 689–695.

Hochberg, J., & Brooks, V. (1962). Pictorial recognition as an unlearned ability: A study of one child's performance. *American Journal of Psychology, 75,* 624–628.

Hoffman, L. W. (1988). Cross-cultural differences in childrearing goals. In R. A. LeVine, P. M. Miller, & M. M. West (Eds.), *Parental behavior in diverse societies. New Directions for Child Development, No. 40.* San Francisco: Jossey-Bass.

Hoffman, L. W. (1989). Effects of maternal employment in the two-parent family. *American Psychologist, 44,* 283–292.

Hoffman, M. L. (1975). Developmental synthesis of affect and cognition and its implications for altruistic motivation. *Developmental Psychology, 11,* 607–622.

Holden, C. (1985). Genes, personality, and alcoholism. *Psychology Today,* January, pp. 38–44.

Holden, C. (1987). The genetics of personality. *Science, 237,* 598–601.

Holden, C. (1988). Doctor of sexology. *Psychology Today,* May, pp. 45–48.

Holinger, P. C., Offer, D., & Zola, M. A. (1988). A prediction model of suicide among youth. *Journal of Nervous and Mental Disease, 176,* 275–279.

Holland, J. L. (1985). *Making vocational choices: A theory of vocational personalities and work environments* (2nd ed.). Englewood Cliffs, N.J.: Prentice Hall.

Holmes, H. B. (1988). In vitro fertilization: Reflections on the state of the art. *Birth, 15,* 134–145.

Honig, A. S. (1988). Humor development in children. *Young Children,* May, pp. 60–73.

Hopkins, J., Campbell, S. B., & Marcus, M. (1987). Role of infant-related stressors in postpartum depression. *Journal of Abnormal Psychology, 96,* 237–241.

Hopkins, J., Marcus, M., & Campbell, S. (1984). Postpartum depression: A critical review. *Psychological Bulletin, 95,* 498–515.

Horner, M. S. (1969). Fail: Bright women. *Psychology Today,* November, pp. 36–38.

Horobin, K., & Acredolo, L. P. (1986). The role of attentiveness, mobility history, and separation of hiding sites on Stage IV search behavior. *Journal of Experimental Child Psychology, 41,* 114–127.

Householder, J., Hatcher, R., Burns, W., & Chasnoff, I. (1982). Infants born to narcotic-addicted mothers. *Psychological Bulletin, 92,* 453–468.

Houts, A. C., & Liebert, R. M. (1984). *Bedwetting.* Springfield, Ill.: Charles C Thomas.

Hover, S. J., & Gaffney, L. R. (1988). Factors associated with smoking behavior in adolescent girls. *Addictive Behaviors, 13,* 139–145.

Howes, C. (1985). Sharing fantasy: Social pretend play in toddlers. *Child Development, 56,* 1253–1258.

Howes, C. (1987). Social competence with peers in young children: Developmental sequences. *Developmental Review, 7,* 252–272.

Howes, C., & Olenick, M. (1986). Family and child care influences on toddler's compliance. *Child Development, 57,* 202–216.

Howrigan, G. A. (1988). Fertility, infant feeding, and change in Yucatán. In R. A. LeVine, P. M. Miller, & M. M. West (Eds.), *Parental behavior in diverse societies. New Directions for Child Development, No. 40.* San Francisco: Jossey-Bass.

Hubel, D. H., & Wiesel, T. N. (1970). The period of susceptibility to the physiological effects of unilateral eye closure in kittens. *Journal of Physiology, 206,* 419–436.

Hudson, L. M., Forman, E. A., & Brion-Meisels, S. (1982). Role-taking as a predictor of prosocial behavior in cross-age tutors. *Child Development, 53,* 1320–1329.

Huesmann, L. R., Eron, L. D., & Yarmel, P. W. (1987). Intellectual functioning and aggression. *Journal of Personality and Social Psychology, 52,* 232–240.

Humphrey, L. L. (1984). Children's self-control in relation to perceived social environment. *Journal of Personality and Social Psychology, 46,* 178–188.

Humphreys, A. P., & Smith, P. K. (1987). Rough and tumble, friendship, and dominance in schoolchildren: Evidence for continuity and change with age. *Child Development, 58,* 201–212.

Hunter, F. T., McCarthy, M. E., MacTurk, R. H., & Vietze, P. M. (1987). Infants' social-constructive interactions with mothers and fathers. *Developmental Psychology, 23,* 249–254.

Huntington, G. E. (1981). Children of the Hutterites. *Natural History,* February, pp. 34–47.

Hunziker, U. A., & Barr, R. G. (1986). Increased carrying reduces infant crying: A randomized control trial. *Pediatrics, 77,* 641–648.

Huyghe, P. (1989). The big yawn. *Discover,* June, pp. 79–81.

Hyman, R. (1989). The psychology of deception. *Annual Review of Psychology, 40,* 133–154.

Hymel, S. (1986). Interpretations of peer behavior: Affective bias in childhood and adolescence. *Child Development, 57,* 431–445.

Inhelder, B., & Piaget, J. (1958). *The growth of logical thinking from childhood to adolescence.* New York: Basic Books.

Istvan, J. (1986). Stress, anxiety, and birth outcomes: A critical review of the evidence. *Psychological Bulletin, 100,* 331–348.

Jacklin, C. N. (1989). Female and male: Issues of gender. *American Psychologist, 44,* 127–133.

Jackson, A. W., & Hornbeck, D. W. (1989). Educating young adolescents: Why we must restructure middle grade schools. *American Psychologist, 44,* 831–836.

Jackson, J. F., & Jackson, J. H. (1978). *Infant culture.* New York: Thomas Y. Crowell.

Jackson, N. E. (1988). Precocious reading ability: What does it mean? *Gifted Child Quarterly, 32*(1), 200–204.

Jacobson, J. L., Jacobson, S. W., Fein, G. G., Schwartz, P. M., & Dowler, J. K. (1984). Prenatal exposure to an environmental toxin: A test of the multiple effects model. *Developmental Psychology, 20,* 523–532.

Jagacinski, C. M., LeBold, W. K., & Salvendy, G. (1988). Gender differences in persistence in computer-related fields. *Journal of Educational Computing Research, 4,* 185–202.

Jaroff, L. (1989). The gene hunt. *Time,* March 20, pp. 62–71.

Jasnow, M., & Feldstein, S. (1986). Adult-like temporal characteristics of mother–infant vocal interactions. *Child Development, 57,* 754–761.

Jensen, A. R. (1969). How much can we boost IQ and scholastic achievement? *Harvard Educational Review, 39,* 1–123.

Jensen, A. R. (1981). *Straight talk about mental tests.* New York: Free Press.

Jessor, R., Costa, F., Jessor, L., Donovan, J. E. (1983). Time of first intercourse: A prospective study. *Journal of Personality and Social Psychology, 44,* 608–626.

Jiao, S., Ji, G., & Jing, Q. (1986). Comparative study of behavioral qualities of only children and sibling children. *Child Development, 57,* 357–361.

Johnson, C. L., Klee, L., & Schmidt, C. (1988). Conceptions of parentage and kinship among children of divorce. *American Anthropologist, 90,* 135–144.

Johnson, E. S., & Meade, A. C. (1987). Developmental patterns of spatial ability: An early sex difference. *Child Development, 58,* 725–740.

Jones, D. C., Swift, D. J., & Johnson, M. A. (1988). Nondeliberate memory for a novel event among preschoolers. *Developmental Psychology, 24,* 641–645.

Jones, G., & Smith, P. K. (1984). The eyes have it: Young children's discrimination of age in masked and unmasked facial photographs. *Journal of Experimental Child Psychology, 38,* 328–337.

Jones, M. C. (1924). The elimination of children's fears. *Journal of Experimental Psychology, 7,* 383–390.

Jouriles, E. N., Pfiffner, L. J., & O'Leary, S. G. (1988). Marital conflict, parenting, and toddler conduct problems. *Journal of Abnormal Child Psychology, 16,* 197–206.

Julesz, B. (1971). *Foundations of cyclopean perception.* Chicago: University of Chicago Press.

Jurich, A. P., & Jurich, J. A. (1975). The lost adolescence syndrome. *Family Coordinator, 24,* 357–361.

Jussim, L. (1989). Teacher expectations: Self-fulfilling prophecies, perceptual biases, and accuracy. *Journal of Personality and Social Psychology, 57,* 469–480.

Kagan, J. (1965). Impulsive and reflective children: Significance of conceptual tempo. In J. D. Krumboltz (Ed.), *Learning and the educational process.* Chicago: Rand McNally.

Kagan, J. (1978). The baby's elastic mind. *Human Nature,* January, pp. 66–73.

Kagan, J. (1979). Family experience and the child's development. *American Psychologist, 34,* 886–891.

Kagan, J. (1984). *The nature of the child.* New York: Basic Books.

Kagan, J., Reznick, J. S., & Snidman, N. (1988). Biological bases of childhood shyness. *Science, 240,* 167–171.

Kagan, J., Reznick, J. S., Snidman, N., Gibbons, J., & Johnson, M. O. (1988). Childhood derivatives of inhibition and lack of inhibition to the unfamiliar. *Child Development, 59,* 1580–1589.

Kagan, J., Rosman, B. L., Day, D., Albert, J., & Phillips, W. (1964). Information processing in the child: Significance of analytic and reflective attitudes. *Psychological Monographs, 78* (1, Whole No. 578).

Kagitcibasi, C., & Berry, J. W. (1989). Cross-cultural psychology: Current research and trends. *Annual Review of Psychology, 40,* 493–531.

Kahn, S., Zimmerman, G., Csikszentmihalyi, M., & Getzels, J. W. (1985). Relations between identity in young adulthood and intimacy at midlife. *Journal of Personality and Social Psychology, 49,* 1316–1322.

Kandel, D. B. (1980). Drug and drinking behavior among youth. *Annual Review of Sociology, 6,* 235–286.

Kanner, L. (1951). The conception of wholes and parts in early infantile autism. *American Journal of Psychiatry, 108,* 23–26.

Kazdin, A. E. (1987). Treatment of antisocial behavior in children: Current status and future directions. *Psychological Bulletin, 102,* 187–203.

Keeney, T. J., Cannizzo, S. R., & Flavell, J. H. (1967). Spontaneous and induced verbal rehearsal in recall tasks. *Child Development, 38,* 953–966.

Keller, Heidi, & Schölmerich, A. (1987). Infant vocalizations and parental reactions during the first 4 months of life. *Developmental Psychology, 23,* 62–67.

Keller, Helen (1905). *The story of my life.* New York: Grosset & Dunlap.

Kellman, P. J., & Spelke, E. S. (1983). Perception of partly occluded objects in infancy. *Cognitive Psychology, 15,* 483–524.

Kellogg, R. (1969). *Analyzing children's art.* Palo Alto, Calif.: National Press.

Kelly, A. (1988). Gender differences in teacher-pupil interactions: A meta-analytic review. *Research in Education, 39,* 1–23.

Kelly, M. (1988). Very active tot likes to be "in the action." Asbury Park [N.J.] Press, December 11, p. C19.

Kennedy, E., Spence, S. H., & Hensley, R. (1989). An examination of the relationship between childhood depression and social competence among primary school children. *Journal of Child Psychology and Psychiatry, 30,* 561–573.

Kennedy, J. H. (1989). Determinants of peer social status: Contributions of physical appearance, reputation, and behavior. Paper presented at the April meeting of the Society for Research in Child Development, Kansas City.

Keogh, J. (1973). Development in fundamental motor tasks. In C. B. Corbin (Ed.), *A textbook of motor development.* Dubuque, Ia.: William C. Brown.

Kermoian, R., & Campos, J. J. (1988). Locomotor experience: A facilitator of spatial cognitive development. *Child Development, 59,* 908–917.

Kershner, J. R., & Ledger, G. (1985). Effect of sex, intelligence, and style of thinking on creativity: A comparison of gifted and average IQ children. *Journal of Personality and Social Psychology, 48,* 1033–1040.

Kidd, A. H., & Kidd, R. M. (1987). Reactions of infants and toddlers to live and toy animals. *Psychological Reports, 61,* 455–464.

Kimball, M. M. (1989). A new perspective on women's math achievement. *Psychological Bulletin, 105,* 198–214.

Kingsbury, N. M., & Minda, R. B. (1988). An analysis of three expected intimate relationship states: Commitment, maintenance, and termination. *Journal of Social and Personal Relationships, 5,* 405–422.

Klahr, D., & Wallace, J. G. (1976). *Cognitive development: An information processing view.* Hillsdale, N.J.: Erlbaum.

Klass, P. (1989). AIDS: The youngest victims. *New York Times Magazine,* June 18, pp. 35, 56–58.

Klaus, M. H., & Kennell, J. H. (1978). Parent-to-infant attachment. In J. H. Stevens, Jr., & M. Mathews (Eds.), *Mother/child, father/child relationships.* Washington, D.C.: National Association for the Education of Young Children.

Kleinman, J. C., Pierre, M. B., Jr., Madans, J. H., Land, G. H., & Schramm, W. F. (1988). The effects of maternal smoking on fetal and infant mortality. *American Journal of Epidemiology, 127,* 274–282.

Kleinman, P. H., Wish, E. D., Deren, S., Rainone, G., & Morehouse, E. (1988). Daily marijuana use and problem behaviors among adolescents. *International Journal of the Addictions, 23*(1), 87–107.

Klinnert, M. D., Emde, R. N., Butterfield, P., & Campos, J. J. (1986). Social referencing: The infant's use of emotional signals from a friendly adult with mother present. *Developmental Psychology, 22,* 427–432.

Kohlberg, L. (1981). *Essays on moral development, Vol. 1: The philosophy of moral development.* New York: Harper & Row.

Kohlberg, L. (1984). *Essays on moral development, Vol. 2: The psychology of moral development.* New York: Harper & Row.

Kohlberg, L., Yaeger, J., & Hjertholm, E. (1968). Private speech: Four studies and a review of theories. *Child Development, 39,* 817–826.

Kolata, G. (1987). Associations or rules in learning language? *Science, 237,* 133–134.

Kolata, G. (1988a). Fetuses treated through umbilical cords. *New York Times,* March 29, p. C3.

Kolata, G. (1988b). Surgery on fetuses reveals they heal without scars. *New York Times,* August 16, pp. C1, C3.

Kolata, G. (1989). Survival of the fetus: A barrier is reached. *New York Times,* April 18, pp. C1, C5.

Kolata, G. (1990). Rush is on to capitalize on testing for gene causing cystic fibrosis. *New York Times,* February 6, p. C3.

Kolb, B. (1989). Brain development, plasticity, and behavior. *American Psychologist, 44,* 1203–1212.

Koluchová, J. (1972). Severe deprivation in twins: A case study. *Journal of Child Psychology and Psychiatry, 13,* 107–114.

Koluchová, J. (1976). The further development of twins after severe and prolonged deprivation: A second report. *Journal of Child Psychology and Psychiatry, 17,* 181–188.

Konner, M. (1977a). Evolution of human behavior development. In P. H. Leiderman, S. R. Tulkin, & A. Rosenfeld (Eds.), *Culture and infancy: Variations in the human experience.* New York: Academic Press.

Konner, M. (1977b). Infancy among the Kalahari Desert San. In P. H. Leiderman, S. R. Tulkin, & A. Rosenfeld (Eds.), *Culture and infancy: Variations in the human experience.* New York: Academic Press.

Kopp, C. B. (1989). Regulation of distress and negative emotions: A developmental view. *Developmental Psychology, 25,* 343–354.

Kopp, C. B., & Kaler, S. R. (1989). Risk in infancy: Origins and implications. *American Psychologist, 44,* 224–230.

Korner, A. F. (1974). The effect of the infant's state, level of arousal, sex, and ontogenetic state on the caregiver. In M. Lewis & L. A. Rosenblum (Eds.), *The effect of the infant on its caregiver.* New York: Wiley.

Kovacs, M. (1989). Affective disorders in children and adolescents. *American Psychologist, 44,* 209–215.

Krasnoff, A. G., Walker, J. T., & Howard, M. (1989). Early sex-linked activities and interests related to spatial abilities. *Personality and Individual Differences, 10,* 81–85.

Krebs, D., & Gillmore, J. (1982). The relationship among the first stages of cognitive development, role-taking abilities, and moral development. *Child Development, 53,* 877–886.

Kreutzer, M. A., Leonard, C., & Flavell, J. H. (1975). An interview study of children's knowledge about memory. *Monographs of the Society for Research in Child Development, 40* (1, Serial No. 159).

Kropp, J. P., & Haynes, O. M. (1987). Abusive and nonabusive mothers' ability to identify general and specific signals of infants. *Child Development, 58,* 187–190.

Kruper, J. C., & Uzgiris, I. C. (1987). Fathers' and mothers' speech to young infants. *Journal of Psycholinguistic Research, 16,* 597–614.

Kruse, L. R. (1985). The jurors will decide what happened to Swain children. *The* [Monmouth County, N.J.] *Register,* November 21, pp. 1A–2A.

Kuczynski, L., Kochanska, G., Radke-Yarrow, M., & Girnius-Brown, O. (1987). A developmental interpretation of young children's noncompliance. *Developmental Psychology, 23,* 799–806.

Kupersmidt, J. B. (1989). Socially rejected children: Bullies, victims, or both? Paper presented at the April meeting of the Society for Research in Child Development, Kansas City.

Kurdek, L. A., & Schmitt, J. P. (1986). Early development of relationship quality in heterosexual married, heterosexual cohabiting, gay, and lesbian couples. *Developmental Psychology, 22,* 305–309.

Kutner, L. (1988). Parent and child: A child's scream in the night may be quite normal. *New York Times,* March 31, p. C8.

Lab, S. P., & Whitehead, J. T. (1988). An analysis of juvenile correctional treatment. *Crime and Delinquency, 34,* 60–83.

Labaree, D. F. (1987). Politics, markets, and the compromised curriculum. *Harvard Educational Review, 57,* 483–494.

Ladd, G. W., Price, J. M., & Hart, C. H. (1988). Predicting preschoolers' peer status from their playground behaviors. *Child Development, 59,* 986–992.

Lamaze, F. (1958). *Painless childbirth.* London: Burke.

Lamb, M. E. (1978). The father's role in the infant's social world. In J. H. Stevens, Jr., & M. Mathews (Eds.), *Mother/child, father/child relationships.* Washington, D.C.: National Association for the Education of Young Children.

Lamb, M. E. (1987). The emergent American father. In M. E. Lamb (Ed.), *The father's role: Cross-cultural perspectives.* Hillsdale, N.J.: Erlbaum.

Landau, E. (1983). *Why are they starving themselves? Understanding anorexia nervosa and bulimia.* New York: Julian Messner.

Landesman, S., & Ramey, C. (1989). Developmental psychology and mental retardation: Integrating scientific principles with treatment practices. *American Psychologist, 44,* 409–415.

Lane, H. (1976). *The wild boy of Aveyron.* Cambridge: Harvard University Press.

Lane, S., & Bergan, J. R. (1988). Effects of instructional variables on language ability of preschool children. *American Educational Research Journal, 25*(2), 271–283.

Lansky, V. (1988). *Fat-proofing your children so that they never become diet-addicted adults.* New York: Bantam Books.

LaRossa, R. (1988). Fatherhood and social change. *Family Relations, 37,* 451–457.

LaRossa, R., & LaRossa, M. M. (1981). *Transition to parenthood: How infants change families.* Beverly Hills, Calif.: Sage Publications.

Leboyer, F. (1975). *Birth without violence.* New York: Knopf.

Lee, R. V. (1988). Parasites and pregnancy: The problems of malaria and toxoplasmosis. *Clinics in Perinatology, 15,* 351–363.

Lee, V. E., Brooks-Gunn, J., & Schnur, E. (1988). Does Head Start work? A 1-year follow-up comparison of disadvantaged children attending Head Start, no preschool, and other preschool programs. *Developmental Psychology, 24,* 210–222.

Leiderman, P. H., & Leiderman, G. F. (1977). Economic change and infant care in an East African agricultural community. In P. H. Leiderman, S. R. Tulkin, & A. Rosenfeld (Eds.), *Culture and infancy: Variations in the human experience.* New York: Academic Press.

Lepper, M. R. (1988). Motivational considerations in the study of instruction. *Cognition and Instruction, 5,* 289–309.

Lepper, M. R., Greene, D., & Nisbett, R. E. (1973). Undermining children's intrinsic interest with extrinsic reward: A test of the "overjustification" hypothesis. *Journal of Personality and Social Psychology, 28,* 129–137.

Lepper, M. R., & Gurtner, J.-L. (1989). Children and computers: Approaching the twenty-first century. *American Psychologist, 44,* 170–178.

Lerner, J. V., Hertzog, C., Hooker, K. A., Hassibi, M., & Thomas, A. (1988). A longitudinal study of negative emotional states and adjustment from early childhood through adolescence. *Child Development, 59,* 356–366.

Levin, I. (1982). The nature and development of time concepts in children: The effects of interfering cues. In W. J. Friedman (Ed.), *The developmental psychology of time.* New York: Academic Press.

Levin, I., Wilkening, F., & Dembo, Y. (1984). Development of time quantification: Integration and nonintegration of beginnings and endings in comparative durations. *Child Development, 55,* 2160–2172.

Leviton, A. (1988). Caffeine consumption and the risk of reproductive hazards. *Journal of Reproductive Medicine, 33,* 175–178.

Levy, J. (1985). Right brain, left brain: Fact and fiction. *Psychology Today,* May, pp. 38–44.

Lewis, M., & Brooks, J. (1975). Infants' social perception: A constructivist view. In L. B. Cohen & P. Salapatek (Eds.), *Infant perception: From sensation to cognition* (Vol. 2). New York: Academic Press.

Lewis, M., Feiring, C., McGuffog, C., & Jaskir, J. (1984). Predicting psychopathology in six-year-olds from early social relations. *Child Development, 55,* 123–136.

Liben, L. S., & Belknap, B. (1981). Intellectual realism: Implications for investigations of perceptual perspective taking in young children. *Child Development, 52,* 921–924.

Licht, B. G., & Dweck, C. S. (1984). Determinants of academic achievement: The interaction of children's achievement orientations with skill area. *Developmental Psychology, 20,* 628–636.

Light, P., & Foot, T. (1986). Partial occlusion in children's drawings. *Journal of Experimental Child Psychology, 41,* 38–48.

Light, P., & Nix, C. (1983). "Own view" versus "good view" in a perspective-taking task. *Child Development, 54,* 480–483.

Lindsay, D. S., & Creedon, C. F. (1985). "Magic" revisited: Children's responses to apparent violations of conservation. *Journal of Experimental Child Psychology, 40,* 338–349.

Linn, S., Lieberman, E., Schoenbaum, S. C., Monson, R. R., Stubblefield, P. G., & Ryan, K. J. (1988). Adverse outcomes of pregnancy in women exposed to diethylstilbestrol in utero. *Journal of Reproductive Medicine, 33,* 3–7.

Linney, J. A., & Seidman, E. (1989). The future of schooling. *American Psychologist, 44,* 336–340.

Lipsitt, L. P. (1980). Taste, smell, and other pleasures of sensation. In A. W. Brann & J. J. Volpe (Eds.), *Neonatal neurological assessment and outcome.* Report of the 77th Ross Conference on Pediatric Research. Columbus, Ohio: Ross Laboratories.

Livesley, W. J., & Bromley, D. B. (1973). *Person perception in childhood and adolescence.* New York: Wiley.

Lockheed, M., & Harris, A. (1984). Cross-sex collaborative learning in elementary classrooms. *American Educational Research Journal, 21,* 275–294.

Loehlin, J. C., Willerman, L., & Horn, J. M. (1988). Human behavior genetics. *Annual Review of Psychology, 39,* 101–133.

Loewenberg, P. (1988). Einstein in his youth. *Science, 239,* 510–512.

Londerville, S., & Main, M. (1981). Security of attachment, compliance and maternal training methods in the second year of life. *Developmental Psychology, 17,* 289–299.

Longstreth, L. E. (1980). Human handedness: More evidence for genetic involvement. *Journal of Genetic Psychology, 137,* 275–283.

Lorber, J. (1981). The disposable cortex. *Psychology Today,* April, p. 126.

Lorch, E. P., & Horn, D. G. (1986). Habituation of attention to irrelevant stimuli in elementary school children. *Journal of Experimental Child Psychology, 41,* 184–197.

Lorenz, K. (1971). *Studies in animal and human behaviour* (Vol. 2). Cambridge: Harvard University Press.

Lovejoy, C. O. (1988). Evolution of human walking. *Scientific American,* November, 118–125.

Lovko, A. M., & Ullman, D. G. (1989). Research on the adjustment of latchkey children: Role of background/demographic and latchkey situation variables. *Journal of Clinical Child Psychiatry, 18,* 16–24.

Lowe, G. D., & Smith, R. R. (1987). Gender, marital status, and mental well-being: A retest of Bernard's his and her marriages. *Sociological Spectrum, 7,* 301–307.

Lowrey, G. H. (1978). *Growth and development of children* (7th ed.). Chicago: Year Book Medical Publishers.

Lozoff, B. (1989). Nutrition and behavior. *American Psychologist, 44,* 231–236.

Lueptow, L. B., Guss, M. B., & Hyden, C. (1989). Sex role ideology, marital status, and happiness. *Journal of Family Issues, 10,* 383–400.

Lütkenhaus, P., Grossmann, K. E., & Grossmann, K. (1985). Infant–mother attachment at twelve months and style of interaction with a stranger at the age of three years. *Child Development, 56,* 1538–1542.

Lyman, R. (1989). A twist of fate—in triplicate. *Asbury Park* [N.J.] *Press,* February 12, p. D22.

Lyons-Ruth, K., Connell, D. B., Zoll, D., and Stahl, J. (1987). Infants at social risk: Relations among infant maltreatment, maternal behavior, and infant attachment behavior. *Developmental Psychology, 23,* 223–232.

Maccoby, E. E. (1990). Gender and relationships: A developmental account. *American Psychologist, 45,* 513–520.

Maccoby, E. E., & Jacklin, C. N. (1974). *The psychology of sex differences.* Stanford, Calif.: Stanford University Press.

Maccoby, E. E., & Jacklin, C. N. (1980). Sex differences in aggression: A rejoinder and reprise. *Child Development, 51,* 964–980.

Maccoby, E. E., & Jacklin, C. N. (1987). Gender segregation in childhood. In *Advances in Child Development and Behavior,* Vol. 20. New York: Academic Press.

MacDonald, K. (1985). Early experience, relative plasticity, and social development. *Developmental Review, 5,* 99–121.

Macfarlane, A. (1977). *The psychology of childbirth.* Cambridge: Harvard University Press.

Macfarlane, J., Allen, L., & Honzik, M. P. (1954). *A developmental study of the behavior problems of normal children between twenty-one months and fourteen years.* Berkeley: University of California Press.

Mackey, W. C. (1989). A decade after the transfiguration: The father-myth continues. Paper presented at the April meeting of the Society for Research in Child Development, Kansas City.

MacKinnon, C. E. (1989). An observational study of sibling interactions in married and divorced families. *Developmental Psychology, 25,* 36–44.

Mannuzza, S., Klein, R. G., Bonagura, N., Konig, P. H., & Shenker, R. (1988). Hyperactive boys almost grown up: II. Status of subjects without a mental disorder. *Archives of General Psychiatry, 45,* 13–18.

Marcia, J. E. (1966). Development and validation of ego identity status. *Journal of Personality and Social Psychology, 3,* 551–558.

Marcia, J. E. (1976). Identity six years after: A follow-up study. *Journal of Youth and Adolescence, 15,* 150–153.

Marcos, A. C., & Bahr, S. J. (1988). Control theory and adolescent drug use. *Youth and Society, 19*(4), 395–425.

Markman, E. M., & Wachtel, G. F. (1988). Children's use of mutual exclusivity to constrain the meanings of words. *Cognitive Psychology, 20,* 121–157.

Markman, H. J., & Kadushin, F. S. (1986). Preventive effects of Lamaze training for first-time parents: A short-term longitudinal study. *Journal of Consulting and Clinical Psychology, 54,* 872–874.

Markoff, J. (1989). Computing in America: A masculine mystique. *New York Times,* February 13, pp. A1, B10.

Marlatt, G. A., Baer, J. S., Donovan, D. M., & Kivlahan, D. R. (1988). Addictive behaviors: Etiology and treatment. *Annual Review of Psychology, 39,* 223–252.

Martin, C. L. (1989). Children's use of gender-related information in making social judgments. *Developmental Psychology, 25,* 80–88.

Martin, P. M. (1989). Kids of the '90s. *Asbury Park* [N.J.] *Press,* October 24–25, pp. B5–B13.

Marvinney, D., & Fury, G. (1989). Sibling relations and peer competence. Paper presented at the April meeting of the Society for Research in Child Development, Kansas City.

Masten, A. S. (1986). Humor and competence in school-aged children. *Child Development, 57,* 461–473.

Masten, A. S. (1989). Humor appreciation in children: Individual differences and response sets. *Humor: International Journal of Humor Research, 2–4,* 365–384.

Masters, J. C., & Furman, W. (1981). Popularity, individual friendship selection, and specific peer interaction among children. *Developmental Psychology, 17,* 344–350.

Matas, L., Arend, R., & Sroufe, L. A. (1979). Continuity of adaptation in the second year: The relationship between quality of attachment and later competence. *Child Development, 49,* 547–556.

Matheny, A. P., Jr. (1987). Psychological characteristics of childhood accidents. *Journal of Social Issues, 43,* 45–60.

Mauer, M. (1990). A lost generation. *Time,* March 12, p. 25.

Maurer, D. (1975). Infant visual perception: Methods of study. In L. B. Cohen & P. Salapatek (Eds.), *Infant perception: From sensation to cognition* (Vol. 1). New York: Academic Press.

Maurer, D., & Maurer, C. (1988). *The world of the newborn.* New York: Basic Books.

Maziade, M. (1988). Child temperament as a developmental or an epidemiological concept: A methodological point of view. *Psychiatric Development, 3,* 195–211.

McCall, R. B. (1979). *Infants.* Cambridge: Harvard University Press.

McCall, R. B., Appelbaum, M. I., & Hogarty, P. S. (1973). Developmental changes in mental performance. *Monographs of the Society for Research in Child Development, 38* (3, Serial No. 150).

McCartin, R., & Meyer, K. A. (1988). The adolescent, academic achievement, and college plans: The role of family variables. *Youth and Society, 19,* 378–394.

McCartney, K. (1984). Effect of day care environment on children's language development. *Developmental Psychology, 20,* 244–260.

McCartney, K., Harris, M. J., & Bernieri, F. (1990). Growing up and growing apart: A developmental meta-analysis of twin studies. *Psychological Bulletin, 107,* 226–237.

McGraw, M. B. (1967). Swimming behavior in the human infant. In Y. Brackbill & G. G. Thompson (Eds.), *Behavior in infancy and early childhood.* New York: Free Press. (Originally published in 1939.)

McGue, M. (1989). Nature–nurture and intelligence. *Nature, 340,* 507–508.

McLeod, B. (1986). The Oriental Express. *Psychology Today,* July, pp. 48–52.

McLeod, H. R. (1989). From the double bind to the double burden: Women and the "Fear of Success." *Radcliffe Quarterly,* June, pp. 6–7.

McLoyd, V. C., Thomas, E. A. C., & Warren, D. (1984). The short-term dynamics of social interaction in preschool triads. *Child Development, 55,* 1051–1070.

McShane, J. (1980). *Learning to talk.* New York: Cambridge University Press.

Mead, M. (1955). *Male and female.* New York: Mentor.

Meaney, M. (1988). Cuddle that rat. *Discover,* July, p. 6.

Mednick, S. A., Gabrielli, W. F., Jr., & Hutchings, B. (1984). Genetic influences in criminal convictions: Evidence from an adoption cohort. *Science, 224,* 891–894.

Meltzoff, A. N. (1988). Infant imitation and memory: Nine-month-olds in immediate and deferred tasks. *Child Development, 59,* 217–225.

Meltzoff, A. N., & Moore, M. K. (1983). Newborn infants imitate adult facial gestures. *Child Development, 54,* 702–709.

Merikangas, K. R., Weissman, M. M., Prusoff, B. A., & John, K.

(1988). Assortative mating and affective disorders: Psychopathology in offspring. *Psychiatry, 51,* 48–57.

Miller, B. C., & Bingham, C. R. (1989). Family configuration in relation to the sexual behavior of female adolescents. *Journal of Marriage and the Family, 51,* 499–506.

Miller, B. C., & Jorgensen, S. R. (1988). Adolescent fertility-related behavior and its family linkages. In D. M. Klein & J. Aldous (Eds.), *Social stress and family development.* New York: Guilford Press.

Miller, B. C., McCoy, J. K., Olson, T. D., & Wallace, C. M. (1986). Parental discipline and control attempts in relation to adolescent sexual attitudes and behavior. *Journal of Marriage and the Family, 48,* 503–512.

Miller, B. C., & Sneesby, K. R. (1988). Educational correlates of adolescents' sexual attitudes and behavior. *Journal of Youth and Adolescence, 17,* 521–530.

Miller, G. A., & Gildea, P. M. (1987). How children learn words. *Scientific American,* September, 94–99.

Miller, J. G. (1986). Early cross-cultural commonalities in social explanation. *Developmental Psychology, 22,* 514–520.

Miller, N. E., & Dollard, J. (1941). *Social learning and imitation.* New Haven: Yale University Press.

Miller, P. H. (1989). *Theories of developmental psychology* (2nd ed.). New York: W. H. Freeman.

Miller, P. H., & Aloise, P. A. (1989). Young children's understanding of the psychological causes of behavior: A review. *Child Development, 60,* 257–285.

Miller, P. H., Danaher, D. L., & Forbes, D. (1986). Sex-related strategies for coping with interpersonal conflict in children aged five to seven. *Developmental Psychology, 22,* 543–548.

Miller, P. H., Kessel, F. S., and Flavell, J. H. (1970). Thinking about people thinking about people thinking about. . .: A study of social-cognitive development. *Child Development, 41,* 613–623.

Miller, P. H., & Weiss, M. G. (1982). Children's and adults' knowledge about what variables affect selective attention. *Child Development, 53,* 543–549.

Milunsky, A. (1987). *How to have the healthiest baby you can.* New York: Simon and Schuster.

Minsky, M. (1989). The intelligence transplant. *Discover,* October, pp. 52–58.

Mischel, W. (1974). Processes in delay of gratification. In L. Berkowitz (Ed.), *Advances in experimental psychology* (Vol. 7). New York: Academic Press.

Mischel, W., Shoda, Y., & Rodriguez, M. L. (1989). Delay of gratification in children. *Science, 244,* 933–938.

Miura, I. T., & Okamoto, Y. (1989). Comparisons of U.S. and Japanese first graders' cognitive representation of number and understanding of place value. *Journal of Educational Psychology, 81,* 109–113.

Miyake, K., Chen, S.-J., & Campos, J. J. (1985). Infant temperament, mother's mode of interaction, and attachment in Japan: An interim report. In I. Bretherton & E. Waters (Eds.), *Growing points of attachment theory and research. Monographs of the Society for Research in Child Development, 50* (1–2, Serial No. 209).

Moffitt, T. E., & Silva, P. A. (1988a). IQ and delinquency: A direct test of the differential detection hypothesis. *Journal of Abnormal Psychology, 97*(3), 1–4.

Moffitt, T. E., & Silva, P. A. (1988b). Neuropsychological deficit and self-reported delinquency in an unselected birth cohort. *Journal of the American Academy of Child and Adolescent Psychiatry, 27,* 233–240.

Money, J., & Ehrhardt, A. (1972). *Man and woman, boy and girl.* Baltimore: Johns Hopkins University Press.

Montemayor, R., & Eisen, M. (1977). The development of self-conceptions from childhood to adolescence. *Developmental Psychology, 13,* 314–319.

Moore, D. (1987). Parent–adolescent separation: The construction of adulthood by late adolescents. *Developmental Psychology, 23,* 298–307.

Moore, E. G. J. (1986). Family socialization and the IQ test performance of traditionally and transracially adopted black children. *Developmental Psychology, 22,* 317–326.

Moore, V. (1986). The relationship between children's drawings and preferences for alternative depictions of a familiar object. *Journal of Experimental Child Psychology, 42,* 187–198.

Moran, G. F., & Vinovskis, M. A. (1985). The great care of godly parents: Early childhood in Puritan New England. In A. B. Smuts & J. W. Hagen (Eds.), History and research in child development. *Monographs of the Society for Research in Child Development, 50* (4–5, Serial No. 211).

Morgan, N. H. (1988). Part-time dad. *Princeton Alumni Weekly,* October 12, pp. 13–14.

Morgan, V., & Dunn, S. (1988). Chameleons in the classroom: Visible and invisible children in nursery and infant classrooms. *Educational Review, 40,* 3–12.

Morris, J. (1974). *Conundrum.* New York: Harcourt Brace Jovanovich.

Moslock, J. A. (1989). Dealing with Down syndrome more goal-directed today. *Asbury Park* [N.J.] *Press,* October 1, pp. D1, D7.

Mounts, N. S., Lamborn, S. D., & Steinberg, L. (1989). Relations between family processes and school achievement in different ethnic contexts. Paper presented at the April meeting of the Society for Research in Child Development, Kansas City.

Muir, D. W. (1985). The development of infants' auditory spatial sensitivity. In S. Trehub & B. Schneider (Eds.), *Auditory development in infancy.* New York: Plenum.

Muir, D. W., & Field, J. (1979). Newborn infants orient to sounds. *Child Development, 50,* 431–436.

Murstein, B. I., Chalpin, M. J., Heard, K. V., & Vyse, S. A. (1989). Sexual behavior, drugs, and relationship patterns on a college campus over thirteen years. *Adolescence, 24,* 125–139.

Myers, B. J. (1984). Mother–infant bonding: The status of this critical-period hypothesis. *Developmental Review, 4,* 240–274.

Naeye, R. L. (1980). Sudden infant death. *Scientific American,* April, pp. 56–62.

Navelet, Y., Payan, C., Guilhaume, A., & Benoit, O. (1984). Nocturnal sleep organization in infants "at risk" for sudden infant death syndrome. *Pediatric Research, 18,* 654–657.

Neal, A. G., Groat, H. T., & Wicks, J. W. (1989). Attitudes about having children: A study of 600 couples in the early years of marriage. *Journal of Marriage and the Family, 51,* 313–328.

Nelson, K. (1973). Structure and strategy in learning to talk. *Monographs of the Society for Research in Child Development, 38* (1–2, Serial No. 149).

Nelson, K., & Gruendel, J. M. (1981). Generalized event representations: Basic building blocks of cognitive development. In A. Brown & M. Lamb (Eds.), *Advances in developmental psychology* (Vol. 1). Hillsdale, N.J.: Erlbaum.

Nesher, P. (1986). Learning mathematics: A cognitive perspective. *American Psychologist, 41,* 1114–1122.

New, R. S. (1988). Parental goals and Italian infant care. In R. A. LeVine, P. M. Miller, & M. M. West (Eds.), *Parental behavior in diverse societies. New Directions for Child Development, No. 40.* San Francisco: Jossey-Bass.

Newcomb, M. D., & Bentler, P. M. (1989). Substance use and abuse among children and teenagers. *American Psychologist, 44,* 242–248.

Newcomb, M. D., Fahy, B. N., & Skager, R. (1988). Correlates of cocaine use among adolescents. *Journal of Drug Issues, 18,* 327–354.

Ney, P. G. (1988). Transgenerational child abuse. *Child Psychiatry and Human Development, 18,* 151–168.

Ninio, A., & Rinott, N. (1988). Fathers' involvement in the care of their infants and their attributions of cognitive competence to infants. *Child Development, 59,* 652–663.

Nolen-Hoeksema, S., Girgus, J. S., & Seligman, M. E. P. (1986). Learned helplessness in children: A longitudinal study of depression, achievement, and explanatory style. *Journal of Personality and Social Psychology, 51,* 435–442.

Nyhan, W. L. (1976). *The heredity factor.* New York: Grosset & Dunlap.

O'Brien, S. F., & Bierman, K. L. (1988). Conceptions and perceived influence of peer groups: Interviews with preadolescents and adolescents. *Child Development, 59,* 1360–1365.

Offer, D., Ostrov, E., & Howard, K. I. (1989). Adolescence: What is normal? *American Journal of Diseases of Children, 143,* 731–736.

Oliwenstein, L. (1988). The perils of pot. *Discover,* June, p. 18.

Olson, D. R., & Astington, J. W. (1987). Seeing and knowing: On the ascription of mental states to young children. *Canadian Journal of Psychology, 41,* 399–411.

Olszewski-Kubilius, P. M., Kulieke, M. J., & Krasney, N. (1988). Personality dimensions of gifted children and adolescents. *Gifted Child Quarterly, 32*(4), 347–352.

O'Mahony, J. F. (1986). Development of person description over adolescence. *Journal of Youth and Adolescence, 15,* 389–403.

O'Mahony, J. F. (1989). Development of thinking about things and people: Social and nonsocial cognition during adolescence. *Journal of Genetic Psychology, 150,* 217–224.

O'Malley, P. M., & Bachman, J. G. (1983). Self-esteem: Change and stability between ages 12 and 23. *Developmental Psychology, 19,* 257–268.

Oppenheimer, V. K. (1988). A theory of marriage timing. *American Journal of Sociology, 94,* 563–591.

Orr, D. P., Brack, C. J., & Ingersoll, G. (1988). Pubertal maturation and cognitive maturity in adolescents. *Journal of Adolescent Health Care, 9,* 273–279.

Osgood, D. W., Johnston, L. D., O'Malley, P. M., & Bachman, J. G. (1988). The generality of deviance in late adolescence and early adulthood. *American Sociological Review, 53,* 81–93.

Ostrov, E., Offer, D., & Howard, K. I. (1989). Gender differences in adolescent symptomatology: A normative study. *Journal of the American Academy of Child and Adolescent Psychiatry, 28,* 394–398.

Otto, L. B. (1988). America's youth: A changing profile. *Family Relations, 37,* 385–391.

Park, C. C. (1967). *The siege.* New York: Harcourt Brace Jovanovich.

Parker, J. G., & Asher, S. R. (1987). Peer relations and later personal adjustment: Are low-accepted children at risk? *Psychological Bulletin, 102,* 357–389.

Parmelee, A. H., Jr. (1986). Children's illnesses: Their beneficial effects on behavioral development. *Child Development, 57,* 1–10.

Parpal, M., & Maccoby, E. (1985). Maternal responsiveness and subsequent child compliance. *Child Development, 56,* 1326–1334.

Parsons, J. E., Adler, T. F., & Kaczala, C. M. (1982). Socialization of achievement attitudes and beliefs: Parental influences. *Child Development, 53,* 310–321.

Parten, M. B. (1932). Social participation among pre-school children. *Journal of Abnormal and Social Psychology, 27,* 243–269.

Passman, R. H. (1987). Attachments to inanimate objects: Are children who have security blankets insecure? *Journal of Consulting and Clinical Psychology, 1987, 55,* 825–830.

Pastor, D. (1981). The quality of mother–infant attachment and its relationship to toddlers' initial sociability with peers. *Developmental Psychology, 17,* 326–335.

Patterson, D. (1987). The causes of Down syndrome. *Scientific American,* August, pp. 52–60.

Patterson, G. R., & Bank, L. (1989). Some amplifying mechanisms for pathologic processes in families. In M. R. Gunnar & E. Thelen (Eds.), *Systems and Development: The Minnesota Symposia on Child Psychology* (Vol. 22). Hillsdale, N.J.: Erlbaum.

Patterson, G. R., DeBaryshe, B. D., & Ramsey, E. (1989). A developmental perspective on antisocial behavior. *American Psychologist, 44,* 329–335.

Patterson, G. R., Littman, R. A., & Bricker, W. (1967). Assertive behavior in children: A step toward a theory of aggression. *Monographs of the Society for Research in Child Development, 32* (5, Serial No. 113).

Patterson, G. R., & Stouthamer-Loeber, M. (1984). The correlation of family management practices and delinquency. *Child Development, 55,* 1299–1307.

Patton, C. G. (1988). The spectrum of eating disorders in adolescence. *Journal of Psychosomatic Research, 32,* 579–584.

Pawl, J. (1987). Working with infants, toddlers, and their families: What we do and how we keep going. *Bulletin of National Center for Clinical Infant Programs, 7*(5), 13–17.

Pedersen, E., Faucher, T. A., & Eaton, W. W. (1978). A new perspective on the effects of first-grade teachers on children's subsequent adult status. *Harvard Educational Review, 48,* 1–31.

Pellegrini, D. S., Masten, A. S., Garmezy, N., & Ferrarese, M. J. (1987). Correlates of social and academic competence in middle childhood. *Journal of Child Psychology and Psychiatry, 28,* 699–714.

Penner, S. G. (1987). Parental responses to grammatical and ungrammatical child utterances. *Child Development, 58,* 376–384.

Perry, D. G. (1989). Social learning theory. Paper presented at the April meeting of the Society for Research in Child Development, Kansas City.

Perry, D. G., & Bussey, K. (1984). *Social development.* Englewood Cliffs, N.J.: Prentice Hall.

Perry, D. G., Perry, L. C., Bussey, K., English, D., & Arnold, G. (1980). Processes of attribution and children's self-punishment following misbehavior. *Child Development, 51,* 545–551.

Perry, D. G., Perry, L. C., & Weiss, R. J. (1989). Sex differences in the consequences that children anticipate for aggression. *Developmental Psychology, 25,* 312–319.

Persson-Blennow, I., & McNeil, T. F. (1988). Frequencies and stability of temperament types in childhood. *Journal of the American Academy of Child and Adolescent Psychiatry, 27,* 619–622.

Petersen, A. C. (1988). Adolescent development. *Annual Review of Psychology, 39,* 583–607.

Pettit, G. S., & Bates, J. E. (1989). Family interaction patterns and children's behavior problems from infancy to 4 years. *Developmental Psychology, 25,* 413–420.

Phelps, R. E., Huntley, D. K., Valdes, L. A., & Tompson, M. C. (1987). Parent–child interactions and child social networks in one-parent families. *Advances in Family Intervention, Assessment, and Theory, 4,* 143–163.

Phillips, D. A. (1987). Socialization of perceived academic competence among highly competent children. *Child Development, 58,* 1308–1320.

Phillips, J. L., Jr. (1975). *The origins of intellect: Piaget's theory* (2nd ed.). San Francisco: W. H. Freeman.

Piaget, J. (1926). *The language and thought of the child* (M. Worden, Trans.). New York: Harcourt Brace Jovanovich.

Piaget, J. (1928). *Judgement and reasoning in the child* (M. Worden, Trans.). London: Routledge & Kegan Paul.

Piaget, J. (1929). *The child's conception of the world* (J. & A. Tomlinson, Trans.). New York: Harcourt Brace Jovanovich.

Piaget, J. (1932). *The moral judgment of the child* (M. Worden, Trans.). New York: Harcourt Brace Jovanovich.

Piaget, J. (1952). *The origins of intelligence in children* (M. Cook, Trans.). New York: International Universities Press.

Piaget, J. (1954). *The construction of reality in the child* (M. Cook, Trans.). New York: Basic Books.

Piaget, J. (1962). Play, dreams, and imitation in childhood (C. Gattegno & F. M. Hodgson, Trans.). New York: Norton.

Piaget, J. (1964). Mother structures and the notion of number. In R. E. Ripple & V. N. Rockcastle (Eds.), *Piaget rediscovered.* Ithaca, N.Y.: Cornell University Press.

Piaget, J. (1965). *The child's conception of number* (C. Gattegno & F. M. Hodgson, Trans.). New York: Norton.

Piaget, J. (1969). *The child's conception of time* (A. J. Pomerans, Trans.). London: Routledge & Kegan Paul.

Piaget, J. (1977). The first year of life of the child. In H. E. Gruber & J. J. Vonèche (Eds. and Trans.), *The essential Piaget.* New York: Basic Books. (Originally published in 1927.)

Piaget, J., & Inhelder, B. (1941). *Le développement des quantités chez l'enfant.* Neuchâtel: Delachaux & Niestle.

Piaget, J., & Inhelder, B. (1956). *The child's conception of space.* (F. J. Langdon & E. L. Lunzer, Trans.). London: Routledge & Kegan Paul.

Piedmont, R. L. (1988). An interactional model of achievement motivation and fear of success. *Sex Roles, 19,* 467–490.

Pillow, B. H. (1988). Young children's understanding of attentional limits. *Child Development, 59,* 38–46.

Pillow, B. H., & Flavell, J. H. (1986). Young children's knowledge about visual perception: Projective size and shape. *Child Development, 57,* 125–135.

Pines, M. (1981). The civilizing of Genie. *Psychology Today,* September, pp. 28–34.

Pipp, S., Shaver, P., Jennings, S., Lamborn, S., & Fischer, K. W. (1985). Adolescents' theories about the development of their relationships with parents. *Journal of Personality and Social Psychology, 48,* 991–1001.

Plomin, R. (1989). Environment and genes: Determinants of behavior. *American Psychologist, 44,* 105–111.

Plomin, R., & Daniels, D. (1987). Why are children in the same family so different from one another? *Behavioral and Brain Sciences, 10,* 1–60.

Plomin, R., McClearn, G. E., Pedersen, N. L., Nesselroade, J. R., & Bergeman, C. S. (1988). Genetic influence on childhood family environment perceived retrospectively from the last half of the life span. *Developmental Psychology, 24,* 738–745.

Pollack, S. (1989). Solving the lead dilemma. *Technology Review, 92*(7), 22–31.

Pollock, V. E., Schneider, L. S., Gabrielli, W. F., Jr., & Goodwin, D. W. (1987). Sex of parent and offspring in the transmission of alcoholism. *Journal of Nervous and Mental Diseases, 175,* 668–673.

Porter, F. L., Miller, R. H., & Marshall, R. E. (1986). Neonatal pain cries: Effect of circumcision on acoustic features and perceived urgency. *Child Development, 57,* 790–802.

Powers, S. I., Hauser, S. T., & Kilner, L. A. (1989). Adolescent mental health. *American Psychologist, 44,* 200–208.

Pressley, M., Levin, J. R., Ghatala, E. S., & Ahmad, M. (1987). Test monitoring in young grade school children. *Journal of Experimental Child Psychology, 43,* 96–111.

Provence, S., & Lipton, R. C. (1962). *Infants in institutions.* New York: International Universities Press.

Pulakos, J. (1987). Brothers and sisters: Nature and importance of the adult bond. *Journal of Psychology, 121,* 521–522.

Putallaz, M. (1987). Maternal behavior and children's sociometric status. *Child Development, 58,* 324–340.

Putallaz, M., & Gottman, J. M. (1981). Social skills and group acceptance. In S. R. Asher & J. M. Gottman (Eds.), *The development of children's friendships.* New York: Cambridge University Press.

Radkey, A. L., & Enns, J. T. (1987). Da Vinci's window facilitates drawings of total and partial occlusion in young children. *Journal of Experimental Child Psychology, 44,* 222–235.

Radke-Yarrow, M., Cummings, E. M., Kuczynski, L., & Chapman, M. (1985). Patterns of attachment in two- and three-year-olds in normal families and families with parental depression. *Child Development, 56,* 884–893.

Radke-Yarrow, M., Zahn-Waxler, C., & Chapman, M. (1983). Children's prosocial dispositions and behavior. In E. M. Hetherington (Ed.), *Handbook of child psychology* (Vol. 4): *Socialization, personality, and social development* (P. H. Mussen, General Editor). New York: Wiley.

Rainone, G. A., Deren, S., Kleinman, P. H., & Wish, E. D. (1987). Heavy marijuana users not in treatment: The continuing search for the "pure" marijuana user. *Journal of Psychoactive Drugs, 19*(4), 353–359.

Raring, R. H. (1975). *Crib death.* Hicksville, N.Y.: Exposition Press.

Ratio of Sexes (1987). Based on data from the U.S. Bureau of the Census. Asbury Park [N.J.] Press, August 23, p. B14.

Ratner, N. B. (1988). Patterns of parental vocabulary selection in speech to very young children. *Journal of Child Language, 15,* 481–492.

Rauh, V. A., Achenbach, T. M., Nurcombe, B., Howell, C. T., & Teti, D. M. (1988). Minimizing the effects of low birthweight: Four-year results of an early intervention program. *Child Development, 59,* 544–553.

Rauste-von Wright, M. (1989). Body image satisfaction in adolescent girls and boys: A longitudinal study. *Journal of Youth and Adolescence, 18,* 71–83.

Raymond, C. L., & Benbow, C. P. (1986). Gender differences in mathematics: A function of parental support and student sex typing? *Developmental Psychology, 22,* 808–819.

Read, D., Adams, G. R., & Dobson, W. R. (1984). Ego-identity status, personality, and social-influence style. *Journal of Personality and Social Psychology, 46,* 169–177.

Reich, P. A. (1986). *Language development.* Englewood Cliffs, N.J.: Prentice Hall.

Reis, S. M. (1989). Reflections on policy affecting the education of gifted and talented students. *American Psychologist, 44,* 399–408.

Resnick, L. B. (1989). Developing mathematical knowledge. *American Psychologist, 44,* 162–169.

Revkin, A. C. (1989). Crack in the cradle. *Discover,* Sept., pp. 62–69.

Reznick, J. S., Kagan, J., Snidman, N., Gersten, M., Baak, K., & Rosenberg, A. (1986). Inhibited and uninhibited children: A follow-up study. *Child Development, 57,* 660–680.

Rice, M. L., & Woodsmall, L. (1988). Lessons from television: Children's word learning when viewing. *Child Development, 59,* 420–429.

Richards, D. D., & Siegler, R. S. (1986). Children's understandings of the attributes of life. *Journal of Experimental Child Psychology, 42,* 1–22.

Richardson, J. L., Dwyer, K., & others (1989). Substance use among eighth-grade students who take care of themselves after school. *Pediatrics, 84,* 556–566.

Richman, A. L., LeVine, R. A., New, R. S., Howrigan, G. A., Welles-Nystrom, B., & LeVine, S. E. (1988). Maternal behavior to infants in five cultures. In R. A. LeVine, P. M. Miller, & M. M. West (Eds.), *Parental behavior in diverse societies. New Directions for Child Development, No. 40.* San Francisco: Jossey-Bass.

Richman, A. L., Miller, P. M., & Solomon, M. J. (1988). The socialization of infants in suburban Boston. In R. A. LeVine, P. M. Miller, & M. M. West (Eds.), *Parental behavior in diverse societies. New Directions for Child Development, No. 40.* San Francisco: Jossey-Bass.

Ricks, M. H. (1985). The social transmission of parental behavior: Attachment across generations. In I. Bretherton & E. Waters (Eds.), Growing points of attachment theory and research. *Monographs of the Society for Research in Child Development, 50* (1–2, Serial No. 209).

Ridenour, M. V. (1978). Programs to optimize infant motor development. In M. V. Ridenour (Ed.), *Motor development: Issues and applications.* Princeton, N.J.: Princeton Book Co. Reprinted from Wickstrom, R. L. (1983). *Fundamental Motor Patterns* (3rd ed.). Philadelphia: Lea & Febiger.

Riese, M. L. (1987). Temperament stability between the neonatal period and 24 months. *Developmental Psychology, 23,* 216–222.

Rimland, B. (1964). *Infantile autism: The syndrome and its implications for a neural theory of behavior.* New York: Meredith Publishing.

Rizzo, T. A., & Corsaro, W. A. (1988). Toward a better understanding of Vygotsky's process of internalization: Its role in the development of the concept of friendship. *Developmental Review, 8,* 219–237.

Roberts, S. B., Savage, J., Coward, W. E., & others (1988). Energy expenditure and intake in infants born to lean and overweight mothers. *New England Journal of Medicine, 318,* 461–466.

Roberts, W. L. (1987). Two-career families: Demographic variables, parenting, and competence in young children. *Canadian Journal of Behavioral Science, 19,* 347–356.

Robson, K. (1968). The role of eye-to-eye contact in maternal-infant attachment. In S. Chess & A. Thomas (Eds.), *Annual progress in child psychiatry and child development.* New York: Brunner/Mazel.

Roche, A. F. (1979). Secular trends in stature, weight, and maturation. In A. F. Roche (Ed.), Secular trends in human growth, maturation, and development. *Monographs of the Society for Research in Child Development, 44* (Serial No. 179).

Rocklin, R., & Lavett, D. K. (1987). Those who broke the cycle: Therapy with nonabusive adults who were physically abused as children. *Psychotherapy, 24,* 769–777.

Rodgers, J. L., & Rowe, D. C. (1988). Influence of siblings on adolescent sexual behavior. *Developmental Psychology, 24,* 722–728.

Roedell, W. C., & Slaby, R. G. (1977). The role of distal and proximal interaction in infant social preference formation. *Developmental Psychology, 13,* 266–273.

Roffwarg, H. P., Muzio, J. N., & Dement, W. C. (1966). Ontogenetic development of the human sleep–dream cycle. *Science, 152,* 604–619.

Rosch, E., & Mervis, C. B. (1978). Children's sorting: A reinterpretation based on the nature of abstraction in natural categories. In M. S. Smart & R. C. Smart (Eds.), *Preschool children: Development and relationships.* New York: Macmillan.

Roscoe, B., Cavanaugh, L. E., & Kennedy, D. R. (1988). Dating infidelity: Behaviors, reasons, and consequences. *Adolescence, 23,* 35–43.

Roscoe, B., Kennedy, D., & Pope, T. (1987). Adolescents' views of intimacy: Distinguishing intimate from nonintimate relationships. *Adolescence, 22,* 512–516.

Rosen, T. S., & Johnson, H. L. (1988). Drug-addicted mothers, their infants, and SIDS. *Annals of the New York Academy of Sciences, 533,* 89–95.

Rosenkoetter, L. I. (1973). Resistance to temptation: Inhibitory and disinhibitory effects of models. *Developmental Psychology, 8,* 80–84.

Rosenstein, D., & Oster, H. (1988). Differential facial responses to four basic tastes in newborns. *Child Development, 59,* 1555–1568.

Rosenthal, E. (1990). New insights on why some children are fat offers clues on weight loss. *New York Times,* January 4, p. B8.

Rosenthal, J. A. (1988). Patterns of reported child abuse and neglect. *Child Abuse & Neglect, 12,* 263–271.

Rosenthal, R., & Jacobson, L. (1968). *Pygmalion in the classroom.* New York: Holt, Rinehart & Winston.

Rosenzweig, M. R. (1966). Environmental complexity, cerebral change, and behavior. *American Psychologist, 21,* 321–332.

Rosinski, R. R. (1977). *The development of visual perception.* Santa Monica, Calif.: Goodyear Publishing.

Ross, G., Kagan, J., Zelazo, P., & Kotelchuck, M. (1975). Separation protest in infants in home and laboratory. *Developmental Psychology, 11,* 256–257.

Rotenberg, K. J., & Sliz, D. (1988). Children's restrictive disclosure to friends. *Merrill-Palmer Quarterly, 34,* 203–215.

Rothbaum, F. (1988). Maternal acceptance and child functioning. *Merrill-Palmer Quarterly, 34,* 163–184.

Rowe, D. C. (1981). Environmental and genetic influences on dimensions of perceived parenting: A twin study. *Developmental Psychology, 17,* 203–208.

Rozin, P., & Gleitman, L. R. (1977). The structure and acquisition of reading. II.: The reading process and the acquisition of the alphabetic principle. In A. S. Reber & D. S. Scarborough (Eds.), *Toward a psychology of reading.* Hillsdale, N.J.: Erlbaum.

Rozin, P., Poritsky, S., & Sotsky, R. (1971). American children with reading problems can easily learn to read English represented by Chinese characters. *Science, 171,* 1264–1267.

Rubin, J. (1989). Brain changes. *Psychology Today,* March, p. 26.

Rubin, Z. (1980). *Children's friendships.* Cambridge: Harvard University Press.

Ruble, D. N., & Brooks-Gunn, J. (1982). The experience of menarche. *Child Development, 53,* 1557–1566.

Ruble, D. N., Fleming, A. S., Hackel, L. S., & Stangor, C. (1988). Changes in the marital relationship during the transition to first time motherhood: Effects of violated expectations concerning division of household labor. *Journal of Personality and Social Psychology, 55,* 78–87.

Rumberger, R. (1987). High school dropouts: A review of issues and evidence. *Review of Educational Research, 57*(2), 101–121.

Rushton, J. P., Fulker, D. W., Neale, M. C., Nias, D. K. B., & Eysenck, H. J. (1986). Altruism and aggression: The heritability of individual differences. *Journal of Personality and Social Psychology, 50,* 1192–1198.

Russell, A. T., Bott, L., & Sammons, C. (1989). The phenomenology of schizophrenia occurring in childhood. *Journal of the American Academy of Child and Adolescent Psychiatry, 28,* 339–407.

Russell, G., & Russell, A. (1987). Mother–child and father–child relationships in middle childhood. *Child Development, 58,* 1573–1585.

Rutter, D. R., & Durkin, K. (1987). Turn-taking in mother–infant interaction: An examination of vocalizations and gaze. *Developmental Psychology, 23,* 54–61.

Rutter, M. (1974). *The qualities of mothering: Maternal deprivation reassessed.* New York: Jason Aronson.

Rutter, M. (1978). Diagnosis and definition of childhood autism. *Journal of Autism and Childhood Schizophrenia, 8,* 139–161.

Rutter, M. (1979). Maternal deprivation, 1972–1978: New findings, new concepts, new approaches. *Child Development, 50,* 283–305.

Rutter, M. (1983). School effects on pupil progress: Research findings and policy implications. *Child Development, 54,* 1–29.

Salt, P., Galler, J. R., & Ramsey, F. C. (1988). The influence of early malnutrition on subsequent behavioral development. VII. The effects of maternal depressive symptoms. *Journal of Developmental and Behavioral Pediatrics, 9,* 1–5.

Savin-Williams, R. C. (1988). Theoretical perspectives accounting for adolescent homosexuality. *Journal of Adolescent Health Care, 9,* 95–104.

Savola, K. (1989). Psychologist studies relationship of body image to depression in adolescent girls. *Radcliffe News,* Summer, p. 4.

Saxe, G. B., Guberman, S. R., and Gearhart, M. (1987). Social processes in early number development. *Monographs of the Society for Research in Child Development, 52* (2, Serial No. 216).

Saxe, G. B., & Sicilian, S. (1981). Children's interpretation of their counting accuracy: A developmental analysis. *Child Development, 52,* 1330–1332.

Scarborough, H. S. (1989). Prediction of reading disability from familial and individual differences. *Journal of Educational Psychology, 81,* 101–108.

Scarr, S., & McCartney, K. (1983). How people make their own environments: A theory of genotype → environment effects. *Child Development, 54,* 424–435.

Scarr, S., Phillips, D., & McCartney, K. (1989). Working mothers and their families. *American Psychologist, 44,* 1402–1409.

Scarr, S., & Weinberg, R. A. (1986). The early childhood enterprise: Care and education of the young. *American Psychologist, 41,* 1140–1146.

Schachter, F. F., & Stone, R. K. (1985). Difficult sibling, easy sibling: Temperament and the within-family environment. *Child Development, 56,* 1335–1344.

Schaefer, C. E. (1969). Imaginary companions and creative adolescents. *Developmental Psychology, 1,* 747–749.

Schaefer, M. R., Sobieraj, K., & Hollyfield, R. L. (1988). Prevalence of childhood physical abuse in adult male veteran alcoholics. *Child Abuse & Neglect, 12,* 141–149.

Schaffer, H. R., & Emerson, P. E. (1964). Patterns of response to physical contact in early human development. *Journal of Child Psychology and Psychiatry, 5,* 1–13.

Schaie, K. W., & Willis, S. L. (1986). Can decline in adult intellectual functioning be reversed? *Developmental Psychology, 22,* 223–232.

Schneider, W., Körkel, J., & Weinert, F. E. (1989). Domain-specific knowledge and memory performance: A comparison of high- and low-aptitude children. *Journal of Educational Psychology, 81,* 306–312.

Schneider, W., & Sodian, B. (1988). Metamemory-memory behavior relationships in young children: Evidence from a memory-for-location task. *Journal of Experimental Child Psychology, 45,* 209–233.

Schneider-Rosen, K., Braunwald, K. G., Carlson, V., & Cicchetti, D. (1985). Current perspectives in attachment theory: Illustration from the study of maltreated infants. In I. Bretherton & E. Waters (Eds.), Growing points of attachment theory and research. *Monographs of the Society for Research in Child Development, 50* (1–2, Serial No. 209).

Schofield, J. W. (1981). Complementary and conflicting identities: Images and interaction in an interracial school. In S. R. Asher & J. M. Gottman (Eds.), *The development of children's friendships.* New York: Cambridge University Press.

Schuman, W. (1985). The baby workout: Does your infant really need it? *Parents,* May, pp. 72–76.

Schwarcz, S. K., & Rutherford, G. W. (1989). Acquired Immunodeficiency Syndrome in infants, children, and adolescents. *Journal of Drug Issues, 19,* 75–92.

Schweickart, R., & Warshall, P. (1980). Urination and defecation in zero-g: There ain't no graceful way. In S. Brand (Ed.), *The next whole earth catalog.* Sausalito, Calif.: Point.

Scott, K. G., & Carran, D. T. (1987). The epidemiology and prevention of mental retardation. *American Psychologist, 42,* 801–804.

Searleman, A., Porac, C., & Coren, S. (1989). Relationship between birth order, birth stress, and lateral preferences: A critical review. *Psychological Bulletin, 105,* 397–408.

Sedlak, A. J. (1989). *Supplementary analyses of data on the national incidence of child abuse and neglect.* Rockville, Md.: Westat, Inc.

Seligman, M. E. P. (1972). Phobias and preparedness. In M. E. P. Seligman & J. L. Hager (Eds.), *Biological boundaries of learning.* Englewood Cliffs, N.J.: Prentice Hall.

Seligman, M. E. P. (1975). *Helplessness: On depression, development, and death.* San Francisco: W. H. Freeman.

Selman, R. (1981). The child as friendship philosopher. In S. R. Asher & J. M. Gottman (Eds.), *The development of children's friendships.* New York: Cambridge University Press.

Selman, R., Beardslee, W., Schultz, L. H., Krupa, M., & Podorefsky, D. (1986). Assessing adolescent interpersonal negotiation strategies: Toward the integration of structural and functional models. *Developmental Psychology, 22,* 450–459.

Serbin, L. A., & Sprafkin, C. (1986). The salience of gender and the process of sex-typing in three- to seven-year-old children. *Child Development, 57,* 1188–1199.

Shaffer, D., Garland, A., Gould, M., Fisher, P., & Trautman, P. (1988). Preventing teenage suicide: A critical review. *Journal of the American Academy of Child and Adolescent Psychiatry, 27,* 675–687.

Shane, P. G. (1989). Changing patterns among homeless and runaway youth. *American Journal of Orthopsychiatry, 59*(2), 208–214.

Sharabany, R., Gershoni, R., & Hofman, J. E. (1981). Girlfriend, boyfriend: Age and sex differences in intimate friendship. *Developmental Psychology, 17,* 800–808.

Shenkman, R. (1988). *Legends, lies, and cherished myths of American history.* New York: William Morrow.

Shirley, M. M. (1933). The first two years: A study of twenty-five babies (Vol. 2). *Institute of Child Welfare Monograph No. 7.* Minneapolis: University of Minnesota Press.

Shore, C. (1986). Combinatorial play, conceptual development, and early multiword speech. *Developmental Psychology, 22,* 184–190.

Siegal, M. (1988). Children's knowledge of contagion and contamination as causes of illness. *Child Development, 59,* 1353–1359.

Siegal, M., & Barclay, M. S. (1985). Children's evaluations of fathers' socialization behavior. *Developmental Psychology, 21,* 1090–1096.

Siegel, M. (1987). Are sons and daughters treated more differently by fathers than by mothers? *Developmental Review, 7,* 183–209.

Siegler, R. S. (1986). *Children's thinking.* Englewood Cliffs, N.J.: Prentice Hall.

Siegler, R. S. (1989). Mechanisms of cognitive development. *Annual Review of Psychology, 40,* 353–379.

Siegler, R. S., Liebert, D. E., & Liebert, R. M. (1973). Inhelder and Piaget's pendulum problem: Teaching preadolescents to act as scientists. *Developmental Psychology, 9,* 97–101.

Siegler, R. S., & Liebert, R. M. (1975). Acquisition of formal scientific reasoning by 10- and 13-year-olds: Designing a factorial experiment. *Developmental Psychology, 11,* 401–402.

Siegler, R. S., & Shrager, J. (1984). Strategy choices in addition and subtraction: How do children know what to do? In C. Sophian (Ed.), *Origins of cognitive skills.* Hillsdale, N.J.: Erlbaum.

Sigman, M., Cohen, S. E., Beckwith, L., & Parmelee, A. H. (1986). Infant attention in relation to intellectual abilities in childhood. *Developmental Psychology, 22,* 788–792.

Simpson, J. A. (1987). The dissolution of romantic relationships: Factors involved in relationship stability and emotional distress. *Journal of Personality and Social Psychology, 53,* 683–692.

Simpson, J. A., Campbell, B., & Berscheid, E. (1986). The association between romantic love and marriage: Kephart twice revisited. *Personality and Social Psychology Bulletin, 12*(3), 363–372.

Sincoff, J. B., & Sternberg, R. J. (1988). Development of verbal fluency abilities and strategies in elementary-school-age children. *Developmental Psychology, 24,* 646–653.

Singer, J. L., & Singer, D. G. (1981). *Television, imagination, and aggression: A study of preschoolers.* Hillsdale, N.J.: Erlbaum.

Skinner, B. F. (1979). *The shaping of a behaviorist.* New York: Knopf.

Slaby, R. G. (1975). Verbal regulation of aggression and altruism. In W. Hartup & J. De Wit (Eds.), *Determinants and origins of aggressive behavior.* The Hague: Mouton.

Slackman, E., & Nelson, K. (1984). Acquisition of an unfamiliar script in story form by young children. *Child Development, 55,* 329–340.

Slavin, R. E. (1987). Ability grouping and student achievement in elementary schools: A best-evidence synthesis. *Review of Educational Research, 57*(3), 293–336.

Slugoski, B. R., Marcia, J. E., & Koopman, R. F. (1984). Cognitive and social interactional characteristics of ego identity statuses in college males. *Journal of Personality and Social Psychology, 47,* 646–661.

Smith, J. D., & Nelson, D. G. K. (1988). Is the more impulsive child a more holistic processor? A reconsideration. *Child Development, 59,* 719–727.

Smith, M. S. (1990). An evolutionary perspective on grandparent–grandchild relationships. In P. K. Smith (Ed.), *The psychology of grandparenthood: An international perspective.* London: Routledge.

Smolak, L. (1986). *Infancy.* Englewood Cliffs, N.J.: Prentice Hall.

Smollar, J., & Youniss, J. (1989). Transformations in adolescents' perceptions of parents. *International Journal of Behavioral Development, 12,* 71–84.

Snarey, J. R. (1985). Cross-cultural universality of social–moral development: A critical review of Kohlbergian research. *Psychological Bulletin, 97,* 202–232.

Snarey, J. R., & Vaillant, G. E. (1985). How lower- and working-class youth become middle-class adults: The association between ego defense mechanisms and upward social mobility. *Child Development, 56,* 899–910.

Snow, C. E.. (1977). The development of conversation between mothers and babies. *Journal of Child Language, 4,* 1–22.

Sommer, R. (1988). Two decades of marijuana attitudes: The more it changes, the more it is the same. *Journal of Psychoactive Drugs, 20(1),* 67–70.

Sonenstein, F. L. (1987). Teenage childbearing . . . in all walks of life. *Brandeis Review, 7(1),* 25–28.

Sonnenschein, S. (1986). Development of referential communication: Deciding that a message is uninformative. *Developmental Psychology, 22,* 164–168.

Sonnenschein, S. (1988). The development of referential communication: Speaking to different listeners. *Child Development, 59,* 694–702.

Sophian, C., & Stigler, J. W. (1981). Does recognition memory improve with age? *Journal of Experimental Child Psychology, 32,* 343–353.

Sorce, J. F., Emde, R. N., Campos, J., & Klinnert, M. D. (1985). Maternal emotional signaling: Its effect on the visual cliff behavior of 1-year-olds. *Developmental Psychology, 21,* 195–200.

Speece, M. W., & Brent, S. B. (1984). Children's understanding of death: A review of three components of a death concept. *Child Development, 55,* 1671–1686.

Speer, J. R. (1984). Two practical strategies young children use to interpret vague instructions. *Child Development, 55,* 1811–1819.

Spelke, E. S. (1982). Perceptual knowledge of objects in infancy. In J. Mehler, E. C. T. Walker, & M. Garrett (Eds.), *Perspectives on mental representation.* Hillsdale, N.J.: Erlbaum.

Spelke, E. S., & Cortelyou, A. (1981). Perceptual aspects of social knowing: Looking and listening in infancy. In M. E. Lamb & L. R. Sherrod (Eds.), *Infant social cognition: Empirical and theoretical considerations.* Hillsdale, N.J.: Erlbaum.

Spence, J. T., & Helmreich, R. L. (1978). *Masculinity and femininity: Their psychological dimensions, correlates, and antecedents.* Austin: University of Texas Press.

Spiker, C. C., Gerjuoy, I. R., & Shepard, W. O. (1956). Children's concept of middle-sizedness and performance on the intermediate size problem. *Journal of Comparative and Physiological Psychology, 49,* 416–419.

Spirito, A., Brown, L., Overholser, J., & Fritz, G. (1989). Attempted suicide in adolescence: A review and critique of the literature. *Clinical Psychology Review, 9,* 335–363.

Sroufe, L. A. (1985). Attachment classification from the perspective of infant-caregiver relationships and infant temperament. *Child Development, 56,* 1–14.

Sroufe, L. A., Fox, N. A., & Pancake, V. R. (1983). Attachment and

dependency in developmental perspective. *Child Development, 54,* 1615–1627.

Stamps, L. E., & Clark, C. L. C. (1987). Relations between the Type A behavior pattern and intelligence in children. *Journal of Genetic Psychology, 148,* 529–531.

Stanovich, K. E. (1988). The right and wrong places to look for the cognitive locus of reading disability. *Annals of Dyslexia, 38,* 154–177.

Stark, E. (1989). Teen boys get condom sense. *Psychology Today,* October, pp. 62–63.

Stark, E., Flitcraft, A., Zuckerman, D., Grey, A., Robison, J., & Frazier, W. (1981). Wife abuse in the medical setting. *Domestic Violence Monograph Series, 7,* 7–41.

Stechler, G., & Halton, A. (1982). Prenatal influences on human development. In B. B. Wollman, G. Stricker, S. J. Ellman, P. Keith- Spiegel, & D. S. Palermo (Eds.), *Handbook of developmental psychology.* Englewood Cliffs, N.J.: Prentice Hall.

Steen, L. A. (1987). Mathematics education: A predictor of scientific competitiveness. *Science, 237,* 300–302.

Steen, S. N., Oppliger, R. A., & Brownell, K. D. (1988). Metabolic effects of repeated weight loss and regain in adolescent wrestlers. *Journal of the American Medical Association, 260(1),* 47–50.

Steffenburg, S., Gillberg, C., Hellgren, L., Andersson, I., Gillberg, C., Jakobsson, G., & Bohman, M. (1989). A twin study of autism in Denmark, Finland, Iceland, Norway and Sweden. *Journal of Child Psychology and Psychiatry, 30,* 405–416.

Steinberg, L. (1986) Latchkey children and susceptibility to peer pressure: An ecological analysis. *Developmental Psychology, 22,* 433–439.

Steinberg, L. (1987a). Impact of puberty on family relations: Effects of pubertal status and pubertal timing. *Developmental Psychology, 23,* 451–460.

Steinberg, L. (1987b). Single parents, stepparents, and the susceptibility of adolescents to antisocial peer pressure. *Child Development, 58,* 269–275.

Steinberg, L. (1988). Reciprocal relation between parent–child distance and pubertal maturation. *Developmental Psychology, 24,* 122–128.

Steiner, J. E. (1979). Human facial expression in response to taste and smell stimulation. In H. W. Reese & L. P. Lipsett (Eds.), *Advances in Child Development and Behavior* (Vol. 13). New York: Academic Press.

Stern, D. N. (1974). Mother and infant at play: The dyadic interaction involving facial, vocal, and gaze behaviors. In M. Lewis & L. A. Rosenblum (Eds.), *The effect of the infant on its caregiver.* New York: Wiley.

Stern, D. N. (1977). *The first relationship.* Cambridge: Harvard University Press.

Stern, M., & Hildebrandt, K. A. (1986). Prematurity stereotyping: Effects on mother–infant interaction. *Child Development, 57,* 308–315.

Stevens, J. H. (1988). Shared knowledge about infants among fathers and mothers. *Journal of Genetic Psychology, 149,* 515–525.

Stevenson, M. R., & Black, K. N. (1988). Paternal absence and sex-role development: A meta-analysis. *Child Development, 59,* 793–814.

Stevenson, H. W. (1972). *Children's learning.* Englewood Cliffs, N.J.: Prentice Hall.

Stewart, M., & Kelso, J. (1987). A two-year follow-up of boys with aggressive conduct disorder. *Psychopathology, 20,* 296–304.

Stewart, R. B., Mobley, L. A., Van Tuyl, S. S., & Salvador, M. A.

(1987). The firstborn's adjustment to the birth of a sibling: A longitudinal assessment. *Child Development, 58,* 341–355.

Stigler, J. W., Lee, S.-Y., & Stevenson, H. W. (1987). Mathematics classrooms in Japan, Taiwan, and the United States. *Child Development, 58,* 1272–1285.

Stivers, C. (1988). Parent–adolescent communication and its relationship to adolescent depression and suicide proneness. *Adolescence, 23,* 291- 295.

St James-Robert, I. (1989). Annotation: Persistent crying in infancy. *Journal of Child Psychology and Psychiatry, 30,* 189–195.

Stocker, C., Dunn, J., & Plomin, R. (1989). Sibling relationships: Links with child temperament, maternal behavior, and family structure. *Child Development, 60,* 715–727.

Stockwell, E. G., Swanson, D. A., & Wicks, J. W. (1987). Trends in the relationship between infant mortality and socioeconomic status. *Sociological Focus, 20,* 319–327.

Stoneman, Z., Brody, G. H., & MacKinnon, C. (1984). Naturalistic observations of children's activities and roles while playing with their siblings and friends. *Child Development, 55,* 617–627.

Straus, M. A. (1983). Ordinary violence, child abuse, and wife beating: What do they have in common? In D. Finkelhor, R. J. Gelles, G. T. Hotaling, & M. A. Straus (Eds.), *The dark side of families: Current family violence research.* Beverly Hills, Calif.: Sage Publications.

Streeter, L. (1976). Language perception of two-month-old infants shows effects of both innate mechanisms and experience. *Nature, 259,* 39–41.

Streissguth, A. P., Barr, H. M., Sampson, P. D., Darby, B. L., & Martin, D. C. (1989). IQ at age 4 in relation to maternal alcohol use and smoking during pregnancy. *Developmental Psychology, 25,* 3–11.

Streri, A., & Spelke, E. S. (1988). Haptic perception of objects in infancy. *Cognitive Psychology, 20,* 1–23.

Strickland, B. R. (1988). Sex-related differences in health and illness. *Psychology of Women Quarterly, 12,* 381–399.

Stunkard, A. J. (1988). Some perspectives on human obesity: Its causes. *Bulletin of the New York Academy of Medicine, 64,* 902–923.

Sullivan, B. (1987). Smoking habit on rise among younger women. *Asbury Park [N.J.] Press,* January 10, 1987, p. C8.

Surra, C. A. (1985). Courtship types: Variations in interdependence between partners and social networks. *Journal of Personality and Social Psychology, 49,* 357–375.

Susman, E. J., Inoff-Germain, G., Nottelmann, E. D., Loriaux, D. L., Cutler, G. B., Jr., & Chrousos, G. P. (1987). Hormones, emotional dispositions, and aggressive attributes in young adolescents. *Child Development, 58,* 1114–1134.

Sutton-Smith, B. (1985). The child at play. *Psychology Today,* October, pp. 64–65.

Sutton-Smith, B. (1988). War toys and childhood aggression. *Play and Culture, 1,* 57–69.

Suzuki-Slakter, N. S. (1988). Elaboration and metamemory during adolescence. *Contemporary Educational Psychology, 13,* 206–220.

Swaim, R. C., Oetting, E. R., Edwards, R. W., & Beauvais, F. (1989). Links from emotional distress to adolescent drug use: A path model. *Journal of Consulting and Clinical Psychology, 57,* 227–231.

Swanson, H. L. (1984). Semantic and visual memory codes in learning disabled readers. *Journal of Experimental Child Psychology, 37,* 124–140.

Swedo, S. E., Rapoport, J. L., Leonard, H., Lenane, M., & Cheslow, D. (1989). Obsessive-compulsive disorder in children and adolescents. *Archives of General Psychology, 46,* 335–341.

Tambs, K., Sundet, J. M., Magnus, P., & Berg, K. (1989). Genetic and environmental contributions to the covariance between occupational status, educational attainment, and IQ: A study of twins. *Behavior Genetics, 19,* 209–222.

Tan, L. E. (1985). Laterality and motor skills in four-year-olds. *Child Development, 56,* 119–124.

Tanner, J. M. (1974). Variability of growth and maturity in newborn infants. In M. Lewis & L. A. Rosenblum (Eds.), *The effect of the infant on its caregiver.* New York: Wiley.

Tanner, J. M. (1978). *Foetus into man: Physical growth from conception to maturity.* Cambridge: Harvard University Press.

Task Force on Pediatric AIDS (1989). Pediatric AIDS and human immunodeficiency virus infection. *American Psychologist, 44,* 258–264.

Taylor, E. (1989). Time is not on their side. *Time,* February 27, p. 74.

Taylor, M. (1988). Conceptual perspective taking: Children's ability to distinguish what they know from what they see. *Child Development, 59,* 703–718.

Taylor, M., & Bacharach, V. R. (1981). The development of drawing rules: Metaknowledge about drawing influences performance on nondrawing tasks. *Child Development, 52,* 373–375.

Teberg, A. J., Walther, F. J., & Pena, I. C. (1988). Mortality, morbidity, and outcome of the small-for-gestational age infant. *Seminars in Perinatology, 12,* 84–94.

Tedesco, L. A., & Gaier, E. L. (1988). Friendship bonds in adolescence. *Adolescence, 23,* 127–135.

Teeple, J. (1978). Physical growth and maturation. In M. V. Ridenour (Ed.), *Motor development: Issues and applications.* Princeton, N.J.: Princeton Book Co.

Tellegen, A., Lykken, D. T., Bouchard, T. J., Wilcox, K., Segal, N., & Rich, S. (1988). Personality similarity in twins reared apart and together. *Journal of Social and Personality Psychology, 54,* 1031–1039.

Teller, D. Y., & Bornstein, M. H. (1987). Infant color vision and color perception. In P. Salapatek & L. B. Cohen (Eds.), *Handbook of infant perception* (Vol. 1): *From sensation to perception.* New York: Academic Press.

Teltsch, T., & Breznitz, Z. (1988). The effect of school entrance age on academic achievement and social-emotional adjustment of children. *Journal of Genetic Psychology, 149,* 471–483.

Terman, L. M. (1954a). The discovery and encouragement of exceptional talent. *American Psychologist, 9,* 221–230.

Terman, L. M. (1954b). Scientists and nonscientists in a group of 800 gifted men. *Psychological Monographs, 68,* 1–44.

Terrace, H. S. (1979). *Nim.* New York: Knopf.

Terrace, H. S. (1985). In the beginning was the "name." *American Psychologist, 40,* 1011–1028.

Tesser, A., Forehand, R., Brody, G., & Long, N. (1989). Conflict: The role of calm and angry parent–child discussion in adolescent development. *Journal of Social and Clinical Psychology, 8,* 317–330.

Teti, D. M., & Lamb, M. (1989). Socioeconomic and marital outcomes of adolescent marriage, adolescent childbirth, and their co-occurrence. *Journal of Marriage and the Family, 51,* 203–212.

Teti, D. M., Lamb, M., & Elster, A. B. (1987). Long-range socioeconomic and marital consequences of adolescent marriage in three cohorts of adult males. *Journal of Marriage and the Family, 49,* 499–506.

Tharp, R. G. (1989). Psychocultural variables and constants:

Effects of teaching and learning in schools. *American Psychologist, 44,* 349–359.

Thelen, E. (1981). Rhythmical behavior in infancy: An ethological perspective. *Developmental Psychology, 17,* 237–257.

Thomas, A., & Chess, S. (1977). *Temperament and development.* New York: Brunner/Mazel.

Thomas, J. R., & French, K. E. (1985). Gender differences across age in motor performance: A meta-analysis. *Psychological Bulletin, 98,* 260–282.

Thompson, K. M., & Wilsnack, R. W. (1987). Parental influence on adolescent drinking: Modeling, attitudes, or conflict? *Youth and Society, 19*(1), 22–43.

Thompson, M. S., Alexander, K. L., & Entwisle, D. R. (1988). Household composition, parental expectations, and school achievement. *Social Forces, 67,* 424–451.

Thompson, R. A., & Lamb, M. E. (1983). Security of attachment and stranger sociability in infancy. *Developmental Psychology, 19,* 184–191.

Thompson, S. K. (1975). Gender labels and early sex-role development. *Child Development, 46,* 339–347.

Thompson, W. R. (1954). The inheritance and development of intelligence. *Research Publications of the Association for Research in Nervous and Mental Disease, 33,* 209–331.

Thompson, W. R., & Grusec, J. E. (1970). Studies of early experience. In P. H. Mussen (Ed.), *Carmichael's manual of child psychology.* New York: Wiley.

Thornton, A., & Camburn, D. (1989). Religious participation and adolescent sexual behavior and attitudes. *Journal of Marriage and the Family, 51,* 641–653.

Tomasello, M., & Farrar, M. J. (1986). Joint attention and early language. *Child Development, 57,* 1454–1463.

Tomasello, M., Mannle, S., & Kruger, A. C. (1986). Linguistic environment of 1- to 2-year-old twins. *Developmental Psychology, 22,* 169–176.

Toner, I. J., & Smith, R. A. (1977). Age and verbalization in delay maintenance behavior in children. *Journal of Experimental Child Psychology, 24,* 123–128.

Toufexis, A. (1989). Shortcut to the Rambo look. *Time,* January 30, p. 78.

Treffert, D. A. (1988). The idiot savant: A review of the syndrome. *American Journal of Psychiatry, 145,* 563–572.

Trickett, P. K., & Kuczynski, L. (1986). Children's misbehaviors and parental discipline strategies in abusive and nonabusive families. *Developmental Psychology, 22,* 115–123.

Tronick, E. Z. (1989). Emotions and emotional communication in infants. *American Psychologist, 44,* 112–119.

Tuma, J. M. (1989), Mental health services for children: The state of the art. *American Psychologist, 44,* 188–199.

Turecki, S., & Tonner, L. (1985). *The difficult child.* New York: Bantam Books.

Turner, J. S., & Helms, D. B. (1979). *Life span development.* Philadelphia: W. B. Saunders.

Turner, W. J. (1954). *Mozart: The man and his work.* Garden City, N.Y.: Doubleday.

Udry, J. R., & Billy, J. O. G. (1987). Initiation of coitus in early adolescence. *American Sociological Review, 52,* 841–855.

U.S. Bureau of the Census (1987). *Statistical abstract of the United States.* Washington, D.C.: U.S. Government Printing Office.

U.S. Environmental Protection Agency, Office of Air and Radiation (1989). *Indoor air facts: Environmental tobacco smoke.* Washington, D.C.: Public Information Center.

Utech, D. A., & Hoving, K. L. (1969). Parents and peers as competing influences in the decisions of children of differing ages. *Journal of Social Psychology, 78,* 267–274.

Valdez-Menchaca, M. C., & Whitehurst, G. J. (1988). The effects of incidental teaching on vocabulary acquisition by young children. *Child Development, 59,* 1451–1459.

Vandell, D. L., & Wilson, K. S. (1987). Infants' interactions with mother, sibling, and peer: Contrasts and relations between interaction systems. *Child Development, 58,* 176–186.

Vasta, R. (1982). Physical child abuse: A dual-component analysis. *Developmental Review, 2,* 125–149.

Veenhoven, R., & Verkuyten, M. (1989). The well-being of only children. *Adolescence, 24*(93), 155–165.

Vemer, E., Coleman, M., Ganong, L. H., & Cooper, H. (1989). Marital satisfaction in remarriage: A meta-analysis. *Journal of Marriage and the Family, 51,* 713–725.

Victor, J. B., Halverson, C. F., Jr., & Montague, R. B. (1985). Relations between reflection-impulsivity and behavioral impulsivity in preschool children. *Developmental Psychology, 21,* 141–148.

Vogel, J. M. (1989). Shifting perspectives on the role of reversal errors in reading disability. Paper presented at the April meeting of the Society for Research in Child Development, Kansas City.

Vogel, S. A., & Walsh, P. C. (1987). Gender differences in cognitive abilities of learning-disabled females and males. *Annals of Dyslexia, 37,* 142–165.

von Hofsten, C., & Fazel-Zandy, S. (1984). Development of visually guided hand orientation in reaching. *Journal of Experimental Child Psychology, 38,* 208–219.

von Noordern, G. K. (1985). Amblyopia: A multi-disciplinary approach. *Investigative Ophthalmology and Visual Science, 26,* 1704–1716.

Vygotsky, L. S. (1962). *Thought and language.* Cambridge: MIT Press.

Waas, G. A. (1988). Social attributional biases of peer-rejected and aggressive children. *Child Development, 59,* 969–975.

Wagner, R. C., & Torgerson, J. K. (1987). The nature of phonological processing and its causal role in the acquisition of reading skills. *Psychological Bulletin, 101,* 192–212.

Walker, A. S. (1982). Intermodal perception of expressive behaviors by human infants. *Journal of Experimental Child Psychology, 33,* 514–535.

Walker, C. E., Milling, L. S., & Bonner, B. L. (1988). Incontinence disorders: Enuresis and encopresis. In D. K. Routh (Ed.), *Handbook of pediatric psychology.* New York: Guilford Press.

Wallerstein, J. S. (1985). The overburdened child: Some long-term consequences of divorce. *Social Work, 30,* 116–123.

Walsh, B. T. (1988). Antidepressants and bulimia: Where are we? *International Journal of Eating Disorders, 7,* 421–423.

Walsh, D. J., Price, G. G., & Gillingham, M. G. (1988). The critical but transitory importance of letter naming. *Reading Research Quarterly, 23*(1), 108–122.

Walters, R. H., & Brown, M. (1963). Studies of reinforcement of aggression. Part III: Transfer of responses to an interpersonal situation. *Child Development, 34,* 563–572.

Walters, R. H., & Brown, M. (1964). A test of the high-magnitude theory of aggression. *Journal of Experimental Child Psychology, 1,* 376–387.

Warden, C. J. (1931). *Animal motivation: Experimental studies on the albino rat.* New York: Columbia University Press.

Warren-Leubecker, A., & Carter, B. W. (1988). Reading and

growth in metalinguistic awareness: Relations to socioeconomic status and reading readiness skills. *Child Development, 59,* 728–742.

Watson, J. B. (1924). *Behaviorism.* New York: Norton.

Watson, J. B., & Rayner, M. (1920). Conditioned emotional reactions. *Journal of Experimental Psychology, 3,* 1–4.

Weinberg, R. A. (1989). Intelligence and IQ: Landmark issues and great debates. *American Psychologist, 44,* 98–104.

Weisfeld, C. C., Weisfeld, G. E., & Callaghan, J. W. (1982). Female inhibition in mixed-sex competition among young adolescents. *Ethology and Sociobiology, 3,* 29–42.

Weisfeld, G. E., & Billings, R. L. (1988). Observations on adolescence. In K. B. MacDonald (Ed.), *Sociobiological perspectives on human development.* New York: Springer-Verlag.

Weiss, M. J., Zelazo, P. R., & Swain, I. U. (1988). Newborn response to auditory stimulus discrepancy. *Child Development, 59,* 1530–1541.

Weiss, S. (1989). New York's dropouts-to-be: A grim class portrait. *New York Times,* April 11, pp. B1, B4.

Wellen, C. (1985). Effects of older siblings on the language young children hear and produce. *Journal of Speech and Hearing Disorders, 50,* 84–99.

Wendel, G. D. (1988). Gestational and congenital syphilis. *Clinics in Perinatology, 15,* 287–303.

Werner, E. E. (1989). High-risk children in young adulthood: A longitudinal study from birth to 32 years. *American Journal of Orthopsychiatry, 59,* 72–81.

Werner, L. (1989). School today. *USA Weekend,* August 18–20, pp. 4–5.

Wertheimer, M. (1961). Psycho-motor coordination of auditory-visual space at birth. *Science, 134,* 1692.

Whitbourne, S. K., & Tesch, S. A. (1985). A comparison of identity and intimacy statuses in college students and alumni. *Developmental Psychology, 21,* 1039–1044.

White, T. G. (1982). Naming practices, typicality, and underextension in child language. *Journal of Experimental Child Psychology, 33,* 324–346.

Whiteside, M. F. (1988). Remarried systems. In L. Combrinck-Graham (Ed.), *Child in family contexts: Perspectives on treatment.* New York: Guilford Press.

Whiting, J. W. M., & Child, I. L. (1953). *Child training and personality: A cross-cultural study.* New Haven: Yale University Press.

Whitley, B. E., Schofield, J. W., & Snyder, H. N. (1984). Peer preferences in a desegregated school: A round robin analysis. *Journal of Personality and Social Psychology, 46,* 799–810.

Whittaker, S. J. (1988). Success and maintenance of memory strategies by preschoolers. *International Journal of Behavioral Development, 11,* 345–358.

Wideman, M. V., & Singer, J. E. (1984). The role of psychological mechanisms in preparation for childbirth. *American Psychologist, 39,* 1357–1371.

Widnall, S. E. (1988). AAAS Presidential Lecture: Voices from the pipeline. *Science, 241,* 1740–1745.

Wiesel, T. N. (1975). Monkey visual cortex. II. Modifications induced by visual deprivation. Friedenwald Lecture presented at May meeting of Association for Research in Vision and Ophthalmology, Sarasota, Fla.

Wiesenfeld, A. R., Whitman, P. B., & Malatesta, C. Z. (1984). Individual differences among adult women in sensitivity to infants: Evidence in support of an empathy concept. *Journal of Personality and Social Psychology, 46,* 118–124.

Williams, H. G. (1983). *Perceptual and motor development.* Englewood Cliffs, N.J.: Prentice Hall.

Williams, J. D., & Jacoby, A. P. (1989). The effects of premarital heterosexual and homosexual experience on dating and marriage desirability. *Journal of Marriage and the Family, 51,* 489–497.

Williams, T. (1986). What I would have done differently. *Parents Magazine,* March, pp. 84–87.

Willits, F. K. (1988). Adolescent behavior and adult success and well-being. *Youth and Society, 20,* 68–87.

Wilson, J. Q., & Herrnstein, R. J. (1985). *Crime and human nature.* New York: Simon and Schuster.

Wilson, R. S. (1985). Risk and resilience in early mental development. *Developmental Psychology, 21,* 795–805.

Winick, M. (1980). The web of hunger. *Natural History,* December, pp. 6-13.

Winner, E. (1986). Where pelicans kiss seals. *Psychology Today,* August, pp. 24–35.

Witelson, S. F. (1987). Neurobiological aspects of language in children. *Child Development, 58,* 653–688.

Wolfe, D. A. (1985). Child-abusive parents: An empirical review and analysis. *Psychological Bulletin, 97,* 462–482.

Wolfe, D. A., Wolfe, V. V., & Best, C. L. (1988). Child victims of sexual abuse. In V. B. VanHasselt, R. L. Morrison, A. S. Bellack, & M. Herson (Eds.), *Handbook of family violence.* New York: Plenum Press.

Wolfenstein, M. (1967). Trends in infant care. In Y. Brackbill & G. G. Thompson (Eds.), *Behavior in infancy and early childhood.* New York: Free Press.

Worobey, J., & Blajda, V. M. (1989). Temperament ratings at 2 weeks, 2 months, and 1 year: Differential stability of activity and emotionality. *Developmental Psychology, 25,* 257–263.

Wynn, K. (1990). Children's understanding of counting. *Cognition, 36,* 155–193.

Wyrwicka, W. (1988). Imitative behavior: A theoretical view. *Pavlovian Journal of Biological Science, 23,* 125–131.

Yalislove, D. (1976). The effect of riddle structure on children's comprehension of riddles. *Developmental Psychology, 14,* 173–180.

Yamamoto, K., Soliman, A., Parsons, J., & Davies, O. L., Jr. (1987). Voices in unison: Stressful events in the lives of children in six countries. *Journal of Child Psychology and Psychiatry, 28,* 855–864.

Yarrow, M. R., Scott, P. M., & Waxler, C. Z. (1973). Learning concern for others. *Developmental Psychology, 8,* 240–260.

Yonas, A. (1979). Studies of space perception in infancy. In A. D. Pick (Ed.), *Perception and its development: A tribute to Eleanor J. Gibson.* Hillsdale, N.J.: Erlbaum.

Zahn-Waxler, C., Radke-Yarrow, M., & King, R. A. (1979). Child rearing and children's prosocial initiations toward victims of distress. *Child Development, 50,* 319–330.

Zajonc, R. B. (1976). Family configuration and intelligence. *Science, 192,* 227–236.

Zajonc, R. B., & Hall, E. (1986). Mining new gold from old research. *Psychology Today,* February, pp. 46–51.

Zajonc, R. B., & Markus, G. B. (1975). Birth order and intellectual development. *Psychological Review, 82,* 74–88.

Zelazo, P. R. (1983). The development of walking: New findings and old assumptions. *Journal of Motor Behavior, 15,* 99–137.

Zuger, B. (1988). Is early effeminate behavior in boys early homosexuality? *Comprehensive Psychiatry, 29,* 509–519.

Photo Credits

Name Index

Subject Index

About the Authors

Judy Harris got her master's degree from Harvard University, where she studied under B. F. Skinner but somehow failed to become a behaviorist. Her research and earlier publications were on visual perception and information processing. She became interested in child development as a result of her experiences in rearing two daughters, one adopted and one biological.

Bob Liebert is Professor of Psychology at the State University of New York at Stony Brook, where his teaching time is split between advanced clinical supervision and introductory level psychology courses. He earned his Ph.D. at Stanford University and went on to do research on many topics discussed in this book, including the effects of television on children, the nature and course of moral development, and bed-wetting. His other books include *Personality* and *The Early Window.*